Lecture Notes in Computer Science 16911

Advanced Research in Computing and Software Science

Subline of Lecture Notes in Computer Science

More information about this series at https://link.springer.com/bookseries/558

Pascal Lenzner · Daniel Schmand
Editors

Algorithmic Game Theory

19th International Symposium, SAGT 2026
Augsburg, Germany, September 15–18, 2026
Proceedings

Springer

Editors
Pascal Lenzner
University of Augsburg
Augsburg, Germany

Daniel Schmand
University of Bremen
Bremen, Germany

ISSN 0302-9743 ISSN 1611-3349 (electronic)
Lecture Notes in Computer Science
ISBN 978-3-032-38781-3 ISBN 978-3-032-38782-0 (eBook)
https://doi.org/10.1007/978-3-032-38782-0

This Springer imprint is published by the registered company Springer Nature Switzerland AG
The registered company address is: Gewerbestrasse 11, 6330 Cham, Switzerland

Preface

This volume contains all papers presented at the 19th International Symposium on Algorithmic Game Theory (SAGT 2026). SAGT 2026 was held as an in-person event from September 15–18, 2026, organized at the University of Augsburg, Germany.

Over the last 19 years, the SAGT conference series has become a leading interdisciplinary forum for the exchange of ideas and scientific progress across continents on incentives and computation arising in diverse areas, such as theoretical computer science, artificial intelligence, economics, operations research, and applied mathematics. SAGT 2026 was built on the success of previous editions of SAGT, which were held annually from 2008 onward.

We tried, for the first time, a double-blind review system. The Program Committee had 63 researchers. The committee reviewed 81 submissions and decided to accept 25 papers. Each paper had exactly three reviews.

We are very grateful to all members of the Program Committee and the external subreviewers for their insightful reviews and discussions. We thank EasyChair for providing a virtual platform to organize the review process. We also thank Springer for providing the proceedings and offering support for Best Paper and Best Student Paper Awards. Also, many thanks to IOG Singapore and the Deutsche Forschungsgemeinschaft (DFG Grant 589844284) for supporting the conference.

In addition to the contributed talks, the program included three invited talks by leading researchers in the field:

- Martin Bichler (Technical University of Munich, Germany),
- Tim Roughgarden (Columbia University, USA),
- Tami Tamir (Reichman University, Israel).

Our special thanks go to the local organization team, in particular Paraskevi Machaira and Marcus Wunderlich.

July 2026

Pascal Lenzner
Daniel Schmand

Organization

General Chairs

Pascal Lenzner	University of Augsburg, Germany
Daniel Schmand	University of Bremen, Germany

Program Committee Chairs

Pascal Lenzner	University of Augsburg, Germany
Daniel Schmand	University of Bremen, Germany

Steering Committee

Elias Koutsoupias	University of Oxford, UK
Marios Mavronicolas	University of Cyprus, Cyprus
Dov Monderer	Technion, Israel
Burkhard Monien	University of Paderborn, Germany
Christos Papadimitriou	Columbia University, USA
Giuseppe Persiano	University of Salerno, Italy
Paul Spirakis (Chair)	University of Liverpool, UK

Program Committee

Andreas Abels	Heinrich-Heine-Universität Düsseldorf, Germany
Elliot Anshelevich	Rensselaer Polytechnic Institute, USA
Davide Bilò	University of L'Aquila, Italy
Vittorio Bilò	University of Salento, Italy
Georgios Birmpas	University of Liverpool, UK
Martin Bullinger	University of Bristol, UK
Javier Cembrano	Universidad de Chile, Chile
Ágnes Cseh	University of Bayreuth, Germany
Bart de Keijzer	King's College London, UK
Argyrios Deligkas	Royal Holloway, University of London, UK
Angelo Fanelli	CNRS, France

Yiding Feng	Hong Kong University of Science and Technology, China
Diodato Ferraioli	Università degli Studi di Salerno, Italy
Aris Filos-Ratsikas	University of Edinburgh, UK
Dimitris Fotakis	National Technical University of Athens, Greece
Paul Goldberg	University of Oxford, UK
Lukas Graf	University of Passau, Germany
Svenja Griesbach	RWTH Aachen University, Germany
Sushmita Gupta	Institute of Mathematical Sciences, India
Guillaume Haeringer	Baruch College, USA
Kristoffer Arnsfelt Hansen	Aarhus University, Denmark
Martin Hoefer	RWTH Aachen University, Germany
Anthony Kim	Standford University, USA
Pieter Kleer	Tilburg University, The Netherlands
Max Klimm	Technische Universität Berlin, Germany
Dušan Knop	Czech Technical University in Prague, Czech Republic
Piotr Krysta	Augusta University, USA
Pascal Lenzner	University of Augsburg, Germany
Bo Li	Hong Kong Polytechnic University, China
Minming Li	City University of Hong Kong, China
Tao Lin	Chinese University of Hong Kong, Shenzhen, China
Ankur Mani	University of Minnesota, USA
David Manlove	University of Glasgow, UK
Evangelos Markakis	Athens University of Economics and Business, Greece
Francisco Javier Marmolejo Cossio	Harvard University, USA
Claudio Mezzetti	University of Queensland, Australia
Tim Oosterwijk	Vrije Universiteit Amsterdam, The Netherlands
Sigal Oren	Ben-Gurion University of the Negev, Israel
Maria Polukarov	King's College London, UK
Baharak Rastegari	University of Southampton, UK
Doron Ravid	University of Michigan, USA
Rebecca Reiffenhäuser	University of Amsterdam, The Netherlands
Shaul Rosner	Tel-Aviv University, Israel
Jörg Rothe	Heinrich-Heine-Universität Düsseldorf, Germany
Šimon Schierreich	Czech Technical University in Prague, Czech Republic
Daniel Schmand	University of Bremen, Germany
Ulrike Schmidt-Kraepelin	Technical University of Eindhoven, The Netherlands

Additional Reviewers

Distributionally Robust Contract Design with Deferred Inspection

Halil İbrahim Bayrak and Martin Bichler

Department of Computer Science, Technical University of Munich, Boltzmannstr. 3, Garching, Germany
{halil.bayrak,m.bichler}@tum.de

Abstract. We study a robust contract design problem with deferred inspection, in which a principal allocates a scarce resource to an agent, observes the agent's realized outcome ex post at negligible cost, and conditions transfers on this information through rewards. The principal faces ambiguity about the agent's value distribution: she knows its support and the first moments and seeks to maximize worst-case expected revenue subject to incentive compatibility and limited liability. In contrast to existing work on inspection mechanisms, which relies on common-prior assumptions, we adopt a distributionally robust approach based on moment information. We first focus on the single agent and first moment case and show the existence of a robustly optimal mechanism, which is more practical compared to its non-robust, prior-dependent counterpart. That is, robust optimality can be achieved with a concave allocation rule and a linear payment rule. We further show that robustness does not uniquely pin down transfers: we characterize a Pareto robustly optimal contract that preserves the same allocation rule while extracting the maximal feasible payment from every type. This mechanism achieves the same worst-case guarantee but yields strictly higher revenue under non-adversarial distributions. Numerical experiments show that the Pareto robustly optimal mechanism remains close to the ex-post optimal prior-dependent benchmark while substantially outperforming it under sufficiently severe distributional misspecification. Finally, we derive structural results for multi-agent extensions, for which we focus on dominant-strategy incentive compatible mechanisms. For ambiguity sets defined by the first N moments, we show that robust optimality requires aggregate payments to be lower bounded by a multi-dimensional polynomial of degree N. However, unlike the single-agent case, robust multi-agent mechanisms are substantially more complex: simple monotone mechanisms are no longer tractable, and worst-case distributions may involve correlated types or degenerate to a Dirac distribution at the mean. These results highlight a sharp contrast between robust contract design and robust multi-agent mechanism design with inspection. The full version of the paper is available at https://arxiv.org/abs/2506.04767.

Fair Division with Binary Valuations: Characterizations

Florian Brandl[1], Warut Suksompong[2], and Nicholas Teh[3]

[1] University of Bonn, Germany
fbrandl@uni-bonn.de
[2] National University of Singapore, Singapore
warut@comp.nus.edu.sg
[3] University of Oxford, UK
nicholas.teh@cs.ox.ac.uk

The fair allocation of resources is a central problem at the intersection of economics and computer science. When the resources are indivisible, a popular allocation method is the *maximum Nash welfare (MNW)* rule, which selects an allocation maximizing the product of the agents' values. Under additive valuations, MNW has been characterized as the unique rule within the class of welfarist rules that ensures the fairness property of *envy-freeness up to one good (EF1)* [3].

An important subclass of additive valuations is the class of *binary valuations*, where each agent's value for each good is either 0 or 1. Under binary valuations, MNW is known to satisfy several desirable properties which they fail under additive valuations [1, 2]. Moreover, it coincides with the leximin rule as well as any additive welfarist rule with a strictly concave function. We further strengthen the case in favor of this rule in the domain of binary valuations by providing two characterizations of it within the space of all rules.

1. For any number of agents, this rule is the only rule that satisfies EF1, strategyproofness, neutrality, minimal completeness, and invariance under disapproving unassigned goods (IDU).
2. As an alternative characterization for two agents, IDU can be replaced by non-redundancy and resource-monotonicity.

We also establish the necessity of all axioms in both characterizations.

The full version of the paper is available at https://arxiv.org/pdf/2607.10064. This work was partially supported by the Singapore Ministry of Education under grant number MOE-T2EP20221-0001, by the DFG under the Excellence Strategy EXC-2047, and by an NUS Start-up Grant.

References

1. Halpern, D., Procaccia, A.D., Psomas, A., Shah, N.: Fair division with binary valuations: one rule to rule them all. In: Proceedings of the 16th Conference on Web and Internet Economics (WINE), pp. 370–383 (2020)
2. Suksompong, W., Teh, N.: On maximum weighted Nash welfare for binary valuations. Math. Soc. Sci. **117**, 101–108 (2022)
3. Yuen, S.M., Suksompong, W.: Extending the characterization of maximum Nash welfare. Econ. Lett. **224**, 111030 (2023)

Robustness of Persuasion to Receiver Preferences

Ronen Brandl[1], Fengming Hu[2], and Rann Smorodinsky[3]

[1] University of Haifa, Haifa, Israel
fbrandl@uni-bonn.de
[2] Technion – Israel Institute of Technology, Haifa, Israel
fengming.hu@campus.technion.ac.il
[3] Technion – Israel Institute of Technology, Haifa, Israel
rgradwohl@econ.haifa.ac.il

Abstract. We study the robustness of Bayesian persuasion to uncertainty about the receiver's preferences. We analyze two conceptually distinct notions: *continuity*, in which only the modeler lacks precise knowledge; and *robustness*, in which the sender also lacks precise knowledge. Continuity captures the idea that the modeler's predictions remain accurate when the modeler's specification of the receiver's preferences is infinitesimally inaccurate. Robustness also accounts for the sender's ignorance in addition to the modeler's—it captures the idea that the outcome of the simpler, complete information setting remains approximately valid in the more complex setting with infinitesimal ignorance about receiver's preferences. We model preference uncertainty as infinitesimally small, non-probabilistic (Knightian) uncertainty, and model the sender as either minimizing the regret or maximizing the minimum utility.

We characterize necessary and sufficient conditions for continuity and robustness under both behavior criteria. Our characterization establishes that continuity holds if and only if robustness holds, so that the three notions—continuity, max-min robustness, and regret-minimizing robustness—are equivalent. We also show that continuity and robustness hold generically. Thus, while some instances of Bayesian persuasion are fragile, typical instances are both continuous and robust with respect to a small amount of ignorance.

The full version is available at https://arxiv.org/abs/2605.28265.

Keywords: Bayesian persuasion · robustness · regret · max-min utility

Acknowledgements. Gradwohl gratefully acknowledges support from the Israel Science Foundation, Grant 2039/24. Hu and Smorodinsky gratefully acknowledge support from the German Research Foundation, Grant 514505843 and the Israel Science Foundation, Grant 2646/22. Hu additionally acknowledges the generous financial support from Israel Planning and Budgeting Committee (VATAT).

Contents

Perpetually Fair Assignments Via Balanced Sequences of Permutations

Terrence Adams[1(✉)] and Erel Segal-Halevi[2]

[1] University at Albany, State University of New York, 1400 Washington Avenue, Albany, NY 12222, USA
terry@ieee.org
[2] Ariel University, Ariel 40700, Israel

Abstract. There is a set of n indivisible items (goods or chores), and a set of n players. Each day, a single item should be assigned to each player. Assignments based on latin squares guarantee fairness after every n days; our goal is to ensure fairness after every single day.

We present two 'balance' conditions on latin squares. Informally, a latin square is balanced if its top rows and leftmost columns contain all n labels; this ensures that all n players receive one of the top items in one of the early days. One such condition can always be satisfied, but is arguably too weak; a second condition is strong, and can be satisfied for all $n \leq 12$, but cannot be satisfied for some larger values of n, including all $n > 108$.

We show that the second balance condition guarantees that the cumulative assignment is always *proportional up to one item (PROP1)*, where proportionality holds in a strong ordinal sense—for every valuations that are consistent with the item ranking. Finally, we present a weaker balance condition on a sequence, that guarantees ordinal proportionality up to two items (PROP2).

All appendices are available in the full version, which is available at https://arxiv.org/abs/2602.21687.

Keywords: Fair division · Repeated assignment · latin squares · Proportionality · Balanced sequences

1 Introduction

Some n house-mates need to divide the n daily house-chores among them. Each housemate must do exactly one chore per day. What would be a fair way to assign the chores? Ideally, a fair allocation would give each housemate the same amount of work. But this might be impossible, as some chores are easier and some are harder; in every single day, some housemates must do the hard chores. However, if the same housemates do the same unwanted chores day after day, they will rightfully complain that this *repeated assignment* is unfair.

A similar problem may arise in different contexts. For example, suppose grandpa wants to divide sweets to his grandchildren each weekend. He has to

P. Lenzner and D. Schmand (Eds.): SAGT 2026, LNCS 16911, pp. 1–18, 2027.
https://doi.org/10.1007/978-3-032-38782-0_1

decide who gets the sweets first, who is second, and so on. Each week, the children who are last to get their sweets might feel somewhat unhappy; but if the same children are last in the line week after week, they will naturally feel that the allocation is unfair. Similar considerations are applicable when assigning seats in classroom to pupils—a task which may be repeated in different terms.

In all these settings, the same assignment problem repeats many times. Whereas some inequality can be tolerated in every single assignment, we expect it to eventually "cancel out" as the same process repeats long enough. We call this problem *Fair Repeated Assignment.*

In Sect. 2 below we define the problem formally. In the following Sects. 3–6 we present our main results on existence and non-existence of fair repeated assignments. In Sect. 7 we discuss various other fair allocation settings studied in the literature and compare them to our setting.

2 Setting

There is a set N of n *players*, $N := \{A_1, \ldots, A_n\}$. There is a set M of n indivisible *items*, $M := [n] = \{1, \ldots, n\}$. We assume that 1 is the best item (e.g. the easiest chore), 2 is the second-best item, etc. This does not lose much generality, as instead of dividing the actual items, we can divide positions in a sequence by which the players pick items, so that the player who receives "1" is the first to pick an item, the player who receives "2" picks second, etc. Clearly, an earlier position in the picking sequence is better for each player.[1]

An *assignment* is a bijection between M and N; equivalently, a permutation of M. A *repeated assignment* is a finite sequence of assignments. We say that each assignment is implemented in a different *day.* The multiset of items that a particular player i has after a repeated assignment is called a *bundle.* The bundle of i after day t is denoted Z_i^t. The multiset of all items allocated up to day t is denoted $Z_N^t := \uplus_{i \in N} Z_i^t =$ the items $1, \ldots, n$, each with multiplicity t.

We often present a repeated assignment in a table in which each column represents a day and each row represents an item. The number in column t and row j represents the player who receives item j in day t; see Table 1.

For any bundle Z and any $k \leq |Z|$, we denote by $Z[k]$ the k-th highest valued item in Z, so that $Z[1]$ is the best item in Z, $Z[2]$ the second-best, etc. The matching between the players and their bundles is called an *allocation.*

[1] This is essentially the "Identical Order Transformation" introduced by Bouveret and Lemaître [12]. Cookson et al. [23] prove that this transformation preserves the approximate proportionality condition PROP1.

Table 1. Examples of permutation sequences (repeated assignments) of 6 items (left) and 8 items (right). Each column represents an assignment in a single day; each row represents the players who get a single item throughout all days.

1	6	5	4	3	2
2	1	6	5	4	3
3	2	1	6	5	4
4	3	2	1	6	5
5	4	3	2	1	6
6	5	4	3	2	1

1	8	5	4	3	6	7	2
2	7	6	3	4	5	8	1
3	6	7	2	1	8	5	4
4	5	8	1	2	7	6	3
5	4	1	8	7	2	3	6
6	3	2	7	8	1	4	5
7	2	3	6	5	4	1	8
8	1	4	5	6	3	2	7

3 Fairness After n Days: Latin Square

We are looking for a formal condition that captures the intuitive notion of "fairness". First, suppose that we are now at the end of day n, and we consider the aggregate bundle of n items that is held by each player. We define the allocation at that point as "fair" if and only if each player has exactly one copy of each item. It is easy to agree that this condition is sufficient for fairness, as it implies that all players have exactly the same bundle. We claim that it is also necessary. This is because we make no assumptions on how much exactly item 1 is better than item 2, 2 is better than 3, etc. Hence, we cannot assume e.g. that a player who received no copy of item 1, can be compensated by receiving two copies of item 2. Only allocations that give each item to each player exactly once are guaranteed to be fair.

This condition is satisfied in both examples in Table 1, where each row is a permutation of $[n]$. As each column is also a permutation of $[n]$, the entire repeated assignment table is a *latin square*. There are many ways to construct latin squares, so this requirement is easy to satisfy.

Clearly, in fewer than n days, it is impossible to give all players exactly the same bundle. Suppose item 1 is very valuable (a diamond) and the other items are much less valuable (stones). Then at any day before the n-th day, some players (those who did not get the diamond so far) will naturally feel that they did not get their fair share. We could tell these players to wait patiently until day n; but n days may be too much to wait. We would like the allocation to be "as fair as possible" after each day—not only after day n.

Below, we explore different ways to define what this fairness means.

4 Fairness After Every Day: Top-Balance

A natural fairness requirement is to require that the top items are allocated among the players in a "balanced" way: in the first two days, each player should get at least one item from the top half (the highest-valued $\lceil n/2 \rceil$ items); in the first three days, each player should get at least one item from the top third (the highest-valued $\lceil n/3 \rceil$ items); and so on.[2] We now state this succinctly.

Definition 1. *A permutation sequence is called* top-balanced *if after every day* $t \in [n]$*, every player* i *has at least one item from the top* $\lceil n/t \rceil$*. Formally,*

$$Z_i^t[1] \leq \lceil n/t \rceil .$$

In terms of the latin square, top-balance means that, for all $t \in [n]$, the top-left rectangle with t columns and $\lceil n/t \rceil$ rows must contain all integers $1, \ldots, n$. The condition is violated by the sequences of Table 1: for $n = 6$ and $t = 2$, the top-left 3×2 rectangle does not contain 5; for $n = 8$ and $t = 3$, the top-left 3×3 rectangle does not contain 4. Are there other sequences that satisfy it? The answer is yes, and moreover, the condition can be satisfied in combination with the latin square requirement.

Theorem 1. *For every positive integer* n*, there exists an* $n \times n$ *latin square that is also top-balanced.*

The proof uses two known results about completing incomplete latin squares. A *latin rectangle* is a rectangle with n rows and $t < n$ columns, such that each integer in $\{1, \ldots, n\}$ appears exactly once in each column, and at most once in each row. Marshall Hall [28], using Philip Hall's marriage theorem, proved that any latin rectangle can be extended, one column at a time, to produce a latin square. In our setting, columns correspond to days; we will construct a top-balanced latin-square sequence one day at a time. We will also use Theorem 4 from [26] to iteratively extend columns from a partial latin rectangle to a full latin rectangle. For convenience, we restate it here as Lemma 1.

Lemma 1 (Column completion lemma, Theorem 4 in [26]). *Let* L *be an* $n \times t$ *latin rectangle where* $t < n$*.*

Suppose that some ℓ *distinct labels are entered into some* ℓ *distinct rows in column* $t+1$*. If we can insert the* $n-\ell$ remaining labels *into the* $n-\ell$ remaining rows *such that the outcome is an* $n \times (t+1)$ *latin rectangle, then we say that column* $t+1$ *is* completable.

The column is completable if and only if any subset I *of the remaining labels is contained in at most* $(n - \ell - |I|)$ *of the remaining rows.*

Equivalently: For any subset I *of remaining labels, there are at least* $|I|$ *remaining rows that do not contain* I*.*

Remark 1. Since L is a latin rectangle with t columns, any subset I of labels can be contained in at most t rows of L (by the pigeonhole principle). Hence, a sufficient condition for completability is that $n - \ell - |I| \geq t$. Moreover, the condition holds trivially when $|I| > t$, so it is sufficient to check the condition for $|I| \leq t$. Hence, it is sufficient to prove that $n - \ell - t \geq t$.

[2] The top-balance condition is asymmetric with respect to time, as it assesses fairness based only on the first t days, and not on the last t days or any other t consecutive days. This asymmetry makes sense when the allocated items are physical items that the players keep, so after t days, each player owns a bundle of t items, which should be sufficiently valuable.

Proof (Proof of Theorem 1). First, we show how to define the assignment for the first half of the days, namely for columns $t \in \{1, \dots \lceil \frac{n}{2} \rceil\}$, and for the top portion of each of these columns (representing the assignment of the top items). After the top-balance condition is satisfied for all these columns, we show how to append the remaining columns such that the entire sequence is a latin square and top-balanced.

Step 1: Constructing a top-balanced partial latin rectangle. We build the top-balanced sequence and partial latin square inductively in the columns t. We want to establish the following two claims inductively in t.

1. The set of labels in the top-$\lceil \frac{n}{t} \rceil$ rows in columns $1, \dots, t$ contains $[n]$, and
2. The labels in the top-$(\lceil \frac{n}{t} \rceil - 1)$ rows in columns $1, \dots, t$ are all unique.

For the induction base, column $t = 1$ is filled by $1, \dots, n$. Column $t = 2$ is filled by $\lceil \frac{n}{2} \rceil + i$ for $1 \le i \le \lfloor \frac{n}{2} \rfloor$, and then by i for $1 \le i \le \lceil \frac{n}{2} \rceil$. This construction clearly satisfies both claims.

Suppose we have filled columns $1, \dots, t$ for $2 \le t < n$ such that claims (1) and (2) hold. We show how to progress to the next column $t + 1$. There are two cases to consider.

Case #1: $\left\lceil \frac{n}{t+1} \right\rceil \le \lceil \frac{n}{t} \rceil - 1$. Then by the induction hypothesis the labels in the top-$\left\lceil \frac{n}{t+1} \right\rceil$ rows and first t columns are unique. In column $t + 1$, fill the top $\left\lceil \frac{n}{t+1} \right\rceil - 1$ cells by labels not in this collection; This is possible since $(t + 1)(\left\lceil \frac{n}{t+1} \right\rceil - 1) < n$. The labels in the top- $(\lceil \frac{n}{t+1} \rceil - 1)$ rows in the first $t + 1$ columns are still unique, so claim (2) is satisfied.

Since $(t+1)\lceil \frac{n}{t+1} \rceil \ge n$, at most one label does not appear in a top-$\left\lceil \frac{n}{t+1} \right\rceil$ row yet; put that label in cell $\left\lceil \frac{n}{t+1} \right\rceil$. Now, all n labels appear in a top-$\left\lceil \frac{n}{t+1} \right\rceil$ row in the first $t + 1$ columns, so claim (1) is satisfied too.

Case #2: $\lceil \frac{n}{t+1} \rceil = \lceil \frac{n}{t} \rceil$. Then by the induction assumption all labels already appear in a top-$\lceil \frac{n}{t+1} \rceil$ row in columns $1, \dots, t$, so claim (1) is already satisfied. We only have to ensure uniqueness. Take any labels that did not appear in a top $(\lceil \frac{n}{t+1} \rceil - 1)$ row yet, and put them in the top cells of column $t + 1$. Since $(t + 1)(\lceil \frac{n}{t+1} \rceil - 1) < n$, all labels in one of the top $\lceil \frac{n}{t+1} \rceil - 1$ rows in the first $t + 1$ columns are unique, and claim (2) is satisfied too.

Step 2: Completing the columns to a full latin rectangle. For each $t \in \{1, \dots, \lceil \frac{n}{2} \rceil - 1\}$, we will show how to complete column $t + 1$, such that the rectangle consisting of days $1, \dots, t+1$ is a latin rectangle. Step 1 already handles $t = 1$, so we can assume $t \ge 2$. In Sect. 5, we will present a fairness notion stronger than both latin square and top-balance; in Theorem 2, we will show that it can be satisfied for all $n \le 11$. Hence, we can assume here that $n \ge 12$.

To complete column $t+1$, we apply Lemma 1 with ℓ being the number of cells filled in Step 1. Note, we have that $\left\lceil \frac{n}{t+1} \right\rceil - 1 \leq \ell \leq \left\lceil \frac{n}{t+1} \right\rceil$. If $t = 2$,

$$n - \ell - t \geq n - \left\lceil \frac{n}{t+1} \right\rceil - t > n - \left(\frac{n}{3} + 1\right) - 2 = \frac{2n}{3} - 3 \geq 5 > t,$$

which is sufficient by Remark 1. Similarly, if $t = 3$, then

$$n - \ell - t \geq n - \left\lceil \frac{n}{t+1} \right\rceil - t > n - \left(\frac{n}{4} + 1\right) - 3 = \frac{3n}{4} - 4 \geq 5 > t.$$

Now, for $n \geq 12$, $t \geq 4$ and $t \leq \lceil \frac{n}{t+1} \rceil$,

$$n - \ell - t \geq n - 2\left\lceil \frac{n}{t+1} \right\rceil > \frac{3n}{5} - 2 > \frac{n}{5} + 1 \geq \left\lceil \frac{n}{t+1} \right\rceil \geq t.$$

Again, by Remark 1, Lemma 1 is satisfied and we are able to complete column $t+1$. Finally, we handle $t > \left\lceil \frac{n}{t+1} \right\rceil$. We consider two cases.

Case #1: n is even (and $n \geq 12$). Recall $\left\lceil \frac{n}{t+1} \right\rceil - 1 \leq \ell \leq \left\lceil \frac{n}{t+1} \right\rceil$. The construction of Step 1 ensures that all n labels appear at least once in the top $\left\lceil \frac{n}{t+1} \right\rceil$ rows of the first $t+1$ columns. Hence, any set I of labels that do not already appear in the top ℓ rows of column $t+1$, must appear in the top $\left\lceil \frac{n}{t+1} \right\rceil$ rows of the first t columns at least once. If $|I| = t$, since $t > \left\lceil \frac{n}{t+1} \right\rceil$, there exists an element $a \in I$ such that a appears in the top ℓ rows and the first t columns. Thus, the element a can only appear at most $t-1$ times in the bottom $n-\ell$ rows. Hence, to apply Lemma 1, it is sufficient to show a slightly weaker condition than that of Remark 1: $n - \ell - |I| \geq t - 1$. As $|I| \leq t$, it is sufficient to show that $n - \ell - t \geq t - 1$.

On the other hand, if $|I| \leq t-1$, then it is sufficient to show $n - \ell - (t-1) \geq t$ which also implies it is sufficient to show $n - \ell - t \geq t - 1$.

Substituting an upper bound for ℓ and rearranging terms leads to the following sufficient condition:

$$n - \left(\frac{n}{t+1} + 1\right) - t - (t-1) = n - \frac{n}{t+1} - 2t \geq 0.$$

We know for $n \geq 12$ and $t = 1$, $n - \frac{n}{t+1} - 2t > 0$. Solving $n - \frac{n}{t+1} - 2t = 0$ gives $t = \frac{n}{2} - 1$ or $t = 0$ (recall that n is even). By Bolzano's Theorem [9], this implies the Lemma 1 condition holds for $0 \leq t \leq \frac{n}{2} - 1$. Hence, we can complete all columns up to column $\frac{n}{2}$.

Case #2: n is odd (and $n \geq 13$). By the argument of Case #1, we can complete column $t+1$ for all $t \leq \frac{n}{2} - 1$, which for odd n means $t \leq \frac{n-3}{2}$. Thus, the first $\frac{n-1}{2}$ columns can be completed.

It remains to complete column $\frac{n+1}{2} = \lceil \frac{n}{2} \rceil$. As $n-1$ labels have already appeared in the top two rows and the first $\frac{n-1}{2}$ columns, the construction of Step 1 has to put only the single remaining label at the top row of column $\frac{n+1}{2}$, so we can take $\ell = 1$. As $t = \frac{n-1}{2}$, we get

$$n - \ell - t = n - 1 - \frac{n-1}{2} = \frac{n-1}{2} = t.$$

The condition in Remark 1 is satisfied, so column $\frac{n+1}{2}$ can be completed.

Step 3: Completing the rectangle to a full latin square. At this point, we have a top-balanced latin rectangle with $\lceil \frac{n}{2} \rceil$ columns. Apply Hall's theorem [28] to complete the final $\lfloor \frac{n}{2} \rfloor$ columns and obtain a latin square.

Since $\lfloor \frac{n}{2} \rfloor$ labels have not appeared at row 1 in the first $\lceil \frac{n}{2} \rceil$ columns, these labels must appear in the first row in the last $\lfloor \frac{n}{2} \rfloor$ columns to obtain a latin square. This implies that the resulting latin square remains top-balanced. □

5 Stronger Fairness After Every Day: Full-Balance

The top-balance condition considers only the top items for each player. The allocations of other items can be arbitrary, and thus unfair. The condition can be strengthened as follows:

- In the first two days, each player should receive at least one item from the top $\lceil n/2 \rceil$ items—this condition is the same as in top-balance.
- In the first three days, each player should receive at least one item from the top $\lceil n/3 \rceil$ items, *and at least two items from the top* $\lceil 2n/3 \rceil$ *items*—the latter condition is new.
- In general, in the first t days, for every $j \in \{1, \dots, t\}$, each player should receive at least j items from the highest-valued $\lceil jn/t \rceil$ items.

All these conditions are formalized succinctly below.

Definition 2. *A permutation sequence is called* fully-balanced *if after every day* $t \in [n]$, *the bundle* Z_i^t *of every player* i *satisfies the following for every* $j \in [t]$:

$$Z_i^t[j] \leq \lceil jn/t \rceil . \tag{1}$$

We denote by $\text{BAL}(t, j)$ the condition (1) for some particular $t \in [n]$ and $j \in [t]$. So a repeated assignment is fully-balanced if it satisfies $\text{BAL}(t, j)$ for every day $t \in [n]$ and item $j \in [t]$.

Remark 2. (a) $\text{BAL}(t = n, j)$ implies that, after n days, the j-best highest item of each player is item j; this implies that each player has exactly one copy of each item, which is the Latin-square condition of Sect. 3.

(b) $\text{BAL}(t, j = 1)$ is exactly the top-balance condition of Sect. 4.

(c) $\text{BAL}(t = 1, \cdot)$ and $\text{BAL}(t, j = t)$ hold trivially, so in fact we only have to check $t \in \{2, \dots, n\}$ and $j \in \{1, \dots, t-1\}$.

Do fully-balanced sequences exist for all n?

It is easy to find fully-balanced sequences for $n \in \{3,4,5,6\}$; the readers may want to try it themselves before looking at Table 2. To verify that a permutation sequence is fully-balanced, one should check, for each $t \in [n]$ and $j \in [t]$, that the top-right rectangle with t columns and $\lceil jn/t \rceil$ rows contains each integer in $1,\ldots,n$ at least j times. For example, for $n = 6$ and $t = 4$, we check that the 2×4 top-left rectangle contains $1,\ldots,6$ at least once; the 3×4 top-left rectangle contains $1,\ldots,6$ at least twice; and the 5×4 top-left rectangle contains $1,\ldots,6$ at least three times.

Table 2. Fully-balanced permutation sequences for $n \in \{3,4,5,6\}$.

1	2	3
2	3	1
3	1	2

1	4	3	2
2	3	4	1
3	2	1	4
4	1	2	3

1	4	2	3	5
2	5	3	4	1
3	1	4	5	2
4	2	5	1	3
5	3	1	2	4

1	4	3	5	2	6
2	5	6	4	1	3
3	6	2	1	4	5
4	1	5	6	3	2
5	2	1	3	6	4
6	3	4	2	5	1

We were able to handcraft sequences for $n \leq 8$. For larger values of n, we implemented a backtracking algorithm, and found such sequences for all $n \leq 11$. Appendix A shows the fully-balanced sequences that we found for $7 \leq n \leq 11$.

Theorem 2. *For all $n \leq 11$, a fully-balanced permutation sequence exists.*

Twelve (12) is the first natural number that does not admit a fully-balanced sequence. Below we show there are infinitely many natural numbers with no fully-balanced sequence, including $n = 12$.

Proposition 1. *There is no fully-balanced sequence of length $n = 6k$ for $k \geq 2$.*

Proof. Let A_i represent the player who goes i^{th} in the first day. Let B_i represent the player who goes i^{th} in the second day; C_i the player who goes i^{th} in the third day and D_i the player who goes i^{th} in the fourth day. We will show that balance must break down within the fourth day. Notice that for $k \geq 2$, $\lceil \frac{6k}{4} \rceil < 2k$. Here is the list of implications that prevent balance:

1. $\{A_i : 3k+1 \leq i \leq 6k\} = \{B_i : 1 \leq i \leq 3k\}$ by BAL(2, 1). Each player that appears in the second half in the first day must appear in the first half in the second day, since $\lceil \frac{6k}{2} \rceil = 3k$.
2. $\{A_i : 1 \leq i \leq 3k\} = \{B_i : 3k+1 \leq i \leq 6k\}$. This follows by (1).
3. $\{C_i : 1 \leq i \leq 2k\} = \{A_i : 2k+1 \leq i \leq 3k\} \cup \{B_i : 2k+1 \leq i \leq 3k\}$ by BAL(3, 1). Since $\lceil \frac{6k}{3} \rceil = 2k$, each player must go at least once in the top $2k$ positions after the first 3 days. But, $\{A_i : 2k+1 \leq i \leq 3k\} \cup \{B_i : 2k+1 \leq i \leq 3k\}$ are $2k$ distinct players that have not gone in the top $2k$ positions after the first 2 days.

4. $\{C_{2k}\} \subset \{D_i : 1 \leq i \leq 3k\}$ by BAL(4, 1). Let $z := \lceil \frac{6k}{4} \rceil$. Since $z < 2k$, then player C_{2k} did not get any of the top z items in any of the first three days. Thus, $C_{2k} \in \{D_i : 1 \leq i \leq z\}$ (Moreover, $\{C_i : z+1 \leq i \leq 2k\} \subseteq \{D_i : 1 \leq i \leq z\}$).
5. $\{C_i : 3k+1 \leq i \leq 6k\} \subseteq \{D_i : 1 \leq i \leq 3k\}$ by BAL(4, 2). Each player is in the first $3k$ positions in the first or second day, but not both days. This follows from (1) and (2). Since $\frac{2(6k)}{4} = 3k$, then each player goes in the top $3k$ positions at least twice in the first 4 days. But, each of $C_{3k+1}, \ldots, C_{6k}$ have gone once in the first 3 days.

But there is no room for all of $C_{2k}, C_{3k+1}, \ldots, C_{6k}$ to go in the top $3k$ positions in the fourth day. That is,

$$|\{C_{2k}, C_{3k+1}, C_{3k+2}, \ldots, C_{6k}\}| = |\{D_1, D_2, \ldots, D_{3k}\}| + 1$$

which leads to a contradiction.

Proposition 1 can be extended to all n. The proof varies with the remainder of n divided by 6, so there are six different proofs (including Proposition 1). The table below shows the lower bounds for each remainder j in $\{0, 1, 2, 3, 4, 5\}$. The proofs are given in Appendix B.

Table 3. Values of $n = 6k + j$ with no fully-balanced sequence

n	$6k$	$6k+1$	$6k+2$	$6k+3$	$6k+4$	$6k+5$
bounds on k	$k \geq 2$	$k \geq 11$	$k \geq 3$	$k \geq 8$	$k \geq 4$	$k \geq 9$
bounds on n	$n \geq 12$	$n \geq 67$	$n \geq 20$	$n \geq 51$	$n \geq 28$	$n \geq 59$

Table 3 shows there are at most finitely many values n which admit a fully-balanced sequence. In particular, the following theorem follows from Table 3.

Theorem 3. *There exist finitely many n such that there is a fully-balanced sequence of length n. Moreover, there is no fully-balanced sequence for $n > 61$.*

Proof. Since every natural number can be expressed uniquely in the form $n = 6k + j$ for $j = 0, 1, 2, 3, 4, 5$, then we can list the natural numbers that fall under the bounds in Table 3. It is straightforward to check that $n = 61$ is the largest natural number which possibly has a fully-balanced sequence. See the Appendix B for a proof of Table 3 and this theorem.

6 Valuations and Proportionality: Weak Full-Balance

As the concept of a fully-balanced sequence is too strong, we would like to relax it. To do so (and also to link our balance concepts to the literature on fair allocation), we assume that each item $j \in [n]$ has a *value* $v_j \in \mathbb{R}$, such that $v_1 > v_2 > \cdots > v_n$.[3] The total value of any bundle (multiset of items) Z is denoted $v(Z) := \sum_{k \in Z} v_k$.

A natural fairness concept is that each player should receive a bundle of items that is worth at least $1/n$ of the total value, that is, $v(Z_i^t) \geq v(Z_N^t)/n$.[4] This concept is prominent both in law and in the literature on fair division ever since its inception [47]. Nowadays, it is called *proportionality* [16,42]. We require a strong variant of proportionality, which holds not only for specific valuations but for *any* valuations that satisfy the condition $v_1 > \cdots > v_n$. We call this variant *ordinal proportionality*, as it is based only on the order among items rather than on their exact values.[5]

Given the latin square constraint (Sect. 3), the allocation after day n is ordinally proportional. This is because the bundle of every player i satisfies $v(Z_i^n) = \sum_{j \in M} v_j$ and the total value of all items is $v(Z_N^n) = n \cdot \sum_{j \in M} v_j$. However, before day n it is impossible to guarantee ordinal proportionality. For example, if v_1 is very high and the other item values are very low, then at any day before the n-th day, the value of some players (those who did not get item 1 so far) will be below the proportionality threshold.

A natural relaxation of proportionality for indivisible items is *proportionality up to c items*, abbreviated PROPc [17,21,22,27,33]. It means that, for each player i, if we add to i's bundle some c items not allocated to i yet, then i's value will be at least $1/n$ of the total value. This definition implicitly assumes that all items are goods (have positive values); we use a more symmetric definition, that applies equally to items with positive or negative values: instead of just adding c items, we both add and remove the same number of items.

Definition 3. *Let $c \geq 1$ be an integer.*

(a) A repeated assignment is called perpetually PROPc for valuation v *if for every time $t \in [n]$ and player i, there is a set $C' \subseteq N \setminus Z_i^t$ and a set $C'' \subseteq Z_i^t$, with $|C''| = |C'| \leq c$, such that $v(Z_i^t \setminus C'' \cup C') \geq v(Z_N^t)/n$.*

(b) A repeated assignment is called perpetually ordinally PROPc *if it is perpetually PROPc for every valuation v satisfying $v_1 > \cdots > v_n$.*

Note that, when all values are positive, Definition 3(a) implies the standard definition of PROPc, as removing items only makes the value smaller.

The sequence for $n = 6$ at Table 1 fails ordinal PROP1 already after the second day. This is because the total value allocated up to this time is $2 \cdot (v_1 + v_2 + v_3 + v_4 + v_5 + v_6)$, whereas the bundle of player 5 is $\{5, 6\}$. Even if we add

[3] The literature on fair division studies a more general setting, in which different players may have different rankings and different valuations over the items. In Appendix E we prove that our main theorem holds in this more general setting too.

[4] The phrase "at least" comes from the more general setting (footnote 5). In the case of a common valuation, proportionality implies that each player receives exactly $1/n$ of the total value.

[5] Ordinal fairness is also known as *necessary fairness* or *stochastic-dominance fairness (sd-fairness)*. Ordinal fairness in item allocation has been studied e.g. by Bouveret et al. [3,10,14,15,41,45].

the most valuable item 1, the resulting bundle value is $v_1 + v_5 + v_6$, which might be smaller than 1/6 of the total value (e.g. if $v_5 = v_6 = 0$ and $v_1 = \cdots = v_4 = 1$). Hence, the repeated assignment at Table 1 is not perpetually ordinally PROP1. Below we relate full balance to perpetual proportionality.

Theorem 4. *A fully-balanced permutation sequence generates a perpetually ordinally PROP1 repeated assignment.*

Theorem 4 follows directly from Theorem 5 below, which shows that ordinal PROP1 follows from an a slightly weaker balance condition.

Definition 4. *A permutation sequence is called* weakly fully-balanced *if for all $t \in [n]$, the bundle Z_i^t of every player i satisfies the following for all $j \in [t]$:*

$$Z_i^t[j] \leq \lfloor jn/t + 1 \rfloor . \tag{2}$$

We call this condition $\text{WeakBal}(t, j)$.

Note that $\text{WeakBal}(t, j)$ is weaker than $\text{Bal}(t, j)$ only when jn/t is an integer; otherwise they are equivalent.

Theorem 5. *A weakly fully-balanced permutation sequence generates a perpetually ordinally PROP1 repeated assignment.*

Proof. We fix a day t, and prove that the cumulative allocation up to day t satisfies ordinal PROP1.

So far, nt items have been allocated, so $|Z_N^t| = nt$. Note that the multiset Z_N^t contains exactly t clones of every item in $1, \dots, n$.

Fix a player i. Let us add to i's bundle Z_i^t a copy of the highest-valued item (1), and remove the least-valuable item from i's bundle, so that i's new bundle still has t items overall. Denote this new bundle C_i. To show PROP1, it is sufficient to show that the $v(C_i) \geq v(Z_N^t)/n$. Construct a new multiset D_i, containing n clones of each item in C_i; now, it is sufficient to show that $v(D_i) \geq v(Z_N^t)$. We do this by showing a bijection $f : D_i \to Z_N^t$, such that $x \leq f(x)$ for all $x \in D_i$; hence $v(x) \geq v(f(x))$ for all $x \in D_i$.

We first show the bijection for the special case that n/t is an integer.

- We first map the n clones of item 1 in D_i (the added item). We map them to the t clones of items $1, 2, \dots, n/t$ in Z_N^t.
- Next, we map the n clones of the best item held by i, denoted $Z_i^t[1]$. By $\text{WeakBal}(t, j = 1)$, $Z_i^t[1] \leq \lfloor n/t + 1 \rfloor = n/t + 1$. Hence, we can map it to the t clones of items $n/t + 1, 2, \dots, 2n/t$ in Z_N^t.
- Similarly, by $\text{WeakBal}(t, j)$ for all $j \in [t-1]$, $Z_i^t[j] \leq jn/t + 1$; hence, we can map the n clones of $Z_i^t[j]$ to the t clones of items $jn/t+1, 2, \dots, (j+1)n/t$ in Z_N^t.

When n/t is not an integer, the mapping works as follows:

- The n clones of item 1 in D_i are mapped to the t clones of items $1, 2, \dots, \lfloor n/t \rfloor$ in Z_N^t, as well as to some $n\%t$ clones of item $\lfloor n/t + 1 \rfloor$ (here % denotes the integer remainder operation).

- The n clones of $Z_i^t[1]$ in D_i, which is at most $\lfloor n/t+1 \rfloor$ by WEAKBAL$(t, j = 1)$, are mapped to the remaining $t - n\%t$ clones of item $\lfloor n/t+1 \rfloor$ in Z_N^t, as well as to the t clones of $\lfloor n/t+2 \rfloor$ and some lower-valued items. Overall, the $2n$ clones of 1 and $Z_i^t[1]$ in D_i are mapped to the t clones of items $1, \ldots, \lfloor 2n/t \rfloor$ as well as to some clones of $\lfloor 2n/t+1 \rfloor$ in Z_N^t.
- Similarly, for all $j \in [t-1]$, the $(j-1)n$ clones of items $1, Z_i^t[1], \ldots, Z_i^t[j-1]$ in D_i are mapped to the t clones of items $1, \ldots, \lfloor jn/t \rfloor$, as well as to some clones of $\lfloor jn/t+1 \rfloor$ in Z_N^t. By WEAKBAL(t, j) $Z_i^t[j] \leq \lfloor jn/t+1 \rfloor$, so the clones of $Z_i^t[j]$ can be mapped to the remaining clones of $\lfloor jn/t+1 \rfloor$ and to lower-valued items.

Table 4. Example for the proof of Theorem 5. Here $n = 10, t = 6$.

1	1	1	1	1	1
2	2	2	2	2	2
3	3	3	3	3	3
4	4	4	4	4	4
5	5	5	5	5	5
6	6	6	6	6	6
7	7	7	7	7	7
8	8	8	8	8	8
9	9	9	9	9	9
10	10	10	10	10	10

Z_N^t

1	1	1	1	1	1
1	1	1	1	2	2
2	2	2	2	2	2
2	2	4	4	4	4
4	4	4	4	4	4
6	6	6	6	6	6
6	6	6	6	7	7
7	7	7	7	7	7
7	7	9	9	9	9
9	9	9	9	9	9

D_i

For illustration, Table 4 shows the items in Z_N^t (left), and the items 1 and $\lfloor jn/t+1 \rfloor$ for $j \in [t-1]$ in D_i (right) for $n = 10, t = 6$. One can see that each item in the D_i table is at least as good as the item at the same location in the Z_N^t table, as required.

We proved in Sect. 4 that there is no fully-balanced sequence for $n = 12$. In contrast, we could find a weakly-fully-balanced sequence for $n = 12$ does exist; see Table 8 in Appendix A.

Corollary 1. *A perpetually ordinally PROP1 repeated assignment exists for all* $n \leq 12$.

Unfortunately, the impossibility result for a fully-balanced sequence extends to weakly-fully-balanced sequences, though for larger values of n, as shown in Table 5. The proof is in Proposition 3 in Appendix C.

7 Related Work

7.1 Fair Division

The literature on fair division is very large, with new papers appearing every several weeks. See Amanatidis et al. [2], Aziz et al. [4], Nguyen and Rothe [40],

Table 5. Values of $n = 6k + j$ with no weakly fully-balanced sequence

n	$6k$	$6k+1$	$6k+2$	$6k+3$	$6k+4$	$6k+5$
bounds on k	$k \geq 19$	$k \geq 11$	$k \geq 16$	$k \geq 12$	$k \geq 17$	$k \geq 9$
bounds on n	$n \geq 114$	$n \geq 67$	$n \geq 98$	$n \geq 75$	$n \geq 106$	$n \geq 59$

Lang and Rothe [35] for some recent surveys. Most works on fair allocation consider a one-round division, but in recent years there is a growing interest in multiple-round division. Below we present several settings that are related to ours. They are ordered by increasing difficulty—from the "easiest" ones (where strongest fairness guarantees are possible) to the "hardest" ones (where only weak fairness guarantees are possible).

Repeated Fair Assignment. This setting is most closely related to ours, as it involves a single assignment problem (of exactly one item to each player) that is repeated every day. It was recently studied by Micheel and Wilczynski [38]. They studied the computational complexity of three separate fairness notions: (a) *Mirrored envy*: if some player envies another player a certain number of times, then the latter envied them the same number of times. (b) *Equal treatment of equals*: players with the same preferences should get exactly the same final bundle. (c) *Minimizing the number of times a player is envious.*

Caragiannis and Narang [20] study a generalization of repeated fair assignment, in which the value of a player for an item may depend on the number of rounds the item was previously used by the same player. In this setting, even obtaining fairness at the last day becomes challenging, as the round-robin technique might not work. They study the run-time of computing an allocation that maximizes the sum of values ("utilitarian"), and present some special cases in which it is possible to ensure EF1 (envy-free up-to one item) at the last day.

Lim et al. [36] study the computational problem of finding a repeated allocation that maximizes the smallest utility overall, or every individual day. This is NP-hard in general, but can be solved efficiently in some special cases.

Repeated Fair Allocation. This setting is more general than ours, as it allows the number of items allocated each day to be different than the number of players, and do not require that each player receives exactly one item per day [30]. Naturally, the attainable fairness guarantees are more restricted. In particular: (a) When $n \geq 3$ and the number of days is fixed in advance (as in our setting), only last-day fairness is guaranteed, and only when the number of days is a multiple of n; there are no guarantees on fairness after each day. (b) When $n = 2$ and the number of days is fixed in advance and is even, there are repeated allocations that are envy-free after the last day, and in addition, the allocation in each individual day satisfies a weak variant of EF1. (c) When the number of rounds can be chosen by the algorithm, there are sequences that are simultaneously last-day envy-free and Pareto-efficient, and individual-day PROP1.

Cookson et al. [23] strengthen their results to *ordinal fairness*, as in our setting. They show polynomial-time algorithms that guarantee the following: (a) For $n = 2$ players: ordinal EF1 after each day, as well as in each individual day; (b) For $n \geq 3$ players: ordinal EF1 at each individual day, as well as ordinal PROP1 after the last day. They also prove that, for $n \geq 3$, ordinal EF1 after each day cannot be guaranteed even when all players have identical preferences.

In contrast to these works, we focus on the important special case of one item per player per day, and consider ordinal fairness guarantees that should hold after each day, for any n.

Temporal Fair Allocation. This setting is even more general, as it allows the number and values of items to be different in each day. The guarantees are naturally weaker; see He et al. [29], Elkind et al. [25], Cookson et al. [23]. Still, the fact that the same players participate in each daily allocation is advantageous, as it allows us to compensate players who got a low value in early days, by giving them a higher value in later days.

One-Shot Allocation. The most well-studied fair division setting involves a one-shot allocation (a single day). For this setting, there are several algorithms that attain an allocation that is *envy-free up to one item (EF1)*—a condition stronger than PROP1 [18,19,37]. These cannot be applied in our setting, as they might allocate more than one item to the same player in the same day.

One-Shot Assignment. Here, each player must receive a single item. In this setting every allocation is trivially PROP1 (and EF1), which makes these conditions uninteresting. Fairness is usually attained either by randomization or by monetary transfers; see Basteck [5] and Segal-Halevi [44] respectively for some recent surveys. In our *repeated* assignment setting, we expect to attain fair outcomes even without randomization or money.

One-Shot Allocation with Cardinality Constraints. Here, items are partitioned into pre-specified categories, and each player can receive at most a fixed number of items (called the "capacity") of each category [8,24,46]. The repeated assignment setting can be reduced to this setting: define, for each day, a category containing all items allocated at that day, with a capacity of 1. There are algorithms that guarantee EF1 (hence also PROP1), but only for specific numeric valuations. For example, the algorithm of Biswas and Barman [8], translated to our setting, works as follows: (1) Assign the items in day 1 arbitrarily. (2) In each day $t \geq 2$, order the players by ascending value, from the player with the smallest to the one with the largest total value; give item 1 to the first player in the order, item 2 to the second player, etc. Suppose that, after some day t, some player i has a smaller value than some other player j, i.e., $v(Z_i^t) < v(Z_j^t)$. Let t' be the maximum $t' < t$ in which $v(Z_i^{t'}) \geq v(Z_j^{t'})$ held. Then at day $t'+1$, player j received an item with a higher value than i, and at days $t'+2, \ldots, t$, player i received an item with an equal-or-higher value than j. Hence, if the item of day $t'+1$ is removed from j's bundle, i does not envy. Hence, the allocation is EF1.

In contrast, our aim is to guarantee *ordinal approximate fairness*—a condition that holds simultaneously for all numeric valuations consistent with the ranking. Another advantage of this approach is that our algorithms do not need to know the valuations, as they can allocate positions in a picking sequence.

Picking Sequences. The output of our algorithms can also be understood as a *picking sequence*—an order by which each player picks a favorite item from the remaining items. Picking sequences have a very low informational requirements, as players do not have to reveal their valuations—they only have to pick the best remaining item when their turn arrives [11,13,43].

Online Fair Allocation. This is the hardest setting studied, as it assumes that the items and their valuations are *not known in advance* (in contrast to temporal fair division). Each day, a new item arrives, and must be allocated immediately and irrevocably to one of the players. As the future is not known, the algorithm might make allocations that are bad in hindsight. This translates to much weaker fairness guarantees. It is not possible to guarantee PROPc for any constant c, even in the last round; such a guarantee is possible only if c grows at least like $\sqrt{t}$. See e.g.Benade et al. [6], Benadè et al. [7], Kahana and Hazon [32], He et al. [29], Neoh et al. [39], Zeng and Psomas [48], Jiang et al. [31].

Latin Squares. Kawase et al. [34] studied an allocation problem with "latin square" constraints. Their goal is not to attain proportionality, but rather to maximize the social welfare.

Acknowledgment. This work has started at the following post on Mathematics Stack Exchange: https://math.stackexchange.com/q/5014281.

Erel is funded by Israel Science Foundation grant no. 1092/24.

The proof of Proposition 3 in Appendix C was written by Aristotle [1] and verified manually by the authors.

Disclosure of Interests. The authors have no competing interests to declare that are relevant to the content of this article.

References

1. Achim, T., e al.: Aristotle: Imo-level automated theorem proving (2025). https://arxiv.org/abs/2510.01346
2. Amanatidis, G., Birmpas, G., Filos-Ratsikas, A., Voudouris, A.A.: Fair division of indivisible goods: A survey. arXiv preprint arXiv:2202.07551 (2022)
3. Aziz, H., Gaspers, S., MacKenzie, S., Walsh, T.: Fair assignment of indivisible objects under ordinal preferences. Artif. Intell. **227**, 71–92 (2015). arXiv:1312.6546
4. Aziz, H., Li, B., Moulin, H., Wu, X.: Algorithmic fair allocation of indivisible items: A survey and new questions. ACM SIGecom Exchanges **20**(1), 24–40 (2022)
5. Basteck, C.: Fair solutions to the random assignment problem. J. Math. Econ. **79**, 163–172 (2018)

6. Benade, G., Kazachkov, A.M., Procaccia, A.D., Psomas, C.A.: How to make envy vanish over time. In: Proceedings of the 2018 ACM Conference on Economics and Computation, pp. 593–610, EC '18, Association for Computing Machinery, Ithaca, NY, USA (2018). ISBN: 978-1-4503-5829-3
7. Benadè, G., Kazachkov, A.M., Procaccia, A.D., Psomas, A., Zeng, D.: Fair and efficient online allocations. Oper. Res. **72**(4), 1438–1452 (2024). ISSN 0030-364X
8. Biswas, A., Barman, S.: Fair division under cardinality constraints. In: Proceedings of the 27th International Joint Conference on Artificial Intelligence, pp. 91–97 (2018)
9. Bolzano, B.: Rein analytischer Beweis des Lehrsatzes, das zwischen je zwey Werthen, die ein entgegengesetzes Resultat gewähren, wenigstens eine reelle Wurzel der Gleichung liege, (1817). gedruckt bei Gottlieb Haase
10. Bouveret, S., Endriss, U., Lang, J.: Fair division under ordinal preferences: Computing envy-free allocations of indivisible goods. In: Proceedings of the 2010 Conference on ECAI 2010: 19th European Conference on Artificial Intelligence, pp. 387–392, IOS Press, NLD (2010). ISBN: 978-1-60750-605-8
11. Bouveret, S., Lang, J.: A general elicitation-free protocol for allocating indivisible goods. In: IJCAI 2011 (2011)
12. Bouveret, S., Lemaître, M.: Characterizing conflicts in fair division of indivisible goods using a scale of criteria. Auton. Agent. Multi-Agent Syst. **30**(2), 259–290 (2016)
13. Brams, S.J., Kaplan, T.R.: Dividing the indivisible. J. Theor. Polit. **16**(2), 143 (2004)
14. Brams, S.J., Kilgour, D.M., Klamler, C.: Two-person fair division of indivisible items when envy-freeness is impossible. In: Operations Research Forum, vol. 3, p. 24, Springer, Cham (2022)
15. Brams, S.J., Kilgour, D.M., Klamler, C.: Fair division of indivisible items: Envy-freeness vs. efficiency revisited. Games **17**(1), 4 (2026)
16. Brams, S.J., Taylor, A.D.: Fair Division: From cake-cutting to dispute resolution, Cambridge University Press (1996)
17. Bu, X., Li, Z., Liu, S., Song, J., Tao, B.: Fair division with allocator's preference. In: International Conference on Web and Internet Economics (WINE 2023), pp. 77–94 (2023)
18. Budish, E.: The combinatorial assignment problem: Approximate competitive equilibrium from equal incomes. J. Polit. Econ. **119**(6), 1061–1103 (2011)
19. Caragiannis, I., Kurokawa, D., Moulin, H., Procaccia, A.D., Shah, N., Wang, J.: The unreasonable fairness of maximum nash welfare. ACM Trans. Econ. Comput. (TEAC) **7**(3), 1–32 (2019)
20. Caragiannis, I., Narang, S.: Repeatedly matching items to agents fairly and efficiently. Theoret. Comput. Sci. **981** (2024). ISSN 0304-3975, arXiv:2207.01589
21. Chakraborty, M., Igarashi, A., Suksompong, W., Zick, Y.: Weighted envy-freeness in indivisible item allocation. ACM Trans. Econ. Comput. **9**(3), 1–39 (2021)
22. Conitzer, V., Freeman, R., Shah, N.: Fair public decision making. In: Proceedings of the 2017 ACM Conference on Economics and Computation, pp. 629–646 (2017)
23. Cookson, B., Ebadian, S., Shah, N.: Temporal fair division. In: Proceedings of the AAAI Conference on Artificial Intelligence, Vol. 39, no. (13), pp. 13727–13734 (2025). ISSN: 2374-3468
24. Dror, A., Feldman, M., Segal-Halevi, E.: On fair division under heterogeneous matroid constraints. J. Artif. Intell. Res. **76**, 567–611 (2023)
25. Elkind, E., Lam, A., Latifian, M., Neoh, T.Y., Teh, N.: Temporal fair division of indivisible items (2024). to appear in the Proceedings of AAMAS 2025

26. Euler, R.: On the completability of incomplete latin squares. Eur. J. Combinatorics **31**(2), 535–552 (2010). ISSN: 0195-6698, combinatorics and Geometry
27. Gourvès, L., Lesca, J., Wilczynski, A.: On Fairness via Picking Sequences in Allocation of Indivisible Goods. In: Fotakis, D., Ríos Insua, D. (eds.) ADT 2021. LNCS (LNAI), vol. 13023, pp. 258–272. Springer, Cham (2021). https://doi.org/10.1007/978-3-030-87756-9_17
28. Hall, M.: An existence theorem for latin squares. Bull. Am. Math. Soc. **51**(6), 387–388 (1945)
29. He, J., Procaccia, A.D., Psomas, A., Zeng, D.: Achieving a fairer future by changing the past. In: Proceedings of the Twenty-Eighth International Joint Conference on Artificial Intelligence, IJCAI 2019, pp. 343–349, Macao, China (2019). ISBN: 978-0-9992411-4-1
30. Igarashi, A., Lackner, M., Nardi, O., Novaro, A.: Repeated fair allocation of indivisible items. In: Proceedings of the AAAI Conference on Artificial Intelligence, Vol. 38, no. (9), pp. 9781–9789 (2024). ISSN: 2374-3468, arXiv:2304.01644
31. Jiang, H., Kulkarni, J., Singla, S.: Online geometric discrepancy for stochastic arrivals with applications to envy minimization (2019)
32. Kahana, I., Hazon, N.: The leximin approach for a sequence of collective decisions. In: ECAI 2023, pp. 1198–1206, Frontiers in Artificial Intelligence and Applications, IOS Press (2023). ISBN 978-1-64368-436-9, arXiv:2305.18024
33. Kahana, I., Segal-Halevi, E., Hazon, N.: Perpetual fully-online approximate fairness. arXiv preprint arXiv:2605.19844 (2026)
34. Kawase, Y., Roy, B., Sanpui, M.A.: Resource allocation under the latin square constraint (2025)
35. Lang, J., Rothe, J.: Fair division of indivisible goods. In: Economics and Computation: An Introduction to Algorithmic Game Theory, Computational Social Choice, and Fair Division, pp. 605–680, Springer, Cham (2024). https://doi.org/10.1007/978-3-662-47904-9_8
36. Lim, E., Neoh, T.Y., Teh, N.: Fairness in repeated matching: A maximin perspective. In: Proceedings of the AAAI Conference on Artificial Intelligence, pp. 17111–17119 (2026)
37. Lipton, R.J., Markakis, E., Mossel, E., Saberi, A.: On approximately fair allocations of indivisible goods. In: Proceedings of the 5th ACM Conference on Electronic Commerce - EC '04, p. 125 (2004). ISBN: 1-58113-771-0
38. Micheel, K.J., Wilczynski, A.: Fairness in repeated house allocation. In: 27th European Conference on Artificial Intelligence (ECAI 2024), Frontiers in Artificial Intelligence and Applications, IOS Press (2024). ISBN: 978-1-64368-548-9
39. Neoh, T.Y., Peters, J., Teh, N.: Online fair division with additional information (2025)
40. Nguyen, T.T., Rothe, J.: Complexity results and exact algorithms for fair division of indivisible items: a survey. In: Proceedings of the Thirty-Second International Joint Conference on Artificial Intelligence, pp. 6732–6740 (2023)
41. Pruhs, K., Woeginger, G.J.: Divorcing Made Easy. In: Kranakis, E., Krizanc, D., Luccio, F. (eds.) FUN 2012. LNCS, vol. 7288, pp. 305–314. Springer, Heidelberg (2012). https://doi.org/10.1007/978-3-642-30347-0_30
42. Robertson, J., Webb, W.: Cake-cutting algorithms: Be fair if you can, AK Peters/CRC Press (1998)
43. Segal-Halevi, E.: Competitive equilibrium for almost all incomes: existence and fairness. Auton. Agents Multi-Agent Syst. **34**(1), 26 (2020). ISSN: 1573-7454, arXiv:1705.04212

44. Segal-Halevi, E.: Generalized rental harmony. Am. Math. Mon. **129**(5), 403–414 (2022)
45. Segal-Halevi, E., Hassidim, A., Aziz, H.: Fair allocation with diminishing differences. J. Artif. Intell. Res. **67**, 471–507 (2020)
46. Shoshan, H., Hazon, N., Segal-Halevi, E.: Efficient nearly-fair division with capacity constraints. In: Proceedings of the 2023 International Conference on Autonomous Agents and Multiagent Systems, pp. 206–214 (2023)
47. Steinhaus, H.: The problem of fair division. Econometrica **16**, 101–104 (1948)
48. Zeng, D., Psomas, A.: Fairness-efficiency tradeoffs in dynamic fair division. In: Proceedings of the 21st ACM Conference on Economics and Computation, pp. 911–912, EC '20, Association for Computing Machinery, Virtual Event, Hungary (2020). ISBN: 978-1-4503-7975-5, arXiv:1907.11672

On the Power of Deception in Repeated Games

Saba Ahmadi, Avrim Blum, Dimitar Chakarov, and Melissa Dutz(✉)

Toyota Technological Institute at Chicago, Chicago, USA
{saba,avrim,chakarov,melissa}@ttic.edu

Abstract. In repeated games, opponents often predict what we'll do next by looking at what we have done so far. This allows us to deceive them: we can deliberately behave one way for a period of time to shape their expectations, then switch strategies to profit from the induced response. We study deception in repeated two-player normal-form games against *count-based* learners, whose behavior depends only on how often we have played each action in the past. We formalize deceptive and non-deceptive play, and introduce the notion of a *deception bonus*, the payoff gain of the best deceptive strategy over the best fixed mixed strategy. We establish structural results on deception in general-sum games. We design exact dynamic programs for optimizing against any count-based learner when the action space or opponent's memory is small, and develop approximation algorithms for settings where the opponent's memory or the time horizon is large. We also provide an approximation algorithm for learning to deceive an opponent whose count-based learning rule is unknown. To complement our algorithmic results, we show that approximating the optimal deceptive payoff against the classic Empirical Risk Minimization (ERM) learning rule is NP-hard, including obtaining any constant-factor approximation or even a T^{α}-additive approximation for any $0 < \alpha < 1$. Finally, we empirically measure the deception bonus in random games with i.i.d. payoffs.

Keywords: Strategic Deception · Repeated Games · Learning in Games · Stackelberg Equilibrium

1 Introduction

In this paper, we propose and explore a game-theoretic model of *deception*, and consider the power of deceptive play in repeated, normal-form, two-player games. What constitutes deceptive play? To deceive someone is to cause them to believe something which is untrue, so to study *deceiving* an opponent requires some model of what the opponent "believes." Here, we model the opponent as believing our past play is predictive of our future play: we study deceiving "count-based" learners, whose behavior is a function of the empirical counts (i.e. empirical distribution) of our past actions. We have a special focus on opponents who use the classic Empirical Risk Minimization algorithm (and a limited-memory

P. Lenzner and D. Schmand (Eds.): SAGT 2026, LNCS 16911, pp. 19–38, 2027.
https://doi.org/10.1007/978-3-032-38782-0_2

variant). Empirical Risk Minimization (ERM) is widely used in settings where one believes the world is stochastic. Using ERM, the opponent plays the action which would have achieved the highest cumulative payoff against our past actions. This models an opponent who believes our next action will be drawn from the empirical distribution of our historical actions (ERM is an optimal strategy in that case). ERM is also known as "Follow-the-Leader" in strategic games; we refer to it as ERM here to reflect the opponent's incorrect belief in the stochasticity of the interaction. A deceptive player could take advantage of ERM by playing a strategic sequence of actions to effectively lure their opponent into playing a favorable action, in order to then deviate from the opponent's expectations and reap a big payoff. In practice, for example, this could capture the behavior of a "pool shark": someone who pretends to be unskilled at pool by playing poorly in order to lure an opponent into playing for money, then surprises their opponent by playing well and winning the money.

In this setting, we ask, how can the deceptive player—who we refer to as "the optimizer"—achieve the highest possible payoff? How much does the optimizer stand to gain by deception over what can be gained by "non-deceptive" play? This raises the question of what, in general, constitutes "non-deceptive" play.

Announcing which action one will play next would certainly be transparent. But this clearly leaves one open to exploitation; in many zero-sum games, for example, the only minimax optimal strategies are mixed. What about announcing a mixed strategy? Randomization does serve to "hide" what one will do; is this deceptive? Previous works often model deception as randomization; for example, randomization is used to model bluffing in the Kuhn poker model [17]. In this work, however, we will consider using randomization to be simply a form of unpredictability, and not deceptive in and of itself. We define our non-deceptive benchmark to be the maximum payoff one could achieve by announcing and playing according to a fixed mixed strategy. In particular, playing a minimax-optimal strategy is *not* deceptive in our model.

1.1 Our Contributions

In the real world, deception often unfolds over time, initially building up trust or shaping expectations to lure someone into a vulnerable position, and then taking advantage. We introduce a new model of deception which aims to capture this kind of multi-stage deception. By contrast, existing works tend to model deception as a one-shot use of randomization (as mentioned above, bluffing in Kuhn poker is an example of this).

We also introduce a new notion of non-deceptive play and a "deception bonus," which measures the additional payoff deceptive play could garner over non-deceptive play.

We begin by establishing structural results for deception in general-sum games. We then design dynamic programming algorithms for exactly optimizing against any count-based learner when the game or the opponent's memory is small, as well as approximation algorithms for memory-limited count-based learners when the opponent's memory or the number of rounds is large. We also provide an algorithm for learning to approximately optimize against an opponent whose specific count-based learning rule is unknown. Complementing our algorithmic results, we show that approximating the optimal payoff against ERM even in zero-sum games is NP-hard, improving on results of [2]. Finally, we measure the deception bonus in random zero- and general-sum games.

1.2 Related Work

Optimizing Against Bounded Players. [13] studied playing against computationally bounded players whose strategies must be realizable by finite automata or polynomial-time Turing machines. They showed that for the games Prisoner's Dilemma and Matching Pennies, there exist dominant strategies for playing against a polynomial-time opponent. [14] extended this line of work by giving a polynomial-time algorithm to learn approximately optimal play against any finite automaton with probabilistic state transitions. Building on that, they further established that if transitions of the (probabilistic state) automaton can be randomized, finding an approximately optimal strategy is PSPACE-complete.

Optimizing against Online Learners. Recent work has established computational hardness for optimizing against opponents who use specific online learning algorithms. [2] show that optimizing against ERM is computationally intractable in general-sum games. In contrast, our hardness result from Sect. 7 shows that the problem is hard even for zero-sum games, and further establishes hardness of approximation up to additive T^{α} for $0 < \alpha < 1$. A complementary line of work [7,8,12,18] studies how to optimize against no-regret online learners. In particular, [12] show that in general-sum games, the optimizer can gain higher cumulative utility when strategizing against a no-regret learner compared to the Stackelberg equilibrium utility. In other words, [12] show that a deception bonus exists in games where the opponent has more than two actions and is playing a certain kind of no-regret strategy which limits the probability mass on actions that would have performed sufficiently sub-optimally in hindsight (also known as a "mean-based" strategy). In contrast, [18] characterize the class of learning algorithms that limit the optimizer's payoff to at most the Stackelberg value. That is, they study the class of learning rules that permit no deception bonus.

Other Notions of Deception. Previous works study deception in Stackelberg games, where the follower misreports their type [15] or commits to a fake payoff matrix [19,20] in order to elicit a specific response from the leader. Later works explore how the follower can optimally deceive a learning leader [6] or learn a good deceptive payoff matrix [11]. In hidden-role games [1,9], where players are assigned private team roles and have to recognize and cooperate with their own team members, deception arises in choosing what information to reveal to the other players. In contrast to these notions where deception involves commitment to false information or concealment of private information, our work models deception over time by capturing how a player can strategically choose a sequence of actions to manipulate and exploit the opponent's learning algorithm.

In a different direction, [5] investigated diversified strategies that protect against deceptive play by bounding the maximal probability of a single action.

2 Model

We consider a repeated normal-form game with two players—A (the optimizer) and B (the opponent)—played for T rounds. The optimizer A has k_A actions $\mathcal{A} = \{a_1, \ldots, a_{k_A}\}$ and the opponent B has k_B actions $\mathcal{B} = \{b_1, \ldots, b_{k_B}\}$. Let $u^A, u^B : \mathcal{A} \times \mathcal{B} \to \mathbb{R}$ be the utility functions of A and B, respectively. Notice that utility is a function of a single pair of actions, i.e. each player receives utility once per round.

Definition 1. (Expected payoff for player A). *For $a \in \mathcal{A}$ and $\beta \in \Delta(\mathcal{B})$ (where $\Delta(\mathcal{B})$ denotes the set of mixed actions available to player B), the* expected payoff *for player A is*

$$\bar{u}^A(a, \beta) \triangleq \mathop{\mathbb{E}}_{b \sim \beta}\left[u^A(a, b)\right] = \sum_{j=1}^{k_B} \beta(b_j) u^A(a, b_j).$$

2.1 Opponent Strategies

Throughout the paper, we focus on deceiving opponents who use *count-based* learning rules.

Definition 2 (Count-based learning rule). *A count-based learning rule for the opponent, player B, is a function $f : \mathbb{N}^{k_A} \to \Delta(\mathcal{B})$ that maps counts $c_1 \ldots c_{k_A}$, where c_i is the number of times A has played action a_i, to a mixed strategy over the action space $\mathcal{B}$. When f outputs pure strategies, we write $f : \mathbb{N}^{k_A} \to \mathcal{B}$. At the beginning of round t, if the opponent has limited memory length m, c_i is the number of times A played a_i in the last m rounds, and $\sum_{i \in [k_A]} c_i = \min(m, t-1)$. Otherwise, $\sum_{i \in [k_A]} c_i = t - 1$.*

While a count-based learning rule does not depend on the time-order of actions in the sense that the mixed action it plays is a function only of the action counts, by convention, we also write $f([a_1, \ldots, a_t])$ to denote the mixed strategy obtained by applying f to the counts induced by the action sequence $[a_1, \ldots, a_t]$. For limited-memory count-based learning rules, access to the sequence is used exclusively to maintain accurate action counts over a sliding window of the past m rounds: at each time step, the opponent must know which action was played m steps ago in order to know which count to decrement next. The strategy itself remains a function only of the action counts.

Remark 1. For a given count-based learning rule, we assume in our algorithmic results that we can compute its output given historical counts in $O(k_A k_B)$ time. This allows constant-time computations involving all k_A counts for each of the opponent's k_B actions. If a given count-based algorithm can be computed faster or requires more time, this factor would change accordingly in our runtimes.

For our structural and hardness results, we focus on the Empirical Risk Minimization (ERM) learning rule and its memory-limited variant, which are both contained in the class of count-based learning rules.

Definition 3. (Empirical Risk Minimization, ERM). *At time step t, the learning rule* Empirical Risk Minimization $\mathsf{ERM} : \mathcal{A}^{t-1} \to \mathcal{B}$ *outputs the action in $\mathcal{B}$ that achieves the best cumulative utility in hindsight, so*

$$\mathsf{ERM}([a_1, \ldots, a_{t-1}]) = \arg\max_{b \in \mathcal{B}} \sum_{i=1}^{t-1} u^B(a_i, b),$$

with ties broken deterministically according to a fixed order (e.g. lexicographically). Because ERM *does not use the time-order of the actions in its input, we also use $\mathsf{ERM}(c_1, \ldots, c_{k_A}) = \arg\max_{b \in \mathcal{B}} \sum_{i=1}^{k_A} c_i \cdot u^B(a_i, b)$, where c_i is the number of times action $a_i \in \mathcal{A}$ was used by player A in the last $t = \sum_{i=1}^{k_A} c_i$ steps.*

Definition 4. (Limited-memory Empirical Risk Minimization, ERM_m). *At time step t, the learning rule* Empirical Risk Minimization with memory m $\mathsf{ERM}_m : \mathcal{A}^{\min(m,t-1)} \to \mathcal{B}$ *outputs the action in $\mathcal{B}$ that achieves the best cumulative utility over the last m actions of A, so*

$$\mathsf{ERM}_m([a_{\max(1,t-m)}, \ldots, a_{t-1}]) = \arg\max_{b \in \mathcal{B}} \sum_{i=\max(1,t-m)}^{t-1} u^B(a_i, b).$$

Similarly to Definition 3, we use

$$\mathsf{ERM}_m(c_1, \ldots, c_{k_A}) = \arg\max_{b \in \mathcal{B}} \sum_{i=1}^{k_A} c_i u^B(a_i, b)$$

for $\sum_{i=1}^{k_A} c_i \leq m$.

When discussing ERM and ERM_m, it will be helpful to refer to the *score* of an action, defined below.

Definition 5 (Score of an action or column). *The* score *of an action $b \in \mathcal{B}$ for player B given that player A has played the sequence $a_1, \ldots, a_t$ is $\sum_{i=1}^{t} u^B(a_i, b)$, where $t \leq m$ when the opponent has memory limit m. Using this definition, an opponent playing* ERM *or* ERM_m *selects the action which has the maximum score. When working with a payoff matrix, since player B is the column player, we also refer to the score of an action as the score of a column.*

2.2 Deception and the Non-deceptive Benchmark

Definition 6 (Non-deceptive play). *Playing according to a fixed, publicly-known mixed strategy.*

By this definition of non-deceptive play, the best non-deceptive strategy would be the Stackelberg leader strategy, the utility-maximizing mixed strategy against the best response of player B. We refer to any additional payoff a player could achieve against a particular opponent in a given game compared to the best non-deceptive strategy (i.e., a Stackelberg leader strategy) as the *deception bonus.*

Definition 7 (Deception bonus). *Let* $\mathbf{a}$ *be player* A*'s Stackelberg leader strategy, i.e. a utility-maximizing mixed strategy against the best response of player* B*. Let* $\mathbf{b} = \arg\max_{b \in \mathcal{B}} \mathbb{E}_{a' \sim \mathbf{a}}\left[u^B(a', b)\right]$ *be the best response of player* B*. Then the* deception bonus *of using an optimal sequence of actions as opposed to* $\mathbf{a}$ *is*

$$\left[\max_{\{a_t\}_{t=1}^T} \sum_{t=1}^{T} \bar{u}^A(a_t, b_t)\right] - T \cdot E_{a' \sim \mathbf{a}}\left[u^A(a', \mathbf{b})\right],$$

where b_t *is the mixed action of player* B *at time* t.

In Definition 7, if player B implements ERM, then $b_t = \mathsf{ERM}([a_1, \ldots, a_{t-1}])$, and if player B implements ERM_m, then $b_t = \mathsf{ERM}_m([a_{\max(1,t-m)}, \ldots, a_{t-1}])$. Note that in the limit as $T \to \infty$, for any game whose payoffs are fixed (i.e. not dependent on T), if player A played a fixed mixed strategy without announcing it in advance, ERM would be best responding.

3 Structural Properties of Deception

We begin with structural results about the existence of deception and size of the deception bonus. In this section, we consider exclusively opponents who use ERM as their learning algorithm. The rows of each game matrix correspond to the optimizer's actions, and columns correspond to the opponent's actions. We assume the opponent breaks ties between actions (columns) by choosing the leftmost tied column. Each game is played for T rounds.

Table 1. Game with arbitrarily large deception bonus.

	a	b	c
a	$(-1, 1)$	$(1, -1)$	$(0, \frac{\varepsilon}{T})$
b	$(1, -1)$	$(-1, 1)$	$(0, \frac{\varepsilon}{T})$
c	$(0, 0)$	$(0, 0)$	$(B, -B)$

Proposition 1. *The deception bonus can be arbitrarily large.*

Proof. Consider the game shown in Table 1. If a appears more than b in the optimizer's history, the opponent will play a, and vice versa. If the history includes only a and b an equal number of times, the opponent will play c, and the optimizer can also play c to get a payoff of B, where B is some arbitrarily large number. Playing b, a, c followed by best responding in the remaining $T-3$ rounds, the optimizer (row player) achieves a utility of at least $(T-1)+B$. On the other hand, the Stackelberg leader strategy is to put equal probability on a and b, and a small enough probability p_c on c such that c is a best response for the column player; in particular, $p_c = \frac{\varepsilon}{\varepsilon+BT}$. The expected utility of the Stackelberg leader strategy over T rounds is $p_c \cdot B \cdot T = \frac{\varepsilon \cdot B \cdot T}{\varepsilon+BT}$ which approaches ε as $B, T \to \infty$.

Table 2. Game where the deception bonus is $\Omega(T)$, even when payoffs are bounded by a constant.

	a	b	c
a	$(-1,1)$	$(1,-1)$	$(0,\frac{\varepsilon}{T})$
b	$(1,-1)$	$(-1,1)$	$(0,\frac{\varepsilon}{T})$

Proposition 2. *The deception bonus can be $\Omega(T)$ even when payoffs are bounded by a constant.*

Proof. Consider the game shown in Table 2. In this game, the Stackelberg leader strategy for the row player is to play a and b with probability $1/2$ each, resulting in an expected overall payoff of 0. However, if the optimizer (row player) plays $baba\ldots$, then ERM will play $abcbc\ldots$, with bc repeating indefinitely, resulting in $\Omega(T)$ utility for the optimizer.

Table 3. Game with no deception bonus.

	a	b
a	(0, 1)	(10, 0)
b	(1, 1)	(0, 0)

Proposition 3. *There exist games with no deception bonus.*

Proof. Consider the game in Table 3. Action a is strictly dominant for the opponent. Hence, regardless of the optimizer's action history, the opponent plays a. Therefore, the optimizer cannot benefit from deviating from playing the best response to a (b), which is also the Stackelberg leader strategy.

Table 4. Game where best-responding in every round does not yield the optimal utility for the optimizer (row player).

	a	b
a	$(0,0)$	$(0,1)$
b	$(1,1+\frac{\varepsilon}{T})$	$(B,0)$

Proposition 4. *There exist games where myopically best-responding to the opponent's next action does not yield optimal (or near-optimal) utility.*

Proof. Consider the game in Table 4. Let B be arbitrarily large. If the optimizer best-responds to the adversary's next move, the optimizer never plays action a: a has 0 payoff no matter what the opponent plays, while b always has a positive payoff. Playing action b every round gives the optimizer a payoff of 1 per round. However, if the optimizer plays $ababab...$, they get 0 in each round they play a and B in each round they play b. Therefore, the optimizer needs to plan ahead to get the optimal (or even near-optimal) utility.

In Proposition 4, although myopically best-responding to the opponent's next action was not sufficient to achieve the optimal payoff, there was a small cycle (ab) which was. It is natural to wonder whether one could always do at least nearly optimally by repeatedly playing some small cycle, a cycle with length polynomial in the number of actions and payoff values. Proposition 5 shows that this is not always possible.

Table 5. Game where no small cyclical strategy gives optimal utility.

	P_{12}	P_{21}	$\cdots$	P_{1k}	P_{k1}	Done
P_1	$(0,p_1)$	$(0,-p_1)$	$\cdots$	$(0,p_1)$	$(0,-p_1)$	$(0,\frac{\varepsilon}{T})$
P_2	$(0,-p_2)$	$(0,p_2)$	$(0,0)$	$(0,0)$	$(0,0)$	$(0,\frac{\varepsilon}{T})$
$\vdots$	$(0,0)$	$(0,0)$	$\ddots$	$(0,0)$	$(0,0)$	$(0,\frac{\varepsilon}{T})$
P_k	$(0,0)$	$(0,0)$	$(0,0)$	$(0,-p_k)$	$(0,p_k)$	$(0,\frac{\varepsilon}{T})$
Done	$(0,0)$	$(0,0)$	$(0,0)$	$(0,0)$	$(0,0)$	$(B,-B)$

Proposition 5. *There exist games where no small (i.e., polynomial in the number of actions and the payoff values) repeating cycle of actions can achieve any positive-factor multiplicative approximation or fixed-error additive approximation of the optimal payoff.*

Proof. Consider the game shown in Table 5 for some $k \geq 2$. For each $i \in \{2,\ldots,k\}$, row P_i has corresponding columns P_{1i} and P_{i1}; row P_1 has entries

$(0, p_1)$ and $(0, -p_1)$ in these columns, respectively, and has entry $(0, \frac{\varepsilon}{T})$ in column Done. Each other row P_i has entry $(0, -p_i)$ in column P_{1i}, $(0, p_i)$ in column P_{i1}, $(0, \frac{\varepsilon}{T})$ in column Done, and $(0, 0)$ elsewhere. All other entries are as shown. Let $p_1, \ldots, p_k$ be distinct primes, let $\varepsilon \in (0, 1)$, and let $B > 1$ be arbitrarily large.

The optimizer's payoff is 0 at every entry except at (Done, Done), where it is B, so any strategy obtaining a positive-factor multiplicative or additive-C approximation must, for $B > C$, induce the opponent to play Done.

Let t denote the current round. The opponent plays Done if and only if $t > 1$, all columns besides Done have score 0, and Done has not been played before. When $t = 1$, all columns have score 0 so the opponent plays the leftmost action P_{12}. When $t > 1$, if Done has not been played before, the Done column has score $(t-1) \cdot \frac{\varepsilon}{T} > 0$, so if all other columns have score 0, the opponent will play Done. Suppose in this case another column P_{ij} has a nonzero score. If P_{ij} has a positive score, it must be ≥ 1 because it is a difference of integers. There are T rounds total, so the Done column will always have a score $\leq \varepsilon < 1$, and the opponent would prefer P_{ij} over Done. If P_{ij} has a negative score, its paired column P_{ji} must have a positive score, so the reasoning above holds for P_{ji}. When $t > 1$ and all non-Done columns have score 0, but Done has been played before, the opponent will not play Done as it has score $< -B + \varepsilon < 0$.

In order to zero out every column P_{ij} while playing at least one non-Done action, P_1 must be played some number of times such that its contribution to each column's score is a common multiple of $p_2, p_3, \ldots, p_k$. Because they are all primes, P_1 must therefore be played at least $\prod_{j=2}^{k} p_j$ times. Then, to cancel out the score in each column from playing P_1, each other action P_i must be played at least $\frac{\prod_{j=1}^{k} p_j}{p_i}$ times. If we play each action exactly the number of times specified above, we can see that each column will have a score of $\prod_{j=1}^{k} p_j - \prod_{j=1}^{k} p_j = 0$. After this sequence, the opponent will play Done as its score is positive. The minimum number of rounds required to induce Done is therefore $1 + \sum_{i=1}^{k} \frac{\prod_{j=1}^{k} p_j}{p_i}$.[1]

Interestingly, in contrast to Proposition 5, in Sect. 5.1 we are able to develop a constant-factor approximation against the memory-limited learning rule ERM_m using a small repeating cycle.

4 Exact Dynamic Programs for Count-Based Learners

In this section, we give exact dynamic programs for finding a sequence that maximizes player A's expected cumulative payoff against any count-based learning rule f or its memory-limited variant f_m. For count-based learners, we focus on games where the number of actions is small; for memory-limited

[1] For example, for $k = 4$, $(p_1, p_2, p_3, p_4) = (11, 13, 17, 19)$, and any $B > 1$, 12,901 rounds are required, despite the small action space and payoff values.

variants, we focus on small m. Later, for large m, we give an approximation algorithm in Sect. 5.1. All expectations are over the learner's internal randomness, conditioned on player A's chosen sequence. Because the learner's mixed action at round t depends only on the history, it suffices to maximize $\sum_{t=1}^{T} \bar{u}^A(a_t, f([a_1, \dots, a_{t-1}]))$ over player A's action sequence $a_1, \dots, a_T$. Proofs appear in the full version.

4.1 DP for Count-Based Learners

We propose an exact dynamic programming algorithm with runtime $O(k_A{}^2 k_B T^{k_A})$. Let $V[c_1, \dots, c_{k_A}]$ store the maximum expected cumulative utility for player A over $t = \sum_i c_i$ rounds, given that player A played each action a_i exactly c_i times. The table has $O(T^{k_A})$ entries.

We initialize the table for each entry where the sum of the counts is 1 (corresponding to $t = 1$):

$$V[0, \dots, c_i = 1, \dots, 0] = \bar{u}^A(a_i, f(0, \dots, 0)) \tag{1}$$

This is the expected utility of playing action a_i against whichever mixed action the count-based learning rule f chooses when there are no actions that have been played before.

Next, we fill all entries whose counts sum to t, starting from $t = 2$ and going in ascending order to $t = T$, so that $t = \sum_{i=1}^{k_A} c_i$ and

$$V[c_1, \dots, c_{k_A}] = \max_{i \in [k_A]: c_i \geq 1} \Big[V[c_1, \dots, c_i - 1, \dots, c_{k_A}] + \bar{u}^A(a_i, f(c_1, \dots, c_i - 1, \dots, c_{k_A})) \Big] \tag{2}$$

The optimal overall expected utility for player A is the maximum entry in V where the sum of all counts adds up to T.

Theorem 1. *The Dynamic Program (Eq. 2) computes the maximum expected cumulative payoff for player A when playing against a count-based learner in time $O(k_A{}^2 k_B T^{k_A})$. We recover the optimal sequence via an auxiliary array that stores a sequence, which achieves the payoff in $V[c_1, \dots, c_{k_A}]$.*

4.2 DP for Memory-Limited Count-Based Learners

We give an analogous dynamic programming algorithm to find the maximum expected cumulative payoff for player A when playing against a memory-limited count-based learning rule f_m with runtime $O(k_A{}^{m+2} k_B T)$. We use a table V parametrized by the time step t and the last $\min(m, t)$ actions played by player A.

We initialize V for each action $a_i \in \mathcal{A}$ at time $t = 1$ as follows:

$$V[1, [a_i]] = \bar{u}^A(a_i, f_m([\emptyset])) \tag{3}$$

This is the expected utility of playing action a_i against the mixed action chosen by the learning rule f_m when no actions have been played before.

Next, for $t \leq m$ we use the update rule:

$$V[t, [a_1, \ldots, a_t]] = V[t-1, [a_1, \ldots, a_{t-1}]] + \bar{u}^A(a_t, f_m([a_1, \ldots, a_{t-1}])) \quad (4)$$

While, for $t > m$ the state $[a_1, ..., a_m]$ denotes the last m actions of player A, ordered from least to most recent, and we use the update rule:

$$V[t, [a_1, \ldots, a_m]] = \max_{a \in \mathcal{A}} \Big[V[t-1, [a, a_1, \ldots, a_{m-1}]] + \bar{u}^A(a_m, f_m([a, a_1, \ldots, a_{m-1}])) \Big] \quad (5)$$

The optimal expected cumulative utility for player A is in the maximum entry of V where $t = T$.

Theorem 2. *The Dynamic Program in Eq. 5 computes the maximum expected cumulative payoff for player A against a memory-limited count-based learner in time* $O({k_A}^{m+2} k_B T)$. *We recover the optimal sequence via an auxiliary array that stores a sequence, which achieves the payoff in* $V[t, [a_1, \ldots, a_m]]$.

5 Approximation Algorithms for Memory-Limited Count-Based Learners

The exact algorithm presented previously for memory-limited count-based learners is practical when m is small and T is not too large. In this section, we develop three approximation algorithms for memory-limited count-based learners when m is large, or when m is small but T is very large. All three algorithms assume that player A's payoffs lie in $[0, H]$. Their guarantees and use cases are summarized in Table 6, alongside the previous exact result for comparison.

5.1 1/2-Approximation Algorithm

We propose an algorithm (Algorithm 1) with runtime $O(k_B k_A^3 (m + 2k_A)^{2k_A})$ that guarantees at least half of player A's optimal expected cumulative payoff. We assume $m < T$; otherwise, one can use Eq. 2 directly. Proofs appear in the full version.

The algorithm partitions the horizon into blocks of length m (the last block has length $p = T \bmod m$). The key observation is that A gets at least half of OPT in either the odd- or even-numbered blocks, so optimizing each and taking the better yields a 1/2-approximation. The algorithm requires three subsequences of actions: S_m, a sequence maximizing A's expected payoff over the first m time steps (computed with Eq. 2); S_{2m}, a sequence of length $2m$ maximizing A's expected payoff in the last m time steps; and S_{m+p}, a sequence of length $m + p$ maximizing A's expected payoff in the last p time steps. Below we give a Dynamic Program for computing S_{2m} and S_{m+p}. We leave it as an open question whether a better approximation factor can be achieved in time polynomial in m.

Table 6. Summary of algorithmic results for memory-limited count-based learners. The first row summarizes the previous exact result, while the remaining rows summarize the approximation results from this section. ALG denotes the cumulative expected payoff achieved by the corresponding algorithm for player A, and OPT is the best cumulative expected payoff that can be achieved by player A. Both expectations are over the opponent's internal randomness. ε is a tunable accuracy parameter.

Result	Guarantee	Running Time	Use Case
Thm. 2	$\mathsf{ALG} = \mathsf{OPT}$	$O(()\, {k_A}^{m+2} k_B T)$	m small, T not too large
Thm. 4	$\mathsf{ALG} \geq \mathsf{OPT}/2$	$O(()\, k_B k_A^3 (m + 2k_A)^{2k_A})$	m large
Thm. 5	$\mathsf{ALG} \geq (1-\varepsilon)(\mathsf{OPT} - mH)$	$O(()\, k_A^{\lceil m/\varepsilon \rceil + 1} k_B \lceil m/\varepsilon \rceil)$	m very small, T very large, and want better than 1/2-approximation
Thm. 6	$\mathsf{ALG} \geq \mathsf{OPT} - O(()\, k_A^m H)$	$O(()\, k_A^m (m + k_A^{m+1} + k_A k_B))$	m small, T very large, and the additive loss is acceptable

Dynamic Program for Computing S_{2m} and S_{m+p}. Let $V[c_1, \ldots, c_{k_A}][c'_1, \ldots, c'_{k_A}]$ be the expected payoff of A in the interval $(m, m + \sum_i c'_i]$ where in the time-interval $(m - \sum_i c_i, m]$ each action $a_i \in \mathcal{A}$ is played c_i times, and in the interval $(m, m + \sum_i c'_i]$, each action $a_i \in \mathcal{A}$ is played c'_i times. We initialize the table for each entry where the sum of the counts $c_1, \ldots, c_{k_A}$ is equal to m:

$$V[c_1, \ldots, c_{k_A}][0, \ldots, 0] = 0 \text{ where } \sum_{i=1}^{k_A} c_i = m \tag{6}$$

We fill in the remaining entries according to the following recurrence. Start from $t = m + 1$ and fill out the entries in ascending order up to $2m$, where $t = m + \sum_{i=1}^{k_A} c'_i$. To compute the maximum expected payoff received by A in the interval $(m, t]$, we iterate over all pairs of actions (a_i, a_j) where a_i was played at time step $t - m$ and a_j is played at step t by player A. For a fixed pair (a_i, a_j), A's maximum expected payoff at step t is computed by adding her expected payoff in the current step t where the opponent is a memory-limited count-based learning rule f_m with a count history of $(c_1 + c'_1, \ldots, c_i + c'_i + 1, \ldots, c_j + c'_j - 1 + \cdots + c_{k_A} + c'_{k_A})$, plus A's expected payoff in step $t-1$ where the history of her actions is $(c_1, \ldots, c_i + 1, \ldots, c_{k_A}, c'_1, \ldots, c'_j - 1, \ldots, c'_{k_A})$:

$$\begin{aligned} &V[c_1, \ldots, c_{k_A}][c'_1, \ldots, c'_{k_A}] \\ &\quad = \max_{\substack{(i,j) \in [k_A]^2 \\ c'_j \geq 1}} \Big[V[c_1, \ldots, c_i + 1, \ldots, c_{k_A}][c'_1, \ldots, c'_j - 1, \ldots, c'_{k_A}] \\ &\qquad + \bar{u}^A(a_j, f_m(c_1 + c'_1, \ldots, c_i + c'_i + 1, \ldots, c_j + c'_j - 1, \ldots c_{k_A} + c'_{k_A})) \Big] \end{aligned} \tag{7}$$

To compute S_{2m}, we note that the first count vector $c_1, \ldots, c_{k_A}$ must be fully exhausted, so the optimal payoff over the last m time steps is

Algorithm 1: 1/2-approximation algorithm

Input: Opponent's count-based learning rule f_m, memory m, action spaces $\mathcal{A}$ and $\mathcal{B}$, time horizon T

Output: Action sequence for player A

1 Divide the time horizon into blocks of size m, except for the last block that has size $p = T \bmod m$;

`/* Compute the three optimal sequences below using DP */`

2 $S_m \leftarrow$ sequence maximizing A's expected payoff in first m time steps;

3 $S_{2m} \leftarrow$ sequence of length $2m$ maximizing A's expected payoff in last m time steps;

4 $S_{m+p} \leftarrow$ sequence of length $m+p$ maximizing A's expected payoff in last p time steps;

`/* Player A's payoff is maximized in either odd or even blocks */`

5 Consider these two strategies and play the one with higher expected payoff:

6 **Odd strategy:** Play S_m, then repeatedly play S_{2m}. If a block of length $m+p$ remains, play S_{m+p}. Otherwise, play arbitrary actions until time T;

7 **Even strategy:** Repeatedly play S_{2m}. If a block of length $m+p$ remains, play S_{m+p}. Otherwise, play arbitrary actions until time T;

$\max_{\sum_i c'_i = m} V[0, \ldots, 0][c'_1, \ldots, c'_{k_A}]$. Because $m - p$ actions remain in the first half for S_{m+p}, the optimal payoff over the last p time steps is $\max_{\sum_i c_i = m-p, \sum_i c'_i = p} V[c_1, \ldots, c_{k_A}][c'_1, \ldots, c'_{k_A}]$. In both cases, the corresponding sequence is recovered by backtracking through the table and selecting the optimal action at each step.

Theorem 3. *The Dynamic Program in Eq. 7 finds a sequence of length* $2m$ *that maximizes* A*'s expected payoff in the last* m *time steps against a memory-limited count-based learning rule* f_m*. It runs in* $O\big(k_B k_A^3 (m + 2k_A)^{2k_A}\big)$ *time.*

Theorem 4. *Algorithm 1 guarantees a 1/2-approximation for* A*'s expected cumulative payoff in time* $O\big(k_B k_A^3 (m + 2k_A)^{2k_A}\big)$.

5.2 $(1 - \varepsilon)(\mathsf{OPT} - mH)$-Approximation Algorithm

Our next approximation algorithm (Algorithm 2) computes a sequence for player A guaranteeing expected payoff at least $(1 - \varepsilon)(\mathsf{OPT} - mH)$ against a memory-limited count-based learning rule f_m, in time $O(k_A^{m/\varepsilon+1} k_B (m/\varepsilon))$. The algorithm finds the sequence of length (m/ε) maximizing payoff over its last $m/\varepsilon - m$ time steps, then repeats it for the remaining time steps. This algorithm is particularly useful when m is very small but T is very large. Proofs appear in the full version.

Theorem 5. *Algorithm 2 guarantees expected cumulative payoff of* $(1 - \varepsilon)(\mathsf{OPT} - mH)$ *for player* A *in time* $O(k_A^{\lceil m/\varepsilon \rceil + 1} k_B \lceil m/\varepsilon \rceil)$.

Algorithm 2: $(1-\varepsilon)(\mathsf{OPT}-mH)$-approximation algorithm

Input: Opponent's count-based learning rule f_m, memory m, action spaces $\mathcal{A}$ and $\mathcal{B}$, time horizon T, approximation factor ε

Output: Action sequence for player A

`/* Phase 1: Find optimal sequence for first block */`

$\mathcal{S} \leftarrow$ set of all possible action sequences in the first $\lceil m/\varepsilon \rceil$ time steps;

$s' \leftarrow \arg\max_{s\in\mathcal{S}} \sum_{t=\min(m+1,T)}^{\min(\lceil m/\varepsilon\rceil,T)} \bar{u}^A(s_t,b_t)$ where $b_t = f_m([s_{\max(1,t-m)},\dots,s_{t-1}])$ when Player A plays sequence s;

`/* Phase 2: Repeat optimal sequence for full blocks */`

for $i = 1,\dots,\left\lfloor \frac{T}{\lceil m/\varepsilon\rceil} \right\rfloor$ **do**

  A plays the action sequence s' for time steps $\left((i-1)\lceil \frac{m}{\varepsilon}\rceil, i\lceil\frac{m}{\varepsilon}\rceil\right]$;

end

`/* Phase 3: Handle remaining time steps */`

$\mathcal{S}' \leftarrow$ all possible action sequences for remaining time steps $\left(\left\lfloor \frac{T}{\lceil m/\varepsilon\rceil}\right\rfloor \lceil\frac{m}{\varepsilon}\rceil, T\right]$;

$s' \leftarrow \arg\max_{s\in\mathcal{S}'} \sum_{t=\min\left(\left\lfloor \frac{T}{m/\varepsilon}\right\rfloor\lceil\frac{m}{\varepsilon}\rceil+m,T\right)}^{T} \bar{u}^A(s_t,b_t)$;

Play sequence s' for remaining time steps;

5.3 $O(k_A^m H)$-Additive Approximation Algorithm

Finally, we present a complementary algorithm for any finite memory $m \geq 1$ with expected cumulative payoff of at least $\mathsf{OPT} - O(k_A^m H)$. As $T \to \infty$, this additive penalty becomes asymptotically negligible. The algorithm runs in time $O\big(k_A^{2m+1} + mk_A^{m+1}k_B\big)$. Since the runtime is independent of T but is exponential in m, this algorithm is again useful when m is small and T is large. When m and T are both small, the exact DP (Eq. 5) is preferable; when m and T are both large, the 1/2-approximation (Algorithm 1) is the practical choice.

We modify the approach of repeating action sequences that we already used in Sects. 5.1 and 5.2. We model the memory-limited learning rule as a state space over sequences of m actions. Karp's maximal mean weight cycle algorithm [10,16] allows us to extract an optimal repeating sequence of actions. Repeating this optimal cycle gives that the optimizer only incurs an additive utility loss at the prefix and suffix of the time horizon. Because the state space has size k_A^m, the maximum length of any simple cycle is bounded by k_A^m, so the algorithm loses at most $O(k_A^m H)$ in utility. The formal construction and proofs appear in the full version.

Theorem 6. *There exists an algorithm that guarantees an expected cumulative payoff of at least* $\mathsf{OPT} - O(k_A^m H)$ *for Player A against a memory-limited count-based learning rule f_m, which runs in* $O\big(k_A^{2m+1} + k_A^m(m + k_A k_B)\big)$ *time.*

For instance, for $m = 1$ Theorem 6 gives a $O(k_A H)$-additive approximation in $O\big(k_A^3 k_B\big)$ time.

6 Deceiving an Unknown Opponent

Suppose the optimizer does not know the particular learning rule that the opponent is using, but does know that it belongs to some family $\mathcal{F}$ of count-based learning rules, each with memory length m. Can the optimizer learn to deceive their opponent in this setting?

A natural idea is to try to quickly determine which opponent we are facing, and then play optimally against that opponent. Since a count-based opponent with memory length m chooses their next action based on only the counts of our previous m actions, we might intuitively try something like the following:

1. while we have not yet determined the true opponent:
   (a) play any m actions against which at least two opponents have a different response
   (b) observe the response, eliminating at least one possible opponent
2. compute and play the optimal sequence against the true opponent for the remaining rounds

With some assumptions (similar to those below) this idea can be used for deterministic count-based opponents. The learning process would require up to $O(m|\mathcal{F}|)$ rounds, after which we can use a DP to compute the optimal sequence against the true opponent and play that sequence for the remaining rounds.

However, we would like to handle *any* count-based opponent, including randomized opponents. In that case, we cannot necessarily eliminate any opponent by simply observing the response to a full history: even if two randomized opponents have a different response distribution to a sequence of m actions, it may take many repetitions of that sequence to have high confidence about which we are playing against. This motivates our approach, which leverages existing results for stochastic bandits; this is a natural connection as in both settings we must balance learning about unknown reward distributions against maximizing overall payoff.

We develop a 1/2-approximation up to $O(\sqrt{|\mathcal{F}|mT} + m)$ regret compared to the optimal cumulative payoff against the actual opponent (Algorithm 3), under two assumptions. We assume there exists a "blank" action for which both players always have zero payoff; when played m times, it effectively clears the history, restoring the opponent's behavior to what it would be at the beginning of the game. We also assume that all payoffs for the optimizer lie in $[0, 1]$. This algorithm is practical when m and $|\mathcal{F}|$ are small relative to T (it is an asymptotic 1/2-approximation when we consider them constants).

6.1 1/2-Approximation up to $O(\sqrt{|\mathcal{F}|mT} + m)$ Regret

At a high level, this algorithm combines a similar idea to our 1/2-approximation (Algorithm 1) with a reduction to stochastic bandits.

The guarantee stated in Theorem 7 depends on the specific stochastic bandits algorithm used in Algorithm 3; we assume the use of MOSS from [4] for concreteness and the simplicity of the bound. [4] derive a regret bound of $O(\sqrt{KT})$

Algorithm 3: 1/2-approximation up to $O(\sqrt{|\mathcal{F}|mT} + m)$ regret against an unknown opponent from count-based family $\mathcal{F}$ with memory m

Input: Family of possible opponent learning rules $\mathcal{F}$ (each count-based with memory length m), stochastic bandits algorithm $\mathsf{Alg}_{\mathsf{SB}}$

for f *in* $\mathcal{F}$ **do**
  $S_{f2m} \leftarrow$ sequence maximizing A's expected payoff in the last m time steps if the opponent is using learning rule f
end
$T' \leftarrow \lfloor \frac{T}{2m} \rfloor$
Run $\mathsf{Alg}_{\mathsf{SB}}$ over T' rounds, where we have $|\mathcal{F}|$ arms, pulling arm i is equivalent to playing S_{f2m} and the realized payoff is the realized payoff over the second m steps of S_{f2m}.
Play arbitrary actions for the remaining $T - 2mT'$ time steps.

for the K-armed stochastic bandit problem with bounded rewards. The proof of Theorem 7 appears in the full version.

Theorem 7. *Algorithm 3 gives a 1/2 approximation up to $O(\sqrt{|\mathcal{F}|mT} + m)$ regret to the optimal expected payoff against the actual opponent.*

Remark 2. When m and $|\mathcal{F}|$ do not scale with T, Algorithm 3 achieves an asymptotic 1/2 approximation. In that case, the regret is sublinear in T. Given the opponent's bounded memory and the existence of the "blank" action, any instance with a nonzero optimal value satisfies $\mathsf{OPT} \in \Theta(T)$, so the regret term vanishes in comparison as $T \to \infty$. If $\mathsf{OPT} = 0$ the guarantee holds trivially since all payoffs are non-negative.

7 Hardness Results

In this section we show that computing the optimal action sequence against ERM is NP-hard to approximate. The proof appears in the full version.

Theorem 8. *It is NP-hard to compute a sequence of actions which attains payoff within any constant multiplicative factor or any T^α additive error (for constant $0 < \alpha < 1$) of the optimal payoff against* ERM*, even in zero-sum games.*

Theorem 8 improves upon a hardness result of Assos et al. [2], who show inapproximability within constant additive error in general-sum games. In contrast, our result holds *even* in the case of zero-sum games and strengthens the additive bound to T^α for any constant $0 < \alpha < 1$. In a related line of work, Assos et al. [3] give an $\Omega(T)$ additive hardness bound for a different opponent learning algorithm—Multiplicative Weights Update.

8 Experiments

As we showed in Sect. 3, depending on the game, the deception bonus can be arbitrarily large (Proposition 1), or there might be no gains from deception at all (Proposition 3). To explore what the gains from deception might typically look like, we empirically measured the deception bonus in random zero-sum and general-sum games. The deception bonus is computed with respect to a particular opponent (see Definition 7); for concreteness in these experiments, we used ERM.

Experimental design For a random zero-sum game (described by payoff matrices A and B for each player), payoffs for A are drawn independently and uniformly at random from the real interval $[-1, 1]$, and $B = -A$. For a random general-sum game, payoffs for both A and B are drawn independently and uniformly at random from $[-1, 1]$. Each experiment (corresponding to a point on the plots below) was run for 500 independent trials.[2]

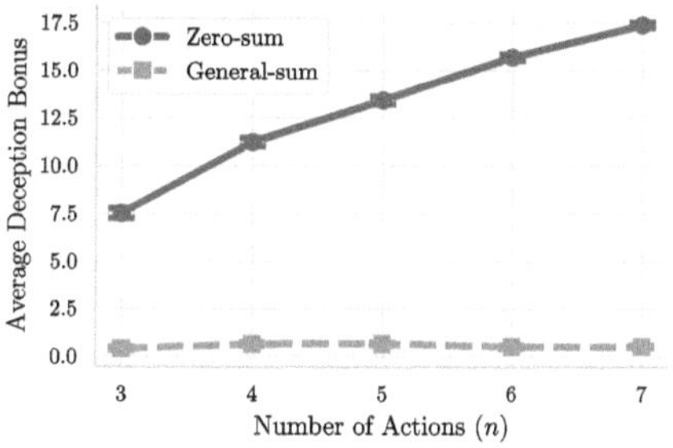

Fig. 1. Deception bonus vs. number of actions for $T = 25$ rounds. Error bars show standard error over 500 trials.

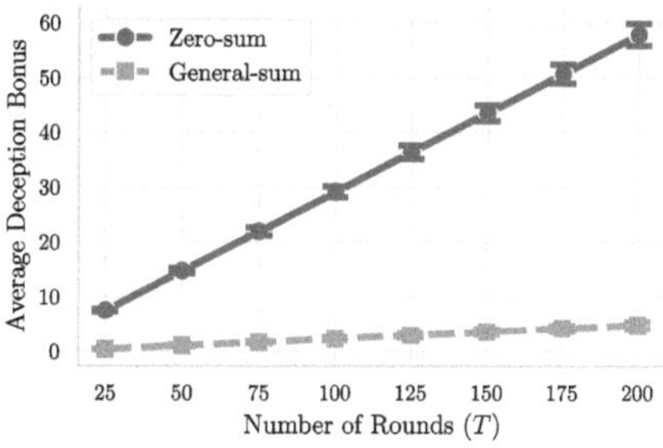

Fig. 2. Deception bonus vs. number of rounds for $n = 3$ actions. Error bars show standard error over 500 trials.

Findings. We summarize our primary findings below.

- The average deception bonus is substantially larger in random zero-sum games than in random general-sum games, where it was consistently low (Figs. 1 and 2). This suggests that on average deception tends to be lucrative in competitive settings while providing little advantage when opportunities for collaboration exist.
- In zero-sum games the deception bonus increases with the number of actions n (Fig. 1). One explanation is that in a random game, as n grows it is more likely that there exists a high-payoff response to each of the opponent's actions; the optimizer can take advantage of this due to the opponent's determinism. In

[2] Source code: https://github.com/dimitarch/deception-code.

general-sum games, however, the deception bonus remains relatively flat as n increases. This may be because larger action spaces also increase the probability of mutually beneficial actions, which reduce the advantage of deceptive play.
- In both zero-sum and general-sum games, the deception bonus is roughly linear in the number of rounds (Fig. 2), indicating that the per-round gains from deception remain relatively constant for a fixed n as the number of rounds varies.

9 Discussion and Future Work

We introduced a new game-theoretic model of deception in repeated games. We provided structural results, a hardness of approximation result for optimizing against Empirical Risk Minimization which holds even in zero-sum games, and experimental results on the deception bonus in random games. We also presented a variety of algorithmic results for optimizing against a count-based opponent: exact dynamic programming algorithms for when the game or the opponent's memory is small, three approximation algorithms—a 1/2-approximation with a time-complexity polynomial in the opponent's memory m, an asymptotic PTAS and an additive-approximation whose runtimes are exponential in m—and an algorithm for learning to optimize against an unknown count-based opponent. Our model captures deception over time, which we believe is an interesting and underexplored direction; we hope it will lead to further work in this area.

Open Questions and Future Work. It remains an open question whether our 1/2-approximation result can be improved while keeping the runtime polynomial in m. Furthermore, while we present an initial result on learning to deceive an opponent whose learning rule is unknown, it would be interesting to explore whether stronger results can be obtained in that setting—perhaps by leveraging knowledge about the opponent's possible learning rules that is not exploited by our reduction to stochastic bandits. Finally, it remains open whether (approximately) optimizing against ERM is still NP-hard in the special case of zero-sum games in which all payoffs are integers bounded by $o(T)$.

Acknowledgment. This work was supported in part by the National Science Foundation under grants CCF-2212968 and ECCS-2216899 and through an NSF CSGrad4US Fellowship under grant 2313998, by the Simons Foundation under the Simons Collaboration on the Theory of Algorithmic Fairness, and by the Office of Naval Research MURI Grant N000142412742. The views expressed in this work do not necessarily reflect the position or the policy of the Government and no official endorsement should be inferred.

References

1. Aitchison, M., Benke, L., Sweetser, P.: Learning to deceive in multi-agent hidden role games. In: Deceptive AI (DeceptAI), pp. 55–75. Springer, Cham (2021). https://doi.org/10.1007/978-3-030-91779-1_5
2. Assos, A., Dagan, Y., Daskalakis, C.: Maximizing utility in multi-agent environments by anticipating the behavior of other learners. NeurIPS (2024)
3. Assos, A., Dagan, Y., Rajaraman, N.: Computational intractability of strategizing against online learners. In: PMLR, pp. 169–199. COLT (2025)
4. Audibert, J.Y., Bubeck, S.: Minimax policies for adversarial and stochastic bandits. In: COLT, pp. 217–226 (2009)
5. Balcan, M.F., Blum, A., Chen, S.T.: Diversified strategies for mitigating adversarial attacks in multiagent systems. In: AAMAS, pp. 407–415 (2018)
6. Birmpas, G., Gan, J., Hollender, A., Marmolejo, F., Rajgopal, N., Voudouris, A.: Optimally deceiving a learning leader in stackelberg games. NeurIPS **33**, 20624–20635 (2020)
7. Braverman, M., Mao, J., Schneider, J., Weinberg, M.: Selling to a no-regret buyer. In: EC, pp. 523–538 (2018)
8. Brown, W., Schneider, J., Vodrahalli, K.: Is learning in games good for the learners? NeurIPS **36**, 54228–54249 (2023)
9. Carminati, L., Zhang, B.H., Farina, G., Gatti, N., Sandholm, T.: Hidden-role games: Equilibrium concepts and computation. In: EC, pp. 106–107 (2024)
10. Chaturvedi, M., McConnell, R.M.: A note on finding minimum mean cycle. Inf. Process. Lett. **127**, 21–22 (2017)
11. Chen, Y., Deng, X., Gan, J., Li, Y.: Learning to manipulate a commitment optimizer. arXiv preprint arXiv:2302.11829 (2023)
12. Deng, Y., Schneider, J., Sivan, B.: Strategizing against no-regret learners. NeurIPS **32** (2019)
13. Fortnow, L., Whang, D.: Optimality and domination in repeated games with bounded players. In: STOC, pp, pp. 741–749 (1994)
14. Freund, Y., Kearns, M., Mansour, Y., Ron, D., Rubinfeld, R., Schapire, R.E.: Efficient algorithms for learning to play repeated games against computationally bounded adversaries. In: FOCS, pp. 332–341. IEEE (1995)
15. Gan, J., Xu, H., Guo, Q., Tran-Thanh, L., Rabinovich, Z., Wooldridge, M.: Imitative follower deception in stackelberg games. In: EC, pp. 639–657 (2019)
16. Karp, R.M.: A characterization of the minimum cycle mean in a digraph. Discret. Math. **23**(3), 309–311 (1978)
17. Kuhn, H.W.: A Simplified Two-Person Poker, pp. 97–104. Princeton University Press, Princeton (1951). https://doi.org/10.1515/9781400881727-010
18. Mansour, Y., Mohri, M., Schneider, J., Sivan, B.: Strategizing against learners in bayesian games. In: Loh, P.L., Raginsky, M. (eds.) COLT. PMLR, vol. 178, pp. 5221–5252 (2022)

19. Nguyen, T., Xu, H.: Imitative attacker deception in stackelberg security games. In: IJCAI, pp. 528–534 (2019)
20. Nguyen, T.H., Butler, A., Xu, H.: Tackling imitative attacker deception in repeated bayesian stackelberg security games. In: ECAI, pp. 187–194 (2020)

Improved Approximation Guarantees for Groupwise Maximin Share Fairness

Georgios Amanatidis[1,2(✉)], Anna Korfiati[1], Evangelos Markakis[1,2,3], and Christodoulos Santorinaios[1,2]

[1] Athens University of Economics and Business, Athens, Greece
{g.d.amanatidis,ann.korfiati,markakis,santgchr}@aueb.gr
[2] Archimedes, Athena Research Center, Athens, Greece
[3] Input Output Group (IOG), Athens, Greece

Abstract. We study the problem of fairly allocating a set of indivisible goods to a set of n agents with additive valuation functions. We focus on the very demanding notion of *groupwise maximin share fairness* (GMMS), which requires that each agent i receives value comparable to her maximin share, where the latter is computed *with respect to any subset of agents that contains* i. We show that it is possible to compute $(\phi - 1)$-approximate GMMS allocations in polynomial time, where $\phi \approx 1.618$ is the golden ratio. This improves on the previously known guarantee of 4/7 of Chaudhury et al. [10] and Amanatidis et al. [5]. We propose a simple algorithm that maintains the same main properties as the Draft-and-Eliminate algorithm of Amanatidis et al. [5] and we improve on the approximation guarantee analysis by carefully bounding the maximin share value within any subinstance induced by the restriction of our allocation to a subset of agents. Our analysis is asymptotically tight for algorithms that share these properties and has the additional benefit of giving improved guarantees for restricted settings; in particular, when the agents agree on the top-n goods or when the number of agents is small. To illustrate the challenges of going beyond the guarantees of our algorithm, we also present a variant with an improved approximation of $(\sqrt{10} - 1)/3 \approx 0.72$ for the case of three agents. To achieve this improvement we partially characterize the maximin share guarantees of short picking sequences for a small number of goods.

Keywords: Groupwise Maximin Share · Discrete Fair Division · Approximation Algorithms

1 Introduction

Fair division is concerned with the problem of partitioning a set of resources among agents with diverse preferences in a manner that is considered *fair* by the agents. The study of this fundamental problem has a rich history, originating in the work of Steinhaus (with the contribution of Banach and Knaster) [23] and has since attracted sustained attention across economics, mathematics, and

P. Lenzner and D. Schmand (Eds.): SAGT 2026, LNCS 16911, pp. 39–56, 2027.
https://doi.org/10.1007/978-3-032-38782-0_3

computer science. While the early literature focused primarily on the allocation of *divisible* resources—where proportionality [23] and envy-freeness [15,24] serve as the central fairness benchmarks—the fair allocation of *indivisible* goods has emerged as a highly active research frontier in recent years (see, e.g., [2]).

In the indivisible setting, strong fairness guarantees are in general unattainable: when a single valuable item must be assigned to one of several agents, no allocation can be fair to all. This has motivated the study of appropriate *relaxations*, most notably *envy-freeness up to one good* (EF$_1$) [8,19], *envy-freeness up to any good* (EFX) [9], and *maximin share fairness* (MMS) [8]. In particular, the maximin share of an agent is the best value she can guarantee to herself by partitioning the goods into n bundles (where n is the total number of agents) and receiving her least preferred one; an MMS allocation assigns every agent at least her maximin share. While such allocations need not always exist [13,18], a flourishing line of work has established that constant-factor approximations are always achievable [16,18]. A natural strengthening of MMS is *groupwise maximin share fairness* (GMMS), introduced by Barman et al. [6], which demands that the MMS guarantee holds not only with respect to the whole set but within every subgroup of agents. This stronger requirement captures collective fairness on a richer level, yet its approximability is significantly less understood. In this paper, we study the existence and efficient computation of approximate GMMS allocations for agents with additive valuation functions.

Note that even checking whether an allocation is approximately GMMS seems nontrivial, and this is not just because computing the maximin shares is hard; even if we had an oracle for the latter, it is still unclear how to efficiently verify that MMS guarantees hold for every single subset of agents. Given this, it is surprising that there are any positive results on the existence and computation of allocations that approximately satisfy GMMS fairness. In particular, Barman et al. [6] showed how to efficiently compute 1/2-GMMS allocations, and this approximation factor was later improved to 4/7 [5,10]. Since then, it has remained open whether better approximations are possible.

Our Contributions. We show that, for agents with additive valuation functions, $(\phi-1)$-GMMS allocations always exist and can be efficiently computed. For this, we revisit the algorithm of Amanatidis et al. [5], along with a closely related algorithm for computing approximately EFX allocations by Farhadi et al. [12], in order to present a simpler version with the desirable approximation guarantee with respect to GMMS. For restrictions of the setting, we obtain significant improvements. In particular,

- We present an algorithm that computes $\min\left\{\frac{2}{3}, \frac{\sqrt{5n^2-4n}-n}{2n-2}\right\}$-GMMS allocations (Theorem 3). For $n \in \{3,4\}$ this factor is $2/3$ and as n grows it gracefully degrades to $\phi - 1 \approx 0.618$. The allocations computed by our algorithm are also EF$_1$ and—with a small parameter adjustment—$(\phi-1)$-EFX (Theorem 2).
- When all n agents agree on the set of the best n items, we improve the ratio to $2/3$ (Theorem 5), matching the known ratio for EFX for this case. This setting

generalizes two particularly well-studied special cases: i) identical agents, and ii) agents with a common ranking over all items.
- For the fundamental case of three agents, we show that it is possible to go beyond 2/3 and efficiently compute 0.72-GMMS allocations (Theorem 6).

All missing proofs are deferred to the full version of this work [4].

Technical Considerations. Our main algorithm itself (Algorithm 1) is relatively simple, following the general framework of the state-of-the-art algorithms for computing approximately EFX allocations. Our main contribution here is our novel analysis that tightly bounds the proportional share after performing a series of reductions on an extended set of "problematic" items. Interestingly, our analysis can be transferred with small adaptations to either one of the two known efficient algorithms for computing $(\phi - 1)$-EFX allocations.

In our proofs we often use the *proportional share* (i.e., the average value) of an agent, restricted to any given subset of agents and the union of their bundles, as a *proxy* quantity for her corresponding maximin share value. This alone, however, is too weak to properly bound the performance of the algorithm. As an additional step, we use known monotonicity properties of the maximin share to reduce our instances to "nicer" ones. The most standard such reduction is to ignore all agents who have a bundle consisting of a single good [7], but even this cannot show a factor strictly greater than 1/2. What allowed Chaudhury et al. [10] and Amanatidis et al. [5] to obtain a guarantee of 4/7 is a technique of Amanatidis et al. [3] that removes one agent at a time along with *two* "bad" items as long as there are sufficiently many such items. Crucially, we broaden the definition of such items (that we call *problematic* in the proof of Lemma 5). As a result, we obtain reduced instances with better structure. Further, we use a different, much more refined, approach with respect to bounding the total value of a reduced instance, leading to a tight analysis of Algorithm 1 (Theorem 4).

To improve our results for $n = 3$, we introduce a very particular modification of the envy graph that depends on the initial allocation of our algorithm and we perform a thorough case analysis on the possible configurations with two or three agents. As an intermediate result, we characterize the MMS guarantees of allocating a small number of items via specific picking sequences.

Related Work. Gamow and Stern [15] were the first to introduce the problem of envy-freeness, which was more formally defined later on by Foley [14] and Varian [24]. The first relaxations, MMS and EF_1, were both defined by Budish [8] while the stronger relaxations, GMMS and EFX, were defined by [6,9] respectively. Lipton et al. [19] implicitly defined EF_1 and designed the *envy cycle elimination* algorithm to compute it in polynomial time. On the contrary, MMS allocations were shown not to exist in [18], whereas the current upper bounds are $\frac{39}{40}$ for 3 agents and $1 - \frac{1}{n^4}$ for a general number of agents, both due to [13]. Both bounds apply to GMMS allocations, and are currently the best known. Regarding positive results, Barman et al. [6] provided a 1/2 approximation factor which was improved to the current state of the art of 4/7 independently by Amanatidis et al. [5] and Chaudhury et al. [10].

Ordered and Top-n Instances. Ordered instances, where the agents agree on a universal ranking of the items, induce a well-motivated setting that often offers an avenue for improved positive results. In the context of EFX allocations, Plaut and Roughgarden [22] showed existence for additive valuations while for MMS the existence in general settings reduces to the existence in ordered ones [7]. However, the former does not imply a factor better than 4/7 for GMMS while the analogous reduction for GMMS is not known to hold. A top-n instance is a mild relaxation of an ordered one where the n agents agree on the set of the top-n items, but not necessarily their order. It was introduced by Markakis and Santorinaios [21] and has led to improved positive results in a variety of fair division problems [1,11,20].

2 Preliminaries

A discrete fair division instance can be described by the triplet (N, M, V) where $N = [n] = \{1, \ldots, n\}$ is a set of n agents and M a set of m indivisible items. The set $V = \{v_1, \ldots, v_n\}$ corresponds to the *additive* valuation functions of the agents, i.e., $v_i(S) = \sum_{g \in S} v_i(\{g\})$. We assume that all the items are *goods*, i.e., $v_i(\{g\}) \geq 0$ for every agent $i \in N$ and item $g \in M$. Hence, the valuation functions are also *monotone*. For the sake of readability, in what follows, we write $v_i(g)$ instead of $v_i(\{g\})$, for $g \in M$.

A complete *allocation* of M to the n agents is a partition, $\mathcal{A} = (A_1, \ldots, A_n)$, where $A_i \cap A_j = \emptyset$ and $\cup_i A_i = M$. By $\Pi_n(M)$ we denote the set of all partitions of a set M into n bundles. If $\mathcal{A}$ is a partial allocation we use $\mathcal{P}(\mathcal{A}) := M \setminus \bigcup_{i \in N} A_i$ to denote the *pool* of unallocated items. As a first step in our Algorithm 1, we use a partial allocation $\mathcal{F}$, such that $|F_i| \leq 1$, for all $i \in N$, and the product $\prod_{i \in N: |F_i|=1} v_i(F_i)$ is maximized. We refer to $\mathcal{F}$ as a *NSW-maximizing matching allocation*, as it corresponds to a matching between agents and items that maximizes the Nash social welfare. Such allocations can be computed efficiently [12].

In fair division, most fairness notions can be categorized into two large families: *share-based* and *envy-based* notions. In the former category, agents perceive fairness by comparing their bundles to the complete set of items while in the latter they compare bundles with each other. As our work focuses on a notion that combines both aspects in a very strong sense, we provide below the necessary definitions from both areas, as well as some tools originally developed for envy-based notions.

2.1 Share-Based Fairness Notions

Definition 1. *Given n agents, and a subset $S \subseteq M$ of goods, the n-maximin share of agent i with respect to S is* $\boldsymbol{\mu}_i(n, S) = \max_{\mathcal{A} \in \Pi_n(S)} \min_{A_j \in \mathcal{A}} v_i(A_j)$.

From the definition, it follows that $n \cdot \boldsymbol{\mu}_i(n, S) \leq v_i(S)$. When $S = M$, this quantity is just called the *maximin share* of agent i. An allocation $\mathcal{A}$ is an *n-maximin share defining partition* for agent i, if $\min_{A_j \in \mathcal{A}} v_i(A_j) = \boldsymbol{\mu}_i(n, M)$.

When it is clear from context what n and M are, we simply write $\boldsymbol{\mu}_i$ instead of $\boldsymbol{\mu}_i(n, M)$. *Maximin share fairness* asks for a partition that gives each agent her (approximate) maximin share.

Definition 2. *An allocation* $\mathcal{A} = (A_1, \ldots, A_n)$ *is called an* α-MMS *(*α*-maximin share) allocation if* $v_i(A_i) \geq \alpha \cdot \boldsymbol{\mu}_i$ *, for every* $i \in N$.

Variations of maximin share fairness have also been proposed. Here, we focus on a strengthening of the notion, by demanding an allocation to have an MMS-type guarantee for *any subset* of agents. That is, for an agent i and any S with $i \in S$, we can think of i as considering the merged bundle of all items received by members of S and requesting to receive at least her $|S|$-maximin share of this bundle as if it were reallocated among S. This is referred to as *groupwise maximin share fairness*, introduced by Barman et al. [6].

Definition 3. *An allocation* $\mathcal{A} = (A_1, \ldots, A_n)$ *is called an* α-GMMS *(*α*-groupwise maximin share) allocation if for every subset of agents* $N' \subseteq N$ *and any agent* $i \in N'$, $v_i(A_i) \geq \alpha \cdot \boldsymbol{\mu}_i(|N'|, \cup_{j \in N'} A_j)$.

In Definitions 2 and 3, when $\alpha = 1$, we refer to the corresponding allocations as MMS and GMMS allocations respectively. It is clear that the notion of GMMS is significantly stronger than MMS.

Before proceeding to the envy-based notions we present some useful lemmas we will repeatedly invoke in the sequel. The first is a monotonicity lemma that allows removing agents and items from an instance, without reducing the maximin share of an agent. Similar statements are standard in the literature of MMS allocations and are used to reduce general instances to more structured ones.

Lemma 1 ([3]). *Suppose* $\mathcal{A} \in \Pi_n(M)$ *is an* n*-maximin share defining partition for agent* i*. Then, for any set of goods* S*, such that there exists some* j *with* $S \subseteq A_j$*, it holds that* $\boldsymbol{\mu}_i(n-1, M \setminus S) \geq \boldsymbol{\mu}_i(n, M)$.

An immediate corollary of this reduction lemma is that singleton bundles do not pose an obstacle to obtaining GMMS approximations. The latter also follows from a monotonicity lemma of [7], which is a special case of Lemma 1.

We conclude this section with another simple monotonicity lemma. Intuitively, if we start with an α-MMS allocation and only agent i receives new items, the allocation remains α-MMS from agent i's perspective.

Lemma 2. *Let* $\mathcal{A} = (A_1, \ldots, A_n)$ *be an allocation of* $M' = \cup_{j \in N} A_j \subsetneq M$ *such that* $v_i(A_i) \geq \alpha \cdot \boldsymbol{\mu}_i(n, M')$ *for some agent* $i \in N$ *and some* $\alpha \in (0, 1]$*. Then, for any* $g \in \mathcal{P}(\mathcal{A})$*, we have* $v_i(A_i \cup \{g\}) \geq \alpha \cdot \boldsymbol{\mu}_i(n, M' \cup \{g\})$.

2.2 Envy-Based Fairness Notions

We begin our exposition with the notion of envy.

Definition 4 (α**-envy).** *For any* $\alpha \geq 1$*, we say that agent* i α*-envies agent* j *if* $v_i(A_j) > \alpha \cdot v_i(A_i)$.

When $\alpha = 1$, we simply say that agent i envies agent j. To address the issue of allocating an indivisible item to two (or more) agents, envy-based notions involve the hypothetical removal of item(s) from agents' bundles. This is reflected in the following definition.

Definition 5. *An allocation $\mathcal{A} = (A_1, \ldots, A_n)$ is an*

a) α-EF1 *allocation (α-envy-free up to one good), if for every pair $i, j \in N$, with $A_j \neq \emptyset$, there exists a good $g \in A_j$, such that $v_i(A_i) \geq \alpha \cdot v_i(A_j \setminus \{g\})$.*
b) α-EFX *allocation (α-envy-free up to any good), if for every pair $i, j \in N$, with $A_j \neq \emptyset$ and every good $g \in A_j$, it holds that $v_i(A_i) \geq \alpha \cdot v_i(A_j \setminus \{g\})$.*

Of course, for $\alpha = 1$ we obtain precisely the notions of envy-freeness up to one good (EF1) [8,19] and envy-freeness up to any good (EFX) [9]. In words, α-EFX dictates that agent i does not α-envy any proper subset of agent's j bundle while α-EF1 is satisfied if the envy vanishes for some maximal proper subset.

It is well known that EF1 allocations can be computed in polynomial time, by Lipton et al. [19], with the celebrated Envy-Cycle-Elimination algorithm, which we also use as a crucial algorithmic component. This is by now a standard algorithm in the literature of fair division but, for the sake of completeness, we provide here a brief presentation and refer to [4] for the full details. A central concept of this algorithm is the *envy graph*. Given a partial allocation $\mathcal{A} = (A_1, \ldots, A_n)$, the envy graph is a directed graph $G_{\mathcal{A}} = (N, E_{\mathcal{A}})$, where $(i, j) \in E_{\mathcal{A}}$ if and only if agent i currently envies agent j, i.e., $v_i(A_i) < v_i(A_j)$. The key observation of the algorithm is that a source node in $G_{\mathcal{A}}$ corresponds to a non-envied agent in the partial allocation $\mathcal{A}$, and this agent can receive one item without disrupting the EF1 property. If no such agent exists, then there is an envy cycle. By repeatedly reallocating the bundles to the agents backwards along envy cycles, the valuation of each agent (weakly) improves, until a source node eventually arises. The fact that the agents' valuations do not decrease is crystallized in the following statement.

Theorem 1 (Follows by [19]). *Let A_i be the bundle assigned to an agent $i \in N$ at the beginning of some iteration of the Envy-Cycle-Elimination algorithm. If A_i' is assigned to i at the end of any future iteration, then $v_i(A_i') \geq v_i(A_i)$.*

We frequently need to reason about an agent's value compared to a good in the pool of unallocated items. For this matter, the next definition is helpful.

Definition 6 (α-content). *For a partial allocation $\mathcal{A}$ and any $\alpha \geq 1$, we say that agent i is α-content with respect to $\mathcal{A}$ if $v_i(A_i) \geq \alpha \cdot v_i(g)$ for any $g \in \mathcal{P}(\mathcal{A})$.*

Throughout the execution of any of our algorithms, we assume that whenever the allocation $\mathcal{A}$ changes, $\mathcal{P}(\mathcal{A})$ and $G_{\mathcal{A}}$ are silently updated.

3 A Simple Algorithm and a ($\phi - 1$)-GMMS Guarantee

In order to obtain an improved approximation guarantee for GMMS, we revisit the two known algorithms with the currently best guarantee for EFX, namely Algorithm 3 in Amanatidis et al. [5] and Algorithm 2 in Farhadi et al. [12][1]. We present Match-Draft-and-Eliminate (Algorithm 1), a simplified hybrid version of these two algorithms.

We briefly explain the formal description of the algorithm. Within the pseudocode, we refer to three (partial) allocations: $\mathcal{F}, \mathcal{S}$ and $\mathcal{A}$. The first one, $\mathcal{F}$, is a NSW-maximizing matching allocation produced in line 1. Recall that in such an $\mathcal{F}$ each agent receives at most one item and, because the product of values is maximized, $G_{\mathcal{F}}$ must be acyclic. For the sake of presentation, we assume that $\mathcal{F}$ assigns to each agent exactly one item. To see that this is without loss of generality, note that any agent i with $F_i = \emptyset$ values positively less than n goods and each of those goods is allocated to a different agent via $\mathcal{F}$; so, any subsequent allocation would be 1-GMMS for agent i, even if she receives no items. Thus, we may safely ignore such agents; if this includes all agents, then no good has a positive value for any agent and any allocation is GMMS.

Then, our algorithm identifies the set R of agents who are not reachable in $G_{\mathcal{F}}$ from any θ-envied agent, and allocates to them one more item, according to their preferences. It is crucial that agents who are envious themselves get their second item early on, hence we follow a topological ordering of a restriction of the envy graph. This step is completed after line 9 and forms the second allocation, $\mathcal{S} = (S_1, \ldots, S_n)$. Thus, so far each agent has received at most two items. Then, the final allocation, $\mathcal{A}$, is computed via the Envy-Cycle-Elimination algorithm of Lipton et al. [19] run on $\mathcal{S}$ and $\mathcal{P}(\mathcal{S})$. Any ties during the execution of Algorithm 1 are resolved lexicographically.

Algorithm 1: Match-Draft-and-Eliminate(N, M, θ)

---

1 Let $\mathcal{F} = (\{f_1\}, \ldots, \{f_n\})$ be a NSW-maximizing matching allocation
2 Set $R = \{i \in N :$ agent i is not reachable in $G_{\mathcal{F}}$ from a θ-envied agent$\}$
3 Let σ be a topological ordering of the envy graph induced by agents in R
4 $\mathcal{S} = \mathcal{F}$
5 **for** *each agent* $i \in R$ *with respect to* σ **do**
6     $s_i = \arg\max_{g \in \mathcal{P}(\mathcal{S})} v_i(g)$
7     $S_i = \{f_i\} \cup \{s_i\}$
8 **for** *each agent* $i \notin R$ **do**
9     $S_i = \{f_i\}$
10 $\mathcal{A} =$ Envy-Cycle-Elimination($N, \mathcal{S}, \mathcal{P}(\mathcal{S})$)
11 **return** $\mathcal{A}$

Similarities and differences of Algorithm 1 *with* [5] *and* [12]. All algorithms share the same structure, in the sense that they are divided into three phases. First, they allocate one item to each agent. In the second phase they identify a set of

[1] We refer to Algorithm 2 in the arxiv version of their work.

agents R that receives a second item. The final phase is to proceed with Envy-Cycle-Elimination. Conceptually, the algorithm we analyze is closer to Algorithm 2 of Farhadi et al. [12], albeit simpler in its description, as it avoids the nontrivial notion of envy-rank. Moreover, the second phase is simpler and more similar to the algorithm of Amanatidis et al. [5]. Namely, for a suitable renaming of the agents, our allocation $\mathcal{S}$ can be constructed using two (partial) passes of the simple Round Robin algorithm.

Our main result is the following theorem.

Theorem 2. *Match-Draft-and-Eliminate(N, M, ϕ) returns in polynomial time an allocation $\mathcal{A}$ which is $(\phi - 1)$-GMMS, EF$_1$, and $(\phi - 1)$-EFX.*

We break down the proof of the GMMS guarantee into two lemmata. In Lemma 4 we focus on the easier case of agents in $N \setminus R$, who start as θ-content. The trickier case of agents in R is treated in Lemma 5 and uses all the machinery about monotonicity of the maximin share and reductions. For both cases, the analysis is carried out parametrically, based on θ. Then, in the proof of Theorem 2 (as well as in the proof of Theorem 3) we combine the two cases and balance the resulting factors to obtain our guarantees.

Remark 1. Our analysis on the approximation guarantees of Theorem 2 is also valid for the two aforementioned algorithms in [5,12]. We have chosen to present it for our version, as the presentation is simpler.

We begin our analysis with a simple lemma regarding the properties of a NSW-maximizing matching allocation.

Lemma 3. *Let $\mathcal{F}$ be a NSW-maximizing matching allocation. For $\theta \geq 1$ and $i, j \in N$ such that agent i θ-envies agent j, we have that any agent k reachable from agent j in the envy graph $G_{\mathcal{F}}$ is θ-content.*

Next, we state a corollary of the lemma that translates the properties of a NSW-maximizing matching in the context of our algorithm. The first and third part of this lemma form the analog of Lemma 4.1 of [5] (up to the use of strict inequalities).

Corollary 1. *If $\mathcal{S}$ is the allocation completed in line 9 of Algorithm 1, we have*

a) $v_i(f_i) \geq \theta \cdot v_i(g)$, *for any* $i \notin R$ *and* $g \in \mathcal{P}(\mathcal{F})$,
b) $v_i(f_i) \geq v_i(f_j)$, *for any* $i \notin R$ *and* $j \in R$,
c) $\theta \cdot v_i(f_i) \geq v_i(f_j)$, *for any* $i, j \in R$,
d) $v_i(f_i) \geq v_i(s_j)$, *for any* $i \in N, j \in R$,
e) if $v_i(f_i) < v_i(f_j)$, *then* $v_i(s_i) \geq v_i(s_j)$, *for any* $i, j \in R$.

Lemma 4. ***(Agents in $N \setminus R$).*** *Fix any $\theta \geq 1$ and let $\mathcal{A}$ be the output of Match-Draft-and-Eliminate(N, M, θ). Then, for any $i \in N \setminus R$ and for any $N' \subseteq N$ with $i \in N'$, it holds that*

$$v_i(A_i) \geq \frac{\theta}{\theta + 1 - 1/n'} \cdot \boldsymbol{\mu}_i(n', M'),$$

where $n' = |N'|$ *and* $M' = \bigcup_{j \in N'} A_j$.

Proof. Let N' be a set as in the statement. We first claim that it is without loss of generality to assume that $|A_j| \geq 2$ for all $j \in N' \setminus \{i\}$. Indeed, if $|A_j| = 1$ for some $j \in N' \setminus \{i\}$, then the restriction of $\mathcal{A}$ on $N' \setminus \{j\}$ is an allocation of $M' \setminus A_j$ to $N' \setminus \{j\}$ and, by Lemma 1, $\boldsymbol{\mu}_i(n'-1, M' \setminus A_j) \geq \boldsymbol{\mu}_i(n', M')$. Thus, any guarantee shown with respect to $N' \setminus \{j\}$ directly holds for N' as well. As a result, in what follows we assume that $|A_j| \geq 2$ for all $j \in N' \setminus \{i\}$.

Let A_ℓ, $\ell \in N'$, be some bundle envied by agent i. If no items were added to A_ℓ during the Envy-Cycle-Elimination step then we can write $A_\ell = \{f_k, s_k\}$, where $k \in R$ is the agent to whom the initial version of this bundle originally belonged. By part b) of Corollary 1, $v_i(f_i) \geq v_i(f_k)$ and, hence agent i envies A_ℓ only after the addition of its second, and last, item, s_k. The same property holds when items were added to A_ℓ during the Envy-Cycle-Elimination step in line 10; agent i envies A_ℓ after the addition of its last item. In any case, call g the last item added to A_ℓ. By the discussion above, $v_i(A_i) \geq v_i(A_\ell \setminus \{g\})$.

By part a) of Corollary 1, we also have that $v_i(g) \leq v_i(f_i)/\theta$, as g was unallocated in $\mathcal{F}$, and thus $v_i(g) \leq v_i(A_i)/\theta$, by the monotonicity of Envy-Cycle-Elimination (Theorem 1). Combining these, we get

$$v_i(A_\ell) \leq \frac{\theta+1}{\theta} \cdot v_i(A_i).$$

Given that the same bound trivially holds for non-envied agents, we can now bound the maximin share $\boldsymbol{\mu}_i(n', M')$ via the total value of M' for agent i:

$$\begin{aligned}\boldsymbol{\mu}_i(n', M') &\leq \frac{1}{n'} v_i(M') = \frac{1}{n'}\left[v_i(A_i) + \sum_{k \in N' \setminus \{i\}} v_i(A_k)\right] \\ &\leq \frac{1}{n'}\left[1 + (n'-1)\frac{\theta+1}{\theta}\right] v_i(A_i) = \frac{n'\theta + n' - 1}{n'\theta} v_i(A_i).\end{aligned}$$

Therefore, $v_i(A_i) \geq \dfrac{\theta}{\theta + 1 - 1/n'} \boldsymbol{\mu}_i(n', M')$.

□

We next move on to the much more challenging case of agents in R. Lemma 5 heavily uses reductions and monotonicity properties of the maximin share.

Lemma 5. ***(Agents in*** R***).*** *Fix any* $\theta \geq \frac{3}{2}$ *and let* $\mathcal{A}$ *be the output of Match-Draft-and-Eliminate*(N, M, θ)*. Then, for any* $i \in R$ *and for any* $N' \subseteq N$ *with* $i \in N'$*, it holds that*

$$v_i(A_i) \geq \frac{1}{\theta} \cdot \boldsymbol{\mu}_i(n', M'),$$

where $n' = |N'|$ *and* $M' = \bigcup_{j \in N'} A_j$.

Proof. We first consider the intermediate allocation $\mathcal{S}$, i.e., before the execution of Envy-Cycle-Elimination. For brevity, we set $v_i(f_i) = x$; then $v_i(s_i) = \delta \cdot v_i(f_i) = \delta x$, for some $\delta \in [0, 1]$, by part d) of Corollary 1. Now, for agent i's final bundle, A_i, we know that $v_i(A_i) \geq v_i(\{f_i, s_i\})$, by Theorem 1. Thus

$$v_i(A_i) \geq (1+\delta)x. \tag{1}$$

Let N' be a set as in the statement. Without loss of generality—as we showed in the beginning of the proof of Lemma 4—we may assume that $|A_j| \geq 2$ for all $j \in N' \setminus \{i\}$. Also, before we go any further, notice that if $v_i(A_i) = 0$, then there are less than n positively valued items for agent i and are all allocated in $\mathcal{F}$. Thus, $\boldsymbol{\mu}_i(n', M') = 0$ and the statement trivially holds for agent i. So, we assume that $v_i(A_i) > 0$.

Next, we will argue about the value agent i has for any other bundle A_ℓ, $\ell \in N'$, in the final allocation. We categorize the other agents of N' into three groups N_1, N_2 and N_3 based on how their bundles received their last item and, thus, how agent i's envy towards them may have formed. The set N_1 contains all agents of $N' \setminus \{i\}$ whose bundle received an item for the last time during the Envy-Cycle-Elimination step in line 10. This means that the sets N_2 and N_3 contain the agents of $N' \setminus \{i\}$ whose bundle received a second item in lines 5–7 and was never augmented by Envy-Cycle-Elimination. In particular, if a bundle received its second and last item *after* agent i received s_i, then its final owner is in N_2, whereas if a bundle received its second and last item *before* agent i received s_i, then its final owner is in N_3.

We argue about agents of different types separately. In general, although we want to refer to a bundle A_ℓ owned by $\ell \in N'$ in the final allocation, when A_ℓ received its last item (which determines whether ℓ is in N_1, N_2 or N_3) it might have belonged to another agent $k \in N$. To avoid cumbersome notation, as we examine the different cases for such an agent $\ell \in N'$ below, we will consistently assume that A_ℓ belonged to agent $k \in N$ when it received its last item and use $\mathcal{B} = (B_1, \ldots, B_n)$ to denote the allocation at the time.

- $\ell \in N_1$. That is, $A_\ell = B_k$ and agent k received the last item, say g, in line 10. Then we have that $v_i(A_\ell) = v_i(B_k) \leq v_i(B_i) + v_i(g) \leq v_i(A_i) + \delta x$. To see this, at the time agent i was not envious of agent k before item g was added (as k must have been a source of the envy graph), i.e., $v_i(B_i) \geq v_i(B_k \setminus \{g\})$. Further, we know that $v_i(g) \leq v_i(s_i) = \delta x$ (or agent i would have picked g instead of s_i in lines 5–7). Using (1) we get that

$$v_i(A_k) \leq \frac{1 + 2\delta}{1 + \delta} v_i(A_i). \tag{2}$$

- $\ell \in N_2$. That is, $A_\ell = B_k = \{f_k, s_k\}$ and s_k was allocated after s_i. Then we have that $\theta \cdot v_i(f_i) \geq v_i(f_k)$ by part c) of Corollary 1 and $v_i(s_k) \leq v_i(s_i) = \delta x$ (or agent i would have picked s_k instead of s_i in lines 5–7) Thus, in total $v_i(A_\ell) = v_i(B_k) \leq (\theta + \delta)x$. Again, using (1) we get that

$$v_i(A_k) \leq \frac{\theta + \delta}{1 + \delta} v_i(A_i). \tag{3}$$

- $\ell \in N_3$. That is, $A_\ell = B_k = \{f_k, s_k\}$ and s_k was allocated before s_i. Now, we have that agent i prefers neither f_k (or else i would be before k in the topological ordering σ in line 3 and s_i would have been allocated before s_k) nor s_k (by part d) of Corollary 1) to f_i. Thus $v_i(A_\ell) = v_i(B_k) \leq 2x$ and using

(1) we get that

$$v_i(A_k) \leq \frac{2}{1+\delta} v_i(A_i). \tag{4}$$

Our next step is to further reduce the instance. Let n_1, n_2, n_3 be the cardinalities of N_1, N_2, N_3 respectively.

We will say that an item is *problematic* if it belongs to some agent in N_3 or if it is the first item added (via $\mathcal{F}$) to a bundle that belongs to some agent in N_2. The number of problematic items is $p := 2n_3 + n_2$, by definition.

We claim that as long as p is larger than the total number of agents, $n' = n_1 + n_2 + n_3 + 1$, we can remove a pair of problematic items and an agent without ever reducing the maximin share of agent i. Indeed, consider a n'-maximin share defining partition $\mathcal{C}$ for agent i with respect to M'. By the pigeonhole principle, if $p > n'$, then there is a bundle of $\mathcal{C}$ containing two problematic goods, say g_1, g_2. We remove those two goods and reduce the number of agents by one; by Lemma 1, we have $\boldsymbol{\mu}_i(n'-1, M' \setminus \{g_1, g_2\}) \geq \boldsymbol{\mu}_i(n', M')$.

So, we may assume that we have already performed these reductions up to the point where there are no more problematic items than agents in the reduced instance. Next, we claim that the remaining items can be partitioned in a *virtual* allocation that closely resembles the restriction of $\mathcal{A}$ on N' after the removal of agents with singletons, and crucially shares the same properties with respect to the bounds derived above in (2), (3) and (4). Indeed, if $\ell \in N_1 \cup \{i\}$, then A_ℓ has remained intact; if $\ell \in N_2$ and A_ℓ lost its problematic item, this can be replaced by an arbitrary problematic item originally belonging to some agent of N_2; and, finally, if there are more problematic items, these can be arbitrarily partitioned in sets of size 2 and be given to (some of the) agents of N_3.

To avoid introducing additional notation for essentially the same thing, from this point onward, we are going to use $N', M', N_1, N_2, N_3, n', n_1, n_2, n_3$ for the final reduced instance. The virtual allocation described above will be denoted by $\mathcal{A}' = (A'_1, \dots, A'_n)$. As we mentioned above, and easily follows by their definition, the bundles of $\mathcal{A}'$ satisfy (2), (3) and (4), whereas $A'_i = A_i$. Further, since the instance is reduced, we now have $2n_3 + n_2 \leq n_1 + n_2 + n_3 + 1$ or, equivalently, $n_3 \leq n_1 + 1$.

Next, we will bound the total value of agent i for M' in this reduced instance.

$$\begin{aligned} v_i(M') &= \sum_{k \in N_1} v_i(A'_k) + \sum_{k \in N_2} v_i(A'_k) + \sum_{k \in N_3} v_i(A'_k) + v_i(A_i) \\ &\leq n_1 \frac{1+2\delta}{1+\delta} v_i(A_i) + n_2 \frac{\theta+\delta}{1+\delta} v_i(A_i) + n_3 \frac{2}{1+\delta} v_i(A_i) + v_i(A_i). \end{aligned}$$

By dividing with $v_i(A_i)$ and rearranging some terms, we get

$$\begin{aligned}\frac{v_i(M')}{v_i(A_i)} &\le n_1\frac{1+2\delta}{1+\delta}+n_2\frac{\theta+\delta}{1+\delta}+n_3\frac{2}{1+\delta}+1\\ &= n_1\frac{1+2\delta}{1+\delta}+(n'-n_1-n_3-1)\frac{\theta+\delta}{1+\delta}+n_3\frac{2}{1+\delta}+1\\ &= n'\frac{\theta+\delta}{1+\delta}+n_1\frac{1+\delta-\theta}{1+\delta}+n_3\frac{2-\delta-\theta}{1+\delta}-\frac{\theta-1}{1+\delta}\end{aligned}$$

Now we have cases based on the sign of the coefficients of n_1 and n_3. Since $\theta \ge 3/2$ and at most one of $1+\delta$ or $2-\delta$ can be greater than $3/2$, at most one term is positive. If they are both negative, then we immediately obtain:

$$\frac{v_i(M')}{v_i(A_i)} \le n'\frac{\theta+\delta}{1+\delta} \implies v_i(A_i) \ge \frac{1+\delta}{\theta+\delta}\frac{v_i(M')}{n'} \ge \frac{1}{\theta}\boldsymbol{\mu}_i(n',M'),$$

where the last inequality follows from the fact that $\frac{1+\delta}{\theta+\delta}$ as a function of $\delta \in [0,1]$ is minimized for $\delta = 0$.

Next, if the coefficient of n_3 is negative, we have that

$$\begin{aligned}\frac{v_i(M')}{v_i(A_i)} &\le n'\frac{\theta+\delta}{1+\delta}+n_1\frac{1+\delta-\theta}{1+\delta}\\ &\le n'\frac{\theta+\delta}{1+\delta}+n'\frac{1+\delta-\theta}{1+\delta}=n'\frac{1+2\delta}{1+\delta} \implies\\ v_i(A_i) &\ge \frac{1+\delta}{1+2\delta}\frac{v_i(M')}{n'} \ge \frac{2}{3}\boldsymbol{\mu}_i(n',M') \ge \frac{1}{\theta}\boldsymbol{\mu}_i(n',M'),\end{aligned}$$

where the second to last inequality follows from the fact that $\frac{1+\delta}{1+2\delta}$ as a function of $\delta \in [0,1]$ is minimized for $\delta = 1$.

Finally, if the coefficient of n_3 is positive, we have that

$$\begin{aligned}\frac{v_i(M')}{v_i(A_i)} &\le n'\frac{\theta+\delta}{1+\delta}+n_1\frac{1+\delta-\theta}{1+\delta}+(n_1+1)\frac{2-\delta-\theta}{1+\delta}-\frac{\theta-1}{1+\delta}\\ &= n'\frac{\theta+\delta}{1+\delta}+n_1\frac{3--2\theta}{1+\delta}+\frac{3-2\theta-\delta}{1+\delta} \le n'\frac{\theta+\delta}{1+\delta} \implies\\ v_i(A_i) &\ge \frac{1+\delta}{\theta+\delta}\frac{v_i(M')}{n'} \ge \frac{1}{\theta}\boldsymbol{\mu}_i(n',M').\end{aligned}$$

Since both reductions (removing a bundle of cardinality 1 along with the corresponding agent and removing 2 problematic items along with an agent in N_2) weakly increase the maximin share of agent i, our $1/\theta$ guarantee holds for any arbitrary $N' \subseteq N$. □

Although the proof of Theorem 2 is deferred to the full version of our work [4], its most relevant part, the calculation of the GMMS approximation, is essentially the same as the one in the proof of Theorem 3 below. We present this one here as it results in an improved factor for any fixed n (at the expence of the EFX approximation) (Fig. 1).

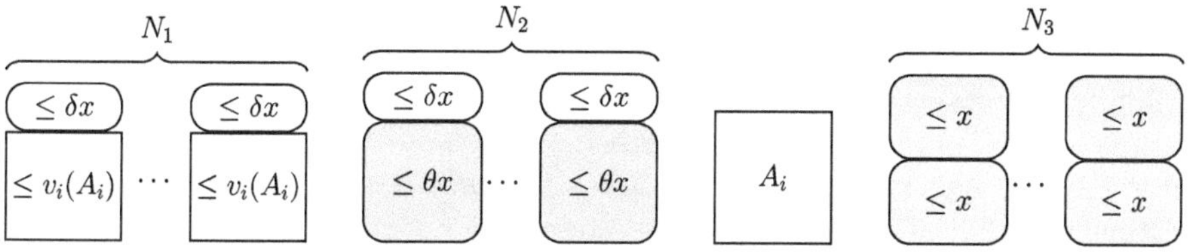

Fig. 1. The structure of the allocation in the proof of Lemma 5 after the reductions that remove agents with singleton bundles, where square boxes denote bundles while rounded ones correspond to a single item. This, however, is also the structure of the virtual allocation $\mathcal{A}'$ we reconstruct after the reductions that remove agents along with pairs of problematic items. The latter are colored; orange for N_2 and pink for N_3.

Theorem 3. *Set* $\theta_n = \max\left\{\frac{3}{2}, \frac{1+\sqrt{5-4/n}}{2}\right\}$. *Then, the allocation* $\mathcal{A}$ *returned by Match-Draft-and-Eliminate*(N, M, θ_n) *is* $\min\left\{\frac{2}{3}, \frac{\sqrt{5n^2-4n}-n}{2n-2}\right\}$-GMMS.

Proof. We invoke Lemma 4 for the agents of $N \setminus R$ and Lemma 5 for the agents of R with parameter $\theta_n \geq 3/2$. Thus, the approximation factor of the final allocation with respect to GMMS is

$$\min\left\{\frac{\theta_n}{\theta_n + 1 - \frac{1}{n}}, \frac{1}{\theta_n}\right\}.$$

Equating the two quantities gives

$$\theta_n^2 - \theta_n - 1 + \frac{1}{n} = 0 \implies \theta_n = \frac{1 \pm \sqrt{5 - 4/n}}{2}$$

Of course, to satisfy the condition $\theta_n \geq 3/2$ we keep the larger solution. Moreover, note that for $n \leq 4$, we have $\frac{1+\sqrt{5-4/n}}{2} \leq 3/2$, thus we must set $\theta_n = 3/2$ to obtain the approximation factor $2/3$. For $n \geq 5$, by setting $\theta_n = \frac{1+\sqrt{5-4/n}}{2}$ we obtain the factor $\frac{\sqrt{5n^2-4n}-n}{2n-2}$. □

Using the proportional share, i.e., the $1/n$-th of the total value, as a proxy for maximin share is very convenient but, more often than not, results in rather loose bounds. Although our analysis leading to $\phi - 1$ is very detailed, it is still surprising that it is tight, as shown below. The proof of Theorem 4, which is deferred to the full version of our paper [4], can easily be adjusted to show that corresponding algorithms of Amanatidis et al. [5] and Farhadi et al. [12] cannot go beyond an approximation factor of $\phi - 1$ either.

Theorem 4. *Let* $\delta > 0$ *and* $\theta \geq 1$. *Algorithm 1 with parameter* θ *does not always produce* $(\phi - 1 + \delta)$-GMMS *allocations.*

4 Improved Guarantees for Restricted Settings

In this section we exhibit some interesting special cases where we can have even better approximation guarantees for GMMS.

4.1 Agreement on the n Most Desirable Items

A family of instances that has recently attracted more attention in the literature is the class we refer to as top-n instances. In a top-n instance, all agents agree on the set of their n most desirable items (but not necessarily on their value or on their ranking of these items). The main motivation for examining this class is that it is a relaxation of ordered valuations (where the agents agree on the ranking of all items), which has been extensively studied in the fair division literature. Additionally, recent works have established improved approximation guarantees for top-n instances for various fairness notions, see e.g., [1,11,20,21].

The work of Markakis and Santorinaios [21] proposed an algorithm that achieves a 2/3-EFX guarantee for top-n instances, improving upon the best-known $(\phi - 1)$ approximation of EFX for additive instances. Our main result in this subsection is that we can have the same improvement for GMMS as well. This is achieved by a slight modification of the algorithm in [21], and its pseudocode is presented as Algorithm 2. The main difference is the condition in line 6. This is similar in spirit but simpler than Algorithm 1, in the sense that again each agent receives one or two items before Envy-Cycle-Elimination begins.

Algorithm 2: Select-and-Eliminate(N, M)

---

1 Let T be the set of the n most desirable items and set $B = M \setminus T$
2 **for** *each agent* $i = 1, \ldots, n$ **do**
3     $f_i^+ = \arg\max_{g \in T} v_i(g)$
4     $f_i^- = \arg\min_{g \in T} v_i(g)$
5     $s_i = \arg\max_{g \in B} v_i(g)$
6   **if** $v_i(f_i^-) + v_i(s_i) \geq v_i(f_i^+)$ **then**
7         $A_i = \{s_i\}$
8         $B = B \setminus \{s_i\}$
9   **else**
10         $A_i = \{f_i^+\}$
11         $T = T \setminus \{f_i^+\}$
12 **for** *each agent* $i = n, \ldots, 1$ **do**
13   **if** $A_i = \{s_i\}$ **then**
14         $f_i = \arg\max_{g \in T} v_i(g)$
15         $A_i = A_i \cup \{f_i\}$
16 $\mathcal{A} =$ Envy-Cycle-Elimination$(N, \mathcal{A}, B)$
17 **return** $\mathcal{A}$

Lemma 6. *Let T be the set of the n most desirable items. Then, all agents are 2-content after all items of T get allocated.*

Proof. First, observe that all items from T are eventually allocated after the execution of the second for-loop, and each agent receives exactly one from that set. Let $\mathcal{A}$ be the allocation produced right after the second for-loop. Now, we have two cases based on whether agent i receives s_i first (through the if condition) or f_i^+ first. If she first receives s_i then she will also receive in line 15 some item f_i, which she values at least as much as f_i^-. Then $v_i(A_i) \geq v_i(\{f_i^-, s_i\}) \geq 2 \cdot v_i(s_i) \geq 2 \cdot v_i(g)\ \forall g \in \mathcal{P}(\mathcal{A})$. Similarly, if she receives f_i^+ then $v_i(A_i) = v_i(f_i^+) > v_i(\{f_i^-, s_i\})$, due to line 6. We then conclude as in the first case. □

Theorem 5. *In top-n instances, Select-and-Eliminate(N, M) returns in polynomial time an allocation $\mathcal{A}$ which is* 2/3-GMMS, EF1*, and* 2/3-EFX.

Corollary 2. *In ordered instances, Select-and-Eliminate(N, M) returns in polynomial time an allocation which is* 2/3-GMMS.

Remark 2. A similar construction as in the proof of Theorem 4 can be used to show that the approximation analysis of Select-and-Eliminate is also tight.

4.2 Three Agents

Here we present a variant of Match-Draft-and-Eliminate and an improved analysis tailored to the fundamental case of $n = 3$ The algorithm is identical to Algorithm 1, except it runs the Envy-Cycle-Elimination subroutine in it using a modification of the envy graph defined below. This construction is inspired by, but not identical to, the modified envy graph used by Kurokawa [17].

Let $\mathcal{S}$ be the allocation completed in line 9 of Algorithm 1. For any partial allocation $\mathcal{B} = (B_1, \dots, B_n)$ from this point onward, we define the *η-modified envy graph* $H_{\mathcal{B},\eta} = (N, E_{\mathcal{B},\eta})$, where an edge $(i, j) \in E_{\mathcal{B},\eta}$ if and only if

- $v_i(B_j) > (1 + \eta) \cdot v_i(B_i)$, when *all* of the following hold
  - $i \in R$,
  - $v_i(s_i) < \eta \cdot v_i(f_i)$,
  - $B_i \supseteq \{f_i, s_i\}$,
  - $\exists k \in N$ such that k's bundle received a second item in lines 5–7 *before* i received s_i and has not been augmented by Envy-Cycle-Elimination yet;
- $v_i(B_j) > v_i(B_i)$, otherwise.

In what follows we are going to set the parameter η equal to the solution to the equation $\frac{2+2\eta}{3+\eta} = \frac{3}{4+\eta}$, i.e., $\eta = \frac{\sqrt{57}-7}{4} \approx 0.1375$. On a high level, for some agents we only add an edge when there is "significant" envy. This is to guarantee that an agent who sees someone else having *two* "somewhat large" items does not end up with a highly divisible bundle (i.e., a bundle with a large number of "small" items from i's perspective) without significantly increasing her value. We call *η-Match-Draft-and-Eliminate* the variant of Algorithm 1 where the Envy-Cycle-Elimination in line 10 uses the η-modified envy graph instead.

Theorem 6. *Let $\theta = \frac{\sqrt{10}+2}{3}$ and $\eta = \frac{\sqrt{57}-7}{4}$. For any instance with three agents, η-Match-Draft-and-Eliminate(N, M, θ) outputs a $\frac{\sqrt{10}-1}{3}$-*GMMS *allocation.*

We may observe that the last condition for modifying some agent i's outgoing envy edges in $H_{\mathcal{B},\eta}$ is reminiscent of the way agents of the set N_3 were defined within the proof of Lemma 5. Indeed, we need a similar categorization of the agents in $N \setminus \{i\}$. So, given $i \in N$, we partition $N \setminus \{i\}$ to N_1, N_2, N_3 as follows:

- N_1 contains all agents of $N \setminus \{i\}$ whose bundle in $\mathcal{A}$ received an item for the last time during the Envy-Cycle-Elimination step in line 10;
- N_2 contains all agents of $N \setminus \{i\}$ whose bundle in $\mathcal{A}$ received its second and last item *after* agent i received s_i;
- N_3 contains all agents of $N \setminus \{i\}$ whose bundle in $\mathcal{A}$ received its second and last item *before* agent i received s_i.

Like before, by n_1, n_2, n_3 we denote the cardinalities of N_1, N_2, N_3 respectively. Consider a subset $S \subseteq N$ and fix some $i \in S$. If necessary, we reduce the subinstance induced by S to get rid of agents with bundles of cardinality 1 (along with their bundles), as discussed in the beginning of the proof of Lemma 4. The result is a new instance on $N' \subseteq S$ with $|N'| = n'$, so that there is no $j \in N' \setminus \{i\}$ such that $|A_j| = 1$. Depending whether i is in R or not, as well as on the values of n', n_1, n_2, n_3, we consider a number of distinct cases. As the proof is long and technical, we do not present it here (see [4]) but, to give an overview, Table 1 summarizes all the cases along with the corresponding approximation ratio and a pointer to the proposition handling this case.

Table 1. Summary of approximation factors for each case, evaluated at $\theta = \frac{\sqrt{10}+2}{3}$ and $\eta = \frac{\sqrt{57}-7}{4} \approx 0.1375$.

Case	Description	Factor	Value ($\theta = \frac{\sqrt{10}+2}{3}$, $\eta = \frac{\sqrt{57}-7}{4}$)
1	$i \in N \setminus R$, $n' \in [3]$	$\dfrac{3\theta}{3\theta+2}$	**0.72076**
2.1	$n' = 2$, $n_1 = 1$	$3/4$	0.75
2.2	$n' = 2$, $n_2 = 1$	$\dfrac{2}{1+\theta}$	0.73509
2.3	$n' = 2$, $n_3 = 1$	$\dfrac{2+2\eta}{3+\eta}$	0.72508
3.1	$n' = 3$, $n_1 = 2$	$3/4$	0.75
3.2	$n' = 3$, $n_2 = 2$	$\dfrac{2+\theta}{3\theta}$	**0.72076**
3.3	$n' = 3$, $n_3 = 2$	1	1
3.4	$n' = 3$, $n_1 = n_2 = 1$	$3/4$	0.75
3.5	$n' = 3$, $n_1 = n_3 = 1$	$\dfrac{3}{4+\eta}$	0.72508
3.6	$n' = 3$, $n_2 = n_3 = 1$	$3/4$	0.75
Overall (minimum)			**0.72076**

5 Discussion

In this work we show that $(\phi - 1)$-GMMS allocations always exist and can be efficiently computed, for any number of agents with additive valuation functions. For small values of n or for instances where the agents agree about their top-n goods, we obtain significant improvements. This is the first improvement on GMMS allocations since the works of Chaudhury et al. [10] and Amanatidis et al. [5], indicating how challenging the problem is. A main reason for this is that the notion of GMMS fairness seems to combine characteristics of both share-based and envy-based notions, without fitting well with either of them. Besides the obvious direction of improving our results (computationally or existentially), showing upper bounds, or extending the study of GMMS fairness beyond the additive domain, there is a less well-defined but very intriguing direction. There is a strong underlying connection between the notions of GMMS and EFX: approximately EFX allocations are approximately GMMS [3], exact GMMS allocations are EFX (albeit for a slightly weaker version of EFX) [6], the state-of-the-art approximation algorithms for the two notions are the same and, as it turns out now, with the same exact approximation ratio. Given the significance of EFX-related questions in the recent development of the fair division literature, we believe that the connection between the two notions should be further explored.

Acknowledgment. This work was supported by the project MIS 5154714 of the National Recovery and Resilience Plan "Greece 2.0" funded by the European Union under the NextGenerationEU Program.

Disclosure of Interests. The authors have no competing interests.

References

1. Akrami, H., Reichert, T.: Simultaneous ordinal maximin share and envy-based guarantees. CoRR **abs/2602.15566** (2026). https://doi.org/10.48550/arXiv.2602.15566
2. Amanatidis, G., et al.: Fair division of indivisible goods: Recent progress and open questions. Artif. Intell. **322**, 103965 (2023)
3. Amanatidis, G., Birmpas, G., Markakis, V.: Comparing approximate relaxations of envy-freeness. In: Proceedings of the Twenty-Seventh International Joint Conference on Artificial Intelligence, IJCAI 2018, pp. 42–48. ijcai.org (2018)
4. Amanatidis, G., Korfiati, A., Markakis, E., Santorinaios, C.: Improved approximation guarantees for groupwise maximin share fairness. CoRR **abs/2606.04731** (2026). https://doi.org/10.48550/arXiv.2606.04731
5. Amanatidis, G., Markakis, E., Ntokos, A.: Multiple birds with one stone: Beating 1/2 for EFX and GMMS via envy cycle elimination. Theoret. Comput. Sci. **841**, 94–109 (2020)
6. Barman, S., Biswas, A., Murthy, S.K.K., Narahari, Y.: Groupwise maximin fair allocation of indivisible goods. In: Proceedings of the Thirty-Second AAAI Conference on Artificial Intelligence, (AAAI-18), pp. 917–924. AAAI Press (2018)

7. Bouveret, S., Lemaître, M.: Characterizing conflicts in fair division of indivisible goods using a scale of criteria. Auton. Agent. Multi-Agent Syst. **30**(2), 259–290 (2016)
8. Budish, E.: The combinatorial assignment problem: Approximate competitive equilibrium from equal incomes. J. of Polit. Econ. **119**(6), 1061–1103 (2011)
9. Caragiannis, I., Kurokawa, D., Moulin, H., Procaccia, A.D., Shah, N., Wang, J.: The unreasonable fairness of maximum Nash welfare. ACM Trans. Econ. Comput. **7**(3), 12:1–12:32 (2019)
10. Chaudhury, B.R., Kavitha, T., Mehlhorn, K., Sgouritsa, A.: A little charity guarantees almost envy-freeness. SIAM J. Comput. **50**(4), 1336–1358 (2021)
11. Christoforidis, V., Santorinaios, C.: On the pursuit of EFX for chores: Non-existence and approximations. In: Proceedings of the 33rd International Joint Conference on Artificial Intelligence, IJCAI 2024, pp. 2713–2721. ijcai.org (2024)
12. Farhadi, A., Hajiaghayi, M.T., Latifian, M., Seddighin, M., Yami, H.: Almost envy-freeness, envy-rank, and Nash social welfare matchings. In: 35th AAAI Conference on Artificial Intelligence, AAAI 2021, pp. 5355–5362. AAAI Press (2021)
13. Feige, U., Sapir, A., Tauber, L.: A Tight Negative Example for MMS Fair Allocations. In: Feldman, M., Fu, H., Talgam-Cohen, I. (eds.) WINE 2021. LNCS, vol. 13112, pp. 355–372. Springer, Cham (2022). https://doi.org/10.1007/978-3-030-94676-0_20
14. Foley, D.K.: Resource allocation and the public sector. Yale Econ. Essays **7**, 45–98 (1967)
15. Gamow, G., Stern, M.: Puzzle-Math. Viking press (1958)
16. Heidari, E., Kaviani, A., Seddighin, M., Shahrezaei, A.: Improved maximin share guarantee for additive valuations. In: Proceedings of the 2026 Annual ACM-SIAM Symposium on Discrete Algorithms, SODA 2026, pp. 2239–2290. SIAM (2026)
17. Kurokawa, D.: Fair Division in Game Theoretic Settings, Ph.D. thesis. Carnegie Mellon University (2017)
18. Kurokawa, D., Procaccia, A.D., Wang, J.: Fair enough: Guaranteeing approximate maximin shares. J. ACM (JACM) **65**(2), 1–27 (2018)
19. Lipton, R.J., Markakis, E., Mossel, E., Saberi, A.: On approximately fair allocations of indivisible goods. In: Proceedings 5th ACM Conference on Electronic Commerce (EC-2004), pp. 125–131. ACM (2004)
20. Mancho, A., Markakis, E., Protopapas, N.: Fairness under equal-sized bundles: Impossibility results and approximation guarantees. In: 18th International Symposium on Algorithmic Game Theory, SAGT 2025, pp. 191–208 (2025)
21. Markakis, E., Santorinaios, C.: Improved EFX approximation guarantees under ordinal-based assumptions. In: Proceedings of the 22nd International Conference on Autonomous Agents and Multiagent Systems, AAMAS 2023, pp. 591–599 (2023)
22. Plaut, B., Roughgarden, T.: Almost envy-freeness with general valuations. In: Proceedings of the Twenty-Ninth Annual ACM-SIAM Symposium on Discrete Algorithms, SODA 2018, pp. 2584–2603. SIAM (2018)
23. Steinhaus, H.: Sur la division pragmatique. Econometrica **17**(Supplement), 315–319 (1949)
24. Varian, H.R.: Equity, envy and efficiency. J. Econ. Theory **9**, 63–91 (1974)

Single-Agent Stability in Additively Separable Hedonic Games with Constrained Coalition Sizes

Martin Bullinger[1](✉), Adam Dunajski[2], Edith Elkind[3], and Matan Gilboa[4]

[1] University of Bristol, Bristol, United Kingdom
martin.bullinger@bristol.ac.uk
[2] University of Edinburgh, Edinburgh, United Kingdom
a.dunajski@sms.ed.ac.uk
[3] Northwestern University, Evanston, Illinois, USA
edith.elkind@northwestern.edu
[4] University of Oxford, Oxford, United Kingdom
matan.gilboa@cs.ox.ac.uk

Abstract. We study stability in additively separable hedonic games when coalition sizes have to respect a fixed lower bound λ and upper bound μ. We consider four classic notions of stability based on single-agent deviations, namely, Nash stability, individual stability, contractual Nash stability, and contractual individual stability. For each stability notion, we consider two variants: in one, the coalition left behind by a deviator must still be of size at least λ, and in the other there is no such constraint. We provide a full picture of the existence of stable outcomes with respect to given parameters λ and μ. Additionally, when there are only upper bounds on coalition sizes, we fully characterize the computational complexity of the associated existence problem. In particular, we obtain polynomial-time algorithms for contractual individual stability and contractual Nash stability, where the latter requires $\mu = 2$. We obtain further results for Nash stability and contractual individual stability when $\lambda \geq 2$.

Keywords: Algorithmic game theory · Coalition formation · Hedonic games · Stability

1 Introduction

Imagine you are tasked with splitting undergraduate students into groups for a collaborative coursework project. Clearly, the groups should not be too large. Moreover, students may additionally need to gain experience in working as a team, and thus there may also be a lower bound on the size of each group. Ideally, the partition of the students into groups should also be robust to students wishing to switch groups, as any such switch contributes to administrative overhead.

P. Lenzner and D. Schmand (Eds.): SAGT 2026, LNCS 16911, pp. 57–75, 2027.
https://doi.org/10.1007/978-3-032-38782-0_4

Similar scenarios arise in several other settings. These include assigning desks to faculty in a department with multi-person offices, assigning participants to hiking groups on Duke of Edinburgh expeditions (which are required to have groups of four to seven participants), organizing seating plans for conference dinners and so on.

Such scenarios can be captured by the framework of *hedonic games*, first presented by Drèze and Greenberg [21]. We study the combination of the two key aspects of the above examples, namely prominent deviation-based stability concepts and the natural constraint of coalition-size bounds. The latter has received little attention so far in the widely used framework of additively separable utilities [8]: Lower and upper bounds have been studied in a mechanism design perspective by Wright and Vorobeychik [36] and group stability and welfare maximization have been studied for upper bounds [23,30].

By contrast, we investigate additively separable hedonic games under stability concepts involving deviations by single agents, including Nash stability (NS), individual stability (IS), contractual Nash stability (CNS), and contractual individual stability (CIS). We only allow deviations into coalitions of size smaller than the upper bound, i.e., the welcoming coalition must be feasible after the deviation, which is a natural assumption. However, it is not as clear whether the size of the abandoned coalition should be constrained in the same way: On the one hand, a selfish agent might not care about the feasibility of the abandoned coalition, while on the other hand, in some settings such deviations may be prohibited (e.g., students are only allowed to leave their project group if the remaining group is large enough). To capture this, we introduce two variants of each stability notion distinguished by an asterisk: a *standard* notion (e.g., NS) where deviations (e.g., a Nash deviation) may render the abandoned coalition infeasible and a *feasible* notion (e.g., NS*) where a deviation must maintain the feasibility of the abandoned coalition.

Table 1. Existence and computational complexity of stability for given size bounds λ and μ. SYM means existence only for symmetric ASHGs while nonexistence (✗) also holds for symmetric ASHGs. Red cells indicate NP-completeness and green cells polynomial-time computability. In the cells, we indicate conditions on the parameters under which these hold. We use inequalities to refer to any parameter satisfying the inequality. CIS* partitions for any size-bound parameters can also be computed in polynomial time for nonzero and nonnegative ASHGs.

	NS	IS	CNS	CIS	NS*	IS*	CNS*	CIS*
Existence	✗	✗	✗	✗	SYM	SYM	SYM	✓
Complexity for (λ, μ)	$(1, \geq 2)$ $(\leq 3, \geq 4)$	$(1, \geq 2)$	$(1, 2)$ $(1, \geq 3)$	$(1, \geq 2)$	$(1, \geq 2)$	$(1, \geq 2)$	$(1, 2)$ $(1, \geq 3)$	$(1, \geq 2)$

An overview of our results is provided in Table 1. We begin with some preliminary considerations about the existence of coalition structures that satisfy the size constraints. We provide a simple characterization and apply it to show that outcomes satisfying fixed size constraints always exist for a sufficiently large number of agents. Our main objective is then to study the existence of *stable* outcomes and the computational complexity of deciding whether one exists. We fully classify existence for all mentioned stability concepts: Akin to similar settings, symmetric valuations lead to existence of NS*, the strongest feasible stability concept. By contrast, even for symmetric 0/1-valuations, CIS outcomes, i.e., the weakest standard stability notion, may not exist. Note that NS* does not imply any standard stability notion, cf. Example 1. Moreover, for nonsymmetric valuations, only CIS* outcomes are guaranteed to exist.

We continue with establishing a complete complexity picture for the setting where coalition sizes are only constrained by an upper bound μ. In particular, we provide a polynomial-time algorithm for CIS, amending an algorithm by Aziz et al. [4]. In addition, we present a polynomial-time algorithm for the construction of CNS outcomes when $\mu = 2$. For all other upper bounds (and a lower bound of $\lambda = 1$) and all other stability concepts, we obtain NP-completeness of the existence of stability.

We conclude with results for a nontrivial lower bound $\lambda \geq 2$. We show NP-completeness for Nash stability for any size constraints satisfying $\mu \geq 4$ and $\lambda < \mu$. Finally, we present polynomial-time algorithms for CIS* for any λ and μ when the additively separable valuations are nonzero or nonnegative.

All proofs missing from the paper are available on arXiv [11].

2 Related Work

Hedonic games were first introduced by Drèze and Greenberg [21], and started to receive continuous and extensive attention since the introduction of additively separable hedonic games (ASHGs) by Bogomolnaia and Jackson [8] two decades later. The book chapters by Aziz and Savani [5] and Bullinger et al. [12] present introductory texts.

A main goal in hedonic games is to consider the existence and computability of stable outcomes. The stability notions based on single-agent deviations that we consider are well understood for ASHGs under unconstrained coalition sizes. The existence problem for NS, IS, and CNS is known to be NP-complete [10,34], while CIS admits a polynomial-time algorithm [4].[1] Notions of group stability as measured by the core or strict core, and popularity are even known to be Σ_2^p-complete [13,35]. By contrast, some positive results are known, in particular for restricted domains of valuations. First, symmetric valuations lead to Nash-stable outcomes [8], a common result in hedonic games that we will extend to coalition size bounds. Moreover, if the range of valuations contains only one nonpositive or one nonnegative value, then existence of IS and CNS is guaranteed [10]. These restrictions encompass, in particular, subclasses of ASHGs based on the distinction of friends and enemies, for which even group-stable outcomes exist

[1] Unfortunately, we identify an inaccuracy in this algorithm that we rectify in our treatment of CIS.

[20]. Notably, our counterexamples to existence even hold under these preference restrictions. Finally, IS and CNS exist and are efficiently computable in random ASHGs, while NS does not exist with high probability [14].

We next discuss related work on hedonic games with constraints on coalition sizes. Levinger et al. [30] study ASHGs under both welfare maximization and stability based on group deviations. They find hardness for maximizing welfare as well as for the existence of an outcome in the core or strict core. By contrast, an outcome in the contractual strict core exists and can be computed in polynomial time. In addition, Fioravantes et al. [23] provide a more nuanced picture of the parameterized complexity of welfare maximality. Both of these focus on upper bounds on the coalition size. Wright and Vorobeychik [36] have lower and upper bounds and study the compatibility of incentive compatibility with high welfare and fairness in the sense of envy-freeness. Our work complements these works by studying prominent stability notions based on deviations by single agents.

In principle, ASHGs with coalition-size bounds can be modeled in fully expressive preference models, e.g., when explicitly listing coalition rankings [6] or encoding them with Boolean formulae [22]. However, since the reduced games in their hardness constructions do not fulfill our size constraints, their proofs do not extend to our setting. Another way to capture arbitrary hedonic games is via hedonic diversity games with an arbitrary number of colors [26]. However, their positive results mostly hold for a small number of colors (with the exception of a lemma concerning parameterized complexity) and thus do not have implications for our work.

Moreover, ASHGs with upper-bounded coalition sizes are a special case of topological distance games [15,19]. There, players are assigned to the vertices of a topology graph and obtain preferences based on additively separable valuations and their distance on the topology graph. The notion of jump stability for topological distance games is akin to NS for ASHGs. For this notion, Bullinger and Suksompong [15] obtain positive results for special valuations and topology graphs, most of which do not correspond to ASHGs. The only result that applies to our setting is for the severe restriction of nonnegative valuations where positive valuations form an acyclic graph. Furthermore, upper bounds on coalition sizes were also considered for online ASHGs [16,25].

We conclude with more loosely related models. Somewhat similar to bounded coalition sizes, Bilò et al. [7] require outputs of fixed coalition sizes. However, this means that coalitions are always at their upper size cap and, instead of single-agent deviations, stability is based on swaps. Another related question that implicitly enforces coalition bounds is to ask for a partition into a given number of coalitions [1,18,31]. This leads to lower bounds in particular when partitions have to be balanced, i.e., coalitions have to be of similar size. However, in this model the coalition size bounds depend on the total number of agents, while our bounds are global parameters. Note that Li et al. [31] and Agarwal et al. [1] only consider simple, i.e., unweighted, ASHGs. Moreover, these works consider different solution concepts, mostly inspired by envy-freeness in the fair division literature. Further developing this model, Fioravantes et al. [24] study partitioning into k coalitions, each of which may be constrained by a lower and an upper bound. They obtain a detailed (parameterized) complexity picture of individual rationality. This simple solution concept merely requires that agents are as well off as on their own. Finally, beyond ASHGs, Darmann et al. [17] consider coalition bounds for group activity selection, a model related to anonymous hedonic games [8].

3 Preliminaries

In this section, we define our model. Given a positive integer $i \in \mathbb{N}$, we use the notation $[i] := \{1, \ldots, i\}$.

3.1 Hedonic Games

Coalition formation is concerned with partitioning a set of agents into disjoint coalitions according to their preferences. We consider a finite set of agents N. A nonempty subset of N is called a *coalition*. We want coalitions to be within given *size bounds*. Let $\lambda, \mu \in \mathbb{N}$ with $\lambda \leq \mu$. A coalition $C \subseteq N$ with $\lambda \leq |C| \leq \mu$ is called a (λ, μ)-coalition. If $|C| = \mu$, we say that C is *full*. A *coalition structure* or *partition* of N is a set of pairwise disjoint coalitions whose union is N. Given a partition $\mathfrak{C}$, we denote by $\mathfrak{C}(a)$ the coalition containing agent a. A partition is called a (λ, μ)-partition if it consists of (λ, μ)-coalitions only.

Let $\mathcal{N}_a$ denote all possible coalitions containing agent a, i.e., $\mathcal{N}_a := \{C \subseteq N : a \in C\}$. A *hedonic game* is defined by a tuple $(N, \succsim)$, where N is an agent set and $\succsim = (\succsim_a)_{a \in N}$ is a tuple of weak orders $\succsim_a$ over $\mathcal{N}_a$. There, $\succsim_a$ represents the preferences of agent a. Let $C, C' \in \mathcal{N}_a$. We say that *a weakly prefers* C over C' if $C \succsim_a C'$. The strict part of $\succsim_a$ is denoted by $\succ_a$, i.e., $C \succ_a C'$ if and only if $C \succsim_a C'$ and not $C' \succsim_a C$. We say that *a prefers* C over C' if $C \succ_a C'$. We extend the preference order to partitions by setting $\mathfrak{C} \succsim_a \mathfrak{C}'$ if and only if $\mathfrak{C}(a) \succsim_a \mathfrak{C}'(a)$.

An important subclass of hedonic games are additively separable hedonic games as first considered by Bogomolnaia and Jackson [8]. They are encoded by a pair (N, v), where N is an agent set and $v = (v_a)_{a \in N}$ is a tuple of valuation functions $v_a \colon N \setminus \{a\} \to \mathbb{R}$. The *utility* of an agent $a \in N$ for coalition $C \in \mathcal{N}_a$ is defined as

$$u_a(C) := \sum_{b \in C \setminus \{a\}} v_a(b).$$

Note that this implies $u_a(\{a\}) = 0$. Utilities again extend to partitions by setting $u_a(\mathfrak{C}) := u_a(\mathfrak{C}(a))$. The *additively separable hedonic game* (ASHG) induced by (N, v) is the hedonic game $(N, \succsim)$, where for all $a \in N$ and $C, C' \in \mathcal{N}_a$,

$$C \succsim_a C' \text{ if and only if } \sum_{b \in C \setminus \{a\}} v_a(b) \geq \sum_{b \in C' \setminus \{a\}} v_a(b).$$

Hence, $C \succsim_a C'$ if and only if $u_a(C) \geq u_a(C')$.

Every ASHG can be naturally represented by a complete directed graph $G = (N, E)$ with weight $v_a(b)$ on arc (a, b). An ASHG is said to be *symmetric* if $v_a(b) = v_b(a)$ for all $a, b \in N$, and can be represented by a complete undirected graph with weight $v(a, b) = v_a(b)$ on edge $\{a, b\}$. An ASHG is said to be *simple* if $v_a(b) \in \{0, 1\}$ for all $a, b \in N$. Simple symmetric ASHGs can be represented by unweighted undirected graphs.

3.2 Useful Agent Sets

We continue with notation for certain sets of agents that will be important in our algorithms. Assume that we are given an ASHG (N, v) together with an agent $a \in N$.

We first introduce a notation for choosing a subset of most preferred agents among a given subset of agents. Let $A \subseteq N$ and $k \in \mathbb{N}$. If $k > |A \setminus \{a\}|$, we set $\mathrm{top}_a(k, A) = A \setminus \{a\}$. Otherwise, let $\mathrm{top}_a(k, A)$ be a subset of k agents among $A \setminus \{a\}$ that maximizes a's utility among subsets of size k from $A \setminus \{a\}$. We explicitly allow that $a \in A$ but a is never contained in $\mathrm{top}_a(k, A)$. Moreover, we can easily find $\mathrm{top}_a(k, A)$ in time polynomial in $n = |N|$: simply order agents in $A \setminus \{a\}$ by decreasing valuation for a and take the first k agents in the obtained order. Note that the obtained set is not necessarily unique, but our algorithms work for any such set.

Next, we want a notation for agents valued positively and negatively by a single agent or set of agents. Given $a, b \in N$, we say that b is a *friend* (or *enemy*) of a if $v_a(b) > 0$ (or $v_a(b) < 0$). Moreover, given an agent $a \in N$ and subsets $A, B \subseteq N$, we define $\mathrm{Fr}(a, B) := \{b \in B : v_a(b) > 0\}$, $\mathrm{Fr}(A, B) := \bigcup_{a \in A} \mathrm{Fr}(a, B)$, $\mathrm{En}(a, B) := \{b \in B : v_a(b) < 0\}$, and $\mathrm{En}(A, B) := \bigcup_{a \in A} \mathrm{En}(a, B)$. Hence, these sets capture the friends and enemies of an agent or a set of agents in B. Note that agents b with $v_a(b) = 0$ are neither friends nor enemies.

3.3 Single-Deviation Stability

Stability captures the absence of beneficial deviations by agents joining other coalitions or forming a new coalition. We focus on deviations by single agents. A *single-agent deviation* performed by agent a transforms a partition $\mathfrak{C}$ into a partition $\mathfrak{C}'$ where $\mathfrak{C}(a) \neq \mathfrak{C}'(a)$ and, for all agents $b \neq a$, it holds that $\mathfrak{C}(b) \setminus \{a\} = \mathfrak{C}'(b) \setminus \{a\}$. We write $\mathfrak{C} \xrightarrow{a} \mathfrak{C}'$ to denote such a single-agent deviation.

In the presence of size bounds, a deviating agent should, however, only end up in a coalition that obeys the bounds. A single-agent deviation $\mathfrak{C} \xrightarrow{a} \mathfrak{C}'$ is said to be *(λ, μ)-permissible* if $\lambda \leq |\mathfrak{C}'(a)| \leq \mu$. Hence, an agent is only allowed to form a new coalition if $\lambda = 1$, and an agent can only join a nonempty coalition of size at most $\mu - 1$.

We now introduce standard stability concepts based on single-agent deviations [8, 33]. However, in contrast to the known definitions for partitions without size constraints, our definition of stability is based on permissible deviations. We assume that we are given a fixed hedonic game $(N, \succsim)$ and size bounds $\lambda, \mu \in \mathbb{N}$ with $\lambda \leq \mu$.

A *Nash deviation* is a single-agent deviation $\mathfrak{C} \xrightarrow{a} \mathfrak{C}'$ such that $\mathfrak{C}'(a) \succ_a \mathfrak{C}(a)$. A (λ, μ)-partition $\mathfrak{C}$ is said to be *Nash-stable* (NS) if no agent can perform a (λ, μ)-permissible Nash deviation.

Since Nash stability disregards the preferences of agents apart from the deviating agent, various refinements have been proposed that additionally require the consent of the abandoned and the joined agents. An *individual deviation* is a Nash deviation $\mathfrak{C} \xrightarrow{a} \mathfrak{C}'$ such that $\{b \in \mathfrak{C}'(a) : \mathfrak{C}(b) \succ_b \mathfrak{C}'(b)\} = \emptyset$. Similarly, a *contractual deviation* is a Nash deviation $\mathfrak{C} \xrightarrow{a} \mathfrak{C}'$ such that $\{b \in \mathfrak{C}(a) : \mathfrak{C}(b) \succ_b \mathfrak{C}'(b)\} = \emptyset$. Moreover, $\mathfrak{C} \xrightarrow{a} \mathfrak{C}'$ is called a *contractual individual deviation* if it is both an individual and a contractual deviation. A (λ, μ)-partition is said to be *individually stable* (IS), *contractually Nash-stable* (CNS), or *contractually individually stable* (CIS) if it allows for no (λ, μ)-permissible individual, contractual, or contractual individual deviation, respectively. Since stability against a superset of deviations is harder to satisfy, NS implies IS and CNS, both of which in turn imply CIS. We refer to NS, IS, CNS, and CIS as *standard stability concepts.*

Still, even though a (λ, μ)-permissible single-agent deviation results in a (λ, μ)-coalition for the deviator, it can result in a partition that is not a (λ, μ)-partition, because the abandoned coalition might have been of size exactly λ and $\lambda \geq 2$. We say that a single-agent deviation $\mathfrak{C} \xrightarrow{a} \mathfrak{C}'$ is (λ, μ)*-feasible* if $\mathfrak{C}'$ is a (λ, μ)-partition. Hence, (λ, μ)-feasible deviations require that a coalition can only be abandoned if it remains within the size bounds, i.e., if it has a size of at least $\lambda + 1$ before it is abandoned or any size if $\lambda = 1$. Each of our stability concepts gives rise to a related concept based on feasible instead of permissible deviations. We speak of the associated *feasible* stability concepts and indicate them by a star in the abbreviated notation, e.g., we say feasible Nash stability and denote it by NS*. As feasible stability concepts prevent a subset of deviations, they result in the logically weaker stability concepts, e.g., NS implies NS*. An overview of our stability concepts is given in Figure 1. Arrows indicate logical relationships between them. It is easy to see that apart from the depicted implications and the ones implied by transitivity, there are no further relationships. For example, there are NS* partitions that are not CIS partitions (cf. Example 1). For all abbreviations α of our solution concepts, e.g., $\alpha =$ NS, we speak of an α deviation to refer to the associated deviation, e.g., NS deviation.

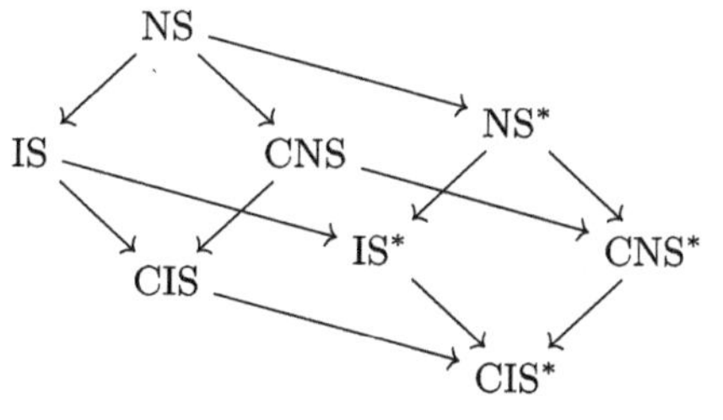

Fig. 1. Overview and logical implications of stability concepts. Each standard stability concept is associated with a feasible stability concept indicated by a star.

Finally, a fundamental desideratum beyond stability is that an agent wants to end up in a coalition at least as good as being on their own. This is captured by individual rationality. A coalition $C \in \mathcal{N}_a$ is said to be *individually rational* for agent a if $C \succsim_a \{a\}$. For ASHGs, this requires that $u_a(C) \geq 0$. Finally, a partition $\mathfrak{C}$ is individually rational if for all $a \in N$, $\mathfrak{C}(a)$ is individually rational.

Clearly, since IS and IS* deviations do not prevent an agent from abandoning a coalition with negative utility, IS and IS* (and, therefore, also the stronger notions of NS and NS*) imply individual rationality if $\lambda = 1$. Indeed, in this case, an agent with negative utility can abandon a coalition of negative utility and form a new singleton coalition. However, when $\lambda \geq 2$, individual rationality is not even implied by NS. We will demonstrate this in Example 1.

4 Feasible Partitions

In contrast to games with unconstrained or upper-bounded coalition sizes, lower bounds may preclude the existence of partitions in which all coalitions satisfy the size constraints. For example, a group of 8 agents cannot form a $(5, 7)$-partition. Hence, as a preliminary consideration, we first consider the existence of (λ, μ)-partitions.

Proposition 1. *Let $\lambda, \mu, n \in \mathbb{N}$ with $\lambda \leq \mu$. A (λ, μ)-partition of n agents exists if and only if $n \leq \left\lfloor \frac{n}{\lambda} \right\rfloor \mu$.*

Proof. Let $\lambda, \mu \in \mathbb{N}$ with $\lambda \leq \mu$ and $n \in \mathbb{N}$. Assume that there exists a (λ, μ)-partition $\mathfrak{C}$ of n agents. As each coalition in $\mathfrak{C}$ is of size at least λ, we know that $|\mathfrak{C}| \leq \left\lfloor \frac{n}{\lambda} \right\rfloor$. Hence, $n \leq \sum_{C \in \mathfrak{C}} |C| \leq \sum_{C \in \mathfrak{C}} \mu = |\mathfrak{C}|\mu \leq \left\lfloor \frac{n}{\lambda} \right\rfloor \mu$.

Conversely assume that n satisfies $n \leq \left\lfloor \frac{n}{\lambda} \right\rfloor \mu$. It holds that $n = \lambda \frac{n}{\lambda} \geq \lambda \left\lfloor \frac{n}{\lambda} \right\rfloor$. Hence, we can use $\lambda \left\lfloor \frac{n}{\lambda} \right\rfloor$ agents to form $\left\lfloor \frac{n}{\lambda} \right\rfloor$ coalitions of size λ. These coalitions have space for $\left\lfloor \frac{n}{\lambda} \right\rfloor \mu$ agents to constitute a (λ, μ)-partition. Hence, since $n \leq \left\lfloor \frac{n}{\lambda} \right\rfloor \mu$, they have space for the remaining agents to form a (λ, μ)-partition. □

Note that the condition $n \leq \left\lfloor \frac{n}{\lambda} \right\rfloor \mu$ excludes the case where $n < \lambda$ (in which case we could not form any coalition of size at least λ), as then this condition reads $n \leq 0$, which is false for any $n \in \mathbb{N}$. Also, $\left\lfloor \frac{n}{\lambda} \right\rfloor$ is the largest number of coalitions that can be created with n agents so that each coalition has size at least λ. Hence, Proposition 1 implies that there exists a (λ, μ)-partition of n agents if and only if there exists such a partition into the largest possible number of coalitions. In fact, we can use it to characterize precisely for which numbers k there exists a (λ, μ)-partition into k coalitions.

Proposition 2. *Let $\lambda, \mu \in \mathbb{N}$ with $\lambda \leq \mu$ and $k, n \in \mathbb{N}$. Then there exists a (λ, μ)-partition of n agents into k coalitions if and only if $k\lambda \leq n \leq k\mu$.*

Proof. Assume first that there exists a (λ, μ)-partition $\mathfrak{C}$ of n agents into k coalitions. As each coalition in $\mathfrak{C}$ is of size at least λ, we know that $k\lambda = |\mathfrak{C}|\lambda \leq n$. Moreover, $n \leq \sum_{C \in \mathfrak{C}} |C| \leq \sum_{C \in \mathfrak{C}} \mu = |\mathfrak{C}|\mu = k \cdot \mu$.

Conversely, assume that $k\lambda \leq n \leq k\mu$. Then, since k is an integer, $k \leq \frac{n}{\lambda}$ implies $k \leq \lfloor \frac{n}{\lambda} \rfloor$. Combining this with $n \leq k\mu$ implies that $n \leq \lfloor \frac{n}{\lambda} \rfloor \mu$. Hence, by Proposition 1, there exists some (λ, μ)-partition $\mathfrak{C}$ of n agents, say $\mathfrak{C} = \{C_1, \dots, C_\ell\}$, where $\ell = |\mathfrak{C}|$. Assume that $|\mathfrak{C}| > k$. Then, since $n \leq k\mu$, we have $k\mu - \sum_{i=1}^{k} |C_i| \geq n - \sum_{i=1}^{k} |C_i| = \sum_{i=k+1}^{\ell} |C_i|$. Hence, there is enough space in the first k coalitions to add the agents in the coalitions $C_{k+1}, \dots, C_\ell$ to obtain a (λ, μ)-partition of the n agents into k coalitions. □

Proposition 1 can be applied to prove another useful fact about the existence of (λ, μ)-partitions. Clearly, if $\lambda = \mu$, then a (λ, μ)-partition exists if and only if μ divides n. Otherwise, we next show that a (λ, μ)-partition exists for a sufficiently large number of agents.

Proposition 3. *Let $\lambda, \mu \in \mathbb{N}$ with $\lambda < \mu$. Then a (λ, μ)-partition exists whenever $n \geq \frac{\lambda-1}{\mu-\lambda}\mu$.*

Proof. Let $\lambda < \mu$. Assume that $n \geq \frac{\lambda-1}{\mu-\lambda}\mu$. Multiplication by $\frac{\mu-\lambda}{\lambda}$ implies that

$$\frac{n}{\lambda}\mu - n = \frac{\mu-\lambda}{\lambda}n \geq \frac{\lambda-1}{\lambda}\mu \Leftrightarrow \left[\frac{n}{\lambda} - \frac{\lambda-1}{\lambda}\right] \cdot \mu \geq n. \tag{1}$$

Hence,

$$\left\lfloor\frac{n}{\lambda}\right\rfloor \cdot \mu = \left[\frac{n}{\lambda} + \left(\left\lfloor\frac{n}{\lambda}\right\rfloor - \frac{n}{\lambda}\right)\right] \cdot \mu \geq \left[\frac{n}{\lambda} - \frac{\lambda-1}{\lambda}\right] \cdot \mu \geq n.$$

For the first inequality, note that the remainder of division by λ is an integer in $\{0, 1, \dots, \lambda - 1\}$. Hence, rounding down $\frac{n}{\lambda}$ can decrease this number by at most $\frac{\lambda-1}{\lambda}$. In the second inequality, we applied Equation (1). Thus, by Proposition 1, there exists a feasible partition. □

While Proposition 1 allows us to check for the existence of a (λ, μ)-partition with a few elementary operations, Proposition 3 implies that the nonexistence of (λ, μ)-partitions is not an algorithmic issue if we fix size bounds. For instance, since hardness reductions construct games with an unbounded number of agents, our hardness results for stability do not rely on the nonexistence of stability for small agent numbers (in fact, all games in our reductions admit partitions for the considered size bounds).

5 Existence of Stable Partitions

We turn to the consideration of stability. We start with an example that highlights basic relationships of stability concepts once we have a nontrivial lower bound.

Example 1. Let $\lambda = 2$, $\mu \geq 3$, and $k \in \mathbb{N}$. We define two ASHGs (N, v) and (N, v') where $N = \{a_i, b_i : i \in [k]\}$. Symmetric valuations v are given by $v(a_i, b_i) = -1$ for all $i \in [k]$ and $v(a, b) = 1$ for any other pair of agents. Symmetric valuations v' are given by $v'(a, b) = -1$ for all pairs of agents $a, b \in N$. We illustrate (N, v) in Figure 2. For both games, we consider the partition $\mathfrak{C} = \{\{a_i, b_i\} : i \in [k]\}$.

For the ASHG (N, v), $\mathfrak{C}$ is an NS* (λ, μ)-partition because no agent can perform a (λ, μ)-feasible deviation when $\lambda = 2$. However, $\mathfrak{C}$ is not a CIS (λ, μ)-partition as each deviation of any agent to any other nonempty coalition is a (λ, μ)-permissible CIS deviation. Hence, even our strongest feasible stability concept does not imply our weakest standard stability concept.

For the ASHG (N, v'), $\mathfrak{C}$ clearly is an NS (λ, μ)-partition. Indeed, every (λ, μ)-permissible deviation is to join another nonempty coalition which is always worse for the deviator. Hence, even our strongest stability concept does not imply individual rationality for any agent.

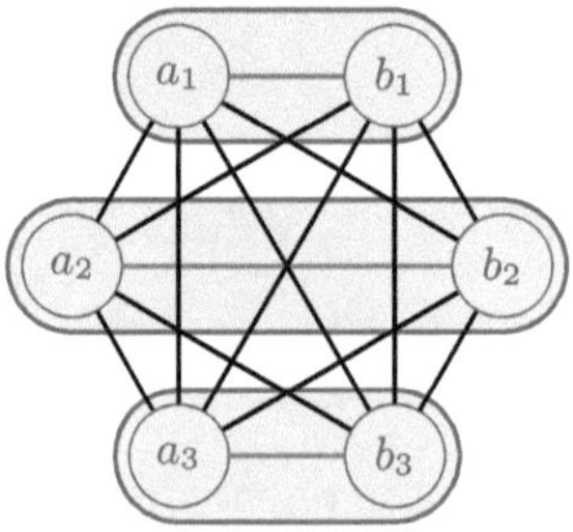

Fig. 2. Illustration of the game (N, v) in Example 1 for the case $k = 3$. Black and red edges indicate a symmetric valuation of 1 and -1, respectively. The partition $\mathfrak{C}$ is indicated in blue.

For the rest of this section, we are concerned with the existence of stable partitions. Our first observation is that feasible stability notions can be satisfied under symmetric valuations. This is a standard result for unconstrained coalition sizes [8] and has also been observed for upper-bounded coalition sizes [23,29] and models related to ASHGs [7,15]. The idea is that a partition maximizing social welfare is stable.

Proposition 4. *Let $\lambda, \mu \in \mathbb{N}$ with $\lambda \leq \mu$. Any symmetric ASHG that admits a (λ, μ)-partition also admits an NS* (λ, μ)-partition.*

By contrast, if we consider (λ, μ)-permissible instead of (λ, μ)-feasible deviations, then stability is not even guaranteed for our weakest standard stability notion, even if valuations are simple and symmetric. Indeed, simple symmetric ASHGs whose valuations evolve from a star graph have this property.

Proposition 5. *Let $2 \leq \lambda < \mu$. Then there exists a simple symmetric ASHG that admits a (λ, μ)-partition but contains no CIS (λ, μ)-partition.*

Propositions 4 and 5 provide a complete picture about the existence of our stability concepts for symmetric ASHGs. While even the strongest feasible stability concept can be satisfied, the weakest standard stability concept cannot. This leads us to the question whether feasible stability is still guaranteed for nonsymmetric valuations. First, since (λ, μ)-feasible deviations lead to (λ, μ)-partitions and increase the social welfare, CIS* partitions exist provided some (λ, μ)-partition exists.

Observation 1. *Let $\lambda, \mu \in \mathbb{N}$ with $\lambda \leq \mu$. Any ASHG that admits a (λ, μ)-partition also admits a CIS* (λ, μ)-partition.*

However, existence for stronger feasible stability concepts is not guaranteed anymore. For IS*, examples are given by instances where the positive valuations form a directed cycle.

Proposition 6. *Let $2 \leq \lambda < \mu$. Then there exists an infinite family of simple ASHGs that admit a (λ, μ)-partition but contain no IS* (λ, μ)-partition.*

Similarly, without symmetry, we lose existence of CNS* on a simple set of instances. To see this, we consider instances where most valuations are zero, except for three agents forming a directed cycle with negative valuations and a partitioning of the other agents into pairs with mutual negative valuations.

Proposition 7. *Let $2 \leq \lambda < \mu$. Then there exists an ASHG that admits a (λ, μ)-partition but contains no CNS* (λ, μ)-partition.*

Notably, the nonexistence results of Propositions 5, 6, and 7 assume a lower bound of $\lambda \geq 2$. In the next section, we will obtain a complete complexity picture of all stability notions when $\lambda = 1$ and thereby also exactly characterize the existence of stability in this case.

6 Computation of Stable Partitions

We now consider the computational complexity of deciding whether there exist stable (λ, μ)-partitions in a given ASHG. We obtain positive results in the form of efficient algorithms as well as NP-completeness results for the corresponding decision problem of whether a stable (λ, μ)-partition exists. Note that for all of our stability notions, membership in NP is straightforward: a stable partition can easily be verified in polynomial time, by considering all potential permissible or feasible deviations from any agents to any coalition (possibly including the empty coalition if $\lambda = 1$). Hence, we will omit this from all completeness proofs.

In the first part of this section, we consider settings with $\lambda = 1$, i.e., partitions only have to satisfy upper bounds on their size. We will obtain a complete picture for the computational complexity for all possible parameters μ. In the second part of the section, we provide results for a nontrivial lower bound of $\lambda \geq 2$.

6.1 Upper-Bounded Coalition Sizes

We start with the consideration of settings where $\lambda = 1$. Note that, under this restriction, permissible and feasible deviations are the same because abandoning a coalition cannot result in an infeasible coalition. In particular, abandoning a singleton coalition leads to the removal of a coalition. Hence, all results for this section hold for both standard stability concepts and their feasible counterparts. For simplicity, we state them all for standard stability concepts. In addition, a $(1, \mu)$-partition of any number of agents always exists as, for example, the singleton partition is such a partition. Hence, we are not concerned with the nonexistence of feasible partitions in this section.

We start with the consideration of CIS. There, we obtain a polynomial-time algorithm for any fixed upper bound. We remark that Aziz et al. [4] present an algorithm to compute CIS partitions in ASHG without size bounds. Their algorithm works by iteratively choosing a leader among agents not assigned to coalitions yet. The idea then is to let the leader either form a new coalition with all their friends or, if this yields a higher utility, joining an existing coalition. When joining an existing coalition, further agents, so called latecomers, are added if this is beneficial for members in this coalition while not harming any agent there. Unfortunately, their algorithm is not correct. The high-level reason is that, when joining a coalition, an agent might prefer joining a different coalition because of the utility gain through latecomers. In the full version of the paper, we present a concrete example where the algorithm does not return a CIS partition [11].

Our algorithm fixes their construction by changing the condition of joining coalitions to immediately take into consideration the gains of other agents that can join as well. We additionally modify it to work for an arbitrary upper bound on coalition sizes. However, note that the algorithm can also be used to compute CIS partitions for ASHGs without size constraints by running it for $\mu = n$.

Theorem 1. *Let $\mu \geq 2$. Then there exists a polynomial-time algorithm that computes CIS $(1, \mu)$-partitions in ASHGs.*

Proof. Consider an ASHG (N, v). We apply Algorithm 1. Note that the algorithm uses notation for agent sets as defined in Section 3.2. The algorithm initializes a counter i capturing the number of already created coalitions. Moreover, it keeps track of a set A of still available agents.

The idea is to iteratively create coalitions S_i based on the preferences of certain *decision makers*, which are stored in a set $\widetilde{S}_i$. These add as many friends as the capacity of a coalition allows to that coalition. Intuitively, the resulting partition is a CIS partition because decision makers obtain a best coalition among the remaining available options whereas agents that are not decision makers are prevented from leaving their coalition by a decision maker whose friend they are.

We start by selecting an available agent $a \in A$, and call them the *leader* of the first coalition S_1. We try to form a coalition that is as good as possible for the leader. For this, we consider the up to $\mu - 1$ best available agents among

Algorithm 1 Contractually individually stable $(1, \mu)$-partitions in ASHGs.

Input: ASHG (N, v), parameter μ
Output: $(1, \mu)$-partition

$i \leftarrow 0$, $A \leftarrow N$ ▷ Coalition counter, available agents
while $A \neq \emptyset$ **do**
  Select any agent $a \in A$
  $h \leftarrow u_a(\{a\} \cup \text{top}_a(\mu - 1, \text{Fr}(a, A)))$ ▷ Utility a gets from creating their best new coalition
  $z \leftarrow i + 1$ ▷ Indicating coalition chosen by a.
  for all $k \in [i]$ with $|S_k| \leq \mu - 1$ and $a \notin \text{En}(\widetilde{S}_k, A)$ ▷ Skipped for $i = 0$ as $[0] = \emptyset$ **do**
    $P_k \leftarrow \text{Fr}(a, A) \cap \left(A \setminus \text{En}(\widetilde{S}_k, A)\right)$
    $h' \leftarrow u_a(S_k \cup \{a\} \cup \text{top}_a(\mu - |S_k| - 1, P_k))$ ▷ Utility when joining S_z with best helpers
    if $h < h'$ **then**
      $h \leftarrow h'$, $z \leftarrow k$
  if $z = i + 1$ **then**
    $S_z \leftarrow \{a\} \cup \text{top}_a(\mu - 1, \text{Fr}(a, A))$ ▷ Create best new coalition
    $\widetilde{S}_z \leftarrow \{a\}$ ▷ New coalition's decision makers
    $A \leftarrow A \setminus S_z$
    $i \leftarrow i + 1$
  else
    $S_z \leftarrow S_z \cup \{a\} \cup \text{top}_a(\mu - |S_z| - 1, P_z)$
    $\widetilde{S}_z \leftarrow \widetilde{S}_z \cup \{a\}$
    $A \leftarrow A \setminus (\{a\} \cup \text{top}_a(\mu - |S_z| - 1, P_z))$
return $\mathfrak{C} = \{S_1, \ldots, S_i\}$

the friends of a, i.e., $\text{top}_a(\mu - 1, \text{Fr}(a, A))$. As a first coalition, we form $S_1 = \{a\} \cup \text{top}_a(\mu - 1, \text{Fr}(a, A))$ and indicate that a is a decision maker of this coalition by setting $\widetilde{S}_1 = \{a\}$. We call the agents enforced to join the coalition by a decision maker the *helpers*.

In subsequent iterations, we start by selecting a new leader $a \in A$. However, apart from creating a new coalition, a may also join an existing coalition, while bringing along friends, provided that they do not violate the upper bound and that both they and their friends are not enemies of a decision maker in the joined coalition. Under these conditions, a either creates a new coalition or joins an existing coalition to maximize their utility. If a joins an existing coalition, we refer to a as a *latecomer* and add them as a decision maker. Additionally, we refer to the friends they bring along as *helpers*, analogous to the helpers of the first leader. Finally, we update the set of available agents by removing a and a's helpers. We continue selecting new agents to become leaders or latecomers until the set A of remaining agents is empty.

Clearly, the algorithm runs in polynomial time. Each agent is processed at most once as a leader and we have to compute at most $n = |N|$ possible options for them. Finding the best k agents among a set and performing the updates of the coalition structure are all straightforward.

We now show that the algorithm produces a CIS $(1, \mu)$-partition $\mathfrak{C}$. Clearly, no created coalition contains more than μ agents, so we create a $(1, \mu)$-partition. It remains to show that no agent can perform a $(1, \mu)$-permissible CIS deviation. For this, we consider potential deviating agents case by case, and show that no agents can make such a deviation.

First, for every helper b, there exists a decision maker $a \in \mathfrak{C}(b)$ with $b \in \mathrm{Fr}(a, N)$, i.e., $v_a(b) > 0$. Hence, b is denied by a to perform a CIS deviation.

Now, consider a decision maker a. Consider the iteration of the while loop during which a was the decision maker and the set of available agents was A. We refer to the partial partition of the subset of agents that were assigned to a coalition after this iteration as $\mathfrak{C}'$. Note that, after a formed a new coalition or joined a coalition, no enemy of a could have joined this coalition. Hence, we have that

$$u_a(\mathfrak{C}) \geq u_a(\mathfrak{C}'). \tag{2}$$

This implies that a is individually rational, and thus does not wish to deviate to a singleton coalition.

It remains to show that a cannot perform a CIS deviation into an existing coalition. Let $C \in \mathfrak{C} \setminus \{\mathfrak{C}(a)\}$ be some coalition, and define $C' = \{b \in C \colon \exists D \in \mathfrak{C}' \text{ with } b \in D\}$. Thus, C' is the subset of agents of C that were in a coalition after the iteration with leader a. Note that C' is either a nonempty coalition of $\mathfrak{C}'$ or it is the empty set, indicating that C was only created after this iteration.

We consider two cases. First, assume that $C' = \emptyset$. Since a had the opportunity to create $\{a\} \cup \mathrm{top}_a(\mu - 1, \mathrm{Fr}(a, A))$, they have a higher utility than for this coalition. Hence, $u_a(\mathfrak{C}') \geq u_a(\{a\} \cup \mathrm{top}_a(\mu - 1, \mathrm{Fr}(a, A))) \geq u_a(\{a\} \cup C)$.

Second, assume $C' \neq \emptyset$. If $|C'| = \mu$, then $C = C'$ and a deviation to C is not allowed. Hence, assume that $|C'| \leq \mu - 1$. Let $\widetilde{S} \subseteq C'$ be the set of decision makers in C'. If $a \in \mathrm{En}(\widetilde{S}, N)$, then a is denied to enter C' and therefore C. Thus a cannot make a CIS deviation to C. Hence, assume that $a \notin \mathrm{En}(\widetilde{S}, N)$

Note that $C \subseteq C' \cup (A \setminus \mathrm{En}(\widetilde{S}, A))$, as by design C cannot contain enemies of its own decision makers. Additionally, a had the opportunity to form the coalition $D = C' \cup \{a\} \cup \mathrm{top}_a(\mu - |C'| - 1, P)$ where $P = \mathrm{Fr}(a, A) \cap \left(A \setminus \mathrm{En}(\widetilde{S}, A)\right)$. Hence, $u_a(\mathfrak{C}') \geq u_a(D) \geq u_a(\{a\} \cup C)$.

Thus, whenever a is not denied entry to C by a decision maker of C', we have obtained $u_a(\mathfrak{C}') \geq u_a(\{a\} \cup C)$. Combining this with Equation (2), we obtain that $u_a(\mathfrak{C}) \geq u_a(\{a\} \cup C)$. Hence, a cannot perform a CIS deviation. □

We next consider the computation of CNS partitions. For $\mu = 2$, we obtain an efficient algorithm based on sequentially considering agents and greedily forming their best available coalition of size 2.

Proposition 8. *There exists a polynomial-time algorithm that computes CNS $(1, 2)$-partitions in ASHGs.*

Unfortunately, as we show next, Proposition 8 does not extend to larger upper bounds. Our proof is inspired by the existing hardness result for the existence of CNS partitions in ASHGs with unconstrained coalition sizes [10, Theorem 3]. However, we apply crucial modifications to avoid the formation of coalitions of size larger than 3. The reduction is from the NP-complete problem EXACT COVER BY 3-SETS (X3C) [27]. An instance of X3C is a pair $\langle R, \mathfrak{S} \rangle$, where R is a ground set of size 3ρ and $\mathfrak{S}$ is a collection of 3-element subsets of R; it is a Yes-instance if and only if there exists a subset $\mathfrak{S}' \subseteq \mathfrak{S}$ that partitions R.

The high-level proof idea is to encode an instance of $\langle R, \mathfrak{S} \rangle$ as an ASHG by representing the elements in R and $\mathfrak{S}$ as gadgets. Each of the gadgets contains a subgame corresponding to a known ASHG without a CNS partition [33]. Notably, this property is even true for any upper bound $\mu \geq 2$. By carefully linking these subgames with auxiliary agents, one can enforce that, in every CNS $(1, \mu)$-partition, some agent in every gadget representing an element $r \in R$ has to be in a coalition with an agent in a gadget representing a set in $\mathfrak{S}$ containing r. Moreover, either agents in all or none of the three gadgets corresponding to the elements in a set in $S \in \mathfrak{S}$ have to be in a coalition with the agents in the gadget representing S. This leads to a correspondence of Yes-instances.

Theorem 2. *Let $\mu \geq 3$. Then it is* NP*-complete to decide whether a CNS $(1, \mu)$-partition exists in ASHGs.*

Next, it is known that it is NP-complete to determine whether there exists a Nash-stable or individually stable matching, which are the same as $(1, 2)$-partitions [2]. A similar approach works for any other upper bound. Interestingly, our reduction allows for a simultaneous treatment of NS and IS. As Aziz [2], we reduce from the NP-complete problem MINIMUM MAXIMAL MATCHING [28].

Theorem 3. *Let $\mu \geq 2$. Then it is* NP*-complete to decide whether an NS (or IS) $(1, \mu)$-partition exists in ASHGs.*

6.2 Coalitions with Nontrivial Lower Bound

We now turn to the consideration of finding stable (λ, μ)-partitions, when $\lambda \geq 2$. First, we show a negative result for NS for any pair (λ, μ) with $\mu \geq 4$.

Theorem 4. *Let $\mu \geq 4$ and $\lambda < \mu$. Then it is* NP*-complete to decide whether an NS (λ, μ)-partition exists in an ASHG.*

The combination of Theorem 3 and 4 implies that computing NS (λ, μ)-partitions is NP-hard for all combinations of λ and μ with $\lambda < \mu$ except for the case $(\lambda = 2, \mu = 3)$, where we leave the complexity open.

Finally, we work towards achieving CIS* for a nontrivial lower bound on coalition sizes $\lambda \geq 2$. As a first result, we present an algorithm for ASHGs (N, v) with nonzero valuations, i.e., $v_i(j) \neq 0$ for all $i, j \in N$. Such games are sometimes referred to as *strict* ASHGs [4]. The idea is similar as for Algorithm 1: We iteratively choose leaders to form their best possible coalitions. However, we have to form coalitions of size at least λ and, therefore, the formed coalitions might have to contain enemies of the leader. Still, we assign them their best coalition of size λ (and possibly larger if space permits). The remaining agents are added in an order that ensures that only later-assigned leaders, which cannot join coalitions of earlier-assigned leaders, may be forced to accommodate enemies.

Theorem 5. *There exists a polynomial-time algorithm that, given an ASHG with nonzero valuations, any* $1 \leq \lambda \leq \mu$, *and* $k \in \mathbb{N}$, *computes a CIS** (λ, μ)*-partition into k coalitions, or determines that no such partition exists.*

Next, we consider ASHGs (N, v) with nonnegative valuations. Hence, an agent would never deny an agent to enter their coalition and, therefore, CIS* equals CNS*. The algorithmic idea is similar to Algorithm 1, however, we have to ensure that there are enough agents to reach a size of λ for all coalitions, which further restricts how many friends an agent might take to join a coalition.

Theorem 6. *There exists a polynomial-time algorithm that, given an ASHG with nonnegative valuations, any* $1 \leq \lambda \leq \mu$, *and* $k \in \mathbb{N}$, *computes a CNS** (λ, μ)*-partition into k coalitions, or determines that no such partition exists.*

7 Conclusion

We have investigated stability based on deviations by single agents in additively separable hedonic games, where the output coalitions are restricted to be within given size bounds. Since size bounds are ubiquitous in coalition formation applications, we think that our paper presents a valuable step to understand the tractability of coalition formation.

Notably, the existence of stability can only be guaranteed when the deviating agent is only allowed to abandon a coalition that is larger than the required minimum size. Otherwise, we cannot even guarantee our weakest stability concept of contractual individual stability. This is an interesting contrast to the unconstrained case, where CIS deviations are Pareto improvements. While they are also Pareto improvements in our setting, they may, however, leave the space of feasible partitions. Hence, CIS partitions may not exist when all Pareto-optimal outcomes of the unconstrained game do not satisfy the size bounds. Once we restrict solution concepts to feasible deviations, we have the existence of CIS* partitions, and have presented polynomial-time algorithms to extract them when the lower bound is equal to 1, or when valuations are nonzero or nonnegative.

We complement our analysis of existence properties by an investigation of computational complexity. There, we present a complete picture when the lower bound is equal to 1. In addition to the polynomial-time solvability of CIS, the only tractable case is CNS when the upper bound on coalitions size is 2. For a nontrivial lower bound, we present an almost complete picture for NS, leaving only the case of coalitions bounded between 2 and 3 open. Further open problems concern the complexity of IS and CNS for a lower bound of at least 2, or CIS* on the complete domain of valuations. Other interesting avenues for future work within our bounded-coalition framework include investigating other classes of hedonic games, such as fractional hedonic games [3], or other solution concepts such as popularity [4,9]. For fractional hedonic games, comprehensive results are known for Nash stability when $\lambda = 1$ and $\mu \in \{2, 3, 4\}$ [32], which leaves many further directions open.

Acknowledgements. Most of this work was done when Martin Bullinger and Edith Elkind were at the University of Oxford, where they were supported by the AI Programme of The Alan Turing Institute. Adam Dunajski was supported by the University of Edinburgh School of Mathematics. Matan Gilboa was supported by the Engineering and Physical Sciences Research Council under grant EP/W524311/1.

References

1. Agarwal, P., Agarwal, H., Raj, V., Nath, S.: Harmonious balanced partitioning of a network of agents. In: Proceedings of the 24th International Conference on Autonomous Agents and Multiagent Systems (AAMAS). pp. 41–49 (2025)
2. Aziz, H.: Stable marriage and roommate problems with individual-based stability. In: Proceedings of the 12th International Conference on Autonomous Agents and Multiagent Systems (AAMAS), (2013)
3. Aziz, H., Brandl, F., Brandt, F., Harrenstein, P., Olsen, M., Peters, D.: Fractional hedonic games. ACM Trans. Econ. Comput. **7**(2), 1–29 (2019)
4. Aziz, H., Brandt, F., Seedig, H.G.: Computing desirable partitions in additively separable hedonic games. Artif. Intell. **195**, 316–334 (2013)
5. Aziz, H., Savani, R., Brandt, F., Conitzer, V., Endriss, U., Lang, J.: Hedonic games. In: Procaccia, A.D. (ed.) Handbook of Computational Social Choice, chap. 15, Cambridge University Press (2016)
6. Ballester, C.: NP-completeness in hedonic games. Games Econom. Behav. **49**(1), 1–30 (2004)
7. Bilò, V., Monaco, G., Moscardelli, L.: Hedonic games with fixed-size coalitions. In: Proceedings of the 36th AAAI Conference on Artificial Intelligence (AAAI), pp. 9287–9295. (2022)
8. Bogomolnaia, A., Jackson, M.O.: The stability of hedonic coalition structures. Games Econom. Behav. **38**(2), 201–230 (2002)
9. Brandt, F., Bullinger, M.: Finding and recognizing popular coalition structures. Journal of Artificial Intelligence Research **74**, 569–626 (2022)
10. Brandt, F., Bullinger, M., Tappe, L.: Stability based on single-agent deviations in additively separable hedonic games. Artif. Intell. **334**, 104160 (2024)
11. Bullinger, M., Dunajski, A., Elkind, E., Gilboa, M.: Single-deviation stability in additively separable hedonic games with constrained coalition sizes (2025), https://arxiv.org/abs/2510.12641
12. Bullinger, M., Elkind, E., Rothe, J.: Cooperative game theory. In: Rothe, J. (ed.) Economics and Computation: An Introduction to Algorithmic Game Theory, Computational Social Choice, and Fair Division, chap. 3, pp. 139–229. Springer (2024)
13. Bullinger, M., Gilboa, M.: Settling the complexity of popularity in additively separable and fractional hedonic games. In: Proceedings of the 34th International Joint Conference on Artificial Intelligence (IJCAI), pp. 3771–3779. (2025)

14. Bullinger, M., Kraiczy, S.: Stability in random hedonic games. In: Proceedings of the 25th ACM Conference on Economics and Computation (ACM-EC). p. 212 (2024)
15. Bullinger, M., Suksompong, W.: Topological distance games. Theoret. Comput. Sci. **981**, 114238 (2024)
16. Cohen, S., Agmon, N.: Egalitarianism in online coalition formation (extended abstract). In: Proceedings of the 24th International Conference on Autonomous Agents and Multiagent Systems (AAMAS), pp. 2475–2477. (2025)
17. Darmann, A., Döcker, J., Dorn, B., Schneckenburger, S.: Simplified group activity selection with group size constraints. Internat. J. Game Theory **51**(1), 169–212 (2022)
18. Deligkas, A., Eiben, E., Ioannidis, S.D., Knop, D., Schierreich, Š.: Balanced and fair partitioning of friends. In: Proceedings of the 39th AAAI Conference on Artificial Intelligence (AAAI). pp. 13754–13762 (2025)
19. Deligkas, A., Eiben, E., Knop, D., Schierreich, Š.: Individual rationality in topological distance games is surprisingly hard. In: Proceedings of the 33rd International Joint Conference on Artificial Intelligence (IJCAI). pp. 2782–2790 (2024)
20. Dimitrov, D., Borm, P., Hendrickx, R., Sung, S.C.: Simple priorities and core stability in hedonic games. Soc. Choice Welfare **26**(2), 421–433 (2006)
21. Drèze, J.H., Greenberg, J.: Hedonic coalitions: Optimality and stability. Econometrica **48**(4), 987–1003 (1980)
22. Elkind, E., Wooldridge, M.: Hedonic coalition nets. In: Proceedings of the 8th International Conference on Autonomous Agents and Multiagent Systems (AAMAS), pp. 417–424. (2009)
23. Fioravantes, F., Gahlawat, H., Melissinos, N.: Exact algorithms and lower bounds for forming coalitions of constrained maximum size. In: Proceedings of the 39th AAAI Conference on Artificial Intelligence (AAAI), pp. 13847–13855. (2025)
24. Fioravantes, F., Gahlawat, H., Melissinos, N., Schierreich, Š.: Individual rationality in constrained hedonic games: Additively separable and fractional preferences. In: Proceedings of the 25th International Conference on Autonomous Agents and Multiagent Systems (AAMAS). pp. 2848–2857 (2026)
25. Flammini, M., Monaco, G., Moscardelli, L., Shalom, M., Zaks, S.: On the online coalition structure generation problem. Journal of Artificial Intelligence Research **72**, 1215–1250 (2021)
26. Ganian, R., Hamm, T., Knop, D., Schierreich, Š, Suchý, O.: Hedonic diversity games: A complexity picture with more than two colors. Artif. Intell. **325**, 104017 (2023)
27. Garey, M.R., Johnson, D.S.: Computers and Intractability: A Guide to the Theory of NP-Completeness. Freeman, W. H (1979)
28. Horton, J.D., Kilakos, K.: Minimum edge dominating sets. SIAM Journal of Discrete Mathematics **6**(3), 375–387 (1993)
29. Levinger, C., Azaria, A., Hazon, N.: Social aware coalition formation with bounded coalition size (extended abstract). In: Proceedings of the 22nd International Conference on Autonomous Agents and Multiagent Systems (AAMAS), pp. 2667–2669. (2023)
30. Levinger, C., Hazon, N., Simola, S., Azaria, A.: Coalition formation with bounded coalition size. In: Proceedings of the 23rd International Conference on Autonomous Agents and Multiagent Systems (AAMAS), pp. 1119–1127. (2024)
31. Li, L., Micha, E., Nikolov, A., Shah, N.: Partitioning friends fairly. In: Proceedings of the 37th AAAI Conference on Artificial Intelligence (AAAI), pp. 5747–5754. (2023)

32. Monaco, G., Moscardelli, L.: Nash stability in fractional hedonic games with bounded size coalitions. In: Proceedings of the 19th International Conference on Web and Internet Economics (WINE), pp. 509–526 (2023)
33. Sung, S.C., Dimitrov, D.: On myopic stability concepts for hedonic games. Theor. Decis. **62**(1), 31–45 (2007)
34. Sung, S.C., Dimitrov, D.: Computational complexity in additive hedonic games. Eur. J. Oper. Res. **203**(3), 635–639 (2010)
35. Woeginger, G.J.: A hardness result for core stability in additive hedonic games. Math. Soc. Sci. **65**(2), 101–104 (2013)
36. Wright, M., Vorobeychik, Y.: Mechanism design for team formation. In: Proceedings of the 29th AAAI Conference on Artificial Intelligence (AAAI), (2015)

Control and Bribery in Stable Marriage and Stable Roommates: A Complete Complexity Landscape

Jiehua Chen[1](✉) and Ildikó Schlotter[2,3]

[1] TU Wien, Vienna, Austria
jiehua.chen@ac.tuwien.ac.at
[2] ELTE Centre for Economic and Regional Studies, Budapest, Hungary
schlotter.ildiko@krtk.elte.hu
[3] Budapest University of Technology and Economics, Budapest, Hungary

Abstract. We study control and bribery problems for stable matchings: a central authority (the *controller*, resp., *briber*) may add agents, delete agents, delete acceptable pairs, swap two adjacent agents in some agent's preference list, or arbitrarily reorder some agent's preference list, in an instance of STABLE MARRIAGE or STABLE ROOMMATES. We extend previous work on control and bribery in stable matchings by Boehmer et al. [8]. We consider goals capturing individual and pair inclusion, stability, and uniqueness requirements: matching a designated agent (MA), matching a designated pair (MP), realizing a stable matching consistent with a given matching (MS), making a given matching the unique stable matching (USM), or guaranteeing that a stable (resp., perfect and stable) matching exists (∃SM/∃PSM). We provide a unified complexity map for all non-trivial action–goal combinations in both settings, consolidating known results and extending the study to the roommates model, where stable matchings need not exist.

1 Introduction

STABLE ROOMMATES deals with the division of human or non-human agents into pairs, where agents have preference lists describing their desires about whom they want to be matched with. More precisely, an instance of STABLE ROOMMATES consists of a set U of agents, with each agent $u \in U$ having a strict preference list over the subset of the remaining agents that u finds *acceptable*. The goal is to decide whether there is a *stable matching*, that is, a set M of pairwise disjoint pairs of agents for which *no* blocking pair exists. Herein, a *blocking pair* for M is a pair of distinct agents u and w who are not matched together by M such that

(i) u is either unmatched by M or prefers w to its partner in M and
(ii) w is either unmatched by M or prefers u to its partner in M.

Note that each STABLE ROOMMATES instance induces an *acceptability graph* where the vertices correspond to the agents and there is an edge between two

P. Lenzner and D. Schmand (Eds.): SAGT 2026, LNCS 16911, pp. 76–94, 2027.
https://doi.org/10.1007/978-3-032-38782-0_5

vertices if both consider each other acceptable. A well-known special case of Stable Roommates called Stable Marriage is the *bipartite* variant where agents are partitioned into two disjoint subsets such that each agent's preference list consists of agents of the opposite subset, and each agent can only be assigned a partner from that subset. The acceptability graph of an instance of Stable Marriage is then bipartite. Due to a celebrated result by Gale and Shapley [18], we know that in the marriage setting a stable matching always exists and can be found in time linear in the input size. However, for the roommates setting, a stable matching is not guaranteed to exist and, more than two decades after the seminal paper by Gale and Shapley [18], Irving [22] provided a polynomial-time algorithm to decide whether a given instance of Stable Roommates admits a stable matching.

Bartholdi III et al. [3,4] introduced a framework for considering questions of manipulation and control in the context of elections, and their approach was adopted by Boehmer et al. [8] to investigate issues of manipulation, control, and bribery in the context of Stable Marriage. In their framework, an external agent (the *controller*, also called the *briber* when modifications affect preferences directly) aims to achieve a specific *goal* by applying as few *actions* as possible.

Example 1.1 ([13]). Suppose that Anna (a), Belle (b), Chris (c), and David (d) are attending a dance class, and need to form opposite-sex couples. Their preferences are as follows:

$$a\colon c \succ d, \qquad b\colon c \succ d, \qquad c\colon a \succ b, \qquad d\colon b \succ a.$$

The only stable matching in this instance is $\{\{a, c\}, \{b, d\}\}$. However, Belle's friend, evil Eve, is among the teachers of the class, and her goal is to match Belle with her top-choice partner, Chris. She considers three options to achieve her goal: (1) declaring that Chris is too short for Anna and hence cannot dance with her, (2) stepping on Anna's toes with her high heels, thereby sending her off to ER, or (3) inviting her attractive friend, Frodo (f), whom Anna prefers to Chris. She decides on option (3), and obtains the following instance:

$$a\colon f \succ c \succ d, \quad b\colon c \succ f \succ d, \quad c\colon a \succ b, \quad d\colon b \succ a, \quad f\colon b \succ a.$$

Yet, Eve is not entirely satisfied, as now there are two stable matchings, namely $M_1 = \{\{a, f\}, \{b, c\}\}$ and $M_2 = \{\{a, c\}, \{b, f\}\}$. Hence, she declares that Frodo is too tall for Belle, ensuring that M_1 becomes the only stable matching.

Example 1.1 illustrates a few of the manipulative actions and goals examined in the literature on control and bribery for stable matchings. However, despite the apparent simplicity of the underlying space of action–goal–setting combinations, *previous work has so far only addressed disjoint fragments of it*: Boehmer et al. [8] consider five manipulative actions, but only three goals, and exclusively in the bipartite Stable Marriage setting; Bérczi et al. [5] consider two further (existence-based) goals, but only for the action of deleting agents and in Stable Roommates; and individual action–goal cases have appeared under different names in work on almost-stable [1,7], maximum-cardinality stable [26,28], and covering-constraint stable [25] matchings. The result is a *patchwork* of partial results, with no unified picture of which combinations are tractable, which are hard, and how the marriage and roommates settings relate.

In this paper, we close this gap. We *unify* these strands into a single coherent framework, considering *all* five manipulative actions of Boehmer et al. under *six* goals, in *both* the marriage and the non-bipartite roommates settings. Following the terminology of Boehmer et al., we organize the five actions into two complementary paradigms.

Control Actions. In many matching markets, an organizer, platform, or regulator can change *participation* and *feasibility* without rewriting preferences: participants may enter or leave the market, and certain pairs may be ruled out (e.g., due to conflicts of interest or policy restrictions); moreover, unlike direct preference manipulation, such interventions can often be justified by external rules. We therefore consider the following control actions, showcased in Example 1.1:

- AddAg: adding agents (e.g., inviting Frodo),
- DelAg: deleting agents (e.g., removing Anna from the class), and
- DelAcc: deleting acceptability (e.g., declaring constraints on who cannot dance with whom).

As in classic control models in computational social choice, we minimize the number of actions, capturing intervention cost and market disruption.

Bribery Actions. A complementary type of intervention models agents who can be *bribed*, i.e., convinced to misreport their preferences; it is captured by the following two actions of Boehmer et al. [8]:

- Swap: swapping two adjacent agents in some agent's preference list (modeling a briber who pays per "small" modification),
- Reorder: arbitrarily permuting some agent's preference list (modeling a briber who pays per fully "bought" agent).

As with control actions, we minimize the number of bribery operations.

Goals. The goals we study correspond to common individual and pair inclusion, stability, and uniqueness requirements. Formally, given an instance of STABLE ROOMMATES, we consider the goals:

- MA: a given agent is matched in some stable matching,
- MP: a given pair is contained in some stable matching,
- MS: there exists a stable matching consistent with a given matching M (i.e., using only pairs from M),
- USM: a given matching M is the unique stable matching,
- ∃SM: a stable matching exists, or
- ∃PSM: a perfect and stable matching exists.

Among these, MP, MS, and USM were studied (under different names) by Boehmer et al. [8], ∃SM and ∃PSM by Bérczi et al. [5], and MA has been studied in a slightly different context by Mnich and Schlotter [25].

Our Problems. For each action $\mathcal{A} \in \{\text{AddAg}, \text{DelAg}, \text{DelAcc}, \text{Swap}, \text{Reorder}\}$ and each goal $\mathcal{G} \in \{\text{MA}, \text{MP}, \text{MS}, \text{USM}, \exists\text{SM}, \exists\text{PSM}\}$, the CONTROL FOR STABLE ROOMMATES-$\mathcal{A}$-$\mathcal{G}$ (abbreviated as CSR-$\mathcal{A}$-$\mathcal{G}$) problem asks for a minimum number of actions of type $\mathcal{A}$ necessary to achieve the goal $\mathcal{G}$ in a given STABLE ROOMMATES instance. When restricted to the bipartite marriage setting, we call these problems CONTROL FOR STABLE MARRIAGE-$\mathcal{A}$-$\mathcal{G}$ (abbreviated as CSM-$\mathcal{A}$-$\mathcal{G}$).

Table 1. Complexity results for CONTROL FOR STABLE MARRIAGE (or ROOMMATES)-$\mathcal{A}$-$\mathcal{G}$ problems. The problems CSM-$\mathcal{A}$-∃SM, marked "—", are trivial, as a stable matching always exists in an instance of SM. "NPc" stands for NP-complete. Hardness results for CSR that carry the mark of a result shown for CSM follow from that result, since STABLE MARRIAGE is a special case of STABLE ROOMMATES (membership in NP is straightforward in each such case). Additionally, we use the following notation: [$\blacklozenge$] and [$\lozenge$] mark results by Boehmer et al. [8] and easy consequences thereof, respectively; [†] marks results by Tan [26,28]; [♡] marks results by Mnich and Schlotter [25]; [⋆] marks results by Abraham et al. [1]; [♠] marks results by Biró et al. [7]; [**] marks results by Chen, Skowron, and Sorge [15]. Previously known results are typeset in gray; results new to this paper are typeset in **bold** black.

	AddAg		DelAg		DelAcc		Reorder		Swap	
	CSM	CSR	CSM	CSR	CSM	CSR	CSM	CSR	CSM	CSR
MA	**NPc** [T3.2]	**NPc** [C3.3]	in P$^{\lozenge}$ [T3.1]	**in P** [T3.1]	NPc$^{\heartsuit}$	NPc$^{\heartsuit}$	**NPc** [T4.1]	**NPc** [T4.1]	**NPc** [P4.2]	**NPc** [P4.2]
MP	NPc$^{\blacklozenge}$	NPc$^{\blacklozenge}$	in P$^{\blacklozenge}$	**in P** [T3.1]	NPc$^{\blacklozenge}$	NPc$^{\blacklozenge}$	NPc$^{\blacklozenge}$	NPc$^{\blacklozenge}$	NPc$^{\blacklozenge}$	NPc$^{\blacklozenge}$
MS	in P$^{\blacklozenge}$	**NPc** [T3.4]	NPc$^{\blacklozenge}$	NPc$^{\blacklozenge}$	in P$^{\blacklozenge}$	in P$^{\lozenge}$ [P3.5]	in P$^{\blacklozenge}$	**NPc** [P4.5]	in P$^{\blacklozenge}$	**NPc** [T4.4]
USM	NPc$^{\blacklozenge}$	NPc$^{\blacklozenge}$	NPc$^{\blacklozenge}$	NPc$^{\blacklozenge}$	in P$^{\blacklozenge}$	**NPc** [T3.7]	NPc$^{\blacklozenge}$	NPc$^{\blacklozenge}$	NPc$^{\blacklozenge}$	NPc$^{\blacklozenge}$
∃SM	—	**NPc** [T3.6]	—	in P†	—	NPc*	—	**NPc** [T4.6]	—	**NPc** [T4.6]
∃PSM	**NPc** [T3.2]	**NPc** [T3.6]	in P†	in P†	NPc$^{\spadesuit}$	NPc$^{\spadesuit}$	NPc$^{\blacklozenge}$	NPc$^{\blacklozenge}$	NPc**	NPc**

Our Contributions. Table 1 summarizes the computational complexity of all non-trivial action–goal–setting combinations. The majority of these results are not new: they either appear explicitly in the prior literature on stable-matching control/manipulation, or they follow via transfer arguments (in particular, from CSM to CSR or by standard reductions from known "almost stable" and deletion problems). Our main technical contributions are (i) introducing and studying the control goal MA (ensuring that a designated agent is matched in some stable outcome), which was not part of the previously studied stable-matching control goal sets, and (ii) settling the remaining cases not implied by existing results or immediate transfers (highlighted in Table 1), yielding a complete and coherent landscape for these actions and goals in both CSM and CSR. For the tractable new cases we provide polynomial-time algorithms, and for the intractable ones we give matching NP-hardness proofs.

Outline. Section 2 introduces notation and formalizes our control problems. Sections 3 and 4 contain our results for control actions (AddAg, DelAg, and DelAcc), and for bribery actions (Reorder and Swap), respectively. We conclude in Sect. 5. Proofs of results marked by ($\star$) are deferred to the full version [14].

Related Work. Control was introduced in computational social choice for elections by Bartholdi III et al. [3] and brought to stable matchings by Boehmer et al. [8], who study multiple actions/goals (including unique stability) for Stable Marriage. A broader unifying perspective is provided by the IJCAI 2025 survey of Chen et al. [13], which reviews control across COMSOC (including voting, fair allocation, cooperative games, and matching under preferences) and helps situate stable-matching control among related structural-intervention models.

Several earlier lines of work coincide with special cases of our action/goal combinations under different motivations. Tan [26,28] studies maximum stable matchings for Stable Roommates, which corresponds to deleting as few agents as possible so that the remaining instance admits a perfect and stable matching (i.e., CSR-DelAg-∃PSM). Problems of the form CSR-DelAcc-$\mathcal{G}$ are closely related to *almost stable* matchings: Deleting k acceptable pairs can be viewed as removing up to k potential blocking pairs. Abraham et al. [1] prove strong inapproximability for minimizing blocking pairs in Stable Roommates, and Biró et al. [7] show even stronger inapproximability for maximizing size while minimizing blocking pairs; their hardness already applies to the marriage setting with a perfect target, implying intractability for CSM-DelAcc-∃PSM. Mnich and Schlotter [25] study covering distinguished agents subject to a bound on blocking pairs; in particular, their hardness for covering even a single distinguished agent implies hardness for CSM-DelAcc-MA. Further intractability and parameterized results include Chen et al. [12] (parameterized analysis for DelAcc variants), Gupta and Jain [20] (weighted/destructive variants), and Kamiyama [23] (agent deletion to achieve super-stability with ties).

Finally, control by adding/deleting agents has recently been extended to coalition formation: Chen et al. [11] initiate the study of control in hedonic games under several stability notions and goals. This underlines that participation-based interventions form a common algorithmic theme across COMSOC models; our results give a complete picture for the classical stable matching setting.

2 Preliminaries

For a positive integer t, we write $[t] := \{1, \ldots, t\}$. In the following, we first introduce the basic concepts of the standard model for STABLE ROOMMATES, and then define the control problems we study.

2.1 Model for Stable Roommates

Formally, an instance I of STABLE ROOMMATES consists of a set U of agents and a collection $(\succ_u)_{u \in U}$ of preferences where each preference list $\succ_u$ is a strict linear order over the set $A(u) \subseteq U \setminus \{u\}$ of agents that u finds *acceptable*. We assume that the acceptability relation is symmetric, meaning that x finds y acceptable if and only if y finds x acceptable. For the acceptability relation of each instance I, there exists an *associated undirected graph* $G = (U, E)$ over the set of agents such that two agents are connected by an edge of E if and only if they find each other acceptable. We use $E(I)$ to denote the set of all acceptable pairs in I.

A *matching* in I is a subset $M \subseteq E$ of pairwise disjoint edges. For a pair $\{u, v\} \in M$, we will use the notation $M(u) = v$ and $M(v) = u$ to denote the partner of u and v, respectively. Consequently, we say that M *covers* u and v. It is *perfect* for I if every agent in I is covered. We write $M(u) = \emptyset$ to indicate that u is *unmatched* by M, that is, M does not cover agent u. A *blocking pair* for some matching M in I is a pair $\{u, v\} \in E$ of agents such that

(i) either $M(u) = \emptyset$ or $v \succ_u M(u)$, and similarly,
(ii) either $M(v) = \emptyset$ or $u \succ_v M(v)$.

A matching is *stable* if it admits no blocking pair.

Given an instance $I = (U, (\succ_u)_{u \in U})$ of STABLE ROOMMATES and a subset W of agents, $I - W$ is the instance obtained by *deleting the agents* in W from I, that is, we let $I - W := (U \setminus W, (\succ'_u)_{u \in U \setminus W})$ where $\succ'_u$ is the restriction of $\succ_u$ to $U \setminus W$. Similarly, given a subset $F \subseteq E$ of agent pairs, the instance obtained from I by *deleting the acceptability* for the pairs in F is $I - F := (U, (\succ'_u)_{u \in U})$, where for each agent $u \in U$, the set of acceptable agents becomes $A'(u) := A(u) \setminus \{v \colon \{u, v\} \in F\}$ and thus $\succ'_u$ is the restriction of $\succ_u$ to $A'(u)$.

Stable Marriage. The STABLE MARRIAGE model is the bipartite special case of STABLE ROOMMATES: The agent set is partitioned into two sides, and acceptability edges only go across the partition. Following tradition, we refer to agents on the two sides as *men* and *women*. Each agent ranks its acceptable partners on the opposite side in strict order, and a matching pairs men and women. Stability is defined identically (no blocking pair of mutually preferred partners), but unlike in STABLE ROOMMATES, a stable matching always exists in STABLE MARRIAGE and can be found by the Gale–Shapley algorithm [18].

2.2 Problem Definitions

We now formally define problem CSR-$\mathcal{A}$-$\mathcal{G}$ for each action $\mathcal{A} \in \{\mathsf{AddAg}, \mathsf{DelAg}, \mathsf{DelAcc}, \mathsf{Swap}, \mathsf{Reorder}\}$ and each goal $\mathcal{G} \in \{\mathsf{MA}, \mathsf{MP}, \mathsf{MS}, \mathsf{USM}, \exists\mathsf{SM}, \exists\mathsf{PSM}\}$.

Adding Agents. We first focus on the control action of agent addition AddAg. For this control action, the input not only contains the *original* set U of agents but also a set U' of *addable* agents, and the preferences of the agents are given for the whole market over $U \cup U'$. For the control goals ∃SM and ∃PSM, the definitions are as follows:

CSR-AddAg-∃SM (resp. CSR-AddAg-∃PSM)
Input: An instance $I = (U \cup U', (\succ_u)_{u \in U \cup U'})$ of Stable Roommates, where U denotes the set of *original* agents and U' the set of *addable* agents, and an integer *budget* ℓ.
Question: Is there a subset $W \subseteq U'$ with $|W| \leq \ell$ such that $I - (U' \setminus W)$ admits a stable (resp., *perfect* and stable) matching?

For the control goals MA and MP, we require an additional input:

CSR-AddAg-MA (resp. CSR-AddAg-MP)
Input: An instance $I = (U \cup U', (\succ_u)_{u \in U \cup U'})$ of Stable Roommates, an integer *budget* ℓ, and an agent $u^* \in U$ (resp., a pair $e^* \in E(I)$ of agents).
Question: Is there a subset $W \subseteq U'$ with $|W| \leq \ell$ such that $I - (U' \setminus W)$ admits a stable matching that covers u^* (resp., contains e^*)?

Finally, for the goals MS and USM, following Boehmer et al. [8], the additional input is a *perfect* matching, which covers not only the original agents but also the addable agents. The reason for this is that the control action AddAg may alter the set of matched agents in an instance.

CSR-AddAg-MS (resp. CSR-AddAg-USM)
Input: An instance $I = (U \cup U', (\succ_u)_{u \in U \cup U'})$ of Stable Roommates, an integer *budget* ℓ, and a perfect matching M of I.
Question: Is there a subset $W \subseteq U'$ with $|W| \leq \ell$ such that $I - (U' \setminus W)$ admits a stable matching M' with $M' \subseteq M$ (resp., a *unique* stable matching M' with $M' \subseteq M$)?

Deleting Agents. The control problems regarding the control action of deleting agents are defined analogously, so we omit their definitions here, except for the goal MS, where we again assume the input matching to be perfect:

CSR-DelAg-MS
Input: An instance $I = (U, (\succ_u)_{u \in U})$ of Stable Roommates, an integer *budget* ℓ, and a perfect matching M of I.
Question: Is there a subset $W \subseteq U$ of at most ℓ agents such that $I - W$ admits a stable matching M' with $M' \subseteq M$?

Deleting Acceptability. The control problems CSR-DelAcc-$\mathcal{G}$ are defined analogously: instead of a set of at most ℓ agents $W \subseteq U$, we ask for a set of at most ℓ edges $F \subseteq E(I)$ so that the instance $I - F$ satisfies our goals. For brevity, we omit these problem definitions. We remark that, contrasting the previous two control actions, the input matching for CSR-DelAcc-MS is simply a matching, because deleting acceptability does not change the set of agents:

CSR-DelAcc-MS
Input: An instance $I = (U, (\succ_u)_{u \in U})$ of STABLE ROOMMATES, an integer *budget* ℓ, and a matching M in I.
Question: Is there a subset $F \subseteq E(I)$ with $|F| \leq \ell$ such that $I - F$ admits a stable matching M' with $M' \subseteq M$?

Swapping Agents in a Preference List. We further consider the manipulative action Swap, introduced by Boehmer et al. [8] as a *bribery* action: in contrast to the three previous actions, Swap does not change the set of agents nor the acceptability relation, but instead modifies the preference orders themselves. Formally, given an instance $I = (U, (\succ_u)_{u \in U})$ of STABLE ROOMMATES, a *swap operation* is a triple $\sigma = (u, v, v')$ where $u \in U$ and $v, v' \in A(u)$ appear consecutively in $\succ_u$, that is, $v \succ_u v'$ and no $x \in A(u)$ satisfies $v \succ_u x \succ_u v'$. Applying σ to I yields the instance $I_\sigma = (U, (\succ'_u)_{u \in U})$ in which $\succ'_u$ is identical to $\succ_u$ except that the relative order of v and v' is reversed, while $\succ'_x = \succ_x$ holds for each $x \in U \setminus \{u\}$. Modeling a briber whose cost grows with the distance an agent must move in another agent's preferences, Swap is the most fine-grained of the bribery actions. Given a sequence S of swap operations, we write $I \oplus S$ for the instance obtained by applying the operations of S to I one after the other (each subsequent operation is interpreted in the already partially modified instance).

Reordering Preference Lists. The second bribery action we adopt from Boehmer et al. [8] is Reorder, which models a briber capable of fully "buying" an agent: a single operation may replace an agent's preference list with an arbitrary strict order over the same acceptable set. Formally, a *reorder operation* is a pair $\rho = (u, \succ^\circ_u)$ where $u \in U$ and $\succ^\circ_u$ is a strict linear order over $A(u)$. Applying ρ to I replaces $\succ_u$ with $\succ^\circ_u$ and leaves every other agent's preference list intact. Given a set R of reorder operations, with at most one per agent, we again write $I \oplus R$ for the resulting instance.

Restriction for the Goals MA *and* MP. As already observed by Boehmer et al. [8, Section 2.4] for the goal corresponding to MP, allowing the briber to act on the distinguished agents themselves trivializes the problem (e.g., a constant number of reorders on u^* and v^* would already make them each other's top choice). They therefore explicitly forbid reordering the preference list of any agent in the distinguished pair, and we adopt the same restriction for the goal MP. For the goal MA, however, protecting only the distinguished agent u^* itself is not enough: a single reorder operation placing u^* at the top of the preference list of an arbitrary agent $w \in A(u^*)$ already forces u^* to be matched in every stable matching, as otherwise $\{u^*, w\}$ would form a blocking pair. To prevent the briber from promoting the distinguished agent indirectly in this way, we additionally forbid operations on the agents that u^* finds acceptable. Formally, given an instance I, a swap or reorder operation acting on an agent u is *admissible* if

- for the goal MA with distinguished agent $u^* \in U$: $u \neq u^*$ and $u \notin A(u^*)$;
- for the goal MP with distinguished pair $e^* = \{u^*, v^*\}$: $u \notin \{u^*, v^*\}$.

For the goals MS, $\exists\mathsf{SM}$, $\exists\mathsf{PSM}$, and USM, every swap and reorder operation is admissible.

For each bribery action $\mathcal{A} \in \{\mathsf{Swap}, \mathsf{Reorder}\}$ and each goal $\mathcal{G} \in \{\mathsf{MA}, \mathsf{MP}, \mathsf{MS}, \exists\mathsf{SM}, \exists\mathsf{PSM}, \mathsf{USM}\}$, the problem CSR-$\mathcal{A}$-$\mathcal{G}$ asks whether the goal can be achieved by at most ℓ admissible operations of type $\mathcal{A}$. We illustrate the formal definitions with two representative cases.

CSR-Swap-MA (resp. CSR-Swap-MP)
Input: An instance $I = (U, (\succ_u)_{u \in U})$ of STABLE ROOMMATES, an integer *budget* ℓ, and an agent $u^* \in U$ (resp., a pair $e^* \in E(I)$).
Question: Is there a sequence S of at most ℓ admissible swap operations on I such that $I \oplus S$ admits a stable matching that covers u^* (resp., contains e^*)?

CSR-Reorder-$\exists$SM (resp. CSR-Reorder-$\exists$PSM)
Input: An instance $I = (U, (\succ_u)_{u \in U})$ of STABLE ROOMMATES and an integer *budget* ℓ.
Question: Is there a set R of at most ℓ reorder operations on I such that $I \oplus R$ admits a stable (resp., *perfect* and stable) matching?

We omit the analogous definitions for the other action–goal combinations. The marriage variants of our problems are defined analogously, with the input containing an instance of STABLE MARRIAGE instead of STABLE ROOMMATES.

We conclude this section with the following simple observation.

Observation 2.1 ($\star$). *For every control action $\mathcal{A} \in \{\mathsf{AddAg}, \mathsf{DelAg}, \mathsf{DelAcc}\}$, there is a polynomial-time Turing reduction from CSR-$\mathcal{A}$-MA to CSR-$\mathcal{A}$-MP, and from CSM-$\mathcal{A}$-MA to CSM-$\mathcal{A}$-MP.*

We remark that Observation 2.1 does not extend directly to the bribery actions Swap and Reorder, since the admissibility restrictions of the two problems differ: an operation that is admissible for the goal MP with distinguished pair $\{u^*, w^*\}$ may act on an agent in $A(u^*) \setminus \{w^*\}$ and is then inadmissible for the goal MA with distinguished agent u^*.

3 Control Actions

We first focus on control by adding or deleting agents, or deleting acceptability. Within the section, we organize our results based on the goal we aim to achieve.

Matching an Agent or a Pair of Agents. We start with our main algorithmic result which shows that even in an instance of STABLE ROOMMATES, we can efficiently decide whether, by deleting at most ℓ agents, we can obtain an instance in which some stable matching pairs two designated agents together. Naturally, this also implies an algorithm for ensuring via agent deletions that a given agent is matched in some stable matching—it suffices to try all its possible partners.

Boehmer et al. [8] showed that, in the marriage setting, it is polynomial-time solvable to make a given pair part of some stable matching. From this, the polynomial-time solvability of CSM-DelAg-MA follows using Observation 2.1. We now extend the approach by Boehmer et al. [8] to the roommates setting. The crucial idea is to use the concept of stable partitions by Tan [28] and a result by Tan and Hsu [29] regarding deleting an agent; see also [24, Sections 4.3.2 and 4.3.4] for the necessary background on stable partitions.

Theorem 3.1. *CSR*-DelAg-MP *and CSR*-DelAg-MA *are in* P.

Proof. We present a polynomial-time algorithm for the CSR-DelAg-MP problem. By Observation 2.1, this implies the polynomial-time solvability of CSR-DelAg-MA as well. As already mentioned, we will use the structural properties of stable partitions and ideas from the algorithm given by Boehmer et al. [8] for the bipartite version of our problem, CSM-DelAg-MP.

Let $\mathcal{J} = (I, \ell, \{a, b\})$ be our input instance where I is an instance of Stable Roommates, ℓ is our budget, i.e., the number of agents we are allowed to delete, and $\{a, b\}$ is the (acceptable) pair in I that we aim to include in the desired matching. We say that a set S of agents is a *solution* for $\mathcal{J}$ if removing S from I yields an instance, denoted by $I - S$, where some stable matching contains $\{a, b\}$.

Let $A^\star$ and $B^\star$ be the sets of agents which are preferred by a to b, or by b to a, respectively (note that $A^\star$ and $B^\star$ need not be disjoint). Furthermore, let the edge set F contain those pairs $\{x, y\}$, where

(i) $x \in A^\star$, and $y = a$ or x prefers a to y, or
(ii) $x \in B^\star$, and $y = b$ or x prefers b to y.

Formally, let

$$\begin{aligned} A^\star &= \{x \colon x \succ_a b\},\ F = \{\{x, y\} \colon x \in A^\star, (y = a \text{ or } a \succ_x y)\} \\ B^\star &= \{x \colon x \succ_b a\}, \qquad\quad \cup \{\{x, y\} \colon x \in B^\star, (y = b \text{ or } b \succ_x y)\}. \end{aligned} \tag{1}$$

Note that no pair in F can be included in a stable matching containing $\{a, b\}$, because all such pairs either match a or b (but not via $\{a, b\}$), or result in a blocking pair formed by one of the agents in the pair and an agent in $\{a, b\}$.

Let $I^\star$ denote the instance obtained from I by deleting all pairs in F from the set of acceptable pairs, i.e., $I^\star := I - F$.

Our algorithm is depicted in Algorithm 1. Note that line 3 can be performed in linear time using Tan's algorithm [27] for computing a stable partition. Hence, the algorithm runs in polynomial time. It remains to show its correctness. We start with the following claim.

Claim 3.1. *A set S of agents with $S \cap \{a, b\} = \emptyset$ is a solution for $\mathcal{J}$ if and only if $I^\star - S$ admits a stable matching that matches every agent in $(A^\star \cup B^\star) \setminus S$.*

ALGORITHM 1: Algorithm for solving CSR-DelAg-MP

Input: An instance I of Stable Roommates, a budget ℓ, and a pair of agents $\{a, b\}$
Output: "yes" if there exists a set S of at most ℓ agents such that $I - S$ admits a stable matching that contains $\{a, b\}$; otherwise "no"

1 Compute $A^\star$, $B^\star$, and F as defined in (1)
2 Compute instance $I^\star := I - F$
3 Compute a stable partition Π for $I^\star$
4 Let U_0 denote the set of singleton parties in Π consisting of an agent in $A^\star \cup B^\star$
5 Let r denote the number of odd parties of size at least 3 in Π
6 Return "yes" if $r + |U_0| \leq \ell$; otherwise, return "no."

Proof. Assume that S is a solution for $\mathcal{J}$. Then there exists a stable matching M in $I - S$ containing $\{a, b\}$. First, we show that $M \cap F = \emptyset$. Suppose for the sake of contradiction that $\{x, y\} \in M \cap F$. Then $x \in A^\star \cup B^\star$; by symmetry we may assume $x \in A^\star$. By the definition of F, we infer that either $y = a$ or x prefers a to y. The former is not possible, because $M(a) = b \notin A^\star$; the latter is not possible either, because it would mean that $\{x, a\}$ blocks M: x prefers a to $y = M(x)$ and a prefers x to $M(a) = b$ by the definition of $A^\star$. This contradiction proves that M is a matching disjoint from F, i.e., it is a matching in $I^\star - S$.

It remains to show that M matches every agent in the set $(A^\star \cup B^\star)\setminus S$. Suppose for the sake of contradiction that $x \in (A^\star \cup B^\star)\setminus S$ is unmatched by M. By symmetry, we may assume $x \in A^\star$. However, then the pair $\{x, a\}$ is a blocking pair, a contradiction. Thus, M has the desired property.

For the other direction, assume that for some agent set S with $S \cap \{a, b\} = \emptyset$, the instance $I^\star - S$ admits a stable matching M that matches every agent in the set $(A^\star \cup B^\star) \setminus S$.

In this case, M matches a to b because they are each other's best choice in $I^\star$ due to the deletion of the acceptability of all pairs in F. Moreover, M is stable in $I - S$, because it is stable in $I^\star - S$ and, since all agents in $(A^\star \cup B^\star) \setminus S$ are matched in $I^\star - S$, no pair in F blocks M. ◁

To show the correctness of our algorithm, assume first that it returns "yes". Let S contain an arbitrarily chosen agent from each odd party of size at least 3 in Π and all singleton parties consisting of an agent in $A^\star \cup B^\star$. Note that $a, b \notin S$: since a and b are each other's top choice in $I^\star$, they form a party of size two in Π, so neither belongs to an odd party. Then deleting S from $I^\star$ yields an instance I' whose stable partition Π' has no odd parties of size at least 3 and whose singleton parties are all disjoint from $A^\star \cup B^\star$, due to well-known properties of stable partitions [28] (see also [24, Proposition 4.11]). This means that in all stable matchings for $I^\star - S$, the set of unmatched agents (i.e., those agents that form singletons in Π') is disjoint from $A^\star \cup B^\star$. By Claim 3.1, S is therefore a solution, and since $|S| = r + |U_0| \leq \ell$ by line 6 of Algorithm 1, we obtain that $\mathcal{J}$ is a "yes"-instance.

It remains to prove that whenever S is a solution of size at most ℓ, then the algorithm returns "yes". Clearly, $a, b \notin S$, as some stable matching of $I - S$ must contain the pair $\{a, b\}$. Since S is a solution, by Claim 3.1 we know that $I^\star - S$ admits a stable matching that matches all agents in $(A^\star \cup B^\star)\backslash S$. This means that the stable partition Π_S of $I^\star - S$ contains no odd parties of size at least 3, and contains no singleton odd parties formed by some agent in $(A^\star \cup B^\star)\backslash S$; let us call such odd parties *forbidden*. However, it is known that deleting an agent from an instance of STABLE ROOMMATES results in an instance whose stable partitions contain all odd parties of the original instance except, possibly, for one (see [29, Corollary 3.9]). Since Π has exactly $|U_0| + r$ forbidden odd parties, deleting fewer than $r + |U_0|$ agents from $I^\star$ will result in an instance that has at least one forbidden odd party. This implies $\ell \geq |S| \geq r + |U_0|$, so the algorithm returns "yes" on line 6. □

Let us turn our focus to control by adding agents. Our next result shows that making an agent matched (MA) in a stable matching is no easier than making a pair matched (MP). The reduction is from the NP-complete CLIQUE problem [19] and is inspired by the one given by Boehmer et al. [8] for the MP case, and happens to prove hardness also for CSM-AddAg-∃PSM.

Theorem 3.2 (⋆). *CSM*-AddAg-MA *and CSM*-AddAg-∃PSM *are* NP*-complete.*

Note that CSR-AddAg-MA is in NP, because even in an instance of STABLE ROOMMATES, all stable matchings cover the same set of agents [21, Theorem 4.5.2]. This leads to the following consequence of Theorem 3.2.

Corollary 3.3. *CSR*-AddAg-MA *is* NP*-complete.*

Stabilizing a Matching. Having settled the complexity of using control actions to achieve the goals MA and MP, we next turn to the goal MS of stabilizing a prescribed matching. For STABLE MARRIAGE, AddAg-MS is solvable in polynomial time by Boehmer et al. [8]. The roommates setting is more brittle: even when we are given a perfect "plan" matching and are only allowed to keep pairs from that plan, deciding whether agent additions suffice becomes intractable.

Theorem 3.4 (⋆). *CSR*-AddAg-MS *is* NP*-complete.*

Boehmer et al. [8, Observation 1] observed that for the marriage case, the number of blocking pairs of a given matching M lower-bounds the number of acceptable pairs to delete to make M stable. Since this observation applies to the roommates case as well, the following holds.

Proposition 3.5 (⋆). *CSR*-DelAcc-MS *can be solved in linear time.*

Ensuring the Existence of a (Perfect) Stable Matching. We now move to the existence-oriented goals for AddAg in CSR, where no reference matching is given and the controller only aims to ensure that a stable (or perfect and stable) matching exists after adding agents. Even under this additional freedom, adding agents remains computationally hard in the roommates setting.

Theorem 3.6 (⋆). *CSR*-AddAg-∃SM *and CSR*-AddAg-∃PSM *are* NP*-complete.*

Next, we prove that the polynomial-time algorithm by Boehmer et al. [8] for CSM-DelAcc-USM does not generalize to the roommates setting; we present a reduction from the NP-complete BACK AND FORTH PATHS problem [17].

Theorem 3.7 (⋆). *CSR-DelAcc-USM is NP-complete, even on instances whose underlying graph can be made bipartite by deleting a single edge.*

Proof sketch. Whether an instance of STABLE ROOMMATES admits a unique stable matching can be decided in polynomial time by standard methods [21]. To show NP-hardness, we reduce from the following variant of the NP-complete problem BACK AND FORTH PATHS [17]: given a directed graph $D = (V, E)$ and two arcs (s, s') and (t, t') in D, decide if there exists a cycle through (s, s') and (t, t') in D. We may assume that every vertex in D has indegree at least 2, and that $(s, v) \in E$ for each $v \in V \setminus \{s, s'\}$; see the full version [14] for details.

For some $v \in V$, let d_v denote the indegree of v. We let $V' = V \setminus \{s', t'\}$. For each vertex v, we fix an ordering of the incoming arcs of v, and for each $i \in [\mathsf{d}_v]$ we denote by $\delta(v, i)$ the tail of the i-th arc in this ordering. For simplicity, we let (s, s') and (t, t') be the first arcs among the incoming edges of s' and of t', respectively, so $\delta(s', 1) = s$ and $\delta(t', 1) = t$.

Construction. We construct an instance of STABLE ROOMMATES as follows. For each vertex $v \in V$, we create two sets of agents, $A_v = \{a_v^i : i \in [\mathsf{d}_v]\}$ and $B_v = \{b_v^i : i \in [\mathsf{d}_v]\}$. The preferences of these agents are as follows; throughout the proof, we treat the superscripts of agents in $A_v \cup B_v$ modulo d_v:

$$
\begin{aligned}
&a_v^1 \colon \{b_u^j : \delta(u, j) = v\} \succ b_v^{\mathsf{d}_v} \succ b_v^1 && \text{for all } v \in V,\\
&a_v^i \colon b_v^{i-1} \succ b_v^i && \text{for all } v \in V,\ 2 \le i \le \mathsf{d}_v,\\
&b_v^i \colon a_v^i \succ a_v^{i+1} \succ a_u^1 && \text{for all } v \in V', i \in [\mathsf{d}_v], \delta(v, i) = u,\\
&b_{s'}^1 \colon a_{s'}^1 \succ a_{s'}^2 \succ b_{t'}^1 \succ a_s^1, &&\\
&b_{t'}^1 \colon a_{t'}^1 \succ a_{t'}^2 \succ b_{s'}^1 \succ a_t^1, &&\\
&b_x^i \colon a_x^i \succ a_x^{i+1} \succ a_u^1 && \text{for } x \in \{s', t'\}, 1 < i \le \mathsf{d}_x, \delta(x, i) = u.
\end{aligned}
$$

We set the target matching to $M = \{\{a_v^i, b_v^i\} : v \in V, i \in [\mathsf{d}_v]\}$ and the budget to $\ell = |V|$. Note that the instance I of STABLE ROOMMATES is almost bipartite: deleting the edge $\{b_{s'}^1, b_{t'}^1\}$ yields an instance of STABLE MARRIAGE.

Correctness. First assume that F is a set of at most ℓ edges in $E(I)$ such that M is the unique stable matching in $I' = I - F$. For each $v \in V$, let C_v denote the unique M-alternating cycle over agent set $A_v \cup B_v$. It is not hard to see that $M_v = M \varDelta C_v$ (where $\varDelta$ stands for symmetric difference) is a stable matching in I. Hence, M_v is also a stable matching in I' unless F contains an edge of $C_v \setminus M$. Due to $|F| \le |V|$, we know that F contains exactly one edge from each $C_v \setminus M$; let $\{b_v^{\sigma(v)}, a_v^{\sigma(v)+1}\}$ denote this edge for some $\sigma(v) \in [\mathsf{d}_v]$.

For each $v \in V$, consider the arc (u, v) in D such that $\delta(v, \sigma(v)) = u$; we will use the notation $\alpha(v) = u$. Define $E^\star = \{(\alpha(v), v) \colon v \in V\} \subseteq E$. We are going to show that $E^\star$ contains a cycle traversing both (s, s') and (t, t'). Clearly, $E^\star$

contains some directed cycle C, since each vertex has indegree exactly 1 in $E^\star$. We define an M-alternating cycle $\varphi(C)$ corresponding to C as the union of the paths $P_{(u,v)} = (a_v^1, b_v^1, \ldots, b_v^{\sigma(v)}, a_u^1)$ for $u = \alpha(v)$, taken over each $v \in V(C)$. It can be shown that if C contains at most one arc from $\{(s,s'),(t,t')\}$, then the matching $M' = M \Delta \varphi(C)$ is stable in I', because each agent a_v^i for which $M'(a_v^i) \neq M(a_v^i)$ prefers M' to M, and each agent b_v^i for which $M'(b_v^i) \neq M(b_v^i)$ is matched by M' to its second best choice in I', except possibly for either $b_{s'}^1$ or $b_{t'}^1$; thus, the only possible blocking edge for M' is $e^\star = \{b_{s'}^1, b_{t'}^1\}$, but by our assumption, at least one endpoint of $e^\star$ prefers its partner both in M and in M' to the other endpoint of $e^\star$. Thus, M' is stable in I', a contradiction. This implies that C must be a cycle in D containing both (s,s') and (t,t').

Assume now that C is a cycle in D containing both (s,s') and (t,t'). Let $\alpha(v)$ be the vertex preceding v on C if $v \in V(C)$, and let $\alpha(v) = s$ otherwise; then $\{(\alpha(v), v) : v \in V\} \subseteq E$. We define $F = \{\{b_v^i, a_v^{i+1}\} : v \in V,\ \alpha(v) = \delta(v,i)\}$ and claim that M is the unique stable matching in $I' = I - F$. Since stability of M is clear, it remains to prove the uniqueness in I'.

Assume for contradiction that I' admits a stable matching other than M. By the work of Cheng and Rosenbaum [16], we know that there exists a stable matching M' in I'—namely, a stable matching in I' that is adjacent to M in the median graph of the instance I'—for which $M \Delta M'$ is a single cycle C_Δ. Since deleting $\{b_{s'}^1, b_{t'}^1\}$ yields a bipartite instance, C_Δ cannot contain $\{b_{s'}^1, b_{t'}^1\}$.

We say that some $v \in V$ is *important*, if C_Δ contains a vertex in $A_v \cup B_v$. Note that $V(C_\Delta) \subseteq A_v \cup B_v$ is not possible, because $A_v \cup B_v$ induces a path in I'. Thus, if v is important, then C_Δ needs to contain at least two edges having exactly one endpoint in $A_v \cup B_v$, and at most one such edge can be incident to a_v^1. Thus, at least one edge on C_Δ connects some b_v^i to a_u^1 for some $i \in [\mathsf{d}_v]$ and $u = \delta(v,i)$. However, then $\{b_v^i, a_v^{i+1}\}$ must be in F, as otherwise it blocks M'. This means that $\{b_v^i, a_v^{i+1}\} \in F$ and, therefore, $\alpha(v) = u = \delta(v,i)$.

Moreover, using the structure of our construction and the fact that C_Δ is M-alternating, it can be shown that the edges of C_Δ incident to vertices of $A_v \cup B_v$ are exactly the edges of $P_{(u,v)}$ for $\alpha(v) = u$ and the edge $\{a_v^1, b_z^j\} \in P_{(v,z)}$ where $\alpha(z) = v = \delta(z,j)$. Consequently, C_Δ must be the union of all paths $P_{(\alpha(v),v)}$ over all important vertices v. It follows that the arcs $(\alpha(v), v) \in E$ for each important vertex v form a single cycle in D which, thus, must be the cycle C; in fact, using the notation $\varphi(\cdot)$ for the first part of the proof, we have $\varphi(C) = C_\Delta$. In particular, $\{b_{s'}^1, a_s^1\}$ and $\{b_{t'}^1, a_t^1\}$ are both on $C_\Delta \cap M'$. However, then $\{b_{s'}^1, b_{t'}^1\}$ forms a blocking pair for M', a contradiction to the stability of M'. This proves that M is indeed the unique stable matching in $I' = I - F$, proving the correctness of our reduction. ◁

4 Bribery Actions

In this section, we focus on the bribery actions that manipulate agents' preferences via the Swap or the Reorder actions. Within the section, we again organize our results based on the goal we aim to achieve.

Matching an Agent. Boehmer et al. [8] showed that, already in the marriage setting, it is NP-complete to decide whether reordering at most ℓ preference lists yields a stable matching that contains a given pair (MP). Their hardness for MP does not immediately imply hardness for MA: a straightforward reduction from MP to MA would require one of the agents of the distinguished pair to have only the other as its acceptable partner, since this is the only way to make "the distinguished agent is matched in some stable matching" equivalent to "the distinguished pair is contained in some stable matching". The construction of Boehmer et al. does not enjoy this property. We therefore provide a direct reduction for MA in the marriage setting. Note that in our construction the distinguished agent a^* has a unique acceptable partner b^*, so a stable matching covers a^* if and only if it contains the pair $\{a^*, b^*\}$; moreover, the admissible operations for the goal MA (which must avoid a^* and $A(a^*) = \{b^*\}$) coincide with those for the goal MP with distinguished pair $\{a^*, b^*\}$. Hence, our reduction also serves as a valid reduction for MP, and thus subsumes the hardness of CSM-Reorder-MP proved by Boehmer et al.

Theorem 4.1 ($\star$). *CSM*-Reorder-MA *and CSR*-Reorder-MA *are* NP-*complete.*

The same construction with a larger budget yields hardness for Swap.

Proposition 4.2 ($\star$). *CSM*-Swap-MA *and CSR*-Swap-MA *are* NP-*complete.*

Remark 4.3. The NP-hardness for the swap action in the marriage case can alternatively be derived from Theorem 3.2 via a generic reduction from AddAg to Swap due to Boehmer et al. [8]: for each addable agent p in the source instance, introduce two dummy agents p_d and q_d with preferences $p_d\colon p \succ q_d$ and $q_d\colon p_d$, and prepend p_d to the head of p's preference list; in addition, pad every other preference list with sufficiently many further dummies between consecutive entries so that no swap on any other list fits within the budget. A single swap on p_d's list (from $p \succ q_d$ to $q_d \succ p$) causes $\{p_d, q_d\}$ to be matched, releasing p to participate in the rest of the matching—corresponding exactly to adding p in the source instance, with the budgets coinciding.

Stabilizing a Matching. Next, we consider the goal MS. Boehmer et al. [8] show that both bribery actions Swap and Reorder are polynomial-time solvable for the marriage case. We complement this result by showing that for the roommates setting, both CSR-Swap-MS and CSR-Reorder-MS become NP-complete.

Theorem 4.4 ($\star$). *CSR*-Swap-MS *is* NP-*complete.*

Proof. Membership in NP is straightforward, since checking whether a given matching is stable can be done in polynomial time. To show NP-hardness, we reduce from the following NP-complete variant [6] of the 3SAT problem which we call (2P,2N)-3SAT: given a 3CNF Boolean formula ϕ (i.e., a set of clauses each containing exactly 3 literals) over a variable set X, such that each variable appears *exactly* twice unnegated and twice negated, decide if ϕ is satisfiable.

Let (X, ϕ) be an instance of (2P,2N)-3SAT with $X = \{x_1, \ldots, x_{\hat{n}}\}$ and $\phi = \{C_1, \ldots, C_{\hat{m}}\}$. For each clause C_j, we fix an arbitrary order of its three literals and write $C_j = (l_j^1 \vee l_j^2 \vee l_j^3)$. We construct an instance of CSR-Swap-MS as follows: for each variable $x_i \in X$, we introduce four *variable agents* $x_i, \overline{x}_i, y_i$, and $\overline{y}_i$; for each clause $C_j \in \phi$ and each $z \in [3]$, we introduce two *clause agents* c_j^z and d_j^z. The preferences are as follows (indices for clause agents taken modulo 3):

$$x_i : \overline{x}_i \succ \{c_j^z : l_j^z = x_i\} \succ y_i,\ y_i : x_i,\ \forall i \in [\hat{n}];$$
$$\overline{x}_i : x_i \succ \{c_j^z : l_j^z = \overline{x}_i\} \succ \overline{y}_i,\ \overline{y}_i : \overline{x}_i,\ \forall i \in [\hat{n}];$$
$$c_j^z : c_j^{z+1} \succ c_j^{z+2} \succ l_j^z \succ d_j^z,\ \ d_j^z : c_j^z,\ \forall j \in [\hat{m}],\ z \in [3].$$

Since each literal occurs in exactly two clauses, each set $\{c_j^z : l_j^z = l\}$ has size 2, so the variable agents' preference lists have exactly four entries each. The target matching is $M := \{\{x_i, y_i\}, \{\overline{x}_i, \overline{y}_i\} : i \in [\hat{n}]\} \cup \{\{c_j^z, d_j^z\} : j \in [\hat{m}],\ z \in [3]\}$, and we set the budget to $\ell := 3\hat{n} + 5\hat{m}$.

We now give some intuition on why (X, ϕ) is satisfiable if and only if at most ℓ swaps suffice to obtain an instance with a stable matching $M' \subseteq M$. First, for each $i \in [\hat{n}]$ we need to ensure that $\{x_i, \overline{x}_i\}$ is not a blocking pair, which requires three swaps in the preferences of either x_i or $\overline{x}_i$; this choice corresponds to setting x_i to true or to false. Next, for each $j \in [\hat{m}]$ we need to ensure that no pair $\{c_j^a, c_j^b\}$ for $a, b \in [3]$ is a blocking pair; this requires five swaps and, importantly, leaves the preferences of c_j^z for some $z \in [3]$ unchanged. Since these swaps already use up the budget, for each agent c_j^z with untouched preferences we must have that the corresponding variable agent's preference list must have been changed (so that $\{c_j^z, l_j^z\}$ is not blocking)—this requirement translates to each clause containing a true literal. For the complete proof of correctness, see the full version [14]. □

For the reorder action, the same hardness can be obtained via a reduction from Vertex Cover that re-uses part of the construction from the proof of Theorem 3.4.

Proposition 4.5 (⋆). *CSR-*Reorder-MS *is* NP*-complete.*

Ensuring the Existence of a Stable Matching. Finally, we consider the bribery counterpart of the existence goal ∃SM. In the marriage case, the existence of a stable matching is always guaranteed, so the question is only interesting in the roommates setting.

Theorem 4.6 (⋆). *CSR-*Reorder-∃SM, *CSR-*Reorder-∃PSM, *CSR-*Swap-∃SM, *and CSR-*Swap-∃PSM *are all* NP*-complete.*

Remark 4.7. Hardness for the swap action with the ∃PSM goal is in fact already known in the strictly easier marriage setting: in the context of the trade-off between optimality (size of the matching) and stability, CSM-Swap-∃PSM has been shown to be W[1]-hard parameterized by the swap budget ℓ [15], and this hardness lifts to CSR-Swap-∃PSM since Stable Marriage is a special case of Stable Roommates. The argument above is nonetheless included because it yields the ∃SM variants and the reorder cases in the same construction.

5 Conclusion

We studied *control* and *bribery* for stable matchings under five manipulative actions and six goals, mapping the complete complexity landscape for both the marriage and the roommates settings (Table 1).

Regarding our NP-hardness results, it is important to keep in mind that our results do not necessarily offer a barrier against control in practice. Nevertheless, several of our reductions go beyond classical NP-hardness: those in Theorems 3.2, 3.6, 4.1 and 4.6, Corollary 3.3, and Proposition 4.2 reduce from CLIQUE or INDEPENDENT SET with budget ℓ polynomial in the solution size, yielding W[1]-hardness parameterized by ℓ. The remaining new hardness results do not yield such parameterized lower bounds: the reductions Theorems 3.4, 3.7 and 4.4 have budgets that are not bounded by the source parameter, and Proposition 4.5 reduces from VERTEX COVER, which is fixed-parameter tractable; hence, the parameterized complexity of these cases remains open.

Several directions remain open. First, since several of our intractable cases are already W[1]-hard parameterized by the number ℓ of applied actions, a natural next step is to identify alternative parameters that may yield fixed-parameter tractability, such as bounds on preference-list lengths, structural restrictions of the acceptability graph (e.g., bounded treewidth/vertex cover), distances to restricted domains, or combined parameters (e.g., ℓ together with such a structural bound); the parameterized complexity of the cases that our reductions leave open is itself a concrete target. Second, one can study restricted preference classes (e.g., single-peaked/single-crossing preferences [2,9,10]) that may restore tractability for some action–goal combinations. Finally, it would be interesting to extend the same action/goal palette to richer matching models (ties, many-to-one, matching with contracts, distributional constraints) and to compare systematically with emerging control landscapes in coalition formation settings.

Acknowledgment. We are grateful to Jörg Rothe for enjoyable and fruitful discussions, and for his invitation to prepare a survey on control problems in the area of matching under preferences; the work contained in this paper originated in our efforts to write that survey. J. Chen is supported by the Vienna Science and Technology Fund (WWTF) [10.47379/VRG18012]. I. Schlotter is supported by the Hungarian Academy of Sciences under its Momentum Programme (LP2021-2) and its János Bolyai Research Scholarship.

References

1. Abraham, D.J., Biró, P., Manlove, D.F.: "Almost stable" matchings in the roommates problem. In: Proceedings of the 3rd Workshop on Approximation and Online Algorithms (WAOA 2005). LNCS, vol. 3879, pp. 1–14. Springer, Cham (2006)
2. Ballester, M., Haeringer, G.: A characterization of the single-peaked domain. Soc. Choice Welfare **36**(2), 305–322 (2011)

3. Bartholdi, J., III., Tovey, C., Trick, M.: How hard is it to control an election? Math. Comput. Model. **16**(8/9), 27–40 (1992)
4. Bartholdi, J.J., III., Tovey, C.A., Trick, M.A.: The computational difficulty of manipulating an election. Soc. Choice Welfare **6**(3), 227–241 (1989)
5. Bérczi, K., Csáji, G., Király, T.: Manipulating the outcome of stable marriage and roommates problems. Games Econom. Behav. **147**, 407–428 (2024)
6. Berman, P., Karpinski, M., Scott, A.D.: Approximation hardness of short symmetric instances of MAX-3SAT. Technical report (2003). report no. 49
7. Biró, P., Manlove, D.F., Mittal, S.: Size versus stability in the marriage problem. Theoret. Comput. Sci. **411**(16–18), 1828–1841 (2010)
8. Boehmer, N., Bredereck, R., Heeger, K., Niedermeier, R.: Bribery and control in stable marriage. J. Artif. Intell. Res. **71**, 993–1048 (2021)
9. Bredereck, R., Chen, J., Finnendahl, U.P., Niedermeier, R.: Stable roommate with narcissistic, single-peaked, and single-crossing preferences. Auton. Agent. Multi-Agent Syst. **34**(53), 1–29 (2020)
10. Bredereck, R., Chen, J., Woeginger, G.J.: A characterization of the single-crossing domain. Soc. Choice Welfare **41**(4), 989–998 (2013)
11. Chen, J., Guttmann, J., Mustajbašić, M., Simola, S.: Control in hedonic games. In: Proceedings of the 25th International Conference on Autonomous Agents and Multiagent Systems (AAMAS 2026), pp. 920–928 (2026)
12. Chen, J., Hermelin, D., Sorge, M., Yedidsion, H.: How hard is it to satisfy (almost) all roommates? In: Proceedings of the 45th International Colloquium on Automata, Languages, and Programming (ICALP 2018). LIPIcs, vol. 107, pp. 35:1–35:15. Schloss Dagstuhl – Leibniz-Zentrum für Informatik (2018)
13. Chen, J., Kaczmarek, J., Nüsken, P., Rothe, J., Schlotter, I., Seeger, T.: Control in computational social choice. In: Proceedings of the 34th International Joint Conference on Artificial Intelligence (IJCAI 2025), pp. 10391–10399 (2025). Survey Track
14. Chen, J., Schlotter, I.: Control and bribery in stable marriage and stable roommates: A complete complexity landscape. arXiv:2502.01215 [cs.GT] (2025)
15. Chen, J., Skowron, P., Sorge, M.: Matchings under preferences: strength of stability and tradeoffs. ACM Trans. Econ. Comput. **9**(4) (2021)
16. Cheng, C.T., Rosenbaum, W.: Bridging the gap between stable marriage and stable roommates: A parameterized algorithm for optimal stable matchings. arXiv:2603.26943 [cs.DS] (2026)
17. Fortune, S., Hopcroft, J., Wyllie, J.: The directed subgraph homeomorphism problem. Theoret. Comput. Sci. **10**(2), 111–121 (1980)
18. Gale, D., Shapley, L.S.: College admissions and the stability of marriage. Am. Math. Mon. **69**(1), 9–15 (1962)
19. Garey, M.R., Johnson, D.S.: Computers and Intractability: A Guide to the Theory of NP-Completeness. W. H, Freeman and Company (1979)
20. Gupta, S., Jain, P.: Manipulation with(out) money in matching market. In: Proceedings of the 8th International Conference on Algorithmic Decision Theory (ADT 2024). LNCS, vol. 15248, pp. 273–287 (2025)
21. Gusfield, D., Irving, R.W.: The Stable Marriage Problem: Structure and Algorithms. Foundations of Computing Series MIT Press, Cambridge (1989)
22. Irving, R.W.: An efficient algorithm for the "stable roommates" problem. J. Algorithms **6**(4), 577–595 (1985)
23. Kamiyama, N.: Modifying an instance of the super-stable matching problem. Inf. Process. Lett. **189**, 106549 (2025)

24. Manlove, D.F.: Algorithmics of Matching Under Preferences. Series on Theoretical Computer Science, vol. 2. World Scientific Publishing (2013)
25. Mnich, M., Schlotter, I.: Stable marriage with covering constraints: A complete computational trichotomy. Algorithmica **82**(1), 1136–1188 (2020)
26. Tan, J.J.: A maximum stable matching for the roommates problem. BIT Numer. Math. **30**, 631–640 (1990)
27. Tan, J.J.: A necessary and sufficient condition for the existence of a complete stable matching. J. Algorithms **12**, 154–178 (1991)
28. Tan, J.J.: Stable matchings and stable partitions. Int. J. Comput. Math. **39**, 11–20 (1991)
29. Tan, J.J., Hsueh, Y.C.: A generalization of the stable matching problem. Discret. Appl. Math. **59**, 87–102 (1995)

Temporal Fair Division of Indivisible Goods with Structured Constraints

Kui-Wang Choi(✉) and Minming Li

Department of Computer Science, City University of Hong Kong, Hong Kong, China
kuiwchoi2-c@my.cityu.edu.hk, minming.li@cityu.edu.hk

Abstract. This paper investigates temporal fair division, a setting where items are allocated over multiple rounds and agents require cumulative fairness over time. We focus on dynamic extensions of classic fairness notions: Temporal Envy-Freeness Up to Any Good (TEFX), its α-TEFX approximation, and Temporal Maximin Share (TMMS). Because these strict fairness criteria are known to be generally impossible to satisfy, we analyze the model under constraints to map the boundary between what is possible and what is not.

Our contribution systematically maps the structural boundaries of these temporal fairness notions. Our main technical result introduces a novel dynamic backtracking framework that achieves exact TEFX for Strong Binary Valuations. We prove, via a lexicographical potential function argument, that this bounded historical reallocation systematically resolves temporal envy cycles and terminates in finite time. Finally, we establish tight approximation ratios for α-TEFX under identical valuations and bi-valued goods, alongside targeted impossibility results for TEFX and TMMS, demonstrating exactly where temporal fairness is mathematically unattainable, and properly contextualizing prior algorithms that only implicitly satisfied our newly defined TMMS metric.

Keywords: Fair Division · Resource Allocation · Algorithmic Game Theory

1 Introduction

Fair division is a fundamental problem in multi-agent systems and economics, traditionally focusing on the static allocation of resources, such as splitting a cake or distributing a set of goods at a single point in time [5,6,9,11,12,15,19,20]. However, many real-world allocation problems are dynamic. For example, in food-bank donation, goods often arrive over time and must be allocated online [1]. Although this approach captures the dynamic feature for real-world problems, it ignores the fairness in intermediate allocations. Therefore, the goal of temporal fair division is to maintain fairness cumulatively in each round, rather than just over the long run. This is crucial in some real-world allocation problems, such as in the food bank donation problem, the allocators receive a timeline

P. Lenzner and D. Schmand (Eds.): SAGT 2026, LNCS 16911, pp. 95–112, 2027.
https://doi.org/10.1007/978-3-032-38782-0_6

for the donation in order to plan ahead, such that the receivers can be as fair as possible during the period of donation.

The transition from dynamic to temporal settings introduces significant theoretical challenges. Unlike dynamic fair division, where intermediate allocations need not be fair, temporal mechanisms must account for this. Recent work has painted a bleak picture for this domain: temporal fair allocations are often impossible to guarantee without compromising efficiency or social welfare [13,14,17]. For instance, strong fairness concepts such as Envy-Freeness up to any good (EFX) are often unattainable in temporal settings because an agent's perception of fairness fluctuates wildly as new goods arrive.

Despite these impossibility results, the literature leaves several critical avenues unexplored. Existing impossibilities heavily rely on broad valuation classes. It is unclear whether more structured preferences, such as identical valuations or strong binary valuations, or structured arrival goods, such as identical days, can circumvent these temporal frictions. In addition, when exact temporal fairness is mathematically infeasible, the precise limits of approximate temporal fairness (α-TEFX) and alternative fairness notions, such as Temporal Maximin Share (TMMS), have not been formally mapped.

In this work, we directly address these gaps. We focus on three fairness metrics that have not been considered by previous works:

- **TEFX**: Temporal Envy-freeness Up to Any Good
- α-**TEFX**: Approximation of TEFX
- **TMMS**: Temporal Maximin Share

For each fairness metric, we seek the boundaries on four structured constraints:

- **Identical Days**: The goods that arrive in each round are identical.
- **Strong Binary Valuation**: Each agent values each good either 0 or 1, and no good is valued 0 for every agent.
- **Identical Valuation**: Each agent's valuation profile is identical.
- **Bi-valued Goods**: Each agent values each good either a or b, where a and b are positively constants.

Therefore, our main research question is to *examine the boundaries of temporal fairness under various structured constraints in temporal fair division.*

1.1 Our Contribution

We summarize our detailed results and position them alongside prior work on temporal fair division in Table 1.

In Sect. 3, we present our key contribution: a novel algorithm that returns a TEFX allocation under the strong binary valuation setting.

In Sect. 4, we establish a negative result for TEFX and TMMS under the identical days setting, while showing that a constant 1/2 approximation ratio exists for TEFX when there are two agents.

In Sect. 5 and Sect. 6, we build on the negative result of TEFX [14] under the identical valuation and bi-valued goods setting, providing two algorithms that return a tight approximation ratio for TEFX, respectively. We also construct a counterexample to show that a TMMS allocation may not exist even under both settings simultaneously.

Table 1. Possibilities, impossibilities, and open questions in temporal fair division under various constraints. ✓ indicates a possibility result; ✗ indicates an impossibility; † indicates a tight approximation ratio

	TEFX	α-TEFX	TMMS
Strong Binary Valuation	✓ (Theorem 1)	1	✓ (Corollary 1)
Identical Days	✗ (Theorem 2)	$\frac{1}{2}$ for $n = 2$ (Theorem 3)	✗ (Theorem 4)
Identical Valuation	✗ [14]	$\frac{\min_{g \in O} v(g)}{\max_{g \in O} v(g)}$ † (Theorem 5)	✗ (Theorem 6)
Bi-valued Goods	✗ [14]	$\frac{a}{b}$ † $b \geq a$ (Theorem 7)	✗ (Corollary 2)

1.2 Related Works

Our work is related to online fair division [1,2,8,22], where some (possibly zero) items arrive in consecutive rounds. We study a stronger version of it, known as temporal fair division, in which fairness must hold at every round [13,14,17]. Since the temporal fair division model must allocate items without knowledge of future arrivals, our temporal model operates in a batched online fair allocation setting. He et al. [17] showed that maintaining EF1 for goods is impossible in an uninformed setting without reallocating past items, and proposed a reallocation-based algorithm for two agents. However, they provided a polynomial-time algorithm in which, at each round, the allocation is EF1 in the informed setting with two agents. Elkind et al. [14] formalized temporal fairness for goods and chores, proving that TEFX allocations may not exist and providing TEF1 algorithms for two agents with chores or restricted settings: two item types, generalized binary valuations, and unimodal preferences. Finally, Cookson et al. [13] explored SD-EF1, EF1, and PROP1, focusing on achieving both temporal and daily fairness. They demonstrated that, while per-round SD-EF1 is generally impossible, under the identical days setting, it is always attainable, guaranteeing a final SD-PROP1 allocation.

2 Preliminaries

We study temporal fair division under an informed online fair division setting, denoted by the tuple $\mathcal{I} = \left(N, T, \{O_t\}_{t \in [T]}, v = (v_1, \ldots, v_n)\right)$, where we denote $[T] := \{1, \ldots, T\}$ where $T \in \mathcal{N}$.

We have a set of $N = [n]$ agents, and a set of items $\{O_t\}$ that arrive in round $t \in [T]$, which are to be allocated to the agents.

Denote $O^t = \bigcup_{i=1}^{t} O_i$ as the cumulative set of goods up to round t, and $O = O^T = \bigcup_{i=1}^{T} O_i$ as the set of all goods.

For each agent, there is an additive valuation function $v_i : 2^O \longrightarrow \mathbb{R}$ over the items, where for $S \subseteq O$, $v_i(S) = \sum_{g \in S} v_i(\{g\})$. We slightly abuse the notation and assume that $v_i(g) = v_i(\{g\})$. In addition, this work focuses on goods allocation, i.e. $\forall g \in O, \forall i \in N, v_i(g) \geq 0$.

An allocation $A = (A_1, \ldots, A_n)$ is defined as an ordered partial partition of O, where A_i is the goods allocated to agent i, such that $\forall i, j \in [N]$ where $i \neq j$, $A_i \cap A_j = \emptyset$ and $\bigcup_{i \in \mathcal{N}} A_i = O$.

In addition, under the online fair division setting, denote $A^t = (A_1^t, \ldots, A_n^t)$ as the allocation from round 1 to after round t, that is $A_i^t = A_i^{t-1} \cup (A_i \cap O_t)$.

To evaluate allocations within our temporal framework, we adapt standard fairness notions from static fair division [3]. Because exact Envy-Freeness (EF) [21] cannot be guaranteed with indivisible goods, the literature relies on relaxations: Envy-Freeness Up to Any Good (EFX) [11], its multiplicative approximation α-EFX [20], and the threshold-based Maximin Share (MMS) [9]. In temporal settings, we denote the cumulative enforcement of these properties at every discrete round $t \in [T]$ by prefixing them with "T" (i.e., TEFX, α-TEFX, TMMS) [13,14].

Definition 1 (Envy-Freeness Up to Any Good (EFX)). *An allocation $A = (A_1, \ldots, A_n)$ is envy-free up to any good (EFX) if $\forall i, j \in N, \forall g \in A_j$ s.t. $v_i(A_i) \geq v_i(A_j \backslash \{g\})$.*

Definition 2 (Temporal Envy-Freeness Up to Any Good (TEFX)). *For any $t \in [T]$, an allocation $A^t = (A_1^t, \ldots, A_n^t)$ is temporal envy-free up to any good (TEFX) if $\forall t' \leq t, A^{t'}$ is EFX.*

Definition 3 (Approximately Envy-Freeness Up to Any Good (α - EFX). *Let $\alpha \in (0, 1]$. An allocation $A = (A_1, \ldots, A_n)$ is approximately envy-free up to any good (α-EFX) if $\forall i, j \in N, \forall g \in A_j$ s.t. $v_i(A_i) \geq \alpha \cdot v_i(A_j \backslash \{g\})$.*

Definition 4 (Approximately Temporal Envy-Freeness Up to Any Good (α-TEFX)). *For any $t \in [T]$, an allocation $A^t = (A_1^t, \ldots, A_n^t)$ is approximately temporal envy-free up to any good (α-TEFX) if $\forall t' \leq t, A^{t'}$ is α-EFX.*

Definition 5 (Maximin Share Fairness (MMS)). *Denote $M_n(O)$ to be the collection of all possible allocations of the goods in O to n agents. An allocation $A = (A_1, \ldots, A_n)$ is maximin share fair (MMS) if $\forall i \in N$, we have*

$$v_i(A_i) \geq \mu_i^n(O) = \max_{B \in M_n(O)} \min_{S \in B} v_i(S).$$

Definition 6 (Temporal Maximin Share Fairness (TMMS)). *For any $t \in [T]$, an allocation $A^t = (A_1^t, \ldots, A_n^t)$ is temporal maximin share fair (TMMS) if $\forall t' \leq t, A^{t'}$ is MMS.*

Before we present our contribution, we highlight two important lemmas. First, we show that no algorithm can guarantee a positive constant approximation ratio for TEFX, thus, we provide tight bounds using items values in our paper.

Lemma 1. *There does not exist any algorithm that returns a positive constant approximation for α-TEFX.*

Proof. Assume there exists a solution that computes a k-TEFX allocation. Consider the instance with two agents and three goods $O = \{g_1, g_2, g_3\}$, where agents have identical valuations: $v(g_1) = v(g_2) = 1$ and $v(g_3) = \frac{1}{k} + 1$, where $k > 0$ and is a constant. Let g_i arrive in round i. In order to obtain a k-TEFX allocation at the first round, g_1 and g_2 must be allocated to each agent, respectively. Then, no matter which agent is allocated g_3, we do not obtain a k-TEFX allocation. Without loss of generality, let it be agent 1, and if the good that we theoretically remove from agent 1 is g_1, for agent 2, we have

$$v(g_2) = 1 < k \cdot (v(g_1 \cup g_3) - v(g_1)) = k \cdot (\frac{1}{k} + 1) = k + 1,$$

which contradicts our assumption.

Then, we note a theorem from [14], where they showed that $|O_t| = 1$ for all rounds $t \in [T]$ is the hardest setting, and any positive existence results in this single-item setting also implies a positive result for the general case with multiple items.

Lemma 2. *Let $\mathcal{I}$ be an instance with T rounds and a total of m items, where multiple items can appear in a single round. We can transform $\mathcal{I}$ into an equivalent instance $\mathcal{I}^{=1}$ with exactly m rounds, such that each round has exactly one item. Then, if a temporal fair allocation exists for $\mathcal{I}^{=1}$, a temporal fair allocation also exists for $\mathcal{I}$.*

By this lemma, we assume that $|O_t| = 1$ for all rounds $t \in [T]$ in the following proofs unless specified or implied by the setting (such as the identical days setting).

3 Strong Binary Valuation

To systematically examine the boundaries of temporal fair division, we analyze several structured settings, beginning with a variant of the binary valuation setting [16], named the Strong Binary Valuation setting. Under this setting, agents exhibit strictly dichotomous preferences: an agent values an arriving good at either zero or a fixed positive utility b, with no goods valued at zero for all agents. This mathematical restriction effectively models practical allocation scenarios characterized by strict, needs-based utility. In many real-world contexts, individuals possess highly polarized preferences: they either require a specific resource and derive a standard baseline benefit from it, or they find it entirely useless [10].

Furthermore, this variant aligns more closely with practical deployment environments than unconstrained binary models: a clearinghouse or central coordinator rarely processes resources that are universally worthless to every single agent. In realistic distribution pipelines, such as food bank logistics or cloud server provisioning, items are naturally filtered or curated such that every resource holds value for at least some subset of the population.

Definition 7 (Strong Binary Valuation). *A temporal fair division instance is under the strong binary valuation setting iff* $\forall t \in [T], \forall g \in O_t, \forall i \in [n], v_i(g) \in \{0,1\}$ *and* $\forall g \in O$, $\exists i \in N$, $v_i(g) > 0$.

While the restriction to binary values simplifies the evaluation of individual goods, achieving temporal fairness remains a profound algorithmic challenge. The fundamental friction of the temporal setting is its forward-looking, irrevocable nature. Standard online mechanisms, such as the greedy minimum-utility rule analyzed by Elkind et al. [14], often fall into inescapable structural deadlocks. Because these algorithms cannot foresee future arrivals, a sequence of locally fair allocations can inadvertently alter the relative capacities of the agents, making it mathematically impossible to satisfy the TEFX invariant in a subsequent round without changing the past.

To circumvent this inherent limitation of purely forward-looking mechanisms, we introduce our flagship technical contribution: a *Dynamic Backtracking Framework*. Instead of treating past decisions as permanent, our mechanism actively monitors the system for emerging fairness violations. The moment a TEFX violation is detected at time t, the algorithm triggers a localized, historical revision. It identifies the most recent round containing a jointly liked good that can be swapped to rebalance agent utilities, executes the swap, and reprocesses the intervening suffix sequence using the deterministic greedy rule.

We prove the correctness and finite termination of our dynamic backtracking framework via a global potential function argument, tracking the system's progress using a lexicographical ordering on the agents' sorted utility vectors. When the forward-looking greedy assignment of items inadvertently triggers a temporal fairness violation, the algorithm executes a localized historical swap of a previously allocated item. While this swap temporarily alters individual agents' utilities, we show that sequentially reprocessing the subsequent rounds from that historical point forward forces a strict, monotonic lexicographic increase in the global potential function compared to its state prior to the backtrack. Because the total number of items is finite, the number of distinct utility configurations is bounded; thus, this strict lexicographic improvement ensures the algorithm can never repeat states or loop infinitely, guaranteeing convergence to a valid fair allocation in finite time.

Example 1. Consider the following instance with two agents, and two goods. $O_i = \{g_i\}$. $v_1(g_1) = v_2(g_1) = 1$. $v_1(g_2) = 1$ and $v_2(g_2) = 0$.

First, in round 1, assume we break ties arbitrarily and allocate g_1 to agent 1. The current allocation is EFX.

Algorithm 1. BT

Input: $N, A, \{O_t\}_{t\in[T]}, t, t', i$
Output: Backtracked allocation A
1: **for** $idx = t'$ to t **do**
2: $\quad A \leftarrow A \setminus O_{idx}$ ▷ De-allocate goods
3: **end for**
4: $A_i^t \leftarrow A_i^t \cup O_t$ ▷ After backtrack, should allocate to i

Then, in round 2, since only agent 1 values g_2 positively, we allocate g_2 to agent 1. But now, EFX is violated.

Thus, we backtrack to the past, and for g_1, instead of breaking the ties to favor agent 1, we allocate g_1 to agent 2. The current allocation is EFX.

Then, in round 2, since only agent 1 values g_2 positively, we allocate g_2 to agent 1, and the allocation is EFX.

Theorem 1. *A TEFX allocation under strong binary valuation can be computed in finite time.*

Proof. We assume that in each round exactly one good arrives. [14] has proved that the one-good-per-round setting is stronger than the standard temporal fair division setting. Thus, we will use g and O_t interchangeably to denote the good that arrive in round t.

Invariant 1. For all pairs of agents i and j, at every round t we have

$$v_i(A_i^t) \;\geq\; v_j(A_i^t).$$

In words, an agent's own bundle is never more valuable to another agent than to herself.

Proof. We prove the invariant by considering how the algorithm allocates goods. Let g be any good that belongs to agent i at time t.

According to the algorithm, a good is only allocated to an agent who values it positively; therefore $v_i(g) = 1$. Consequently every good in A_i^t is liked by i, and we have

$$v_i(A_i^t) \;=\; |A_i^t|.$$

For any other agent j,

$$v_j(A_i^t) \;=\; \big|\{\, g \in A_i^t : v_j(g) > 0 \,\}\big| \;\leq\; |A_i^t| \;=\; v_i(A_i^t).$$

Hence $v_i(A_i^t) \geq v_j(A_i^t)$ holds for every pair i, j at any moment of the execution.

Lemma 3. *When the backtracking condition $v_i(A_i^t) < v_i(A_j^t) < v_j(A_j^t)$ occurs, the following two properties hold:*

– *There exist two distinct goods g and g' such that*

$$v_i(g) = v_j(g) = 1 \qquad \textit{and} \qquad v_i(g') = 0,\; v_j(g') = 1.$$

Algorithm 2. Returns a TEFX allocation under the Strong Binary Valuation setting

Input: Strong binary valuation temporal fair division instance $\mathcal{I} = \left(N, T, \{O_t\}_{t\in[T]}, v = (v_1, \ldots, v_n)\right)$
Output: TEFX allocation $\mathcal{A}$

$t \leftarrow 1$
$agent \leftarrow -1$
while $t \leq T$ **do**
  $A^t \leftarrow A^{t-1}$
  $g \leftarrow O_t$
  $S \leftarrow \{i \mid v_i(g) > 0\}$ ▷ agents that like the new good
  minU $\leftarrow \arg\min_{i\in S} v_i(A_i^t)$
  candidates $\leftarrow \{i \in S \mid u_i = \text{minU}\}$
  $i \leftarrow$ arbitrary deterministic agent from candidates ▷ It means, if we have an identical state (Identical instance, identical A^t), then we will always select the same agent
  $A_i^t \leftarrow A_i^t \cup \{g\}$
  backtrack $\leftarrow$ *false*
  if $\exists j \in N \setminus \{i\}$ s.t. $v_j(A_j^t) < v_j(A_i^t) < v_i(A_i^t)$ **then**
    backtrack $\leftarrow$ *true*
  end if
  if backtrack $=$ *false* **then**
    $t \leftarrow t + 1$
  else
    $t' \leftarrow$ latest time $t* < t$ with a good such that $v_i(O_{t*}) = v_j(O_{t*}) = 1$
    $A \leftarrow \text{BT}(N, A, O, t, t', j)$ ▷ Backtrack subprocess
    $t \leftarrow t' + 1$ ▷ Reset the round
  end if
end while

- *The jointly liked good g arrives strictly earlier than the good g' that only agent j likes.*

Proof. Let $u_k = v_k(A_k^t)$ denote the number of goods agent k values positively in her own bundle at time t. The condition $v_i(A_i^t) < v_i(A_j^t) < v_j(A_j^t)$ translates to

$$u_i < v_i(A_j^t) < u_j.$$

Proof of (1). Since $v_i(A_j^t) > u_i$, agent i likes at least one good that belongs to agent j. Pick any such good and call it g; then $v_i(g) = 1$. Because the algorithm only allocates a good to an agent who values it positively, we also have $v_j(g) = 1$, so g is jointly liked.

The inequality $v_i(A_j^t) < u_j$ means that agent i likes strictly fewer goods in A_j^t than agent j owns. Hence, A_j^t must contain at least one good that j likes but i does not. Choose one such good and call it g'; then $v_i(g') = 0$ and $v_j(g') = 1$, and clearly $g \neq g'$.

Proof of (2). We argue by contradiction: suppose g' arrived before g. Consider the moment just before the algorithm processes good g.

First, we have $v_i(A_j) < u_j$, since Lemma 1, and there exists g' in agent j's bundle ($v_i(g') = 0$).

Second, we have $u_i \geq u_j$, otherwise the algorithm would not have allocated g to agent j.

However, after the allocation of g to agent j, by the above two statements, we have $v_i(A_j) \leq u_i$, which contradicts our assumption.

Therefore, g' cannot arrive before g; g must arrive strictly earlier than g'.

Invariant 2. For all pairs agents i and j, $v_i(A_i^t) \geq v_i(A_j^t) - 1$.

Proof. This invariant is a known property of the underlying allocation rule: it always gives a good to an agent with the minimum utility among those who value it.

[14] proved that for online allocation of indivisible goods with binary valuations, a greedy algorithm that allocates each good to a minimum-utility agent who likes it maintains the inequality $v_i(A_i) \geq v_i(A_j) - 1$ at every round.

Our algorithm extends that procedure by adding backtracking steps; however, these backtracking operations only reassign a jointly liked good from a higher-utility agent to a lower-utility one and reprocess later goods in the same minimum-utility fashion.

One can verify that this does not break the invariant: whenever a good is allocated normally, the original guarantee applies, and a backtrack correction moves the allocation closer to the greedy assignment, preserving the invariant.

Lemma 4. *At any round t, the allocation violates EFX if and only if there exist two agents i and j such that*

$$v_i(A_i^t) \; < \; v_i(A_j^t) \; < \; v_j(A_j^t).$$

Proof. We prove both directions separately.

(⇐) Assume $v_i(A_i^t) < v_i(A_j^t) < v_j(A_j^t)$ for some i, j. Since $v_i(A_j^t) < v_j(A_j^t)$, agent j's bundle contains at least one good that j likes but i does not (the algorithm only gives goods to agents who like them, so every good in A_j^t is valued 1 by j). Pick such a good $g \in A_j^t$ with $v_i(g) = 0$ and $v_j(g) = 1$. Removing g from A_j^t leaves i's valuation unchanged:

$$v_i(A_j^t \setminus \{g\}) = v_i(A_j^t).$$

Because $v_i(A_i^t) < v_i(A_j^t)$, we obtain

$$v_i(A_i^t) \; < \; v_i(A_j^t \setminus \{g\}),$$

which directly violates the EFX condition for the pair (i, j).

Hence, the allocation is not EFX.

(⇒) Now suppose the allocation is not EFX. Then there exists a pair (i, j) with $A_j^t \neq \emptyset$ and a good $g \in A_j^t$ such that

$$v_i(A_i^t) \; < \; v_i(A_j^t \setminus \{g\}).$$

We distinguish two cases based on $v_i(g)$.

- **Case 1:** $v_i(g) = 1$. Then $v_i(A_j^t \setminus \{g\}) = v_i(A_j^t) - 1$, so the violation becomes $v_i(A_i^t) < v_i(A_j^t) - 1$. But Invariant 2 states $v_i(A_i^t) \geq v_i(A_j^t) - 1$, a contradiction. Hence this case cannot occur.
- **Case 2:** $v_i(g) = 0$. Then $v_i(A_j^t \setminus \{g\}) = v_i(A_j^t)$, so the violation implies

$$v_i(A_i^t) < v_i(A_j^t). \tag{1}$$

Because g is in A_j^t and $v_i(g) = 0$ while $v_j(g) = 1$, agent j values her own bundle strictly more than i does:

$$v_i(A_j^t) < v_j(A_j^t). \tag{2}$$

Combining (1) and (2) yields exactly $v_i(A_i^t) < v_i(A_j^t) < v_j(A_j^t)$.

Lemma 5. *Algorithm 2 returns an allocation that is TEFX.*

Proof. We proceed by induction on t. For the base case $t = 0$, it is trivial since no goods are allocated, so no agent has a non-empty bundle, and EFX holds vacuously.

For the induction step, assume there exists t such that for all $t' \leq t$, $A^{t'}$ is EFX. We prove that A^{t+1} is EFX. Let g be the good arriving in round $t+1$ (i.e., the good with index t). At the moment cur $= t$, the allocation is A^t. The algorithm processes good g as follows.

Case 1: No Backtrack Is Triggered. The algorithm selects an agent i who values g positively and has minimum utility among all such agents (deterministic tie-breaking), and allocates g to i. Let A^{t+1} be the resulting allocation.

Suppose, for contradiction, that A^{t+1} violates EFX. By Lemma 4, there exist agents x, y with

$$v_x(A_x^{t+1}) < v_x(A_y^{t+1}) < v_y(A_y^{t+1}). \tag{3}$$

Since A^t was EFX, the violation must involve the new good g. The good g was allocated to agent i, so either $x = i$ or $y = i$.

- If $x = i$, then $v_x(A_x^{t+1}) = v_i(A_i^t) + 1$. Inequality (1) gives $v_i(A_i^t) + b < v_i(A_y^{t+1})$. Because A^{t+1} differs from A^t only by adding g to i, the only way $v_i(A_y^{t+1})$ can be larger than $v_i(A_y^t)$ is when $y = i$ and $v_i(g) = 1$. Thus $y = i$, which is impossible because $x = i$ and $y \neq x$.
- If $y = i$, then $v_x(A_y^{t+1}) = v_x(A_i^{t+1})$. Since g was given to i, we have $v_x(A_i^{t+1}) = v_x(A_i^t) + 1$ if $v_x(g) = 1$, or $= v_x(A_i^t)$ if $v_x(g) = 0$.
If $v_x(g) = 0$, the violation already existed in A^t, contradicting the induction hypothesis.
If $v_x(g) = 1$, then $v_x(A_i^{t+1}) = v_x(A_i^t) + 1$. The inequality $v_x(A_x^{t+1}) < v_x(A_i^t) + 1$ together with Invariant 2 ($v_x(A_x) \geq v_x(A_i) - 1$) forces

$$v_x(A_x^t) = v_x(A_i^t) - 1 \quad \text{and} \quad v_x(A_i^t) + 1 < v_i(A_i^t) + 1.$$

Simplifying, $v_x(A_x^t) < v_i(A_i^t)$.
But recall that i was chosen as a minimum-utility agent among those who liked g.
Since x also likes g (as $v_x(g) = 1$), we must have $v_i(A_i^t) \leq v_x(A_x^t)$, a contradiction.

Both cases lead to contradictions; therefore A^{t+1} is EFX.

Case 2: A Backtrack Is Triggered. The backtrack condition identifies agents i, j and a good g' that arrives before t such that $v_i(g') = v_j(g') = 1$, and the sequence leading to the violation is exactly the one described in Lemma 3. We denote the arrival of g' by $t_{g'}$.

The algorithm then:

1. Reassigns g' from i to j,
2. De-allocates all goods from $t_{g'}$ to t,
3. Sets t to $t_{g'}$,
4. Reprocesses the arrival of goods from round $t + 1$ again.

Consider the state *just after the swap*. The allocated goods are the prefix $O_1, \ldots, O_{t_{g'}}$ and good g' now owned by j. All later goods are unallocated. Call this intermediate allocation A'. One can verify directly that A' is EFX: the only change w.r.t. A^t restricted to $O_1, \ldots, O_{t_{g'}}$ is the movement of g' from i to j, and at the moment of the swap the utilities satisfy $v_i(A'_i) = v_j(A'_j)$ (because the backtrack condition together with Lemma 3 forces that after removing the later goods, the two agents had equal utility counts).

The EFX property for A' follows from the induction hypothesis (the prefix $O_1, \ldots, O_{t_{g'}-1}$ was part of A^t, which was EFX) and the fact that the swapped good does not create a new violation due to the equality.

Now the algorithm reprocesses the goods $O_{t_{g'}+1}, \ldots, O_t$ in the original arrival order, starting from the allocation A'.

This is exactly the same situation as if the algorithm were run from time g' onward with the initial allocation A' (which is EFX) and received the remaining goods.

Since the algorithm is deterministic and its decisions depend only on the current allocation and the incoming good, this suffix phase will produce the same result as a fresh execution on the suffix.

By the induction hypothesis applied to the smaller number of already settled goods, the algorithm will eventually output an allocation of these suffix goods that, together with A', is EFX.

When the algorithm processes O_{t+1} for the first time, the resulting allocation A^{t+1} is therefore EFX.

This completes the proof of the inductive step. Hence A^t is EFX for all t.

After all m goods are processed, A^T is the final allocation returned by the algorithm, and it is TEFX.

Lemma 6. *Algorithm 2 terminates.*

Proof. We prove by strong induction on t the statement

$$P(t): \text{Every backtrack that starts at time } t \text{ eventually finishes without repeating any state.}$$

For the base case, round $t = 1$ is trivial, since a backtrack at time 1 would need a good g' that arrives before round 1, which does not exist. Hence $P(0)$ and $P(1)$ hold.

For the induction step, assume $P(s)$ holds for all $s < t$. We prove $P(t)$.

Suppose, for a contradiction, that a backtrack starting at time t causes a repeated state.

Because the set of all states is finite, a repetition implies an infinite cycle of states.

Let C be the set of states that occur while $t' < t$ during this infinite execution.

Since the backtrack started at round t, the cycle must contain a state with t (the triggering state) and a subsequent revert to some $t' < t$.

Consider the smallest time index s for which a backtrack is triggered inside the cycle.

By the induction hypothesis $P(s)$ for $s < t$, no backtrack that starts at a time $< t$ can be part of an infinite cycle; therefore, s cannot be $< t$.

Thus, every backtrack inside the cycle starts exactly at time t.

Now, examine a full cycle iteration. At the beginning of the iteration, we have an allocation $\mathcal{A}^{\text{old}}$ of the first t goods.

The algorithm selects a candidate i and finds an agent j satisfying the backtrack condition.

It then locates the most recent jointly liked good g' that arrives before round t that was allocated to i, reassigns g' to j, de-allocates all goods from the arrival of g' to $t - 1$, and sets t back to the arrival of g'. Denote the arrival of g' to be $t_{g'}$. Afterward, it reprocesses the arrival of goods again.

Because any backtrack during this reprocessing would start at a time $< t$, which is impossible by the induction hypothesis, the reprocessing runs *without any further backtrack.*

During a backtrack-free forward pass, every time a good is allocated, the algorithm uses the normal minimum-utility rule: It gives the good to an agent who likes it and whose current utility (the count of liked goods in her own bundle) is the smallest among all such agents (ties broken deterministically). A standard monotonicity fact for this rule is that the *sorted utility vector*

$$\Phi = (u_{(1)}, u_{(2)}, \ldots, u_{(n)})$$

(where u_k is the number of liked goods owned by agent k) strictly increases lexicographically after each allocation. Consequently, as the suffix is reprocessed, Φ strictly increases at every step.

Let Φ_{start} be the sorted utility vector of the allocation *just after the swap* (goods $O_1, \ldots, O_{t_{g'}}$ allocated, with g' now owned by j), and Φ_{end} be the sorted utility vector when the reprocessing finishes and we return to round t with a new allocation $\mathcal{A}^{\text{new}}$ of the first t goods.

Because the reprocessing consists of a sequence of strict increases, we have

$$\Phi_{\text{end}} >_{\text{lex}} \Phi_{\text{start}}.$$

On the other hand, the allocation $\mathcal{A}^{\text{old}}$ (the one that triggered the backtrack) was itself obtained after some sequence of normal allocations from the state just after the swap (if we compare the two histories, they share the prefix up to $t_{g'} - 1$, diverge at the assignment of g', and then process the same remaining goods with the same rules).

A known property of the minimum-utility rule is that among all ways to break ties at the steps where several agents have the same minimum utility, the rule that picks a fixed deterministic order produces the *lexicographically minimal* final sorted utility vector.

Changing the assignment of g' from i to j (which means we break the tie at time $t_{g'}$ in favor of j instead of i) can only *increase* the final sorted utility vector by Lemma 4.

Formally, one can show that $\mathcal{A}^{\text{new}}$ yields a sorted utility vector that is lexicographically larger than that of $\mathcal{A}^{\text{old}}$. Hence

$$\Phi_{\text{end}} >_{\text{lex}} \Phi_{\text{old}},$$

where Φ_{old} is the vector of $\mathcal{A}^{\text{old}}$.

But Φ_{old} is exactly the vector we had at the previous visit to round t. Therefore, the state at round t in the new iteration is different from the previous one, contradicting the assumption that the cycle contains a repeated state.

The contradiction shows that no infinite cycle can occur; hence, the backtrack starting at t must eventually finish after a finite number of steps. This proves $P(t)$.

Thus, by strong induction, $P(t)$ holds for every t. Consequently, the algorithm never repeats a state. Since the number of possible states is at most $(m+1) \cdot (n+1)^m$, which is finite, the algorithm must return an allocation after a finite number of operations.

Therefore, our algorithm produces a TEFX allocation in finite time.

Given that our algorithm guarantees exact TEFX at every round t, we can exploit a powerful structural relationship unique to binary valuation domains to immediately settle the status of our newly defined temporal maximin share metric.

Corollary 1. *Under strong binary valuations, any TEFX allocation is also a TMMS allocation. Therefore, a TMMS allocation exists and can be computed in finite time.*

Proof. Let A^t be a TEFX allocation at any round t. Under binary valuations, the EFX condition implies that for any pair of agents i and j, agent i's valuation of j's bundle satisfies $v_i(A_j^t) \leq v_i(A_i^t) + b$. Because the utilities are tightly bounded within a single item's value across all agents, agent i is guaranteed to receive at least her maximin share of the items allocated up to time t. Since this holds for every intermediate round, the cumulative allocation satisfies TMMS.

4 Identical Days

The second environment we investigate is the Identical Days setting [18].

Intuitively, this setting dictates that the exact same set of items arrives at every discrete time step. While mathematically rigid, this structure directly models pervasive real-world allocation paradigms characterized by strict periodicity. For example, in cloud computing and network bandwidth distribution, a static pool of server resources or time slots is continuously provisioned and allocated in identical, recurring cycles [7].

Definition 8 (Identical Days). *A temporal fair division instance is under the identical days setting iff* $\forall t, t' \in [T]$*, there is a bijection* $f_{t,t'} : O_t \Rightarrow O_{t'}$ *s.t.* $\forall i \in [n], \forall g \in O_t, v_i(g) = v_i(f_{t,t'}(g))$.

One might expect that the structural predictability of the Identical Days setting would fundamentally simplify temporal fair division, given that the algorithm faces a reliable, recurring sequence of items. Surprisingly, we show that this rigid periodicity is still insufficient to guarantee exact temporal fairness. Even in the highly restrictive domain where only two agents exist and they have completely identical valuations, the strict requirement to maintain envy-freeness for any good at every intermediate time step introduces unavoidable deadlocks. This reveals that structural symmetry in both time and preferences cannot fully overcome temporal frictions, leading to our first major impossibility result.

Theorem 2. *A TEFX allocation is not guaranteed under the identical days setting when* $T > 2$*, even if there are only two agents with identical valuations.*

This impossibility result naturally shifts our focus to the approximation frontiers of temporal envy-freeness in the identical-days setting. As a foundational baseline for this domain, we establish that a 1/2-TEFX allocation always exists and can be efficiently computed for two agents. While this approximation ratio leaves room for future optimization, it serves as a pioneering tractability result that provides crucial structural insights for approximating temporal fairness.

Our algorithmic approach adapts the classical Envy-Cycle Elimination framework [19]. Specifically, we leverage a modified selection rule: rather than assigning an arbitrary unallocated good to an agent who is not envied, our mechanism greedily allocates the most valuable available good to that agent. This variant is known to yield a 1/2-EFX guarantee in static, two-agent environments [12]. By exploiting the temporal symmetry inherent in the identical-days setting, together with this two-agent structural alignment, we prove that this greedy cycle-elimination invariant can be preserved across rounds, yielding a polynomial-time temporal guarantee.

Theorem 3. *A* $\frac{1}{2}$*-TEFX allocation can be computed in polynomial time when there are two agents under the identical days setting.*

The temporal regularity of the identical days setting is similarly insufficient to overcome the structural hurdles of maximin fairness. Despite the predictable recurrence of items, the requirement to maintain the maximin share threshold at each discrete time step remains overly restrictive. We find that the adversarial potential of even a simple, repeating sequence of goods can force a violation of the TMMS requirement. This impossibility holds even under complete preference symmetry, as formalized below.

Theorem 4. *A TMMS allocation for goods under the identical days setting may not exist, even when there are two agents with identical valuations.*

5 Identical Valuation

The next constraint we explore is the Identical Valuation setting [20]. In this scenario, every agent assigns the exact same utility to any given item. This strict symmetry accurately models the distribution of universal commodities, standard-issue resources, or fungible assets, such as monetary grants, where subjective differences in preference are non-existent, and allocations are purely driven by the objective value of the goods.

Definition 9 (Identical Valuation). *A temporal fair division instance is under the identical valuation setting iff* $\forall t \in [T], \forall g \in O_t, \forall i, j \in [n], v_i(g) = v_j(g)$.

Recall from Lemma 1 that even when all agents share perfectly identical valuations, a universal, constant-factor approximation for α-TEFX remains structurally impossible. However, the strict uniformity of preferences in this setting allows us to significantly tighten the value-dependent bound relative to that derived for the general environment. The core intuition behind this stronger result lies in a greedy equalization strategy coupled with the meticulous handling of zero-valued goods. By systematically assigning each arriving item to the agent currently holding the least valuable bundle, and carefully circumventing the algorithmic vulnerabilities introduced by items with zero marginal utility, we can successfully secure the following improved approximation guarantee.

Theorem 5. *A* $\frac{\min_{g \in O, v(g)>0} v(g)}{\max_{g \in O} v(g)}$*-TEFX allocation can be computed in polynomial time under the identical valuation setting, and it is tight.*

This tight approximation result naturally prompts a fundamental question: when relational, envy-based fairness metrics must be relaxed, can we instead guarantee an absolute, share-based threshold? To answer this, we evaluate our newly introduced benchmark, the Temporal Maximin Share (TMMS).

One might intuitively conjecture that this structural constraint would easily yield a positive existence result for TMMS in temporal settings. Surprisingly, the next result reveals a stark, counterintuitive divergence: the relentless requirement to maintain fairness at every intermediate step introduces temporal friction so severe that even perfect preference alignment cannot guarantee absolute guarantees.

Theorem 6. *A TMMS allocation for goods may not exist under the identical valuation settings.*

6 Bi-Valued Goods

Lastly, we examine the bi-valued goods setting [4]. In this restricted domain, every agent assigns one of two strictly positive constants to each arriving good. We explicitly exclude zero-valued goods from this model; permitting a utility of zero would cause the framework to degenerate into the generalized binary valuation setting analyzed previously.

Definition 10 (Bi-valued Valuation). *A temporal fair division instance is under the bi-valued valuation setting iff* $\forall t \in [T], \forall g \in O_t, \forall i \in [n], v_i(g) \in \{b_1, b_2\}$ *where* $b_1, b_2 \in \mathbb{R}^+$.

By strictly bounding utilities to these two positive tiers, which we denote as a and b, where $b \geq a > 0$, we establish a highly elegant approximation result. We demonstrate that our proposed algorithmic mechanism yields an approximation ratio exactly equal to the proportional gap between these two valuation constants. Furthermore, we prove that this bound is not merely a worst-case guarantee, but a mathematically tight limit for this setting.

Intuitively, we observe that in the bi-valued goods setting, the ratio of goods does not exceed b/a. Therefore, if two agents have bundles with the same size, the ratio of the bundle's values also does not exceed b/a.

Theorem 7. *For bi-valued goods valued* $b \geq a$, *a* $\frac{a}{b}$*-TEFX allocation can be computed in polynomial time, and it is tight.*

As considered in the previous section, the instance used in Theorem 6 is also bi-valued. Therefore, the following corollary is obtained.

Corollary 2. *A TMMS allocation may not exist under the bi-valued setting.*

7 Discussion and Future Works

In this work, we explored the boundaries of temporal fair division with structured constraints. Our primary technical contribution is a novel dynamic backtracking framework that utilizes a lexicographical potential function to resolve temporal envy cycles and guarantee exact TEFX under strong binary valuations, proving that the irreversible deadlocks of forward-looking greedy algorithms can be resolved via bounded historical reallocations. Furthermore, we expand the field's conceptual landscape by being the first to define and explicitly consider TMMS. Our structural analysis reveals a fascinating divergence between these fairness concepts: while strong binary valuations yield an elegant alignment in which TEFX naturally guarantees TMMS, identical valuations introduce severe temporal frictions that render exact TMMS impossible and limit relational fairness to our tight approximation ratio for α-TEFX.

Several open questions remain regarding the extension of the temporal fair division framework. One problem is the approximation ratio for TEFX under identical days. The result we have given in this paper is weak. Another key question is the study of temporal fair division with varying strategic behavior among agents. Investigating the compatibility of temporal fairness with strategy-proofness is crucial to ensure that agents cannot manipulate the algorithm through misreporting, which is essential for deploying these mechanisms in competitive environments, such as cloud computing markets.

References

1. Aleksandrov, M., Aziz, H., Gaspers, S., Walsh, T.: Online fair division: analysing a food bank problem. In: Proceedings of the 24th International Conference on Artificial Intelligence, IJCAI 2015, pp. 2540–2546. AAAI Press (2015)
2. Aleksandrov, M., Walsh, T.: Pure Nash equilibria in online fair division. In: Proceedings of the Twenty-Sixth International Joint Conference on Artificial Intelligence (IJCAI-17), pp. 42–48. International Joint Conferences on Artificial Intelligence, Melbourne, Australia (2017)
3. Amanatidis, G., et al.: Fair division of indivisible goods: recent progress and open questions. Artif. Intell. **322**, 103965 (2023)
4. Amanatidis, G., Birmpas, G., Filos-Ratsikas, A., Hollender, A., Voudouris, A.A.: Maximum Nash welfare and other stories about EFX. Theoret. Comput. Sci. **863**, 69–85 (2021)
5. Amanatidis, G., Markakis, E., Ntokos, A.: Multiple birds with one stone: beating 1/2 for EFX and GMMS via envy cycle elimination. Theoret. Comput. Sci. **841**, 94–109 (2020)
6. Aziz, H., Caragiannis, I., Igarashi, A., Walsh, T.: Fair allocation of indivisible goods and chores. In: Proceedings of the 28th International Joint Conference on Artificial Intelligence, pp. 53–59. AAAI Press, Macao, China (2019)
7. Baruah, S., Gehrke, J., Plaxton, C.: Fast scheduling of periodic tasks on multiple resources. In: Proceedings of 9th International Parallel Processing Symposium, pp. 280–288 (1995). https://doi.org/10.1109/IPPS.1995.395946
8. Benade, G., Kazachkov, A.M., Procaccia, A.D., Psomas, A., Zeng, D.: Fair and efficient online allocations. Oper. Res. **72**(4), 1438–1452 (2024)
9. Budish, E.: The combinatorial assignment problem: approximate competitive equilibrium from equal incomes. J. Polit. Econ. **119**(6), 1061–1103 (2011)
10. Camacho, F., Fonseca-Delgado, R., Pino Pérez, R., Tapia, G.: Generalized binary utility functions and fair allocations. Math. Soc. Sci. **121**, 50–60 (2023)
11. Caragiannis, I., Kurokawa, D., Moulin, H., Procaccia, A.D., Shah, N., Wang, J.: The unreasonable fairness of maximum Nash welfare. ACM Trans. Econ. Comput. **7**(3), 12:1–12:32 (2019)
12. Chan, H., Chen, J., Li, B., Wu, X.: Maximin-aware allocations of indivisible goods. In: Proceedings of the 28th International Joint Conference on Artificial Intelligence, pp. 137–143. AAAI Press, Macao, China (2019)
13. Cookson, B., Ebadian, S., Shah, N.: Temporal fair division. In: Proceedings of the Thirty-Ninth AAAI Conference on Artificial Intelligence and Thirty-Seventh Conference on Innovative Applications of Artificial Intelligence and Fifteenth Symposium on Educational Advances in Artificial Intelligence. AAAI Press, Pennsylvania, USA (2025)
14. Elkind, E., Lam, A., Latifian, M., Neoh, T.Y., Teh, N.: Temporal fair division of indivisible items. In: Proceedings of the 24th International Conference on Autonomous Agents and Multiagent Systems, pp. 676–685. International Foundation for Autonomous Agents and Multiagent Systems, Richland, SC (2025)

15. Gourvès, L., Monnot, J., Tlilane, L.: Near fairness in matroids. In: Proceedings of the Twenty-First European Conference on Artificial Intelligence, pp. 393–398. IOS Press, Prague, Czech Republic (2014)
16. Halpern, D., Procaccia, A.D., Psomas, A., Shah, N.: Fair division with binary valuations: one rule to rule them all. In: Web and Internet Economics: 16th International Conference. WINE 2020, Beijing, China, 7–11 December 2020, Proceedings, pp. 370–383. Springer-Verlag, Heidelberg (2020)
17. He, J., Procaccia, A.D., Psomas, A., Zeng, D.: Achieving a fairer future by changing the past. In: Proceedings of the Twenty-Eighth International Joint Conference on Artificial Intelligence (IJCAI-19), pp. 343–349. International Joint Conferences on Artificial Intelligence Organization, Macao, China (2019)
18. Igarashi, A., Lackner, M., Nardi, O., Novaro, A.: Repeated fair allocation of indivisible items. In: Proceedings of the Thirty-Eighth AAAI Conference on Artificial Intelligence and Thirty-Sixth Conference on Innovative Applications of Artificial Intelligence and Fourteenth Symposium on Educational Advances in Artificial Intelligence, pp. 9781–9789. AAAI Press, Vancouver, Canada (2024)
19. Lipton, R., Markakis, E., Mossel, E., Saberi, A.: On approximately fair allocations of indivisible goods. In: Proceedings of the 5th ACM Conference on Electronic Commerce (EC), pp. 125–131. ACM, New York, USA (2004)
20. Plaut, B., Roughgarden, T.: Almost envy-freeness with general valuations. SIAM J. Discret. Math. **34**(2), 1039–1068 (2020)
21. Varian, H.R.: Equity, envy, and efficiency. J. Econ. Theory **9**, 63–91 (1974)
22. Wang, Y., Wei, T.: Online fair allocations with binary valuations and beyond. In: Proceedings of the 40th AAAI Conference on Artificial Intelligence, pp. 1–8. Association for the Advancement of Artificial Intelligence, Singapore (2026)

Network Allocation Games with Anonymous Preferences

Argyrios Deligkas[1], Eduard Eiben[1], Šimon Schierreich[2,3](✉), and Alexandros A. Voudouris[4]

[1] Royal Holloway, University of London, Egham, UK
{argyrios.deligkas,eduard.eiben}@rhul.ac.uk
[2] AGH University of Krakow, Krakow, Poland
schiesim@fit.cvut.cz
[3] Czech Technical University in Prague, Prague, Czech Republic
[4] University of Southern Denmark, Vejle, Denmark
voudouris@imada.sdu.dk

Abstract. We study network allocation games in which a set of agents must be allocated to (a subset of) the vertices of a graph topology. The agents are anonymous and strategic: Each of them aims to maximize her utility, which is a function of the number of agents in the neighborhood of their allocated vertex. We focus on the existence and the computation of stable allocations under various notions of stability. More specifically, we study *swap-based* stability notions, where agents can exchange locations between them, and *jump-based* stability notions, where agents can jump to an empty vertex of the graph. For almost all stability notions we consider, we provide dichotomies between existence and intractability that depend on the structure of the utility functions of the agents and the topology. In addition, we prove strong intractability results for computing allocations that are Pareto optimal, or that maximize various notions of social welfare.

Keywords: network allocation · anonymous preferences · jump stability · swap stability · envy-freeness

1 Introduction

Imagine your university has just opened a new campus aiming to expand, and you, as an already senior member of your department, have been assigned the important task of deciding how to allocate your newly-recruited colleagues in the available offices. Interestingly, the building in the new campus is a refurbished old factory, and the office space is quite unusual and does not resemble a grid; instead, trying to optimize the number of people it can fit, the space was partitioned like a pretty arbitrary graph. In addition, you do not really know your new colleagues, and, maybe with a few exceptions, they do not know each other either. So the only information you can get about their preferences is about how

P. Lenzner and D. Schmand (Eds.): SAGT 2026, LNCS 16911, pp. 113–131, 2027.
https://doi.org/10.1007/978-3-032-38782-0_7

comfortable they would be with how many people have neighboring offices, or even are in shared rooms. In other words, they express anonymous preferences that assign values depending on the number of their neighbors. Your task then boils down to assigning offices such that the resulting allocation is "stable", i.e., none of your colleagues has any incentive to request a change.

This toy, and, of course, completely imaginary example, leads to an interesting network allocation game, which, to the best of our knowledge, has not been studied in the past. Beyond office allocation, similar considerations arise in many other settings, such as assigning jobs to the interconnected machines in a computing cluster, where a job's performance depends on the number of busy neighboring machines. More formally, in the game, we have a set of agents that must be allocated to (a subset of) the vertices of a graph. Crucially, though, the agents are *anonymous* and *strategic*. Each of them aims to maximize her utility, which is a function of the *number* of agents in the neighborhood of her allocated vertex, but *not* of their identity. Then, the goal is to find a *stable allocation* of the agents to the vertices, if such an allocation exists. Put simply, we want an allocation such that no agent can improve by (ex)changing her position.

This network allocation game shares common characteristics with two important classes of games that have attracted significant attention, that of *Hedonic games* (e.g., see [4,7,13]) and that of *Schelling games* (e.g., see [1,20]). In Hedonic games, the objective is to compute a partition of the agents into groups that is stable with respect to the preferences of the agents over the members of their groups. In Schelling games, the agents have types, and the objective is to compute an allocation of them to the vertices of a graph that is stable, given that each agent aims to optimize a function of the number of agents of the same type in their neighborhood. In both cases, two main stability notions have been studied: *swap-stability*, where no pair of agents can mutually benefit by exchanging their locations, and *jump-stability*, where no agent has incentives to unilaterally move to another group or empty vertex (possibly under some restrictions).

Despite their similarities, neither of these models fully captures the one we study in this work. In Hedonic games, there is no underlying topology, whereas in Schelling games, the preferences of the agents are not anonymous. By embedding anonymous hedonic preferences into a graph structure, our model captures both the richness of network topology and the simplicity of aggregate-based preferences, leading to our question of interest: *What type of stable outcomes exist for anonymous network allocation games, and how difficult is it to find them?*

1.1 Our Contribution

We study the existence and complexity of finding stable outcomes in anonymous network allocation games with respect to three dimensions: a) the stability notion; b) the structure of the utility functions of the agents; c) the structure of the topology graph. For the majority of possible combinations of the restrictions mentioned above, we provide dichotomies with respect to the existence of stable allocations *and* the complexity of computing them: either the stability concept always exists and can be computed in polynomial time, or it does not always exist and deciding whether an instance admits a solution is an intractable problem.

We begin by studying various notions of swap-based stability. We first prove that swap-stable allocations (in which no pair of agents wants to exchange their locations) always exist, independently of the topology graph and the utility functions of the agents, and can be found in quadratic time, with respect to the number of agents, via natural swap dynamics (Theorem 1). In fact, the same proof shows the same result even for *weak* swap-stable allocations, where at least one agent strictly increases her utility from the swap. We also consider envy-free allocations (in which no agent prefers the vertex allocated to a different agent more than her own); envy-freeness is the most prominent fairness notion and is stronger than swap-stability since it requires that all agents are completely satisfied with the allocation. Because of this, besides the notable case of two agents, we show that envy-free allocations do not always exist when there are at least three agents (Proposition 1), and it is, in general, NP-complete to decide their existence (Theorem 2). In fact, we show that our NP-completeness result holds for two other cases: approximately envy-free allocations, and β-hurting swap-stable allocations, a notion that interpolates between weak swap-stability and envy freeness. Our hardness result holds for any non-trivial approximation in both cases, even for restricted utility functions. On the positive side, we prove that both problems are FPT parameterized by the number of agents (Theorem 3).

We next jump (sic) to jump-based stability notions. We first observe that the structure of the utility functions of the agents plays a crucial role in the existence and computation of jump-stable allocations. When agents have binary utilities, jump-stable allocation do not always exist, even when the graph topology is a path and we have two agents (Proposition 2) and in general it is NP-complete to compute them (Theorem 5). On the contrary, when the utility functions are monotone, a jump-stable allocation can always be reached via the natural dynamics in polynomial time (Theorem 4).

We also show several results for the more restrictive notion of ℓ-jump-stability according to which no agent has an incentive to jump to an empty vertex at a distance of at most ℓ from her current location. In particular, we show that, under binary utilities, a 1-jump-stable allocation always exists on tree topologies and can be computed efficiently via a simple greedy algorithm (Theorem 8), but does not necessarily exist when the graph contains cycles, even for identical binary, or single peaked, utilities (Theorem 6). In addition, we prove that it is NP-complete to decide the existence of a 2-jump-stable allocation when agents have binary utilities (Theorem 7). The complexity of 1-jump stable allocations remains open.

We finally consider the problem of maximizing social welfare for several different definitions. Specifically, we focus on the utilitarian social welfare (USW; the total utility of the agents), the egalitarian social welfare (ESW; the minimum utility over all agents), the Nash social welfare (NSW; the geometric mean of the agents' utilities), and Pareto optimality (PO; according to this notion, there is no other allocation such that an agent has strictly larger utility and no other agent is worse off). We first show that it is NP-complete and W[1]-hard with respect to the number of agents to compute welfare-maximizing allocations for USW, ESW, and NSW (Theorem 9). We then observe that even though a PO allocation always exists, it is coNP-hard and coW[1]-hard under the same parameterization to verify if an allocation is indeed PO (Theorem 10). We complement these strong impossibilities with an XP algorithm that solves all these optimization problems and is optimal under the ETH (Theorem 11).

1.2 Related Work

As already stressed, most closely related to our model are *Schelling games* [1,9–11,17,19,20,25,33,34,41,42] and *anonymous hedonic games* [4,7,13,21,28]. In contrast to Schelling games, where the agents are partitioned into types and their utilities are only implicitly determined by the type composition of their neighborhood[1], we work directly with explicit utility functions, allowing each agent an arbitrary function of the number of occupied neighbors. In contrast to anonymous hedonic games, which likewise involve no types but partition the agents into disjoint coalitions, our agents are placed on a topology in which their neighborhoods overlap. A similar contrast applies to *load balancing games* [27,45], where an agent's cost depends on the number (or load) of agents assigned to the same machine: the machines are disjoint bins with no topology among them, which is the key reason why stable outcomes there are guaranteed by potential-function arguments, whereas in our game they may fail to exist.

A related class of problems is the so-called *refugee housing* [35,37,43,44], where agents are likewise placed on the empty vertices of a graph topology and an agent's satisfaction depends on the number of agents in her neighborhood. The crucial difference is that these models feature a set of preallocated agents (the inhabitants) who are fixed in place, whereas in our game, every agent is free to deviate. This property makes both classes very different. Moreover, the anonymous preferences studied in refugee housing take the form of approved sets or upper bounds on the number of accepted neighbors, while we allow for much more general classes of utility functions.

A further group of games places agents on a structure and derives the utility of an agent from the agents located near her. In the *seat arrangement problem* [8,12,18,46], agents are assigned to seats and care about who exactly is placed next to them, whereas in *social distance games* [5,6,15,30,32], an agent's utility aggregates her distances to the other agents in her connected component. Finally, in *topological distance games* [16,24] and *distance preservation games* [3,22], the utility of an agent depends on her graph distances to specific other agents. In contrast to all these distance-based models, the utility in our game is *anonymous* and *local*: it is determined solely by the number of occupied vertices in an agent's immediate neighborhood.

[1] The vast majority of papers focus on agents with homophilic preferences. However, recently, diversity- and variety-seeking preferences were also considered [38,39].

2 The Model

We consider a network allocation game $\Gamma = (G, N, (\mathrm{u}_i)_{i \in N})$ consisting of a set N of n *agents* and an undirected graph $G = (V, E)$ with $|V| \geq n$ to which we refer as the *topology*. By $N_G(v) = \{u \in V \mid uv \in E\}$ we denote the *neighborhood* of a vertex $v \in V$, i.e., the set of all vertices adjacent to v. The goal is to assign the agents to the vertices of the topology. Formally, an *allocation* is an injective function $\pi \colon N \to V$ that assigns to each agent her host vertex; we also call it the *location* of the agent. Observe that, by injectivity, every vertex hosts at most one agent; that is, the agents cannot share a vertex. Additionally, each agent $i \in N$ is associated with a *utility function* $\mathrm{u}_i \colon [n-1]_0 \to \mathbb{R}_0^+$. Intuitively, the function returns the utility agent i experiences if there are $x \in [n-1]_0$ agents allocated to her direct neighborhood. We naturally extend the notation from numbers to allocations and set $\mathrm{u}_i(\pi) = \mathrm{u}_i(|\{j \in N \mid \pi(j) \in N_G(\pi(i))\}|)$. We say that the utility function u_i is:

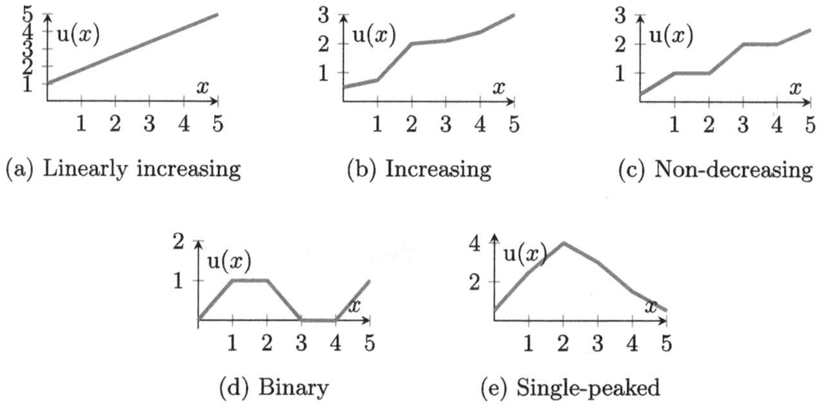

Fig. 1. Illustrations of the restrictions of utility functions used throughout the paper. Additionally, we define linearly decreasing, decreasing, and non-increasing utilities, which are natural counterparts of linearly increasing, increasing, and non-decreasing utilities, respectively.

- *linearly increasing* if there exist $a \in \mathbb{N}$ and $b \in \mathbb{N}_0$ such that $\mathrm{u}_i(x) = a \cdot x + b$ for every $x \in [n-1]_0$;
- *increasing* if $\mathrm{u}_i(x) < \mathrm{u}_i(y)$ whenever $x < y$;
- *non-decreasing* if $\mathrm{u}_i(x) \leq \mathrm{u}_i(y)$ whenever $x < y$;
- *linearly decreasing* if there exist $a \in \mathbb{N}$ and $b \in \mathbb{N}_0$ with $b \geq a \cdot (n-1)$ such that $\mathrm{u}_i(x) = b - a \cdot x$ for every $x \in [n-1]_0$;
- *decreasing* if $\mathrm{u}_i(x) > \mathrm{u}_i(y)$ whenever $x < y$;
- *non-increasing* if $\mathrm{u}_i(x) \geq \mathrm{u}_i(y)$ whenever $x < y$;
- *binary* if $\mathrm{u}_i(x) \in \{0, 1\}$ for every $x \in [n-1]_0$;

- *single-peaked* if there exists $z^* \in [n-1]_0$ such that for every $x, y \in [0, z^*]$, $x < y$, it holds that $\mathrm{u}_i(x) < \mathrm{u}_i(y)$, and for every $x, y \in [z^*, n-1]$, $x < y$, we have $\mathrm{u}_i(x) > \mathrm{u}_i(y)$.

See Fig. 1 for an illustration of the restrictions of utility functions defined above and Fig. 2 for their relationships. Additionally, we say that the utility function is *monotone* if it is non-decreasing or non-increasing.

Binary utilities correspond to the well-studied dichotomous (approval) preferences [40]: an agent simply approves a set of acceptable neighborhood sizes. Single-peaked utilities capture an ideal amount of social interaction, with satisfaction decreasing in either direction away from the peak; single-peakedness is a classic domain restriction that was recently also studied in Schelling games [29].

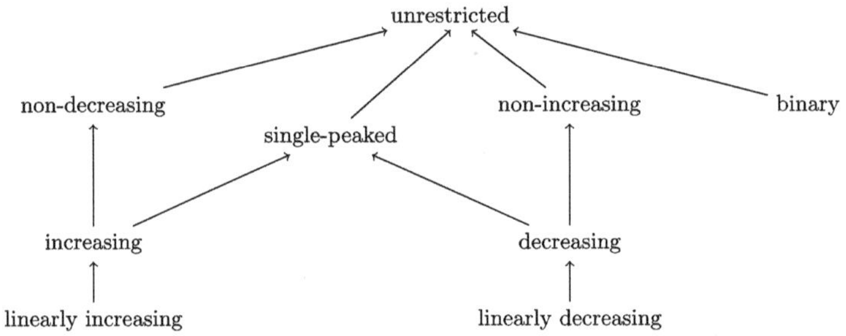

Fig. 2. Relationships between our utility restrictions. An arrow from A to B means that whenever a utility function satisfies restriction A, it also satisfies B.

Stability Notions. We are interested in allocations that are *stable*. The first notion of stability we study is that of *envy-freeness*, which is extensively studied in the fair division literature [2], but was recently also considered in settings similar to ours; see, e.g., [22,23,36]. For $\alpha \in [0,1]$, we say that agent i *α-envies* agent $j \neq i$ if $\mathrm{u}_i(\pi) < \alpha \cdot \mathrm{u}_i(\pi^{i\leftrightarrow j})$, where $\pi^{i\leftrightarrow j}$ is the allocation obtained from π by swapping only the locations of i and j. An allocation without α-envious agents is called *α-envy-free.* If $\alpha = 1$, we will say that agent i *envies* agent j instead of i 1-envies j, and an allocation is *envy-free* instead of 1-envy-free, respectively.

One can argue that the requirement of envy-freeness, i.e., that no agent prefers another's location to her own, is too demanding, as it ignores whether the swap would be agreeable to the other party. Therefore, we also study a weaker notion of stability, in which both agents must agree to the potential swap of locations. Formally, a pair of agents i, j admits a *swap deviation* if $\mathrm{u}_i(\pi) < \mathrm{u}_i(\pi^{i\leftrightarrow j})$ and $\mathrm{u}_j(\pi) < \mathrm{u}_j(\pi^{i\leftrightarrow j})$. An allocation in which no pair of agents admits a swap deviation is called *swap stable.* A *weak swap deviation* is then defined analogously, but we allow two agents to swap their locations when neither of them is worse off and at least one of them is strictly better off. Finally, an agent i can perform a β-hurting swap deviation, $\beta \in [0,1]$, with an agent j

if $u_i(\pi) < u_i(\pi^{i \leftrightarrow j})$ and $u_j(\pi^{i \leftrightarrow j}) \geq (1 - \beta) \cdot u_j(\pi)$, i.e., if i strictly improves her utility and the utility of j decreases by at most a factor of β. Observe that if $\beta = 0$, then β-hurting swap deviations are equivalent to weak swap deviations, and when $\beta = 1$, then a β-hurting swap deviation is equivalent to i envying j.

Finally, we say that an agent i admits a *jump deviation* to an empty vertex v if $u_i(\pi) < u_i(\pi^{i \mapsto v})$, where $\pi^{i \mapsto v}$ is the allocation obtained from π by changing the location of i to v. An allocation with no jump deviating agent is called *jump stable.* We additionally restrict the space of possible jump deviations by introducing a parameter ℓ. Formally, an *ℓ-jump deviation* is a jump deviation of agent i to a vertex v such that $\text{dist}_G(\pi(i), v) \leq \ell$, where $\text{dist}_G(u, w)$ is the length of the shortest path between u and w in G; we set $\text{dist}_G(u, w) = \infty$ if no such path exists. Then, an allocation is *ℓ-jump stable* if there is no ℓ-jump deviation.

Efficiency Notions. We also study several notions of economic efficiency, which are based on aggregating the utilities of the agents. In particular, we say that an allocation π

- *maximizes the utilitarian social welfare* (USW) if, for every allocation π',
$$\text{USW}(\pi) :- \sum_{i \in N} u_i(\pi) \geq \text{USW}(\pi').$$
- *maximizes the egalitarian social welfare* (ESW) if, for every allocation π',
$$\min_{i \in N} u_i(\pi) \geq \min_{i \in N} u_i(\pi').$$
- *maximizes the Nash social welfare* (NSW) if, for every allocation π',
$$\text{NSW}(\pi) :- \prod_{i \in N} u_i(\pi) \geq \text{NSW}(\pi').$$
- is *Pareto optimal* (PO) if there is no allocation π' such that
$$\forall i \in N\colon\ u_i(\pi') \geq u_i(\pi) \quad \text{and} \quad \exists i \in N\colon\ u_i(\pi') > u_i(\pi).$$

3 Swap-Based Deviations

In this section, we study swap-based stability solutions, and we prove a dichotomy that depends on the solution concept; see Fig. 3.

We begin by proving that swap stable allocations always exist no matter the utility functions of the agents, and can be efficiently found via natural dynamics.

Theorem 1. *Every network allocation game Γ admits at least one (weakly) swap stable allocation. Moreover, the allocation can be found in polynomial time.*

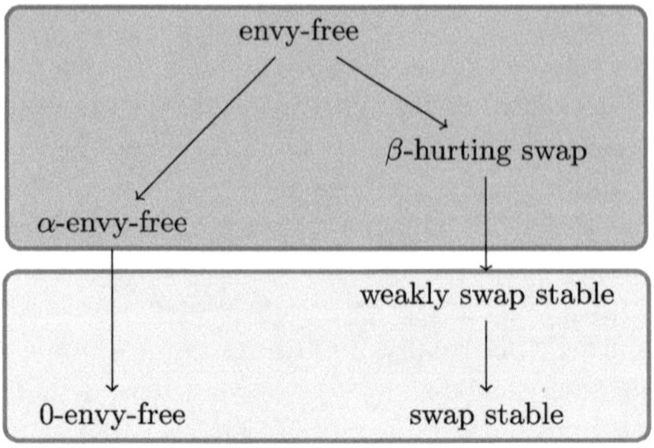

Fig. 3. An overview of our results for swap-based deviations. A red background indicates non-existence and NP-hardness (even if the utilities are binary, linearly increasing, or linearly decreasing); a green background indicates existence and polynomial-time solvability (even for unrestricted utilities). (Color figure online)

Proof. Starting from an arbitrary allocation, we repeatedly allow a pair of agents i, j to swap locations if their utility (or at least one of them in the case of weak swap stability) increases. Clearly, if there is no (weakly) profitable swap, then the allocation is already swap stable. Moreover, observe that the utilitarian social welfare (the total utility of the agents) increases with each swap: i and j increase their utility, and the utility of any agent different than i and j remains the same (since it only depends on the number of her neighbors, which does not change once i and j swap their locations). Consequently, the dynamics converges to a swap stable allocation. Furthermore, since the utility function of each agent takes n distinct values and her utility increases with each swap she participates in, the dynamics converges to a swap-stable allocation after $\mathcal{O}(n^2)$ swaps. □

We note that our proof implies a stronger result. In every anonymous network allocation game, applying (weak) swap dynamics in any initial allocation converges to a (weak) swap stable allocation after at most n^2 steps.

Next, we switch our attention to envy-free allocations. We begin by observing that when there are only two agents, any allocation is trivially envy-free; this follows from the fact that the two locations are symmetric, i.e., they either both have zero neighbors, or one.

Observation 1. *If there are two agents, any allocation is envy-free.*

On the other hand, though, as we show next, when there are three or more agents, envy-free allocations fail to exist even in the approximate sense, for any non-trivial approximation.

Proposition 1. *For any $\alpha \in (0, 1]$, an α-envy-free allocation is not guaranteed to exist, even with three agents and identical utilities that are either binary, linearly increasing, or linearly decreasing.*

Trivially, if the factor α from the previous proposition is equal to zero, which is the only missing case, then by the non-negativity of utilities, we obtain that any allocation is 0-envy-free.

Observation 2. *Any allocation is* 0*-envy-free.*

Next, we show that the dichotomy between (weak) swap-stability and (relaxations) of envy-freeness extends beyond the landscape of existence and also includes computational aspects of these notions. Specifically, in sharp contrast to weakly swap stable solutions, deciding whether an instance admits an α-envy-free allocation for some $\alpha \in (0, 1]$, or a β-hurting swap stable allocation for some $\beta \in (0, 1)$ is NP-complete, even for the most restricted models of preferences.

Theorem 2. *It is NP-complete to decide whether an instance $\mathcal{I}$ admits at least one envy-free allocation, even if the utilities are (i) binary, (ii) linearly increasing, or (iii) linearly decreasing. The same reduction also shows NP-completeness for α-envy-freeness, $\alpha \in (0, 1]$, and β-hurting swap stability, $\beta \in (0, 1)$, but only if the preferences are increasing, decreasing, or, in the case of α-envy-freeness, binary.*

We conclude the section with one more positive result. Specifically, we show that the computational hardness of the problem crucially stems from a strategic decision of how to allocate a large number of agents. It turns out that, when the number of agents is small, deciding the existence becomes tractable.

Theorem 3. *Deciding whether an α-envy-free, $\alpha \in (0, 1]$, or a β-hurting swap stable, $\beta \in [0, 1)$, allocation exists is fixed-parameter tractable when parameterized by the number of agents n.*

Proof. Let $R(n, n)$ denote the Ramsey number: the smallest ν such that every graph on ν vertices contains either a clique of size n or an independent set of size n. By the Erdős-Szekeres bound [26], $R(n, n) \leq 4^n$, and a homogeneous set of size n can be found in time polynomial in $|V(G)|$, whenever $|V(G)| \geq R(n, n)$. We distinguish two cases based on $|V(G)|$.

First, let $|V(G)| \geq R(n, n)$. Then, by the previous arguments, we can find either a clique K or an independent set I of size n in G. Let π be any bijective allocation of the agents onto the vertices of K or I. In either case, every agent has the same number of allocated neighbors as every other agent in π and in every allocation $\pi^{i \leftrightarrow j}$ obtained by swapping a pair of agents. Hence, $\mathrm{u}_i(\pi) = \mathrm{u}_i(\pi^{i \leftrightarrow j})$ for every $i, j \in N$, so the allocation is 1-envy-free and 0-hurting swap stable.

Now, let $|V(G)| < R(n, n)$. Since $R(n, n) < 4^n$, the number of allocations is at most $|V(G)|^n < 4^{n^2}$. We enumerate all allocations and, for each of them, check whether it is α-envy-free (respectively β-hurting swap stable) by examining all $\mathcal{O}(n^2)$ ordered pairs of agents in polynomial time. The total running time is $4^{n^2} \cdot |V(G)|^{\mathcal{O}(1)}$, which is FPT with respect to the number of agents n. □

4 Jump-Based Deviations

We now switch to jump-stable allocations; recall that, in such an allocation, no agent has incentive to deviate to an empty vertex. Unfortunately, in contrast to swap-stable allocations, jump-stable allocations do not necessarily always exist (Fig. 4).

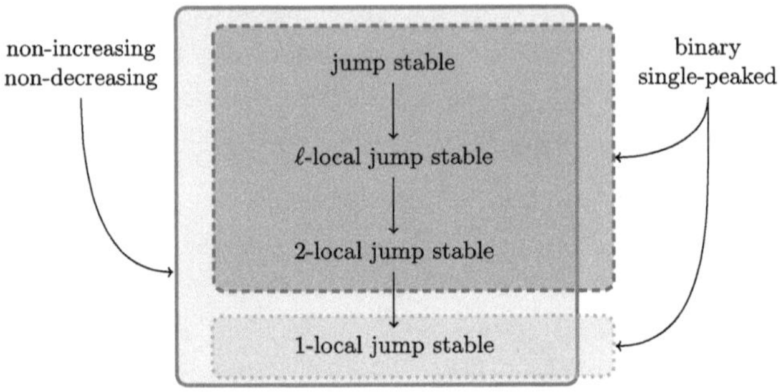

Fig. 4. An overview of our solution concepts based on the jumps of single agents, together with the corresponding existence and complexity results. The three shaded, overlapping regions indicate: existence guaranteed and polynomial-time solvable (green, solid outline); non-existence and NP-complete (Color figure online) (red, dashed outline); and non-existence with complexity status open (yellow, dotted outline). For single-peaked preferences, only non-existence is known.

Proposition 2. *Jump-stable allocations may fail to exist, even if there are two agents, the topology is a simple path, and the utilities are single-peaked or binary.*

Proof. Consider a game with a line graph G consisting of 5 vertices, and two agents. The utility function of agent 1 is $u_1(0) = 1$ and $u_1(1) = 0$, whereas the utility function of agent 2 is $u_2(0) = 0$ and $u_2(1) = 1$. To maximize her utility, agent 2 aims to be a neighbor of agent 1. In contrast, agent 1 aims to have no neighbors. Hence, in any possible allocation, at least one agent has an incentive to jump (either agent 2 jumps to be a neighbor of agent 1, or agent 1 jumps to not be a neighbor of agent 2). □

On the positive side, when the utility functions are monotone, a jump-stable allocation exists and can be computed efficiently via a natural dynamics.

Theorem 4. *If the utility functions are all monotone of the same type (increasing or decreasing), a jump stable allocation is guaranteed to exist and can be found in polynomial time.*

Proof. For any allocation π, let $O(\pi) = \{z \in V \mid \exists j \in N : \pi(j) = z\}$ be the set of non-empty vertices. In addition, for any vertex $z \in V$, let $n_z(\pi) = |\{j \in N \mid \pi(j) \in N_G(z)\}|$ be the number of agents that occupy vertices that are neighboring z. Hence, if an agent i occupies v in π, she obtains utility $u_i(\pi) = u_i(n_v(\pi))$. We claim that the function

$$\Phi(\pi) = \sum_{z \in O(\pi)} n_z(\pi),$$

or its negation $-\Phi$, is an ordinal potential function. Intuitively, $\Phi(\pi)$ equals twice the number of edges of G with both endpoints occupied: an improving jump of an agent with a non-decreasing utility function strictly increases the number of agents neighboring her location and, by symmetry, also this number of edges, while under non-increasing utilities the opposite holds. Consider two allocations π and π' that only differ in the vertex that some agent i occupies; in particular, i occupies v in π and $v' \neq v$ in π', while all other agents occupy the same vertices in the two allocations. Observe that v' is empty in π, and v is empty in π'. Let O be the set of non-empty vertices different than v and v' in the two allocations; clearly, these vertices are the same among the two allocations, that is, $O = O(\pi) \setminus \{v\} = O(\pi') \setminus \{v'\}$. For an arbitrary vertex $z \in O$, we have:

- If $z \notin N_G(v) \cup N_G(v')$ then i is not a neighbor of z in both allocations, and thus $n_z(\pi) = n_z(\pi')$;
- If $z \in N_G(v) \cap N_G(v')$, then i is a neighbor of z in both allocations, and thus $n_z(\pi) = n_z(\pi')$;
- If $z \in N_G(v) \setminus N_G(v')$, then i is a neighbor of z in π but not in π', and thus $n_z(\pi) = n_z(\pi') + 1$;
- If $z \in N_G(v') \setminus N_G(v)$, then i is a neighbor of z in π' but not in π, and thus $n_z(\pi) = n_z(\pi') - 1$.

Therefore,

$$\begin{aligned}\Phi(\pi) - \Phi(\pi') &= n_v(\pi) - n_{v'}(\pi') + \sum_{z \in O} \Big(n_z(\pi) - n_z(\pi')\Big) \\ &= n_v(\pi) - n_{v'}(\pi') + |O \cap (N_G(v) \setminus N_G(v'))| - |O \cap (N_G(v') \setminus N_G(v))| \\ &= n_v(\pi) - n_{v'}(\pi') + n_v(\pi) - n_{v'}(\pi') = 2\Big(n_v(\pi) - n_{v'}(\pi')\Big).\end{aligned}$$

If the utility function is non-decreasing, $\mathrm{u}_i(\pi) > \mathrm{u}_i(\pi')$ implies that $n_v(\pi) > n_{v'}(\pi')$, and thus Φ is a potential function. If the utility function is non-increasing, $\mathrm{u}_i(\pi) > \mathrm{u}_i(\pi')$ implies that $n_v(\pi) < n_{v'}(\pi')$, and thus $-\Phi$ is a potential function. This completes the proof. □

We next show that it is hard to decide if a game admits a jump-stable allocation. The reduction is inspired by the reduction of [40, Theorem 9] showing that it is NP-hard to decide whether a given *Anonymous Hedonic Game with Dichotomous Preferences* admits a Nash stable solution.

Theorem 5. *It is NP-complete to decide whether a network allocation game* Γ *admits a jump stable allocation, even if all utility functions are binary.*

Proof Sketch. To show NP-hardness, we reduce from the RESTRICTED EXACT COVER BY 3-SETS (RX3C) problem, which is known to be NP-complete [31]. In this problem, we are given a universe $\mathcal{U} = \{e_1, \ldots, e_{3p}\}$ and a family $\mathcal{S} = \{S_1, \ldots, S_{3p}\}$ of 3-element subsets of $\mathcal{U}$ such that every e_i appears in exactly 3 sets of $\mathcal{S}$. We ask whether there exists $X \subseteq \mathcal{S}$ of size p such that $\bigcup_{S \in X} S = \mathcal{U}$.

Given an instance $\mathcal{I} = (\mathcal{U}, \mathcal{S})$ of RX3C, we construct an equivalent game Γ as follows. The high-level idea is that the agents will form clusters in the cliques of the topology, where each cluster represents either a set $S_j \in \mathcal{S}$ chosen for the cover or an auxiliary triplet of leftover set agents; the special agent at the apex acts as a global "anchor", and the guard agent prevents any agent from being alone in a clique. Moreover, every agent except the special agent is also happy when fully isolated; this ensures that no agent other than the special agent can occupy the apex, since anyone else would prefer to move to an empty clique.

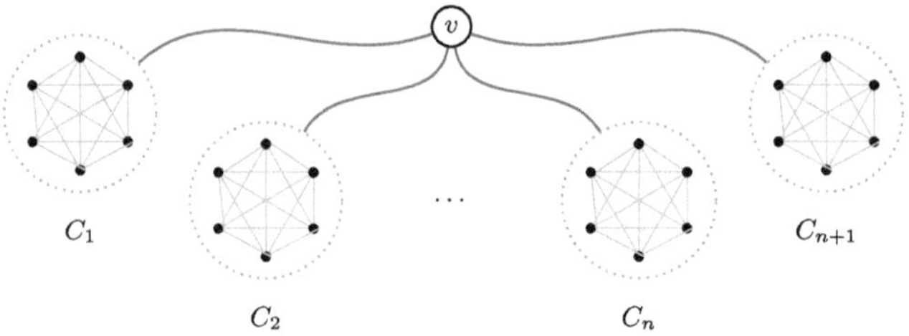

Fig. 5. The topology G used in the reduction of Theorem 5. The apex vertex v is connected to every vertex of every clique $C_1, \ldots, C_{n+1}$, each of size n. Dotted circles represent cliques; bold dots represent vertices.

For every element $e_i \in \mathcal{U}$, we create one *element agent* a_i, which represents the requirement that e_i must be covered. For every set $S_j \in \mathcal{S}$, we create $12j - 3$ *set agents* $s_j^1, \ldots, s_j^{12j-3}$; together with the three element agents corresponding to the elements of S_j, these $12j$ agents will form the "cluster" of S_j when S_j is selected for the cover. The factor $12j$ varies with j to give each set a distinct preferred cluster size, ensuring that an agent in a $12j$-cluster can only be associated with the unique set S_j. To finalize the set of agents, we add one *guard agent* g and one *special agent* s^*. The utilities are as follows:

Element Agent a_i: $\mathrm{u}_{a_i}(x) = 1$ if $x \in \{0, 1\} \cup \{12j \mid e_i \in S_j\}$, and 0 otherwise. That is, a_i is happy fully isolated, alone in a clique (with only the apex agent as a neighbor), or in the cluster of any set containing e_i.

Set Agent s_j^ℓ: $\mathrm{u}_{s_j^\ell}(x) = 1$ if $x \in \{0, 1, 3, 12j\}$, and 0 otherwise. A set agent is happy fully isolated or alone in a clique, in a triplet of set agents (when her set is unselected), or in her full set-cluster of size $12j$ (when her set is selected).

Guard Agent g: $\mathrm{u}_g(x) = 1$ if $x \in \{0, 2\}$, and 0 otherwise. Besides being fully isolated, the guard is happy in a cluster of size exactly 2, which, when the apex is occupied, forces her to "chase" any agent that is alone in a clique—the guard can jump there to form a pair.

Special Agent s^***:** $u_{s^*}(x) = 1$ if $x = n - 1$ (recall that n denotes the total number of agents), and 0 otherwise. The special agent is happy only when adjacent to every other agent, which can be achieved only at the apex of the topology described below.

The topology G consists of $n+1$ disjoint cliques $C_1, \ldots, C_{n+1}$, each of size n, together with an *apex* vertex v adjacent to every vertex of every clique. The role of the apex is to give the special agent a unique location achieving her peak utility, while simultaneously providing every other agent with a constant "+1 neighbor" contribution from s^*. The cliques act as bins for clusters of agents, and having $n + 1$ cliques ensures, by the pigeonhole principle, that at least one clique is empty in every allocation, giving any unhappy agent the option to jump and become a singleton. See Fig. 5 for an illustration.

4.1 Local Jumps

We now focus on the case where agents can only jump a certain distance away from their location. Clearly, for monotone utility functions, such an allocation always exists due to Theorem 4. Our first observation is a strengthening of the non-existence of jump-stable allocation when agents can only jump to vertices that are neighbors of their current location.

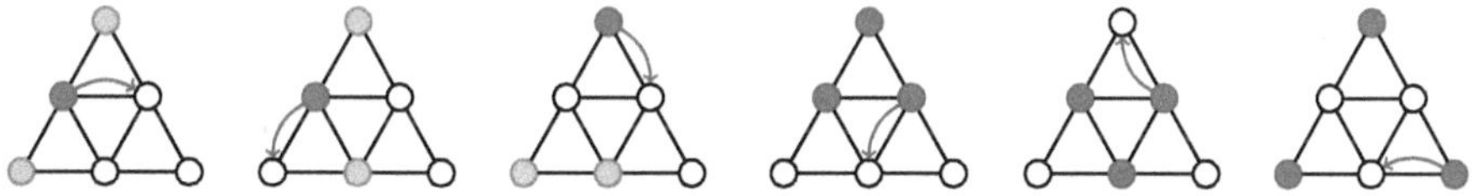

Fig. 6. All possible non-isomorphic allocations in the instance used to prove Theorem 6. Recall that our agents have identical preferences such that utility is 1 if and only if they have exactly one neighbor. We use green (light gray) to highlight agents with utility 1 in an allocation, and red (dark gray) to highlight agents with utility 0. In each case, we depict one possible improving 1-jump deviation.

We begin by showing that 1-jump stable allocations may fail to exist in general. See Fig. 6 for an illustration of the argument.

Theorem 6. *A* 1*-jump stable allocation may fail to exist, even if there are three agents with identical binary/single-peaked utility functions.*

We next observe that the hardness of deciding the existence of jump stable allocations holds, even if we restrict the jump to the distance at most 2.

Theorem 7. *Given a game* Γ*, it is NP-complete to decide whether it admits a* 2*-jump stable allocation.*

The topology constructed in the proof of Theorem 7 is of diameter two. In contrast, when the topology is of diameter one (i.e., G is a complete graph), we have trivial existence even for unrestricted utility functions.

Observation 3. *If G has diameter 1, then every allocation is jump stable.*

To see this, observe that in a complete graph, every agent has exactly $n-1$ occupied neighboring vertices in every allocation; hence, no jump can change the utility of any agent.

We next focus on acyclic graphs and explore the existence of 1-jump-stable and 2-jump-stable allocations.

Theorem 8. *If the topology is a tree and agents have binary utility functions, a 1-jump stable allocation is guaranteed to exist and can be found in polynomial time. On the other hand, a 2-jump stable allocation may fail to exist, even if the topology is a simple path, and the utility functions are identical and binary/single-peaked.*

Proof. Assume that we are given a tree graph T and we have a set of agents with binary utilities. In order to construct a 1-jump stable allocation, we follow the procedure described next.

- We first order the vertices of T with respect to the height of their sub-tree, i.e., leaves have height zero and every other vertex has height equal to the maximum height of its children plus 1.
- We visit the vertices according to this order, and for each vertex v, we check the following.
  - If the number of remaining unvisited vertices (including v) is equal to the number of unallocated agents, then we allocate all unallocated agents to the unvisited vertices in an arbitrary way.
  - Otherwise, we check if there is an unallocated agent that gets utility 1 when allocated to v when the children of v have a fixed allocation and assuming that the parent of v will remain empty. If there is such an agent, we allocate her to v. Otherwise, we leave v empty, and we move to the next vertex of the ordering.

We will prove that indeed the constructed allocation is 1-jump stable. Clearly, if an agent has utility 1, it has no profitable 1-jump. Hence, in what follows, we focus on agents with utility 0 and an empty neighboring vertex.

We begin by considering the agents that are allocated during the last step of the algorithm. Assume that this is agent i that is allocated on vertex v. In order for agent i to have utility 0, it means that the parent vertex of v has been allocated to a different agent; otherwise i would have had utility 1. Observe that agent i cannot 1-jump to the parent vertex of v, since it is occupied. Thus, if there is an empty vertex in the neighborhood of v, it is a child of v. We claim that she has no incentives to jump to such a vertex, which we denote z. To see why this is the case, observe that our procedure has visited z before v, and agent i was not allocated to z. This is because the agent would get utility 0 given the allocated agents on the children of z while having its parent-vertex, i.e., v, empty. Thus, the utility of agent i after the 1-jump from v to z is still 0.

Finally, we consider the agents that were allocated to the unvisited vertices. Observe that the procedure guarantees that all parents of unvisited vertices have an allocated agent. Thus, the only possible 1-jumps are towards child vertices that have been visited in the past. Again, we claim that no agent has incentives to 1-jump to such a vertex, following the reasoning above: if an agent could get utility 1 from jumping to a visited vertex v, then she would have been allocated to this vertex when our procedure was considering v. Hence, no agent overall has a profitable 1-jump, and the constructed allocation is 1-jump stable.

For the second claim of the theorem, consider a path with five vertices and three agents with identical binary utilities. Every agent has utility 1 if she is next to exactly one occupied vertex and 0 otherwise. We claim that in every configuration, at least one agent has a profitable 2-jump.

- If the allocated vertices form an independent set, then all three can move to a neighboring vertex and be next to an occupied vertex, and increase their utility from 0 to 1.
- If the allocated vertices form a path, then the agent at the middle of the path always has a 2-jump that places her next to exactly one occupied vertex, i.e., the occupied vertices form an edge and an independent vertex.
- If the allocated vertices form an edge and an independent vertex, then no matter how the configuration is, the agent that is on the independent vertex is at a distance of at most 2 from the occupied vertices. Thus, she has a profitable 2-jump.

That is, in no configuration is there a stable solution, finishing the proof. □

5 Social Welfare and Pareto Optimality

Now, we shift our focus from stability to efficiency. In this section, we will focus on finding optimal allocations with respect to the efficiency notions introduced in Sect. 2. We start with the case of utilitarian social welfare, egalitarian social welfare, and Nash social welfare, for which we show that, given a bound, it is computationally intractable to decide whether an allocation with welfare at least this bound exists or not. The computational intractability persists, even if the number of agents to allocate is small.

Theorem 9. *It is NP-complete and W[1]-hard when parameterized by the number of agents to decide whether there exists an allocation with utilitarian social welfare at least ζ, even if the utilities are binary, linearly increasing, or linearly decreasing. The same holds for egalitarian and Nash social welfare.*

Proof Sketch. To show the theorem, we reduce from the k-CLIQUE problem. Given an instance $\mathcal{I} = (H, k)$ of the k-CLIQUE problem, we construct an equivalent game Γ as follows. The topology G is identical to the graph H, and we set

$N = \{a_1, \ldots, a_k\}$. The utility function of every agent $i \in N$ is defined as

$$\mathrm{u}_i(x) = \begin{cases} 1 & \text{if } x = k-1 \text{ and} \\ 0 & \text{otherwise.} \end{cases}$$

Clearly, the utilities are identical and binary. To finalize the construction for USW, we set $\zeta = k$. Then, an allocation with utilitarian social welfare at least ζ exists if and only if every agent has all remaining agents in her neighborhood, i.e., the agents occupy a clique of size k in H. The results for the other utility classes and welfare notions follow by adjusting the utilities, the topology, and the bound ζ.

Next, we turn our attention to Pareto optimality. First, observe that a Pareto optimal allocation always exists in our model, regardless of the utility profile. The set of allocations is finite and non-empty, and Pareto domination is a strict partial order on this set. Every finite non-empty strict partial order has a maximal element, and a maximal element under Pareto domination is by definition a Pareto optimal allocation.

Observation 4. *Every game Γ admits at least one Pareto optimal allocation.*

Hence, we focus on the complexity of verifying and finding such allocations rather than their existence. Unfortunately, the result here is very negative: already verifying whether an allocation π is Pareto optimal is computationally hard, even if the number of agents is small.

Theorem 10. *It is coNP-hard and coW[1]-hard when parameterized by the number of agents to verify whether an allocation π is Pareto optimal, even if all utility functions are identical and binary, linearly increasing, or linearly decreasing.*

We conclude this section by presenting XP algorithms for parameterization by the number of agents for all efficiency notions we are interested in, complementing the above hardness results. The algorithms employ a simple brute-force approach, trying all possible allocations. However, interestingly enough, such a naïve enumeration is, under ETH, asymptotically optimal.

Theorem 11. *There is an algorithm running in $|V(G)|^{\mathcal{O}(n)}$ time that, given a game Γ, finds an allocation π that (i) maximizes USW, (ii) maximizes ESW, (iii) maximizes NSW, or (iv) is Pareto optimal. Moreover, unless ETH fails, there is no algorithm solving problems (i)-(iii) in time $f(n) \cdot |V(G)|^{o(n)}$ for any computable function f.*

6 Conclusions

As our results indicate, the existence and tractability of the underlying computational problem change drastically based on the combination of stability notion, utility function, and graph topology. One question that remains open is to provide a complete dichotomy for 1-jump-stability on trees. Our algorithm for binary utilities cannot immediately work for other utility functions, such as single-peaked utilities, although there might exist a sophisticated modification that makes it work.

A different direction is to consider other stability notions, with contractual-based stability notions being prime candidates [14]. This family is a different refinement of jump-stability, where a jump of an agent must be "approved" either by her current neighbors (out-contractual), or by her potential new neighbors after the jump (in-contractual), or both (in-out-contractual). Here, there is ample room for choosing what "approval" actually means: it can be (weak) majority, veto, or a welfare-based function. Although a couple of our results can be extended to a subset of cases, we believe there are novel algorithmic insights that can yield positive results for these notions.

Acknowledgment. This research was supported in part by the National Science Centre, Poland, grant number UMO-2025/58/A/ST6/00371, by the EPSRC grant EP/X039862/1, EPSRC grant UKRI4530, and co-funded by the European Union under the project Robotics and Advanced Industrial Production (reg. no. CZ.02.01.01/00/22_008/0004590).

References

1. Agarwal, A., Elkind, E., Gan, J., Igarashi, A., Suksompong, W., Voudouris, A.A.: Schelling games on graphs. Artif. Intell. **301**, 103576 (2021)
2. Amanatidis, G., et al.: Fair division of indivisible goods: recent progress and open questions. Artif. Intell. **322**, 103965 (2023)
3. Aziz, H., Chan, H., Lederer, P., Narang, S., Walsh, T.: Distance preservation games. In: IJCAI '25. pp. 3735–3743 (2025). ijcai.org
4. Ballester, C.: NP-completeness in hedonic games. Games Econ. Behav. **49**(1), 1–30 (2004)
5. Balliu, A., Flammini, M., Melideo, G., Olivetti, D.: On non-cooperativeness in social distance games. J. Artif. Intell. Res. **66**, 625–653 (2019)
6. Balliu, A., Flammini, M., Melideo, G., Olivetti, D.: On Pareto optimality in social distance games. Artif. Intell. **312**, 103768 (2022)
7. Banerjee, S., Konishi, H., Sönmez, T.: Core in a simple coalition formation game. Soc. Choice Welf. **18**(1), 135–153 (2001)
8. Berriaud, D., Constantinescu, A., Wattenhofer, R.: Stable dinner party seating arrangements. In: WINE '23, vol. 14413, pp. 3–20. Springer (2023)
9. Bilò, D., Bilò, V., Döring, M., Lenzner, P., Molitor, L., Schmidt, J.: Schelling games with continuous types. In: IJCAI '23, pp. 2520–2527 (2023). ijcai.org
10. Bilò, D., Bilò, V., Lenzner, P., Molitor, L.: Topological influence and locality in swap Schelling games. Auton. Agent. Multi-Agent Syst. **36**(2), 1–60 (2022)
11. Bilò, D., Bilò, V., Lenzner, P., Molitor, L.: Tolerance is necessary for stability: single-peaked swap Schelling games. In: IJCAI '22, pp. 81–87. ijcai.org (2022)
12. Bodlaender, H.L., Hanaka, T., Jaffke, L., Ono, H., Otachi, Y., van der Zanden, T.C.: Hedonic seat arrangement problems. Auton. Agent. Multi-Agent Syst. **39**(2), 33 (2025)
13. Bogomolnaia, A., Jackson, M.O.: The stability of hedonic coalition structures. Games Econ. Behav. **38**(2), 201–230 (2002)

14. Brandt, F., Bullinger, M., Tappe, L.: Stability based on single-agent deviations in additively separable hedonic games. Artif. Intell. **334**, 104160 (2024)
15. Brânzei, S., Larson, K.: Social distance games. In: IJCAI '11, pp. 91–96 (2011)
16. Bullinger, M., Suksompong, W.: Topological distance games. Theor. Comput. Sci. **981**, 114238 (2024)
17. Bullinger, M., Suksompong, W., Voudouris, A.A.: Welfare guarantees in Schelling segregation. J. Artif. Intell. Res. **71**, 143–174 (2021)
18. Ceylan, E., Chen, J., Roy, S.: Optimal seat arrangement: what are the hard and easy cases? J. Comput. Syst. Sci. **160**, 103779 (2026)
19. Chan, H., Irfan, M.T., Than, C.V.: Schelling models with localized social influence: a game-theoretic framework. In: AAMAS '20, pp. 240–248. IFAAMAS (2020)
20. Chauhan, A., Lenzner, P., Molitor, L.: Schelling segregation with strategic agents. In: SAGT '18. LNCS, vol. 11059, pp. 137–149. Springer (2018)
21. Constantinescu, A., Lenzner, P., Reiffenhäuser, R., Schmand, D., Varricchio, G.: Solving Woeginger's hiking problem: wonderful partitions in anonymous hedonic games. In: ICALP '24, pp. 48:1–48:18 (2024)
22. Deligkas, A., Eiben, E., Goldsmith, T., Knop, D., Schierreich, Š.: Individual rationality in size-constrained hedonic games: anonymous and diversity preferences. In: WINE '26 (2026)
23. Deligkas, A., Eiben, E., Ioannidis, S.D., Knop, D., Schierreich, Š.: Balanced and fair partitioning of friends. In: AAAI '25, pp. 13754–13762. AAAI Press (2025)
24. Deligkas, A., Eiben, E., Knop, D., Schierreich, Š.: Individual rationality in topological distance games is surprisingly hard. In: IJCAI '24, pp. 2782–2790 (2024)
25. Echzell, H., et al.: Convergence and hardness of strategic Schelling segregation. In: WINE '19. LNCS, vol. 11920, pp. 156–170. Springer (2019)
26. Erdős, P., Szekeres, G.: A combinatorial problem in geometry. Compos. Math. **2**, 463–470 (1935)
27. Even-Dar, E., Kesselman, A., Mansour, Y.: Convergence time to Nash equilibrium in load balancing. ACM Trans. Algorithms **3**(3), 32 (2007)
28. Fioravantes, F., Gahlawat, H., Melissinos, N., Schierreich, Š.: Individual rationality in constrained hedonic games: anonymous and diversity preferences. In: GAIW '26 (2026)
29. Friedrich, T., Lenzner, P., Molitor, L., Seifert, L.: Single-peaked jump Schelling games. In: SAGT '23. LNCS, vol. 14238, pp. 111–126. Springer (2023)
30. Ganian, R., Hamm, T., Knop, D., Roy, S., Schierreich, Š., Suchý, O.: Maximizing social welfare in score-based social distance games. In: TARK '23, pp. 272–286 (2023)
31. Gonzalez, T.F.: Clustering to minimize the maximum intercluster distance. Theor. Comput. Sci. **38**, 293–306 (1985)
32. Kaklamanis, C., Kanellopoulos, P., Patouchas, D.: On the price of stability of social distance games. In: SAGT '18. LNCS, vol. 11059, pp. 125–136. Springer (2018)
33. Kanellopoulos, P., Kyropoulou, M., Voudouris, A.A.: Modified Schelling games. Theor. Comput. Sci. **880**, 1–19 (2021)
34. Kanellopoulos, P., Kyropoulou, M., Voudouris, A.A.: Not all strangers are the same: the impact of tolerance in Schelling games. Theor. Comput. Sci. **971**, 114065 (2023)
35. Knop, D., Schierreich, Š.: Host community respecting refugee housing. In: AAMAS '23, pp. 966–975. IFAAMAS (2023)
36. Li, L., Micha, E., Nikolov, A., Shah, N.: Partitioning friends fairly. In: AAAI '23, pp. 5747–5754. AAAI Press (2023)

37. Lisowski, G., Schierreich, Š.: Stability in newcomers' housing: a story about anonymous preferences and beyond. In: EUMAS '25. LNCS, vol. 16258, pp. 232–249. Springer (2025)
38. Narayanan, L., Opatrny, J., Tummala, S., Voudouris, A.A.: Variety-seeking jump games on graphs. In: IJCAI '25, pp. 4005–4013 (2025). ijcai.org
39. Narayanan, L., Sabbagh, Y., Voudouris, A.A.: Diversity-seeking jump games in networks. Auton. Agent. Multi-Agent Syst. **39**(2), 32 (2025)
40. Peters, D.: Complexity of hedonic games with dichotomous preferences. In: AAAI '16, pp. 579–585. AAAI Press (2016)
41. Schelling, T.C.: Models of segregation. Am. Econ. Rev. **59**(2), 488–493 (1969)
42. Schelling, T.C.: Dynamic models of segregation. J. Math. Sociol. **1**(2), 143–186 (1971)
43. Schierreich, Š.: Refugee housing with restricted preferences: complexity, algorithms, and relaxation. In: ADT '26 (2026)
44. Schierreich, Š.: Two-stage refugee resettlement models: computational aspects of the second stage. In: AIES '24, pp. 50–51. AAAI Press (2024)
45. Vöcking, B.: Selfish Load Balancing, pp. 517–542. Cambridge University Press (2007)
46. Wilczynski, A.: Ordinal hedonic seat arrangement under restricted preference domains: swap stability and popularity. In: IJCAI '23, pp. 2906–2914 (2023). ijcai.org

Distributed Agent-Constrained Truthful Facility Location

Argyrios Deligkas[1], Panagiotis Kanellopoulos[2(✉)], and Alexandros A. Voudouris[3]

[1] Royal Holloway University of London, Egham, UK
argyrios.deligkas@rhul.ac.uk
[2] King's College London, London, UK
panagiotis.kanellopoulos@kcl.ac.uk
[3] University of Southern Denmark, Vejle, Denmark
voudouris@imada.sdu.dk

Abstract. We study a distributed facility location problem in which a set of agents, each with a private position on the real line, is partitioned into a collection of fixed, disjoint groups. The goal is to open k facilities at locations chosen from the set of positions reported by the agents. This decision is made by mechanisms that operate in two phases. In Phase 1, each group selects the position of one of its agents to serve as the group's representative location. In Phase 2, k representatives are chosen as facility locations. Once the facility locations are determined, each agent incurs an individual cost, defined either as the sum of its distances to all facilities (sum-variant) or as the distance to its farthest facility (max-variant). We focus on strategyproof mechanisms, which preclude the agents from benefiting through strategic misreporting, and establish tight bounds on the approximation ratio with respect to the social cost (the group-normalized average individual cost) in both variants.

1 Introduction

Imagine you are the newly elected mayor of a village in which residents live along a single street and value being close to public services. During your campaign, you promised to open several new facilities at sites proposed by the residents themselves. How should you decide where to place them? A natural idea is to ask every resident for her ideal location and place each facility so as to minimize the total walking distance. Two complications get in the way. First, a resident may have an incentive to misreport her ideal location if doing so moves the facilities closer to her actual home. Second, your village is organized into civic associations that each speak with a single voice: within each association, residents' reports are first aggregated into one nominated location, and you make the final decision from those nominations. You weigh the associations equally, judging outcomes by how well each one is served on average. Each of these features has been studied on its own in the truthful facility location literature [13]; in this paper,

P. Lenzner and D. Schmand (Eds.): SAGT 2026, LNCS 16911, pp. 132–150, 2027.
https://doi.org/10.1007/978-3-032-38782-0_8

we study a model in which they appear together, and find that the combination is technically richer than either feature in isolation.

Before describing our model in detail, it is useful to place it within the broader truthful facility location literature, which has explored several largely independent axes of variation. One such axis concerns the number of facilities and the preferences of the agents over them. When a single facility is to be opened, it is natural to assume that every agent would prefer to be as close to it as possible. In the case of multiple facilities, however, the preferences of the agents might depend on the types of services that the facilities provide. A large part of the literature has considered settings where the facilities are homogeneous, and thus agents aim to be close to one of them [27,38,39]. However, when the facilities are heterogeneous, agents might prefer to be close to more than one facility and suffer a cost that is a function of their distances to all facilities. In particular, two main individual cost functions have been proposed: one that considers the sum of an agent's distances to all facilities (known as the *sum-variant*), and another that considers the distance to the farthest facility (known as the *max-variant*).

Another crucial aspect of the problem concerns the feasible locations where facilities can be opened. The earliest works in this area considered the continuous case, in which facilities can be opened at any point on the line. In many real-world applications, however, the setting is discrete, and facility placement is restricted to existing agent locations due to physical, legal, or budgetary constraints, or even due to pre-existing infrastructure. Many different location-constrained models have been proposed and studied in recent years, in which facilities can be opened only at predetermined candidate locations [22,33,42], or at the locations reported by the agents [18]; the latter *agent-constrained* model is also linked to well-studied social choice settings, such as *peer selection* and *sortition*, where agents act as candidates.

There are also several applications, such as federated or regional planning, where collecting input from all agents simultaneously may be logistically too difficult or even prohibited, for instance when agents are partitioned into disjoint administrative regions or belong to different sub-networks. In such scenarios, the decision is typically computed in a distributed manner. Agents are partitioned into groups (e.g., focus groups or subcommittees), and each group locally proposes a single location that is representative of the positions of all agents within the group. The outcome is then computed based on the group proposals; for example, facilities may be opened at a subset of these representative locations. This setting is known as the *distributed facility location* model and was first considered by Filos-Ratsikas *et al.* [23], who focused on the case of a single facility. More recently, Xu *et al.* [47] studied a slightly different distributed model for two facilities, in which each group proposes two locations.

1.1 Our Contribution

In this paper, we consider distributed facility location problems with n *agents* that are partitioned into m disjoint *groups*, and there are $k \leq m$ facilities to open. The agents have *private positions* on the line of real numbers and report them to an algorithm (or, *mechanism*) which decides the locations of the facilities by implementing the following two phases. In Phase 1, for each group, given the positions of the agents therein, the mechanism chooses one of these positions as the representative location of the whole group. In Phase 2, it chooses where to open the facilities from the set of representative locations of all groups. Once the facility locations have been determined, each agent suffers an individual cost, which is either her total distance to the facilities (*sum-variant*), or her distance to the farthest facility (*max-variant*). Naturally, an agent acts as cost-minimizer and can potentially misreport her true position if this can decrease her individual cost. We focus on the design of deterministic *strategyproof* mechanisms that make decisions to eliminate the strategic behavior of the agents and at the same time achieve a good approximation of the minimum possible *social cost*, which we define as a group-normalized average of the agents' individual costs.

We paint an almost complete picture of the best possible approximation ratio that can be achieved by strategyproof mechanisms. In particular, for $k = 2$ facilities, we show a tight bound of $1+\sqrt{2}$ in the sum-variant, and a tight bound of $9/2$ in the max-variant. The $1 + \sqrt{2}$ bound in the sum-variant turns out to not only be the best possible among strategyproof mechanisms, but also among unrestricted algorithms that ignore the strategic behavior of the agents. In the max-variant, a slightly better bound of 4 can be achieved for such unrestricted algorithms. For $k \geq 3$ facilities, we show that the best possible approximation ratio of strategyproof mechanisms is between $3 - 2/k$ and $3 + 2/k$ in the sum-variant (leaving a small gap that diminishes as k increases), and between $2k$ and $2(k + 1)$ in the max-variant. An overview of these results is given in Table 1.

Table 1. Overview of our bounds on the approximation ratio of deterministic strategyproof mechanisms for the different variants (sum- and max-) and the number k of available facilities. Single numbers for $k = 2$ indicate tight bounds.

	$k = 2$	$k \geq 3$
Sum-variant	$1+\sqrt{2}$	$[3-2/k, 3+2/k]$
Max-variant	$9/2$	$[2k, 2(k+1)]$

Our upper bounds follow by strategyproof mechanisms that make choices based on ordered statistics. That is, such mechanisms select the group representative locations based on the ordering of the positions reported by the agents therein, and then decide the final facility location based on the ordering of the representative locations. The Phase 2 rule is related to the Percentile Mechanisms in [26], but operates on representatives generated through an additional local aggregation phase. For two facilities in particular, multiple such mechanisms must be appropriately combined depending on the number of groups, in order to create mechanisms that achieve the best possible approximation ratio bounds. Our lower bounds follow by, in cases quite elaborate, constructions that exploit a locality property of distributed mechanisms which dictates that the same representative location must be chosen for any group with the same number of agents that have the same positions, as well as the fact that all representative locations must be part of the solution when $k = m$.

1.2 Related Work

Over the last decades, truthful facility location problems have been studied extensively within the area of *approximate mechanism design without money*, with early works establishing foundational models and approximation results mainly for settings where the facilities can be opened anywhere on the line [27,38,39]; see also the survey of Chan *et al.* [13]. An ever-growing body of research has investigated different truthful k-facility location models with additional feasibility constraints, most notably when facilities must be chosen from a finite set of candidate locations. This constraint has been explored under various objectives and information models, including the sum- and max-variants that we also consider here [22,29,32,33,37,40–42,45,48]. One crucial aspect in all these works is that the set of candidate locations is fixed and known a priori. In contrast, in our model, the candidate locations are the positions of the agents and are thus dynamically determined once the agents report them, as in the recent work of Deligkas *et al.* [18]. Besides models where the facilities are desirable, there has also been significant work on obnoxious facility location with candidate locations, where agents prefer facilities to be opened as far away as possible [28,31,49]. Another related constraint, which can be thought of as orthogonal to having candidate locations, is requiring a minimum distance between the facilities, aiming for better distribution and fairness [19,46].

Going beyond centralized decision-making and inspired by similar work in voting, Filos-Ratsikas *et al.* [23] were the first to study distributed facility location models, focusing exclusively on the case of one facility. In their model, as in our setting, the agents are partitioned into groups, and each group independently proposes a representative location (which can be any point on the line), and then one of those is chosen to open the facility. Recently, Xu *et al.* [47] considered a setting with two facilities. In their model, the facilities can only be opened on fixed candidate locations, and each group proposes two representative locations. This is in contrast to our model where the facilities can be opened on agent locations and each group only proposes one such location. Complementary to these distributed models, another line of recent work has considered group facility location models, where the agents are partitioned into groups that potentially affect their individual costs, but the decision is centralized [35,36,50].

Our setting is also closely related to *utilitarian voting* where agents have (metric) preferences over a set of candidates, typically expressed via ordinal rankings, and the objective is to select one or more candidates so as to minimize the social cost or maximize the social welfare. We refer to the survey of Anshelevich *et al.* [6] for a comprehensive overview of this literature and the notion of *distortion*. Within this framework, the most related works are those focusing on distributed variants, where, similarly to our facility location model and to the ones mentioned above, agents are grouped together in disjoint districts and communication among agents in different districts is prohibited [1,7,24,43,44]. Amanatidis *et al.* [4] recently studied another related, centralized voting model with unknown groups of agents to evaluate how well outcomes approximate the optimal solution in terms of group-fair objectives.

Another line of research considers, similarly to our work, *peer selection* settings in which agents themselves are the candidates, aiming to model representative selection and social choice among individuals [12,14,15]. A related concept is that of α-*decisiveness* in metric voting, used to capture structured preferences where $\alpha \in [0, 1]$ is a factor indicating how close an agent is to all the candidates compared to how close she is to her top-ranked candidate, with $\alpha = 0$ implying that an agent actually coincides with her top-ranked candidate in the metric space [5,8,30,34]. Finally, a less related setting where agents act as candidates is that of *impartial selection*, where a winner or a small set of winners must be selected from a group of agents who nominate one another, under the constraint that no agent can influence their own chance of being selected [3,11,25].

2 The Model

We consider a distributed facility location model with a set N of $n \geq 2$ agents and $k \geq 2$ facilities. Each agent i has a position $x_i \in \mathbb{R}$ on the line of real numbers. Let $\mathbf{x} = (x_i)_{i \in N}$ be the *position profile* consisting of all agent positions. The agents are partitioned into $m \geq k$ disjoint fixed groups that are known a priori. Let G be the set of all groups, and denote by $n_g = |g|$ the size of group $g \in G$. So, an instance of our problem can be fully described by a tuple $I = (\mathbf{x}, G, k)$ which defines the positions of the agents, the groups of agents, and the number of facilities to be opened.

Our goal is to build all k facilities at k locations chosen from the (multi)set of positions reported by the agents; note that two facilities are allowed to be opened at the same position if there are (at least) two agents with that position. In particular, a solution is a k-tuple $\mathbf{y} = (y_\ell)_{\ell \in [k]}$ indicating the location y_ℓ of facility $\ell \in [k]$, such that $\mathbf{y} \subseteq \mathbf{x}$. In our distributed setting, an algorithm $\mathcal{A}$ works by implementing the following two phases:

- Phase 1: For each group $g \in G$, the algorithm decides the position of an agent $r_g \in g$ as the representative location for the whole group.
- Phase 2: The algorithm chooses k out of the m group representative locations where the k facilities are opened. That is, it outputs a solution $\mathbf{y} \subseteq \bigcup_{g \in G}\{x_{r_g}\}$.

For any instance I, let $\mathcal{A}(I)$ be the solution computed by $\mathcal{A}$. We will typically use $\mathbf{w}_I$ (or simply $\mathbf{w}$ if I is clear from context) to denote the solution of an algorithm in our proofs.

Let $d(i, y) = |x_i - y|$ be the distance of agent i from any point y on the line. Given a solution $\mathbf{y} = (y_\ell)_{\ell \in [k]}$, the *individual cost* of an agent i in instance I is

- **(sum-variant)** the total distance of agent i from all facilities: $\text{cost}_i^{\text{sum}}(\mathbf{y}|I) = \sum_{\ell \in [k]} d(i, y_\ell)$;

– **(max-variant)** the distance of i from the farthest facility: $\text{cost}_i^{\max}(\mathbf{y}|I) = \max_{\ell \in [k]} d(i, y_\ell)$.

When the variant is clear from context, we will simply write $\text{cost}_i(\mathbf{w}|I)$ to denote the individual cost of agent i for $\mathbf{y}$. Since the groups might in general be of different sizes, we define the *social cost* of a solution $\mathbf{y}$ in instance I as the average over groups of the average individual cost of the agents within the groups, i.e.,

$$\text{SC}(\mathbf{y}|I) = \frac{1}{m} \sum_{g \in G} \frac{1}{n_g} \sum_{i \in g} \text{cost}_i(\mathbf{y}|I).$$

We will typically use $\mathbf{o}_I$ (or simply $\mathbf{o}$ if I is clear from context) to denote a solution that minimizes the social cost. Observe that, if we were allowed to open all facilities at the same point, then, to minimize the social cost, that point would be the *weighted median* of the agents. In particular, let π be the ranking of all agents according to their positions (breaking ties arbitrarily). Each agent i in a group g has a weight $\mathrm{v}_i = 1/n_g$. The weighted median i^* is an agent such that $\sum_{i:\pi(i)<\pi(i^*)} \mathrm{v}_i < m/2$ and $\mathrm{v}_{i^*} + \sum_{i:\pi(i)<\pi(i^*)} \mathrm{v}_i \geq m/2$. When the groups are *symmetric* (i.e., they all have the same size n/m), our social cost definition reduces to the *average individual agent cost*, and the weighted median agent reduces to the median agent. For simplicity, if the groups are symmetric, we will calculate the total individual agent cost as the social cost.

The *approximation ratio* $\rho_k(\mathcal{A})$ of an algorithm $\mathcal{A}$ is the worst-case ratio (over all instances with a given number k of facilities) between the social cost of the computed solution and the minimum social cost achieved by any feasible solution, that is

$$\rho_k(\mathcal{A}) = \sup_{I=(\mathbf{x},G,k)} \frac{\text{SC}(\mathcal{A}(I)|I)}{\min_{\mathbf{y} \subseteq \mathbf{x}:|\mathbf{y}|=k} \text{SC}(\mathbf{y}|I)}.$$

In many cases, it is important to avoid strategic manipulations by the agents who aim to minimize their individual costs without any consideration for the social cost. In particular, an algorithm $\mathcal{A}$ (also referred to as *mechanism* in this case) is *strategyproof* if, for any agent i and two instances $I = ((x_i, \mathbf{x}_{-i}), G, k)$ and $J = ((x_i', \mathbf{x}_{-i}), G, k)$ that differ only on the position of agent i, we have that $\text{cost}_i(\mathcal{A}(I)|I) \leq \text{cost}_i(\mathcal{A}(J)|I)$. Our goal is to design *unrestricted algorithms* and *strategyproof mechanisms* with an approximation ratio as small as possible.

3 A Class of Strategyproof Mechanisms for Two Facilities

We start by presenting a class of mechanisms for $k = 2$ facilities. We will argue that all members of this class are strategyproof mechanisms, and show a general bound on the approximation ratio they achieve for both the sum- and the max-variant. For any parameters $\theta, \ell, r \in (0, 1]$ such that $\lceil \ell m \rceil < \lceil rm \rceil$, mechanism $\mathcal{M}_m(\theta, \ell, r)$ works as follows: In Phase 1, for each group $g \in G$, it selects the position of the $\lceil \theta n_g \rceil$-leftmost agent therein as g's representative r_g. In Phase 2, the mechanism opens the facilities at the $\lceil \ell m \rceil$- and $\lceil rm \rceil$-leftmost representative locations. See Mechanism 1 for a description using pseudocode. Note that the constraint $\lceil \ell m \rceil < \lceil rm \rceil$ that we impose on the parameters guarantees that we never co-locate the two facilities unless there are at least two agents there.

Mechanism 1: $\mathcal{M}_m(\theta, \ell, r)$

```
Input: Instance I = (x, G, 2), parameters θ, ℓ, r ∈ (0, 1] such that ⌈ℓm⌉ < ⌈rm⌉;
Output: Facility locations w = (w_1, w_2);
Rep ← ∅;
for each group g ∈ G do
    i_g ← ⌈θn_g⌉-leftmost agent in g;
    r_g ← x_{i_g};
    Rep ← Rep ∪ {r_g};
w_1 ← ⌈ℓm⌉-leftmost location in Rep;
w_2 ← ⌈rm⌉-leftmost location in Rep;
```

We first argue that mechanism $\mathcal{M}_m(\theta, \ell, r)$ is strategyproof, for any (valid) parameters and any of the two variant settings we consider (sum and max).

Theorem 1. *For any $m \geq 2$ and $\theta, \ell, r \in (0, 1]$ with $\lceil \ell m \rceil < \lceil rm \rceil$, mechanism $\mathcal{M}_m(\theta, \ell, r)$ is strategyproof.*

Proof. Consider a group g with representative r_g and an agent $i \in g$ with true position x_i. Suppose that i reports a different position x'_i and let $\mathbf{w}' = (w'_1, w'_2)$ be the resulting solution. If the representative of g does not change after i misreports, then the overall solution does not change, and thus i suffers the same cost as before. Since r_g is a fixed-order statistic, if the representative of g does change to r'_g, then it must be the case that either $x_i \leq r_g < r'_g$ or $r'_g < r_g \leq x_i$. We now switch between different cases depending on the relative locations of w_1, w_2, r_g, x_i and r'_g.

Case 1: $r_g > w_2$. Clearly, the solution does not change if $r'_g > r_g$. Otherwise, if $r'_g < r_g \leq x_i$, since $w_1 \leq w_2 < r_g \leq x_i$, either the solution does not change, or it changes to $\mathbf{w}'$ with $w'_1 \leq w_1$ and $w'_2 \leq w_2$. In any case, the cost of i does not decrease.

Case 2: $r_g < w_1$. This is symmetric to Case 1.

Case 3: $r_g \in (w_1, w_2)$. If $x_i \leq r_g < r'_g$, then the new solution $\mathbf{w}'$ is such that $w'_2 \geq w_2$ and $w'_1 = w_1$. Otherwise, if $r'_g < r_g \leq x_i$, the new solution $\mathbf{w}'$ is such that $w'_1 \leq w_1$ and $w'_2 = w_2$. In both cases, the cost of i may only increase.

Case 4: $r_g \in \{w_1, w_2\}$. Without loss of generality, suppose that $r_g = w_1$. If $r'_g < r_g$, we have $w'_1 \leq w_1$ and $w'_2 = w_2$. As $x_i \geq r_g$, such a change may only increase the cost of agent i. Otherwise, if $r_g < r'_g$, we have $w'_1 \geq w_1$ and $w'_2 \geq w_2$. Since $x_i \leq r_g$, such a change may again only increase the cost of agent i. □

Next, we focus on the approximation ratio that mechanism $\mathcal{M}_m(\theta, \ell, r)$ can achieve as a function of the parameters θ, ℓ and r, as well as the number n of agents and the number m of groups. This will allow us in the next section to identify the best possible combinations of the parameters for the different settings we consider. Before analyzing the approximation ratio, we argue that any instance can be transformed into another with symmetric groups (where each group g has size $n_g = n/m$) such that the mechanism outputs the same solution and the position of the weighted median in the original instance is the same as the position of the median agent in the new instance. Using this, we can without loss of generality focus on bounding the approximation ratio of the mechanism on instances with symmetric groups.

Lemma 1. *For any instance I with m groups, there is another instance J with m symmetric groups such that the representative location chosen by $\mathcal{M}_m(\theta, \ell, r)$ for a group is the same in I and J, and the position of the weighted median agent in I is the same as the position of the median agent in J.*

Proof. Let G_I and G_J be the sets of groups in instance I and instance J, respectively. For every group $g \in G_I$ of size n_g in instance I, we create a group $g' \in G_J$ in instance J of size $\prod_{q \in G_I} n_q$ as follows: For each agent $i \in g$ that is positioned at x_i, g' contains $\prod_{q \in G_I \setminus \{g\}} n_q$ agents at x_i.

It is now not hard to see that the representative of group g' in J is the same as the representative of group g in I: The representative of g' is the position of the $\lceil \theta \prod_{q \in G_I} n_q \rceil$-leftmost agent in g'. Since the position x_i of each agent $i \in g$ is repeated $\prod_{q \in G_I \setminus \{g\}} n_q$ times in g', the representative location of g' is the same as the position of the $\left\lceil \frac{\theta \prod_{q \in G_I} n_q}{\prod_{q \in G_I \setminus \{g\}} n_q} \right\rceil = \lceil \theta n_g \rceil$-leftmost agent in g, which is exactly the position chosen as the representative of g by the mechanism. For the same reason, the position of the median agent in J is the same as the position of the weighted median agent in I. $\square$

We are now ready to bound the mechanism's approximation ratio.

Theorem 2. *Let Y be an indicator variable that is 1 if the setting is the sum-variant, and 0 if the setting is the max-variant. For any $m \geq 2$ and $\theta, \ell, r \in (0, 1]$ with $\lceil \ell m \rceil < \lceil rm \rceil$, mechanism $\mathcal{M}_m(\theta, \ell, r)$ has approximation ratio at most*

$$\max \left\{ \frac{n}{(m+1-\lceil \ell m \rceil)(\frac{n}{m}+1-\lceil \frac{\theta n}{m} \rceil)} - 1, \frac{n}{(1+Y)(m+1-\lceil rm \rceil)(\frac{n}{m}+1-\lceil \frac{\theta n}{m} \rceil)}, \right.$$
$$\left. \frac{n}{\lceil rm \rceil \lceil \frac{\theta n}{m} \rceil} - 1, \frac{n}{(1+Y)\lceil \ell m \rceil \lceil \frac{\theta n}{m} \rceil} \right\}.$$

4 Tight Strategyproof Bounds for Two Facilities

Using Theorem 2, we can now design strategyproof mechanisms that achieve low approximation ratios for both the sum- and the max-variant settings by appropriately choosing the parameters θ, ℓ and r depending on the number m of groups. Since $\mathcal{M}_m(\theta, \ell, r)$ is strategyproof for any $\theta, \ell, r \in (0, 1]$, and the number m of groups is a priori known, running different versions of $\mathcal{M}_m(\theta, \ell, r)$ depending on the value of m leads to a strategyproof mechanism. Taking advantage of this, we will show an upper bound of $1 + \sqrt{2} \approx 2.414$ in the sum-variant, and an upper bound of 9/2 in the max-variant. We will also prove that these are the best possible bounds over all strategyproof mechanisms.

4.1 Sum-Variant

We start with the sum-variant.

Theorem 3. *In the sum-variant, for $k = 2$ facilities, there exists a strategyproof mechanism with approximation ratio at most $1 + \sqrt{2}$.*

Proof. For any $m \neq 3, 5$, we run $\mathcal{M}_m(1/2, \sqrt{2} - 1, 2 - \sqrt{2})$. By Theorem 2, with $Y = 1$ (as we are in the sum-variant setting), using the fact that $xm \leq \lceil xm \rceil \leq xm + 1$ for any $x \in \{\ell, r\}$, we can first simplify the upper bound, and then substitute these values for the parameters θ, ℓ and r, to get an approximation ratio of at most

$$\max\left\{\frac{1}{(1-\ell)(1-\theta)} - 1, \frac{1}{2(1-r)(1-\theta)}, \frac{1}{r\theta} - 1, \frac{1}{2\ell\theta}\right\}$$
$$= \max\left\{\frac{2}{2-\sqrt{2}} - 1, \frac{1}{\sqrt{2}-1}, \frac{2}{2-\sqrt{2}} - 1, \frac{1}{\sqrt{2}-1}\right\} = 1 + \sqrt{2}.$$

Note that for $m \in \{3, 5\}$, $\lceil(\sqrt{2} - 1)m\rceil = \lceil(2 - \sqrt{2})m\rceil$, which means that these parameter values cannot be used for the mechanism. So, we have to treat each of these cases separately using a different combination of parameters.

For $m = 3$, we run $M_3(1/3, 2/3, 1)$. First, observe that for these parameters we have $\lceil 3\ell \rceil < \lceil 3r \rceil$. By Theorem 2, substituting $\theta = 1/3$, $\ell = 2/3$, $r = 1$, and using the fact that $n/9 \leq \lceil n/9 \rceil \leq n/9 + 1$, the approximation ratio is at most

$$\max\left\{\frac{n}{2(\frac{n}{3} + 1 - \lceil\frac{n}{9}\rceil)} - 1, \frac{n}{2(\frac{n}{3} + 1 - \lceil\frac{n}{9}\rceil)}, \frac{n}{3\lceil\frac{n}{9}\rceil} - 1, \frac{n}{4\lceil\frac{n}{9}\rceil}\right\}$$
$$\leq \max\left\{\frac{5}{4}, \frac{9}{4}, 2, \frac{9}{4}\right\} = \frac{9}{4}.$$

Finally, for $m = 5$, we run $M_5(2/5, 3/5, 4/5)$. Again observe that for these values we have $\lceil 5\ell \rceil < \lceil 5r \rceil$. By Theorem 2, substituting $\theta = 2/5$, $\ell = 3/5$, $r = 4/5$, and using the fact that $2n/25 \leq \lceil 2n/25 \rceil \leq 2n/25 + 1$, the approximation ratio is at most

$$\max\left\{\frac{n}{3(\frac{n}{5} + 1 - \lceil\frac{2n}{25}\rceil)} - 1, \frac{n}{4(\frac{n}{5} + 1 - \lceil\frac{2n}{25}\rceil)}, \frac{n}{4\lceil\frac{2n}{25}\rceil} - 1, \frac{n}{6\lceil\frac{2n}{25}\rceil}\right\}$$
$$\leq \max\left\{\frac{16}{9}, \frac{25}{12}, \frac{17}{8}, \frac{25}{12}\right\} = \frac{25}{12}.$$

We conclude that, for any m, the approximation ratio is at most $1 + \sqrt{2}$. $\square$

We will now show that $1 + \sqrt{2}$ is the best possible approximation ratio we can hope for over any algorithm, even non-strategyproof ones.

Theorem 4. *In the sum-variant, for* $k = 2$ *facilities, the approximation ratio of any algorithm is at least* $1 + \sqrt{2} - \varepsilon$*, for any* $\varepsilon > 0$.

4.2 Max-Variant

We now turn to the max-variant. Using Theorem 2 again, we design a strategyproof mechanism with approximation ratio at most $9/2$.

Theorem 5. *In the max-variant, for* $k = 2$ *facilities, there exists a strategyproof mechanism with approximation ratio at most* $9/2$.

Proof. First, by Theorem 2, with $Y = 0$ (as we are in the max-variant setting), for any valid parameters ℓ and r that satisfy the inequality $\lceil \ell m \rceil < \lceil rm \rceil$, the upper bound on the approximation ratio achieved by mechanism $\mathcal{M}_m(\theta, \ell, r)$ can be simplified to

$$\max\left\{\frac{n}{(m+1-\lceil \ell m\rceil)(\frac{n}{m}+1-\lceil\frac{\theta n}{m}\rceil)} - 1, \frac{n}{(m+1-\lceil rm\rceil)(\frac{n}{m}+1-\lceil\frac{\theta n}{m}\rceil)}, \frac{n}{\lceil rm\rceil\lceil\frac{\theta n}{m}\rceil} - 1, \frac{n}{\lceil \ell m\rceil\lceil\frac{\theta n}{m}\rceil}\right\}$$
$$= \max\left\{\frac{n}{(m+1-\lceil rm\rceil)(\frac{n}{m}+1-\lceil\frac{\theta n}{m}\rceil)}, \frac{n}{\lceil \ell m\rceil\lceil\frac{\theta n}{m}\rceil}\right\}.$$

For any even number $m \geq 2$ of groups, we run mechanism $\mathcal{M}_m(1/2, 1/2, 1/2+\varepsilon)$ for a sufficiently small $\varepsilon > 0$. This mechanism opens the facilities at the two median representative locations in Phase 2. The approximation ratio is at most

$$\max\left\{\frac{n}{(m+1-\lceil(\frac{1}{2}+\varepsilon)m\rceil)(\frac{n}{m}+1-\lceil\frac{n}{2m}\rceil)}, \frac{n}{\lceil\frac{m}{2}\rceil\lceil\frac{n}{2m}\rceil}\right\}$$
$$\leq \max\left\{\frac{2n}{m(\frac{n}{m}+1-\lceil\frac{n}{2m}\rceil)}, \frac{2n}{m\lceil\frac{n}{2m}\rceil}\right\} = 4.$$

For any odd number $m \geq 3$ of groups, we run mechanism $\mathcal{M}_m(\frac{m-1}{2m}, \frac{m+1}{2m}, \frac{m+1}{2m} + \varepsilon)$ for a sufficiently small $\varepsilon > 0$. This mechanism opens the facilities at the median representative and the representative directly to its right. The approximation ratio is now at most

$$\max\left\{\frac{n}{(m+1-\lceil(\frac{m+1}{2m}+\varepsilon)m\rceil)(\frac{n}{m}+1-\lceil\frac{n(m-1)}{2m^2}\rceil)}, \frac{n}{\lceil\frac{m+1}{2m}m\rceil\lceil\frac{n(m-1)}{2m^2}\rceil}\right\}$$
$$\leq \max\left\{\frac{2n}{(m-1)(\frac{n}{m}+1-\lceil\frac{n(m-1)}{2m^2}\rceil)}, \frac{2n}{(m+1)\lceil\frac{n(m-1)}{2m^2}\rceil}\right\} \leq \frac{4m^2}{m^2 - -1} \leq \frac{9}{2}.$$

The proof is now complete. □

We complement the above positive result with a tight lower bound of 9/2 on the approximation ratio of any strategyproof mechanism for two facilities in the max-variant. Our construction uses instances with three groups of agents. We should remark at this point that, from the proof of Theorem 5, it follows that we can achieve a better upper bound of 4 when the number of groups is even (in the next section we will actually argue that 4 is the best possible bound over all unrestricted algorithms in the max-variant), so the worst-case necessarily arises when there is an odd number of groups.

Theorem 6. *In the max-variant, for $k = 2$ facilities, the approximation ratio of any strategyproof mechanism is at least* 9/2.

5 Unrestricted Algorithms for Two Facilities

Here we focus on unrestricted algorithms. In the sum-variant, as already mentioned in Sect. 4.1, the lower bound of $1 + \sqrt{2}$ holds even for non-strategyproof mechanisms, implying that $1 + \sqrt{2}$ is the best possible approximation ratio over any algorithm in this setting. In the max-variant, we will show a tight bound of 4. As briefly discussed in Sect. 4.2, the proof of Theorem 5 implies that our strategyproof mechanism achieves this upper bound when the number m of groups is even. The lower bound is implied by Theorem 11 for $k = 2$ which is presented in Sect. 6 and holds for any unrestricted algorithm. So, it suffices to focus on the case of odd m, and show an upper bound of 4; actually, we will show an improved bound of 7/2.

We consider the following algorithm $\mathcal{A}^*_{\text{max}}$ (see Algorithm 2 for a description using pseudocode): In Phase 1, for each group, the algorithm picks the leftmost median agent as the group's representative. In Phase 2, it opens the facilities at the median representative and the representative closest to it.

Algorithm 2: $\mathcal{A}^*_{\text{max}}$

```
Input: Instance I = (x, G, 2);
Output: Facility locations w = (w_1, w_2);
Rep ← ∅;
for each group g ∈ G do
    i_g ← ⌈n_g/2⌉-leftmost agent in g;
    r_g ← x_{i_g};
    Rep ← Rep ∪ {r_g};
w_1 ← ⌈m/2⌉-leftmost location in Rep;
w_2 ← arg min_{r∈Rep\{w_1}} d(r, w_1);
```

Before bounding its approximation ratio, we present a simple instance with three groups showing that $\mathcal{A}^*_{\text{max}}$ is not strategyproof. The first group consists of an agent at 0 and an agent at 0.1, the second group consists of two agents at 0.51, and the third group consists of two agents at 1. Since each group is of size 2, its representative is the position of the leftmost agent therein; so, the representatives are 0, 0.51 and 1. The two facilities are opened at 0.51 (the median representative) and at 1 (the representative closest to the median one). Observe that the agent at 0 in the first group (whose position is selected as that group's representative) has cost 1. By misreporting her position as 0.1, the representative location of the first group becomes 0.1 which is closer to 0.51 than 1 is, and thus the facilities are opened at 0.1 and 0.51. This decreases the cost of the deviating agent from 1 to 0.51, proving that the algorithm is not strategyproof.

We now focus on showing an upper bound of 7/2 on the approximation ratio of the algorithm for odd m.

Theorem 7. *In the max-variant, for $k = 2$ facilities and odd number m of groups, the approximation ratio of algorithm $\mathcal{A}^*_{\max}$ is at most 7/2.*

6 Mechanisms for $k \geq 3$ Facilities

We now turn our attention to the case of more than two facilities. We show that the approximation ratio of strategyproof mechanisms is between $3-2/k$ and $3+2/k$ in the sum-variant, and between $2k$ and $2(k+1)$ in the max-variant; our lower bounds hold even for non-strategyproof algorithms. Our upper bounds follow by mechanisms that are generalizations of the mechanism $\mathcal{M}_m(\theta, \ell, r)$ which was used for the case of $k = 2$ facilities in previous sections: They first choose the group representative locations according to the ordering of the agents in the groups, and then choose the final facility locations according to the ordering of the representatives. Because of this structure, the proof of Theorem 1 can be extended to show that these mechanisms are also strategyproof. Moreover, the same symmetric-group reduction used for Lemma 1 applies, so it suffices to consider instances with symmetric groups to bound their approximation ratio.

6.1 Sum-Variant

We start with the sum-variant and first show the upper bound of $3 + 2/k$. Our mechanism $\mathcal{M}_k^{\text{sum}}$ works as follows: In Phase 1, for each group g, it selects the position of the (leftmost) median agent therein as g's representative. In Phase 2, the mechanism opens the facilities at the $\lceil \frac{\ell m}{k+1} \rceil$-leftmost representative location, for any $\ell \in [k]$; observe that $\lceil \frac{\ell m}{k+1} \rceil < \lceil \frac{(\ell+1)m}{k+1} \rceil$, and hence the computed solution is feasible. See Mechanism 3 for a description using pseudocode.

Mechanism 3: $\mathcal{M}_k^{\text{sum}}$

Input: Instance $I = (\mathbf{x}, G, k)$;
Output: Facility locations $\mathbf{w} = (w_\ell)_{\ell \in [k]}$;
$\texttt{Rep} \leftarrow \varnothing$;
for *each group* $g \in G$ **do**
  $i_g \leftarrow \lceil n_g/2 \rceil$-leftmost agent in g;
  $r_g \leftarrow x_{i_g}$;
  $\texttt{Rep} \leftarrow \texttt{Rep} \cup \{r_g\}$;
for *each* $\ell \in [k]$ **do**
  $w_\ell \leftarrow \lceil \frac{\ell m}{k+1} \rceil$-leftmost location in Rep;

We now present the bound on the approximation ratio of the mechanism.

Theorem 8. *In the sum-variant, for $k \geq 3$ facilities, the approximation ratio of mechanism $\mathcal{M}_k^{sum}$ is at most $3 + 2/k$.*

Proof. First, recall that it suffices to consider only instances with m symmetric groups, i.e., $n_g = n/m$ for any group g. We also assume without loss of generality that m is a multiple of $k+1$.[1] Let $\mathbf{w} = (w_1, \ldots, w_k)$ be the solution computed by the mechanism, and denote by $\texttt{med}$ the position of the overall median agent. For simplicity, also let $w_0 = -\infty$ and $w_{k+1} = +\infty$. Define the sets $L = \{\ell \in [k] : w_\ell \leq \texttt{med}\}$ and $R = \{\ell \in [k] : w_\ell > \texttt{med}\}$. Clearly, L and R define a partition of $[k]$. In addition, for any $\ell \in \{2, \ldots, k\}$, if $\ell \in L$, then $\ell - 1 \in L$, and, similarly, for any $\ell \in \{1, \ldots, k-1\}$, if $\ell \in R$, then $\ell + 1 \in R$. Note that it might be the case that L or R is empty in case $\texttt{med}$ is to the left or to the right of all representative locations that are included in the solution $\mathbf{w}$, respectively.

For any $\ell \in L$, let $S_\ell = \{i \in g : r_g \in (w_{\ell-1}, w_\ell] \wedge x_i \leq r_g\}$ be the set of agents in groups g with representative $r_g \in (w_{\ell-1}, w_\ell]$ with positions weakly to the left of r_g. Similarly, for any $\ell \in R$, let $S_\ell = \{i \in g : r_g \in [w_\ell, w_{\ell+1}) \wedge x_i \geq r_g\}$ be the set of agents in groups g with representative $r_g \in [w_\ell, w_{\ell+1})$ with positions weakly to the right of r_g. By definition, these sets are disjoint. Since for any group g, r_g is the position of the median agent in g, and since there are at least $\frac{m}{k+1}$ group representatives between any two representatives in $\mathbf{w}$ (and also to the left of w_1, i.e., between w_0 and w_1, and to the right of w_k, i.e., between w_k and w_{k+1}), we have that $n_\ell := |S_\ell| \geq \frac{m}{k+1} \cdot \frac{n}{2m} = \frac{n}{2(k+1)}$ for any $\ell \in [k]$.

[1] Observe that for any instance I where m is not a multiple of $k+1$, there is another instance J consisting of $k+1$ copies of each group in I, for which the solution computed by the mechanism is clearly the same (since the representatives are chosen according to equidistant quantiles). In addition, the position of the median agent is the same in I and J since each agent has been copied the same number of times.

Now, using the triangle inequality, the social cost of $\mathbf{w}$ is

$$\begin{aligned}
\text{SC}(\mathbf{w}) &= \sum_{i\in N}\sum_{\ell=1}^{k} d(i, w_\ell) \\
&\leq \sum_{i\in N}\sum_{\ell=1}^{k} \Big(d(i, \texttt{med}) + d(\texttt{med}, w_\ell) \Big) \\
&= k \cdot \sum_{i\in N} d(i, \texttt{med}) + n \cdot \sum_{\ell=1}^{k} d(\texttt{med}, w_\ell). \qquad (1)
\end{aligned}$$

For the optimal social cost, since an agent in S_ℓ needs to travel the distance $d(\texttt{med}, w_\ell)$ to reach from her position to $\texttt{med}$ (note that $x_i \leq r_g \leq w_\ell \leq \texttt{med}$ for $\ell \in L$ and $x_i \geq r_g \geq w_\ell \geq \texttt{med}$ for $\ell \in R$), we have

$$\begin{aligned}
\text{SC}(\mathbf{o}) &\geq k \cdot \sum_{i\in N} d(i, \texttt{med}) \qquad (2) \\
&\geq k \cdot \sum_{\ell=1}^{k}\sum_{i\in S_\ell} d(\texttt{med}, w_\ell) \\
&= k \cdot \sum_{\ell=1}^{k} n_\ell \cdot d(\texttt{med}, w_\ell) \\
&\geq \frac{kn}{2(k+1)} \cdot \sum_{\ell=1}^{k} d(\texttt{med}, w_\ell). \qquad (3)
\end{aligned}$$

Using (2) and (3), (1) gives us that

$$\text{SC}(\mathbf{w}) \leq \text{SC}(\mathbf{o}) + \frac{2(k+1)}{k} \cdot \text{SC}(\mathbf{o}) = \left(3 + \frac{2}{k}\right) \cdot \text{SC}(\mathbf{o}),$$

and the proof is complete. □

Next, we show a lower bound of $3 - 2/k$ on the approximation ratio of any unrestricted algorithm. Combined with the above upper bound, these two results leave a small gap for any $k \geq 3$, which, however, becomes nearly 0 when the number k of facilities is rather large.

Theorem 9. *In the sum-variant, for $k \geq 3$ facilities, the approximation ratio of any algorithm is at least $3 - 2/k$.*

Proof. Without loss of generality, assume that in a group with one agent at 0 and another agent at 1, the algorithm selects 0 as the group's representative. Then, consider an instance with k groups such that the first group has an agent at 0 and another agent at 1, whereas the remaining $k-1$ groups have both agents at 1. The algorithm has no choice but to open a facility at 0 and $k-1$ facilities at 1 for a social cost of $\text{SC}(\mathbf{w}) = 3k - 2$. However, the optimal solution is to open all k facilities at 1 for a social cost of $\text{SC}(\mathbf{o}) = k$, and the claim follows. □

6.2 Max-Variant

We now consider the max-variant and again start by showing the upper bound. Our mechanism $\mathcal{M}_k^{\max}$ works as follows: In Phase 1, for each group g, it selects the position of the (leftmost) median agent therein as g's representative. In Phase 2, the mechanism opens the facilities at the k most central representative locations, i.e., at the $(\lceil \frac{m}{2} \rceil + \ell)$-leftmost representative for $\ell \in \{-(\lceil \frac{k}{2} \rceil - 1), \dots, 0, \dots, \lfloor \frac{k}{2} \rfloor\}$. See Mechanism 4 for a description using pseudocode.

Mechanism 4: $\mathcal{M}_k^{\max}$

```
Input: Instance I = (x, G, k) ;
Output: Facility locations w = (w_ℓ)_{ℓ∈[k]};
Rep ← ∅;
for each group g ∈ G do
    i_g ← ⌈n_g/2⌉-leftmost agent in g;
    r_g ← x_{i_g};
    Rep ← Rep ∪ {r_g};
for each ℓ ∈ [k] do
    w_ℓ ← (⌈m/2⌉ + ℓ − ⌈k/2⌉)-leftmost location in Rep;
```

Theorem 10. *In the max-variant, for $k \geq 3$ facilities, the approximation ratio of mechanism $\mathcal{M}_k^{max}$ is at most $2(k+1)$.*

Finally, we show a lower bound of $2k$ for any unrestricted algorithm, which holds even for $k = 2$. Overall, this implies that 4 is the best possible approximation ratio over unrestricted algorithms for $k = 2$ (but not over strategyproof mechanisms, for which the bound is $9/2$), and mechanism $\mathcal{M}_k^{\max}$ is asymptotically best possible for large k.

Theorem 11. *In the max-variant, for $k \geq 2$ facilities, the approximation ratio of any algorithm is at least $2k$.*

Proof. Let g be a group with one agent at 0 and one agent at 1. Due to symmetry, suppose without loss of generality that the algorithm selects 0 as the representative of g. Consider an instance with g and another $k-1$ groups consisting of two agents at 1. Clearly, 1 is the representative of each of the last $k-1$ groups, and the facilities are therefore opened at 0 and 1. Then, $\text{SC}(\mathbf{w}) = 2k$. However, the optimal solution is to open all k facilities at 1 for a social cost of 1, leading to an approximation ratio of $2k$. □

7 Conclusion and Open Questions

In this work, we considered a truthful distributed facility location model where the goal is to open $k \geq 2$ facilities at locations chosen from the agent positions which are locally reported within their groups. We showed bounds on the best possible approximation ratio of strategyproof mechanisms in both the sum-variant (where the individual cost of an agent is the total distance to all facilities) and the max-variant (where the individual cost is the distance to the farthest facility). Our bounds are tight for $k = 2$ facilities in both variants, but there are small gaps for $k \geq 3$ facilities, which appear to be quite challenging to close.

There are several other future directions for extending our results and model. Our investigation of deterministic strategyproof mechanisms turned out to be quite rich and led to small and mostly tight bounds, but it would also be interesting to investigate whether randomized mechanisms can lead to significantly better approximation bounds. In addition, one can consider alternative modeling assumptions, by changing the social objective or the individual cost definition. For example, one can study alternative objectives such as the sum-of-max or max-of-sum, which have been considered in several other distributed social choice models [4, 7, 23, 43, 47]. The individual cost could alternatively be defined as the distance from the q-th closest facility for $q \in [k]$ (note that the max-variant corresponds to the case $q = k$), similarly to previous work on the distortion of metric multiwinner voting [10], peer selection [12], and sortition [20]. Finally, another direction could be to consider models with (possibly inaccurate) predictions about, for example, the optimal facility location or the agent positions, following the learning-augmented framework [2, 9, 16, 17, 21].

References

1. Abam, M.A., Kareshki, D., Nilipour, M., Paydar, M.H., Seddighin, M.: Tight bounds on the distortion of randomized and deterministic distributed voting. In: Proceedings of the 39th Annual Conference on Neural Information Processing Systems (NeurIPS) (2025)
2. Agrawal, P., Balkanski, E., Gkatzelis, V., Ou, T., Tan, X.: Learning-augmented mechanism design: leveraging predictions for facility location. Math. Oper. Res. **49**(4), 2626–2651 (2024)
3. Alon, N., Fischer, F.A., Procaccia, A.D., Tennenholtz, M.: Sum of Us: strategyproof selection from the selectors. In: Proceedings of the 13th Conference on Theoretical Aspects of Rationality and Knowledge (TARK), pp. 101–110 (2011)
4. Amanatidis, G., Anshelevich, E., Jerrett, C., Voudouris, A.A.: Metric distortion under group-fair objectives. In: Proceedings of the 18th International Symposium on Algorithmic Game Theory (SAGT), pp. 465–482 (2025)
5. Anshelevich, E., Bhardwaj, O., Elkind, E., Postl, J., Skowron, P.: Approximating optimal social choice under metric preferences. Artif. Intell. **264**, 27–51 (2018)
6. Anshelevich, E., Filos-Ratsikas, A., Shah, N., Voudouris, A.A.: Distortion in social choice problems: the first 15 years and beyond. In: Proceedings of the 30th International Joint Conference on Artificial Intelligence (IJCAI), pp. 4294–4301 (2021)

7. Anshelevich, E., Filos-Ratsikas, A., Voudouris, A.A.: The distortion of distributed metric social choice. Artif. Intell. **308**, 103713 (2022)
8. Anshelevich, E., Postl, J.: Randomized social choice functions under metric preferences. J. Artif. Intell. Res. **58**, 797–827 (2017)
9. Balkanski, E., Gkatzelis, V., Shahkarami, G.: Randomized strategic facility location with predictions. In: Proceedings of the 38th Annual Conference on Neural Information Processing Systems (NeurIPS) (2024)
10. Caragiannis, I., Shah, N., Voudouris, A.A.: The metric distortion of multiwinner voting. Artif. Intell. **313**, 103802 (2022)
11. Cembrano, J., Fischer, F.A., Klimm, M.: Improved bounds for single-nomination impartial selection. In: Proceedings of the 24th ACM Conference on Economics and Computation (EC), p. 449 (2023)
12. Cembrano, J., Shahkarami, G.: Metric distortion in peer selection. CORR arxiv:abs/2502.21084 (2025)
13. Chan, H., Filos-Ratsikas, A., Li, B., Li, M., Wang, C.: Mechanism design for facility location problems: a survey. In: Proceedings of the Thirtieth International Joint Conference on Artificial Intelligence (IJCAI), pp. 4356–4365 (2021)
14. Cheng, Y., Dughmi, S., Kempe, D.: Of the people: voting is more effective with representative candidates. In: Proceedings of the 2017 ACM Conference on Economics and Computation (EC), pp. 305–322 (2017)
15. Cheng, Y., Dughmi, S., Kempe, D.: On the distortion of voting with multiple representative candidates. In: Proceedings of the 32nd AAAI Conference on Artificial Intelligence (AAAI), pp. 973–980 (2018)
16. Christodoulou, G., Sgouritsa, A., Vlachos, I.: Mechanism design augmented with output advice. In: Proceedings of the 38th Annual Conference on Neural Information Processing Systems (NeurIPS) (2024)
17. Deligkas, A., Eiben, E., Klumper, S., Schäfer, G., Tsikiridis, A.: Mechanism design with outliers and predictions. CORR arxiv:abs/2509.09561 (2025)
18. Deligkas, A., Lotfi, M., Voudouris, A.A.: Agent-constrained truthful facility location games. J. Comb. Optim. **49**(2), 24 (2025)
19. Duan, L., Gong, Z., Li, M., Wang, C., Wu, X.: Facility location with fractional preferences and minimum distance. In: Proceedings of the 27th International Conference on Computing and Combinatorics (COCOON), pp. 499–511 (2021)
20. Ebadian, S., Kehne, G., Micha, E., Procaccia, A.D., Shah, N.: Is sortition both representative and fair? In: Proceedings of the 36th Annual Conference on Neural Information Processing Systems (NeurIPS) (2022)
21. Fang, J., Fang, Q., Liu, W., Nong, Q., Voudouris, A.A.: Mechanism design with predictions for facility location games with candidate locations. J. Comb. Optim. **49**(5), 74 (2025)
22. Feldman, M., Fiat, A., Golomb, I.: On voting and facility location. In: Proceedings of the 2016 ACM Conference on Economics and Computation (EC), pp. 269–286 (2016)
23. Filos-Ratsikas, A., Kanellopoulos, P., Voudouris, A.A., Zhang, R.: The distortion of distributed facility location. Artif. Intell. **328**, 104066 (2024)
24. Filos-Ratsikas, A., Micha, E., Voudouris, A.A.: The distortion of distributed voting. Artif. Intell. **286**, 103343 (2020)
25. Fischer, F.A., Klimm, M.: Optimal impartial selection. SIAM J. Comput. **44**(5), 1263–1285 (2015)
26. Fotakis, D., Gourvès, L., Monnot, J.: Conference program design with single-peaked and single-crossing preferences. In: Proceedings of the 12th International Conference on Web and Internet Economics (WINE), pp. 221–235 (2016)

27. Fotakis, D., Tzamos, C.: On the power of deterministic mechanisms for facility location games. ACM Trans. Econ. Comput. **2**(4), 15:1–15:37 (2014)
28. Gai, L., Liang, M., Wang, C.: Obnoxious facility location games with candidate locations. In: Proceedings of the 16th International Conference Algorithmic Aspects in Information and Management (AAIM), vol. 13513, pp. 96–105 (2022)
29. Gai, L., Liang, M., Wang, C.: Two-facility-location games with mixed types of agents. Appl. Math. Comput. **466**, 128479 (2024)
30. Gkatzelis, V., Halpern, D., Shah, N.: Resolving the optimal metric distortion conjecture. In: Proceedings of the 61st IEEE Annual Symposium on Foundations of Computer Science (FOCS), pp. 1427–1438 (2020)
31. Kanellopoulos, P., Voudouris, A.A.: Constrained truthful obnoxious two-facility location with optional preferences. Algorithmica **88**, 42 (2026)
32. Kanellopoulos, P., Voudouris, A.A., Zhang, R.: On discrete truthful heterogeneous two-facility location. SIAM J. Discret. Math. **37**, 779–799 (2023)
33. Kanellopoulos, P., Voudouris, A.A., Zhang, R.: Truthful two-facility location with candidate locations. Theoret. Comput. Sci. **1024**, 114913 (2025)
34. Kizilkaya, F.E., Kempe, D.: Plurality veto: a simple voting rule achieving optimal metric distortion. In: Proceedings of the 31st International Joint Conference on Artificial Intelligence (IJCAI), pp. 349–355 (2022)
35. Li, J., Li, M., Chan, H.: Strategyproof mechanisms for group-fair obnoxious facility location problems. In: Proceedings of the 38th AAAI Conference on Artificial Intelligence (AAAI). pp. 9832–9839 (2024)
36. Li, M., Peng, C., Wang, Y., Zhou, H.: Group-fair facility location games with externalities. In: Proceedings of the 24th International Conference on Autonomous Agents and Multiagent Systems (AAMAS), pp. 2615–2617 (2025)
37. Lotfi, M., Voudouris, A.A.: On truthful constrained heterogeneous facility location with max-variant cost. Oper. Res. Lett. **52**, 107060 (2024)
38. Lu, P., Sun, X., Wang, Y., Zhu, Z.A.: Asymptotically optimal strategy-proof mechanisms for two-facility games. In: Proceedings of the 11th ACM Conference on Electronic Commerce (EC), pp. 315–324 (2010)
39. Procaccia, A.D., Tennenholtz, M.: Approximate mechanism design without money. ACM Tran. Econ. Comput. **1**(4), 18:1–18:26 (2013)
40. Serafino, P., Ventre, C.: Heterogeneous facility location without money. Theoret. Comput. Sci. **636**, 27–46 (2016)
41. Sui, X., Boutilier, C.: Approximately strategy-proof mechanisms for (constrained) facility location. In: Proceedings of the 2015 International Conference on Autonomous Agents and Multiagent Systems (AAMAS), pp. 605–613 (2015)
42. Tang, Z., Wang, C., Zhang, M., Zhao, Y.: Mechanism design for facility location games with candidate locations. In: Proceedings of the 14th International Conference on Combinatorial Optimization and Applications (COCOA), pp. 440–452 (2020)
43. Voudouris, A.A.: Tight distortion bounds for distributed metric voting on a line. Oper. Res. Lett. **51**(3), 266–269 (2023)
44. Voudouris, A.A.: Metric distortion of obnoxious distributed voting. Inf. Process. Lett. **189**, 106559 (2025)
45. Walsh, T.: Strategy proof mechanisms for facility location at limited locations. In: Proceedings of the 8th Pacific Rim International Conference on Artificial Intelligence (PRICAI), pp. 113–124 (2021)
46. Xu, X., Li, B., Li, M., Duan, L.: Two-facility location games with minimum distance requirement. J. Artif. Intell. Res. **70**, 719–756 (2021)

47. Xu, X., Liu, W., Fang, Q.: Constrained distributed heterogeneous two-facility location problems with max-variant cost. In: Proceedings of the 19th Annual Conference on Theory and Applications of Models of Computation (TAMC), pp. 121–134 (2025)
48. Zhao, Q., Liu, W., Nong, Q., Fang, Q.: Constrained heterogeneous facility location games with max-variant cost. J. Comb. Optim. **45**(3), 90 (2023)
49. Zhao, Q., Liu, W., Nong, Q., Fang, Q.: Constrained heterogeneous two-facility location games with sum-variant. J. Comb. Optim. **47**(4), 65 (2024)
50. Zhou, H., Li, M., Chan, H.: Strategyproof mechanisms for group-fair facility location problems. In: Proceedings of the 31st International Joint Conference on Artificial Intelligence (IJCAI), pp. 613–619 (2022)

Nucleolus Computation by Non-Zero-Constrained Optimization

Daniel Ebert([✉]) and Antonia Ellerbrock

Research Institute for Discrete Mathematics, University of Bonn, Bonn, Germany
{ebert,ellerbrock}@dm.uni-bonn.de

Abstract. We extend the list of games where the nucleolus is computable in polynomial time. Based on the classical MPS scheme, nucleolus computation can be reduced to the problem of finding a coalition with minimum excess that does not belong to a given linear subspace. We call this problem LSA-MinExcess, and show that it is equivalent to NZ-MinExcess: Given integral values per player, find a coalition with minimum excess whose player values do not sum up to 0. Exploiting this representation, we prove that the nucleolus is computable in polynomial time for arboricity games, network strength games, and certain b-matching games. Along these lines, we show that for b-matching games with $b \leq 2$, LSA-MinExcess is polynomially equivalent to Shortest Non-Zero Cycle. Further, we prove that in general, linear subspace avoidance strictly increases the complexity of the minimum excess problem, even for monotone games. We still provide a reduction that trades linear subspace avoidance against an arbitrarily small approximation error. Finally, we show that the nucleolus is unstable in the following sense: A small change in the value function of the game can lead to a change in the nucleolus that is exponential in the number of players.

1 Introduction

A *cooperative game* is a pair (P, v) of a finite set of *players* P and a value function $v : 2^P \to \mathbb{R}$ on *coalitions* $S \subseteq P$ with $v(\emptyset) = 0$. (P, v) is called *monotone* if $v(S) \leq v(T)$ for all $S \subseteq T \subseteq P$, and *superadditive* if $v(S \cup T) \geq v(S) + v(T)$ for all $S, T \subseteq P$. Usually, v is not given explicitly, but by some combinatorial optimization problem, e.g., as the maximum weight of a matching in the subgraph $G[S]$ of some weighted graph G for $S \subseteq P$ [8]. Such an input (e.g. a weighted graph) defines the *encoding* of the game (P, v), whose size is typically polynomial in $|P|$. Given a cooperative game (P, v), a *cost allocation* is a vector $y \in \mathbb{R}^P$. We will write $y(S) := \sum_{p \in S} y_p$ for $S \subseteq P$. The *nucleolus* by Schmeidler [32] defines a unique and supposedly fair cost allocation. For a formal definiton, let $y \in \mathbb{R}^P$, and consider the excess vector $\theta(y)$ that contains all coalitional *excess* values $(y(S) - v(S))_{S \subseteq P}$ in non-decreasing order. The *nucleolus* is the unique cost allocation that lexicographically maximizes the excess vector $\theta(y)$ among all $y \in \mathbb{R}^P$ with $y(P) = v(P)$ and $y(\{p\}) \geq v(\{p\})$ for all $p \in P$.

P. Lenzner and D. Schmand (Eds.): SAGT 2026, LNCS 16911, pp. 151–168, 2027.
https://doi.org/10.1007/978-3-032-38782-0_9

1.1 Our Results

We study the cost allocation concept of the nucleolus for cooperative games. Its computation can be reduced to separating over the polytopes in the classical Maschler-Peleg-Shapley (MPS) scheme: For a proposed cost allocation, we have to find a coalition with smallest excess that is not yet fixed. The latter requirement results in a linear subspace avoidance constraint. We show that linear subspace avoidance (LSA) is polynomially equivalent to requring a *non-zero* (NZ) coalition in the following sense: Given integral values per player, the total sum of these values in our coalition cannot be 0.

Proposition 1. *The problems* LSA-MINEXCESS *and* NZ-MINEXCESS *are polynomially equivalent.*

This representation proves to be extremely powerful. While linear subspace avoidance has not received much attention beyond applications in game theory, non-zero constraints have appeared in various fields. For example, we can make use of previous results about non-zero matroid basis computation [17] and non-zero submodular function minimization [15]. Thereby, we extend the list of games for which the nucleolus can be computed in polynomial time, and simplify existing proofs:

Theorem 1. *The nucleolus can be computed in polynomial time for*

- *b-matching games with $b \leq 2$, if $b = 2$ for only constantly many vertices,*
- *b-matching games with $b \leq 2$, if* SHORTEST NON-ZERO CYCLE *can be solved in polynomial time,*
- *arboricity games,*
- *network strength games.*

The SHORTEST NON-ZERO CYCLE problem is closely related to the SHORTEST ODD CYCLE problem, which is conjectured to be polynomially solvable [31]. Therefore, this seems like a promising approach to compute the nucleolus of general b-matching games with $b \leq 2$.

Beyond these applicational results, we study linear subspace avoidance from a more general perspective. It was known before that linear subspace avoidance constraints strictly increase the complexity of minimum excess problems in general, unless P = NP [21]. The reduction relies on a non-monotone game. We show that the same complexity increase occurs for the class of monotone games, even if P = NP. On the positive side, we provide a polynomial-time reduction from LSA-MINEXCESS to MINEXCESS that trades the linear subspace avoidance constraints against an arbitrarily small approximation error. Unfortunately, such an error might propagate exponentially in the MPS scheme. The nucleolus defines a continuous mapping based on the value function of a coooperative game [32]. We show that this mapping is generally unstable, even when restricting to monotone and superadditive games, in the following sense:

Theorem 8. *Let $n \in \mathbb{N}$ and $\varepsilon > 0$. There are monotone, superadditive games (P, v) and $(P, \tilde{v})$ with $|P| = O(n)$ such that $|v(S) - \tilde{v}(S)| \leq \varepsilon$ for all $S \subseteq P$ but the nucleoli of (P, v) and $(P, \tilde{v})$ differ by $2^n \cdot \varepsilon$ for some players.*

Some proofs are omitted in this version and can be found in the full version [10]. This concerns Theorem 2 to 4, 6 and 8 Lemma 2.

1.2 Related Work

Since its definition by Schmeidler in 1969 [32], the nucleolus and its computability have received much attention in the context of cooperative game theory. The first positive result, i.e., an algorithm that computes the nucleolus in polynomial time, was attained by Littlechild [25] for minimum cost spanning tree games on line graphs. More games followed, e.g., convex games [14] and spanning connectivity games [4]. On the other hand, the first negative result, i.e., a proof of NP-hardness of nucleolus computation, was attained by Faigle, Kern, and Kuipers [13] for general minimum cost spanning tree games. Over the years, both lists have grown and are still extended.

We contribute positive results for arboricity games, network strength games, and certain b-matching games. For both arboricity and network strength games, the nucleolus was previously known to be computable in polynomial time in case of a non-empty core due to Xiao and Fang [35] and Baïou and Barahona [5], respectively. We will show that the same is possible for all instances, while simultaneously simplifying the proofs. Note that moving from instances with non-empty core to general instances is often non-trivial [6,20,30]. For b-matching games, nucleolus computation was shown to be NP-hard by Könemann, Toth, and Zhou [22], even for bipartite graphs and $b \leq 3$. The general case of $b \leq 2$ is still open. Certain special cases were solved in [22]. We will provide a detailed overview over past work in Section 3.1.

Next to results for specific games, there are also structural findings such as the MPS scheme for nucleolus computation by Kopelowitz [23] and Maschler, Peleg, and Shapley [26], and a framework by Könemann and Toth [21] that requires a certain structure of a game. Part of our work follows this line of research. We will provide a detailed discussion comparing our work with [21] in Section 2.3. Stability of the nucleolus has not been studied thoroughly, but an example of Kumabe and Yoshida [24] implies that changing the value function of a game by a constant may change the nucleolus by $\Omega(|P|)$. We show that this change can even be exponential in $|P|$.

Finally, we want to mention that all our results carry over to cooperative games defined by a *cost* function (instead of a *value* function), as well as related solution concepts which also lexicographically maximize the excess vector, but require a different total value $y(P)$ [2,6,12,27].

2 Nucleolus Computation by Constrained Optimization

In this section, we study separation over the polytopes of the classical Maschler-Peleg-Shapley (MPS) scheme for nucleolus computation, which gives rise to the following problem:

Problem 1. (*LSA*-MinExcess). Given a cooperative game (P, v), a cost allocation $y \in \mathbb{R}^P$, and a linear subspace $L \subsetneq \mathbb{R}^P$ (described by a basis), find a coalition $S \subseteq P$ with $S \notin L$ that minimizes $y(S) - v(S)$.

When writing $S \notin L$, we identify S with its incidence vector $\mathbb{1}_{\{p \in S\}} \in \mathbb{R}^P$. We show that linear subspace avoidance is equivalent to non-zero constraints:

Problem 2. (*NZ*-MinExcess). Given a cooperative game (P, v), a cost allocation $y \in \mathbb{R}^P$, and $a \in \mathbb{Z}^P$, find a coalition $S \subseteq P$ with $a(S) := \sum_{p \in S} a_p \neq 0$ that minimizes $y(S) - v(S)$.

We will compare this formulation to previous work by Könemann and Toth [21] that relied on congruency constraints, and show that the latter are strictly harder than linear subspace avoidance (and therefore also than non-zero constraints).

2.1 MPS Scheme

As shown by Maschler, Peleg, and Shapley [26], the nucleolus can be computed by solving a sequence of linear programs. An improved variant which needs at most a linear number of iterations was proposed by Solymosi [33], see Figure 1.

In order to apply this scheme, we need to be able to solve the linear program (LP). Except for the constraints

$$y(S) \geq v(S) + \xi \qquad \text{for } S \in 2^P \setminus \text{span}(\mathcal{S}_{\text{fixed}}) , \tag{1}$$

the LP has only a polynomial number of constraints and variables (note that $\mathcal{S}_{\text{fixed}}$ contains at most $|P|$ sets). Hence, if the constraints (1) can be separated (i.e., given an LP solution, find a violated constraint if it exists) in polynomial time, then we can also solve (LP) and its dual [16], and therefore compute the nucleolus. This motivates the following well-known result:

Proposition 1. *If we can solve* LSA-MinExcess *for a cooperative game (P, v) in polynomial time in the encoding size of (P, v), then the nucleolus of (P, v) can also be computed in polynomial time.* □

Step 1: Let $\mathcal{S}_{\text{fixed}} \leftarrow \emptyset$.

Step 2: Compute a pair of optimum primal and dual solutions $((\xi, y), z)$ to (LP), where $\text{span}(\mathcal{S}_{\text{fixed}})$ denotes the linear subspace of $\mathbb{R}^P$ generated by the incidence vectors of coalitions in $\mathcal{S}_{\text{fixed}}$.

$$
\begin{array}{llcll}
\max \ \xi & & & & \\
\text{s.t.} & y(S) & = & v(S) + \xi^*_S & \text{for } S \in \mathcal{S}_{\text{fixed}} \\
& y(S) & \geq & v(S) + \xi & \text{for } S \in 2^P \setminus \text{span}(\mathcal{S}_{\text{fixed}}) \\
& y(P) & = & v(P) & \\
& y(\{p\}) & \geq & v(\{p\}) & \text{for } p \in P \\
& \xi & \in & \mathbb{R} & \\
& y & \in & \mathbb{R}^P &
\end{array}
\tag{LP}
$$

Step 3: For each $S \in 2^P \setminus \text{span}(\mathcal{S}_{\text{fixed}})$ with $z_S \neq 0$, $\mathcal{S}_{\text{fixed}} \leftarrow \mathcal{S}_{\text{fixed}} \cup \{S\}$, $\xi^*_S \leftarrow \xi$.

Step 4: Repeat Steps 2 and 3 until $\text{span}(\mathcal{S}_{\text{fixed}}) = \mathbb{R}^P$. Return y.

Fig. 1. MPS scheme.

2.2 Introducing Non-Zero Constraints

We will reformulate linear subspace avoidance to a non-zero constraint, which we believe easier to handle and think about. Such a non-zero constraint already appeared in optimization outside of game theory [17,19,34], but was not connected to subspace avoidance so far.

Proposition 2. *The problems* LSA-MINEXCESS *and* NZ-MINEXCESS *are polynomially equivalent.*

Proof. For a vector $a \in \mathbb{Z}^P$ that is not 0 everywhere,

$$L \; = \; \text{span}(\{S \subseteq P \ : \ a(S) = 0\})$$

defines a proper linear subspace of $\mathbb{R}^P$, so finding a non-zero coalition is a special case of linear subspace avoidance, namely the special case of an $(n-1)$-dimensional linear subspace. Transforming L into basis representation can be done in polynomial time by Gaussian elimination.

Given a general linear subspace L, represented by a basis, this can be expressed by the null space of a matrix $A \in \mathbb{Q}^{k \times |P|}$, i.e.,

$$L \; = \; \{x \in \mathbb{R}^P \ : \ \langle a_i \, , \, x \rangle = 0 \quad \forall i = 1, \ldots, k\} \ ,$$

where a_i are the rows of A and $k = |P| - \dim L$. By scaling everything up, we can additionally require $a_i \in \mathbb{Z}^P$. It then suffices to compute a minimum-excess coalition $S_i \subseteq P$ with $a_i(S_i) \neq 0$ for all $i = 1, \ldots, k$, and choose the best one. The matrix A can be computed in polynomial time by Gaussian elimination. □

2.3 Congruency-Constrained Optimization

Könemann and Toth [21] also considered LSA-MinExcess to compute the nucleolus. They proved that it can be reduced to a congruency-constrained problem. Additionally, if an optimization problem can be solved via dynamic programming, then so can its congruency-constrained variant. We restate the first result here, since it will be useful for the proof of Theorem 3 in Section 3.1.

Lemma 1 (Könemann and Toth [21]). *Let M be a finite set, $f : 2^M \to \mathbb{R}$, and $L \subseteq \mathbb{R}^M$ a linear subspace (given by a basis). Then, $S \subseteq M$ with $S \notin L$ that maximizes $f(S)$ can be computed by solving a polynomial (in $|M|$) number of problems of the form*

$$\max\{f(S) \ : \ a(S) \equiv k \mod p\} \ ,$$

where p is a polynomially (in $|M|$) bounded prime, $a \in (\mathbb{Z}_p)^M$, and $k \in \mathbb{Z}_p$. □

We remark that the congruency constraint $a(S) \equiv k \mod p$ is in general more difficult to handle than the constraint $a(S) \neq 0$ of NZ-MinExcess: Given a matroid on a ground set E, $a \in \mathbb{Z}^E$, and a target number $k \in \mathbb{Z}$, finding a basis B of the matroid with $a(B) = k$ is not possible with a polynomial number of calls to an independence oracle, even if a and k are polynomially bounded [9]. In contrast, finding a basis B with $a(B) \neq 0$ can be done in oracle polynomial time [17]. In fact, the tractability of a similar non-zero-constrained matroid problem is the foundation for our results in Section 3.2.

This example shows that, while LSA-MinExcess and NZ-MinExcess are equivalent, the congruency-constrained variant of Könemann and Toth [21] is sometimes harder, even for monotone games. For this reason, we focus our attention on the NZ-MinExcess problem.

3 Application to Specific Classes of Games

In this section, we focus on LSA-MinExcess for specific classes of games. Our proofs rely on the equivalent formulation as NZ-MinExcess, cf. Lemma 1. Recall that if we can solve LSA-MinExcess in polynomial time, we can also compute the nucleolus in polynomial time by Proposition 1. Our positive results are summarized in Theorem 1, which is a consequence of Theorem 2,4 and 5.

Further, we can recover previous positive results on nucleolus computability: LSA-MinExcess is solvable in polynomial time for *convex games* and *spanning connectivity games*. For both, polynomial time computability of the nucleolus was known before, but derived differently. Convex games are characterized by a supermodular value function. We can solve NZ-MinExcess due to a result by Goemans and Ramakrishnan [15] on submodular functions, and the fact that non-zero coalitions constitute what they call a *parity family*. Spanning connectivity games [3] are based on the graphic matroid, and fall under Theorem 5. Figure 2 summarizes our findings.

	LSA-MinExcess	Nucleolus
Matching	**this paper**	known [20]
b-Matching, $b \leq 2$, $b = 2$ constantly often	**this paper**	**this paper**
Arboricity	**this paper**	**this paper**
Network Strength	**this paper**	**this paper**
Spanning Connectivity	**this paper**	known [4]
Convex	**this paper**	known [14]

Fig. 2. Games for which LSA-MinExcess and Nucleolus can be solved in polynomial time. Results of this paper are highlighted.

3.1 b-Matching Games

In the following part, we will study LSA-MinExcess for b-matching games:

Definition 1. *Let $G = (V, E)$ be an undirected graph with edge weights $w \in \mathbb{R}^E$ and vertex values $b \in \mathbb{N}^V$. The* b-matching game *associated with (G, w, b) is the value game (P, v) with $P := V$. For $S \subseteq V$,*

$$v(S) := \max\{w(M) : M \subseteq E(G[S]) , |\delta(v) \cap M| \leq b(v) \ \forall v \in V\}$$

is the maximum weight of a b-matching in the induced subgraph $G[S]$.

It is known that computing the nucleolus of b-matching games is NP-hard even for bipartite graphs and $b \leq 3$ [22]. Thus, we focus on $b \leq 2$, where the nucleolus is so far known to be computable in polynomial time for certain instances on bipartite graphs [22]. We show that LSA-MinExcess for b-matching games with $b \leq 2$ is equivalent to Shortest Non-Zero Cycle:

Problem 3. (Shortest Non-Zero Cycle). Given an undirected graph $G = (V, E)$ with conservative edge costs $c \in \mathbb{R}^E$ (i.e., no c-negative cycles) and $a \in \mathbb{Z}^E$, compute a cycle C with $a(C) \neq 0$ that minimizes $c(C)$.

This is closely related to Shortest Odd Cycle, where one asks for a cycle with odd (instead of non-zero) total value. In fact, both problems are a special case of a non-zero constraint in a commutative group, for the groups $\mathbb{Z}$ and $\mathbb{Z}_2$. Problems with a non-zero constraint in a group have been studied e.g. for shortest path [18,19] and matroid problems [17].

Schlotter and Sebö [31] showed that Shortest Odd Cycle is NP-hard if one additionally requires the cycle to contain a specified vertex. Their construction can trivially be adapted to show that the same is true for Shortest Non-Zero Cycle. However, the complexity of both problems without this constraint is still open. Schlotter and Sebö [31] conjecture that Shortest Odd Cycle can be solved in polynomial time. Their main reason for this is the fact that it can be solved in randomized polynomial time for polynomially bounded weights, which is also true for Shortest Non-Zero Cycle, see Theorem 3 and 2. Therefore, it seems likely that Shortest Non-Zero Cycle is solvable in polynomial time, which would immediately imply an algorithm to compute the nucleolus of general b-matching games with $b \leq 2$ in polynomial time.

Finally, we show that LSA-MinExcess for b-matching games with $b \leq 2$ can be solved in some new special cases. If the weights and cost allocation are polynomially bounded, then the problem can be solved in randomized polynomial time. Additionally, we show that it can be solved in polynomial time if $b = 2$ only for a constant number of vertices. For this class of games, the nucleolus was previously not known to be computable in polynomial time.

Problem 4. (Maximum Weight Non-Zero Matching). Given an undirected graph $G = (V, E)$ with edge weights $w \in \mathbb{R}^E$ and $a \in \mathbb{Z}^E$, compute a matching M with $a(M) \neq 0$ that maximizes $w(M)$.

Theorem 2. *The following problems are polynomially equivalent:*

(i) LSA-MinExcess *for b-matching games with* $b \leq 2$

(ii) Maximum Weight Non-Zero Matching

(iii) Shortest Non-Zero Cycle

Additionally, this equivalence also holds when restricting to instances with polynomially bounded weights. More precisely, we require w *and* y *(for problem (i)),* w *(for problem (ii)), and* c *(for problem (iii)) to be polynomially bounded.*

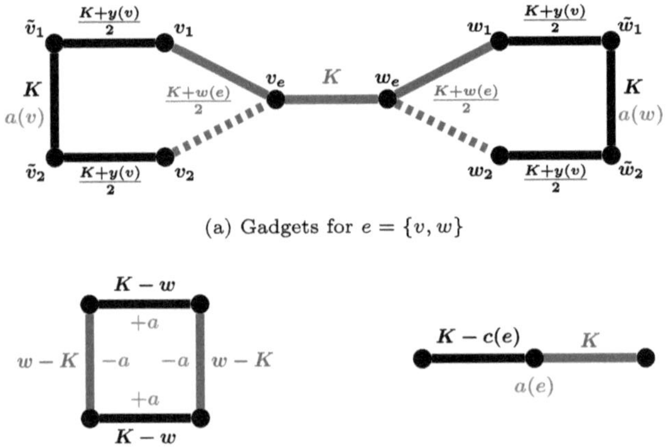

(a) Gadgets for $e = \{v, w\}$

(b) Augmenting cycle

(c) Gadget for e

Fig. 3. Reductions in the proof of Theorem 2.

We present the main ideas of the reductions in the following proof sketch.

Proof (sketch.). All reductions work with a sufficiently large constant $K \in \mathbb{R}_{\geq 0}$ that dominates the objective.

(a) Reducing (i) to (ii):
We create node and edge gadgets as illustrated in Figure 3 (a). A solution S to NZ-MinExcess with associated b-matching M corresponds to the matching in the constructed graph that contains all the edges $\{\tilde{v}_1, \tilde{v}_2\}$ for $v \in S$, the pairs of edges $\{v_1, \tilde{v}_1\}$, $\{v_2, \tilde{v}_2\}$ for $v \notin S$, one of the edges $\{v_i, v_e\}$, $i \in \{1, 2\}$, for every $e \in M$ and $v \in e$, and all the edges $\{v_e, w_e\}$ for $e = \{v, w\} \notin M$.

Note that every maximum weight (non-zero) matching in the constructed graph contains edges with total weight $\approx K$ in every node and edge gadget, which ensures that it corresponds to a coalition in the b-matching game.

(b) Reducing (ii) to (iii):
We start by computing a maximum weight matching $\overline{M}$. If $a(\overline{M}) \neq 0$, then it is an optimum solution, and we are done. Otherwise, $\overline{M} \Delta M^*$ can be decomposed into paths and cycles, where M^* is an optimum solution. By adding trivial edges, we can restrict to cycles.

Augmenting along these cycles can only decrease the weight, and at least one of them, say C, satisfies $a(C \cap \overline{M}) \neq a(C \cap M^*)$. It therefore suffices to find a shortest non-zero cycle in a modified graph, see Figure 3 (b). The same techniques were used in a slightly different context in [11].

(c) Reducing (iii) to (i):
We replace every edge e by a path of length 2 with an additional vertex v_e, setting $a(v_e) := a(e)$ and $a := 0$ for all other vertices, as shown in Figure 3 (c). One of the path edges gets a cost of $K - c(e)$, the other one a cost of K. By setting $b \equiv 2$ and $y \equiv K$, we can ensure that every optimum solution to NZ-MinExcess for the b-matching game corresponds to a set of disjoint cycles. Since c is conservative, only one of these cycles is non-trivial, and therefore an optimum solution to the Shortest Non-Zero Cycle problem. (□)

Theorem 3. LSA-MinExcess *for b-matching games with $b \leq 2$ can be solved in randomized polynomial time if w and y are polynomially bounded.*

This follows from Theorem 2 and the randomized exact matching algorithm by [28] applied to the congruency-constrained problem formulation by Könemann and Toth [21] described in Lemma 1.

Theorem 4. LSA-MinExcess *for b-matching games with $b \leq 2$ can be solved in polynomial time if $b(v) = 2$ only for a constant number of vertices v.*

We prove this based on the reductions from (i) to (iii) in the proof of Theorem 2, and a total enumeration argument.

3.2 Arboricity and Network Strength Games

Next, we will study games with an underlying matroid structure, and show how to solve LSA-MinExcess in polynomial time based on results by Hörsch et al. [17] on non-zero matroid bases. We will reduce to the following problem:

Problem 5. (Maximum Weight Non-Zero Independent Set).
Given a matroid $(E, \mathcal{F})$ (by a polynomial-time independence oracle), weights $w \in \mathbb{R}^E$, and $a \in \mathbb{Z}^E$, find $F \in \mathcal{F}$ with $a(F) \neq 0$ that maximizes $w(F)$.

Specifically, we will study *arboricity games* and *network strength games*:

Definition 2. *Let $G = (V, E)$ be an undirected graph and $P := E$. The* arboricity game *associated with G is the cost game (P, c), where for $S \subseteq E$,*

$$c(S) \ := \ \min\{k \ : \ S \textit{ can be covered by } k \textit{ forests}\} \ .$$

The network strength game *associated with G is the value game (P, v), where for $S \subseteq E$,*

$$v(S) \ := \ \max\{k \ : \ S \textit{ contains } k \textit{ disjoint spanning trees}\} \ .$$

For cost games, the nucleolus is defined analogously to value games, but the excess of a coalition $S \subseteq P$ is now given by $c(S) - y(S)$.

Theorem 5. *Consider a cooperative game for which* LSA-MinExcess *can be polynomially reduced to* Maximum Weight Non-Zero Independent Set. *Then,* LSA-MinExcess *can be solved in polynomial time.*

Especially, this holds for

(a) arboricity games,

(b) network strength games.

Proof. By a simple matroid basis exchange argument, a maximum weight non-zero basis can be computed in polynomial time for every matroid given by a polynomial-time independence oracle [17]. This immediately implies that we can also find a maximum weight non-zero independent set: Consider the k-truncation of $(E, \mathcal{F})$, i.e., the restriction to independent sets of size at most k, for every $1 \leq k \leq |E|$. This is again a matroid, and a polynomial-time independence oracle can easily be constructed. Thus, we can compute a maximum weight non-zero basis in polynomial time. Now every independent set of $(E, \mathcal{F})$ is a basis of some k-truncation, so we can simply choose the best computed solution. In total, we can solve Maximum Weight Non-Zero Independent Set in polynomial time. If LSA-MinExcess polynomially reduces to the latter, it can therefore also be solved in polynomial time. For the specific games, we will use the equivalence established in Lemma 1 and reduce NZ-MinExcess:

(a) Arboricity games:
Let (V, E) be an undirected graph, $y \in \mathbb{R}^E$, $a \in \mathbb{Z}^E$, and $k \in \mathbb{N}$. We will compute a coalition $S \subseteq E$ with $c(S) \leq k$ and $a(S) \neq 0$ that maximizes $y(S)$. Doing this for all $1 \leq k \leq |E|$ suffices to solve NZ-MinExcess.

Let $(E, \mathcal{F})$ be the k-fold sum of the graphic matroid on (V, E), i.e.,

$$\mathcal{F} := \{F \subseteq E \ : \ F \text{ can be partitioned into } k \text{ forests}\} \ .$$

By Nash-Williams [29], this is a matroid, and it has a polynomial-time independence oracle via matroid intersection. It suffices to solve Maximum Weight Non-Zero Independent Set with weights y over $\mathcal{F}$.

(b) Network strength games:
Let (V, E) be an undirected graph, $y \in \mathbb{R}^E$, $a \in \mathbb{Z}^E$, and $k \in \mathbb{N}$. Again, by enumerating all relevant values for k, NZ-MinExcess reduces to finding a set $S \subseteq E$ with $a(S) \neq 0$ that contains at least k disjoint spanning trees (i.e., $v(S) \geq k$) and minimizes $y(S)$. Without loss of generality, $a(E) = 0$, otherwise add a new edge e' such that $a(E \cup \{e'\}) = 0$ and $y(e')$ sufficiently large.

We define the matroid $(E, \mathcal{F})$ as before by

$$\mathcal{F} := \{F \subseteq E \ : \ F \text{ can be partitioned into } k \text{ forests}\} \ .$$

We can assume that the bases of $(E, \mathcal{F})$ are exactly the disjoint unions of k spanning trees, otherwise there is no coalition S with $v(S) \geq k$. Let $(E, \mathcal{F}^*)$ be the dual of $(E, \mathcal{F})$, i.e.,

$$\mathcal{F}^* := \{F \subseteq E \ : \ E \setminus F \text{ contains a basis of } (E, \mathcal{F})\} \ .$$

This is again a matroid with a polynomial-time independence oracle. Solving Maximum Weight Non-Zero Independent Set with weights y over $\mathcal{F}^*$ yields an independent set $F \in \mathcal{F}^*$ with $a(F) \neq 0$ and $y(F)$ maximum. Then, $E \setminus F$ contains k disjoint spanning trees, $a(E \setminus F) = -a(F) \neq 0$, and $y(E \setminus F)$ is minimum. So $S = E \setminus F$ is our wanted coalition. □

4 LSA-MinExcess for General Games

In this section, we study the hardness of linear subspace avoidance, that is, the complexity gap between LSA-MinExcess and MinExcess:

Problem 6. (MinExcess). Given a cooperative game (P, v) and a cost allocation $y \in \mathbb{R}^P$, find a coalition $S \subseteq P$ that minimizes $y(S) - v(S)$.

It was known before that for non-monotone games, linear subspace avoidance might increase complexity from polynomial-time solvability to NP-hardness [21].

We extend this result to monotone games, using completely new ideas. Then, we provide a reduction from LSA-MinExcess to MinExcess that incurs an arbitrarily small additive error in the approximation guarantee, which is the best we can hope for. Finally, we show that any such tiny error might propagate exponentially in the MPS scheme, so the reduction does not imply satisfying guarantees for approximate nucleolus computation. In fact, this leads to a general instability result for the nucleolus as a mapping of the value function of a cooperative game, even if we restrict to monotone and superadditive games.

4.1 Hardness of Linear Subspace Avoidance

For non-monotone games, linear subspace avoidance constraints can increase the complexity of MinExcess: Computing a shortest s_1-t_2-path in a directed graph is easy, but by forcing the inclusion of an artificial edge (t_1, s_2), subspace-avoidance constraints can encode the NP-hard Directed Two Disjoint Paths problem [21]. Note that the value function of this game is not monotone, as it must strictly distinguish feasible paths from s_1 to t_2. Further, for monotone games, enforcing a single player is easy: Simply set its y-value to 0 and add it to the result of MinExcess. Thus, we need new ideas for monotone games.

Theorem 6. *There exists no algorithm that solves* LSA-MinExcess *for a general monotone game* (P, v) *with at most* $|P|^{O(1)}$ *oracle calls to an oracle that solves* MinExcess.

4.2 Reducing LSA-MinExcess to MinExcess

In the following, we show how to approximate LSA-MinExcess for monotone games where MinExcess can be approximated. The reduction incurs an arbitrarily small additional error in the approximation guarantee. The intuitive notion of approximation, i.e., requiring a solution whose excess is at most α times the optimum excess, does not make much sense, since the optimum excess might well be zero or negative. Instead, we define:

Definition 3 (α-approximation). *Let $\mathcal{F}$ be a family of monotone cooperative games with non-negative value functions, and $\alpha \geq 1$. An α-*approximation algorithm *for* MinExcess *or* LSA-MinExcess *for $\mathcal{F}$ is an algorithm that, given $(P, v) \in \mathcal{F}$, $y \in \mathbb{R}^P_{\geq 0}$ and a linear subspace $L \subsetneq \mathbb{R}^P$, computes in polynomial time a feasible solution $S \subseteq P$ and a lower value bound $\lambda \leq v(S)$ such that*

$$y(S) - \lambda \ \leq \ \alpha \cdot y(S^*) \ - \ v(S^*) \ ,$$

where S^* is an optimum solution.

For $\alpha = 1$, it is clear that $\lambda = v(S)$ and the algorithm computes a solution with minimum excess. For $\alpha > 1$, the computed solution may have larger excess than the optimum one. In this case, we allow $\lambda < v(S)$, which is relevant for games where the value function cannot be computed exactly in polynomial time. This is e.g. the case for maximum independent set games and maximum clique games as defined in [8]. For technical reasons, we assume that $\max_{S \subseteq P} v(S)$ is polynomially bounded in the input size.

Lemma 2. *Let $\mathcal{F}$ be a family of monotone cooperative games and $\alpha \geq 1$ such that there is an α-approximation algorithm for* MinExcess *for $\mathcal{F}$. Let $(P, v) \in \mathcal{F}$, $y \in \mathbb{R}^P_{\geq 0}$, and $A, B \subseteq P$ disjoint subsets. We can find an α-approximate solution to* MinExcess *restricted to coalitions S with $A \subseteq S \subseteq P \setminus B$ in polynomial time.*

This follows easily by modifying y appropriately. For general monotone games, Theorem 6 shows that LSA-MinExcess cannot be reduced to MinExcess without loss. We present a reduction that incurs an arbitrarily small additional error:

Theorem 7. *Let $\mathcal{F}$ be a family of monotone cooperative games and $\alpha \geq 1$ such that there exists an α-approximation algorithm for* MinExcess *for $\mathcal{F}$. Fix $\varepsilon > 0$. There exists an $(\alpha + \varepsilon)$-approximation algorithm for* LSA-MinExcess *for $\mathcal{F}$.*

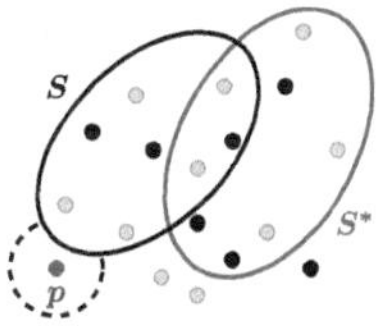

(a) $p \in (P' \setminus S^*)$ satisfies (2). S and $S \cup \{p\}$ are cheap and at least one of them is feasible.

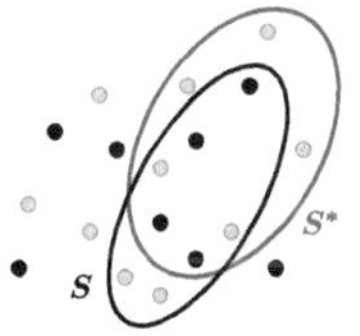

(b) No $p \in (P' \setminus S^*)$ satisfies (2). S is cheap and feasible since it agrees with S^* on P'.

Fig. 4. An illustration of the proof of Theorem 7. Players in P' are drawn as black points, all others gray. S^* is an optimum solution to the subspace-avoiding problem. The solution(s) found by our algorithm are shown in blue.

Proof. Let (P, v, y, L) be an instance of LSA-MinExcess with $(P, v) \in \mathcal{F}$ and $y \in \mathbb{R}^P_{\geq 0}$. Let

$$P' := \{p \in P : \{p\} \notin L\}$$

and $K := \lceil \frac{1}{\varepsilon} \rceil$. Note that $P' \neq \emptyset$. Let S^* be an optimum solution. We proceed differently depending on whether there exists $p \in (P' \setminus S^*)$ with low y-value

$$y_p \leq \varepsilon \cdot y(S^*) \ . \tag{2}$$

If not, we want to work with a certain *in-set* $I \subseteq S^*$ of bounded size $|I| \leq K$. Even though we have to try all possibilities for p and I (because we do not know S^*), the procedure takes only polynomial time because K is constant. Figure 4 illustrates the following two cases.

(a) $p \in (P' \setminus S^*)$ satisfies (2).
Let (S, λ) be an α-approximate solution to MinExcess restricted to coalitions that do not contain p. This can be computed in polynomial time by Lemma 2. By $p \notin S^*$,

$$y(S) - \lambda \leq \alpha \cdot y(S^*) - v(S^*) \ .$$

By $p \in P'$, we have $S \notin L$ or $(S \cup \{p\}) \notin L$. We claim that both solutions are sufficiently cheap, so we can simply return whichever is feasible. Since λ remains valid for $S \cup \{p\}$ by monotonicity of (P, v), and p satisfies (2),

$$\begin{aligned} y(S \cup \{p\}) - \lambda &= y_p + y(S) - \lambda \\ &\leq (\alpha + \varepsilon) \cdot y(S^*) - v(S^*) \ , \end{aligned}$$

where we used that S^* is an optimum solution to the restricted problem.

(b) No $p \in (P' \setminus S^*)$ satisfies (2).
We assume to have found $I \subseteq (S^* \cap P')$ of size $|I| = \min\{K, |S^* \cap P'|\}$ that maximizes $y(I)$, and define the *out-set*

$$O := \begin{cases} \{p \in (P' \setminus I) \ : \ y_p > \min_{q \in I} y_q\} & \text{if } |I| = K \ , \\ P' \setminus I & \text{if } |I| < K \ . \end{cases}$$

We claim that $P' \setminus S^* = O$. This is trivial for $|I| < K$ by definition of I and O. Otherwise, $O \subseteq (P' \setminus S^*)$ because I maximizes $y(I)$ inside $S^* \cap P'$. Additionally, $(P' \setminus S^*) \subseteq O$, because for every $p \in (P' \setminus S^*)$, (2) does not hold, and thus, using $y \geq 0$ for the third inequality,

$$y_p > \varepsilon \cdot y(S^*) \geq \frac{1}{K} \cdot y(S^*) \geq \frac{1}{K} \cdot y(I) \geq \min_{q \in I} y_q \ .$$

Let (S, λ) be an α-approximate solution to MinExcess restricted to coalitions S with $S \cap P' = S^* \cap P' = P' \setminus O$, again using Lemma 2. Then, $S^* \notin L$ implies $S \notin L$, so S is feasible. Additionally, $y(S) - \lambda \leq \alpha \cdot y(S^*) - v(S^*)$, because S^* is an optimum solution to the restricted problem. □

Remark 1. An analogous result holds for cost games. Given a cost game (P, c), where $c : 2^P \to \mathbb{R}$ is monotonically non-decreasing, and $y \in \mathbb{R}^P_{\geq 0}$, an α-approximation for MinExcess or LSA-MinExcess asks for a coalition $S \subseteq P$ such that $c(S) + y(P \setminus S)$ is at most α times the minimum possible value. This is sometimes called a *prize-collecting* problem, and combining a proof analogous to that of Theorem 7 with known results [1,7] shows that there is a 1.599-approximation algorithm for LSA Symmetric Prize-Collecting TSP, and a 1.7995-approximation algorithm for LSA Prize-Collecting Steiner Tree.

4.3 Nucleolus Instability

If MINEXCESS can be solved in polynomial time, Theorem 7 implies that LSA-MINEXCESS can be solved with an arbitrarily small relative error. However, this does not immediately imply an approximation scheme for computing the nucleolus because errors may accumulate during the MPS scheme. We will demonstrate that even small errors when solving LSA-MINEXCESS can result in large errors in the nucleolus. Thus, solving the separation problem approximately by Theorem 7 cannot lead to a reasonable nucleolus approximation in general.

More precisely, we show that changing the value function by some ε may change the nucleolus of the game by $\varepsilon \cdot 2^{\Omega(|P|)}$ per player. This relates to Theorem 7 in the following way: An oracle for LSA-MINEXCESS with a relative error of ε can essentially be viewed as an exact oracle for a slightly different game, whose value function differs by at most $\varepsilon \cdot y(S^*)$ from the original value function. Here, S^* denotes an optimum solution to LSA-MINEXCESS.

Theorem 8. *Let $n \in \mathbb{N}$ and $\varepsilon > 0$. There are monotone, superadditive games (P, v) and $(P, \tilde{v})$ with $|P| = O(n)$ such that $|v(S) - \tilde{v}(S)| \leq \varepsilon$ for all $S \subseteq P$ but the nucleoli of (P, v) and $(P, \tilde{v})$ differ by $2^n \cdot \varepsilon$ for some players.*

For the proof, we define (P, v) and $(P, \tilde{v})$ as *packing games*: For a family of sets $\mathcal{S} \subseteq 2^P$ with set weights $w : \mathcal{S} \to \mathbb{R}$,

$$v(S) := \max \left\{ \sum_{i=1}^{k} w(S_i) \ : \ S_1, \ldots, S_k \in \mathcal{S} \text{ are pairwise disjoint subsets of } S \right\}$$

for $S \subseteq P$, and $\tilde{v}$ analogously (based on $\tilde{w} : \mathcal{S} \to \mathbb{R}$), illustrated in Figure 5.

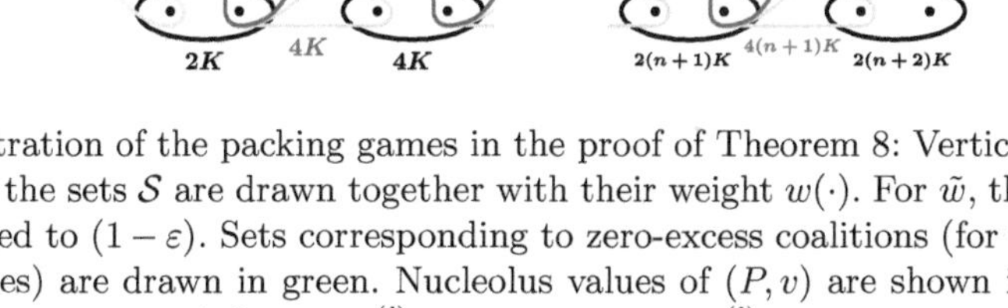

Fig. 5. Illustration of the packing games in the proof of Theorem 8: Vertices illustrate players, and the sets $\mathcal{S}$ are drawn together with their weight $w(\cdot)$. For $\tilde{w}$, the weight of $\{r\}$ is changed to $(1 - \varepsilon)$. Sets corresponding to zero-excess coalitions (for the nucleoli of both games) are drawn in green. Nucleolus values of (P, v) are shown in blue. For $(P, \tilde{v})$, they increase by $2^{l-2} \cdot \varepsilon$ for $p_i^{(l)}$, and decrease for $q_i^{(l)}$. K may be any sufficiently large constant.

5 Conclusion

We have introduced the NZ-MinExcess problem and shown that it can be used to compute the nucleolus. This relates nucleolus computation to results on non-zero-constrained optimization. We demonstrated the power of this approach by applying it to arboricity and network strength games. This strengthens previous results on these games (which require a non-empty core), while at the same time being much simpler. We believe that computing the nucleolus for more classes of games by solving NZ-MinExcess is a promising direction for further research.

For b-matching games with $b \leq 2$, we showed that LSA-MinExcess is equivalent to the Shortest Non-Zero Cycle problem. The complexity of this, and of the related Shortest Odd Cycle problem, are still unknown. Since there is already some interest in this from different areas, these are important open problems. While the general case is still open, we showed that the nucleolus of b-matching games with $b \leq 2$ can be computed if $b = 2$ only for a constant number of vertices. This also gives a new proof that the nucleolus for matching games can be computed in polynomial time. For bounded weights and cost allocations, we showed that LSA-MinExcess can be solved in randomized polynomial time. However, turning this into an algorithm to compute the nucleolus for instances with bounded weights would require a strong bound on the bit complexity of the b-matching nucleolus. We are not aware of any such bound.

We also provided insights into LSA-MinExcess for general monotone games, including a reduction to MinExcess that incurs an arbitrarily small error, which is best possible. The nucleolus, however, was shown to be very unstable under slight changes in the value function.

References

1. Ahmadi, A., Gholami, I., Hajiaghayi, M. T., Jabbarzade, P., Mahdavi, M.: Prize-Collecting Steiner Tree: a 1.79 Approximation. In: Proceedings of the 56th Annual ACM Symposium on Theory of Computing, pp. 1641–1652 (2024)
2. Aziz, H., Brandt, F., Harrenstein, P.: Monotone Cooperative Games and their Threshold Versions. In: Proceedings of the 9th International Conference on Autonomous Agents and Multiagent Systems, pp. 1017–1024 (2010)
3. Aziz, H., Lachish, O., Paterson, M., Savani, R.: Power Indices in Spanning Connectivity Games. In: Algorithmic Aspects in Information and Management, pp. 55–67 (2009)
4. Aziz, H., Lachish, O., Paterson, M., Savani, R.: Wiretapping a Hidden Network. In: Proceedings of the International Workshop on Internet and Network Economics, pp. 438–446 (2009)
5. Baïou, M., Barahona, F.: Network Strength Games: the Core and the Nucleolus. Math. Program. **180**, 117–136 (2020)
6. Blauth, J., Ellerbrock, A., Traub, V., Vygen, J.: Cost Allocation for Set Covering: The Happy Nucleolus. In: Operations Research Letters, vol. 57, 107158, pp. 1–8 (2024)

7. Blauth, J., Klein, N., Nägele, M.: A Better-Than-1.6-Approximation for Prize-Collecting TSP. In: Mathematical Programming, vol. 216, pp. 87–109 (2025)
8. Deng, X., Ibaraki, T., Nagamochi, H.: Algorithmic Aspects of the Core of Combinatorial Optimization Games. In: Mathematics of Operations Research, vol. 24.3, pp. 751–766 (1999)
9. Doron-Arad, I., Kulik, A., Shachnai, H.: Lower Bounds for Weighted Matroid Problems. In: ACM Transactions on Algorithms, vol. 22.2, 20, pp. 1–21 (2026)
10. Ebert, D., Ellerbrock, A.: Nucleolus Computation by Non-Zero-Constrained Optimization. In: arXiv:2605.29571 (2026). Extended abstract in SAGT 2026
11. El Maalouly, N., Haslebacher, S., Taubner, A., Wulf, L.: On Finding l-th Smallest Perfect Matchings. In: Leibniz International Proceedings in Informatics, vol. 351 (19), pp. 1–15 (2025)
12. Engevall, S., Göthe-Lundgren, M., Värbrand, P.: The Heterogeneous Vehicle-Routing Game. In: Transportation Science, vol. 38.1, pp. 71–85 (2004)
13. Faigle, U., Kern, W., Kuipers, J.: Note: computing the Nucleolus of Min-Cost Spanning Tree Games is NP-Hard. Internat. J. Game Theory **27**, 443–450 (1998)
14. Faigle, U., Kern, W., Kuipers, J.: On the Computation of the Nucleolus of a Cooperative Game. Internat. J. Game Theory **30**, 79–98 (2001)
15. Goemans, M. X., Ramakrishnan, V. S.: Minimizing Submodular Functions over Families of Sets. In: Combinatorica, vol. 15.4, pp. 499–513 (1995)
16. Grötschel, M., Lovász, L., Schrijver, A.: The Ellipsoid Method and its Consequences in Combinatorial Optimization. In: Combinatorica, vol. 1.2, pp. 169–197 (1981)
17. Hörsch, F., Imolay, A., Ryuhei, M., Oki, T., Schwarcz, T.: Problems on Group-Labeled Matroid Bases. In: Proceedings of the 51st International Colloquium on Automata, Languages, and Programming, Article 86, pp. 1–20 (2024)
18. Iwata, Y., Yamaguchi, Y.: Finding a Shortest Non-Zero Path in Group-Labeled Graphs. In: Combinatorica, vol. 42 Suppl(2), pp. 1253–1282 (2022)
19. Kobayashi, Y., Toyooka, S.: Finding a Shortest Non-Zero Path in Group-Labeled Graphs via Permanent Computation. In: Algorithmica, vol. 77.4, pp. 1128–1142 (2017)
20. Könemann, J., Pashkovich, K., Toth, J.: Computing the nucleolus of weighted cooperative matching games in polynomial time. Math. Program. **183**, 555–581 (2020)
21. Könemann, J., Toth, J.: A General Framework for Computing the Nucleolus via Dynamic Programming. In: Proceedings of the 13th International Symposium on Algorithmic Game Theory, pp. 307–321 (2020)
22. Könemann, J., Toth, J., Zhou, F.: On the Complexity of Nucleolus Computation for Bipartite b-Matching Games. In: Theoretical Computer Science, vol. 998, Article 114476, pp. 1–17 (2024)
23. Kopelowitz, A.: Computation of the Kernels of Simple Games and the Nucleolus of n-Person Games. Tech. rep. RM-31, Department of Mathematics. Hebrew University of Jerusalem (1967)
24. Kumabe, S., Yoshida, Y.: Lipschitz Continuous Allocations for Optimization Games. In: Proceedings of the 51st International Colloquium on Automata, Languages, and Programming, Article 102, pp. 1–16 (2024)
25. Littlechild, S.C.: A simple expression for the nucleolus in a special case. Internat. J. Game Theory **3**, 21–29 (1974)
26. Maschler, M., Peleg, B., Shapley, L. S.: Geometric Properties of the Kernel, Nucleolus, and Related Solution Concepts. In: Mathematics of Operations Research, vol. 4.4, pp. 303–338 (1979)

27. Meir, R., Rosenschein, J. S., Malizia, E.: Subsidies, Stability, and Restricted Cooperation in Coalitional Games. In: Proceedings of the 2nd Workshop on Cooperative Games in MultiAgent Systems, pp. 14–26 (2011)
28. Mulmuley, K., Vazirani, U. V., Vazirani, V. V.: Matching is as Easy as Matrix Inversion. In: Proceedings of the 19th Annual ACM Symposium on Theory of Computing, pp. 345–354 (1987)
29. Nash-Williams, C. S. J. A.: An Application of Matroids to Graph Theory. In: Theory of Graphs – International Symposium, pp. 263–265 (1967)
30. Pashkovich, K.: Computing the nucleolus of weighted voting games in pseudo-polynomial time. Math. Program. **195**, 1123–1133 (2022)
31. Schlotter, I., Sebő, A.: Odd paths, cycles, and T-joins: connections and algorithms. SIAM J. Discret. Math. **39**, 484–504 (2025)
32. Schmeidler, D.: The Nucleolus of a Characteristic Function Game. In: SIAM Journal on Applied Mathematics, vol. 17.6, pp. 1163–1170 (1969)
33. Solymosi, T.: On Computing the Nucleolus of Cooperative Games, PhD thesis. University of Illinois at Chicago (1993)
34. Thomas, R., Yoo, Y.: Packing cycles in undirected group-labelled graphs. J. Comb. Theory **161**, 228–267 (2023)
35. Xiao, H., Fang, Q.: Arboricity Games: the core and the nucleolus. Math. Program. **198**, 1–25 (2023)

Efficiently Restructuring Sovereign Debt via Arctic Auctions with Convex Costs

Jugal Garg[1], Edwin Lock[2](✉), and Vijay V. Vazirani[3]

[1] University of Illinois Urbana-Champaign, Urbana, IL, USA
jugal@illinois.edu
[2] King's College London, London, UK
edwin.lock@kcl.ac.uk
[3] University of California, Irvine, USA
vazirani@ics.uci.edu

Abstract. We study the problem of computing competitive equilibria in the Arctic product-mix auction, originally developed for the Icelandic government for exchanging blocked financial accounts, and more recently proposed by IMF staff for sovereign debt restructuring. From the buyers' perspective, the Arctic auction is equivalent to the quasi-linear Fisher market. However, unlike the standard Fisher model, the seller can express rich supply preferences through explicit supply-side costs and constraints. Despite extensive algorithmic literature on Fisher markets, the seller side has not received much attention, and no polynomial-time algorithm was previously known for computing competitive equilibrium when sellers face nontrivial costs.

We look at the natural and expressive regime of separable, stepwise-increasing marginal costs, which underlie the above-stated applications. Using polyhedral theory techniques, we first show that rational inputs lead to rational-valued competitive equilibria. Motivated by this result, we develop the first polynomial-time algorithm for this setting based on a non-trivial extension of classic primal-dual balanced-flow techniques for linear Fisher markets. Our work provides a robust computational foundation for auctions with sophisticated preferences, paving the way for flexible and institutionally feasible market designs in global finance.

Keywords: Arctic auctions · Product-mix auctions · Fisher markets · Competitive equilibrium · Polynomial-time algorithms

1 Introduction

The Arctic Product-Mix Auction was originally designed by Paul Klemperer for the Icelandic Government to exchange blocked accounts for other financial assets, e.g., cash or bonds.[1] More recently, IMF staff have proposed using the Arctic

J. Garg—Supported by NSF Grant CCF-2334461.

[1] For Klemperer's original description of the Arctic auction, see Klemperer [11]. The Arctic auction belongs to the family of Product-Mix Auctions, originally designed for the Bank of England to provide liquidity to financial institutions following the UK financial crisis of 2008-9.

P. Lenzner and D. Schmand (Eds.): SAGT 2026, LNCS 16911, pp. 169–186, 2027.
https://doi.org/10.1007/978-3-032-38782-0_10

auction for the purpose of sovereign debt restructuring [15]. In this mechanism, creditors bid to exchange their claims for alternative debt instruments. Importantly, the auctioneer (sovereign), and possibly outside sellers offering additional funds, can specify supply costs which govern the quantity of goods they are willing to produce at given market prices. Both the Icelandic Government and the sovereign debt restructuring mechanism pursued the approach of computing competitive equilibria for (many) different supply schedules, and then selecting the most desirable equilibrium among these.[2] For this approach to be practicable, efficient algorithms for computing equilibria are necessary.

The most useful market model that underlies these applications is the Arctic auction in which the auctioneer has a stepwise increasing marginal cost curve for each good. The objective is to find equilibrium prices and allocations: each buyer should obtain a utility-maximizing bundle of goods at current prices and the auctioneer should maximize his profit. This paper develops the first efficient algorithm for computing such a competitive equilibrium, in the general regime where one or more sellers have separable convex costs for each good.

From the buyer's perspective, the Arctic auction is equivalent to a variant of the linear Fisher market in which buyers have quasi-linear utilities: the preferences expressed by buyers in the Arctic auction can be interpreted as the aggregate demand of one or more bidders in such a Fisher market. The linear Fisher market occupies a special place in algorithmic game theory not only because of its widespread applications (see the full version [8]), but also because of its strong algorithmic properties and its connections to convex optimization. For this market model, Devanur et al. [4] gave an exact polynomial-time algorithm, henceforth referred to as *the DPSV algorithm*. The primal–dual balanced-flow techniques from this classic algorithm will also play a key role in our work. Equilibrium allocations and prices for this model are captured by the celebrated Eisenberg–Gale convex program [5]. However, this program was not sufficient to derive an efficient algorithm for computing an *exact equilibrium*—that needed an algorithm for Diophantine approximation, which was given later in [10]. Later, Orlin [12] provided the first strongly polynomial algorithm for computing equilibria of the linear Fisher market.

While buyer preferences have been extensively studied, the *seller side* of Fisher markets remains comparatively underexplored. For Arctic-auction applications in central banking and sovereign debt restructuring, however, seller costs are essential. Separable, stepwise increasing marginal costs are both practically natural and theoretically expressive: sufficiently fine steps approximate arbitrary separable convex costs. The only prior efficient algorithmic treatment of seller costs that we are aware of handles the simpler case of constant marginal costs [14].

Due to these applications, the Arctic auction has begun to receive algorithmic attention in recent years. Fichtl [6] analyzed an algorithm proposed by Klemperer and DotEcon that solves the Arctic auction with stepwise increasing separable marginal costs by computing equilibria via explicit enumeration, which does

[2] The precise criteria for choosing the optimal competitive equilibrium are confidential.

not scale well with the number of goods. Baldwin et al. [2] develop reductions from Arctic auctions with stepwise increasing marginal costs to auctions without costs, and to linear Fisher markets. Vazirani [14] showed that equilibrium computation in the setting without costs reduces to a *rational convex program* [13] and obtained a polynomial-time algorithm by modifying the DPSV algorithm. Most recently, Garg et al. [9] built on the work of Orlin [12] to develop a strongly polynomial algorithm for the Arctic auction without costs.

In the classical setting, the supply of each good is fixed and buyers are endowed with fixed budgets; equilibrium computation can therefore proceed by adjusting prices alone. In contrast, in our setting the supply of each good must be endogenously adjusted by the algorithm in response to prices and demand, and buyers have quasi-linear preferences, so their effective spending is not fixed in advance but depends on prices and allocations. As a result, unlike the DPSV algorithm, which updates only prices, our algorithm must jointly update prices, supplies, and buyers' remaining budgets. The main difficulty is not only that supplies change, but that the algorithm must reason about two notions of supply. During the primal-dual process, it maintains an upper bound on the amount of each good that may be sold at the current price. However, at final prices, seller optimality also imposes lower bounds: at a marginal-cost breakpoint, the seller is indifferent over an interval of quantities, while in the interior of a segment, the seller requires the full segment quantity to be sold. Thus, the usual DPSV min-cut invariant cannot be applied.

Our solution separates the fixed-supply part of the DPSV analysis from the new seller-side bookkeeping. Within an iteration of the outer loop, the algorithm scales prices while holding actual supply fixed, so the balanced-flow and surplus-reduction arguments from the fixed-supply Arctic auction can be adapted locally. Globally, we maintain a hybrid min-cut invariant on an auxiliary network that uses actual supply on the goods currently being repriced and profitable supply on the rest. Splitting the network this way is what lets the local balanced-flow analysis run while the seller's global requirements still hold. At termination, a lower-bounded flow chooses quantities between these upper and lower supplies, reconciling buyer clearing with seller profit maximization.

Finally, because marginal costs increase in discrete steps, the algorithm must adjust prices continuously without skipping over an equilibrium price. We exploit the structure of the cost functions: at the *kinks* between consecutive cost segments, prices can be increased continuously while holding supply fixed. Within these fixed-supply intervals the DPSV-style balanced-flow machinery can be adapted, while the hybrid invariant handles transitions between intervals.

Due to space constraints, full proofs and additional material are deferred to the full version of this paper [8]. In particular, we refer to the full version for further details on the Iceland and sovereign debt restructuring mechanism, as well as other related work.

Notation. Vectors are written in bold. We write $[k]$ for the set $\{1, 2, \ldots, k\}$, and $\boldsymbol{e}^i$ for the ith standard basis vector. We use $\mathbb{Q}$, $\mathbb{Q}_{\geq 0}$, and $\mathbb{Q}_{>0}$ to denote the rationals, the non-negative rationals, and the strictly positive rationals respectively, and analogously use $\mathbb{R}$, $\mathbb{R}_{\geq 0}$, and $\mathbb{R}_{>0}$ for the reals. We use the convention $1/\infty = 0$.

2 The Arctic Auction with Costs

In the Arctic auction, bidders submit one or more *Arctic bids* consisting of a budget and a value vector for the set G of n goods. Each bid has the same demand as a buyer in the Fisher market with quasi-linear utilities, and the total demand of a bidder in the Arctic auction is given by the (Minkowski) sum of the demands of her individual bids. Accordingly, let B denote the set of individual Arctic bids, and view these as buyers in the Fisher market. Let $m = |B|$. After computing an allocation in this market, the allocation to an original Arctic bidder is recovered by summing the allocations to her individual bids.

Formally, we assume that each buyer $i \in B$ has a value $u_{ij} \in \mathbb{Q}_{\geq 0}$ for good $j \in G$, and a budget $m_i \in \mathbb{Q}_{>0}$. Her utility $u_i(\boldsymbol{x}_i, \boldsymbol{p})$ for bundle $\boldsymbol{x}_i = (x_{ij})_{j \in G} \in \mathbb{R}^G_{\geq 0}$ of goods at prices $\boldsymbol{p} \in \mathbb{R}^G_{>0}$ is

$$u_i(\boldsymbol{x}_i, \boldsymbol{p}) = \begin{cases} m_i + \sum_{j \in G} u_{ij} x_{ij} - \sum_{j \in G} p_j x_{ij}, & \text{if } \sum_{j \in G} p_j x_{ij} \leq m_i, \\ -\infty, & \text{otherwise.} \end{cases}$$

Thus the buyer always prefers a bundle that does not exceed her budget. Throughout, we restrict attention to strictly positive prices.

Definition 1. *The bang per buck of buyer i for good j at price p_j is $\frac{u_{ij}}{p_j}$. The buyer's maximum bang per buck (mbpb) at prices $\boldsymbol{p}$ is*

$$\alpha_i := \max_{j \in G} \frac{u_{ij}}{p_j}.$$

The goods that give the buyer a bang per buck of α_i are her maximum bang per buck goods (or mbpb goods) at $\boldsymbol{p}$.

Given fixed prices $\boldsymbol{p}$, each buyer's utility $u_i(\boldsymbol{x}_i, \boldsymbol{p})$ is linear in $\boldsymbol{x}_i$ over the affordable region $\{\boldsymbol{x}_i \in \mathbb{R}^G_{\geq 0} \mid \sum_{j \in G} p_j x_{ij} \leq m_i\}$. Hence, any bundle $\boldsymbol{x}_i$ which maximizes the utility of buyer i at prices $\boldsymbol{p}$ contains only mbpb goods, i.e., $x_{ij} > 0$ implies $\frac{u_{ij}}{p_j} = \alpha_i$. Moreover, the buyer may choose not to spend all her money precisely when $\alpha_i \leq 1$. For instance, if $u_{ij} < p_j$ for all goods $j \in G$, then it is immediate that $u_i(\boldsymbol{x}_i, \boldsymbol{p})$ is maximized by the empty bundle $\mathbf{0}$. It follows that the buyer spends all her budget m_i if $\alpha_i > 1$, a portion of her budget if $\alpha_i = 1$, and none of her budget if $\alpha_i < 1$.

For any buyer i and prices $\boldsymbol{p}$, define the set $M_i(\boldsymbol{p}) := \{j \in G \mid \frac{u_{ij}}{p_j} = \alpha_i \geq 1\}$ containing the buyer's mbpb goods at $\boldsymbol{p}$ if $\alpha_i \geq 1$ and the empty set $\emptyset$ otherwise.

Lemma 1. **([7, Lemma 1]).** *Fix a buyer $i \in B$ and prices $\boldsymbol{p}$, and let $D^i(\boldsymbol{p})$ be the set of bundles the buyer demands at $\boldsymbol{p}$.*

1. *If $\alpha_i > 1$, then $D^i(\boldsymbol{p}) = \operatorname{conv}\left\{\frac{m_i}{p_j}\boldsymbol{e}^j \mid j \in M_i(\boldsymbol{p})\right\}$.*

2. *If* $\alpha_i = 1$, *then* $D^i(\boldsymbol{p}) = \operatorname{conv}\left(\{\mathbf{0}\} \cup \left\{\frac{m_i}{p_j}\boldsymbol{e}^j \mid j \in M_i(\boldsymbol{p})\right\}\right)$.
3. *If* $\alpha_i < 1$, *then* $D^i(\boldsymbol{p}) = \{\mathbf{0}\}$.

An *outcome* $(\boldsymbol{p}, \boldsymbol{x})$ consists of a price p_j for each good $j \in G$ and an allocation x_{ij} of good j to buyer i, for every good $j \in G$ and every buyer $i \in B$. An outcome is *feasible* if each buyer receives a utility-maximizing bundle, that is, a bundle they demand. For convenience, we define $y_j = \sum_{i \in B} x_{ij}$ as the total quantity of good j sold by the auctioneer.

The auctioneer has separable supply costs given by a stepwise increasing marginal cost function for each good.

Definition 2. *The auctioneer's production costs are given by the separable function* $c(\boldsymbol{y}) = \sum_{j \in G} c_j(y_j)$. *For each good* $j \in G$, *the function* c_j *is specified by a sequence of* K_j *breakpoints* $b_{j1} < \cdots < b_{j,K_j}$ *and marginal costs* $0 \leq d_{j1} < \cdots < d_{j,K_j}$. *The* k*th segment is the interval* $(b_{j,k-1}, b_{jk}]$, *on which* c_j *has constant marginal cost* d_{jk}; *supplying beyond* b_{j,K_j} *is infeasible. For notational convenience, we define* $b_{j0} = 0$, $d_{j,K_j+1} = \infty$, *and* $c_j(0) = 0$. *For* $y_j > 0$, *define*

$$c_j(y_j) = \begin{cases} \displaystyle\sum_{k=1}^{s-1} d_{jk}(b_{jk} - b_{j,k-1}) + d_{js}(y_j - b_{j,s-1}), & \text{if } y_j \leq b_{j,K_j}, \\ \infty, & \text{if } y_j > b_{j,K_j}, \end{cases}$$

where s *is the unique index in* $[K_j]$ *such that* $y_j \in (b_{j,s-1}, b_{js}]$. *See Fig. 1 for an illustration.*

The last breakpoint b_{j,K_j} is an explicit supply cap for good j. In applications, this cap can be chosen so that it never binds at equilibrium. Throughout, we assume that $d_{j1} > 0$ for every good $j \in G$. The case $d_{j1} = 0$ can be treated separately and is omitted here.[3]

The auctioneer's profit from selling aggregate quantities $\boldsymbol{z} \in \mathbb{R}^G_{\geq 0}$ at prices $\boldsymbol{p}$ is his income from $\boldsymbol{z}$ minus his cost,

$$\sum_{j \in G} p_j z_j - \sum_{j \in G} c_j(z_j).$$

As the cost functions are separable, the auctioneer's profit-maximizing quantity for each good j at fixed prices $\boldsymbol{p}$ can be determined independently.

Lemma 2. *If* $p_j < d_{j1}$, *the auctioneer wants to sell* $z_j = 0$. *If* $p_j \in [d_{jk}, d_{j,k+1})$ *for some* $k \in [K_j]$, *then the profit-maximizing quantities are* $z_j \in [b_{j,k-1}, b_{jk}]$ *when* $p_j = d_{jk}$, *and* $z_j = b_{jk}$ *when* $p_j \in (d_{jk}, d_{j,k+1})$.

Now that we have defined the buyers' demand and the auctioneer's profit, we can formulate competitive equilibrium.

---

3 Assuming $d_{j2} > 0$, a good j with $d_{j1} = 0$ can be handled by initializing its price to any rational $p_j \in (0, d_{j2})$ and its supply to $t_j = b_{j1}$, then running the algorithm unchanged. Since demand exceeds supply at this small initial price, the algorithm raises p_j until equilibrium is reached, exactly as in the $d_{j1} > 0$ case.

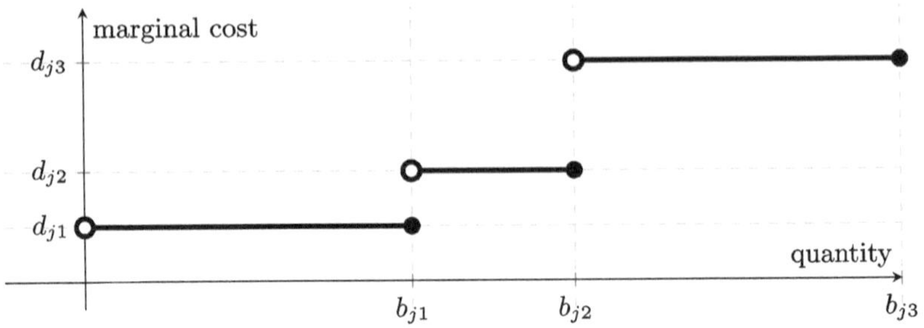

Fig. 1. A stepwise increasing marginal cost curve c'_j for good j with three segments, given by breakpoints b_{j1}, b_{j2}, b_{j3} and segment heights d_{j1}, d_{j2}, d_{j3}.

Definition 3. *An outcome* $(\boldsymbol{p}, \boldsymbol{x})$ *(with aggregate quantities* $\boldsymbol{y}$*) is a competitive equilibrium if it is feasible and selling* $\boldsymbol{y}$ *at* $\mathbf{p}$ *maximizes the auctioneer's profit among all possible bundles* $\boldsymbol{z} \in \mathbb{R}^G_{\geq 0}$.

Note that the auctioneer's maximization problem in this definition is independent of the buyers' budgets, as $\boldsymbol{z}$ can be any bundle of goods; quantities above the cap b_{j,K_j} are simply infeasible because they incur infinite cost.

Our first result establishes that rational inputs guarantee a rational-valued competitive equilibrium, a property that is not immediate with seller costs.

Theorem 1. *Suppose the utilities and budgets of the buyers, as well as the coefficients of the cost functions, are rational numbers. If a competitive equilibrium exists, there exists a competitive equilibrium that is rational-valued, with prices and allocation quantities having bit size polynomial in the bit size of the input parameters.*

Our polynomial-time algorithm (Theorem 2) in fact constructs such a rational-valued equilibrium, so Theorem 1 also follows from our algorithmic results. We nonetheless give a direct, self-contained proof via polyhedral theory, as the argument is short and may be of independent interest.

In the proof, we fix an arbitrary competitive equilibrium $(\boldsymbol{p}^*, \boldsymbol{x}^*)$, and record only its combinatorial type: each buyer's mbpb goods, whether her maximum bang per buck is strictly greater than 1, and the cost segment containing the aggregate quantity sold of each good. In inverse-price variables $q_j = 1/p_j$, these choices define a rational polyhedron whose constraints require allocated goods to remain mbpb, buyers to satisfy the spending conditions in Lemma 1, and aggregate supplies to remain in the corresponding seller-optimal intervals. The original equilibrium gives a feasible point with $q_j > 0$ for every good, and every feasible point with positive inverse prices gives a competitive equilibrium of the same type. Adding a variable ϵ and constraints $q_j \geq \epsilon$ lets us optimize for a positive lower bound on all inverse prices over a rational polyhedron. Standard rational linear-programming bit-complexity bounds then give a basic feasible solution with polynomially many bits. We defer the precise construction to the full version [8].

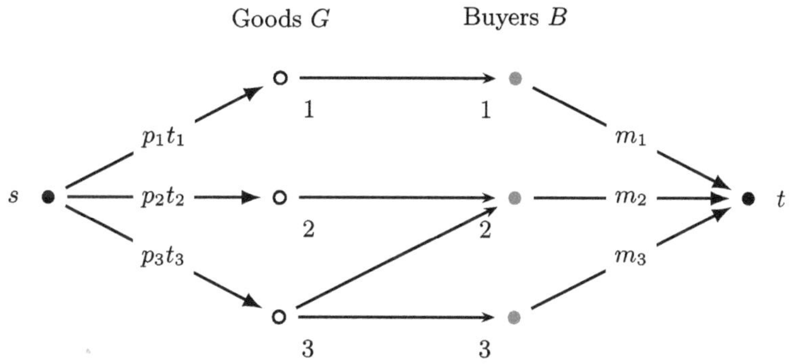

Fig. 2. The expenditure network $N(\boldsymbol{p}, \boldsymbol{m}, \boldsymbol{t})$ with the arcs labeled with their capacities. The arcs from goods to buyers have capacity ∞.

3 The Algorithm

The existence of a rational-valued competitive equilibrium motivates the design of a polynomial-time algorithm to find one. We propose a primal-dual algorithm for solving the Arctic auction with stepwise increasing marginal costs, building upon the work of [4,14] for linear Fisher markets and Arctic auctions without costs. However, our algorithm requires several key extensions. In fixed-supply markets, the same supply vector both limits the flow during the algorithm and describes seller-side feasibility at equilibrium. With stepwise increasing marginal costs these roles separate: actual supplies are upper bounds during the algorithm, while seller optimality at final prices imposes profitable lower bounds. We handle this by maintaining a hybrid min-cut invariant and recovering the final allocation through a lower-bounded flow. The structural lemmas proving this invariant are deferred to the full version [8]; the main text below states the algorithm and records only the consequences needed for correctness and running time.

We use standard network-flow terminology throughout this section. The definitions and basic facts needed for the algorithm, including residual graphs, min-cuts, lower-bounded flows, and Hoffman's circulation criterion, are collected in [8, Appendix A]; see also Ahuja et al. [1] for further details.

Definition 4. *For any prices $\boldsymbol{p} \in \mathbb{Q}^G_{>0}$, budgets $\boldsymbol{m} \in \mathbb{Q}^B_{>0}$, and supply $\boldsymbol{t} \in \mathbb{Q}^G_{\geq 0}$, let the expenditure network $N(\boldsymbol{p}, \boldsymbol{m}, \boldsymbol{t})$ be the flow network with vertices consisting of a source s, a sink t, the buyers B, and the goods G. These vertices are connected by*

- *an arc from the source s to each good j with capacity $\mathrm{cap}(s, j) = p_j t_j$;*
- *an arc from each buyer i to the sink t with capacity $\mathrm{cap}(i, t) = m_i$;*
- *an arc from good j to buyer i with capacity $\mathrm{cap}(j, i) = \infty$ if j is a mbpb good for buyer i at prices $\boldsymbol{p}$.*

We illustrate this network in Fig. 2.

The algorithm makes use of balanced flows. Intuitively, such a flow distributes the surplus (the unspent money) of the buyers as equitably as possible.

Definition 5. *The surplus* $\gamma(f)$ *of flow* f *in network* $N(\boldsymbol{p}, \boldsymbol{m}, \boldsymbol{t})$ *is given by* $\gamma(f)_i = m_i - f(i, t)$ *for each buyer* $i \in B$. *A balanced flow of network* $N(\boldsymbol{p}, \boldsymbol{m}, \boldsymbol{t})$ *is a max flow of* $N(\boldsymbol{p}, \boldsymbol{m}, \boldsymbol{t})$ *that minimizes* $\|\gamma(f)\|_2^2$.

For a feasible flow f in a network N, we write $R_N(f)$ for the *restricted residual graph*: the residual graph restricted to the buyer and good vertices $B \cup G$, with s, t, and all their incident arcs removed. We will also use a standard residual-graph property of balanced flows from Devanur et al. [4], stated as [8, Lemma 3] in the full version.

Balanced flows can be computed in polynomial time. Devanur et al. [4] designed a divide-and-conquer method that uses a linear number of max flow computations to find a balanced flow. Later, Darwish and Mehlhorn [3] introduced a parametric flow one-shot method for computing balanced flows using $O(\log |V(N)|)$ max flow computations. Since the expenditure network has $|V(N)| = m + n + 2$ vertices, this gives $O(\log(m + n))$ max flow computations in our setting.

Next, we introduce the notion of *tight sets*. For any subset $S \subseteq B$ of buyers, let $\Gamma(S)$ be the set of goods adjacent to S in $N(\boldsymbol{p}, \boldsymbol{m}, \boldsymbol{t})$. Similarly, for any subset $S \subseteq G$ of goods, let $\Gamma(S)$ be the set of buyers adjacent to S in $N(\boldsymbol{p}, \boldsymbol{m}, \boldsymbol{t})$.

Definition 6. *A subset* $S \subseteq G$ *of goods is* tight *if* $\sum_{j \in S} p_j t_j \geq \sum_{i \in \Gamma(S)} m_i$.

3.1 An Overview of the Algorithm

The algorithm combines the fixed-supply balanced-flow machinery from the Arctic auction without costs with explicit updates to supplies and buyers' remaining budgets. In the primal steps, the algorithm scales up a judiciously chosen subset of goods by a common factor, causing prices to increase monotonically. In the dual steps, the algorithm computes a balanced flow in the expenditure network, in which each buyer is connected only to her current mbpb goods. When a buyer's maximum bang per buck drops to 1, her budget is partially or fully returned; in the latter case, she is removed from the market entirely.

Formally, let $\widehat{B}$ denote the original buyer set of the instance. On the buyer side, the algorithm maintains the active buyer set $B \subseteq \widehat{B}$ and current budgets $(m_i)_{i \in B}$, initialized from the input; the expenditure network $N(\boldsymbol{p}, \boldsymbol{m}, \boldsymbol{t})$ is always built only on the active buyers, and removed buyers receive zero allocation in the final output.

On the seller side, the algorithm maintains a segment index seg_j for each good j, recording which segment of the cost function the current price lies on, and a supply vector $\boldsymbol{t}$: each good's supply is initialized to the maximum the seller is willing to sell at the starting price and is increased only when the price reaches the next marginal-cost breakpoint, ensuring the auctioneer never sells more than is profitable at current prices. The proof simultaneously tracks the *profitable supply* vector $\bar{\boldsymbol{t}}$, which records the lower quantities needed for seller optimality. For the current prices $\boldsymbol{p}$ and segment indices $(\text{seg}_j)_{j \in G}$,

$$\bar{t}_j = \begin{cases} b_{j,\text{seg}_j - 1} & \text{if } p_j = d_{j,\text{seg}_j}, \\ b_{j,\text{seg}_j} & \text{if } p_j \in (d_{j,\text{seg}_j}, d_{j,\text{seg}_j+1}), \end{cases} \qquad \text{for every } j \in G,$$

so $\bar{t}_j$ is the smallest quantity of good j that the seller must sell to maximize profit at current prices. We refer to $N(\boldsymbol{p}, \boldsymbol{m}, \bar{\boldsymbol{t}})$ as the *profitable network* at prices $\boldsymbol{p}$.

The full algorithm is given in Algorithm 1. We now highlight its key features.

Initialization. Note that the auctioneer's stepwise increasing marginal cost curves specify a minimum price d_{j1} at which he is willing to sell any quantity of each good $j \in G$. Therefore, we initialize prices to $p_j = d_{j1}$. At these initial prices, the auctioneer maximizes profit by selling up to a quantity of b_{j1} of good j (by Lemma 2), so supply is set to $t_j = b_{j1}$. Since buyers with a maximum bang per buck of less than 1 demand nothing at the initial prices, and prices increase monotonically throughout the algorithm, these buyers are removed. If this empties B, the algorithm immediately returns zero allocation at prices $\boldsymbol{p}$: every removed buyer demands the empty bundle since $\alpha_i < 1$, and the auctioneer is satisfied by zero supply since prices are at the first breakpoint ($\bar{t}_j = b_{j0} = 0$), so this is a competitive equilibrium. Otherwise the algorithm maintains the invariant that only buyers with maximum bang per buck at least 1, at the current prices $\boldsymbol{p}$, remain in the market.

The Inner and Outer Loops. The main part of the algorithm consists of an outer and an inner loop. We call each execution of the inner loop body an *inner iteration*, and a *phase* consists of one iteration of the outer loop together with all the inner iterations it spawns. Each iteration of the outer loop begins by rebuilding the full expenditure network $N = N(\boldsymbol{p}, \boldsymbol{m}, \boldsymbol{t})$ at the current prices, budgets, and supply, and computing a balanced flow of this network. If this balanced flow has zero surplus for every buyer, then the outer loop terminates and enters the final processing step. Otherwise, we let I be the set of buyers with the largest surplus, and let J be the goods adjacent to I in the expenditure network. The algorithm then removes all the arcs in N from goods in J to buyers not in I, and identifies all newly *isolated* buyers $Z \subseteq B \setminus I$ in N. Here, a buyer is considered isolated if they have no incoming arcs from any good in G. We refer to the restricted subnetwork induced by $\{s\} \cup J \cup I \cup \{t\}$ after these deletions as the current *phase component*.

The algorithm then enters the inner loop, which scales up the prices of goods J by a common factor $\theta \geq 1$. Conceptually, we determine θ by continuously increasing it from 1 upwards, until one of Events 1 to 6 occurs. Formally, we compute, for each event e, the smallest $\theta_e \geq 1$ for which the event holds, and set $\theta = \min_{e \in [6]}\{\theta_e\}$. The value θ_1 may be infinite if every good in J already lies on its last segment, and some of the other event values may also be infinite when the relevant set of buyers or goods is empty. Nevertheless, θ is well-defined: unless an earlier event occurs, the buyers in I eventually reach maximum bang per buck 1, triggering Event 6. In each inner iteration, the algorithm executes only the

Algorithm 1. Solving Arctic auctions with stepwise increasing marginal costs.

Input: Arctic auction instance $(\widehat{B}, G, \boldsymbol{u}, \boldsymbol{m}, \boldsymbol{b}, \boldsymbol{d})$.
Output: Competitive equilibrium $(\boldsymbol{p}, \boldsymbol{x})$.

Set $B = \widehat{B}$.
For each good $j \in G$, set price $p_j = d_{j1}$, initial supply $t_j = b_{j1}$ and $\text{seg}_j = 1$.
Remove all buyers i with $\alpha_i = \max_{j \in G} \frac{u_{ij}}{p_j} < 1$ from B.
if $B = \emptyset$ **then** set $x_{ij} = 0$ for all $i \in \widehat{B}$, $j \in G$; **return** $(\boldsymbol{p}, \boldsymbol{x})$.
Outer Loop
  Build $N = N(\boldsymbol{p}, \boldsymbol{m}, \boldsymbol{t})$ and compute a balanced flow f.
  if $\max_{i \in B} \gamma(f)_i = 0$ **then break** out of outer loop.
  Let $I = \arg\max_{i \in B} \gamma(f)_i$.
  Let $J = \Gamma(I)$, delete all edges from goods J to buyers $B \setminus I$ in N, and let $Z = \{i \in B \setminus I \mid \Gamma(\{i\}) = \emptyset\}$.
  Inner Loop
    Compute the smallest scaling factor $\theta \geq 1$ at which one of Events 1–6 occurs.
    Scale up prices of goods in J by setting $p_j = \theta p_j$.
    if Event 1 ($p_j = d_{j,\text{seg}_j+1}$ for some $j \in J$ with $\text{seg}_j < K_j$) **then**
      Let $H = \{j \in J \mid \text{seg}_j < K_j \text{ and } p_j = d_{j,\text{seg}_j+1}\}$.
      For each $j \in H$, set $t_j = b_{j,\text{seg}_j+1}$, $\text{cap}(s,j) = p_j t_j$, and $\text{seg}_j \leftarrow \text{seg}_j + 1$; **break** out of inner loop.
    else if Event 2 (buyer $i \in I$ starts demanding good $j \in G \setminus J$ at $\boldsymbol{p}$) **then**
      Add arc (j,i) with capacity ∞ to N and recompute balanced flow f.
      if $\max_{i \in B} \gamma(f)_i = 0$ **then break** out of both loops.
      Let I' be all buyers $i' \in B \setminus I$ with a directed path from i' to I in $R_N(f)$; set $I \leftarrow I \cup I'$, $J \leftarrow \Gamma(I)$, delete all edges from J to $B \setminus I$, and recompute Z.
    else if Event 3 (buyer $i \in Z$ starts demanding good $j \in G \setminus J$ at $\boldsymbol{p}$) **then**
      Add arc (j,i) with capacity $\text{cap}(j,i) = \infty$ to N and remove i from Z.
    else if Event 4 (a buyer $i \in Z$ becomes indifferent: $\alpha_i = 1$) **then**
      Set $B \leftarrow B \setminus \{i\}$ and delete i and its incident arcs.
    else if Event 5 (a goods subset $\emptyset \subsetneq S \subseteq J$ goes tight: $\sum_{j \in S} p_j t_j \geq \sum_{i \in \Gamma(S)} m_i$) **then**
      break out of inner loop.
    else if Event 6 (buyer $i \in I$ becomes indifferent: $\alpha_i = 1$) **then**
      Let $N_{I,J}^{(i,0)}$ be the restricted network on $\{s\} \cup J \cup I \cup \{t\}$, with buyer arc (i,t) capacity set to 0.
      if $(\{s\}, J \cup I \cup \{t\})$ is an s-t min-cut in $N_{I,J}^{(i,0)}$ **then**
        Set $B \leftarrow B \setminus \{i\}$ and delete i and its incident arcs.
      else
        Find a maximal source-side min-cut with good side S and buyer side T in $N_{I,J}^{(i,0)}$, and set $m_i \leftarrow \sum_{j \in S} p_j t_j - \sum_{i' \in T \setminus \{i\}} m_{i'}$.
      break out of inner loop.
Rebuild $N = N(\boldsymbol{p}, \boldsymbol{m}, \boldsymbol{t})$. For each good $j \in G$, compute $\bar{\boldsymbol{t}}$ as $\bar{t}_j = b_{j,\text{seg}_j-1}$ if $p_j = d_{j,\text{seg}_j}$, and $\bar{t}_j = b_{j,\text{seg}_j}$ if $p_j \in (d_{j,\text{seg}_j}, d_{j,\text{seg}_j+1})$.
Let $\overline{N}$ be N with bounds $[p_j \bar{t}_j, p_j t_j]$ on (s,j), $[m_i, m_i]$ on (i,t), and $[0, \infty]$ on (j,i). Find a feasible flow f of $\overline{N}$.
For $i \in \widehat{B}$ and $j \in G$, set $x_{ij} = f(j,i)/p_j$ if $(j,i) \in N$, and $x_{ij} = 0$ otherwise.
return $(\boldsymbol{p}, \boldsymbol{x})$.

smallest-index event attaining this minimum scaling factor. It is straightforward to compute the values $\theta_1, \ldots, \theta_4$ and θ_6 in linear time. For Event 5, we need to compute the smallest scaling factor $\theta_5 \geq 1$ for which some nonempty subset $S \subseteq J$ becomes tight, that is, $\sum_{i \in \Gamma(S)} m_i \leq \sum_{j \in S} \theta_5 p_j t_j$.

The value θ_5 may equal 1 immediately after an Event 2 restoration, in which case no positive price scaling is needed before Event 5 can end the phase. Otherwise the same subroutines as in Devanur et al. [4] compute θ_5 using at most n max flow computations. Several event-level facts used below, including the restoration property of Event 2 and the slack condition before Event 6, are proved in the full version [8]. We now describe the events.

Event 1. This event fires when the prices p_j of one or more goods newly reach their next supply breakpoints. For each such good j with current segment $\text{seg}_j = k < K_j$ and price $p_j = d_{j,k+1}$, the auctioneer is willing to sell up to quantity $b_{j,k+1}$, so we increase the supply to $t_j = b_{j,k+1}$ and update the current segment to $\text{seg}_j = k+1$. This may create temporary oversupply in the expenditure network, but that is harmless: source capacities are only upper bounds during the algorithm, and the final lower-bounded flow enforces the seller's actual profit-maximizing quantities.

Event 2. As the prices of goods J increase, the goods not in J become more desirable relative to those in J. This event fires when some buyer $i \in I$ starts demanding a good $j \in G \setminus J$. We add the arc (j, i) to the network N and recompute the balanced flow. If this balanced flow has zero surplus on every buyer, then the outer loop terminates and we enter the algorithm's final processing steps. Otherwise, we add to I every buyer $i' \in B \setminus I$ that has a directed path to I in the restricted residual graph $R_N(f)$. We update J to be all the goods adjacent to I in N, remove all arcs from goods in the new set J to buyers in $B \setminus I$, and recompute the set Z of isolated buyers. By the full version [8, Lemma 4], the set J strictly increases and every arc deleted in this restoration step carries zero flow in the recomputed balanced flow.

Event 3. Similarly to Event 2, this event fires when some buyer $i \in Z$ starts demanding a good $j \in G \setminus J$. We add the arc (j, i) to N and remove i from Z (but not from B).

Event 4. As prices increase, the maximum bang per buck of buyers decreases monotonically. This event fires when a buyer $i \in Z$ reaches maximum bang per buck $\alpha_i = 1$. She becomes indifferent between receiving an empty bundle and receiving any bundle containing only mbpb goods, so we remove buyer i from the market. Since prices will continue to rise, such a buyer will always be willing to accept an empty bundle in the future.

Event 5. This event fires when a nonempty subset $S \subseteq J$ of goods becomes tight. The current phase ends and a new phase begins. The algorithm does not need to identify a particular tight set explicitly, since the next outer-loop iteration rebuilds the full expenditure network from scratch.

Event 6. Similarly to Event 4, this event fires when a buyer $i \in I$ reaches $\alpha_i = 1$. We form the restricted phase network $N_{I,J}^{(i,0)}$ induced by $\{s\} \cup J \cup I \cup \{t\}$, with the current source capacities $p_j t_j$ on J, the current mbpb edges between

J and I, and buyer i's sink capacity temporarily set to 0. If the source-side cut $(\{s\}, J \cup I \cup \{t\})$ is a min-cut of $N_{I,J}^{(i,0)}$, we remove the buyer. Otherwise, we compute the unique inclusion-wise maximal source-side min-cut of $N_{I,J}^{(i,0)}$ with good side $S \subseteq J$ and buyer side $T \subseteq I$; uniqueness holds because the union of the source sides of source-side min-cuts is again the source side of a min-cut. We set

$$m'_i = \sum_{j \in S} p_j t_j - \sum_{i' \in T \setminus \{i\}} m_{i'}$$

and update $m_i \leftarrow m'_i$. Since Event 5 has priority over Event 6, the full version [8, Lemma 5] shows that $\sum_{j \in S} p_j t_j < \sum_{i' \in \Gamma(S)} m_{i'}$ for every $S \subseteq J$ at the moment Event 6 fires. This implies $m'_i < m_i$, so the budget strictly decreases. Since the source-side cut has capacity $C = \sum_{j \in J} p_j t_j$ and is not a min-cut of $N_{I,J}^{(i,0)}$, the chosen min-cut has capacity $C - m'_i < C$, hence $m'_i > 0$, so the updated budget remains positive.

The Final Phase. The outer loop terminates once some balanced-flow computation yields zero surplus for every remaining buyer. At that moment, the current prices already support full spending by all buyers on their mbpb goods. Before the final processing step, we rebuild the full expenditure network $N(\boldsymbol{p}, \boldsymbol{m}, \boldsymbol{t})$ at these final prices, budgets, and supply. As the supply of a good only increases once prices are sufficiently high, the auctioneer never sells more than they wish at $\boldsymbol{p}$. However, at the final prices the seller also requires a minimum quantity of each good to be sold in order to maximize profit; this is exactly the final profitable supply $\bar{\boldsymbol{t}}$. The final processing step computes a feasible flow in the lower-bounded network $\overline{N}$ obtained from N by giving each source arc (s, j) lower bound $p_j \bar{t}_j$ and upper bound $p_j t_j$, each mbpb arc (j, i) upper bound ∞, and each buyer arc (i, t) lower and upper bounds both equal to m_i.

4 Correctness of the Algorithm

We now establish that, whenever the algorithm terminates, the returned prices and allocation form a competitive equilibrium. The complete structural treatment is deferred to the full version [8]; here we give a proof overview.

Proposition 1. *The algorithm returns a competitive equilibrium if it terminates.*

Let $\boldsymbol{p}$, $\boldsymbol{m}$, $\boldsymbol{t}$, and $(\text{seg}_j)_{j \in G}$ be the final prices, budgets, supplies, and segments. Let $\bar{\boldsymbol{t}}$ be the final profitable supply vector and let $\overline{N}$ be the lower-bounded network used in the final processing step.

The structural lemmas in the full version [8] use an inductive argument to establish the invariant that, at the start of every outer-loop iteration and after termination, the source-side cut is a min-cut of the profitable network. In concrete terms, at the final prices, every set of goods has enough adjacent buyer budget to absorb the minimum quantity that the seller must sell for profit maximization. When the outer loop terminates, the rebuilt expenditure network also has a zero-surplus balanced flow, so every set of buyers can spend its budget on adjacent goods without exceeding actual supply. Together, these two Hall-type conditions imply by Hoffman's criterion that the final lower-bounded network admits a feasible flow f (see [8, Lemma 9]). The algorithm returns $x_{ij} = f(j,i)/p_j$ on arcs (j,i) of $\overline{N}$, and $x_{ij} = 0$ otherwise, including for buyers removed earlier.

The arcs of $\overline{N}$ go only from goods to buyers for whom the good is mbpb at the final prices, and every remaining buyer spends her entire final budget because $\overline{N}$ enforces $f(i,t) = m_i$. We check the three cases of Lemma 1. If $\alpha_i < 1$ at the final prices, then buyer i must have been removed during initialization or when she reached $\alpha_i = 1$ in Event 4 or Event 6; she receives the empty bundle, which she demands. If $\alpha_i = 1$, then either she was removed and receives the empty bundle, or she remains in the market and receives an affordable bundle of mbpb goods. Both are demanded when $\alpha_i = 1$. If $\alpha_i > 1$, then she was never removed and never affected by Event 6, so her final budget is her original budget; she receives only mbpb goods and spends that whole budget, as required.

Finally, feasibility of f in $\overline{N}$ gives $\bar{t}_j \le y_j \le t_j$ for every good j, where $y_j = \sum_{i \in \widehat{B}} x_{ij}$. By the definitions of $\bar{\boldsymbol{t}}$ and $\boldsymbol{t}$, this means $y_j \in [b_{j,\mathrm{seg}_j - 1}, b_{j,\mathrm{seg}_j}]$ when $p_j = d_{j,\mathrm{seg}_j}$, and $y_j = b_{j,\mathrm{seg}_j}$ when $p_j \in (d_{j,\mathrm{seg}_j}, d_{j,\mathrm{seg}_j + 1})$. By Lemma 2, these are exactly the profit-maximizing quantities for the auctioneer at prices $\boldsymbol{p}$. Thus the returned outcome is a competitive equilibrium.

5 The Running Time

Together with Proposition 1, the following theorem completes the proof that the algorithm computes a competitive equilibrium in polynomial time.

Theorem 2. *Suppose $\mathcal{A} = (B, G, u, \boldsymbol{m}, \boldsymbol{b}, \boldsymbol{d})$ is an Arctic auction instance with rational utilities, budgets, and marginal cost steps. Let $n = |G|$, $m = |B|$, $K = \sum_{j \in G} K_j$, and let L be the maximum bit length of the numerator or denominator of any input rational appearing in $\boldsymbol{u}$, $\boldsymbol{m}$, $\boldsymbol{b}$, or $\boldsymbol{d}$. Algorithm 1 solves $\mathcal{A}$ with at most*

$$O((m+K)(m+n)^5(L+\log(m+n)))$$

outer loop iterations, and performs at most

$$O((m+K)mn(n+\log(m+n))(m+n)^5(L+\log(m+n)))$$

max flow computations.

The bound on our algorithm's running time is likely to be pessimistic; we optimize for a clean polynomial rather than sharp exponents.

Our running-time analysis starts from the squared-surplus potential used by Vazirani [14] and Devanur et al. [4], which maps any network flow f and budgets

$\boldsymbol{m}$ to the sum of the squared surpluses of all buyers:

$$\Phi(f, \boldsymbol{m}) = \sum_{i \in B} (m_i - f(i,t))^2.$$

Recall that a phase is an iteration of the outer loop together with all its inner iterations. A phase is *nonterminal* if its last inner iteration enters Event 1, 5, or 6; it is a *terminal phase* if the outer loop terminates during it, either because a balanced-flow computation at the start of the outer-loop iteration yields zero surplus on every buyer, or because an Event 2 inner iteration yields zero surplus on every buyer. In the latter case the terminal phase has no closing Event 1, 5, or 6, and is charged as a single additional phase for the purposes of Proposition 2. We subdivide Event 6 into Event 6a, in which a buyer is removed, and Event 6*b*, in which we retain the buyer and only partially return her budget. This leads to the following four types of nonterminal phases:

Type 1: A phase that ends with an inner iteration entering Event 1, during which the supply of some good is increased.

Type 5: A phase that ends with an inner iteration entering Event 5 during which a nonempty subset of goods goes tight.

Type 6a: A phase that ends with an inner iteration entering Event 6 during which a buyer is removed.

Type 6b: A phase that ends with an inner iteration entering Event 6 during which a buyer is not removed but her budget is reduced.

In the fixed-supply Arctic auction of Vazirani [14], source capacities are fixed multiples of current prices and buyer budgets remain fixed until exit. Here, source capacities are products of prices and endogenous supplies, supplies may jump at marginal-cost breakpoints, and Event 6*b* can partially refund a buyer rather than remove her. Accordingly, the bit-complexity step tracks new rationality certificates, while the potential-decrease step handles the new event types.

Let m_i^{init} denote buyer i's initial budget, let $M = \sum_{i \in B} m_i^{\text{init}}$, and let $h = m + n$. Budgets only decrease, so every feasible flow satisfies $0 \le \Phi(f, \boldsymbol{m}) \le M^2$.

The proof has four parts.

Step 1: Potential Checkpoints. We first lower-bound every nonzero value of the potential at the balanced-flow checkpoints where the algorithm evaluates it. This requires a new certificate of rationality for the current prices, source capacities, and active budgets: in addition to mbpb equations and breakpoint anchors, the certificate must keep historical tight-set equations and the cut equations created by partial refunds. The resulting bit-complexity bound gives the following separation from zero; its proof is deferred to the full version [8].

Lemma 3. *At every state immediately after a balanced-flow computation, either* $\Phi = 0$ *or*

$$\Phi \ge 2^{-O((m+n)^2 (L + \log(m+n)))}.$$

Step 2: Reset and Decrease Phases. The phases that do not fit a monotone potential-decrease argument are controlled directly: a Type 1 phase advances a supply segment, and a Type 6*a* phase removes a buyer.

Lemma 4. *There are at most $\sum_{j \in G} K_j$ phases of Type 1 (which increases the supply of a good), and at most m phases of Type 6a (which removes a buyer).*

All remaining nonterminal phases end with Event 5 or Event 6*b*. Their analysis is local to intervals in which the actual supplies on the active phase are fixed. On such intervals the balanced-flow surplus-reduction mechanism from Vazirani [14] can still be used, but only after isolating the restricted phase network and checking that the extra operations of our algorithm preserve the relevant comparison. Event 2 restores the phase component by adding residually reachable buyers and deleting only zero-flow arcs; Event 6*b* changes the budget vector and must be compared through an explicit post-refund feasible flow. These adaptations yield the following multiplicative decrease; the proof is in the full version [8].

Lemma 5. *Every Type 5 phase reduces Φ to at most a $(1 - 1/h^3)$ fraction of its previous value, and every Type 6b phase reduces Φ to at most a $(1 - 1/(4h^3))$ fraction of its previous value.*

Step 3: Counting Phases. The lower bound from Step 1 and the multiplicative decrease from Step 2 bound the number of Type 5 and Type 6*b* phases between two reset phases. Since the reset phases themselves are bounded by Lemma 4, we obtain the total number of phases.

Proposition 2. *The number of phases in the algorithm is bounded by $O((m + K)(m + n)^5(L + \log(m + n)))$.*

Proof. Suppose there are R consecutive phases of Type 5 or 6*b*, and let Φ_{before} and Φ_{after} denote the value of the potential function at the balanced-flow checkpoints immediately before and immediately after this block of phases. At the beginning of such a block, either the algorithm has just started or the preceding phase ended with Event 1 or Event 6*a*; in all cases the general bound above gives $\Phi_{\text{before}} \leq M^2$. By Lemma 5, each phase reduces the potential to at most a $(1 - \frac{1}{4h^3})$ fraction of its previous value. Therefore,

$$\Phi_{\text{after}} \leq \left(1 - \frac{1}{4h^3}\right)^R \Phi_{\text{before}} \leq \left(1 - \frac{1}{4h^3}\right)^R M^2.$$

If $\Phi_{\text{after}} = 0$, the outer loop terminates. Otherwise, Lemma 3 gives

$$2^{-O((m+n)^2(L+\log(m+n)))} \leq \left(1 - \frac{1}{4h^3}\right)^R M^2.$$

Since $\log M = O(L + \log(m + n))$, taking logarithms and using $\ln(1 - x) \leq -x$ gives

$$R = O(h^3(m + n)^2(L + \log(m + n))) = O((m + n)^5(L + \log(m + n))).$$

By Lemma 4, there are at most $m + K$ reset phases, i.e., phases of Type 1 or 6a. Removing these reset phases partitions the remaining nonterminal phases of Type 5 and 6b into at most $m+K+1$ consecutive blocks, and the bound above applies to each block. There may also be one terminal phase, which does not affect the asymptotic bound. Hence the total number of phases is

$$O\big((m + K)(m + n)^5(L + \log(m + n))\big).$$

□

Step 4: Work Inside a Phase. It remains to bound the number of inner iterations per phase and the number of max flow computations required per inner iteration.

Proposition 3. *Each phase consists of at most $O(mn)$ inner iterations, and each inner iteration performs at most $O(n+\log(m+n))$ max flow computations.*

Proof. At the start of each phase, the computation time is dominated by computing a balanced flow of the expenditure network. At the start of each inner iteration, computing the scaling factor θ is dominated by computing the factor θ_5 (for Event 5). As discussed in the algorithm overview, this requires at most n max flow computations. In addition, an inner iteration may trigger Event 2, which requires recomputing a balanced flow, or Event 6, which requires one max flow/min-cut computation in the restricted network $N_{I,J}^{(i,0)}$ to classify the step as removal or refund. Using the parametric method of Darwish and Mehlhorn [3], each balanced flow can be computed with $O(\log(m+n))$ max flow computations. Hence each inner iteration uses at most $O(n + \log(m + n))$ max flow computations.

Each phase consists of $O(mn)$ inner iterations. This follows because the only events after which the algorithm remains in the inner loop are Events 2, 3, and 4. By the full version [8, Lemma 4], Event 2 strictly enlarges J, so it can occur at most n times in a phase. Between two Event 2 updates, the set Z only shrinks: Event 3 removes one buyer from Z, and Event 4 removes one buyer from the market entirely. Since Z is recomputed after each Event 2 update, there can be $O(m)$ Events 3 and 4 after each of the $O(n)$ Event 2 updates. Therefore, the number of max flow computations per phase is $O(mn(n + \log(m + n)))$. After the outer loop terminates, the final lower-bounded-flow instance can be reduced to $O(1)$ ordinary max flow computations by the standard circulation reduction recalled in [8, Appendix A]; see also Ahuja et al. [1]. Thus it does not affect the asymptotic bound. This completes the proof. □

We are now ready to prove the polynomial running time bound.

Proof (of Theorem 2). By Proposition 2, the algorithm executes at most

$$O((m + K)(m + n)^5(L + \log(m + n)))$$

outer-loop iterations. By Proposition 3, each such phase contains $O(mn)$ inner iterations, and each inner iteration uses at most $O(n+\log(m+n))$ max-flow computations. The final lower-bounded-flow computation uses only $O(1)$ additional max-flow computations by the standard reduction to circulation [1]. Multiplying these bounds gives

$$O((m+K)mn(n+\log(m+n))(m+n)^5(L+\log(m+n)))$$

max-flow computations in total. The outer loop therefore terminates within the claimed number of iterations, and Proposition 1 shows that the outcome returned after final processing is a competitive equilibrium. □

6 Discussion

Our algorithm shows that Arctic auctions can accommodate sophisticated separable seller costs without losing polynomial-time computability. This removes a significant computational barrier for applications such as central-bank liquidity provision and sovereign debt restructuring, where institutions must compare many feasible supply schedules before choosing an outcome. More broadly, it shows that seller-side objectives can be incorporated into a Fisher-style auction framework without abandoning exact equilibrium computation.

A natural next question is whether Arctic auctions with piecewise linear costs admit a strongly polynomial algorithm, as was recently achieved for the auction without costs [9]. The present model keeps seller costs separable across goods. Natural extensions include non-separable constraints that capture cross-instrument dependencies, such as aggregate maturity targets, currency exposure, or portfolio risk limits. Whether rationality of equilibrium prices and polynomial-time computability survive in such settings remains open, and may require new ideas beyond the hybrid min-cut invariant used here.

References

1. Ahuja, R.K., Magnanti, T.L., Orlin, J.B.: Network Flows: Theory, Algorithms, and Applications. Prentice Hall, Englewood Cliffs, NJ (1993)
2. Baldwin, E., Klemperer, P., Lock, E.: Solving the "Arctic" Product-Mix Auction (2026). https://edwinlock.com/pdfs/solving-arctic-pma.pdf. Working paper
3. Darwish, O., Mehlhorn, K.: Improved balanced flow computation using parametric flow. Inf. Process. Lett. **116**(9), 560–563 (2016). https://doi.org/10.1016/j.ipl.2016.04.008
4. Devanur, N.R., Papadimitriou, C.H., Saberi, A., Vazirani, V.V.: Market equilibrium via a primal-dual algorithm for a convex program. J. ACM **55**(5) (2008). https://doi.org/10.1145/1411509.1411512
5. Eisenberg, E., Gale, D.: Consensus of subjective probabilities: the Pari-Mutuel method. Ann. Math. Stat. **30**(1), 165–168 (1959). https://doi.org/10.1214/aoms/1177706369
6. Fichtl, M.: Computing candidate prices in budget-constrained Product-Mix auctions (2022). https://arxiv.org/abs/2208.02633
7. Finster, S., Goldberg, P.W., Lock, E.: Competitive and revenue-optimal pricing with budgets. Theor. Econ. **20**(4), 1135–1153 (2025). https://doi.org/10.3982/TE5913

8. Garg, J., Lock, E., Vazirani, V.V.: Efficiently restructuring sovereign debt via Arctic Auctions with convex costs (2026). https://arxiv.org/abs/2606.09631
9. Garg, J., Taherijam, S., Vazirani, V.V.: A strongly polynomial algorithm for Arctic Auctions (2026). https://arxiv.org/abs/2604.24756
10. Jain, K.: A polynomial time algorithm for computing an Arrow-Debreu market equilibrium for linear utilities. SIAM J. Comput. **37**(1), 303–318 (2007). https://doi.org/10.1137/S0097539705447384
11. Klemperer, P.: Product-Mix auctions. Tech. Rep. 2018-W07, Nuffield College (2018). https://www.nuffield.ox.ac.uk/economics/Papers/2018/2018W07_productmix.pdf, Economics Paper
12. Orlin, J.B.: Improved algorithms for computing Fisher's market clearing prices. In: Proceedings of the Forty-Second ACM Symposium on Theory of Computing, pp. 291–300 (2010). https://doi.org/10.1145/1806689.1806731
13. Vazirani, V.V.: The notion of a rational convex program, and an algorithm for the Arrow-Debreu Nash bargaining game. J. ACM **59**(2) (2012). https://doi.org/10.1145/2160158.2160160
14. Vazirani, V.V.: Arctic Auctions, linear Fisher markets, and rational convex programs (2025). https://arxiv.org/abs/2511.21637
15. Willems, T.: An auction-based sovereign debt restructuring mechanism (2021). https://www.imfconnect.org/content/dam/imf/Spring-Annual%20Meetings/SM21/openevents/An%20Auction-Based%20Sovereign%20Debt%20Restructuring%20Mechanism.pdf. Working paper

Minimizing Cumulative Envy in Allocating a Sequence of Items

Paul W. Goldberg, Isaac Robinson, and Nicholas Teh(✉)

University of Oxford, Oxford, UK
{paul.goldberg,isaac.robinson,nicholas.teh}@cs.ox.ac.uk

Abstract. We study temporal fair division with indivisible goods that arrive sequentially and must be allocated irrevocably. In contrast to the usual online model, we assume that valuations and future arrivals are known in advance, and ask how unfairness evolves during the process. We introduce *cumulative maximum envy*: the sum, over all rounds, of the maximum pairwise envy at that round. Equivalently, this is the area under the worst-envy curve, and it captures both the magnitude and the duration of envy. For a fixed arrival order, we show that the corresponding decision problem is strongly NP-complete and that minimizing this objective admits no constant-factor approximation unless P = NP, even under identical valuations and even under binary valuations. We complement these hardness results with a dynamic program that gives pseudopolynomial-time solvability for a constant number of agents, polynomial-time algorithms in further restricted settings, and an FPTAS for fixed n under identical integer valuations. We then study a sequencing variant where the algorithm may choose the arrival order. This variant remains NP-complete even for two agents with identical valuations; however, a simple greedy algorithm achieves a 3/2-approximation for $n = 2$ agents, an $n/(n-1)$-approximation for any number of agents, and an additive guarantee depending on the maximum value of any good.

1 Introduction

Fair division of indivisible goods is a fundamental, well-studied problem at the intersection of computer science and economics [9,30], with applications ranging from divorce settlements to distributed load balancing. A central fairness notion in this context is *envy-freeness*, which requires that every agent values their allocated bundle at least as much as any other agent's bundle. However, this strong requirement is not always achievable; consider, for example, the case of two agents and a single good that both value positively, which must be allocated to one of them. As a result, recent years have seen considerable interest in relaxations of envy-freeness. Arguably, the two most prominent relaxations are *envy-freeness up to one good (EF1)* and *envy-freeness up to any good (EFX)*. An allocation is EF1 if, for any pair of agents, any envy can be eliminated by removing one good from the envied agent's bundle, where goods are compared using the envious agent's valuation; in particular, removing a most-valued good

P. Lenzner and D. Schmand (Eds.): SAGT 2026, LNCS 16911, pp. 187–204, 2027.
https://doi.org/10.1007/978-3-032-38782-0_11

is sufficient. It is EFX if the envy is eliminated even after removing a least-valued good.

The concept of EF1 originates from the seminal work of Lipton et al. [28], which introduced the first algorithmic approach for computing approximately envy-free allocations of indivisible goods. Their *envy-cycle elimination* algorithm remains a foundational tool and has since been used as a building block in tackling some of the most challenging problems in fair division, including the recent breakthrough on the existence of EFX allocations for three agents [10]. Interestingly, EF1 emerged from an effort to bound envy: if each agent's maximum envy can be bounded by the largest value of a single good, then a polynomial-time algorithm can achieve this relaxed form of envy-freeness. This same line of reasoning also motivates the optimization problem of minimizing envy, which was considered by Lipton et al. [28]. The optimization perspective has received comparatively less attention than discrete relaxations such as EF1 and EFX.

While most prior works study the fair division problem in the *offline* setting (i.e., all goods are immediately available and are allocated to agents in a single-shot), many real-world systems do not allocate all resources at once. Instead, indivisible goods become available over time and must be assigned as they appear: affordable housing units are completed in phases, public extraction permits are issued across multiple periods, and platforms assign arriving tasks or opportunities to workers. In such settings, stakeholders care not only about the *final* allocation, but also about the *trajectory*: large early imbalances can create lasting disadvantages, distort downstream behavior, or erode trust.

Several recent works have considered an *online* model where goods arrive one at a time, and must immediately and irrevocably be allocated to agents. This captures numerous application scenarios where goods need to be allocated in a sequential manner, such as assigning donations to food banks [1], allocating resources in cloud computing environments [6], or allocating impressions in recommendation systems [31]. In the standard online fair division model, it is usually assumed that each good's valuation is not known until its arrival. Most work on online fair division evaluates fairness only at the end of the process, once all goods have arrived and been allocated. In practice, agents experience the allocation process as it unfolds, and limiting unfairness throughout the process can be important for maintaining balance, participation, and trust, especially in long-term allocation systems.

This motivation is central to recently-studied *temporal fair division* model [11,14], where the goal is to guarantee fairness not merely at the end, but at *every prefix* during the allocation process given information about future arrivals and valuations for each good-agent pair. This perspective provides a different lens on sequential fair division. In the standard and commonly-studied online model, agents have limited to no information about future arrivals, and fairness is evaluated only at the end (after all goods have arrived). In contrast to these standard online models with unknown future arrivals, the temporal fair division model assumes complete information about valuations and future arrivals while striving for typically stronger, *cumulative* fairness guarantees [11,14].[1] Consider the allocation of pre-built affordable housing units that become available over time: while the housing authority knows when each unit will be ready, ensuring equitable distribution throughout the multi-year process—not just at the end—is essential for maintaining public trust and preventing systematic disadvantage to any group. Similarly, when allocating extraction rights for public natural resources across multiple time periods to private companies, temporal fairness ensures that no firm gains disproportionate early advantages that could distort market competition.

To quantify experienced unfairness over time, we take an optimization view rooted in classic envy minimization [28]. For an allocation process, let A_i^t denote agent i's bundle after the first t goods, and define $\mathrm{envy}_{i,j}^t := \max\{0, v_i(A_j^t) - v_i(A_i^t)\}$. Let $c_t := \max_{i,j \in N} \mathrm{envy}_{i,j}^t$ be the maximum envy after the first t goods have been allocated. The sequence $(c_1, \ldots, c_m)$ is the worst-envy curve of the process. Our objective is $\sum_{t=1}^m c_t$, the area under this curve. This objective is a simple, parameter-free baseline: it uses the standard maximum-envy measure at each round and aggregates it over time, so it penalizes both large envy and envy that persists for many rounds. We do not claim that this is the only meaningful temporal objective. Rather, it is a natural optimization counterpart to prefix-based temporal fairness notions, and it remains meaningful even when maintaining a strong fairness guarantee at every prefix is impossible.

For each agent i, let $e_i^t := \max_{j \in N} \mathrm{envy}_{i,j}^t$ and $E_i := \sum_{t=1}^m e_i^t$. Since $c_t = \max_{i \in N} e_i^t$, we have $\max_{i \in N} E_i \le \sum_{t=1}^m c_t \le \sum_{i \in N} E_i \le n \max_{i \in N} E_i$. Thus, our objective upper-bounds the cumulative envy experienced by every agent and is within a factor n of the largest individual cumulative envy. In either of our two models, an optimal solution for our objective is therefore an n-approximation for directly minimizing $\max_{i \in N} E_i$ over the same feasible allocation processes. However, our objective need not distribute envy evenly across agents. Directly minimizing $\max_{i \in N} E_i$, $\sum_{i \in N} E_i$, or weighted versions of these quantities is a natural direction for future work. It would also be useful to study objectives that directly minimize the largest or total individual cumulative envy.

We investigate cumulative maximum envy minimization in two related settings. First, we study the standard temporal model where the arrival order is fixed and may be adversarially chosen as part of the input. Second, we study a sequencing variant in which the algorithm may choose the order of the goods before allocating them. This models settings where all goods are known and can be held briefly before release; for example, a food bank may have several donated pallets in storage and choose which pallet to allocate next, or a public agency may choose the order in which approved permits are issued.

[1] Note that without this "cumulative fairness" consideration, the problem reduces to the standard offline model.

1.1 Our Contributions

We begin in Sect. 3 by presenting several intractability results. We show that the fixed-order problem is NP-complete even under identical valuations and even under binary valuations. In both cases, we also prove that no constant-factor approximation is possible unless $\mathsf{P} = \mathsf{NP}$.

Motivated by these hardness results, in Sect. 4 we give a dynamic programming algorithm that computes an optimal allocation sequence in time $\mathcal{O}((m+1)(V_{\max}m^2+1)(mV_{\max}+1)^{n^2} \cdot n^3)$, where n is the number of agents, m is the number of goods, and $V_{\max}$ is the maximum value of any good to any agent. This gives pseudopolynomial-time solvability when n is constant, and polynomial-time solvability under binary valuations for constant n. If the number of goods is constant, an optimal solution can also be found by direct enumeration. We further show that binary identical valuations admit a simple polynomial-time optimal algorithm, and that identical integer valuations admit an FPTAS for every fixed n.

In Sect. 5, we explore a natural variant of the model in which the algorithm is allowed to choose the arrival order of goods (while an adversary pre-selects the agents' valuations over the goods). We show that this variant remains NP-complete even for just two agents and identical valuations. On the positive side, when agents have identical valuations, we design a polynomial-time algorithm that achieves: (i) a 3/2-approximation for $n = 2$ agents, (ii) a $n/(n-1)$-approximation for general n, and (iii) a $\frac{n-1}{n} V_{\max}$-additive approximation to the optimal cost.

1.2 Related Work

We highlight the works most relevant to our focus on envy minimization in the temporal setting.

Offline Fair Division. In the offline fair division model, all goods are available simultaneously and allocated at once. Lipton et al. [28] investigate envy minimization in this setting, aiming to bound the maximum envy between any pair of agents. They introduce the well-known envy cycle elimination algorithm, which runs in polynomial time and guarantees an allocation where the *maximum envy* is at most the highest value of any good. This result also gives rise to the well-known EF1 concept.

Online Fair Division. In the online fair division model, goods arrive sequentially in a fixed order, and the algorithm has no knowledge of future items. Due to this uncertainty, most works on this model focus on ensuring fairness guarantees at the final round, once all goods have arrived and been allocated. Several works look at minimizing the maximum envy in this setting. Benade et al. [7] study a fully adversarial setting in which item values are chosen adaptively: an adversary observes the algorithm and all decisions made thus far, and selects the value of each incoming good to maximize envy at the end. They prove that any online algorithm must incur a maximum envy of at least $\Omega(\sqrt{m})$, where m is the number of goods, even with just two agents.

Recognizing that adaptive adversaries may be unrealistically powerful, Halpern et al. [22] consider an *oblivious adversary* model, where item values are fixed in advance and chosen to be worst-case with respect to the algorithm, but do not depend on the actual allocation decisions made in previous rounds. In this setting, they show connections to the *online multicolor discrepancy* problem and, in the special case of two agents, to *online vector balancing* [33].

In contrast, our work assumes full information about the values of all goods from the outset, and focuses on cumulative envy minimization, aligning more with the temporal fair division model than with adversarial online models.

Temporal Fair Division. In the temporal fair division model (sometimes also referred to as the *fully informed* online fair division model), the sequence of goods is known in advance, allowing the algorithm to make allocation decisions with full knowledge of future arrivals. This setting enables us to introduce the study of fairness guarantees that are cumulative over time, rather than only at the final round. Cookson et al. [11] introduce temporal fair division and give existence/algorithmic guarantees for achieving EF1-type fairness simultaneously at multiple points in time, with stronger positive results in special cases (e.g., two agents or structured preferences). Elkind et al. [14] formalize temporal EF1 (TEF1) for sequential item arrivals, showing that TEF1 need not exist in general and that deciding existence is NP-hard, while providing polynomial-time algorithms in several structured cases. He et al. [23] maintain EF1 at every round by allowing limited reallocations (or what they call adjustments), and quantify how many such changes are necessary (including separations between informed vs. uninformed settings). In contrast to this constraint-based line of work (maintaining temporal EF1 at every prefix), we take an optimization view and minimize the cumulative "area under the envy curve", which remains meaningful even when strong prefix-fairness constraints are infeasible. Micheel and Wilczynski [29] study a related repeated house allocation model in which every round is a complete matching, so each agent receives one object. They focus on envy-based fairness across the repeated assignments, together with Pareto efficiency in each round. Their model differs from ours in two main ways: they make a complete assignment in every round, whereas we allocate one indivisible good irrevocably at each step; and they study fairness conditions across repeated assignments, whereas we minimize cumulative maximum envy.

2 Preliminaries

For each positive integer z, we denote $[z] := \{1, \ldots, z\}$. An instance of the *fair division* problem is a tuple $\mathcal{I} = (N, G, \mathbf{v} = (v_1, \ldots, v_n))$, where $N = [n]$ is the set of (fixed) *agents*, G is a set of m goods, and for each $i \in N$, the function $v_i \colon 2^G \to \mathbb{R}_{\geq 0}$ is the *valuation function* of agent i. We write v instead of v_i when all agents have identical valuation functions. In the *temporal fair division* problem, goods arrive sequentially according to some order π, and we must allocate each good (to an agent) as it arrives. Let Π denote the space of all such arrival orders. In this work, we consider both the setting where π is chosen by an adversary (i.e., the standard temporal fair division setting) and the setting where π can be chosen by the algorithm.

As with most works in the fair division literature, we assume that valuation functions are *additive*, i.e., for any subset of goods $B \subseteq G$, $v_i(B) = \sum_{g \in B} v_i(\{g\})$. For convenience, we write $v_i(g)$ instead of $v_i(\{g\})$ for a single good g. Every subset of goods in G can also be referred to as a *bundle*. An *allocation* $\mathcal{A} = (A_1, \ldots, A_n)$ is a partition of the goods into bundles, with agent $i \in N$ receiving bundle A_i. For each $i \in N$ and $t \in [m]$, let A_i^t denote the partial allocation of agent i *after* the t-th arriving good is allocated to an agent and let $A_i^0 = \varnothing$ be the initial empty allocation, and $A_i^m = A_i$. Equivalently, we can represent an allocation by an allocation sequence $S = (s_1, \ldots, s_m) \in N^m$, where for each $t \in [m]$, the t-th entry s_t specifies the agent that the t-th arriving good is allocated to. Let the space of all such sequences be $\mathcal{S}$.

Next, we define *envy* and the *envy minimization* objective. Let S be the allocation sequence corresponding to $\mathcal{A}$, given some order π. Then, for any $t \in [m]$, the *envy* of agent $i \in N$ toward agent $j \in N \setminus \{i\}$ is $\text{envy}_{i,j}^t(S, \pi) := \max\{0, v_i(A_j^t) - v_i(A_i^t)\}$; in particular, $\text{envy}_{i,i}^t(S, \pi) = 0$. The *per-round cost* is $c_t(S, \pi) := \max_{i,j \in N} \text{envy}_{i,j}^t(S, \pi)$, and the *cumulative maximum envy* is $\mathsf{cost}(S, \pi) := \sum_{t=1}^{m} c_t(S, \pi)$, which we seek to minimize.

Maximum envy is a standard quantitative objective in both offline envy minimization [28] and online envy minimization [8,22]. In most online models, fairness is evaluated only after the last item has been allocated. In the fully informed temporal model, however, future arrivals and valuations are known, so it is natural to ask for fairness over the trajectory of the allocation, not just at the end. One stronger requirement would be to optimize every prefix simultaneously, or to impose a fairness constraint at every prefix as in temporal EF1. We instead optimize the total area under the worst-envy curve. This permits short-term imbalances when they are compensated later, but penalizes imbalances that are large or long-lasting. This matches settings where temporary disparities are acceptable but prolonged severe unfairness is not.

Finally, optimizing only the final maximum envy can be badly misaligned with minimizing cumulative exposure to envy. Example 1 gives a linear separation even under identical valuations; conversely, cumulative maximum envy always controls final envy because $c_m(S, \pi)$ is one of the terms in $\sum_t c_t(S, \pi)$.

Example 1. Consider an instance with $n = 2$ and identical valuation function v. Fix any integer $q \geq 2$, let $m := 2q + 1$ and $\varepsilon := \frac{99}{2q}$. Then m is odd and $(m - 1)\varepsilon = 99$. Let $\pi = (g_1, \ldots, g_m)$ be a fixed arrival order where $v(g_t) = \varepsilon$ for every $t \leq m - 1$ and $v(g_m) = 100$. For $n = 2$, we have $c_t(S, \pi) = |v(A_1^t) - v(A_2^t)|$ for every $t \in [m]$.

- *An allocation minimizing the final round cost.* Allocate $\{g_1, \ldots, g_{m-1}\}$ to agent 1 and g_m to agent 2. Then $v(A_1^m) = 99$ and $v(A_2^m) = 100$, so $c_m(S, \pi) = 1$ (and no allocation can have $c_m(S, \pi) < 1$ since $v(G) = 199$). Moreover, for each $t \leq m - 1$ we have $v(A_1^t) = t\varepsilon$ and $v(A_2^t) = 0$, so $c_t(S, \pi) = t\varepsilon$. Thus,

$\text{cost}(S, \pi) = \sum_{t=1}^{m-1} t\varepsilon + 1 = \varepsilon\frac{m(m-1)}{2} + 1 = \frac{99\,m}{2} + 1$, which grows linearly in m.

- *An allocation with much smaller cumulative cost.* Alternately allocate the first $m-1$ goods between the agents. Then for every $t \leq m-1$, we maintain $|v(A_1^t) - v(A_2^t)| \leq \varepsilon$, so $c_t(S, \pi) \leq \varepsilon$; more precisely, $c_t(S, \pi) = \varepsilon$ on odd t and $c_t(S, \pi) = 0$ on even t. Since $m-1$ is even, $\sum_{t=1}^{m-1} c_t(S, \pi) = \frac{m-1}{2}\varepsilon$. Allocating g_m gives $c_m(S, \pi) = 100$, so $\text{cost}(S, \pi) = \frac{m-1}{2}\varepsilon + 100 = \frac{99}{2} + 100 = \frac{299}{2} < \frac{99\,m}{2} + 1$ for all $m > 3$.

3 Intractability Results

We first present several results highlighting the computational intractability of envy minimization as an objective in the temporal fair division setting.

We begin by formalizing the decision problem.

TEMPORAL-ENVYMIN

Given an instance $\mathcal{I} = (N, G, \mathbf{v})$, an order $\pi = (g_1, \ldots, g_m)$ over the goods in G, and an integer $\gamma \in \mathbb{Z}_{\geq 0}$, can we find an allocation sequence S such that $\mathsf{cost}(S, \pi) \leq \gamma$?

Then, we show that the problem is computationally intractable even in the restricted setting where agents have *identical valuation functions*—that is, for any pair of agents $i, j \in N$ and good g, we have $v_i(g) = v_j(g) = v(g)$. Moreover, we go one step further by showing that a constant-factor approximation algorithm is unlikely to exist.

Theorem 1. *TEMPORAL-ENVYMIN is strongly NP-complete even when agents have identical valuations. Moreover, in this setting, there exists no constant-factor approximation algorithm, unless P = NP.*

Proof. We reduce from the 3-PARTITION problem, which is known to be strongly NP-complete [17]. An instance of 3-PARTITION is given by a multiset of positive integers $X = \{x_1, \ldots, x_{3k}\}$ (with $\sum_{j=1}^{3k} x_j = kT$); it is a yes-instance if there exists a partition of X into k subsets $X_1', \ldots, X_k'$ (each containing three integers) such that $\sum_{x \in X_j'} x = T$ for all $j \in [k]$, and a no-instance otherwise. Note that for each integer $x \in X$, we can without loss of generality assume that $x < T$ (otherwise it is trivially a no-instance).

Construct an instance of our problem, where $N = [k+2]$ and we have $m := 9k+7$ goods arriving in the order $\pi = (g_1, g_2, \ldots, g_{3k+1}, g_{3k+2}, g_{3k+3}, \ldots, g_{9k+7})$, with valuations defined as follows:

$$v(g_j) = \begin{cases} 10T & \text{if } j = 1; \\ x_{j-1} + 3T & \text{if } j \in \{2, \ldots, 3k+1\}; \\ 10T & \text{if } j = 3k+2; \\ 0 & \text{if } j \in \{3k+3, \ldots, 9k+7\}. \end{cases}$$

We first show that TEMPORAL-ENVYMIN is NP-complete (it is easy to see that the problem is in NP, we thus focus on proving NP-hardness). We do so by proving that there exists a solution $X'_1, \ldots, X'_k$ to 3-PARTITION if and only if there exists an allocation $\mathcal{A}$ (and hence corresponding allocation sequence S) such that $\mathsf{cost}(S, \pi) \leq 10T \cdot (3k+1)$ for the above constructed instance.

($\Rightarrow$) Suppose there exists a solution $X'_1, \ldots, X'_k$ to 3-PARTITION. Consider the sequence $S = (s_1, \ldots, s_m)$:

$$s_j = \begin{cases} 1 & \text{if } j \in \{1, 3k+3, \ldots, 9k+7\}; \\ 2 & \text{if } j = 3k+2; \\ \ell + 2 & \text{if } x_{j-1} \in X'_\ell \text{ for } \ell \in [k] \end{cases}$$

Observe that for all $t \in \{1, \ldots, 3k+1\}$, every agent $i \geq 3$ holds at most three positively-valued goods, whose total value is at most $T + 9T = 10T$. Thus, $\max_{i \in N} v(A_i^t) = 10T$ and $\min_{i \in N} v(A_i^t) = 0$, so we have that $c_t(S, \pi) = 10T$. Moreover, since each agent in $N \setminus \{1, 2\}$ has bundle value $T + 3 \cdot 3T = 10T$, we get that $c_{3k+2}(S, \pi) = 0$. Then,

$$\begin{aligned} \mathsf{cost}(S, \pi) &= \sum_{t=1}^{3k+2} c_t(S, \pi) + \sum_{t=3k+3}^{9k+7} c_t(S, \pi) \\ &= 10T \cdot (3k+1) + 0 + 0 = 10T \cdot (3k+1). \end{aligned}$$

($\Leftarrow$) Suppose there does not exist a solution to 3-PARTITION. This means that there does not exist a partition of integers in $X = \{x_1, \ldots, x_{3k}\}$ into k subsets of equal sum T. Equivalently, there is no way to partition the $3k$ goods $\{g_2, \ldots, g_{3k+1}\}$ into k bundles each of total value $10T$.

Let $i^* \in N$ be the agent that receives good g_{3k+2}, i.e., $g_{3k+2} \in A_{i^*}$. We split our analysis into two cases.

Case 1: No good in $\{g_1, \ldots, g_{3k+1}\}$ *allocated to agent* i^*. Let g_1 be allocated to agent $i' \in N \setminus \{i^*\}$. Then, $A^1_{i'} = \{g_1\}$ and $v(A^1_{i'}) = 10T$. Now, since no goods in $\{g_1, \ldots, g_{3k+1}\}$ was allocated to agent i^*, for all $t \in \{1, \ldots, 3k+1\}$, we have that $A^t_{i^*} = \varnothing$, giving us $c_t(S, \pi) \geq 10T$. At round $3k+2$, agent i^* receives a good valued at $10T$ and thus has value exactly $10T$ (since she received nothing earlier). If $c_{3k+2}(S, \pi) = 0$, then every agent must have value exactly $10T$ at round $3k+2$ (since the total value of the first $3k+2$ goods is $10T(k+2)$, equality across $k+2$ agents forces each to have value $10T$). The agent i' holding the first good valued at $10T$ (i.e., g_1) cannot hold any other positively-valued good (each such good has value $> 3T$), else it would exceed $10T$. Therefore, the remaining k agents must partition the $3k$ goods of values $x_{j-1} + 3T$ into k bundles each of value $10T$. Since each such good has value strictly between $3T$ and $4T$, each bundle must contain exactly 3 goods, and the x_j parts in each bundle must sum to T, which is a 3-PARTITION solution, giving us a contradiction. Thus, $c_{3k+2}(S, \pi) \geq 1$, and together with $\sum_{t=1}^{3k+1} c_t(S, \pi) \geq 10T(3k+1)$, we get $\mathsf{cost}(S, \pi) > 10T(3k+1)$.

Case 2: Some good in $\{g_1, \ldots, g_{3k+1}\}$ *allocated to agent* i^*. Let g_1 be allocated to agent $i' \in N$ (note that it could be $i' = i^*$). Since i^* is also allocated good g_{3k+2}, we have that $v(A_{i^*}^{3k+2}) \geq 3T + 10T = 13T$. If $i' = i^*$, then $3k$ goods are distributed among $k+1$ agents, so some agent gets at most two goods from $\{g_2, \ldots, g_{3k+1}\}$. If $i' \neq i^*$, then i^* must have taken at least one of the $3k$ goods (since g_1 went to i'), leaving at most $3k-1$ such goods for the remaining k agents in $N \setminus \{i', i^*\}$; and by pigeonhole one of them gets at most two goods from $\{g_2, \ldots, g_{3k+1}\}$. Now, for each $j \in \{2, \ldots, 3k+1\}$, we know that $v(g_j) < T+3T = 4T$ (by our assumption that $x < T$ for each $x \in X$). Then, $v(A_i^{3k+2}) < 8T$. This means that $c_{3k+2}(S, \pi) \geq v(A_{i^*}^{3k+2}) - v(A_i^{3k+2}) > 13T - 8T = 5T$. There are $6k+5$ zero-valued goods after round $3k+2$, i.e., rounds $t = 3k+3, \ldots, 9k+7$. Since these goods do not change any bundle values, $c_t(S, \pi) = c_{3k+2}(S, \pi)$ for all such t. Thus,

$$\sum_{t'=3k+3}^{9k+7} c_{t'} = (6k+5) \cdot c_{3k+2}(S, \pi) > (6k+5) \cdot 5T > 10\,T(3k+1),$$

which implies $\text{cost}(S, \pi) > 10T(3k+1)$.

Next, we argue that in (the same) setting where agents have identical valuations, there exists no constant-factor approximation algorithm, unless P = NP.

Since 3-Partition is strongly NP-complete, meaning even when $T = \mathsf{poly}(n)$, the problem remains NP-complete. Thus, we can assume $T = \mathsf{poly}(n)$.

Then, note that in the reduction above, we showed that given an instance $\mathcal{I}$ and order π, determining whether we can find an allocation sequence S such that $\mathsf{cost}(S, \pi) \leq 10T \cdot (3k+1)$ is NP-complete. Equivalently,

- any yes-instance admits a sequence S with $\mathsf{cost}(S, \pi) \leq 10T \cdot (3k+1)$, and in particular $c_{3k+2}(S, \pi) = 0$;
- any no-instance will force any sequence S to have $c_{3k+2}(S, \pi) \geq 1$.

Let $B := 10T(3k+1)$ and fix any constant $\alpha \geq 1$. To amplify the gap, append $Z_\alpha := \lceil B(\alpha - 1) \rceil + 1$ zero-valued goods after g_{9k+7}. In a yes-instance, the allocation above still has cost at most B, because the envy is already zero from round $3k+2$ onward. In a no-instance, every allocation has positive envy after round $3k+2$; since all appended goods have value zero, this envy persists through the appended rounds. Thus, every allocation has cost strictly larger than $B + Z_\alpha > \alpha B$. Therefore, given a 3-Partition instance, run the assumed α-approximation on the corresponding Temporal-EnvyMin instance and compare its returned cost with αB. If the original 3-Partition instance is a yes-instance, the returned cost is at most αB. If it is a no-instance, every feasible allocation has cost greater than αB. The assumed approximation algorithm would therefore decide 3-Partition in polynomial time, which is impossible unless $\mathsf{P} = \mathsf{NP}$.

Notably, the above hardness result continues to hold even when the maximum value of any good is bounded by a polynomial in n, owing to the strong NP-completeness property of the 3-Partition problem used in the reduction.

We now turn to a different restricted setting in which agents have *binary valuation functions*—that is, for each agent $i \in N$ and good g, $v_i(g) \in \{0, 1\}$. In this case, we establish a second intractability result by reducing from a known NP-hard problem in the standard (offline) fair division literature: deciding whether there exists a complete envy-free allocation under binary valuations, a problem we refer to as BINARY-EF. This hardness was first shown implicitly by Aziz et al. [3] and later made explicit by Hosseini et al. [24]. As in the previous case, we show that a constant-factor approximation algorithm is unlikely to exist.

Theorem 2. *TEMPORAL-ENVYMIN is NP-complete even when agents have binary valuations. Moreover, in this setting, there exists no constant-factor approximation algorithm, unless P = NP.*

4 Tractability in Restricted Settings

Given the computational hardness of finding an envy-minimizing allocation sequence, even under two distinct restricted settings (identical valuations or binary valuations), a natural follow-up question is whether there exists any restricted setting for which an optimal solution can be computed efficiently.

We begin with a simple warm-up result. The most favorable remaining setting is when valuations are both binary *and* identical. While this does not exactly reduce the problem to one with identically-valued goods,[2] it is closely related. In this case, a straightforward greedy algorithm (which allocates each arriving good to an agent with the currently lowest total bundle value) produces an allocation with minimum cost.

Proposition 1. *Under binary and identical valuations, an optimal sequence can be computed in polynomial time.*

Next, for the main result of this section, we present a dynamic programming algorithm that runs in time $\mathcal{O}((m+1)(V_{\max}m^2+1)(mV_{\max}+1)^{n^2} \cdot n^3)$, where $V_{\max} := \max_{i \in N, g \in G} v_i(g)$ is the maximum value of any good in any agent's view (and we can assume valuations are encoded in unary and scaled to integers). For $t \in \{0, \ldots, m\}$, let $M^t \in \{0, \ldots, m \cdot V_{\max}\}^{n \times n}$ be the *valuation matrix* after the first t goods have arrived: $M^t_{i,j}$ is the value agent i has for agent j's bundle thus far, and M^0 is the all-zero matrix.

The algorithm is presented as follows (Algorithm 1).

Intuitively, the algorithm explores every possible way to assign the first t goods while precisely tracking the valuation matrix M and cost (i.e., envy) incurred c. At each step, it branches on which agent receives the next good, updates the corresponding column of M, accrues the cost incurred, and records a predecessor pointer. At the end (layer m), it scans through all reachable pairs (c, M) and returns the one minimizing cost, reconstructing a witnessing allocation by following the pointers backward. Our result is as follows.

[2] This setting has also been studied in other fair division contexts; see, e.g., Elkind et al. [13].

Algorithm 1. Dynamic programming algorithm that returns an optimal sequence

Input: Instance $\mathcal{I} = (N, G, \mathbf{v})$ and order $\pi = (g_1, \ldots, g_m)$.
Output: Allocation sequence $S = (s_1, \ldots, s_m)$.

1: Let M^0 be the all–zero $n \times n$ matrix
2: Create hash maps $\mathrm{DP}[0], \ldots, \mathrm{DP}[m]$ mapping keys (c, M) to predecessor pointers
3: Initialize $\mathrm{DP}[0][(0, M^0)] \leftarrow \varnothing$
4: **for** $t = 0, \ldots, m-1$ **do**
5:     **for all** states (c, M) in $\mathrm{DP}[t]$ **do**
6:         **for** $s = 1, \ldots, n$ **do**
7:             $M' \leftarrow M$ (deep copy)
8:             **for** $i = 1, \ldots, n$ **do**
9:                 $M'_{i,s} \leftarrow M'_{i,s} + v_i(g_{t+1})$
10:             **end for**
11:             $c' \leftarrow c + \max_{i,j} \max\{0, M'_{i,j} - M'_{i,i}\}$
12:             **if** $(c', M') \notin \mathrm{DP}[t+1]$ **then**
13:                 $\mathrm{DP}[t+1][(c', M')] \leftarrow ((c, M), s)$
14:             **end if**
15:         **end for**
16:     **end for**
17: **end for**
18: Let $(c^*, M^*) := \arg\min_{(c,M) \in \mathrm{DP}[m]} c$
19: Initialize $S = (s_1, \ldots, s_m) = (0, \ldots, 0)$ and $(c, M) \leftarrow (c^*, M^*)$
20: **for** $t = m, \ldots, 1$ **do**
21:     $((c_{\mathrm{prev}}, M_{\mathrm{prev}}), s_t) \leftarrow \mathrm{DP}[t][(c, M)]$
22:     $S[t] \leftarrow s_t$
23:     $(c, M) \leftarrow (c_{\mathrm{prev}}, M_{\mathrm{prev}})$
24: **end for**
25: **return** $S = (s_1, \ldots, s_m)$

Theorem 3. *Algorithm 1 returns an optimal sequence in time* $\mathcal{O}((m+1)(V_{\max} m^2 + 1)(m V_{\max} + 1)^{n^2} \cdot n^3)$.

Proof. We first prove correctness. Observe that the $\{(c, M) : (c, M) \in \mathrm{DP}[m]\}$ is the set of pairs attainable after all goods have arrived. Then, selecting (c^*, M^*) with minimum c^* (Line 18) corresponds to one with minimum cost (or cumulative envy). From there, our algorithm is able to reconstruct a corresponding allocation sequence (Lines 20–24).

Thus, it suffices for us to prove the following invariant. Let $\pi_t := (g_1, \ldots, g_t)$.

Invariant. For every $t \in \{0, \ldots, m\}$ and pair (c, M), $\mathrm{DP}[t][(c, M)]$ exists if and only if there is an allocation sequence X_t for the first t goods (prefix π_t) such that the resulting valuation matrix is M and $c = \sum_{\tau=1}^{t} c_\tau(X_t, \pi_\tau)$. Moreover, the predecessor pointer encodes one such sequence.

We prove the invariant by induction on $t \in \{0, \ldots, m\}$.

For the base case, at $t = 0$, $\mathrm{DP}[t]$ only contains $(0, M^0)$, where M^0 is the all-zero matrix; and the cost is 0. Thus the invariant holds trivially.

Next, we prove the inductive step. Assume the invariant holds for some $t < m$. Since for each round t, $c_t(S, \pi) \leq t \cdot V_{\max}$, we have $\sum_{t=1}^{m} c_t(S, \pi) \leq V_{\max} \cdot m(m+1)/2 < V_{\max} \cdot m^2$.

Consider any state $(c, M) \in \mathrm{DP}[t]$. By the induction hypothesis, there exists an allocation sequence $X_t = (x_1, \ldots, x_t)$ of the first t goods with valuation matrix M and cost $\mathsf{cost}(X_t, \pi_t) = c$. When good g_{t+1} arrives, Algorithm 1 considers every agent $s \in N$ and for each s, constructs M' by increasing column s by $v_i(g_{t+1})$. Hence every feasible extension is represented in $\mathrm{DP}[t+1]$.

Conversely, suppose (c', M') is inserted into $\mathrm{DP}[t+1]$ from predecessor (c, M) using agent s. By the induction hypothesis, (c, M) arises from some allocation sequence $(x_1, \ldots, x_t)$ with matrix M and cost $\mathsf{cost}(X_t, \pi_t)$; extending by $x_{t+1} = s$ gives us matrix M' and updating the cost to c', so (c', M') corresponds to a feasible allocation of $t + 1$ goods. Note that after updating column s, M' is exactly the valuation matrix after $t + 1$ items under the extended sequence. Therefore, the maximum envy at round $t + 1$ is

$$c_{t+1} = \max_{i,j} \max\{0,\ M'_{i,j} - M'_{i,i}\},$$

so the cumulative cost is consistent with Line 11 of the algorithm. Thus the invariant holds for $t + 1$.

By induction, the invariant holds for all $t \leq m$, and optimality follows.

Next, we prove the running time. The state space is indexed by (t, c, M) with $t \in \{0, \ldots, m\}, c \in \{0, \ldots, V_{\max} \cdot m^2\}$, and $M \in \{0, \ldots, m \cdot V_{\max}\}^{n \times n}$. Thus, the number of states is

$$(m + 1) \cdot (V_{\max} \cdot m^2 + 1) \cdot (m \cdot V_{\max} + 1)^{n^2}.$$

From each state, there are n agents the algorithm can consider allocating the incoming good to, updates one column of M and computes the new cost. Both operations (i.e., per transition) take $\mathcal{O}(n^2)$ time. Since there are n transitions per state, it takes $\mathcal{O}(n^3)$ per state. Thus, the total running time is $\mathcal{O}((m + 1)(V_{\max} m^2 + 1)(mV_{\max} + 1)^{n^2} \cdot n^3)$. Reconstruction follows m pointers and is $\mathcal{O}(m)$, which does not change the bound.

This result has two important implications. First, for fixed n, the running time is polynomial in m and $V_{\max}$; thus the algorithm is pseudopolynomial. In particular, if item values are polynomially bounded integers (or given in unary), the algorithm runs in polynomial time.

Corollary 1. *TEMPORAL-ENVYMIN is XP with respect to (n, V_{max}). Equivalently, it is solvable in pseudopolynomial time when n is bounded by a constant.*

Second, in the case of binary valuations,[3] the size of the state space in the dynamic program becomes more structured. Then, the number of agents is constant, the problem is polynomial-time solvable (i.e. slicewise polynomial in n).

[3] Binary valuations are very well-studied in online fair division [1,2,35] and in the broader fair division literature [21,24,34].

Corollary 2. *Under binary valuations,* TEMPORAL-ENVYMIN *is* XP *with respect to* n.

These results show that, despite the general computational hardness of the problem, efficient algorithms are achievable under natural and practically motivated restrictions.

That being said, an intriguing open question remains: is the problem polynomial-time solvable when the number of agents is constant and agents have identical valuation functions? We conjecture that the answer is 'no'.

As a partial positive result, we provide an FPTAS for identical valuations (with integer item values) when n is fixed.

Theorem 4. *For any fixed* $n \geq 2$*, under identical valuations with integer-valued items, and for every* $\varepsilon \in (0, 1)$*, there exists a* $(1 + \varepsilon)$*-approximation algorithm whose running time is polynomial in* m *and* $1/\varepsilon$.

5 Choosing the Arrival Sequence

The results presented in Sect. 3 show that computing a cost-minimizing allocation sequence is generally intractable, even under restricted settings such as identical or binary valuations. While Sect. 4 presents some positive algorithmic results under stronger assumptions, the overall hardness results align with existing impossibility results in the literature on online and temporal fair division: fairness objectives remain elusive in the presence of fixed input sequences. In fact, we illustrate with an example how an adversary deciding the arrival order can make a significant difference when it comes to minimizing cumulative envy.

Example 2. Consider an instance with $n = 2$ and identical valuation function v. Fix any integer $q \geq 2$, let $m := 2q + 1$, and set $\varepsilon := 99/(2q)$. Thus, m is odd and $(m - 1)\varepsilon = 99$. There is one good of value 100 and $m - 1$ goods of value ε.

- If the arrival order is $\pi = (g_1, \ldots, g_m)$ with $v(g_1) = 100$ and $v(g_t) = \varepsilon$ for all $t \geq 2$, then after round 1, $c_1(S, \pi) = 100$ for every allocation sequence S. Furthermore, each subsequent ε-good can reduce the gap $|v(A_1^t) - v(A_2^t)|$ by at most ε, so for $k = 0, 1, \ldots, m - 1$, $c_{1+k}(S, \pi) \geq 100 - k\varepsilon$. Allocating every ε-good to the currently lagging agent achieves equality at every round, and therefore $\min_{S \in \mathcal{S}} \text{cost}(S, \pi) = \sum_{k=0}^{m-1} (100 - k\varepsilon) = 100\,m - \varepsilon\frac{m(m-1)}{2} = \frac{101\,m}{2}$, which is $\Theta(m)$.
- In contrast, if the ε-goods arrive first (e.g., $\pi' = (g_2, \ldots, g_m, g_1)$), then allocating the first $m-1$ goods alternately keeps $c_t(S, \pi') \leq \varepsilon$ for all $t \leq m-1$, and the last step contributes $c_m(S, \pi') = 100$. Consequently, $\text{cost}(S, \pi') = \frac{m-1}{2}\varepsilon + 100 = \frac{299}{2}$, which is $O(1)$ in m.

Thus, when one item dominates in value, placing it early can force cumulative cost that is a factor $\Theta(m)$ larger than an order that places it last.

Motivated by this example, we study a variant in which the algorithm chooses the order of the goods, while the agents' valuations are fixed in advance. This models settings where the full set of goods is known and goods can be held briefly before release. For example, a food bank may have several donated pallets in storage and choose which pallet to allocate next, or a public agency may choose the order in which approved permits are issued. We ask whether control over the order can reduce cumulative envy.[4]

Importantly, this setting is not inherently "stronger" or "weaker" than the standard one; it is simply of a different structure. Although the ability to control the arrival order offers additional flexibility, the benchmark for optimization also shifts: the optimal solution under this new setting may differ from that in the fixed-order setting. As a result, the optimization problem (e.g., obtaining approximation results) does not necessarily become easier—the performance is still measured relative to a stronger baseline, and the underlying computational challenges remain significant.

Observe that the cost objective is cumulative, so even when the final allocation can be envy-free, early rounds may still incur substantial envy. In the special case of identical valuations, Lemma 1 (stated below) implies the universal lower bound $\mathsf{OPT}(\mathcal{I}) \geq (1 - 1/n) \cdot v(G)$. One might hope that by choosing the arrival order, the algorithm could always achieve this bound. Our next result shows that even deciding whether this lower bound is attainable is NP-complete.

TEMPORAL-ENVYMIN-SEQ

Given an instance $\mathcal{I} = (N, G, \mathbf{v})$ and an integer $\gamma \in \mathbb{Z}_{\geq 0}$, can we find a permutation π over the goods in G and an allocation sequence S such that $\mathsf{cost}(S, \pi) \leq \gamma$?

Theorem 5. *TEMPORAL-ENVYMIN-SEQ is NP-complete even for two agents with identical valuations.*

Theorem 5 shows that allowing the algorithm to choose the arrival order does not eliminate computational intractability: the problem remains NP-hard even under identical valuations.[5] Nevertheless, this setting admits simple algorithms with provable approximation and additive guarantees.

We first state a universal lower bound (independent of the chosen order), which will serve as a benchmark for both hardness and approximation results. Importantly, the bound holds for any number of agents, assuming identical valuations. Given an instance $\mathcal{I}$, let $\mathsf{OPT}(\mathcal{I}) := \min_{S \in \mathcal{S}, \pi \in \Pi} \mathsf{cost}(S, \pi)$ denote the min-

---

[4] Many related online problems assume a *random arrival order* as a way to circumvent impossibility results that arise under adversarial input models [4,12,15,16,18,20,26,27].

[5] This setting has also been extensively studied both in sequential fair division models [14,25] and in the broader fair division literature [5,32].

imum possible cost achievable over all arrival orders π and allocation sequence S.

Lemma 1. *For any instance $\mathcal{I} = (N, G, \mathbf{v})$ where $n \geq 2$ and agents have identical valuations, $OPT(\mathcal{I}) \geq (1 - 1/n)\, v(G)$. Moreover, the bound is tight.*

Next, we introduce the following algorithm (Algorithm 2), designed for the setting where agents have identical valuations. The algorithm proceeds by first sorting the goods in increasing order of value (that will be the π), then iteratively allocating each good to the agent with the currently smallest bundle value. Despite its simplicity, we will show that this greedy approach is able to give us several positive approximation guarantees.

Algorithm 2. IDENTICAL-LOWEST-FIRST

Input: Instance $\mathcal{I} = (N, G, \mathbf{v})$.
Output: An order π and allocation sequence $S = (s_1, \dots, s_m)$.

```
Initialize A^(0) ← (∅, ..., ∅) and label goods such that v(g_1) ≤ ··· ≤ v(g_m)
π ← (g_1, ..., g_m)
for t = 1, ..., m do
    Let i* ∈ argmin_{i∈N} v(A_i^{t-1}), with ties broken in favor of the lowest-index agent
    s_t ← i*
    A_{i*}^t ← A_{i*}^{t-1} ∪ {g_t}
    A_i^t ← A_i^{t-1} for all i ∈ N \ {i*}
end for
return π and allocation sequence S = (s_1, ..., s_m)
```

Scheduling interpretation. Under identical valuations, Algorithm 2 has the same steps as shortest-processing-time-first list scheduling on identical machines: goods are jobs, agents are machines, and $v(g)$ is the processing time of job g. The objectives are different, however. List scheduling is usually analyzed using the final makespan, that is, the largest final machine load. In our setting, c_t is the difference between the largest and smallest loads after the first t jobs, and we minimize $\sum_t c_t$. Thus, the 3/2 factor in Theorem 6 does not follow from the usual list-scheduling analysis, although the common greedy rule may help explain why the same constant appears [19].

First, we show that in the case of two agents, we can get a 3/2-approximation to the optimal cost.

Theorem 6. *When $n = 2$ and the agents have identical valuations, Algorithm 2 achieves a 3/2-approximation to the optimal cost.*

We can extend the analysis to any n, obtaining an $\frac{n}{n-1}$-approximation (which approaches 1 as n grows).

Theorem 7. *For all $n \geq 2$, if the agents have identical valuations, then Algorithm 2 achieves a $\frac{n}{n-1}$-approximation to the optimal cost.*

For $n = 2$, the 3/2-approximation guarantee of Theorem 6 is tight; see Appendix C.5. For $n \geq 3$, Appendix C.6 provides an instance on which Identical-Lowest-First achieves approximation ratio $\frac{2n-1}{2n-2}$.

Finally, we complement the multiplicative bounds with an additive approximation guarantee, stated in terms of $V_{\max}$.

Theorem 8. *For all $n \geq 2$, if agents have identical valuations, then Algorithm 2 outputs an order π and allocation sequence S such that $\mathsf{cost}(S, \pi) \leq \mathsf{OPT}(\mathcal{I}) + \left(1 - \frac{1}{n}\right) V_{\max}$.*

In Appendix C.8, we present a matching lower bound.

6 Conclusion

In this paper, we initiated the study of envy minimization in temporal fair division from an optimization perspective, departing from the traditional focus on discrete relaxations like EF1 and EFX and on the prefix-based notions studied in earlier temporal work. In the standard model where the order of goods is adversarially chosen and fixed, we show that minimizing this objective is computationally intractable and cannot be approximated within any constant factor unless $\mathsf{P} = \mathsf{NP}$. In spite of this, we provide a dynamic programming algorithm that computes an optimal solution in several special cases. We then explored a natural variant in which the algorithm is allowed to choose the arrival order of goods, while an adversary pre-selects the valuations. Even with this additional flexibility, we show that the problem remains NP-complete for just two agents and identical valuations. We complement this with efficient approximation algorithms.

Our results contribute to the growing understanding of temporal fairness in sequential allocation problems. Several directions remain open. In particular, it would be interesting to study discounted cumulative envy where recent unfairness matters more than past inequities.

References

1. Aleksandrov, M., Aziz, H., Gaspers, S., Walsh, T.: Online fair division: analysing a food bank problem. In: Proceedings of the 24th International Joint Conference on Artificial Intelligence (IJCAI), pp. 2540–2546 (2015)
2. Aleksandrov, M., Walsh, T.: Pure Nash equilibria in online fair division. In: Proceedings of the 26th International Joint Conference on Artificial Intelligence (IJCAI), pp. 42–48 (2017)
3. Aziz, H., Gaspers, S., Mackenzie, S., Walsh, T.: Fair assignment of indivisible objects under ordinal preferences. Artif. Intell. **227**, 71–92 (2015)

4. Babaioff, M., Immorlica, N., Kempe, D., Kleinberg, R.: A knapsack secretary problem with applications. In: Proceedings of the 10th International Workshop on Approximation (APPROX) and the 11th International Workshop on Randomization, and Combinatorial Optimization. Algorithms and Techniques (RANDOM), pp. 16–28 (2007)
5. Barman, S., Sundaram, R.G.: Uniform welfare guarantees under identical subadditive valuations. In: Proceedings of the 29th International Joint Conference on Artificial Intelligence (IJCAI), pp. 46–52 (2020)
6. Bei, X., Li, Z., Luo, J.: Fair and efficient multi-resource allocation for cloud computing. In: Proceedings of the 18th Conference on Web and Internet Economics (WINE), pp. 169–186 (2022)
7. Benadè, G., Kazachkov, A.M., Procaccia, A.D., Psomas, A., Zeng, D.: Fair and efficient online allocations. Oper. Res. **72**(4), 1438–1452 (2023)
8. Benadè, G., Kazachkov, A.M., Procaccia, A.D., Psomas, C.-A.: How to make envy vanish over time. In: Proceedings of the 19th ACM Conference on Economics and Computation (EC), pp. 593–610 (2018)
9. Brams, S.J., Taylor, A.D.: Fair Division: From Cake-Cutting to Dispute Resolution. Cambridge University Press (1996)
10. Chaudhury, B.R., Garg, J., Mehlhorn, K.: EFX exists for three agents. J. ACM **71**(1), 1–27 (2024)
11. Cookson, B., Ebadian, S., Shah, N.: Temporal fair division. In: Proceedings of the 39th AAAI Conference on Artificial Intelligence (AAAI), pp. 13727–13734 (2025)
12. Devanur, N.R., Hayes, T.P.: The adwords problem: online keyword matching with budgeted bidders under random permutations. In: Proceedings of the 10th ACM Conference on Electronic Commerce (EC), pp. 71–78 (2009)
13. Elkind, E., Igarashi, A., Teh, N.: Fair division of chores with budget constraints. In: Proceedings of the 17th International Symposium on Algorithmic Game Theory (SAGT), pp. 55–71 (2024)
14. Elkind, E., Lam, A., Latifian, M., Neoh, T.Y., Teh, N.: Temporal fair division of indivisible items. In: Proceedings of the 24th International Conference on Autonomous Agents and Multiagent Systems (AAMAS), pp. 676–685 (2025)
15. Feldman, J., Korula, N., Mirrokni, V., Muthukrishnan, S., Pál, M.: Online ad assignment with free disposal. In: Leonardi, S. (ed.) Proceedings of the 5th International Workshop on Internet and Network Economics (WINE), pp. 374–385 (2009)
16. Feldman, J., Mehta, A., Mirrokni, V., Muthukrishnan, S.: Online stochastic matching: beating 1-1/e. In: Proceedings of the 50th Annual IEEE Symposium on Foundations of Computer Science (FOCS), pp. 117–126 (2009)
17. Garey, M.R., Johnson, D.S.: Complexity results for multiprocessor scheduling under resource constraints. SIAM J. Comput. **4**(4), 397–411 (1975)
18. Goel, G., Mehta, A.: Online budgeted matching in random input models with applications to adwords. In: Proceedings of the 19th Annual ACM-SIAM Symposium on Discrete Algorithms (SODA), pp. 982–991 (2008)
19. Graham, R.L.: Bounds for certain multiprocessing anomalies. Bell Syst. Tech. J. **45**, 1563–1581 (1966)
20. Hajiaghayi, M., Khani, M., Panigrahi, D., Springer, M.: Online algorithms for the Santa Claus problem. In: Proceedings of the 36th International Conference on Neural Information Processing Systems (NeurIPS), pp. 30732–30743 (2022)
21. Halpern, D., Procaccia, A.D., Psomas, A., Shah, N.: Fair division with binary valuations: one rule to rule them all. In: Proceedings of the 16th Conference on Web and Internet Economics (WINE), pp. 370–383 (2020). Extended version available at arXiv:2007.06073v2

22. Halpern, D., Psomas, A., Verma, P., Xie, D.: Online envy minimization and multicolor discrepancy: equivalences and separations. In: Proceedings of the 26th ACM Conference on Economics and Computation (EC), p. 188 (2025)
23. He, J., Procaccia, A.D., Psomas, A., Zeng, D.: Achieving a fairer future by changing the past. In: Proceedings of the 28th International Joint Conference on Artificial Intelligence (IJCAI), pp. 343–349 (2019)
24. Hosseini, H., Sikdar, S., Vaish, R., Wang, H., Xia, L.: Fair division through information withholding. In: Proceedings of the 34th AAAI Conference on Artificial Intelligence (AAAI), pp. 2014–2021 (2020)
25. Igarashi, A., Lackner, M., Nardi, O., Novaro, A.: Repeated fair allocation of indivisible items. In: Proceedings of the 38th AAAI Conference on Artificial Intelligence (AAAI), pp. 9781–9789 (2024)
26. Karande, C., Mehta, A., Tripathi, P.: Online bipartite matching with unknown distributions. In: Proceedings of the 43rd Annual ACM Symposium on Theory of Computing (STOC), pp. 587–596 (2011)
27. Kleinberg, R.: A multiple-choice secretary algorithm with applications to online auctions. In: Proceedings of the 16th Annual ACM-SIAM Symposium on Discrete Algorithms (SODA), pp. 630–631 (2005)
28. Lipton, R., Markakis, E., Mossel, E., Saberi, A.: On approximately fair allocations of indivisible goods. In: Proceedings of the 5th ACM Conference on Electronic Commerce (EC), pp. 125–131 (2004)
29. Micheel, K.J., Wilczynski, A.: Fairness in repeated house allocation. In: Proceedings of the 27th European Conference on Artificial Intelligence (ECAI), pp. 3549–3556 (2024)
30. Moulin, H.: Fair Division and Collective Welfare. MIT Press (2003)
31. Murray, R., Kroer, C., Peysakhovich, A., Shah, P.: Robust market equilibria with uncertain preferences. In: Proceedings of the 34th AAAI Conference on Artificial Intelligence (AAAI), pp. 2192–2199 (2020)
32. Plaut, B., Roughgarden, T.: Almost envy-freeness with general valuations. SIAM J. Discret. Math. **34**(2), 1039–1068 (2020)
33. Spencer, J.: Balancing games. J. Comb. Theory Ser. B **23**(1), 68–74 (1977)
34. Suksompong, W., Teh, N.: On maximum weighted Nash welfare for binary valuations. Math. Soc. Sci. **117**, 101–108 (2022)
35. Wang, Y., Wei, T.: Online fair allocations with binary valuations and beyond (2025). arXiv preprint arXiv:2505.24321

Improved Lower Bounds and Output Augmentation for Facility Location Mechanisms

Rafael Gomes[1], Sophie Klumper[1], Guido Schäfer[1,2(✉)], and Jens Schlöter[1]

[1] Centrum Wiskunde and Informatica (CWI), Amsterdam, The Netherlands
{r.silva.jardim.gomes,s.j.klumper,g.schaefer,j.schloter}@cwi.nl
[2] University of Amsterdam, Amsterdam, The Netherlands

Abstract. We study the facility location problem in Euclidean space under the egalitarian objective, where a mechanism selects a facility location based on the reported positions of n strategic agents so as to minimize the maximum distance to any agent. While the line case is well understood, much less is known in higher dimensions: even in the plane the achievable approximation guarantees of randomized mechanisms that are strategyproof in expectation are poorly understood. We prove a lower bound of $1 + \sqrt{d/(2(d+1))}$ on the approximation ratio of any strategyproof in expectation mechanism in any dimension d as $n \to \infty$, improving the previous best lower bound of 1.118 in the plane to 1.577. The construction is based on a simple geometric configuration that extends to higher dimensions. We show that this barrier is driven by large populations: for $n = 2$ we derive a $\sqrt{2}$-approximate mechanism. We then study output augmentation, where the facility may lie outside the agents' domain. For agents on a line and the facility in the plane, we design a deterministic strategyproof $\sqrt{2}$-approximate mechanism with a matching lower bound. This already breaks the 3/2 lower bound for randomized mechanisms without augmentation, establishing that output augmentation allows for strictly more powerful mechanisms. As our main technical result, we obtain a randomized 3/2-approximate mechanism that is group-strategyproof in expectation for agents on the unit circle and the facility in the plane. The mechanism distributes probability mass in a report-dependent way between the optimal facility location and extreme agent locations. We complement this with a lower bound of 2 for deterministic group-strategyproof mechanisms, showing the limitations of output augmentation without randomization.

Keywords: Mechanism Design · Facility Location Problem · Randomized Mechanisms · Egalitarian Social Cost · Output Augmentation

P. Lenzner and D. Schmand (Eds.): SAGT 2026, LNCS 16911, pp. 205–223, 2027.
https://doi.org/10.1007/978-3-032-38782-0_12

1 Introduction

The facility location problem has been a prototypical benchmark for approximate mechanism design without money since its introduction by Procaccia and Tennenholtz [14]. A planner runs a mechanism $\mathcal{M}$ to determine a (random) location Y of a facility to serve a set $N = \{1, \ldots, n\}$ of $n \geq 2$ agents, where each agent $i \in N$ has a private location $x_i \in \mathbb{R}^d$ with $d \geq 1$. Throughout this work, we consider distances in Euclidean space and adopt the egalitarian objective: Given locations $\boldsymbol{x} = (x_1, \ldots, x_n)$, the cost of agent i is the (expected) Euclidean distance $\mathbb{E}[d(x_i, Y)]$ from x_i to $Y = \mathcal{M}(\boldsymbol{x})$. Under the *egalitarian* objective, the mechanism seeks to minimize the maximum distance experienced by any agent, i.e., $\mathrm{MC}(\mathcal{M}, \boldsymbol{x}) = \mathbb{E}[\max_i d(x_i, \mathcal{M}(\boldsymbol{x}))]$. Because agents may misreport their locations to pull the facility closer to their true locations, we are interested in designing mechanisms that incentivize truthfulness: $\mathcal{M}$ is *strategyproof in expectation* if no agent can decrease their expected distance by unilaterally misreporting, and *group-strategyproof in expectation* if no coalition of agents can jointly misreport so that every member decreases their expected distance.

On the real line $\mathbb{R}$, this problem is essentially settled: Procaccia and Tennenholtz [14] established that the optimal egalitarian approximation ratio is 2 for deterministic mechanisms and $3/2$ for randomized mechanisms that are strategyproof in expectation. In higher-dimensional Euclidean space, the picture is far less complete for randomized mechanisms, and the gap between known upper and lower bounds on the approximation guarantee is striking. The best-known randomized mechanism in $\mathbb{R}^d$ is the *Centroid Mechanism* by Tang et al. [17] achieving an approximation ratio of $2 - 1/n$. On the lower bound side, the strongest result prior to this work was a bound of 1.118 in the plane $\mathbb{R}^2$, due to Balkanski et al. [2]. Closing this gap, even in $\mathbb{R}^2$, has remained open.[1]

A second open direction that we address in this paper concerns the design of mechanisms whose output is permitted to lie outside the agents' input domain. Note that this is conceptually different from resource augmentation in the sense of [15]: we do not weaken the benchmark, we enrich the mechanism's output space. Formally, we distinguish between the input space $\mathcal{I}$ where agents' reports live and the output space $\mathcal{O}$ where the facility is placed, with $\mathcal{I} \subseteq \mathcal{O}$. The standard setting in the literature takes $\mathcal{I} = \mathcal{O} = \mathbb{R}^d$; in the *output-augmented setting* we allow $\mathcal{I} \subsetneq \mathcal{O}$. Given reports $\boldsymbol{x} = (x_1, \ldots, x_n) \in \mathcal{I}^n$, the optimum $\mathrm{OPT}(\boldsymbol{x})$ is the radius of the smallest enclosing ball of $\boldsymbol{x}$ in the *output space* $\mathcal{O}$. The approximation ratio of $\mathcal{M}$ is $\sup_{\boldsymbol{x} \in \mathcal{I}^n} \mathrm{MC}(\mathcal{M}, \boldsymbol{x}) / \mathrm{OPT}(\boldsymbol{x})$.

Beyond its theoretical interest, this relaxation is also practically motivated: A radio antenna serves subscribers distributed along a road, but need not stand on the road itself. An offshore wind platform serves towns arranged along a coastal arc, but can be built at sea. Whether output augmentation allows mechanisms to bypass classical lower bounds is the main question we study in this setting.

[1] In higher dimensions, the optimal randomized *utilitarian* approximation ratio also remains open. Recent progress was made in [3] with a *universally* strategyproof mechanism that is $4/\pi$-approximate in $\mathbb{R}^2$, strictly improving upon the achievable guarantee of deterministic strategyproof mechanisms.

Our Contributions. Our results address two settings:

(1) Standard setting ($\mathcal{I} = \mathcal{O} = \mathbb{R}^d$). We prove that, as $n \to \infty$, every randomized mechanism that is strategyproof in expectation for egalitarian facility location in $\mathbb{R}^d$ has an approximation ratio of at least $1+\sqrt{d/2(d+1)}$. For the planar case $d = 2$, this gives a bound of $1 + 1/\sqrt{3} \approx 1.577$, improving the previous best lower bound of 1.118 [2]; the bound tends to $1 + 1/\sqrt{2} \approx 1.707$ as $d \to \infty$. The construction places agents at the vertices of a regular simplex inscribed in the unit sphere and then has one cluster of agents deviate to the boundary of a larger sphere centered at their original position. The new bound makes essential use of infinitely large populations, but in $\mathbb{R}^2$ a discretized argument gives a lower bound that grows with n, exceeding $3/2$ already for $n \geq 15$. For small n we obtain complementary results: a lower bound of 1.277 for $n \geq 3$, and a randomized $\sqrt{2}$-approximation for $n = 2$, which beats the $3/2$ ratio achievable on the line.

(2) Output-Augmented Setting ($\mathcal{I} \subsetneq \mathcal{O}$). We address the question whether output augmentation yields genuinely more powerful strategyproof mechanisms.

For agents on a line $\mathcal{I} = \mathbb{R}$ and the facility in the plane $\mathcal{O} = \mathbb{R}^2$, we design a simple *deterministic* strategyproof mechanism with an approximation ratio of $\sqrt{2}$, matched by a $\sqrt{2}$ lower bound for any deterministic mechanism. Notably, this shows that deterministic mechanisms even beat the classical *randomized* lower bound of $3/2$ for the line without augmentation [14], demonstrating that the augmented framework is strictly more powerful.

Our main technical contribution concerns agents on the unit circle $\mathcal{I} = S^1$ and the facility in the plane $\mathcal{O} = \mathbb{R}^2$. We design a randomized mechanism, the *Chord-Midpoint Mechanism*, that is group-strategyproof in expectation and achieves an approximation ratio of $3/2$. The mechanism identifies two extreme agents A and B that delimit the minimal arc containing all reports, and outputs A, B, or the midpoint of the chord AB according to a probability $\lambda(\alpha)$ that depends on the arc's angular span. The choice of $\lambda(\alpha)$ is delicate: it must be small enough such that agents have an incentive to reveal their true positions, and large enough such that the realized facility remains close to the chord midpoint in expectation. We complement this with a lower bound of 2 for any deterministic, unanimous, group-strategyproof mechanism in the same setting, showing that randomization is necessary to break the barrier.

To the best of our knowledge, studying output-augmented settings in this form is new, particularly when non-trivial input topologies are considered such as $\mathcal{I} = S^1$ and $\mathcal{O} = \mathbb{R}^2$ (see Related Work for prior work on dimension augmentation). We see the study of such concrete topologies as a stepping stone toward designing optimal mechanisms for increasingly rich input domains, which might ultimately lead to a resolution of the general setting.

Techniques. In our lower bounds for the standard setting, we combine symmetric simplex configurations with a cluster-deviation lemma (showing that a coalition of co-located agents cannot reduce their expected distance to their true position) to reduce the analysis to a purely geometric statement about the maximum diameter of a set under a fixed circumradius. A consequence of Jung's theorem is that this strategy is tight for the simplex-based construction, so any further improvement will require a structurally different approach. Given this geometric connection, it remains an intriguing open question whether a matching mechanism exists.

In the setting with reports on the circle $\mathcal{I} = S^1$ and facility in the plane $\mathcal{O} = \mathbb{R}^2$, the report-dependent mixing parameter $\lambda(\alpha)$ allows the mechanism to interpolate smoothly between the deterministic optimum (when the agents fill a semicircle) and a randomization that resembles the classical 3/2-mechanism on the line (when the arc is small). The analysis hinges on a tight factorization of the distance from any agent to the moving chord midpoint (established in Lemma 6). Our proof that the mechanism is group-strategyproof in expectation follows from a decomposition argument that reduces coalitional deviations to a sequence of unilateral arc-expansion and arc-shrinking moves.

Related Work. Following [14], extensive research has investigated truthful mechanisms across various settings. While the literature spans multiple social cost objectives, we focus on the egalitarian objective in this paper. We give a brief overview of further related work and refer to [6] for a more extensive survey.

Facility Location in Higher Dimensions. Moulin [12] showed that the generalized median scheme characterizes all deterministic strategyproof mechanisms on the line $\mathbb{R}$; subsequently, this result was extended to higher dimensions [5,10,13,17]. The characterization of mechanisms that are strategyproof in expectation remains an intriguing open problem. Under the stronger requirement of group-strategyproofness, Tang et al. [17] characterized randomized, translation-invariant mechanisms in strictly convex spaces as 2-dictatorial rules.

Facility Location on Networks. Another line of work embeds the problem on graphs, where agents and facilities both reside along the edges (in contrast to the output-augmented setting of this paper). Schummer and Vohra [16] provided characterizations of deterministic mechanisms showing that strategyproof rules behave similarly to generalized medians on trees but reduce to local dictatorships when restricted to cycles. In the randomized setting, Alon et al. [1] analyzed approximation bounds under the minimax objective, proving a $2 - o(1)$ lower bound for trees and presenting a tight 3/2 approximation mechanism for the circle graph under the egalitarian cost.

Constrained and Augmented Spaces. There is a body of literature studying settings where the agent input space and the facility output space do not coincide. In *constrained facility location*, the output space is a strict subset of the input space, i.e., $\mathcal{O} \subsetneq \mathcal{I}$, orthogonal to the output-augmented setting we consider in this paper. A variety of papers have studied this variant to understand what happens when the facility is restricted to specific sub-regions or discrete candidate locations [4,7,11,18]. Conversely, in *dimension-augmented* settings, the output space strictly encompasses the input space. To the best of our knowledge, the only prior work to explore this paradigm is by Fullerton et al. [8], who investigate the two-facility location problem under the utilitarian objective with $\mathcal{I} = \mathbb{R}$ and $\mathcal{O} = \mathbb{R}^2$.

2 Preliminaries

Let $\boldsymbol{x} \in \mathcal{I}^n$ be a profile of reported locations. We use the standard notation $\boldsymbol{x}_{-i}$ to denote the reports of all agents except agent i, and similarly $\boldsymbol{x}_{-S}$ for the reports of all agents outside a coalition $S \subseteq N$. Throughout the paper, we use $d(x, y)$ and $\|x - y\|$ interchangeably to denote the Euclidean distance between two points x and y.

A (randomized) mechanism $\mathcal{M}$ takes a profile $\boldsymbol{x} \in \mathcal{I}^n$ as input and outputs a (random) location $Y = \mathcal{M}(\boldsymbol{x}) \in \Delta(\mathcal{O})$.[2] $\mathcal{M}$ is deterministic if it outputs a location $y = \mathcal{M}(\boldsymbol{x})$ with probability 1 for each $\boldsymbol{x}$. A deterministic mechanism $\mathcal{M}$ is *strategyproof* if for any profile $\boldsymbol{x}$, agent i, and unilateral deviation $x_i' \in \mathcal{I}$, we have $d(x_i, \mathcal{M}(\boldsymbol{x})) \leq d(x_i, \mathcal{M}(x_i', \boldsymbol{x}_{-i}))$; similarly, a randomized mechanism $\mathcal{M}$ is *strategyproof in expectation* if $\mathbb{E}[d(x_i, \mathcal{M}(\boldsymbol{x}))] \leq \mathbb{E}[d(x_i, \mathcal{M}(x_i', \boldsymbol{x}_{-i}))]$. Furthermore, $\mathcal{M}$ satisfies *group-strategyproofness in expectation* if no coalition $S \subseteq N$ can jointly misreport to a partial profile $\boldsymbol{x}'_S$ such that $\mathbb{E}[d(x_i, \mathcal{M}(\boldsymbol{x}'_S, \boldsymbol{x}_{-S}))] < \mathbb{E}[d(x_i, \mathcal{M}(\boldsymbol{x}))]$ for all $i \in S$.

We say that a mechanism $\mathcal{M}$ is *anonymous* if its outcome is invariant to permutations of the agents' reports. $\mathcal{M}$ is *unanimous* if, whenever all agents $i \in N$ report the same location $x_i = u \in \mathcal{I}$, the facility is placed at u.

A mechanism $\mathcal{M}$ is *α-approximate* if for any $\boldsymbol{x} \in \mathcal{I}^n$: $\mathrm{MC}(\mathcal{M}, \boldsymbol{x}) \leq \alpha \cdot \mathrm{OPT}(\boldsymbol{x})$.

3 Randomized Mechanisms

In this section, we consider the standard setting with $\mathcal{I} = \mathcal{O} = \mathbb{R}^d$, where $d \geq 1$.

3.1 Lower Bound in $\mathbb{R}^d$

We start by proving the following lemma.

Lemma 1. *Let $S = \{x_0, \ldots, x_d\}$ be the vertices of a regular d-simplex in $\mathbb{R}^d$ such that the geometric median O satisfies $d(O, x_k) = 1$ for all $x_k \in S$. Then, given $\boldsymbol{x} = (x_0, \ldots, x_d)$, for any randomized mechanism $Y = \mathcal{M}(\boldsymbol{x})$ there exists a vertex $x_j \in S$ such that $\mathbb{E}[d(Y, x_j)] \geq 1$.*

Proof. For any realized facility location $y \in \mathbb{R}^d$, the sum of the Euclidean distances to the vertices of S is minimized at the geometric median, which for a regular simplex coincides with its circumcenter O. Because the distance from O to each of the $d+1$ vertices is exactly 1, the minimum possible sum of distances is $d+1$. Thus, for any $y \in \mathbb{R}^d$, we have the deterministic bound:

$$\sum_{k=0}^{d} d(y, x_k) \geq \sum_{k=0}^{d} d(O, x_k) = d + 1. \tag{1}$$

[2] We use $\Delta(\mathcal{O})$ to refer to the set of all distributions over $\mathcal{O}$.

Taking the expectation over the randomness of the mechanism $\mathcal{M}$, linearity of expectation yields:

$$\sum_{k=0}^{d} \mathbb{E}\left[d(Y, x_k)\right] = \mathbb{E}\left[\sum_{k=0}^{d} d(Y, x_k)\right] \geq d+1.$$

Because the sum of these $d+1$ expected distances is bounded below by $d+1$, at least one term in the sum must be at least 1. Therefore, there exists an index $j \in \{0, \ldots, d\}$ such that $\mathbb{E}[d(Y, x_j)] \geq 1$. □

The following lemma will be useful below.

Lemma 2. *Let $\mathcal{M}$ be a randomized mechanism that is strategyproof in expectation. Let $\boldsymbol{x}$ be a profile where a subset of k agents share the same true location u. Consider a profile $\boldsymbol{x}'$ where all k agents misreport their locations. Let $Y = \mathcal{M}(\boldsymbol{x})$ and $Y' = \mathcal{M}(\boldsymbol{x}')$. Then $\mathbb{E}[d(Y', u)] \geq \mathbb{E}[d(Y, u)]$.*

Proof. We construct a sequence of profiles $\boldsymbol{x} = \boldsymbol{x}_0, \boldsymbol{x}_1, \ldots, \boldsymbol{x}_k = \boldsymbol{x}'$. For each $i \in \{1, \ldots, k\}$, let $\boldsymbol{x}_i$ be the profile that we obtain after exactly i agents have changed their report from u to the respective misreported location in $\boldsymbol{x}'$. Let $Y_i = \mathcal{M}(\boldsymbol{x}_i)$ be the random outcome of the mechanism for profile $\boldsymbol{x}_i$.

Consider the transition from profile $\boldsymbol{x}_{i-1}$ to $\boldsymbol{x}_i$. The only difference between these two profiles is that a single agent, whose true location is u, changes their reported location. Because the mechanism $\mathcal{M}$ is strategyproof in expectation, this agent cannot decrease their expected distance to their true location u by misreporting, i.e., $\mathbb{E}[d(Y_i, u)] \geq \mathbb{E}[d(Y_{i-1}, u)]$. Chaining these inequalities for all $i \in \{1, 2, \ldots, k\}$, we obtain:

$$\mathbb{E}[d(Y', u)] = \mathbb{E}[d(Y_k, u)] \geq \mathbb{E}[d(Y_{k-1}, u)] \geq \cdots \geq \mathbb{E}[d(Y_0, u)] = E[d(Y, u)].$$

□

Theorem 1. *Any randomized strategyproof mechanism for facility location in $\mathbb{R}^d$, with $d \geq 1$, has an egalitarian approximation ratio of at least $1 + \sqrt{d/2(d+1)}$.*

Proof. Consider the unit sphere $C_O = S^{d-1}$ in $\mathbb{R}^d$ centered at the origin $O = (0, \ldots, 0)$. Let S be a regular simplex inscribed in S^{d-1}, defined by $d+1$ vertices $x_0, x_1, \ldots, x_d$, where we orient the simplex such that $x_0 = (1, 0, \ldots, 0)$. Because the circumradius of S is 1, the distance from the origin to any vertex is $d(O, x_k) = 1$ for all $k \in \{0, 1, \ldots, d\}$. The uniform side length of this regular simplex is given by $a_d = \sqrt{2 + 2/d}$. Therefore, the pairwise distance is $d(x_j, x_k) = a_d$ for all $j \neq k$.

See Fig. 1a for an illustration of the construction for $d = 2$.

Let n be a multiple of $d+1$. Consider an initial profile $\boldsymbol{x}$ of n agents equally distributed among the $d+1$ vertices of S. Let $Y = \mathcal{M}(\boldsymbol{x})$ denote the random facility location chosen by the mechanism. Applying Lemma 1 directly to the vertices of the regular simplex S, the expected distance from the facility to at least one of these vertices is at least 1. W.l.o.g. assume this holds for x_0, i.e.,

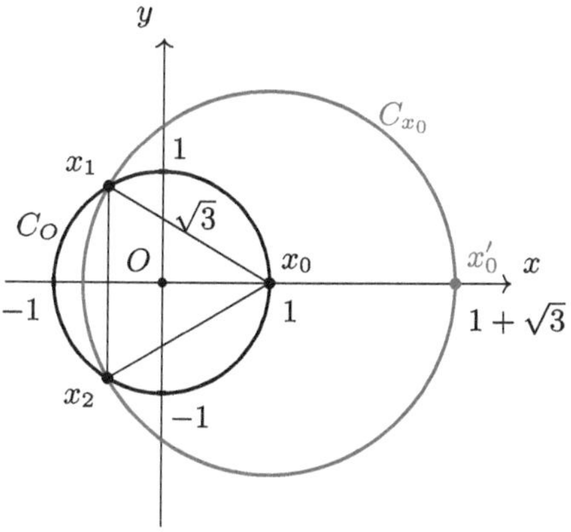

(a)

d	Lower bound
1	$1+\sqrt{1/4}=1.5$
2	$1+\sqrt{2/6}\approx 1.577$
3	$1+\sqrt{3/8}\approx 1.612$
∞	$1+\sqrt{1/2}\approx 1.707$

n	Lower bound ($d=2$)
6	$\sqrt{4/3}\approx 1.155$
9	$\sqrt{4/3+2/\sqrt{3}\cos(\pi/3)}\approx 1.382$
12	$\sqrt{4/3+2/\sqrt{3}\cos(\pi/4)}\approx 1.466$
15	$\sqrt{4/3+2/\sqrt{3}\cos(\pi/5)}\approx 1.506$

(b)

Fig. 1. (a) Lower bound instance for $d = 2$. (b) Asymptotic lower bounds as a function of d (top) and lower bounds for $d = 2$ as a function of n (bottom).

$$\mathbb{E}\left[d(Y, x_0)\right] \geq 1. \tag{2}$$

We now construct a sequence of modified profiles $\boldsymbol{x}'$ as $n \to \infty$. Let C_{x_0} be the $(d-1)$-sphere centered at x_0 with radius a_d. Observe that all other vertices $x_1, \ldots, x_d$ inherently lie on C_{x_0} because $d(x_0, x_k) = a_d$. We modify the profile by having the agents originally located at x_0 uniformly deviate over the surface of C_{x_0}.

Let $Y' = \mathcal{M}(\boldsymbol{x}')$. By Lemma 2, a simultaneous deviation by the subset of agents from their true location x_0 to the boundary of C_{x_0} cannot decrease their expected distance to x_0. Applying (2), we obtain:

$$\mathbb{E}[d(Y', x_0)] \geq \mathbb{E}[d(Y, x_0)] \geq 1.$$

To evaluate the egalitarian cost of $\mathcal{M}$ on $\boldsymbol{x}'$, consider any realized facility location y'. The supremum distance from y' to any point on the sphere C_{x_0} is achieved by extending the line segment from y' through the center x_0 to the far boundary. This supremum is exactly $d(y', x_0) + a_d$. As $n \to \infty$, the discretely distributed deviating agents densely populate C_{x_0}, and the maximum distance to any agent in the profile formally converges to this supremum:

$$\lim_{n\to\infty} \max_{i \in [n]} d(y', x_i') = d(y', x_0) + a_d.$$

Taking the expectation, the asymptotic expected egalitarian cost of the mechanism is bounded below by:

$$\lim_{n\to\infty} \mathrm{MC}(\mathcal{M}(\boldsymbol{x}'), \boldsymbol{x}') = \lim_{n\to\infty} \mathbb{E}\left[\max_{i\in[n]} d(Y', x_i')\right] = \mathbb{E}[d(Y', x_0)] + a_d \geq 1 + a_d.$$

Since the optimal egalitarian cost for the modified profile $\boldsymbol{x}'$ is $\mathrm{OPT}(\boldsymbol{x}') = a_d$, the asymptotic approximation ratio is at least:

$$\frac{1+a_d}{a_d} = 1 + \frac{1}{a_d} = 1 + \sqrt{\frac{d}{2(d+1)}}.$$

□

Remark 1. The established bound represents a natural limit for this specific deviation strategy. The proof requires an initial configuration of agents that are equidistant to its geometric median while maximizing the ratio of its circumradius to its diameter. By Jung's theorem, the maximum possible value of this ratio for any set in $\mathbb{R}^d$ is $\sqrt{d/2(d+1)}$. As the regular simplex achieves this limit, any further improvement to the lower bound will require a different proof strategy.

It is not hard to see that we can parameterize our lower bound construction for $d = 2$ as follows: Suppose in the initial profile $\boldsymbol{x}$ we have $n = 3k$ agents distributed equally over the three vertices, and we let the k agents in x_0 deviate equidistantly to the surface of C_{x_0}. We can then lower bound the maximum distance of y' to any of these points by considering the point x' on C_{x_0} that is nearest to the point that we obtain when projecting y' through the center x_0 onto C_{x_0}. Details are given in the full version of our paper [9]. Figure 1b (bottom table) summarizes the lower bounds we obtain.

Theorem 2. *Any randomized strategyproof mechanism for facility location in* $\mathbb{R}^2$ *has an egalitarian approximation ratio of at least* $\sqrt{4/3 + 2/\sqrt{3}\cos(\pi/(n/3))}$.

3.2 Results for Few Agents

In this subsection, we start by proving a lower bound for $n \geq 3$ agents. The proof is similar to the general lower bound. It relies on the following lemma, which, for a fixed profile, relates the distance from the optimal location to the egalitarian cost, whose proof can be found in the full version [9].

Lemma 3. *Consider the profile* $\boldsymbol{x}' = (x_1', x_2, x_3)$ *with* $x_1' = (0, 1+\sqrt{3})$, $x_2 = (\frac{\sqrt{3}}{2}, -\frac{1}{2})$, *and* $x_3 = (-\frac{\sqrt{3}}{2}, -\frac{1}{2})$. *Let* $L(r)$ *denote the minimum possible egalitarian cost for* $\boldsymbol{x}'$ *subject to the constraint that the facility is located at distance* r *from* $x_1 = (0, 1)$. *For* $r \geq 0$, *this minimal cost function is strictly convex and increasing, and is given by:*

$$L(r) = \sqrt{r^2 + \lambda r + 3}, \quad \textit{where } \lambda = \frac{2\sqrt{3}}{\sqrt{8 + 4\sqrt{3}}}.$$

We are now ready to prove the following:

Theorem 3. *Any randomized strategyproof mechanism for facility location in* $\mathbb{R}^2$ *has an egalitarian approximation ratio of at least* 1.277 *for* $n \geq 3$ *agents.*

Proof. Consider profile $\boldsymbol{x}$ of $n = 3$ agents at the vertices of a regular simplex inscribed in the unit circle: $x_1 = (0, 1)$, $x_2 = (\frac{\sqrt{3}}{2}, -\frac{1}{2})$, and $x_3 = (-\frac{\sqrt{3}}{2}, -\frac{1}{2})$.

By Lemma 1, the expected distance from the facility to at least one of these vertices is at least 1. Without loss of generality, assume $\mathbb{E}[d(\mathcal{M}(\boldsymbol{x}), x_1)] \geq 1$.

Following the deviation argument of Theorem 1, agent 1 shifts outward to $x_1' = (0, 1 + \sqrt{3})$. Now all agents in the new profile $\boldsymbol{x}' = (x_1', x_2, x_3)$ are at distance $\sqrt{3}$ from x_1. Thus, the optimal egalitarian cost for $\boldsymbol{x}'$ is exactly $\sqrt{3}$.

Let $R = d(\mathcal{M}(\boldsymbol{x}'), x_1)$. By strategyproofness, agent 1 cannot decrease their expected distance by misreporting, establishing the bound:

$$\mathbb{E}[R] \geq \mathbb{E}[d(\mathcal{M}(\boldsymbol{x}), x_1)] \geq 1.$$

By Lemma 3, the maximum distance from any realized facility to the agents in $\boldsymbol{x}'$ is bounded below by the convex, increasing function $L(R)$. Applying Jensen's Inequality, the expected cost of $\mathcal{M}$ given $\boldsymbol{x}'$ is bounded by:

$$\mathbb{E}[\mathrm{MC}(\mathcal{M}(\boldsymbol{x}'), \boldsymbol{x}')] \geq \mathbb{E}[L(R)] \geq L(\mathbb{E}[R]) \geq L(1) = \sqrt{4 + \lambda}.$$

Dividing this expected cost by the optimal cost for $\boldsymbol{x}'$ yields the approximation ratio $\alpha \geq \frac{\sqrt{4+\lambda}}{\sqrt{3}} \approx 1.277$. This lower bound extends to $n > 3$ by co-locating any additional agents at the origin. □

We now focus on the two-agent case in $\mathbb{R}^d$ for $d \geq 2$, where we present a randomized mechanism that outperforms the general lower bound of Theorem 1. The optimal facility always lies on the line connecting the two reported locations. Yet, if a mechanism restricts its output to this line, it cannot achieve an approximation ratio better than 1.5 [14]. By placing the facility outside this axis, our mechanism bypasses this restriction to achieve an improved ratio.

Definition 1 (Orthogonal Sphere Mechanism). *Given reports* x_1, x_2*, let* $m = \frac{x_1+x_2}{2}$ *and* $h = \frac{\|x_1-x_2\|}{2}$*. The mechanism outputs* $L = m + \boldsymbol{v}$*, where* $\boldsymbol{v}$ *is drawn uniformly from a* $(d-2)$*-dimensional sphere* $S^{\perp}$ *of radius* h *centered at the origin within the hyperplane orthogonal to the vector* $x_1 - x_2$*. (Note: For* $d = 2$*,* $S^{\perp}$ *consists of two vectors of length* h*, each chosen with probability* $\frac{1}{2}$*.)*

Theorem 4. *The Orthogonal Sphere Mechanism is strategyproof in expectation and has an egalitarian approximation ratio of* $\sqrt{2}$*.*

Proof. The optimal minimax cost is $\mathrm{OPT} = \frac{\|x_1-x_2\|}{2} = h$. Because any $\boldsymbol{v} \in S^{\perp}$ is orthogonal to the segment connecting x_1 and x_2, the mechanism places the facility at a distance $\sqrt{h^2 + \|\boldsymbol{v}\|^2} = \sqrt{h^2 + h^2} = h\sqrt{2}$ from both agents, yielding an approximation ratio of $\sqrt{2}$.

By symmetry, we may assume the true locations are $x_1 = (-R, 0, \ldots, 0)$ and $x_2 = (R, 0, \ldots, 0)$ for $R \geq 0$. Let agent 1 be the deviating agent and, w.l.o.g., rotate its misreport into the xy-plane: $x_1' = (-R+\delta_x, \delta_y, 0, \ldots, 0)$. The mechanism computes midpoint $m = (\frac{\delta_x}{2}, \frac{\delta_y}{2}, 0, \ldots, 0)$ and radius $h = \frac{1}{2}\|x_1' - x_2\|$, giving $h^2 = (R - \frac{\delta_x}{2})^2 + (\frac{\delta_y}{2})^2$. It places the facility at $L = m + \boldsymbol{v}$, with $\boldsymbol{v} = (v_x, v_y, \ldots, v_d)$ drawn uniformly from the $(d-2)$-sphere $S^\perp$ orthogonal to $x_1' - x_2$.

Due to symmetry, we evaluate antipodal pairs $\pm\boldsymbol{v} \in S^\perp$. Their corresponding squared distances to x_1 are $D_\pm = \|(m - x_1) \pm \boldsymbol{v}\|^2 = \|m - x_1\|^2 + \|\boldsymbol{v}\|^2 \pm 2\langle m - x_1, \boldsymbol{v}\rangle$. Since $\|\boldsymbol{v}\|^2 = h^2$, expanding the base cost yields $\|m - x_1\|^2 + h^2 = 2R^2 + \frac{\delta_x^2}{2} + \frac{\delta_y^2}{2}$. Because $\boldsymbol{v} \perp (x_1' - x_2) = (-2R + \delta_x, \delta_y, 0, \ldots, 0)$, we have $v_y\delta_y = (2R - \delta_x)v_x$. Substituting this yields $\langle m - x_1, \boldsymbol{v}\rangle = v_x(R + \frac{\delta_x}{2}) + v_y(\frac{\delta_y}{2}) = 2Rv_x$. Thus, $D_\pm = 2R^2 + \frac{\delta_x^2}{2} + \frac{\delta_y^2}{2} \pm 4Rv_x = 2[(R \pm v_x)^2 + z^2]$, where $z = \sqrt{\frac{\delta_x^2 + \delta_y^2}{4} - v_x^2}$.

To ensure $z \in \mathbb{R}$, note that $v_x^2 + v_y^2 \leq \|\boldsymbol{v}\|^2 = h^2$. Substituting $v_y = ((2R - \delta_x)v_x)/\delta_y$ into $v_x^2 + v_y^2 \leq h^2$ gives $v_x^2[1 + (2R - \delta_x)^2/\delta_y^2] \leq h^2$. Since $(2R - \delta_x)^2 + \delta_y^2 = 4h^2$, this simplifies to $v_x^2(4h^2/\delta_y^2) \leq h^2$, bounding $v_x^2 \leq \delta_y^2/4$.

Defining $p = (v_x, z)$ and focal points $F_{1,2} = (\mp R, 0)$ yields $D_\pm = 2[(R \pm v_x)^2 + z^2] = 2\|p - F_{1,2}\|^2$. The pair's average distance is $\frac{1}{2}(\sqrt{D_+} + \sqrt{D_-}) = \frac{\sqrt{2}}{2}(\|p - F_1\| + \|p - F_2\|) \geq \frac{\sqrt{2}}{2}\|F_1 - F_2\| = \sqrt{2}R$, where the last inequality follows by the triangle inequality. Since every pair satisfies this, $\mathbb{E}[d(L, x_1)] \geq \sqrt{2}R$. Truthful reporting achieves $\sqrt{2}R$; thus, no deviation decreases the expected cost. □

4 Dimension Augmented

We now focus on the output augmented setting where $\mathcal{I} \subsetneq \mathcal{O}$ and $\mathcal{O} = \mathbb{R}^2$, examining two cases: agents on a line and agents on a circle.

4.1 Line Case

The agents' true locations are all in the $y = 0$ line, i.e., $\mathcal{I} = \mathbb{R} \times \{0\}$, and the facility can be placed anywhere in $\mathbb{R}^2$, i.e., $\mathcal{O} = \mathbb{R}^2$.

Inspired by the two-agent mechanism from the previous section, we introduce a strategyproof mechanism for any number of agents that makes use of the extra dimension to achieve an approximation ratio of $\sqrt{2}$. Later in the section we prove that this is best-possible for deterministic mechanisms in this setting. Note that, in contrast the Orthogonal Sphere Mechanism, the following mechanism only has to be strategyproof against deviations on the line. This allows for a simpler deterministic mechanism.

Definition 2 (Augmented Midpoint Mechanism). *Let $\boldsymbol{x} = (x_1, \ldots, x_n) \in \mathbb{R}^n$ be the reported agent coordinates on the x-axis. Let $l = \min_i x_i$ and $r = \max_i x_i$. The mechanism $\mathcal{M}$ outputs the facility location $Y = (\frac{l+r}{2}, \frac{r-l}{2}) \in \mathbb{R}^2$.*

We defer the proof of the following theorem to the full version [9]. Observing that the extreme points dominate the maximum distance, the approximation ratio can be analyzed the same way as in Theorem 4. For the strategyproofness, in contrast to Theorem 4, we only have to take deviations on the line into account but also need to consider non-extreme point agents. However, the latter behave in a similar way to the extreme points, allowing for a simplified proof.

Theorem 5. *The Augmented Midpoint Mechanism is strategyproof and has an egalitarian approximation ratio of* $\sqrt{2}$.

We complement our mechanism with the following matching lower bound.

Theorem 6. *Let* $\mathcal{M} : \mathbb{R}^n \to \mathbb{R}^2$ *be a deterministic, strategyproof mechanism for* $n \geq 2$ *agents that achieves a worst-case egalitarian approximation ratio of* λ. *Then,* $\lambda \geq \sqrt{2}$.

Proof. We first show the statement for $n = 2$ and afterwards argue that it extends to arbitrary $n \geq 2$.

Let $n = 2$. Fix agent 1 at the origin $(0, 0)$ and restrict agent 2 to the positive x-axis such that $x \in (0, \infty)$. For any such profile, the mechanism's outcome defines a curve parameterized by x: $f(x) = \mathcal{M}(0, x) = (u(x), v(x))$.

The optimal facility location is the midpoint $(x/2, 0)$, which yields an optimal maximum cost of $x/2$. Because $\mathcal{M}$ guarantees a λ-approximation, the distance from $f(x)$ to both agents is bounded above by $\lambda x/2$. Squaring these distances establishes two inequalities for all $x > 0$:

$$u(x)^2 + v(x)^2 \leq \frac{\lambda^2 x^2}{4}, \tag{3}$$

$$D(x) := (x - u(x))^2 + v(x)^2 \leq \frac{\lambda^2 x^2}{4}. \tag{4}$$

Let $x, y \in (0, \infty)$. By the strategyproofness constraint, an agent whose true location is x cannot decrease their distance to the facility by reporting y. Thus, $D(x) \leq (x - u(y))^2 + v(y)^2$. Expanding the squared term and substituting the definition of $D(y)$ yields:

$$D(x) - D(y) \leq (x - y)^2 + 2(x - y)(y - u(y)). \tag{5}$$

Symmetrically, for an agent located at y reporting x, we obtain:

$$D(x) - D(y) \geq -(x - y)^2 + 2(x - y)(x - u(x)). \tag{6}$$

Let $[a, b] \subset (0, \infty)$ be an arbitrary compact interval. For any $z \in [a, b]$, inequality (3) ensures $|u(z)| \leq \frac{\lambda}{2} z \leq \frac{\lambda}{2} b$. Dividing (5) and (6) by $|x - y|$ establishes that for any distinct $x, y \in [a, b]$, the difference quotient is bounded: $\left|\frac{D(x)-D(y)}{x-y}\right| \leq |x - y| + 2|x| + 2|y| + 2|u(x)| + 2|u(y)| \leq (b - a) + 4b + 2\lambda b$. Since this upper bound is a finite constant dependent on the interval endpoints, and $[a, b]$ was arbitrary, $D(x)$ is locally Lipschitz on $(0, \infty)$, which implies it is absolutely continuous and differentiable almost everywhere (a.e.).

Let x be a point of differentiability. Dividing (6) by $(x - y)$ and taking the one-sided limits as $y \to x^+$ and $y \to x^-$ yields $D'(x) = 2(x - u(x))$ a.e.

Expanding $D(x)$ and applying (3) gives $D(x) \leq x^2 - 2xu(x) + \frac{\lambda^2 x^2}{4}$. Substituting $2u(x) = 2x - D'(x)$ into this inequality yields $D(x) \leq -x^2 + xD'(x) + \frac{\lambda^2 x^2}{4}$ a.e. Rearranging gives $xD'(x) - D(x) \geq x^2(1 - \lambda^2/4)$. Dividing by x^2 for $x > 0$ forms the derivative of a quotient: $\frac{d}{dx}\left(\frac{D(x)}{x}\right) \geq 1 - \frac{\lambda^2}{4}$ a.e.

Because $D(x)$ is absolutely continuous on $(0, \infty)$, the quotient $D(x)/x$ is absolutely continuous on any interval $[\epsilon, X]$ for $0 < \epsilon < X$. Integrating from ϵ to X preserves the inequality: $\frac{D(X)}{X} - \frac{D(\epsilon)}{\epsilon} \geq \left(1 - \frac{\lambda^2}{4}\right)(X - \epsilon)$.

From (4), we know $0 \leq D(\epsilon) \leq \frac{\lambda^2}{4}\epsilon^2$, which implies $0 \leq \frac{D(\epsilon)}{\epsilon} \leq \frac{\lambda^2}{4}\epsilon$. Taking the limit as $\epsilon \to 0^+$ sends $\frac{D(\epsilon)}{\epsilon}$ to 0. Multiplying the resulting inequality by X and combining it with (4) yields $X^2\left(1 - \frac{\lambda^2}{4}\right) \leq D(X) \leq \frac{\lambda^2 X^2}{4}$. Dividing by X^2 simplifies to $1 - \lambda^2/4 \leq \lambda^2/4$, establishing $\lambda \geq \sqrt{2}$.

It remains to argue that the bound extends to any $n > 2$. If an n-agent mechanism achieved an approximation ratio better than λ, we could construct a strategyproof 2-agent mechanism preserving this improved bound by having it run the n-agent mechanism on a profile where the reports (a, b) are padded with $n - 2$ dummy agents co-located at b. The full formal argument for the extension to $n > 2$ can be found in the full version [9] of the paper. □

4.2 Circle Case

The agents' locations are restricted to the unit circle $\mathcal{I} = S^1 \subset \mathbb{R}^2$ with center $O = (0, 0)$ and $\mathcal{O} = \mathbb{R}^2$ As a main result, we prove the following theorem.

Theorem 7. *There exists a randomized mechanism $\mathcal{M}$ that is group-strategyproof in expectation and achieves an egalitarian approximation ratio of 1.5.*[3]

Our mechanism, formalized by Algorithm 1, is based on the concept of *extreme agents*, defined as follows.

Definition 3 (Extreme Agents). *For any profile of points $\boldsymbol{x}$ on S^1 that is contained entirely within a minimal arc of length $\alpha < \pi$, this spanning arc is unique. The* extreme agents *(or extreme points) A and B are the two agent locations that define the boundaries of this minimal spanning arc.*

The two extreme agents A and B define a spanning arc of some angle α that contains all reported locations. Intuitively, there are two relevant configurations of this spanning arc. If the angle is large ($\alpha \geq \pi$), then the arc spans at least a semicircle implying that OPT $= 1$, achieved by placing the facility in the center of the circle. On the other hand, if the angle is small ($\alpha < \pi$), the optimum is achieved by placing the facility on the midpoint of the chord between A and B.

Let z denote the optimal facility location. A strategyproof mechanism cannot just place the facility on point z as agents would be incentivized to misreport

[3] Note that the mechanism of this theorem is also *strongly group-strategyproof*.

Algorithm 1: Chord-Midpoint Mechanism $\mathcal{M}$

Input: Strategic profile $\boldsymbol{x}$ of reported agent locations

```
Let A and B denote the extreme agents for the reported locations x;
Let α denote the angle of the minimum spanning arc defined by A and B;
if α ≥ π then
    Output the origin O = (0, 0) with probability one;
else
    Compute λ(α) = cos(α/2) / (2(1+cos(α/2)));
    Compute the midpoint z of the chord between A and B;
    Output A and B with prob. λ(α) each, and z with prob. 1 − 2λ(α);
```

their location in order to pull z closer to their true location, in particular when the angle α is small. The key idea of our mechanism is to offset the benefit that an agent might achieve by randomizing between selecting z, A and B according to a carefully selected distribution.

In the following, we first analyze the approximation ratio of our mechanism. Then, we show strategyproofness in expectation and finally extend it to group-strategyproofness in expectation. Together, this will imply Theorem 7.

Analysis of the Approximation Ratio. The following lemma proves a fine-grained guarantee depending on the angle α of the spanning arc between the two extreme agents. For $\alpha \to \pi$, the approximation ratio approaches 1 and, for $\alpha \to 0$, it approaches 1.5. Intuitively, this can be explained by the observation that our mechanism converges to the optimal solution as α increases and to the randomized 1.5-approximation for the problem on the line [14] as α decreases.

Lemma 4. *The Chord-Midpoint Mechanism $\mathcal{M}$ achieves an egalitarian approximation ratio of* $\max\{\frac{1+2\cos(\alpha/2)}{1+\cos(\alpha/2)}, 1\} \leq 1.5$.

Proof. We distinguish between the two configurations of the spanning arc.

Case 1: Assume that $\alpha \geq \pi$. The profile spans at least a semicircle, so $\text{OPT} = 1$. The mechanism outputs the origin, yielding a distance of exactly 1 for all agents $x_i \in S^1$. Thus, $\text{MC}(\mathcal{M}, \boldsymbol{x}) = 1 \leq 1.5 \cdot \text{OPT}$.

Case 2: Assume $\alpha < \pi$. The smallest enclosing circle for $\boldsymbol{x}$ has a diameter equal to the length of the chord AB centered at z. Hence, $\text{OPT} = \frac{1}{2}\|A - B\| = \sin(\alpha/2)$.

The mechanism outputs a facility $Y \in \{A, B, z\}$. As all agents lie within the arc bounded by A and B, the maximum distance d^* from Y to any agent is achieved at one of the extremes: If $Y = A$, then $d^* = \|A - B\| = 2\sin(\alpha/2)$. If $Y = B$, then $d^* = \|B - A\| = 2\sin(\alpha/2)$. If $Y = z$, then $d^* = \|z - A\| = \sin(\alpha/2)$.

Abbreviate $\lambda := \lambda(\alpha) = \frac{\cos(\alpha/2)}{2(1+\cos(\alpha/2))}$. Taking the expectation over the mechanism's randomness, the expected maximum cost is

$$\begin{aligned} \mathrm{MC}(\mathcal{M}, \boldsymbol{x}) &= \lambda(2\sin(\alpha/2)) + \lambda(2\sin(\alpha/2)) + (1-2\lambda)\sin(\alpha/2) \\ &= \sin(\alpha/2)\left[\frac{1+2\cos(\alpha/2)}{1+\cos(\alpha/2)}\right]. \end{aligned}$$

Thus, the approximation ratio is $\frac{\mathrm{MC}(\mathcal{M},\boldsymbol{x})}{\mathrm{OPT}} = \frac{1+2\cos(\alpha/2)}{1+\cos(\alpha/2)}$. For $\alpha \in (0, \pi)$, this expression is strictly decreasing in α and is bounded by its limit as $\alpha \to 0$:

$$\frac{\mathrm{MC}(\mathcal{M}, \boldsymbol{x})}{\mathrm{OPT}} \leq \lim_{\alpha \to 0} \frac{1+2\cos(\alpha/2)}{1+\cos(\alpha/2)} = \frac{3}{2}.$$

□

Strategyproofness. Our next goal is to prove the following lemma. Later, we will use the lemma as a blackbox to prove the stronger notion of group-strategyproofness.

Lemma 5. *The Chord-Midpoint Mechanism $\mathcal{M}$ is strategyproof in expectation.*

Preliminaries. Let the circle S^1 be embedded in $\mathbb{R}^2$ and parameterized by angles in $[0, 2\pi)$. By rotational symmetry, whenever a profile spans a minimal arc of length $\alpha < \pi$, we can fix our coordinate system such that one extreme point, B, is anchored at angle 0, and the other extreme, A, is at angle α. Any agent's true location can then be represented by an angle γ.

Our analysis relies on analyzing the distance of agents to the midpoint that is one possible output of the mechanism when the arc angle is smaller than π. In the full version [9], we prove the following lemma, which allows us to bound such distances.

Lemma 6 (Distance to Midpoint Factorization). *Let A be located at angle α, and let z' be the chord midpoint of the arc $[0, x]$ for some $x \in (0, \pi)$. Then, $D(x)^2 = \|A - z'\|^2$ factors as:*

$$D(x)^2 = \left(\sin\left(\tfrac{\alpha}{2}\right) - \cos\left(\tfrac{x}{2}\right)\sin\left(\tfrac{x-\alpha}{2}\right)\right)^2 + \left(\cos\left(\tfrac{\alpha}{2}\right) - \cos\left(\tfrac{x}{2}\right)\cos\left(\tfrac{x-\alpha}{2}\right)\right)^2.$$

To show strategyproofness, we separately show that neither deviations that expand the minimum spanning arc nor deviations that shrink the minimum spanning arc benefit the deviating agent. We will first analyze such deviations under the assumption that the stationary extreme point B remains an extreme point after the deviation. That is, if the angle of the spanning arc before and after the deviation is smaller than π, we assume that both arcs are of the form $[0, \alpha]$. As a final step, we then analyze deviations past the stationary extreme.

Deviations that Expand the Minimum Spanning arc. As discussed above, we first only consider deviations that expand the spanning arc from $[0, \alpha]$ to $[0, \gamma]$ for some $\gamma > 0$. In the following, we prove the stronger than required property that such a deviation indeed increases the expected distance of *every agent* to the selected facility. This will be helpful when proving group-strategyproofness.

Lemma 7. *Let $\boldsymbol{x}$ be a truthful profile that spans $[0, \alpha]$ with $\alpha < \pi$ and let $\boldsymbol{x}'$ either be a profile that spans $[0, \gamma]$ with $\alpha < \gamma < \pi$ or a profile with spanning angle $\geq \pi$. Then, $\mathbb{E}[d(x_i, \mathcal{M}(\boldsymbol{x}))] < \mathbb{E}[d(x_i, \mathcal{M}(\boldsymbol{x}'))]$ for all $i \in [n]$.*

Proof. Fix an arbitrary x_i. By assumption of the lemma, the angle of x_i is in $[0, \alpha]$. First assume that $\boldsymbol{x}'$ spans the arc $[0, \gamma]$ with $\gamma < \pi$. In the full version [9], we formally prove that $\mathbb{E}[d(x_i, \mathcal{M}(\boldsymbol{x}))] < \mathbb{E}[d(x_i, \mathcal{M}(\boldsymbol{x}'))]$ with the following three steps:

1. Let $u = \gamma/2$ and $v = \beta/2$ where β is the angle of x_i. Using Lemma 6, we show that the distance $D(u) := \|x_i - z'\|$ between x_i and the new chord midpoint z' satisfies $D(u)^2 = A(u)^2 + (1+\cos u)C(u)$, where $A(u) = \sin v - \cos u \sin(u - v)$ and $C(u) = (1 - \cos u)\sin^2(u - v)$.
2. Based on the identities of the first step, we show that the expected distance of x_i to the selected facility for span $[0, \gamma]$ is
$$\mathbb{E}[d(\mathcal{M}(\boldsymbol{x}'), x_i)] = \sin v + \frac{D(u) - A(u)}{1 + \cos u}.$$
Similarly, we observe that $\mathbb{E}[d(\mathcal{M}(\boldsymbol{x}), x_i)]$ can be expressed with the same formula by plugging in $\alpha/2$ for u.
3. We show that the function $y(u) := \frac{D(u)-A(u)}{1+\cos u}$ is strictly increasing in the range $[\alpha/2, \pi/2)$, proving $\mathbb{E}[d(\mathcal{M}(\boldsymbol{x}'), x_i)] > \mathbb{E}[d(\mathcal{M}(\boldsymbol{x}), x_i)]$.

If $\boldsymbol{x}'$ spans an arc of angle $\geq \pi$, then $\mathbb{E}[d(\mathcal{M}(\boldsymbol{x}'), x_i)] = 1$ as the mechanism deterministically outputs the origin. On the other hand, as argued above, $\mathbb{E}[d(\mathcal{M}(\boldsymbol{x}), x_i)] = \sin v + \frac{D(u)-A(u)}{1+\cos u}$ for $u = \alpha/2$. As shown above, this expected distance is strictly increasing. For $u = \frac{\pi}{2}$, the expected distance is one. Since $\alpha < \pi$ by assumption, this implies $\mathbb{E}[d(\mathcal{M}(\boldsymbol{x}), x_i)] < 1$. □

Deviations that Shrink The Minimum Spanning arc. We distinguish whether the angle α of the minimum spanning arc for the truthful profile $\boldsymbol{x}$ is large or small.

Lemma 8. *Let $\boldsymbol{x}$ be a profile with a minimum spanning arc of angle $\alpha \geq \pi$. Let $\boldsymbol{x}' = (x_i', \boldsymbol{x}_{-i})$ be such that the angle of the minimum spanning arc is $\theta < \pi$. Then $\mathbb{E}[d(\mathcal{M}(\boldsymbol{x}), x_i)] < \mathbb{E}[d(\mathcal{M}(\boldsymbol{x}'), x_i)]$.*

Proof. Profile $\boldsymbol{x}$ yields an expected cost of 1. W.l.o.g., assume the reported profile $\boldsymbol{x}'$ spans the arc $W' = [-\theta/2, \theta/2]$. Let $z' = (\cos(\theta/2), 0)$ be its chord midpoint.

Since the truthful profile $\boldsymbol{x}$ has a span $\geq \pi$ and all non-deviating agents lie within W', agent i must lie in the complement interval $[\pi - \theta/2, \pi + \theta/2]$ to maintain the spanning condition. Consequently, the angle γ of agent i satisfies $\cos\gamma \le \cos(\pi - \theta/2) = -\cos(\theta/2)$.

Let $f(X) = \|x_i - X\|$ be the distance to the mechanism's output X. Since f is strictly convex, by Jensen's inequality: $\mathbb{E}[d(\mathcal{M}(\boldsymbol{x}'), x_i)] = \mathbb{E}[\|x_i - X\|] > \|x_i - \mathbb{E}[X]\| = \|x_i - z'\|$. Applying the Law of Cosines with $\|x_i\| = 1$ and $\|z'\| = \cos(\theta/2)$:

$$\begin{aligned}\|x_i - z'\|^2 &= 1^2 + \cos^2(\theta/2) - 2\cos(\theta/2)\cos\gamma \\ &\ge 1 + \cos^2(\theta/2) - 2\cos(\theta/2)(-\cos(\theta/2)) \\ &= 1 + 3\cos^2(\theta/2) > 1.\end{aligned}$$

Thus, $\mathbb{E}[d(\mathcal{M}(\boldsymbol{x}'), x_i)] > 1 = \mathbb{E}[d(\mathcal{M}(\boldsymbol{x}), x_i)]$. □

We defer the proof of the next lemma to the full version [9]. Deviations covered by the lemma only happen if the deviating agent is the extreme agent A. We prove the lemma by (i) computing a lower bound on the distance to the new chord midpoint with Lemma 6, (ii) using it to lower bound $\mathbb{E}[d(\mathcal{M}(\boldsymbol{x}'), A)]$ and (iii) observing that the resulting bound is larger than $\mathbb{E}[d(\mathcal{M}(\boldsymbol{x}), A)]$.

Lemma 9. *Let $\boldsymbol{x}$ be a profile with a minimum spanning arc of angle $\alpha < \pi$. Let $\boldsymbol{x}' = (x_i', \boldsymbol{x}_{-i})$ be such that the angle of the minimum spanning arc is $\gamma < \alpha$. Then $\mathbb{E}[d(\mathcal{M}(\boldsymbol{x}), x_i)] < \mathbb{E}[d(\mathcal{M}(\boldsymbol{x}'), x_i)]$.*

Deviations Past the Stationary Extreme at B. As a final step, we analyze deviations past the stationary extreme point B. We prove the following lemma in the full version [9]. The idea is to analyze such deviations by sequentially applying Lemmas 7 and 9: We first consider the deviation to $[-\gamma, \alpha]$ and apply Lemma 7 (considering α the stationary extreme), then we deviate to $[-\gamma, \beta]$ and apply Lemma 9. Overall, the deviation will turn out non-beneficiary.

Lemma 10. *Let $\boldsymbol{x}$ be a profile with a minimum spanning arc $[0, \alpha]$ for $\alpha < \pi$. Let $\boldsymbol{x}' = (x_i', \boldsymbol{x}_{-i})$ be such that the minimum spanning arc is $[-\gamma, \beta]$ with $\beta \in [0, \alpha)$, $\gamma > 0$, and $\gamma + \beta < \pi$. Then $\mathbb{E}[d(\mathcal{M}(\boldsymbol{x}), x_i)] < \mathbb{E}[d(\mathcal{M}(\boldsymbol{x}'), x_i)]$.*

Lemmas 7 to 10 together imply Lemma 5.

Group-Strategyproofness. We complete the proof of Theorem 7 by proving that our mechanism is group-strategyproof in expectation.

Lemma 11. *The Chord-Midpoint Mechanism $\mathcal{M}$ is group-strategyproof in expectation.*

Proof. Let the truthful profile $\boldsymbol{x}$ span a minimal arc W, and a coalition S deviate to a reported profile $\boldsymbol{x}'$ spanning W'. To prove group-strategyproofness, we must show that if $W \ne W'$, at least one agent in S loses. By the logic of Lemma 7 and of Lemma 8, any deviation that transitions the spanning arc between $< \pi$ and $\ge \pi$ in either direction increases the expected cost for at least one deviator.

Therefore, we restrict our analysis to the case where both W and W' have angles smaller than π. Without loss of generality, let $W = [0, \alpha]$. We partition the analysis based on how many of the true extreme agents (at angles 0 and α) belong to S:

Both Extreme Agents are in S: Under truthful reporting, the mechanism restricts its outputs to the line segment between the extremes. Consequently, the truthful expected cost for each extreme agent is $\sin(\alpha/2)$, and the sum of their expected costs is $2\sin(\alpha/2)$. Because $W' \neq W$, the mechanism's support for the reported profile $\boldsymbol{x}'$ must include points strictly off this line segment. By the triangle inequality, the expected sum of their distances to the new facility exceeds $2\sin(\alpha/2)$. Therefore, at least one of these two deviating extreme agents must incur an expected cost greater than $\sin(\alpha/2)$; thus the coalition fails.

At Least One Extreme Agent is Not in S: We formalize the deviation of S in two sequential steps by constructing an intermediate profile $\boldsymbol{y}$. In profile $\boldsymbol{y}$, only the deviating agents located in the interior of W report their deviations from $\boldsymbol{x}'$, while all other agents (including any deviating extreme agents) report truthfully. Because the honest extreme agent(s) continue to anchor the boundaries, this interior deviation yields an intermediate spanning arc W_y that either expands or remains equal to W.

By Lemma 7, if this intermediate arc expands, the expected cost for every agent in $[0, \alpha]$ increases. If neither extreme agent is in S, then the intermediate profile is the final reported profile, and the required expansion implies the coalition loses.

Alternatively, if exactly one extreme agent (w.l.o.g., the agent at 0) is in S, we evaluate the deviation based on the intermediate arc W_y:

- If W_y expands, agent 0's expected cost increases in the transition to $\boldsymbol{y}$. By individual strategyproofness (Lemma 5), their subsequent unilateral deviation to $\boldsymbol{x}'$ cannot recover this loss.
- If $W_y = W$, the transition to $\boldsymbol{y}$ leaves agent 0's expected cost unchanged. However, because $W' \neq W$, agent 0's unilateral deviation to $\boldsymbol{x}'$ must alter the spanning arc. As established by our boundary lemmas (Lemmas 7 and 9), any unilateral deviation that alters the minimal spanning arc increases the expected cost of the deviating boundary agent.

Thus, in all cases, agent 0 incurs a higher expected cost than in the initial truthful profile, ensuring the coalition fails. □

Lower Bound for Group-Strategyproof Mechanisms. We complement Theorem 7 by showing that randomization is necessary for a group-strategyproof mechanism to achieve an egalitarian approximation ratio strictly smaller than 2. We give the proof in the full version [9]; it is based on adapting ideas from [17, Lemma 3.5] and [14] to our setting.

Theorem 8. *Any deterministic, group-strategyproof, and unanimous mechanism for the 2-agent facility location problem on the unit circle* S^1 *with output augmentation has an egalitarian approximation ratio of at least* 2.

5 Conclusion and Future Directions

In this work, we explored the limits of strategyproof mechanisms for the egalitarian facility location problem under the Euclidean distance. We first established improved lower bounds for randomized mechanisms in standard multidimensional spaces. A related major open problem is to fully close the gap between these new limits and existing mechanisms. A potential path forward involves formally characterizing the class of randomized strategyproof mechanisms; however, given that complete characterizations remain elusive even for the line case, this poses a significant challenge.

We also introduced a dimension-augmented framework, demonstrating that expanding the allowable output space beyond the agents' input domain can fundamentally increase the optimization capabilities of strategyproof mechanisms and bypass classical barriers. This new paradigm naturally presents parallel open questions, making the closure of the remaining approximation bounds in these augmented settings a logical next step. Notably, while we established a tight bound for deterministic mechanisms in the augmented line setting, complete characterizations of deterministic rules remain open for both of the augmented cases we investigated. In particular, for the circle setting, it remains an open question whether there exists any deterministic mechanism that genuinely exploits the output augmentation without simply reducing to a standard strategyproof mechanism defined over the entire $\mathbb{R}^2$ plane.

References

1. Alon, N., Feldman, M., Procaccia, A.D., Tennenholtz, M.: Strategyproof approximation of the minimax on networks. Math. Oper. Res. **35**(3), 513–526 (2010). https://doi.org/10.1287/moor.1100.0457
2. Balkanski, E., Gkatzelis, V., Shahkarami, G.: Randomized strategic facility location with predictions. Adv. Neural. Inf. Process. Syst. **37**, 35639–35664 (2024)
3. Barak, Z.: Facility location mechanism design: breaking the deterministic barrier. CoRR abs/2605.24750 (2026). https://arxiv.org/abs/2605.24750
4. Barberá, S., Massó, J., Neme, A.: Voting under constraints. J. Econ. Theory **76**(2), 298–321 (1997). https://doi.org/10.1006/jeth.1997.2301
5. Border, K.C., Jordan, J.S.: Straightforward elections, unanimity and phantom voters. Rev. Econ. Stud. **50**(1), 153 (1983). https://doi.org/10.2307/2296962
6. Chan, H., Filos-Ratsikas, A., Li, B., Li, M., Wang, C.: Mechanism design for facility location problems: a survey. In: Proceedings of the Thirtieth International Joint Conference on Artificial Intelligence, pp. 4356–4365 (2021)
7. Feldman, M., Fiat, A., Golomb, I.: On voting and facility location. In: Proceedings of the 2016 ACM Conference on Economics and Computation, pp. 269–286 (2016)
8. Fullerton, E.J., Hu, Z., Plaxton, C.G.: Constant-approximate and constant-strategyproof two-facility location. In: International Symposium on Algorithmic Game Theory, pp. 119–136. Springer (2025)
9. Gomes, R., Klumper, S., Schäfer, G., Schlöter, J.: Improved lower bounds and output augmentation for facility location mechanisms. CoRR (2026). https://arxiv.org/abs/2607.20196

10. Kim, K.H., Roush, F.W.: Nonmanipulability in two dimensions. Math. Soc. Sci. **8**(1), 29–43 (1984). https://doi.org/10.1016/0165-4896(84)90059-3
11. Li, W., Zhou, Y.: Locating two facilities on a square with a minimum distance requirement. Theoret. Comput. Sci. **1047**, 115310 (2025). https://doi.org/10.1016/j.tcs.2025.115310
12. Moulin, H.: On strategy-proofness and single peakedness. Public Choice **35**(4), 437–455 (1980). https://doi.org/10.1007/BF00128122
13. Peters, H., Stel, H., Storcken, T.: Range convexity, continuity, and strategy-proofness of voting schemes. ZOR-Methods Models Opera. Res. **38**(2), 213–229 (1993). https://doi.org/10.1007/BF01414216
14. Procaccia, A.D., Tennenholtz, M.: Approximate mechanism design without money. ACM Trans. Econ. Comput. **1**(4), 1–26 (2013). https://doi.org/10.1145/2542174.2542175
15. Roughgarden, T.: Resource augmentation. In: Beyond the Worst-Case Analysis of Algorithms, pp. 72–92. Cambridge University Press (2020)
16. Schummer, J., Vohra, R.V.: Strategy-proof location on a network. J. Econom. Theory **104**(2), 405–428 (2002). https://doi.org/10.1006/jeth.2001.2807
17. Tang, P., Yu, D., Zhao, S.: Characterization of group-strategyproof mechanisms for facility location in strictly convex space. In: Proceedings of the 21st ACM Conference on Economics and Computation, pp. 133–157 (2020)
18. Tang, Z., Wang, C., Zhang, M., Zhao, Y.: Mechanism design for facility location games with candidate locations. In: International Conference on Combinatorial Optimization and Applications, pp. 440–452. Springer (2020)

Stability in Combinatorial Markets with Side Payments

Alexander Grosz and Chiara Vanoli(✉)

Chair of Operations Research, Technical University of Munich, Arcisstraße 21, 80333 Munich, Germany
{alexander.grosz,chiara.vanoli}@tum.de

Abstract. Combinatorial markets provide a general framework for trading bundles of indivisible goods. Building on the combinatorial market models of Bikhchandani & Ostroy [5] and Bichler & Waldherr [3], we introduce explicit side payments, thereby allowing restricted transfers of utility among subsets of agents and capturing different forms of financial collusion.

This extension results in a large number of seemingly distinct market settings. However, we establish a systematic classification of their expressive power. Most notably, we show that higher-order market settings (i.e., those with more personalized prices and less clearinghouse power) are essentially equivalent in terms of market properties when side payments are permitted between buyers. An analogous collapse occurs for the third- and higher-order settings when side payments are permitted between sellers. In contrast, we identify a fundamental structural separation between the second- and third-order settings.

To analyze stability in these environments, we generalize the classical concepts of stability with and without transferable utility (TU and NTU) to a partition-based notion of restricted transferability (the $\mathcal{T}$-core). We relate stable outcomes across different settings to appropriate stability notions, identify market instances in which partially transferable utility yields a better (or any) stable outcome, and show that under personalized pricing, all stability notions collapse to NTU-stability.

Keywords: Combinatorial markets · Core · Stability · Side payments · Transferable utility

1 Introduction

Explaining the behavior of agents in markets where goods are exchanged for money has been an important field of research for the better part of the last century (starting with the seminal contribution by Arrow & Debreu [1]). Such market models can be applied to plenty of real-life scenarios. Our object of interest is a combinatorial market in which agents trade non-divisible items offered and requested as bundles. Such markets have applications, e.g., in logistics

P. Lenzner and D. Schmand (Eds.): SAGT 2026, LNCS 16911, pp. 224–241, 2027.
https://doi.org/10.1007/978-3-032-38782-0_13

for cargo transfer, airport time-slot allocation, spectrum auctions, and energy markets (see, e.g., [4] for references).

The theory of combinatorial markets generalizes the simpler case of assignment markets, in which each buyer and seller trades only a single indivisible item at a time [18]. In combinatorial markets, agents exchange bundles or packages of items, and both the valuation functions and prices can differ structurally from the simple linear case. Computing a socially optimal trade in such markets is NP-hard, even for a single seller, which underscores the structural complexity of combinatorial markets. Additionally, the exhaustive elicitation of preferences poses an interesting problem and has seen various proposed solutions in terms of communication models for valuations [17], including fully expressive OR language or other logically described languages [15], and compact, problem-specific languages [8,13].

Bikhchandani & Ostroy [5] establish four settings for combinatorial markets, distinguished by the degree of control exercised by a central clearinghouse, which can modify the exchange by opening and rebundling packages and relabeling them. These settings also differ in their pricing restrictions, from linear item prices shared across the market to fully individualized package prices. These markets are formulated as integer programs (and the corresponding dual pricing problems) and, as such, allow the identification of pricing equilibria and integral solutions. In general, when pricing equilibria exist, they belong to the core, but not every element of the core may represent an equilibrium. However, in the special case of a single seller (i.e., the combinatorial auction setting), the set of pricing equilibria does coincide with the core, thereby establishing their stability against coalitional deviations.

Building on the work of [5], Bichler & Waldherr [3] introduce a model that combines two extremes from previous settings: the clearinghouse can rearrange packages freely, but bundle prices remain fully personalized. The underlying integer programming model is more verbose than in [5], in that it defines binary variables for every feasible package combination in the full market, rather than modeling the occurrence of each package directly. In this paradigm, they establish that the core coincides with the set of pricing equilibria, whenever any exist. In more recent work, Bichler & Waldherr [4] augment their setting with budget constraints and show that computing welfare-optimal stable outcomes is Σ_2^p-hard.

In related work, [2,9] discuss the existence of equilibria for special valuation structures with the endowment effect, both under strong assumptions that admit equilibria and under weaker assumptions that do not. In [11] (see also [12]), a relaxation of the standard equilibrium notion is introduced in a reduced market to make the problem tractable. There is substantial literature on pricing methods for combinatorial and iterative (dynamic pricing) auctions; see [6] for a comprehensive overview. A different type of combinatorial market is discussed in [7], where goods are divisible, but certain covering constraints must be satisfied. In [10] a mechanism design perspective to address the lack of truthful, revenue-maximizing mechanisms is discussed by relaxing to approximately optimal revenue.

Our Contributions. Our work builds directly on the combinatorial market models of Bikhchandani & Ostroy [5] and their extension by Bichler & Waldherr [3]. Motivated by market environments in which regulators restrict cooperation on one side of the market (e.g., through competition or antitrust laws), or in which informational frictions prevent agents from engaging in strategic coordination, we extend existing market models by introducing explicit side payments. We consider different degrees of transferability, depending on which agents may exchange utility: only buyers, only sellers, buyers and sellers independently within their respective sides (but not across sides), and finally all agents.

To systematically compare the five original settings now extended with (restricted) side payments, we introduce hierarchical equivalence levels. These notions indicate which properties of a given reference setting can also be represented in another setting. While in some cases we can only find a corresponding market outcome that trades the same cumulative bundle for every agent (*item equivalence*), sufficiently verbose settings can realize not just the cumulative prices each agent pays or receives (*price equivalence*), but even the individual prices paid for every traded bundle (*market equivalence*). We consider *payoff equivalence* to be the most relevant property, as it describes when market outcomes exist with the same set of traded items and the same utility for each agent and thereby captures their strategic incentive.

Our first set of results establishes a near-monotonicity principle: increasing the power of the pricing system – either by moving to higher-order market settings, i.e., simultaneously increasing price personalization while reducing the power of the clearinghouse, or by allowing richer side payments – generally expands the set of implementable assignments (Theorem 1, Remark 2). The main exception arises in the second-order setting, where a buyer-seller pair can effectively trade multiple bundles, leading to a qualitative change once personalized prices and labels are introduced (Sect. 3.1).

This structural peculiarity of the second-order setting breaks payoff equivalence when moving to higher-order settings under restrictive transfer regimes. However, payoff equivalence is recovered if sufficiently strong side payments are allowed, including separate transfers between buyers or sellers, or seller-side transfers under compatible restrictions (Lemma 3and 5). Moreover, every second-order assignment remains price equivalent to an assignment in the fourth-order setting, although full market equivalence need not hold.

Beyond this case, tightening side-payment restrictions while increasing the order of the market typically makes it impossible to exceed item-equivalence between settings. The only exception is going from full to separate side payments, which preserves payoff equivalence across all order settings (Lemma 3).

When moving to a lower-order market setting, payoff equivalence is always preserved provided that full or separate side payments are allowed. Intuitively, in these cases, most or all monetary transfers can be implemented through side payments, effectively circumventing the pricing restrictions (Lemma 3). Two further instances where payoff equivalence holds are the following: any assignment with sellers' single or no side payments in the fourth- or fifth-order setting is payoff equivalent to an assignment in the third-order setting with sellers' single side payments (Lemma 5), and any assignment in the fifth-order setting with single or no side payments is payoff equivalent to an assignment in the fourth-order setting with the same or more restrictive side-payment structure (Lemma 4).

We identify settings that are fully equivalent in a strong sense: for certain combinations of market rules and side-payment regimes, payoff equivalence holds in both directions. In these cases, not only the assignments but also the deviations coincide, implying that the core is identical. We identify the following equivalences, which follow directly from the Lemmas outlined above.

Theorem 1.

- *All order settings with full and separate side payments are payoff equivalent.*
- *The fourth-order and the fifth-order settings with buyers' single side payments are payoff equivalent.*
- *The third-, fourth-, and fifth-order settings with sellers' single side payments are payoff equivalent.*

Thus, under sufficiently permissive side-payment regimes, distinctions between several higher-order market rules become immaterial for both payoff implementability and stability. Notice the asymmetry between the buyers' and sellers' side results: this is due to the restriction of the third-order setting to only one of the two possible sides where the labels are disregarded (see Sect. 2 for more detail).

To investigate the solution properties of these new market settings, we turn to the standard notions of TU-stability (transferable utility) as well as NTU-stability (non-transferable utility). While either notion describes solutions that are stable against coalitional deviations, they differ in how such improvements can be achieved: under TU, agents may freely transfer utility, whereas under NTU, each agent's payoff is fixed by the market outcome.

We generalize these notions by the definition of $\mathcal{T}$-RTU-stability (restricted TU) in Sect. 2.2, where $\mathcal{T}$ denotes a partition of the agents, and transfers of money are allowed only between agents in the same partition block. The new notion generalizes both TU-stability and NTU-stability in that it additionally allows us to model stable outcomes that include collusion on one side or two different sides of the market, while restricting all money between the two sides to flow through the market via payments.

These new stability notions are closely related to the side-payment restrictions outlined above. In Sect. 2.3, we show that finding $\mathcal{T}$-RTU-stable outcomes is equivalent to finding an NTU-stable outcome in the market setting that admits a corresponding set of side payments within the market itself. Thus, we can effectively simplify the analysis of different stability notions to NTU-stability with the respective side-payment restrictions.

Theorem 2. *For a given h^{th}-order market $\mathcal{E}_h^r$ with side-payment restriction r and a side-payment partition $\mathcal{T}$, its $\mathcal{T}$-core $\mathcal{C}^{\mathcal{T}}(\mathcal{E}_h^r)$ corresponds to the NTU-core $\mathcal{C}^{\mathcal{T}^{\text{no}}}(\mathcal{E}_h^s)$ of the same economy with side-payment restriction s, i.e.,*

$$\mathcal{C}^{\mathcal{T}}(\mathcal{E}_h^r) = \mathcal{C}^{\mathcal{T}^{\text{no}}}(\mathcal{E}_h^s),$$

where s is the side-payment restriction induced by the join $\mathcal{S}$ of the respective partitions, i.e., $\mathcal{S} = \mathcal{T} \vee \mathcal{T}^r$.

We analyze several properties of stable outcomes under the different stability notions introduced above. By establishing separations between these notions – or, equivalently, between different side-payment regimes – we show that they can lead to stable outcomes with strictly different levels of social welfare (see the full version of this paper [14]). This demonstrates that allowing restricted forms of collusion on one side of the market can fundamentally alter the set of stable outcomes. Thus, our results emphasize the importance of accurately modeling the extent of collusion in combinatorial markets with correlated pricing systems.

In market settings with personalized prices, on the other hand, we identify strong structural properties of stable solutions: We provide a constructive method to eliminate all side payments from a stable outcome (Lemma 8 and 6), showing that in such settings all stability notions provide equivalent outcomes, regardless of which side payments are permitted in the market (Theorem 3).

Theorem 3. *Let $\mathcal{E}$ be an economy and $\mathcal{T}$ an arbitrary partition of its agents. Then, all of the following $\mathcal{T}$-cores $\mathcal{C}^{\mathcal{T}}(\mathcal{E}_h^r)$ for an hth-order market with side-payment restriction r coincide:*

- *for $h \in \{1, \dots, 5\}$, $r \in \{\text{full, sep, buy, sell, no}\}$ and $\mathcal{T}$, such that the join of the respective partitions is at least as coarse as $\mathcal{T}^{\text{sep}}$, i.e., $\mathcal{T} \vee \mathcal{T}^r \succeq \mathcal{T}^{\text{sep}}$,*
- *for $h \in \{4, 5\}$ and $r \in \{\text{full, sep, buy, sell, no}\}$, and*
- *for $h = 3$ and $\mathcal{T}$, such that the join of the respective partitions has the sellers as a group of transferable utility, i.e., $\mathcal{T} \vee \mathcal{T}^r \succeq \mathcal{T}^{\text{sell}}$.*

2 Preliminaries

The following setting for combinatorial markets based on a package assignment model was formally introduced in [5]. The crucial feature of this model of package exchanges is that trades are not directly executed between seller-buyer pairs, but instead routed through a *clearinghouse* that receives bundles from sellers and, under certain restrictions, potentially repackages them into new bundles before shipping them to buyers. It also collects all payments from buyers and distributes them to sellers in accordance with an adequate market pricing system.

The market settings differ in the possible alterations the clearinghouse can make to the packages it receives and in the restrictions on the pricing system. The first four settings were first defined in [5] and the fifth setting was introduced in [3]. We provide a quick overview of the different restrictions in the following table.

Setting	Clearinghouse	Bundle Compatibility	Pricing
1st order	Repackage	Item counts	Linear (item based)
2nd order	Relabel	Bundle counts	Per bundle
3rd order	Relabel sellers	Bundle counts for each buyer	Buyer personalized
4th order	–	Direct trade	Fully personalized
5th order	Repackage	Item counts	Independent

In the first-order setting, the clearinghouse can both repackage and reassign the bundles, while any package labels are completely disregarded. Therefore, only the total item counts on both sides of the market submissions have to coincide. A first-order pricing system is based on *item* prices, independently of the bundle structure. The bundle prices are then derived linearly from the item prices.

In the second-order setting, the clearinghouse is not allowed to open any packages. However, both the sellers' and buyers' labels on the packages can be freely adjusted. The corresponding pricing system is based on common *bundle* prices across all agents.

In the third-order setting, the clearinghouse can only change the labels of one side of the market (and we restrict our discussion to the sellers' labels similarly to [5]). The pricing system becomes *personalized for the buyers*, i.e., the prices for the same bundle sent to any given buyer have to coincide, but a seller may send the same bundle to different buyers at different prices.

For the fourth-order setting, the restrictions on the clearinghouse represent essentially the *direct trade* situation: no labels can be adjusted and the prices are personalized between any buyer-seller pair.

Finally, the fifth-order setting is based on *cumulative bundles*: every agent only offers/requests a cumulative bundle and the prices are personalized to each agent for the entire bundle. This corresponds to the first-order setting in terms of the set of offered items, where only the total count on each market side must coincide. This setting relaxes the interaction between the two sides of the market in the pricing system, so budget balance needs to be explicitly assumed (as compared to the other settings, where it is derived from the interactions given by the pricing system).

We extend the model of [5] by introducing *side payments* so as to make it applicable to economies with coordination issues, externalities, or other frictions that prices alone cannot resolve. Depending on the setting, we allow (a subset of) agents to exchange money outside the combinatorial market and its pricing restrictions. In particular, these payments are a priori available to any pair of agents, not restricted to seller-buyer pairs that trade a bundle.

For an economy $\mathcal{E}$ and $h \in \{1, \ldots, 5\}$, we indicate by $\mathcal{E}_h$ the market with resale restrictions imposed by the hth-order setting. The bundles that are being traded in the market by the agents N are notated as an *allocation* $(\boldsymbol{S}_I, \boldsymbol{Z}_J)$, where each agent specifies the bundle of items they want to offer to or request from each agent on the other side of the market. A *pricing system* is then given by functions p_{ij}, defining the price of bundle $\boldsymbol{\omega}$ when sold by seller $j \in J$ and bought by buyer $i \in I$ as $p_{ij}(\boldsymbol{\omega})$.

We denote by $q_{kl} \in \mathbb{R}$ the amount of money that agent $k \in N$ side-pays to agent $l \in N$. The case of $q_{kl} < 0$ corresponds to k receiving instead of paying the respective side payment. We require consistency between side payments of two agents $k \neq l$, i.e., $q_{lk} = -q_{kl}$, so that each outgoing payment from k is equivalently received by l. For notational ease, we allow side payments q_{kk} of an agent to themselves; $q_{kk} = 0$ follows from consistency.

For every $k \in N$, the individual side payments are denoted by $\boldsymbol{Q}_k = (q_{kl})_{l \in N}$ and the corresponding cumulative side payments by $q_k = \sum_{l \in N} q_{kl}$. The vector of all side payments is denoted by $\boldsymbol{Q}_N = (\boldsymbol{Q}_k)_{k \in N}$.

An *assignment* $((\boldsymbol{S}_I, \boldsymbol{Z}_J), \boldsymbol{p}, \boldsymbol{Q}_N)$ in a market $\mathcal{E}_m$ is the tuple of the allocation, the pricing system, and the side payments. We may omit all side payments with value zero in the notation and use only $\boldsymbol{Q}_C$ in place of $\boldsymbol{Q}_N$ for some $C \subseteq N$ or fully omit $\boldsymbol{Q}_N$, when no side payments are used or allowed. For a given market setting $\mathcal{E}_m$, the set of *admissible* assignments $\mathcal{A}(\mathcal{E}_m)$ is structurally restricted in one of the various ways outlined above. These restrictions will apply to the set of assignments that are valid in the market, as well as to the structure of the pricing system and the side payments.

We naturally extend the definition of quasi-linear utility to include the side payments and denote the agents' *payoff* associated with an assignment as $\pi_i = v_i(\boldsymbol{s}_i) - p_i - q_i$ for every buyer $i \in I$ and $\pi_j = p_j - v_j(\boldsymbol{z}_j) - q_j$ for every seller $j \in J$. Any agent's payoff thus consists of the value they gain for receiving, or lose from selling their cumulative bundle, and the total amount of money they send to or receive from other agents. We will denote the vector of all payoffs as $\boldsymbol{\pi}_N = (\pi_k)_{k \in N}$.

We will specify the different stability notions we use further below (see Sect. 2.2), but a common property and fundamental assumption is the individual rationality of every agent in the outcome, i.e., that they would drop out of the market if they received a negative payoff from the trade. For some of our results, it is therefore reasonable to restrict the set of assignments accordingly.

Definition 1 (Feasible assignment). *The set $\mathcal{F}(\mathcal{E}_m)$ of* feasible assignments *comprises all assignments $((\boldsymbol{S}_I, \boldsymbol{Z}_J), \boldsymbol{p}, \boldsymbol{Q}_N)$ that are admissible in the market $\mathcal{E}_m$ and give non-negative payoff to all agents, $\boldsymbol{\pi}_N \geq \boldsymbol{0}$.*

Because the market settings restrict the structure of the pricing system in specific ways, it might not be possible for every admissible allocation $(\boldsymbol{S}_I, \boldsymbol{Z}_J)$ to achieve a market outcome that is also individually rational for every agent. While the allocations themselves might be used in different settings (under certain modifications), it might not be possible to do the same with the pricing system.

Definition 2 (Priceability of an allocation). *An allocation $(\boldsymbol{S}_I, \boldsymbol{Z}_J)$ is* priceable *in the market $\mathcal{E}_m$ if it is admissible and if there exist an admissible pric-*

ing system and admissible side payments in $\mathcal{E}_m$ *such that* $((\boldsymbol{S}_I, \boldsymbol{Z}_J), \boldsymbol{p}, \boldsymbol{Q}_N) \in \mathcal{F}(\mathcal{E}_m)$.

As already observed by [5], two properties that we can easily deduce from the definitions of the first four settings are the following:

Remark 1. Because the repackaging restrictions increase in $h \in \{1,2,3,4\}$, it holds that if an allocation $(\boldsymbol{S}_I, \boldsymbol{Z}_J)$ is admissible in the hth-order setting, then it is also admissible in the $(h-1)^{\text{th}}$-order setting for every $h \in \{2,3,4\}$.

Conversely, the pricing systems become more individualized in h, so if $\boldsymbol{p}$ is an hth-order pricing system, it naturally induces a $(h+1)^{\text{th}}$-order pricing system for every $h \in \{1,2,3\}$ by applying the same price to all corresponding individual prices.

2.1 Side-Payment Schemes

Independent of how the pricing system is restricted in the five settings, we also differentiate levels of side-payment restrictions in the market. While the definition covers the extent of side payments among any pair of agents, we introduce the following notions and restrictions:

We denote by *full side payments* the unrestricted setting, in which all agents can side-pay each other.

Separate side payments refers to the restriction where the two sides of the market can send and receive side payments among each other, but all side payments between any seller and buyer are zero, i.e., $q_{ij} = 0$ for every $i \in I$ and $j \in J$. This restriction establishes that all payments between the two sides go through the market pricing system and will allow us to differentiate between market settings where side payments can be equivalently realized by adjusting the pricing system accordingly.

Buyers'/sellers' single side payments are an even more severely restricted setting, where we do allow one side of the market to send and receive money among each other, but not the other side. This setting reflects, e.g., the situation of markets in which this type of collusion is prohibited for sellers, but this may not be necessary or enforceable for buyers.

Finally, we consider the setting with *no side payments*, which represents the original market setting in the previous literature.

We use the notation $\mathcal{E}_h^r$ with $h \in \{1, \ldots, 5\}$ and $r \in \{\text{full, sep, buy, sell, no}\}$ to indicate the market $\mathcal{E}_h$ with the respective restriction r on the side payments as outlined above.

The restrictions on the side payments imply a partial ordering of the sets of admissible assignments based on the sets of agents that can exchange side payments: $\mathcal{A}(\mathcal{E}_h^{\text{no}}) \subseteq \mathcal{A}(\mathcal{E}_h^{\text{buy}}) \subseteq \mathcal{A}(\mathcal{E}_h^{\text{sep}}) \subseteq \mathcal{A}(\mathcal{E}_h^{\text{full}})$, and similarly, $\mathcal{A}(\mathcal{E}_h^{\text{no}}) \subseteq \mathcal{A}(\mathcal{E}_h^{\text{sell}}) \subseteq \mathcal{A}(\mathcal{E}_h^{\text{sep}}) \subseteq \mathcal{A}(\mathcal{E}_h^{\text{full}})$. We use the notation $r \preceq \tilde{r}$ to refer to the corresponding partial order on the side-payment restrictions themselves when comparing them, where $\tilde{r}$ admits all side payments that r does.

2.2 Stability

Combinatorial markets can be interpreted as a specific type of *cooperative games*, where agents make binding agreements on which strategy they use and how the payoff gets distributed among them ([16]). For these games, standard solution concepts are stability in the sense of *transferable utility (TU)*, where agents can freely distribute their total utility among each other, and *non-transferable utility (NTU)*, where no payments outside the market are allowed. Both concepts share the solution concept of payoff vectors that admit coalitional stability, i.e., no coalition of agents can strictly increase their individual payoffs by deviating from the agreed-upon global solution. The set of these vectors is commonly referred to as the *core* of the game.

We consider the concepts of TU and NTU as special cases of the following generalization: Let $\mathcal{T} = \{T_1, \dots, T_{|\mathcal{T}|}\}$ be a partition of the set of agents N. The agents in a given block T of the partition can transfer money freely among themselves, but not to agents in a different block. We call this concept *$\mathcal{T}$-restricted transferable utility ($\mathcal{T}$-RTU)*. The classical definitions of TU and NTU are then included in this representation by setting, respectively, $\mathcal{T} = \{N\}$ or $\mathcal{T} = \{\{k\} : k \in N\}$. The notion of stability corresponding to $\mathcal{T}$-RTU is established by the following definition.

Definition 3 ($\mathcal{T}$-core). *A vector $\boldsymbol{\rho}_N \in \mathbb{R}^N$ is in the $\mathcal{T}$-*core *$\mathcal{C}^{\mathcal{T}}(\mathcal{E}_h^r)$ of the market $\mathcal{E}_h^r$ if*

1. *there exists an assignment $((\boldsymbol{S}_I, \boldsymbol{Z}_J), \boldsymbol{p}, \boldsymbol{Q}_N) \in \mathcal{A}(\mathcal{E}_h^r)$ with $\sum_{k \in T} \rho_k = \sum_{k \in T} \pi_k$ for every $T \in \mathcal{T}$, and*
2. *for every coalition $C \subseteq N$ and for every assignment $((\tilde{\boldsymbol{S}}_{C_I}, \tilde{\boldsymbol{Z}}_{C_J}), \tilde{\boldsymbol{p}}, \tilde{\boldsymbol{Q}}_C) \in \mathcal{A}(\mathcal{E}_h^r[C])$,*

$$\exists T \in \mathcal{T} : \sum_{k \in C \cap T} \tilde{\pi}_k \leq \sum_{k \in C \cap T} \rho_k .$$

*We also call such a vector $\mathcal{T}$-*stable *in the market $\mathcal{E}_h^r$.*

A vector in the core is typically also called a *payoff vector* (due to the interpretation of the stability concept as its own game), a notion we have already used for the utility of each player in the assignment of the market setting. If we require disambiguation between the utility from the market itself and the vector we consider in the context of the core, we will refer to the latter as the *payoff after utility transfers*. One assumption necessary to avoid non-optimal stable outcomes is that the agents whose cumulative bundle is empty in an assignment that realizes a core vector and allows for free price readjustment have zero payoff.

The first condition in the definition establishes the transfer of utility within each block of the partition $\mathcal{T}$ among its agents. The second condition can be interpreted in the following way: a vector is $\mathcal{T}$-stable if no coalition $C \subseteq N$ can find an assignment that improves the cumulative payoff for every agent group $C \cap T$, $T \in \mathcal{T}$. Compare this condition to the standard notion of TU-stability, where this holds for the group of all agents, and to NTU-stability, where it applies to every agent individually. A property that immediately follows from the definition is that every vector in the core is non-negative: for the singleton coalition $\{k\}$, that agent will receive a payoff of $\tilde{\pi}_k = 0$ by not trading anything.

For NTU-stability, every vector in $\mathcal{C}^{\mathcal{T}^{\text{no}}}(\mathcal{E}_h^r)$ needs to be exactly realized as the payoff vector of some assignment in the market $\mathcal{E}_h^r$. We can therefore equivalently define the notion of stability directly for the respective assignment.

Definition 4 (NTU-stable assignment). *An assignment* $((\boldsymbol{S}_I, \boldsymbol{Z}_J), \boldsymbol{p}, \boldsymbol{Q}_N) \in \mathcal{A}(\mathcal{E}_h^r)$ *is* NTU-stable *in the market* $\mathcal{E}_h^r$ *if for every coalition* $C \subseteq N$ *and for every assignment* $((\tilde{\boldsymbol{S}}_{C_I}, \tilde{\boldsymbol{Z}}_{C_J}), \tilde{\boldsymbol{p}}, \tilde{\boldsymbol{Q}}_C) \in \mathcal{A}(\mathcal{E}_h^r[C])$, *there exists an agent* $k \in C$ *such that* $\tilde{\pi}_k \leq \pi_k$.

2.3 Relation Between Stability Notions and Side-Payment Settings

Intuitively, the transfer of utility we allow in different settings of $\mathcal{T}$-RTU stability corresponds to the side payments of some specific setting we have established above on a different level of the problem; the former applies the transfer after the market has established its trade, while the latter incorporates it into the strategic considerations within the market. Indeed, we provide a formal discussion of this relation in this section. In particular, the following partitions correspond to the side-payment restrictions we have already defined. Whenever we refer to any of the special partitions defined here, we call the partition $\mathcal{T}$ a *side-payment partition* and conversely emphasize by writing *arbitrary* partition otherwise.

1. *TU-core* when $\mathcal{T}^{\text{full}} = \{N\}$,
2. *sepRTU-core* when $\mathcal{T}^{\text{sep}} = \{I, J\}$,
3. *bRTU-core* when $\mathcal{T}^{\text{buy}} = \{I\} \cup \{\{j\} : j \in J\}$,
4. *sRTU-core* when $\mathcal{T}^{\text{sell}} = \{\{i\} : i \in I\} \cup \{J\}$,
5. *NTU-core* when $\mathcal{T}^{\text{no}} = \{\{k\} : k \in N\}$.

We can consider the natural partial order on the previous partitions based on the refinement, i.e., $\mathcal{T}^{\text{no}} \preceq \mathcal{T}^{\text{buy}} \preceq \mathcal{T}^{\text{sep}} \preceq \mathcal{T}^{\text{full}}$, and similarly $\mathcal{T}^{\text{no}} \preceq \mathcal{T}^{\text{sell}} \preceq \mathcal{T}^{\text{sep}} \preceq \mathcal{T}^{\text{full}}$. Clearly, this is the same partial order as for the side-payment settings, if we identify the partition with the respective setting it represents.

Following the intuition outlined above, we expect a close relation between an r side-payment setting and the corresponding notion of $\mathcal{T}^r$-RTU stability in the sense that we can replace one by the other, i.e., the $\mathcal{T}^r$-core should give the same stable outcomes as the NTU-core for r side payments. We formalize this intuition in the following. In fact, it turns out that an even stronger statement can be proved: When considering $\mathcal{T}$-RTU stability and the partition $\mathcal{T}^r$ that corresponds to the r side-payment setting in the market, we can alternatively consider joining the partitions in the partition lattice to their common least upper bound $\mathcal{S} = \mathcal{T} \vee \mathcal{T}^r$.[1] Then, the original setting corresponds to both $\mathcal{S}$-RTU

[1] We omit a formal discussion of this operator. For comparable elements, the greater one is the least upper bound. The only pair of incomparable partitions we consider is $\mathcal{T}^{\text{buy}} \vee \mathcal{T}^{\text{sell}} = \mathcal{T}^{\text{sep}}$.

stability for the same economy without side payments, as well as NTU-stability on the market that allows side payments according to the partition $\mathcal{S}$.

Lemma 1. *It holds that* $\mathcal{C}^{\mathcal{T}}(\mathcal{E}_h^r) = \mathcal{C}^{\mathcal{S}}(\mathcal{E}_h^{\text{no}})$, *where* $\mathcal{S} = \mathcal{T} \vee \mathcal{T}^r$, *when*

- $\mathcal{T}$ *is a side-payment partition, or*
- $\mathcal{T}$ *and* $\mathcal{T}^r$ *are comparable, i.e.,* $\mathcal{T} \preceq \mathcal{T}^r$ *or* $\mathcal{T}^r \preceq \mathcal{T}$.

Using $\mathcal{T} = \mathcal{T}^{\text{no}} \preceq \mathcal{T}^r$ and $\mathcal{S} = \mathcal{T}^{\text{no}} \vee \mathcal{T}^r = \mathcal{T}^r$ for some side-payment restriction r gives the following corollary.

Corollary 1. $\mathcal{C}^{\mathcal{T}^{\text{no}}}(\mathcal{E}_h^r) = \mathcal{C}^{\mathcal{T}^r}(\mathcal{E}_h^{\text{no}})$.

Combining Corollary 1 and Lemma 1 establishes Theorem 2.

The previous results let us conclude the discussion on stability settings in the following way: By using side payments, every $\mathcal{T}$-RTU stability notion can be equivalently represented by allowing a certain type of side payments in the market and discussing NTU-stability only, or by discussing the appropriate RTU-stability in the market without any side payments. The stability setting itself is then identified by the specific restrictions on side payments. Most importantly, TU-stability immediately corresponds to NTU-stability in the market with the full side payment setting.

3 Equivalences

With the introduction of side payments, the relation between the different order settings becomes more involved. Originally, the pricing systems provided defining restrictions on the structure of the payoff outcomes of the problem. In this section, we investigate how the market settings actually differ from each other after the introduction of side payments, establishing various one-directional results by identifying situations where a market setting can represent all outcomes of another setting, and conversely provide examples when a certain setting's restrictions do not allow another setting's outcomes.

A fundamental requirement for comparing two market settings is whether we can even find an allocation in which each agent offers or requests the same total amount of items. In this case, we call two assignments (or their respective allocations) *item-equivalent.* Already [5, Lemma 2.1] have established that when an allocation is admissible in one of the first four order settings, we can always find an item-equivalent allocation in any of the other settings by greedily reassigning and repackaging the items so as to obtain a fourth-order admissible allocation (which in turn is trivially admissible in all lower order settings). This result can be easily generalized to the fifth-order setting by applying the same reasoning.

The standard equivalence notion we typically want to work with is *payoff equivalence*, where every agent receives the same payoff in the two equivalent assignments. From the perspective of stability, the agents are then indifferent between the assignments.

Stronger notions of equivalence require the agents to pay the same total money to the clearinghouse (*price equivalence*) or even the same bundle prices (*market equivalence*). Clearly, the latter cannot always be maintained when considering a setting in which the pricing system is less flexible.

The combination of the results from Lemmas 2 to 5 below immediately establishes Theorem 1, which states the full equivalence between certain settings in the sense that we can always find assignments using the same items and each agent achieves the exact same utility from the total trade. In the following, we discuss these results on a high level and give intuition (and counterexamples) on why other equivalences do not hold. We refer to the full version [14] for a structured overview of all equivalences we establish.

3.1 Increasing Order Setting

The first results we present consider going from a given order setting to a higher one. Thereby, the pricing system becomes more individualized, but the clearinghouse gets more restricted in terms of how it can reassemble or reassign packages. While the former is clearly relaxing the restrictions for higher settings, it turns out that the latter is in most cases only a formal issue, which does not impede equivalence properties between the settings. We present only a brief summary of the results and refer to the full version [14] for a thorough discussion and proofs.

We start by considering the cases in which, going from one setting to the other, the side-payment restrictions remain the same or are relaxed. If the order setting does not change, market equivalence can be directly established.

Remark 2. As we have already observed in Sect. 2.1, any assignment $((\boldsymbol{S}_I, \boldsymbol{Z}_J), \boldsymbol{p}, \boldsymbol{Q}_N) \in \mathcal{F}(\mathcal{E}_h^r)$ is also feasible in a market with the same order setting but with fewer side-payment restrictions, i.e., $((\boldsymbol{S}_I, \boldsymbol{Z}_J), \boldsymbol{p}, \boldsymbol{Q}_N) \in \mathcal{F}(\mathcal{E}_h^{\tilde{r}})$ for every $\tilde{r} \succeq r$. Therefore, we can immediately deduce that a market equivalent assignment always exists when the only change to the setting is a relaxation of the side-payment restrictions.

We summarize our results for increasing the order setting, when the side-payment restrictions are not refined, as follows:

Lemma 2. *When the side-payments of the original setting remain directly applicable, i.e., $\tilde{r} \succeq r$, the following equivalences hold:*

- *For $\boldsymbol{A} \in \mathcal{F}(\mathcal{E}_1^r)$, there exists a market-equivalent assignment $\tilde{\boldsymbol{A}} \in \mathcal{F}(\mathcal{E}_{\tilde{h}}^{\tilde{r}})$ with $\tilde{h} \in \{2, 3, 4\}$.*
- *For $\boldsymbol{A} \in \mathcal{F}(\mathcal{E}_3^r)$, there exists a market-equivalent assignment $\tilde{\boldsymbol{A}} \in \mathcal{F}(\mathcal{E}_4^{\tilde{r}})$.*
- *For $\boldsymbol{A} \in \mathcal{F}(\mathcal{E}_h^r)$ with $h \in \{1, \ldots, 4\}$, there exists a price-equivalent assignment $\tilde{\boldsymbol{A}} \in \mathcal{F}(\mathcal{E}_5^{\tilde{r}})$.*
- *For $\boldsymbol{A} \in \mathcal{F}(\mathcal{E}_2^r)$, there exists a price-equivalent assignment $\tilde{\boldsymbol{A}} \in \mathcal{F}(\mathcal{E}_4^{\tilde{r}})$.*[2]

[2] Note that for the fifth-order setting, the notion of market-equivalence doesn't apply due to the difference in representation of this model.

The proofs of these results are all based on identifying an appropriate pricing system in the higher-order setting to achieve the same market outcome as before, while identifying the required structure to compile admissible packages with restricted clearinghouse power.

The noteworthy outlier in this discussion is the second-order setting. No market equivalence result holds when going to the third-order setting because the relabeling of the clearinghouse on both sides of the market allows some buyer-seller pairs to effectively trade more than one individual bundle and, thereby, circumvent the price restrictions that would usually apply to the cumulative bundles. Going to the fourth-order setting, however, price-equivalence can be restored.

If we restrict the side payments or change the side of the market where they are allowed, we can't establish the same rich set of equivalence implications. In fact, in most cases, not even payoff equivalence is guaranteed. Again, we refer to our full version [14] for a more detailed discussion.

3.2 Full and Separate Side Payments

The full side-payment setting is the least restrictive one, and every possible distribution of social welfare in a trade is realizable. As a consequence, for any assignment, we can determine a payoff equivalent outcome in any order setting with full side payments by having all money exchanges go through side payments and setting the prices to zero.

This fact can also be generalized to the separate side-payment setting. In this case, we can transfer the money from the buyers to the sellers through the price of a single traded item (while setting the prices of all the other items to zero), and then redistribute the money separately among the two groups so that each agent still attains the same payoff. The following statement summarizes these observations.

Lemma 3. *Let* $((\boldsymbol{S}_I, \boldsymbol{Z}_J), \boldsymbol{p}, \boldsymbol{Q}_N) \in \mathcal{F}(\mathcal{E}_h^r)$*, then for every* $\tilde{h} \in \{1, \ldots, 5\}$ *there exists a payoff-equivalent assignment* $((\tilde{\boldsymbol{S}}_I, \tilde{\boldsymbol{Z}}_J), \tilde{\boldsymbol{p}}, \tilde{\boldsymbol{Q}}_N) \in \mathcal{F}(\mathcal{E}_{\tilde{h}}^{\text{sep}})$.

Price equivalence does not hold in general between the full and separate side-payment settings, unless we go to the same or higher order setting with the same or less restricted side payments, as outlined in Sect. 3.1. See the full version [14] for an extensive discussion.

3.3 Single Side Payments

When only single side payments are allowed, some equivalence properties hold only for sufficient levels of price personalization. We first observe that, if the prices depend only on the items in each bundle or on the bundle itself, then no equivalence relations can be found starting from a setting in which prices are personalized for at least one side of the market.

Remark 3. When going from a higher order setting to the first- or second-order settings with at most single side payments, the rigidity of the pricing system and the restrictions on the side payments do not allow any equivalence result. In fact, we can always consider an economy where there exists a feasible assignment whose pricing system is admissible only in the higher order settings, and any corresponding item-equivalent assignment is not priceable in the first- and second-order settings. In particular, the following modifications of settings do not admit payoff equivalence:

- Going from the hth-order setting with $h \in \{2, \ldots, 5\}$ and any type of side payments to the first-order setting with at most single side payments.
- Going from the hth-order setting with $h \in \{3, 4, 5\}$ and any type of side payments to the second-order setting with at most single side payments.

However, we provide positive results for the more personalized settings in the following. The first result establishes that going from the fifth-order to the fourth-order setting with single side payments preserves payoff equivalence. This is because the money each agent receives or pays in the initial assignment can be distributed through side-payments on the side where this is allowed, and on the other side is redistributed using individualized prices.

Lemma 4. *Let* $((\boldsymbol{s}_I, \boldsymbol{z}_J), \boldsymbol{p}, \boldsymbol{Q}_N) \in \mathcal{F}(\mathcal{E}_5^r)$ *with* $r \in \{\text{buy, sell}\}$*, then there exists a payoff-equivalent assignment* $((\tilde{\boldsymbol{S}}_I, \tilde{\boldsymbol{Z}}_J), \tilde{\boldsymbol{p}}, \tilde{\boldsymbol{Q}}_N) \in \mathcal{F}(\mathcal{E}_4^r)$.[3]

Price equivalence does not hold in this case due to the fully centralized nature of the fifth-order setting, which may allow part of a buyer's cumulative price to be effectively directed to a seller who doesn't offer any item the buyer requests. This indirect exchange of money is not possible in the fourth-order setting, since the price of the empty bundle, which those agents trade with each other, is always normalized to zero.

If instead of maintaining the same single side-payment restrictions we restrict or change the side of the market in which side payments are allowed, i.e., going from the fifth-order setting with at least buyers' or sellers' single side payments to the fourth-order setting with sellers' or buyers' single side payments respectively, then payoff equivalence does not hold for the same reasons as for the setting above. Similarly, going from the fifth-order setting with any type of side payments to the fourth-order setting with no side payments does not admit payoff equivalence.

The second result highlights an interesting property of the third-order setting with sellers' single side payments: Any feasible assignment with at most sellers' single side payments is payoff equivalent to a third-order admissible assignment with sellers' single side payments. This is due to the fact that price personalization only applies to buyers, but not for sellers in the third-order setting. Hence, it is sufficient to adjust the prices so that buyers can pay the exact amount

[3] It follows that every assignment $((\boldsymbol{s}_I, \boldsymbol{z}_J), \boldsymbol{p}, \boldsymbol{Q}_N) \in \mathcal{F}(\mathcal{E}_5^{\text{no}})$ is payoff equivalent to some $((\tilde{\boldsymbol{S}}_I, \tilde{\boldsymbol{Z}}_J), \tilde{\boldsymbol{p}}, \tilde{\boldsymbol{Q}}_N) \in \mathcal{F}(\mathcal{E}_4^r)$ with $r \in \{\text{buy, sell}\}$.

they have to maintain payoff equivalence, and then readjust the sellers' payoffs through side payments.

Lemma 5. *Let* $((\boldsymbol{S}_I, \boldsymbol{Z}_J), \boldsymbol{p}, \boldsymbol{Q}_J) \in \mathcal{F}(\mathcal{E}_h^r)$ *with* $h \in \{2,4,5\}$ *and* $r \in \{\text{sell, no}\}$, *then there exists a payoff-equivalent assignment* $((\tilde{\boldsymbol{S}}_I, \tilde{\boldsymbol{Z}}_J), \tilde{\boldsymbol{p}}, \tilde{\boldsymbol{Q}}_J) \in \mathcal{F}(\mathcal{E}_3^{\text{sell}})$.

Further negative results are discussed in this context are discussed in the full version [14].

4 Stable Solutions

Now that the previous section has established useful relations between the different settings, we continue to investigate their stability properties. Most importantly, the maximum social welfare achievable by an admissible assignment can differ across different settings or stability notions. However, if two markets are payoff equivalent, their $\mathcal{T}$-core coincides for any partition $\mathcal{T}$ of the set of agents, as both the assignments that realize a given payoff vector for the core, just as the possible deviating coalitions, correspond to each other. Therefore, from Theorem 1, we can already deduce the following.

Corollary 2. *Let* $\mathcal{E}$ *be an economy and* $\mathcal{T}$ *an arbitrary partition of its agents.*

- *The* $\mathcal{T}$*-cores of all the order settings with full or separate side payments coincide, i.e.,* $\mathcal{C}^{\mathcal{T}}(\mathcal{E}_h^r) = \mathcal{C}^{\mathcal{T}}(\mathcal{E}_{\tilde{h}}^{\tilde{r}})$ *for every* $h, \tilde{h} \in \{1, \ldots, 5\}$ *and* $r, \tilde{r} \in \{\text{full, sep}\}$.
- $\mathcal{C}^{\mathcal{T}}(\mathcal{E}_4^{\text{buy}}) = \mathcal{C}^{\mathcal{T}}(\mathcal{E}_5^{\text{buy}})$.
- $\mathcal{C}^{\mathcal{T}}(\mathcal{E}_3^{\text{sell}}) = \mathcal{C}^{\mathcal{T}}(\mathcal{E}_4^{\text{sell}}) = \mathcal{C}^{\mathcal{T}}(\mathcal{E}_5^{\text{sell}})$.

From Lemma 1, we know that $\mathcal{C}^{\mathcal{T}}(\mathcal{E}_h^{\text{full}}) = \mathcal{C}^{\mathcal{T}^{\text{no}}}(\mathcal{E}_h^{\text{full}})$. Therefore, we can establish an even stronger result: For the full and separate side-payment settings, regardless of the order setting, all notions of stability coincide. The same structure of solutions is also achieved when the stability notion sufficiently complements the side-payment setting.

Corollary 3. $\mathcal{C}^{\mathcal{T}}(\mathcal{E}_h^r)$ *is the same for every* $h \in \{1, \ldots, 5\}$, $r \in \{\text{full, sep, buy, sell, no}\}$ *and arbitrary partition* $\mathcal{T}$ *such that* $\mathcal{T} \vee \mathcal{T}^r \succeq \mathcal{T}^{\text{sep}}$.

4.1 Separations

The existence of stable vectors is not guaranteed in general market settings. However, if the TU-core is not empty (and consequently, also the $\mathcal{T}$-core for every partition $\mathcal{T} \succeq \mathcal{T}^{\text{sep}}$), all of its vectors achieve the maximum social welfare, independently of the market order setting and side-payment restrictions. However, this is generally not the case for finer partitions and lower order settings, where not only bRTU-core, sRTU-core, and NTU-core stable vectors might not achieve the maximum social welfare, but there also might be stable vectors whose total utility differs from each other.

On the other hand, in some economies in which the TU-core is empty, limiting side payments to one side of the market or completely forbidding them can yield stable outcomes. Moreover, bRTU- and sRTU-stable vectors might achieve a social welfare that is arbitrarily larger than the one of any NTU-stable outcome. Thus, the assumptions on how agents transfer utility outside the market have a critical influence on the achievable total welfare in what can be considered a stable assignment, and the new stability notions meaningfully introduce new solution concepts to these settings. All examples justifying the separations can be found in the full version [14].

4.2 Stability-Equivalent Settings

The differences between the stability notions disappear when the resale restrictions in the market allow for more personalized prices. By using the structural properties of stable outcomes, we are able to establish further equivalence results, that do not hold for general assignments. Specifically, in this section, we discuss how this is the case for the fourth- and fifth-order settings, where side-payments can be effectively entirely disregarded. Note that, by Theorem 2, $\mathcal{T}$-stability in a market $\mathcal{E}_h^r$ only depends on the join of the partitions $\mathcal{S} = \mathcal{T} \vee \mathcal{T}^r$, or in other words, $\mathcal{C}^{\mathcal{T}}(\mathcal{E}_h^r) = \mathcal{C}^{\mathcal{T}^{\text{no}}}(\mathcal{E}_h^s)$ for the side-payment restrictions corresponding to $\mathcal{S}$. Therefore, we will discuss the results by assuming that all the transfers of utility are made inside the market and $\mathcal{T} = \mathcal{T}^{\text{no}}$.

Let's start with the fifth-order setting. We first show that for every stable assignment in the fifth-order setting, we can always find a payoff-equivalent one in $\mathcal{E}_5^{\text{no}}$ by simply including the side payments in the cumulative prices that every agent sends or receives from the clearinghouse.

Lemma 6. *Let $((\boldsymbol{s}_I, \boldsymbol{z}_J), \boldsymbol{p}, \boldsymbol{Q}_N) \in \mathcal{F}(\mathcal{E}_5^r)$ be an NTU-stable assignment in $\mathcal{E}_5^r$, then there exists a payoff-equivalent NTU-stable assignment $((\tilde{\boldsymbol{s}}_I, \tilde{\boldsymbol{z}}_J), \tilde{\boldsymbol{p}}) \in \mathcal{F}(\mathcal{E}_5^{\text{no}})$.*

On the other hand, every assignment that is NTU-stable in the market in $\mathcal{E}_5^{\text{no}}$ is also stable if we allow more side payments. If this were not the case, we could still find a deviating assignment with no side payments in the more general market.

Lemma 7. *Let $((\boldsymbol{s}_I, \boldsymbol{z}_J), \boldsymbol{p}) \in \mathcal{F}(\mathcal{E}_5^{\text{no}})$ be an NTU-stable assignment in $\mathcal{E}_5^{\text{no}}$, then it is also NTU-stable in $\mathcal{E}_5^r$.*

Then, by Lemma 1, we deduce that $\mathcal{C}^{\mathcal{T}}(\mathcal{E}_5^r) = \mathcal{C}^{\mathcal{S}}(\mathcal{E}_5^{\tilde{r}})$ for every $r, \tilde{r} \in \{\text{full, sep, buy, sell, no}\}$ and partitions $\mathcal{T}, \mathcal{S}$. Note that the previous two lemmas can be applied to any type of side-payment restrictions, not only the ones we originally defined.

We now discuss the analogous results for the fourth-order setting. In this case, the proofs are more involved since the role of the clearinghouse is not as powerful as before, and therefore, we need to find appropriate paths in the pricing graph, through which we are able to send the side payments instead.

Lemma 8. *Let* $((\boldsymbol{S}_I, \boldsymbol{Z}_J), \boldsymbol{p}, \boldsymbol{Q}_N) \in \mathcal{F}(\mathcal{E}_4^r)$ *be an NTU-stable assignment in* $\mathcal{E}_4^r$*, hen there exists a payoff-equivalent NTU-stable assignment* $((\tilde{\boldsymbol{S}}_I, \tilde{\boldsymbol{Z}}_J), \tilde{\boldsymbol{p}}) \in \mathcal{F}(\mathcal{E}_4^{\text{no}})$.

As before, any NTU-stable assignment in $\mathcal{E}_4^{\text{no}}$ is also stable with any type of side payments. With a similar construction as in the proof of the previous lemma, we can show that we can otherwise find a deviating coalition C and an assignment with no side payments, where every agent strictly improves their payoff.

Lemma 9. *Let* $((\tilde{\boldsymbol{S}}_I, \tilde{\boldsymbol{Z}}_J), \tilde{\boldsymbol{p}}) \in \mathcal{F}(\mathcal{E}_4^{\text{no}})$ *be an NTU-stable assignment in* $\mathcal{E}_4^{\text{no}}$*, then it is also NTU-stable in* $\mathcal{E}_4^r$.

Since the previous two lemmas are still valid for any type of side payments, by Lemma 1, we can then deduce that $\mathcal{C}^{\mathcal{T}}(\mathcal{E}_4^r) = \mathcal{C}^{\mathcal{S}}(\mathcal{E}_4^{\tilde{r}})$ for every $r, \tilde{r} \in \{\text{full, sep, buy, sell, no}\}$ and partitions $\mathcal{T}, \mathcal{S}$.

Summarizing the results in this section, we can deduce that all the $\mathcal{T}$-cores for the fourth- and fifth-order settings coincide.

Corollary 4. $\mathcal{C}^{\mathcal{T}}(\mathcal{E}_h^r)$ *is the same for every* $h \in \{4, 5\}$, $r \in \{\text{full, sep, buy, sell, no}\}$ *and partition* $\mathcal{T}$.

Combining the observations from above provides the summary result of Theorem 3, stating that if the join partition is coarse enough, or the prices are personalized enough, all the stability notions in an economy $\mathcal{E}$ coincide.

5 Concluding Remarks

We expand well-established combinatorial market models by adding explicit side payments, allowing for different restrictions on utility transfers among agents. To compare the relative strengths of the resulting markets, we introduce a hierarchy of equivalence notions, ranging from item equivalence to market equivalence. This comparison yields near-monotonicity: the set of assignments that can be realized generally increases with more personalized prices or with the allowance of side payments across more groups. However, in the second-order setting, payoff equivalence fails when compared to higher-order settings under restricted utility transfer. This irregularity disappears once sufficiently strong side payments are permitted. We also generalize the classical notions of TU- and NTU-stability to model limits on financial transfers between different groups of agents. The new concept aligns naturally with our models of side payments and also sheds new light on the original notions, especially NTU-stability. In particular, allowing restricted forms of collusion expands the set of stable outcomes, leading to more nuanced solution concepts that reflect different assumptions about agents' ability to coordinate.

Acknowledgment. The authors thank their advisor Andreas S. Schulz for his valuable input. They also thank the anonymous reviewers for their constructive feedback.

References

1. Arrow, K.J., Debreu, G.: Existence of an equilibrium for a competitive economy. Econometrica **22**(3), 265 (1954). https://doi.org/10.2307/1907353
2. Babaioff, M., Dobzinski, S., Oren, S.: Combinatorial auctions with endowment effect. In: Proceedings of the 2018 ACM Conference on Economics and Computation, pp. 73–90. EC '18, ACM, New York, NY, USA (2018).https://doi.org/10.1145/3219166.3219197
3. Bichler, M., Waldherr, S.: Core and pricing equilibria in combinatorial exchanges. Econ. Lett. **157**, 145–147 (2017). https://doi.org/10.1016/j.econlet.2017.06.003
4. Bichler, M., Waldherr, S.: Core pricing in combinatorial exchanges with financially constrained buyers: computational hardness and algorithmic solutions. Oper. Res. **70**(1), 241–264 (2022). https://doi.org/10.1287/opre.2021.2132
5. Bikhchandani, S., Ostroy, J.M.: The package assignment model. J. Econ. Theory **107**(2), 377–406 (2002). https://doi.org/10.1006/jeth.2001.2957
6. Cramton, P., Shoham, Y.: Combinatorial Auctions. Presented at the (2005). https://doi.org/10.7551/mitpress/9780262033428.001.0001
7. Devanur, N.R., Garg, J., Mehta, R., Vazirani, V.V., Yazdanbod, S.: A New Class of Combinatorial Markets with Covering Constraints: Algorithms and Applications, pp. 2311–2325. Society for Industrial and Applied Mathematics, Philadelphia, PA (2018). https://doi.org/10.1137/1.9781611975031.149
8. Emadikhiav, M., Day, R.: Walrasian pricing for combinatorial markets with compact-bidding languages: an application to truckload transportation. Inf. Syst. Res. **36**(3), 1718–1737 (2025). https://doi.org/10.1287/isre.2023.0676
9. Ezra, T., Feldman, M., Friedler, O.: A general framework for endowment effects in combinatorial markets. ACM SIGecom Exchanges **18**(2), 38–44 (2020). https://doi.org/10.1145/3440968.3440973
10. Fadaei, S., Bichler, M.: Truthfulness with value-maximizing bidders: on the limits of approximation in combinatorial markets. Eur. J. Oper. Res. **260**(2), 767–777 (2017). https://doi.org/10.1016/j.ejor.2016.12.031
11. Feldman, M., Gravin, N., Lucier, B.: Combinatorial Walrasian equilibrium. In: Proceedings of the Forty-Fifth Annual ACM Symposium on Theory of Computing, pp. 61–70. STOC '13, Association for Computing Machinery, New York, NY, USA (2013). https://doi.org/10.1145/2488608.2488617
12. Feldman, M., Lucier, B.: Clearing markets via bundles. In: Lavi, R. (ed.) Algorithmic Game Theory, pp. 158–169. Springer, Berlin, Heidelberg (2014)
13. Goetzendorff, A., Bichler, M., Shabalin, P., Day, R.W.: Compact bid languages and core pricing in large multi-item auctions. Manage. Sci. **61**(7), 1684–1703 (2015). https://doi.org/10.1287/mnsc.2014.2076
14. Grosz, A., Vanoli, C.: Stability in combinatorial markets with side payments (2026). https://arxiv.org/abs/2607.19098
15. Nisan, N.: Bidding and allocation in combinatorial auctions. In: Proceedings of the 2nd ACM Conference on Electronic Commerce, pp. 1–12. EC '00, ACM, New York, NY, USA (2000). https://doi.org/10.1145/352871.352872
16. Peleg, B., Sudhölter, P.: Introduction to the Theory of Cooperative games, vol. 34. Springer Science & Business Media, Heidelberg (2007)
17. Sandholm, T.: Algorithm for optimal winner determination in combinatorial auctions. Artif. Intell. **135**(1–2), 1–54 (2002). https://doi.org/10.1016/s0004-3702(01)00159-x
18. Shapley, L.S., Shubik, M.: The assignment game I: the core. Internat. J. Game Theory **1**, 111–130 (1971). https://doi.org/10.1007/bf01753437

Hospitals/Residents with Inseparable Couples: Finding a Coalition-Stable Assignment Is NP-Hard

Zeyuan Hu[1] and C. Gregory Plaxton[2(✉)]

[1] University of California, Los Angeles, USA
zeyuanhu@cs.ucla.edu
[2] University of Texas at Austin, Austin, USA
plaxton@cs.utexas.edu

Abstract. In recent work on course allocation, Rodríguez and Manlove consider the complexity of finding a stable assignment under four notions of stability, including two coalitional notions. In one case, which they call pair-size stability, they show that a stable assignment always exists and they provide a polynomial-time algorithm to find one. In a second case, called pair stability, they observe that an earlier NP-hardness result of McDermid and Manlove holds for a special case of course allocation called *Hospitals/Residents with Sizes* (HRS). In a third case, called first-coalition stability, they use a reduction from HRS to show it is NP-hard to find a stable assignment. They leave open the complexity of finding a stable assignment under so-called coalition stability. Building on ideas from McDermid and Manlove, we resolve the open problem of Rodríguez and Manlove by showing that it is NP-hard to find a coalition-stable assignment for HRS. Indeed, our proof shows that the problem remains NP-hard when the hospital capacities and resident sizes are at most two. Accordingly, our NP-hardness result applies to the special case of HRS known as *Hospitals/Residents with Inseparable Couples* (HRIC). Finally, we introduce a novel and natural notion of coalitional stability for both HRS and course allocation, and we show that our NP-hardness result extends to this notion, which we call unitwise-coalition stability.

Keywords: stable matching · hospitals/residents · course allocation · coalition stability · NP-hardness

1 Introduction

We begin by defining a well-known "hospitals and residents" variant of the classic stable marriage problem [8], which we denote HR.[1] We are given a set of hospitals and a set of residents; the goal is to determine a good assignment of residents to hospitals. Each resident (resp., hospital) has strict preferences over the set

[1] In [8], this is referred to as the college admissions problem.

P. Lenzner and D. Schmand (Eds.): SAGT 2026, LNCS 16911, pp. 242–260, 2027.
https://doi.org/10.1007/978-3-032-38782-0_14

of hospitals (resp., residents) that it finds acceptable.[2] Each hospital h has a positive integer capacity that represents the maximum number of residents that can be assigned to h. An assignment for a given HR instance is a set μ of resident-hospital pairs (if (r, h) belongs to μ, then μ is said to assign resident r to hospital h) subject to the following constraints.

1. Acceptability constraints. If (r, h) belongs to μ, then h is acceptable to r and r is acceptable to h.
2. Resident degree constraints. Any resident appears in at most one pair in μ.
3. Hospital capacity constraints. The number of pairs in μ involving a hospital h is at most the capacity of h.

A resident r is said to be unassigned under μ if no pair in μ involves r. For any assignment μ and any hospital h, we define $\text{res}(\mu, h)$ as $\{r \mid (r, h) \in \mu\}$. A hospital h is said to be under-subscribed under μ if $|\text{res}(\mu, h)|$ is less than the capacity of h. A resident-hospital pair (r, h) is said to be a blocking pair for an assignment μ if (1) r is unassigned under μ or r prefers h to its assigned hospital under μ and (2) h is under-subscribed under μ or h prefers r to its least preferred assigned resident under μ. An assignment is said to be stable if it does not admit a blocking pair.

In this paper we are concerned with a generalization of the HR problem called *Hospitals/Residents with Sizes* (HRS) introduced by McDermid and Manlove [10]. In this generalization, each resident has a positive integer size and the hospital capacity constraints are modified to require that the total size of the residents assigned to a hospital h is at most the capacity of h. McDermid and Manlove consider a resident-hospital pair (r, h) to be a blocking pair for an assignment μ if (1) r is unassigned under μ or r prefers h to its assigned hospital under μ and (2) the size of $\{r' \in \text{res}(\mu, h) \mid h \text{ prefers } r \text{ to } r'\}$ is at least the size of r minus the unused capacity of h under μ. As for the HR problem, an assignment is said to be stable if it does not admit a blocking pair.

Alternative notions of stability have been proposed for HRS. Adopting the terminology of Rodríguez and Manlove [11], we refer to the stability notion investigated by McDermid and Manlove [10] as pair stability. In the concluding remarks of their paper, McDermid and Manlove propose a second notion of stability for HRS in which condition (2) above is replaced by "there exists a subset of $\{r' \in \text{res}(\mu, h) \mid h \text{ prefers } r \text{ to } r'\}$ with total size at most the size of r and at least the size of r minus the unused capacity of h under μ." Rodríguez and Manlove refer to a resident-hospital pair (r, h) satisfying (1) and the modified version of (2) as a size-blocking pair. The associated notion of stability (i.e., absence of size-blocking pair) has subsequently been referred to as pair-size stability [11], occupancy-stability [4], and size-stability [7].[3] In the present paper, we use the term pair-size stability.

[2] Since we will only consider assigning resident r to hospital h if h is acceptable to r and r is acceptable to h, we can assume without loss of generality that h appears on the preference list of r if and only if r appears on the preference list of h.

[3] Delacrétaz studies the special case where the resident sizes belong to $\{1, 2\}$.

Rodríguez and Manlove [11] study a generalization of HRS to the setting of course allocation, where the goal is to assign students to courses. Unlike HRS, where each resident can be assigned to at most one hospital, a student can take many courses and a course can be taken by many students.[4] Rodríguez and Manlove prove that a pair-size stable assignment always exists in the course allocation setting, and they provide a polynomial-time algorithm for finding such an assignment. Independently, Balasundaram et al. [4] obtain the same result for pair-size stability (which they call occupancy stability) in the HRS setting.

Rodríguez and Manlove propose and investigate two "coalitional" notions of stability for course allocation, which they call first-coalition stability and coalition stability. For these notions a blocking coalition is given by a set of courses and a student, as opposed to a course-student pair. These coalitional notions are also applicable to the HRS special case of course allocation. Using notation similar to that introduced by Rodríguez and Manlove, we define HRS-C (resp., HRS-P, HRS-PS, and HRS-FC) as the problem of finding a coalition-stable (resp., pair-stable, pair-size-stable, first-coalition-stable) assignment for a given HRS instance, or reporting correctly that no such assignment exists. McDermid and Manlove show that HRS-P is NP-hard [10]. As discussed earlier, Rodríguez and Manlove provide a polynomial-time algorithm for finding a pair-size stable assignment in the course allocation setting (which generalizes HRS-PS). Rodríguez and Manlove show that HRS-FC is NP-hard, and leave open the complexity of HRS-C.

We now define the two coalitional notions of stability introduced by Rodríguez and Manlove [11]. Given the NP-hardness results discussed in the previous paragraph, we find it sufficient to define these notions in the restricted setting of HRS, as opposed to the more general course allocation setting. Given an assignment μ for an HRS instance, Rodríguez and Manlove define a blocking (resp., first-blocking) coalition for μ as a pair (R, h) where R is a set of residents and h is a hospital such that (1) for all r in R, r is unassigned under μ or r prefers h to its assigned hospital under μ, and (2) there exists a subset of $\{r' \in \text{res}(\mu, h) \mid h \text{ prefers } r \text{ to } r' \text{ for all (resp., some) } r \text{ in } R\}$ with total size at most the total size of R and at least the total size of R minus the unused capacity of h under μ.[5]

Rodríguez and Manlove [11] consider six different problems (e.g., testing whether a given assignment is stable, finding a stable assignment) with respect to each of the four notions of stability discussed above. For some of the resulting 24 problem combinations, there is both an existence question (i.e., whether a stable assignment is guaranteed to exist) and a complexity question (i.e., what is

[4] We can model an HRS instance I as a course allocation instance I' as follows: for each size-k resident in I, we add a unit-capacity k-credit course to I'; for each capacity-k hospital in I, we add a student to I' with credit limit k.

[5] Our definitions of the terms "blocking coalition" and "first-blocking coalition", as well as our earlier definitions of the terms "blocking pair" and "size-blocking pair", are formulated somewhat differently than in earlier work, but are equivalent to the original definitions.

the complexity of finding a stable assignment if one exists) to resolve. Rodríguez and Manlove resolve the questions associated with all 24 problem combinations, except they leave open the question of whether a coalition-stable assignment is guaranteed to exist for any course allocation instance, along with the associated complexity question.[6] In the present paper, we resolve these questions by exhibiting an HRS instance with four residents and three hospitals that does not admit a coalition-stable assignment, and by proving that HRS-C is NP-hard.[7]

We show that HRS-C is NP-hard using the same high-level approach as McDermid and Manlove [10, Theorem 3.8, erratum] used to show that HRS-P is NP-hard. More specifically, we also use a reduction from a special case of 3-SAT called (2, 2)-E3-SAT; this satisfiability variant is formally defined in Sect. 2. The transformation of [10] from (2, 2)-E3-SAT to HRS-P is presented in a somewhat monolithic manner: parameterized sets of agents (residents and hospitals) are listed along with the associated preference lists [10, Figure 1, erratum]. At the same time, like many transformations from 3-SAT variants, the transformation admits a gadget-based interpretation: for each variable (resp., clause) in the given (2, 2)-E3-SAT instance, the resulting HRS-P instance includes a set of agents inducing a copy of a variable (resp., clause) gadget. Moreover, the variable and the clause gadgets are implicitly constructed from smaller gadgets. The variable gadget is constructed from a smaller gadget that admits exactly two stable assignments; in the present paper, we refer to this smaller gadget as a bistable gadget. The clause gadget is constructed using three copies of a smaller gadget, one for each literal in the clause; in the present paper, we refer to this smaller gadget as a literal gadget. The literal gadget is in turn constructed from a smaller gadget that does not admit a stable assignment; in the present paper, we refer to this smaller gadget as an unstable gadget.

We find it useful to present our transformation in a modular and explicitly gadget-based style. To aid the reader's intuition, we present a diagram of each gadget using the digraph representation proposed by Balinski and Ratier [5] and subsequently employed in various works (see, e.g., [1–3]); in the present paper, we refer to such a diagram as a preference digraph.

We now highlight the main new ideas underlying our gadget-based transformation from (2, 2)-E3-SAT to HRS-C. A key difference between our setting and that of [10] is that a blocking coalition involving a hospital h cannot propose to reduce the total size of the set of residents assigned to h. This seems to necessitate a more complicated construction than in [10] for the unstable, literal, and bistable gadgets. In developing our variable gadget from our bistable gadget as in the preference digraph of Fig. 4, we noticed that the corresponding construction in [10] can be streamlined via the same approach. The streamlined construction

[6] Regarding the problem of testing whether a given assignment is coalition-stable, Rodríguez and Manlove establish co-NP-completeness in the context of course allocation; their proof also applies to the HRS special case.

[7] In [11], Rodríguez and Manlove also consider problem variants with so-called "downward-feasible constraints". Our hardness results hold even in the absence of such constraints.

reduces the number of residents from 10 to 8 and the number of hospitals from 6 to 4.

While our literal gadget differs from that of [10], it satisfies similar abstract properties such that the construction of our clause gadget from three copies of the literal gadget can follow precisely the same pattern as is implicit in [10]. Likewise, our variable and clause gadgets satisfy similar abstract properties to those satisfied by the corresponding gadgets of [10], such that our overall construction of the HRS-C instance corresponding to a given (2, 2)-E3-SAT instance follows the pattern implicit in [10]. An advantage of our modular gadget-based presentation is that individual modules may be reusable in proofs of other similar results. In Sect. 5, we discuss a natural coalitional notion of stability that is different from the two notions (first-coalition stability and coalition stability) defined earlier, and we explain why our NP-hardness result related to coalition stability also applies to this third notion, which we call unitwise-coalition stability.

Like the NP-hardness proof of McDermid and Manlove for HRS-P, our NP-hardness proof for HRS-C involves HRS instances where the resident sizes and hospital capacities belong to $\{1, 2\}$. Because the resident sizes belong to $\{1, 2\}$, these NP-hardness results apply to the important special case of HRS called *Hospitals/Residents with Inseparable Couples* (HRIC).

In the foregoing, we have focused our discussion of the prior literature on results that are directly relevant to our NP-hardness proof. For a broader overview of two-sided assignment problems with preferences, we refer the reader to Rodríguez and Manlove [11].

Due to space limitations, some lemmas (Lemmas 2.1 and 2.2, and all lemmas in Sect. 4) are stated without proof; proofs may be found in the full version [9]. The full version also includes two appendices: Appendix A provides a tabular representation of the construction of Sect. 4.3; Appendix B presents preference digraphs for the gadgets implicit in the construction of [10, erratum].

2 Preliminaries

We now give a formal definition of the HRS-C problem discussed in Sect. 1. The input is an HRS instance, which we now describe. An HRS instance I consists of a set of residents, where each resident r has a positive integer size, denoted $\text{size}(r)$, and a set of hospitals, denoted $\text{hosps}(I)$, where each hospital h has a positive integer capacity, denoted $\text{cap}(h)$. For any set of residents R, we define $\text{size}(R)$ as $\sum_{r \in R} \text{size}(r)$. Each resident (resp., hospital) has a strict preference list over the set of hospitals (resp., residents) that it considers to be acceptable. An assignment μ for such an instance I is a set of resident-hospital pairs subject to certain constraints to be defined below. If the resident-hospital pair (r, h) belongs to an assignment μ, we say that r is assigned to h under μ. As in Sect. 1, we define $\text{res}(\mu, h)$ as $\{r \mid (r, h) \in \mu\}$. An assignment μ is required to satisfy the following constraints.

1. Acceptability constraints. If (r, h) belongs to μ, then h is acceptable to r and r is acceptable to h.
2. Resident degree constraints. Any resident appears in at most one pair in μ.
3. Hospital capacity constraints. For any hospital h, we have $\text{size}(\text{res}(\mu, h)) \leq \text{cap}(h)$.

We assume without loss of generality that for any resident r and hospital h, r considers h to be acceptable if and only if h considers r to be acceptable.

Given such an HRS instance I and an assignment μ for I, we say that a set of residents R and a hospital h form a blocking coalition (R, h) for μ in I if the following conditions hold: (1) for all r in R, r is unassigned under μ or r prefers h to its assigned hospital under μ, and (2) there exists a subset R' of $\{r' \in \text{res}(\mu, h) \mid h \text{ prefers } r \text{ to } r' \text{ for all } r \text{ in } R\}$ such that

$$\text{size}(R) - \text{cap}(h) + \text{size}(\text{res}(\mu, h)) \leq \text{size}(R') \leq \text{size}(R).$$

For any HRS instance I and any assignment μ for I, we define $\text{block}(I, \mu)$ as the set of all blocking coalitions for μ in I, and we say that μ is coalition-stable for I if $\text{block}(I, \mu) = \emptyset$. Given an HRS instance I as input, the HRS-C problem asks us to either find a coalition-stable assignment for I, or to report correctly that no such assignment exists. The decision version of HRS-C asks whether a given HRS instance admits a coalition-stable assignment.

Our main result is to show that HRS-C is NP-hard. We obtain this result by presenting a polynomial-time transformation from the known NP-complete problem (2, 2)-E3-SAT to the decision version of HRS-C. The problem (2, 2)-E3-SAT is a special case of the well-known 3-SAT problem that was shown to be NP-complete by Berman et al. [6, Theorem 1] (where (2, 2)-E3-SAT is referred to as (3,B2)-SAT). The input is a 3-CNF formula, that is, a propositional formula that is the conjunction of a number of clauses, where each clause is a disjunction of three distinct literals, and each literal is a variable or the negation of a variable. In addition, we require that each variable occurs exactly four times, twice in negated form and twice in positive (i.e., not negated) form. Given this requirement, any instance of (2, 2)-E3-SAT involves $3n$ variables and $4n$ clauses for some positive integer n.

Let ϕ be an instance of (2, 2)-E3-SAT and let n be a positive integer such that ϕ has $3n$ variables and $4n$ clauses. We index the variables from 1 to $3n$ and the clauses from 1 to $4n$. For any j in $\{1, \ldots, 3n\}$ and any k in $\{1, 2, 3, 4\}$, we define literal (j, k) as follows: if $k = 1$ (resp., $k = 2$) then it is the first (resp., second) positive instance of variable j in ϕ; if $k = 3$ (resp., $k = 4$) then it is the first (resp., second) negative instance of variable j in ϕ.

Our NP-hardness proof involves the construction of various HRS-C "gadgets", some of which are defined in terms of smaller "sub-gadgets". The following additional definitions, along with Lemmas 2.1 and 2.2 below, are useful for reasoning about the interface between a gadget and one of its sub-gadgets. For any HRS-C instance I and any subset H of the hospitals in I, we define $I\big|_H$ as the HRS-C instance obtained from I by removing all residents who do not have at least one acceptable hospital in H, removing all hospitals not in H, and pruning the removed hospitals from the preference lists of the non-removed residents. For any HRS-C instance I, any assignment μ of I, and any subset H of the hospitals in I, we define $\mu\big|_H$ as the assignment $\{(r,h) \in \mu \mid h \in H\}$ for $I\big|_H$, and we define $B\big|_H$ as $\{(R,h) \in B \mid h \in H\}$ where B denotes $\text{block}(I,\mu)$.

Lemma 2.1. *Let I be an HRS-C instance, let μ be an assignment of I, let B denote* $\text{block}(I,\mu)$, *let H be a subset of* $\text{hosps}(I)$, *let I' denote $I\big|_H$, let B' denote $B\big|_H$, let μ' denote $\mu\big|_H$, and let B'' denote* $\text{block}(I',\mu')$. *Then $B' \subseteq B''$.*

For any HRS-C instance I, any subset H of $\text{hosps}(I)$, and any assignment μ of I, we define $\text{bdry}(I,H,\mu)$ as the set of all blocking coalitions (R,h) in $\text{block}(I\big|_H, \mu\big|_H)$ for which there is a resident r in R and a hospital h' in $\text{hosps}(I) \setminus H$ such that r prefers h' to h.

Lemma 2.2. *Let I be an HRS-C instance, let μ be an assignment of I, let B denote* $\text{block}(I,\mu)$, *let H be a subset of* $\text{hosps}(I)$, *let I' denote $I\big|_H$, let B' denote $B\big|_H$, let μ' denote $\mu\big|_H$, and let B'' denote* $\text{block}(I',\mu')$. *Then $B'' \subseteq B' \cup \text{bdry}(I,H,\mu)$.*

3 Building Blocks

In this section, we present three gadgets. The first of these, which we call the unstable gadget, is an HRS-C instance with four residents and three hospitals that does not admit a coalition-stable assignment, thereby providing a negative answer to the question of Rodríguez and Manlove [11] regarding the existence of coalition-stable assignments. The second gadget that we present, which we call the literal gadget, contains a copy of the unstable gadget along with three additional residents and two additional hospitals. (One resident in the unstable gadget has its preference list extended to include one of the two additional hospitals.) In Sect. 4.2, we define a clause gadget that includes three copies of the literal gadget, one for each of the associated literals. The third gadget that we present, which we call the bistable gadget, has five residents and three hospitals and admits exactly two coalition-stable assignments. In Sect. 4.1, we define a variable gadget that includes a copy of the bistable gadget.

Our unstable, literal, and bistable gadgets are analogous to fragments of the monolithic construction presented by McDermid and Manlove [10] in the context of pair stability. Each of these gadgets differs from the corresponding fragment in its detailed design.[8] Throughout the remainder of this section, the only notion of stability we are concerned with is coalition stability. Accordingly, we find it

[8] Using the notation of [10, Figure 1, erratum], the correspondence is as follows: the subinstance induced by the set of residents $\{q_{j,1}^k, q_{j,2}^k, q_{j,3}^k\}$ and the set of hospitals $\{p_{j,1}^k, p_{j,2}^k\}$ is analogous to our unstable gadget; the subinstance induced by the set of residents $\{q_{j,1}^k, q_{j,2}^k, q_{j,3}^k, v(p_{j,3}^k)\}$ and the set of hospitals $\{p_{j,1}^k, p_{j,2}^k, p_{j,3}^k\}$ is analogous to our literal gadget; the subinstance induced by the set of residents $\{r_j^1, r_j^2, r_j^3, r_j^4\}$ and the set of hospitals $\{h_j^1, h_j^2\}$ is analogous to our bistable gadget.

convenient to use the term "stability" (resp., "stable") to mean "coalition stability" (resp., "coalition-stable"). For any HRS-C instance I, any assignment μ of I, and any subset H of hosps(I), we say that μ is H-stable if no blocking coalition in block(I, μ) involves a hospital in H.

3.1 Unstable Gadget

In this section, we present an HRS-C instance that does not admit a stable assignment, thereby settling (in the negative) the open question of Rodríguez and Manlove [11] concerning whether a stable assignment always exists.

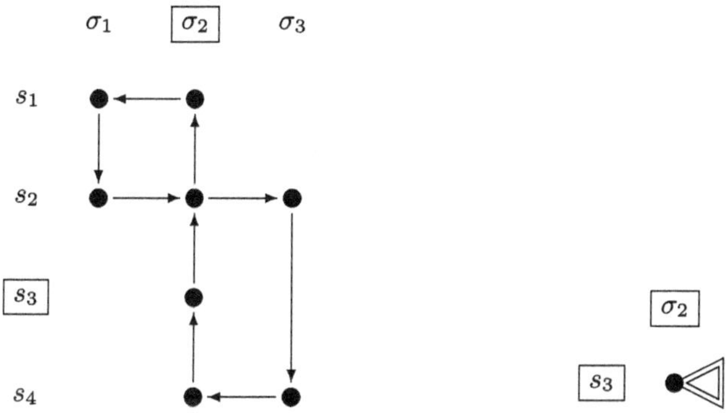

(a) The unstable gadget. (b) The associated icon.

Fig. 1. The preference digraph for the unstable gadget has four residents $s_1, \ldots, s_4$ and three hospitals $\sigma_1, \sigma_2, \sigma_3$ with sizes and capacities as indicated. The unstable gadget icon is used in the preference digraph of Fig. 2(a); the dot in this icon corresponds to the resident-hospital pair (s_3, σ_2).

As discussed in Sect. 1, we find it useful to present all of our gadgets using a preference digraph. Figure 1(a) presents the preference digraph for our unstable gadget: each dot represents a mutually acceptable resident-hospital pair; dots in the same row (resp., column) have the same associated resident (resp., hospital); the symbol associated with each row (resp., column) represents the associated resident (resp., hospital); if the symbol is enclosed in a box then the size (resp., capacity) of the resident (resp., hospital) is 2, otherwise it is 1; the directed edges within a row (resp., column) are used to represent the preference list of the associated resident (resp., hospital). To understand how the directed edges determine preference order, it is sufficient to consider the example of hospital σ_2 in Fig. 1(a). Hospital σ_2 has four acceptable residents s_1, s_2, s_3, and s_4. These four residents are linked together (within column σ_2) by three directed edges forming a simple path from s_4 to s_3 to s_2 to s_1. This path signifies that s_1 (resp., s_2, s_3, s_4) is the first (resp., second, third, fourth) preference of σ_2. Similarly, resident s_2 has three acceptable hospitals σ_1, σ_2, and σ_3, where σ_3 (resp., σ_2, σ_1) is the first (resp., second, third) preference of s_2.

Throughout the remainder of Sect. 3.1, let I denote the unstable gadget of Fig. 1(a). We define the *critical assignment of* I as $\{(s_1, \sigma_1), (s_2, \sigma_3), (s_4, \sigma_2)\}$.

Lemma 3.1. *Instance* I *does not admit a stable assignment, and the critical assignment of* I *is the unique assignment* μ *of* I *such that* $\text{block}(I, \mu) = \{(s_3, \sigma_2)\}$.

Proof. Let μ^* denote the critical assignment of I and let B^* denote $\text{block}(I, \mu^*)$. We first argue that $B^* = \{(s_3, \sigma_2)\}$. It is easy to see that (s_3, σ_2) belongs to B^* and is the unique blocking coalition in B^* that involves resident s_3. Each resident in the set $\{s_1, s_2, s_4\}$ gets its most preferred hospital and so cannot participate in any blocking coalition. Thus $B^* = \{(s_3, \sigma_2)\}$, as required.

Let μ be an assignment for I such that $\text{block}(I, \mu) \subseteq \{(s_3, \sigma_2)\}$. Below we complete the proof by proving that $\mu = \mu^*$. Let B denote $\text{block}(I, \mu)$.

We begin by arguing that (s_1, σ_2) does not belong to μ. Assume for the sake of contradiction that (s_1, σ_2) belongs to μ. Hence (s_3, σ_2) does not belong to μ. In addition, since (s_1, σ_1) does not belong to B, we deduce that (s_2, σ_1) belongs to μ. Hence (s_2, σ_2) does not belong to μ and we conclude that $\text{res}(\mu, \sigma_2) \subseteq \{s_1, s_4\}$. It follows that (s_2, σ_2) belongs to B, a contradiction.

We now argue that (s_3, σ_2) does not belong to μ. Assume for the sake of contradiction that (s_3, σ_2) belongs to μ. Hence $\text{res}(\mu, \sigma_2) = \{s_3\}$. Since (s_4, σ_3) does not belong to B, we deduce that (s_4, σ_3) belongs to μ. Since (s_2, σ_1) does not belong to B, we deduce that (s_2, σ_1) belongs to μ. It follows that s_1 is unassigned in μ and hence $(\{s_1, s_2\}, \sigma_2)$ belongs to B, a contradiction.

Since (s_1, σ_2) and (s_3, σ_2) do not belong to μ, we conclude that $\text{res}(\mu, \sigma_2) \subseteq \{s_2, s_4\}$. Since (s_4, σ_2) does not belong to B, we deduce that (s_4, σ_2) belongs to μ. Hence $\text{res}(\mu, \sigma_3) \subseteq \{s_2\}$. Since (s_2, σ_3) does not belong to B, we deduce that (s_2, σ_3) belongs to μ. Hence $\text{res}(\mu, \sigma_1) \subseteq \{s_1\}$. Since (s_1, σ_1) does not belong to B, we deduce that (s_1, σ_1) belongs to μ. In summary, $\mu = \mu^*$, as required. □

3.2 Literal Gadget

Throughout the remainder of Sect. 3.2, let I denote the literal gadget of Fig. 2(a) and let I' denote the unstable gadget of I. We define the *critical assignment of* I as the union of the critical assignment of I' and $\{(s_3, \tau_2), (t_2, \tau_1)\}$.

Lemma 3.2. *Instance* I *does not admit a stable assignment, and the critical assignment of* I *is the unique assignment* μ *of* I *such that* $\text{block}(I, \mu) = \{(t_1, \tau_1)\}$.

Proof. Let μ^* denote the critical assignment of I, let B^* denote $\text{block}(I, \mu^*)$, let H denote the set of hospitals in I', let μ' denote $\mu^*\big|_{H}$, and let B' denote $\text{block}(I', \mu')$. Thus μ' is the critical assignment of I', and hence Lemma 3.1 implies $B' = \{(s_3, \sigma_2)\}$.

We claim that $B^* = \{(t_1, \tau_1)\}$. It is easy to see that (t_1, τ_1) belongs to B^*. Since resident t_1 has only one acceptable hospital τ_1, and since t_1 has size 1 and τ_1 has capacity 1, resident t_1 cannot belong to any other blocking coalition in B^* apart from (t_1, τ_1). Since residents s_3 and t_2 are each assigned to their

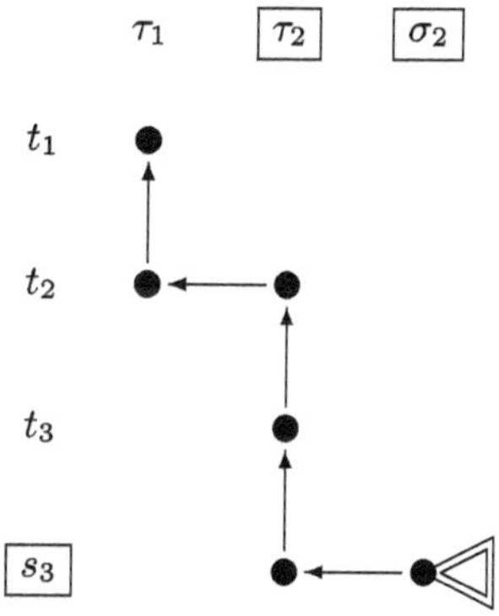

(a) The literal gadget.

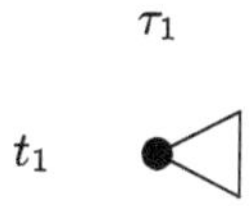

(b) The associated icon.

Fig. 2. The preference digraph for the literal gadget includes a copy of the unstable gadget and has a total of $3 + 4 = 7$ residents and $2 + 3 = 5$ hospitals. Within the literal gadget, resident s_3 has two acceptable hospitals τ_2 and σ_2, with τ_2 being the first preference of s_3 as indicated by the directed edge in row s_3. The literal gadget icon is used in the preference digraph of Fig. 5; the dot in this icon refers to the resident-hospital pair (t_1, τ_1).

most preferred hospital under μ^*, neither s_3 nor t_2 participates in any blocking coalition in B^*. Since resident t_3 has size 1, resident s_3 has size 2, and (s_3, τ_2) belongs to μ^*, we deduce that resident t_3 does not participate in any blocking coalition in B^*. Given the foregoing observations, it is sufficient to argue that μ^* is H-stable. Lemma 2.1 implies $B^*\big|_H \subseteq B'$. Since $B' = \{(s_3, \sigma_2)\}$ and since resident s_3 does not participate in any blocking coalition in B^*, we deduce that μ^* is H-stable.

Let μ_1 be an assignment of I such that $\text{block}(I, \mu_1) \subseteq \{(t_1, \tau_1)\}$ and let B denote $\text{block}(I, \mu_1)$. Below we complete the proof by establishing that $\mu_1 = \mu^*$.

Let B'' denote $\text{block}(I', \mu_1\big|_H)$. Since $\text{bdry}(I, H, \mu_1) \subseteq \{(s_3, \sigma_2)\}$, Lemma 2.2 implies $B'' \setminus \{(s_3, \sigma_2)\} \subseteq B\big|_H \subseteq B$. Since $B \subseteq \{(t_1, \tau_1)\}$, we conclude from Lemma 3.1 that $\mu_1\big|_H = \mu'$. Hence $B'' = \{(s_3, \sigma_2)\}$. Since (s_3, σ_2) does not belong to B, we deduce that (s_3, τ_2) belongs to μ_1. It follows that $\text{res}(\mu_1, \tau_2) = \{s_3\}$. Since $(\{t_2, t_3\}, \tau_2)$ does not belong to B, we deduce that (t_2, τ_1) belongs to μ_1. Thus $\mu_1 = \mu' \cup \{(s_3, \tau_2), (t_2, \tau_1)\} = \mu^*$. □

3.3 Bistable Gadget

Throughout the remainder of Sect. 3.3, let I denote the bistable gadget depicted in Fig. 3(a). We define the *true (resp., false) assignment of* I as $\{(a_1, \alpha_3), (a_2, \alpha_1), (a_3, \alpha_2), (a_5, \alpha_3)\}$ (resp., $\{(a_3, \alpha_1), (a_4, \alpha_3), (a_5, \alpha_1)\}$).

Lemma 3.3. *The true and false assignments of I are stable, and I does not admit any other stable assignments.*

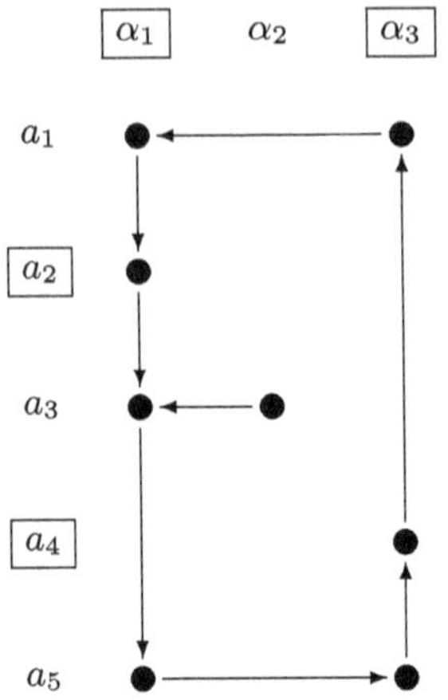

(a) The bistable gadget.

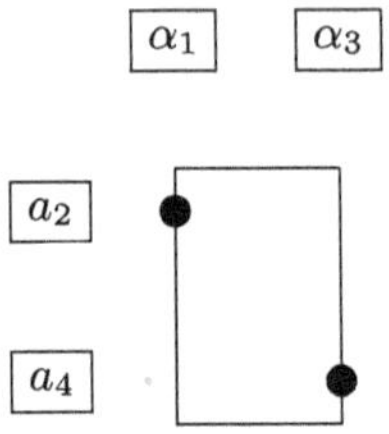

(b) The associated icon.

Fig. 3. The preference digraph for the bistable gadget has five residents $a_1, \ldots, a_5$ and three hospitals $\alpha_1, \alpha_2, \alpha_3$. The bistable gadget icon is used in the preference digraph of Fig. 4; the left (resp., right) dot in this icon corresponds to the resident-hospital pair (a_2, α_1) (resp., (a_4, α_3)).

Proof. Let μ_1 (resp., μ_2) denote the true (resp., false) assignment of I. We begin by arguing that μ_1 is stable for I. Residents a_2 and a_5 are each assigned to their most preferred hospital, and hence cannot belong to a blocking coalition for μ_1. Resident a_1 cannot belong to a blocking coalition for μ_1 because hospital α_1 prefers a_2 to a_1. Because a_2 has size 2, it is straightforward to argue that any blocking coalition involving a_3 and α_1 has to be $(\{a_3, a_5\}, \alpha_1)$. Since resident a_5 cannot belong to a blocking coalition for μ_1, we conclude that resident a_3 cannot belong to a blocking coalition for μ_1. Resident a_4 cannot belong to a blocking coalition for μ_1 because hospital α_3 prefers a_1 to a_4.

Now we argue that μ_2 is stable for I. Hospital α_1 cannot belong to a blocking coalition for μ_2 because $\text{res}(\mu_2, \alpha_1) = \{a_3, a_5\}$ contains the two most preferred residents of α_1. Hospital α_2 cannot belong to a blocking coalition for μ_2 because its lone acceptable resident a_3 is assigned to its most preferred hospital α_1. Hospital α_3 cannot belong to a blocking coalition for μ_2 because resident a_4 has size two and the total size of all residents that α_3 prefers to a_4 is only one.

It remains to argue that μ_1 and μ_2 are the only stable assignments for I. Let μ be a stable assignment for I and let B denote $\text{block}(I, \mu)$. Since μ is stable, B is empty. We consider two cases.

Case 1: (a_3, α_2) belongs to μ. Since (a_3, α_1) does not belong to B, the Case 1 condition implies that $\text{res}(\mu, \alpha_1)$ is either $\{a_2\}$ or $\{a_1, a_5\}$. Since (a_3, α_1) does not belong to B, the Case 1 condition implies (a_1, α_1) does not belong to μ and hence $\text{res}(\mu, \alpha_1) = \{a_2\}$. Since $(\{a_3, a_5\}, \alpha_1)$ does not belong to B, we deduce that (a_5, α_3) belongs to μ. Since (a_1, α_3) does not belong to B, we deduce that

(a_1, α_3) belongs to μ. In summary, under the Case 1 condition, $\mu_1 \subseteq \mu$. Since hospitals α_1, α_2, and α_3 are full under μ_1, we conclude that $\mu = \mu_1$.

Case 2: (a_3, α_2) does not belong to μ. Since (a_3, α_2) does not belong to B, we deduce that (a_3, α_1) belongs to μ and hence (a_2, α_1) does not belong to μ. Thus $\text{res}(\mu, \alpha_1) \subseteq \{a_1, a_3, a_5\}$.

We first argue that (a_5, α_1) belongs to μ. Assume for the sake of contradiction that (a_5, α_1) does not belong to μ. Hence $\text{res}(\mu, \alpha_1) \subseteq \{a_1, a_3\}$. Since (a_1, α_1) does not belong to B, we deduce that (a_1, α_1) belongs to μ. Since (a_4, α_3) does not belong to B, we deduce that (a_4, α_3) belongs to μ. Thus (a_5, α_3) does not belong to μ. Together with our assumption that (a_5, α_1) does not belong to μ, this implies a_5 is unassigned in μ. Since $\text{res}(\mu, \alpha_1) \subseteq \{a_1, a_3\}$, we conclude that (a_5, α_1) belongs to B, a contradiction.

Since (a_3, α_1) and (a_5, α_1) belong to μ, we conclude that $\text{res}(\mu, \alpha_1) = \{a_3, a_5\}$.

We claim that (a_1, α_3) does not belong to μ. Assume for the sake of contradiction that (a_1, α_3) belongs to μ. Thus (a_4, α_3) does not belong to μ. Hence (a_5, α_3) belongs to B, a contradiction.

Since (a_1, α_3) does not belong to μ and (a_4, α_3) does not belong to B, we deduce that (a_4, α_3) belongs to μ. In summary, under the Case 2 condition, $\mu_2 \subseteq \mu$ and $\text{res}(\mu, \alpha_2) = \emptyset$. Since hospitals α_1 and α_3 are full under μ_2, we conclude that $\mu = \mu_2$. □

4 NP-Hardness

In the present section, we use a reduction from (2, 2)-E3-SAT to prove that the decision version of HRS-C is NP-hard. Since course allocation generalizes HRS, we conclude that the problem of finding a coalition-stable assignment for a given instance of course allocation is NP-hard, thereby resolving an open problem of Rodríguez and Manlove [11].

As discussed earlier, the literal gadget of Sect. 3.2 satisfies similar abstract properties to those satisfied by the corresponding fragment of the construction of McDermid and Manlove [10]. Consequently, we can use the approach implicit in [10] to build a clause gadget from three copies of the literal gadget. Similarly, the bistable gadget can be used to build a variable gadget using the approach implicit in [10].[9] Finally, again following the approach implicit in [10], we can build a suitable overall HRS-C instance for a given (2, 2)-E3-SAT formula ϕ

[9] In studying the variable gadget implicit in [10], which is induced by the residents in the set $\{r_j^1, r_j^2, r_j^3, r_j^4, r_j^5, r_j^6, x_j^1, x_j^2, y_j^1, y_j^2\}$ and the hospitals in the set $\{h_j^1, h_j^2, h_j^3, h_j^4, h_j^T, h_j^F\}$, we observed that their construction can be simplified. Specifically, the set of residents can be reduced to $\{r_j^1, r_j^2, r_j^3, r_j^4, x_j^1, x_j^2, y_j^1, y_j^2\}$ and the set of hospitals can be reduced to $\{h_j^1, h_j^2, h_j^T, h_j^F\}$. Figure 4 shows how we construct our variable gadget from our bistable gadget, and the same approach can be used to construct a streamlined version of the variable gadget implicit in [10] from the bistable gadget implicit in [10].

using a copy of the variable gadget for each variable in ϕ and a copy of the clause gadget for each clause in ϕ.

For the sake of completeness, below we provide all of the details concerning the construction of the variable gadget, the clause gadget, and the overall HRS-C instance corresponding to a given (2, 2)-E3-SAT formula ϕ. We emphasize that all of the constructions and arguments in this section precisely mirror elements implicit in the work of McDermid and Manlove [10]. As in Sect. 3, throughout this section we use the term "stability" (resp., "stable") to mean "coalition stability" (resp., "coalition-stable").

4.1 Variable Gadget

Throughout the remainder of Sect. 4.1, let I denote the variable gadget depicted in Fig. 4 and let I' denote the bistable gadget of I. We define the *true (resp., false) assignment of* I as the union of the true (resp., false) assignment of I' and $\{(b_1, \beta_1), (b_2, \beta_1), (a_4, \beta_2)\}$ (resp., $\{(a_2, \beta_1), (b_3, \beta_2), (b_4, \beta_2)\}$).

Lemma 4.1. *The true and false assignments of I are stable, and I does not admit any other stable assignments.*

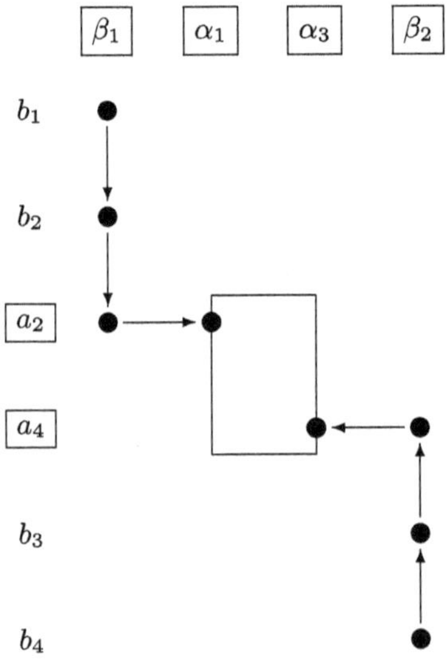

Fig. 4. The preference digraph for the variable gadget includes a copy of the bistable gadget and has a total of $4 + 5 = 9$ residents and $2 + 3 = 5$ hospitals.

4.2 Clause Gadget

In this section, we describe a clause gadget that contains three copies of the literal gadget. The three copies of the literal gadget have pairwise disjoint sets of agents (7 residents and 5 hospitals each); we use a superscript ℓ in $\{1, 2, 3\}$ to identify the agents in copy ℓ. For example, we write t_1^ℓ to refer to the resident t_1 in copy ℓ. See Fig. 5 for a depiction of the clause gadget.

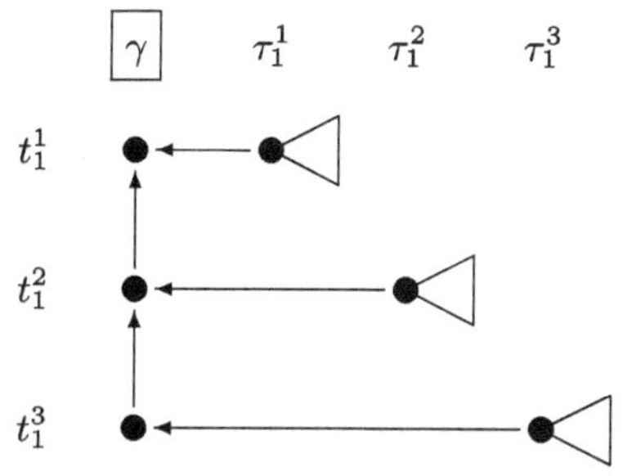

Fig. 5. The preference digraph for the clause gadget includes three copies of the literal gadget and has $3 \times 7 = 21$ residents and $1 + 3 \times 5 = 16$ hospitals.

Throughout the remainder of Sect. 4.2, let I denote the clause gadget of Fig. 5 and for any ℓ in $\{1, 2, 3\}$, let I^ℓ denote literal gadget ℓ of I and let H^ℓ denote hosps(I^ℓ). We say that an assignment μ of I is critical if for all ℓ in $\{1, 2, 3\}$, $\mu\big|_{H^\ell}$ is the critical assignment of I^ℓ. We say that an assignment μ of I is nice if every blocking coalition in block(I, μ) either involves hospital γ or belongs to $\{(t_1^1, \tau_1^1), (t_1^2, \tau_1^2), (t_1^3, \tau_1^3)\}$.

Lemma 4.2. *Let μ be a critical assignment of I, let ℓ belong to $\{1, 2, 3\}$, let B denote* block(I, μ)*, and let B' denote $B\big|_{H^\ell}$. Then $B' \subseteq \{(t_1^\ell, \tau_1^\ell)\}$.*

Lemma 4.3. *Let μ be a nice assignment of I, let ℓ belong to $\{1, 2, 3\}$, and let μ' denote $\mu\big|_{H^\ell}$. Then μ' is the critical assignment of I^ℓ.*

Lemma 4.4. *Let μ be an assignment of I. Then μ is a nice assignment of I if and only if μ is a critical assignment of I.*

4.3 Transformation

Throughout this section, we fix a $(2, 2)$-E3-SAT instance ϕ. Below we describe how to transform ϕ into an instance I of HRS-C so that I admits a stable assignment if and only if ϕ is satisfiable. It will be evident that the transformation is polynomial-time computable.

Let n be a positive integer such that ϕ has $4n$ clauses and $3n$ variables. We index the clauses (resp., variables) from 1 to $4n$ (resp., $3n$). We use two schemes for identifying the $12n$ literals of ϕ. For any i in $\{1, \ldots, 4n\}$ and any ℓ in $\{1, 2, 3\}$, we say that the literal in position ℓ of clause i has A-identifier (i, ℓ). For any j in $\{1, \ldots, 3n\}$, we say that a literal has B-identifier $(j, 1)$ (resp., $(j, 2)$, $(j, 3)$, $(j, 4)$) if it is the first positive (resp., second positive, first negative, second negative) occurrence of variable j in ϕ. In order to translate between these two schemes, we define the bijection $\varphi : \{1, \ldots, 4n\} \times \{1, 2, 3\} \to \{1, \ldots, 3n\} \times \{1, 2, 3, 4\}$ to map any given A-identifier to the corresponding B-identifier. Our instance I will be constructed from $3n$ variable gadgets and $4n$ clause gadgets. Below we discuss these components in greater detail.

As discussed in Sect. 4.1, our variable gadget has 9 residents and 5 hospitals. We create $3n$ copies of this gadget, one for each variable in ϕ; each copy has its own set of 9 residents and 5 hospitals. For any j in $\{1, \ldots, 3n\}$, we define V^j as copy j of the variable gadget. We use a superscript j to identify the agents in V^j. For example, we write a_1^j to refer to the resident corresponding to a_1 in V^j. In our overall instance I, the preference list of each hospital in V^j is the same as in the isolated gadget V^j; likewise, the preference list of each resident in V^j that does not belong to $\{b_1^j, \ldots, b_4^j\}$ is the same as in the isolated gadget V^j. Each resident in $\{b_1^j, \ldots, b_4^j\}$ has a preference list of length 1 in V^j and of length 3 in I: the most preferred hospital of b_k^j in I is its lone acceptable hospital in V^j; the two remaining hospitals on the preference list of b_k^j do not belong to V^j and are specified below.

As discussed in Sect. 4.2, our clause gadget has 21 residents and 16 hospitals. We create $4n$ copies of this gadget, one for each clause in ϕ; each copy has its own set of 21 residents and 16 hospitals. For any i in $\{1, \ldots, 4n\}$, we define C^i as copy i of the clause gadget. We use a superscript i to identify the agents in C^i. For example, we write $t_1^{i,1}$ to refer to the resident corresponding to t_1^1 in C^i. In our overall instance I, the preference list of each hospital in C^i is the same as in the isolated gadget C^i; likewise, the preference list of each resident in C^i that does not belong to $\{t_1^{i,1}, t_1^{i,2}, t_1^{i,3}\}$ is the same as in the isolated gadget C^i.

It remains to describe the preference lists of the residents b_k^j and $t_1^{i,\ell}$ in I. For each A-identifier (i, ℓ), we identify resident $t_1^{i,\ell}$ with the resident b_k^j such that B-identifier (j, k) is equal to $\varphi(i, \ell)$. The preference list of length 3 of resident $t_1^{i,\ell} = b_k^j$ in I is obtained by merging the preference list of b_k^j in V^j with the preference list of $t_1^{i,\ell}$ in C^i, as follows: the top preference is the lone acceptable hospital of b_k^j in V^j; the second and third preferences are the first and second preferences of $t_1^{i,\ell}$ in C^i.

The above completes our description of the HRS-C instance I corresponding to (2, 2)-E3-SAT instance ϕ. We remark that the total number of residents in I is $3n \cdot 9 + 4n \cdot (21 - 3) = 99n$ and the total number of hospitals in I is $3n \cdot 5 + 4n \cdot 16 = 79n$. The resident sizes and hospital capacities all belong to $\{1, 2\}$, and the longest preference list of any resident (resp., hospital) in I is 3 (resp., 4).

In the remainder of this section, we establish the correctness of the polynomial-time transformation described above. That is, we prove that I admits a stable assignment if and only if ϕ is satisfiable.

If Direction. Assume that ϕ is satisfiable, and fix a satisfying truth assignment $\pi = (\pi_1, \ldots, \pi_{3n})$ for ϕ; in other words, π_j is the truth value of variable j under π. We need to prove that HRS-C instance I admits a stable assignment.

We now describe how to use π to construct an assignment μ for I. After describing the construction, we prove that μ is a valid assignment for I (i.e., no resident or hospital is over-subscribed), and then we prove that μ is stable for I.

For each variable j such that π_j is true (resp., false), we include the true (resp., false) assignment of V^j in μ. For each clause i, we include in μ the critical assignment of C^i that, for each ℓ in $\{1, 2, 3\}$, assigns resident $t_1^{i,\ell}$ to hospital γ^i if and only if the literal with A-identifier (i, ℓ) evaluates to false under truth assignment π. This completes the definition of assignment μ.

We now argue that μ is a valid assignment of I. It is easy to see that for any j in $\{1, \ldots, 3n\}$, no hospital in V^j is over-subscribed and that no resident in V^j outside the set $\{b_1^j, \ldots, b_4^j\}$ is over-subscribed. Similarly, it is easy to see that for any i in $\{1, \ldots, 4n\}$, no hospital in C^i apart from γ^i is over-subscribed and no resident in C^i outside the set $\{t_1^{i,1}, t_1^{i,2}, t_1^{i,3}\}$ is over-subscribed. Thus Lemmas 4.5 and 4.7 below imply μ is a valid assignment of I.

Lemma 4.5. *Let i belong to $\{1, \ldots, 4n\}$. Then hospital γ^i is not over-subscribed.*

Lemma 4.6. *Let i belong to $\{1, \ldots, 4n\}$ and let ℓ belong to $\{1, 2, 3\}$. Resident $t_1^{i,\ell}$ is assigned under μ to its most (resp., second most) preferred hospital if and only if literal ℓ of clause i evaluates to true (resp., false) under π.*

Lemma 4.7. *Let i belong to $\{1, \ldots, 4n\}$, let ℓ belong to $\{1, 2, 3\}$, and let (j, k) denote the B-identifier $\varphi(i, \ell)$. Then resident $t_1^{i,\ell} = b_k^j$ is not over-subscribed.*

It remains to prove that μ is stable for I.

Lemma 4.8. *Let i belong to $\{1, \ldots, 4n\}$ and let H denote* $\text{hosps}(C^i)$. *Then μ is an H-stable assignment of I.*

Lemma 4.9. *Let j belong to $\{1, \ldots, 3n\}$ and let H denote* $\text{hosps}(V^j)$. *Then μ is an H-stable assignment of I.*

Lemma 4.10. *Assignment μ is stable for I.*

Only If Direction. Assume that I admits a stable assignment, and fix a stable assignment μ of I. We need to prove that ϕ is satisfiable.

Lemma 4.11. *Let j belong to $\{1, \ldots, 3n\}$, let H denote* $\text{hosps}(V^j)$, *and let μ' denote $\mu|_H$. Then μ' is the true or the false assignment for V^j.*

Let $\pi = (\pi_1, \ldots, \pi_{3n})$ be the truth assignment for ϕ such that π_j is true if and only if $\mu|_{\text{hosps}(V^j)}$ is the true assignment for V^j. Below we complete the "only if" proof by showing that π is a satisfying truth assignment for ϕ.

Lemma 4.12. *Let i belong to $\{1,\ldots,4n\}$ and let ℓ belong to $\{1,2,3\}$. Then the literal of ϕ with A-identifier (i,ℓ) evaluates to true under π if and only if μ assigns resident $t_1^{i,\ell}$ to its most preferred hospital.*

Lemma 4.13. *Let i belong to $\{1,\ldots,4n\}$ and let ℓ belong to $\{1,2,3\}$. Then μ assigns resident $t_1^{i,\ell}$ to one of its two most preferred hospitals.*

Lemma 4.14. *Let i belong to $\{1,\ldots,4n\}$ and let ℓ belong to $\{1,2,3\}$. Then the literal of ϕ with A-identifier (i,ℓ) evaluates to false under truth assignment π if and only if μ assigns $t_1^{i,\ell}$ to γ^i.*

Lemma 4.15. *Truth assignment π satisfies ϕ.*

5 Unitwise-Coalition Stability

As discussed in Sect. 1, Rodríguez and Manlove have considered two coalitional notions of stability in the context of course allocation, namely first-coalition stability and coalition stability, which correspond to HRS-FC and HRS-C in the special-case setting of HRS. Rodríguez and Manlove have shown that HRS-FC is NP-hard and we have shown that HRS-C is NP-hard. In this section, we discuss a third notion of coalitional stability in the context of HRS that is arguably more natural than either first-coalition stability or coalition stability, and we indicate why our NP-hardness result for HRS-C extends to this third notion, which we call unitwise-coalition stability.

To motivate this third coalitional notion of stability, consider the following example. Suppose hospital h has $\text{cap}(h) = 4$ and preference list r_1 (most preferred), r_2, r_3, r_4 (least preferred) where $\text{size}(r_1) = 2$, $\text{size}(r_2) = 1$, $\text{size}(r_3) = 2$, and $\text{size}(r_4) = 3$. Further assume that assignment μ assigns residents r_2 and r_4 to hospital h. In this scenario, it is straightforward to verify that there is no blocking coalition (in the sense of HRS-C) for μ involving hospital h. Under our proposed coalitional notion of stability, we consider $(\{r_1, r_3\}, h)$ to be a blocking coalition because h "should" prefer $\{r_1, r_3\}$ to $\{r_2, r_4\}$: the two units of r_1 are preferred to the single unit of r_2 and one unit of r_4; the two units of r_3 are preferred to the two remaining units of r_4. More generally, the idea is that a hospital h prefers a set of residents R to a set of residents R' (disjoint from R) if $\text{size}(R) \geq \text{size}(R')$ and for all i in $\{1,\ldots,\text{size}(R')\}$, h prefers its ith most preferred unit in R to its ith most preferred unit in R'.

Unitwise-coalition stability admits an equivalent definition in terms of additive utility. Assume that the utility hospital h derives from being assigned a set of residents R is equal to the sum of its utility for each resident r in R, where the utility for each resident is a positive real number. Further assume that the utilities respect the preference list of h, in the following sense: if h prefers r to r', then the per-unit utility of r (i.e., the utility of h for r divided by $\text{size}(r)$) is greater than the per-unit utility of r' (i.e., the utility of h for r' divided by $\text{size}(r')$). We consider hospital h to prefer a set of residents R to a set of residents R' (disjoint from R) if $\text{size}(R) \geq \text{size}(R')$ and the utility of h for R exceeds the utility of h for R' under any utilities that respect the preference list of h. It is straightforward to prove that this utility-based formulation is equivalent to unitwise-coalition stability.

We now indicate why the NP-hardness proof of Sect. 4 also applies to unitwise-coalition stability. Our proof establishes that HRS-C is NP-hard even in the special case where the resident sizes and the hospital capacities belong to $\{1, 2\}$. It is straightforward to verify that in this special case, an assignment is coalition-stable (i.e., stable under HRS-C) if and only if it is unitwise-coalition-stable.

6 Concluding Remarks

In this paper, we presented an instance of HRIC that does not admit a coalition-stable assignment. In addition, we established that it is NP-hard to find a coalition-stable assignment for a given HRIC instance (or correctly report that no such assignment exists), even if every hospital has capacity at most two and the length of the preference list of each resident (resp., hospital) is at most three (resp., four). As discussed in Sect. 5, this hardness result also holds for unitwise-coalition stability. Since HRS generalizes HRIC and course allocation generalizes HRS, our results resolve the open questions of Rodríguez and Manlove [11] related to finding a coalition-stable assignment in the course allocation setting.

As remarked in Sect. 1, Rodríguez and Manlove prove that the problem of testing whether a given assignment is coalition-stable is co-NP-complete for course allocation, and their argument also applies to the HRS special case. On the other hand, we claim that the testing problem for HRIC under pair-size, first-coalition, coalition, and unitwise-coalition stability belongs to P. To show this, we first argue that if there is a blocking coalition involving some hospital h, then there is a blocking coalition (R, h) such that $\text{size}(R) \leq 2$. Furthermore, for any hospital h and any set of residents R such that $\text{size}(R) \leq 2$, it is straightforward to check in polynomial time whether (R, h) is a blocking coalition. Since there are only polynomially many candidate blocking coalitions (R, h) with $\text{size}(R) \leq 2$, the claim follows.

References

1. Baïou, M., Balinski, M.: Many-to-many matching: stable polyandrous polygamy (or polygamous polyandry). Discret. Appl. Math. **101**(1), 1–12 (2000)
2. Baïou, M., Balinski, M.: Erratum: the stable allocation (or ordinal transportation) problem. Math. Oper. Res. **27**(4), 662–680 (2002)
3. Baïou, M., Balinski, M.: Characterizations of the optimal stable allocation mechanism. Oper. Res. Lett. **35**(3), 392–402 (2007)
4. Balasundaram, H., Krishnashree, J.B., Limaye, G., Nasre, M.: Stability notions for hospital residents with sizes. In: Proceedings of the 45th IARCS Annual Conference on Foundations of Software Technology and Theoretical Computer Science, pp. 11:1–11:18 (2025)

5. Balinski, M., Ratier, G.: Of stable marriages and graphs, and strategy and polytopes. SIAM Rev. **39**(4), 575–604 (1997)
6. Berman, P., Karpinski, M., Scott, A.D.: Approximation hardness of short symmetric instances of MAX-3SAT. Tech. Rep. IHES/M/04/28, Institut des Hautes Études Scientifiques (2004)
7. Delacrétaz, D.: Stability in matching markets with sizes (2019). Working paper
8. Gale, D., Shapley, L.S.: College admissions and the stability of marriage. Am. Math. Mon. **69**(1), 9–15 (1962)
9. Hu, Z., Plaxton, C.G.: Hospitals/residents with inseparable couples: Finding a coalition-stable assignment is NP-hard (2026). https://arxiv.org/abs/2607.18634
10. McDermid, E.J., Manlove, D.F.: Keeping partners together: algorithmic results for the hospitals/residents problem with couples. J. Comb. Optim. **19**(3), 279–303 (2010). Our main technical results follow the proof framework of the erratum https://www.dcs.gla.ac.uk/~davidm/HRS-errata.pdf co-authored with K. Cechlárová
11. Rodríguez, J., Manlove, D.: Course allocation with credits via stable matching. In: Proceedings of the 18th International Symposium on Algorithmic Game Theory, pp. 286–303 (2025). Journal version to appear in *ACM Transactions on Economics and Computation*

Bribery's Influence on Ranked Aggregation

Pallavi Jain(✉) and Anshul Thakur

Department of Computer Science and Engineering, IIT Jodhpur, India
pallavijain.t.cms@gmail.com, thakur.17@iitj.ac.in

Abstract. Kemeny Consensus is a well-known rank aggregation method in social choice theory. In this method, given a set of rankings, the goal is to find a ranking Π that minimizes the total Kendall tau distance to the input rankings. Computing a Kemeny consensus is NP-hard, and even verifying whether a given ranking is a Kemeny consensus is coNP-complete. Fitzsimmons and Hemaspaandra [IJCAI 2021] established the computational intractability of achieving a desired consensus through manipulative actions. Kemeny Consensus is an optimization problem related to Kemeny's rule. In this paper, we consider a decision problem related to Kemeny's rule, known as *Kemeny Score*, in which the goal is to decide whether there exists a ranking Π whose total Kendall tau distance from the given rankings is at most k. Computation of Kemeny score is known to be NP-complete. In this paper, we investigate the impact of several manipulation actions on the Kemeny Score problem, in which given a set of rankings, an integer k, and a ranking X, the question is to decide whether it is possible to manipulate the given rankings so that the total Kendall tau distance of X from the manipulated rankings is at most k. We show that this problem can be solved in polynomial time for various manipulation actions. Interestingly, these same manipulation actions are known to be computationally hard for Kemeny consensus.

Keywords: Kemeny Score · Bribery · Rank Aggregation

1 Introduction

Rank aggregation, the task of combining multiple rankings into a single consensus ranking, is a ubiquitous problem with wide-ranging applications. It is a fundamental problem in computational social choice theory and plays a crucial role in various domains such as meta-search engines [21], recommendation systems, machine learning [2], marketing and advertisement, bioinformatics [41], etc. One of the rank aggregation techniques, widely accepted in social choice theory, is *Kemeny's* rule defined by Kemeny in 1959 [36]. In the Kemeny Score problem, given a set of n rankings, say $\mathcal{R}$, and an integer k, the goal is to determine if there exists a ranking X such that the total *Kendall tau distance* (defined later) between the set of rankings in $\mathcal{R}$ and X is at most k [9,34]. Kemeny's rule is interesting in social choice theory as it satisfies the Condorcet extension criterion and is also maximum likelihood estimator for a simple probabilistic model

P. Lenzner and D. Schmand (Eds.): SAGT 2026, LNCS 16911, pp. 261–279, 2027.
https://doi.org/10.1007/978-3-032-38782-0_15

in which individual preferences are noisy estimates of an underlying "true" ranking [9, page 87]. Kemeny Score is well-studied computationally from theoretical computer science viewpoint [4–7,18,30,34,37], machine learning [32], as well as heuristically [17,43,44]. Interestingly, Kemeny Score is polynomial-time solvable for two rankings and NP-hard for four rankings [7], while the case of three rankings is a long-standing open problem.

One of the important directions of research in computational social choice theory is to study the computational complexity of changing the outcome via manipulation, bribery, and various control actions, such as adding or deleting candidates or rankings [1,9,19,24,26,39,40]. To the best of our knowledge, de Haan [33] initiated the study of manipulation for Kemeny in the context of judgment aggregation. Recently, Fitzsimmons and Hemaspaandra [28] studied the computational complexity of manipulation schemes for the Kemeny Consensus problem, where given the set of n rankings, $\mathcal{R}$, and a ranking X, the goal is to manipulate the rankings $\mathcal{R}$ using a manipulative action so that X attains the minimum total Kendall tau distance to the profile among all rankings. The Kendall tau distance between two rankings π and π' over a candidate set $\mathcal{C}$ is the number of pairs of candidates whose relative ordering differs between π and π'. Mathematically,

$$\mathtt{KT}(\pi,\pi') = |\{\{x,y\} \subseteq \mathcal{C} \colon (x \prec_\pi y \wedge y \prec_{\pi'} x) \vee (y \prec_\pi x \wedge x \prec_{\pi'} y)\}|$$

The notation $x \prec_\pi y$ denotes that x is before y in the ranking π. The Kendall tau distance of a ranking π from the set of rankings $\mathcal{R}$ is the summation of distance from π to each ranking in $\mathcal{R}$, i.e., $\sum_{\pi' \in \mathcal{R}} \mathtt{KT}(\pi,\pi')$.

In this paper, we explore the computational complexity of various manipulation schemes for Kemeny Score, which has not been studied so far to the best of our knowledge.

Kemeny Consensus vs Kemeny Score. Kemeny Score is a decision problem of Kemeny's rule and Kemeny Consensus is an optimization problem of Kemeny's rule [9, page 88]. However, interestingly, when manipulation is considered, there is a significant difference between the two problems. In the manipulation problems for KEMENY SCORE, the Kendall tau distance of X should be at most k from $\mathcal{R}$. At the same time, in manipulation problems for KEMENY CONSENSUS it is possible that the distance of X from $\mathcal{R}$ does not change at all; rather, the distance of other rankings increases so that X is the closest one. We explain it using the following example, which is the same as Example 9 in [28].

Example 1. Consider three candidates a, b, c. Suppose there are three rankings $R_1 = R_2 = R_3 = a \succ b \succ c$, two rankings $R_4 = R_5 = a \succ c \succ b$, and one ranking $R_6 = c \succ b \succ a$. Let $X = a \succ c \succ b$. Let $k = 3$. Note that if we delete ranking R_6, then the Kendall tau distance of X from $\mathcal{R} = \{R_1, \ldots, R_5\}$ is 3; while X is not a Kemeny consensus. The Kemeny consensus ranking is $a \succ b \succ c$. However, if we delete R_1, then X is the Kemeny consensus of $\mathcal{R} = \{R_2, \ldots, R_6\}$ while the Kendall tau distance of X from $\mathcal{R}$ is 4.

While many problems, including the Kemeny Consensus and the KEMENY WINNER (the top candidate in the Kemeny consensus is the winner), are not susceptible to various bribery-based manipulation schemes, we have developed polynomial-time algorithms for the KEMENY SCORE under various bribery-based manipulative actions. Formally, we study the following problem.

$\mathfrak{B}$-**KEMENY SCORE**
Input: a set of candidates $\mathcal{C}$, a set of rankings $\mathcal{R}$ over $\mathcal{C}$, a ranking X over $\mathcal{C}$, a cost function $\texttt{cost}_{\mathfrak{B}}$ (depending on the bribery action $\mathfrak{B}$), a budget $\texttt{bgt} \in \mathbb{N}$, and an integer k.
Question: Does there exist a set of rankings $\mathcal{R}'$ that can be obtained by manipulating rankings in $\mathcal{R}$ using bribery action $\mathfrak{B}$ within the budget $\texttt{bgt}$, and the total Kendall tau distance of X from the rankings in $\mathcal{R}'$ is at most k?

We consider the following bribery actions. The cost of bribery is additive for all bribery actions.

\$Bribery. In this manipulation action, a ranking $R \in \mathcal{R}$ can be changed to any arbitrary ranking. Note that for our problem, changing them to X is a better choice rather than anything else, as this makes the distance 0. The cost function is defined as follows: $\texttt{cost}_\$: \mathcal{R} \to \mathbb{N}$. Let $S \subseteq \mathcal{R}$ be the set of rankings that are changed to X. Then, the cost of manipulation is $\sum_{R \in S} \texttt{cost}_\$(R)$.

Swap Bribery. A swap $(c, c')_R$ in the ranking R is called *admissible* if c and c' are consecutive in R. In this manipulation action, we can change a ranking by admissible swaps, and the cost depends on the ranking and the number of swaps. Formally, the cost function is defined as follows: $\texttt{cost}_{\mathsf{SB}} : \mathcal{R} \to \mathbb{N}$. Note that $\texttt{cost}_{\mathsf{SB}}(R)$ denotes the cost of one swap in the ranking R. If l_1 swaps are done on ranking R_1 and l_2 swaps are done on ranking R_2 then the total cost would be $l_1 \cdot \texttt{cost}_{\mathsf{SB}}(R_1) + l_2 \cdot \texttt{cost}_{\mathsf{SB}}(R_2)$

Ranking Deletion. In this manipulation action, we are allowed to delete rankings, and there is a cost associated with the deletion. The cost function is defined as follows: $\texttt{cost}_{\mathsf{RD}} : \mathcal{R} \to \mathbb{N}$.

Candidate Deletion. In this manipulation action, we are allowed to delete candidates. Note that if we delete a candidate $c \in \mathcal{C}$, then it is deleted from all the rankings in $\mathcal{R}$ as well as from X, and it does not change the ordering of other candidates. The cost function is defined as follows: $\texttt{cost}_{\mathsf{CD}} : \mathcal{C} \to \mathbb{N}$.

In the technical sections, we omit the subscript below cost *since each section is dedicated to a specific bribery action. Thus, it will be clear from the context.*

Candidate deletion and ranking deletion are usually considered as control actions. Since we are considering the cost, we consider these manipulative actions also as bribery actions for brevity.

Note that the addition of rankings or candidates is not a meaningful manipulation action for us. This is because adding rankings does not decrease the distance of X from the existing rankings. Additionally, since X is given to us, the addition of candidates is not a meaningful operat thion for us.

We also study the problem when the rankings in $\mathcal{R}$ are not complete, i.e., all the rankings in $\mathcal{R}$ are partial; however, X is a ranking over $\mathcal{C}$. The objective is to complete the rankings in $\mathcal{R}$ so that X is at most k distance away from the new complete rankings over $\mathcal{C}$. Formally, we study the following problem.

Possible Kemeny Score

Input: a set of candidates $\mathcal{C}$, a set of partial rankings $\mathcal{R}$, a ranking X over $\mathcal{C}$, and an integer k.

Question: Can we *extend* rankings in $\mathcal{R}$ using the remaining candidates so that the total Kendall tau distance of X from the extended rankings in $\mathcal{R}$ is at most k?

By *extending* a ranking R, we mean that the candidates of $\mathcal{C} \setminus C'$ are added to R, where R is over C'; however, the relative ordering of the candidates of the set C' in the ranking R does not change.

Table 1 summarizes the complexity of various manipulation schemes for Kemeny Score, Kemeny Consensus, and Kemeny Winner. All the results pertaining to Kemeny Score are build in this paper.

Table 1. Summary of computational complexity of various manipulation schemes for Kemeny Score, Kemeny Consensus, and Kemeny Winner. The computational complexity of the cases marked with "-" are not known to the best of our knowledge and also mentioned in [39].

	Kemeny Score	Kemeny Consensus	Kemeny Winner
$Bribery	P [Theorem 4]	**coNP**-complete [[28], Observation 6]	OPEN
Swap Bribery	P [Theorem 6]	OPEN	OPEN
Ranking Deletion	P [Theorem 5]	Σ_2^P-complete [[28], Conjecture on page 199]	OPEN
Candidate Deletion	$k = 0$: P [Theorem 7] $\lvert\mathcal{R}\rvert = 1$: P [Theorem 8] OPEN (in general)	Σ_2^P-complete [[28], Theorem 8]	Σ_2^P-complete [[29], Theorem 5]
Possible Kemeny Score	P [Theorem 3]	OPEN	OPEN

Related Work. Here, we discuss some more related work. In 1992, Bartholdi et al. [3] initiated the study of manipulating the election by adding/deleting the candidates or voters so that a favorite candidate is the winner. Afterwards, there is a lot of study on the manipulation actions for the several voting rules [1,9,10,12,13,16,19,20,22,25,27,35], with several results pertaining to NP-hardness as well as algorithms.

Manipulation is closely linked to the robustness of voting rules, a connection identified a few years ago [11]. This insight has since inspired research into manipulation from a new perspective [8,14,23,31,42]. This relation also highlights the importance of algorithmic results for these problems.

Road Map. We begin our technical sections from Sect. 3, which is dedicated to a polynomial time algorithm for POSSIBLE KEMENY SCORE. Then, in Sect. 4, we present results for $-Bribery-Kemeny Score and Ranking Deletion-Kemeny Score. Section 5 and Sect. 6 are dedicated to Swap Bribery-Kemeny Score and CANDIDATE DELETION-KEMENY SCORE, respectively. Section 7 concludes the paper with some open questions.

2 Preliminaries

The notation $[n]$ denotes the set of natural numbers $\{1, \ldots, n\}$. Throughout, we let $m = |\mathcal{C}|$ denote the number of candidates and $n = |\mathcal{R}|$ the number of rankings. The Kendall tau distance between two rankings π, π' is denoted as $\texttt{KT}(\pi, \pi')$. Furthermore, we abuse the notations and use $\texttt{KT}(\pi, \mathcal{R})$ to denote the Kendall tau distance of ranking π from the set of rankings $\mathcal{R}$. For a ranking π, let $S(\pi)$ denote the set of elements that are ranked in π, i.e., π is a ranking over $S(\pi)$. We also use $\texttt{KT}(\pi, \pi')$ to denote the distance between π and π' when either $S(\pi) \subseteq S(\pi')$ or $S(\pi') \subseteq S(\pi)$. The distance is computed only for the elements in $S(\pi) \cap S(\pi')$. It will be clear from the context. When we say that a ranking π is k distance away from another ranking π' (or set of rankings $\mathcal{R}$), we mean that $\texttt{KT}(\pi, \pi') \leq k$ (or $\texttt{KT}(\pi, \mathcal{R}) \leq k$). A pair of candidates c, c' disagree in π and π' if their relative ordering differs in π and π'. Let π, π' be two rankings and $S \subseteq S(\pi) \cap S(\pi')$. We say that π and π' *agree* over S if for every $\{c, c'\} \subseteq S$, the relative ordering of c and c' is the same in both π and π', i.e., either c is before c' in π and π' or c' is before c in both rankings. Let π be a ranking. Let $Y \subseteq S(\pi)$. Then, $\pi|_Y$ denotes the ordering π *restricted* to Y, i.e., it is an ordering over Y and the relative ordering of every pair of elements in Y is the same as that in π. We denote the ith element of π as $\pi(i)$ and the number of elements in π as $|\pi|$. The notation $x \prec_\pi y$ denotes that x is before y in the ordering π. The number of *disagreements* with respect to x in π and π' is defined as follows $\#\mathsf{disagree}(\pi, \pi', x) = |\{(x, y) \colon (x \succ_\pi y \wedge y \succ_{\pi'} x) \vee (y \succ_\pi x \wedge x \succ_{\pi'} y)\}|$. We treat the set of rankings $\mathcal{R}$ as an ordered tuple $(R_1, \ldots, R_n)$ for convenience in the technical sections.

For a function $f \colon P \to Q$ and a subset $S \subseteq P$, $f(S) = \cup_{s \in S} f(s)$. For a graph $G = (V, E)$, $V(G)$ denotes the vertex set of G and $E(G)$ denotes the edge set of G. For a subset $S \subseteq V(G)$, $G - S$ denotes the graph on the vertex set $V(G) \setminus S$ and the edge set $\{uv \in E(G) \colon \{u, v\} \subseteq V(G) \setminus S\}$.

3 Possible Kemeny Score

In this section, we design a polynomial-time algorithm for the POSSIBLE KEMENY SCOREproblem. Recall that in POSSIBLE KEMENY SCOREwe need to complete the partial ranking set $\mathcal{R}$ so that the Kendall tau distance between the given ranking X and the extended ranking set of $\mathcal{R}$, say $\mathcal{R}'$, is at most k. Note that there is no cost associated with the extension of rankings. Thus, we first design an algorithm to extend a ranking R over $C' \subseteq \mathcal{C}$ to R' using the candidates in $C'' = \mathcal{C} \setminus C'$ such that $\mathtt{KT}(X, R')$ is minimum among all the extensions of R. We call R' an *optimal* extension of R. We will argue that we can extend all the rankings in $\mathcal{R}$ using this algorithm and return YES if and only if we are given a yes-instance.

The algorithm proceeds as follows. We have a ranking R over $C' \subseteq \mathcal{C}$ as an input. Let $C'' = \mathcal{C} \setminus C'$ and $\Pi = X|_{C''}$. Let $R' = R$. For $i \in [|\mathcal{C}''|]$, we insert $\Pi(i)$ after the candidates $\Pi(1), \ldots, \Pi(i-1)$ in R' at the leftmost position that minimizes the Kendall tau distance of R' from X after inserting $\Pi(i)$. Algorithm 1 describes the procedure formally. By *inserting* a candidate c in the ranking R' at position j, we mean that c is inserted between $R'|_{C'}(j)$ and $R'|_{C'}(j+1)$ and after all the candidates of C'' between $R'|_{C'}(j)$ and $R'|_{C'}(j+1)$ in R'. We denote this operation by $\mathsf{insert}(R', c, j)$. For example, let $C' = \{1, 2, \ldots, 100\}$, $C'' = \{a, b, \ldots, z\}$, and $R = 1 \prec 2 \prec 3 \prec a \prec b \prec c \prec 4 \prec \ldots \prec 100$. Then $\mathsf{insert}(R, d, 3)$ will result in ranking $R' = 1 \prec 2 \prec 3 \prec a \prec b \prec c \prec d \prec 4 \prec \ldots \prec 100$. Note that $\mathsf{insert}(R', c, 0)$ means that c is inserted before $R'|_{C'}(1)$ and $\mathsf{insert}(R', c, |C'|)$ means that c is inserted after the last candidate in $R'|_{C'}$ in R'.

Algorithm 1: Possible-Kemeny-Score

Input: Ranking X, Partial ranking R over $C' \subseteq \mathcal{C}$
Output: a ranking R' over $\mathcal{C}$ which is an extension of R

```
Initialize set C'' = 𝒞 \ C', ranking Π = X|_{C''}, and R'_0 = R
l = 0
for i ∈ [|𝒞''|] do
    S = {l, ..., |C'|}
    q = min(argmin_{j∈S} KT(X, insert(R', Π(i), j)))
    R'_i = insert(R'_{i-1}, Π(i), q)
    l = q
return R'_{|C''|}
```

Before proving that R' is an optimal extension of R, we first prove the following structural property of all optimal extensions, which is crucial for our algorithm.

Lemma 1. *Let $\hat{R}$ be an optimal extension of R. Then $\hat{R}$ and X agree over C''.*

Proof. Let $\hat{R}$ be an optimal extension of R. Suppose that $\{c, c'\} \subseteq C''$ such that $c \prec_X c'$. Towards the contradiction, suppose that $c' \prec_{\hat{R}} c$. Let $R^\star$ be an ordering over $\mathcal{C}$ obtained by swapping c' and c in $\hat{R}$. Clearly, $\mathtt{KT}(X, \hat{R}) \leq \mathtt{KT}(X, R^\star)$ as $\hat{R}$ is an optimal extension. Note that if there is no candidate between c and c' in $\hat{R}$, then $\mathtt{KT}(X, R^\star) < \mathtt{KT}(X, \hat{R})$, which is a contradiction.

Next we consider the case when there exist candidates $c_1, c_2, \ldots, c_n$ between c and c' in $\hat{R}$, i.e., $c' \prec_{\hat{R}} \cdots \prec_{\hat{R}} c_i \prec_{\hat{R}} \cdots \prec_{\hat{R}} c$. Recall that $\{c, c'\}$ contributes to $\mathtt{KT}(X, \hat{R})$, but not to $\mathtt{KT}(X, R^\star)$. Let $c_i \in \{c_1, c_2, \ldots, c_n\}$. If c_i is between c and c' in X, i.e., $c \prec_X c_i \prec_X c'$, then note that $\{c, c_i\}$ and $\{c', c_i\}$ contribute to $\mathtt{KT}(X, \hat{R})$, but not to $\mathtt{KT}(X, R^\star)$. If c_i is after c' in X, i.e., $c \prec_X c' \prec_X c_i$, then $\{c, c_i\}$ contributes to $\mathtt{KT}(X, \hat{R})$ and not to $\mathtt{KT}(X, R^\star)$, while $\{c', c_i\}$ contributes to $\mathtt{KT}(X, R^\star)$ and not to $\mathtt{KT}(X, \hat{R})$. Similarly, if c_i is before c in X, i.e., $c_i \prec_X c \prec_X c'$, then $\{c', c_i\}$ contributes to $\mathtt{KT}(X, \hat{R})$ and not to $\mathtt{KT}(X, R^\star)$, while $\{c, c_i\}$ contributes to $\mathtt{KT}(X, R^\star)$ and not to $\mathtt{KT}(X, \hat{R})$. Since we do not change the position of any other candidates, their relative ordering does not change in $R^\star$. Thus, $\mathtt{KT}(X, R^\star) < \mathtt{KT}(X, \hat{R})$, which is a contradiction. Thus, every optimal extension of R agrees with X over C''. □

Lemma 1 provides the intuition for placing $\Pi(i)$ after $\Pi(1), \ldots, \Pi(i-1)$ in Algorithm 1.

Let A be a ranking over $\mathcal{C}$, such that A and X agree over C''. Let $A_i = A|_{C' \cup \{\Pi(1), \ldots, \Pi(i)\}}$. Before analysing the correctness of Algorithm 1, let us consider the following scenario. Suppose the candidate $\Pi(i)$ is positioned at t_i in the ranking A_i, and there exists a position $t_f \geq t_i$ such that placing $\Pi(i)$ at position t_f minimises the number of disagreements between $\Pi(i)$ and the candidates of C' as measured between A and X compared to any position after t_i. If we move $\Pi(i)$ along with all candidates $\ell > i$, $\Pi(\ell) \in C''$ positioned between t_i and t_f in A to t_f, this operation will not increase Kendall tau distance between A and X as proved in Lemma 2. Note that we conserve the relative order between candidates of C'' in the aforementioned operation. We illustrate this operation and the importance of Lemma 2 using Fig. 1. Note that in the figure, it is clear that moving $\Pi(i)$ from t_i to t_f reduces the number of disagreements involving $\Pi(i)$. However, it is not obvious why moving other candidates of C'' in red squares does not increase the total Kendall tau distance.

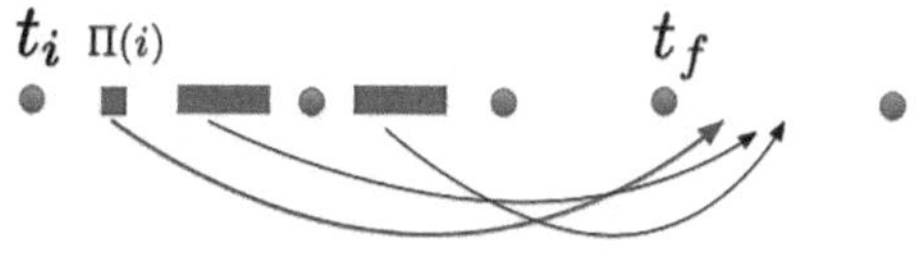

Fig. 1. $\Pi(i), t_i$, and t_f are as discussed in above paragraph. Circles represent the candidates of C' and squares denote the candidates of C''. Big squares denote a chunk of C'' that are consecutive in the ranking.

Lemma 2. *Moving $\Pi(i)$, along with every candidate $\Pi(\ell) \in C''$ for $\ell > i$ that is positioned between t_i and t_f in A, to position t_f does not increase the Kendall tau distance between A and X.*

Proof. To streamline our arguments, we begin by defining a sequential operation that moves $\Pi(i)$ and all the candidates of C'' after $\Pi(i)$ that are positioned between t_i and t_f to t_f in A. The procedure is as follows, first we move all the candidates of C'' after $\Pi(i)$ positioned at t_i to $t_i + 1$, then we move all the candidates of C'' positioned at $t_i + 1$ to $t_i + 2$, note that in the second operation, the candidates of C'' positioned at $t_i + 1$ include all the candidates moved to $t_i + 1$ after the first operation. We continue to do this operation until we move all the candidates $\Pi(\ell) \in C''$, $\ell \geq i$, positioned between t_i and t_f to t_f. We denote the change in the number of disagreements of $c \in C''$ with the candidates in C' when we move a candidate c from its position x to y as $\Delta_{x,y}c$, i.e., $\Delta_{x,y}c$ is the number of disagreements when c is at position y minus the number of disagreements when c is at position x.

Claim 1. *For every $j \in \{i, \ldots, f-1\}$, $\Delta_{t_j,t_j+1}\Pi(\ell) \leq \Delta_{t_j,t_{j+1}}\Pi(i)$, where $\Pi(i)$ and $\Pi(\ell)$ are at position j, $\ell > i$.*

Proof. Note that moving $\Pi(i)$ from t_j to t_{j+1}, either increases or decreases the number of disagreements of $\Pi(i)$ with the candidates in C' by 1. We consider these two cases separately.

Case 1. If moving $\Pi(i)$ to $t_j + 1$ increases the number of disagreements by 1 (i.e., $\Delta_{t_j,t_j+1}\Pi(i) = +1$), this implies that, $\Pi(i) \prec_X A|_{C'}(t_j+1)$. In this case, we cannot definitively predict the effect of moving the candidate $\Pi(\ell)$ forward to $t_j + 1$, as $\Pi(i) \prec_X \Pi(\ell)$. Therefore, $\Delta_{t_j,t_j+1}\Pi(\ell)$ can be either positive or negative 1 when moved. Hence $\Delta_{t_j,t_j+1}\Pi(\ell) \leq \Delta_{t_j,t_j+1}\Pi(i)$

Case 2. If moving $\Pi(i)$ to $t_j + 1$ decreases the number of disagreements by 1 (i.e., $\Delta_{t_j,t_j+1}\Pi(i) = -1$), this implies that, $A|_{C'}(t_j + 1) \prec_X \Pi(i)$. Since $A|_{C'}(t_j+1) \prec_X \Pi(i) \prec_X \Pi(\ell)$, moving $\Pi(\ell)$ up by one position in A will also decrease the number of disagreements by 1 (i.e., $\Delta_{t_j,t_j+1}\Pi(\ell) = -1$). Hence $\Delta_{t_j,t_j+1}\Pi(\ell) \leq \Delta_{t_j,t_j+1}\Pi(i)$.

Due to our sequential procedure and Claim 1, we know that for every $\Pi(\ell)$, where $\ell > i$, at t_{i+p}, where $p \in \{0, \ldots, f-1\}$

$$\sum_{0 \leq j < f-p} \Delta_{t_{i+p+j},t_{i+p+j+1}}\Pi(\ell) \leq \sum_{0 \leq j < f-p} \Delta_{t_{i+p+j},t_{i+p+j+1}}\Pi(i)$$

Therefore, $\Delta_{t_{i+p},t_f}\Pi(\ell) \leq \Delta_{t_{i+p},t_f}\Pi(i)$. Due to definition of t_f, $\Delta_{t_{i+p},t_f}\Pi(\ell) \leq \Delta_{t_{i+p},t_f}\Pi(i) \leq 0$. Thus moving $\Pi(i)$, along with every candidate $\Pi(\ell) \in C''$ for $\ell > i$ that is positioned between t_i and t_f in A, to position t_f does not increase the Kendall tau distance between A and X.

Finally, we are ready to argue that the ranking returned by Algorithm 1 is an optimal extension of R.

Lemma 3. *Let R' be the ranking returned by Algorithm 1. Then, R' is an optimal extension of R.*

Proof. We first claim that R' is an extension of R. Note that $R'|_{C'} = R|_{C'}$ as we do not change the relative ordering of any pair of candidates of C' in the algorithm, i.e., for all $\{c, c'\} \subseteq C'$, if $c \prec_R c'$, then $c \prec_{R'} c'$. Let $\Pi_i = \bigcup_{q=1}^{i} \Pi(q)$ and R'_i be the ranking after i^{th} iteration of Algorithm 1. Next, we argue the optimality in the following claim.

Claim 2. *For all $i \in [|C''|]$, there exists an optimal extension $R^\star$ of R such that and $R^\star|_{C' \cup \Pi_i} = R'_i$*

Proof. We prove this claim using induction on i. For $i = 1$, consider the case where $R^\star|_{C' \cup \Pi_1} \neq R'_1$, which means that $t_1 \neq t'_1$ where t_1 is the position of $\Pi(1)$ in $R^\star$ and t'_1 is the position where $\Pi(1)$ was inserted in R'_1. If we move $\Pi(1)$ to the position t'_1 in $R^\star$, we note that the number of disagreements between $R^\star$ and X do not increase as t'_1 is the position returned by Algorithm 1 such that insertion of $\Pi(1)$ at that position leads to the least number of disagreements between our ranking and X. Let this new ranking be $\tilde{R}$. We can see that $\tilde{R}$ is an optimal extension of R such that $\tilde{R}|_{C' \cup \Pi_1} = R'_1$.

Suppose that Claim 2 holds for $i \leq \ell$. Then there exists an optimal extension $R^\star$ of R such that $R^\star|_{C' \cup \Pi_l} = R'_l$. Next we argue for $i = \ell + 1$. Consider the case where $R^\star|_{C' \cup \Pi_{\ell+1}} \neq R'_{\ell+1}$, which means that $t_{\ell+1} \neq t'_{\ell+1}$ where $t_{\ell+1}$ is the position of $\Pi(\ell + 1)$ in $R^\star$ and $t'_{\ell+1}$ is the position where $\Pi(\ell + 1)$ was inserted in $R'_{\ell+1}$. So let us assume the case where $t'_{\ell+1} < t_{\ell+1}$. Note that $t_\ell = t'_\ell \leq t'_{\ell+1}$ as $R^\star|_{C' \cup \Pi_l} = R'_\ell$. We can always move $\Pi(\ell + 1)$ to $t'_{\ell+1}$ in $R^\star$ and it does not change the relative ordering of candidates of C''. If we move $\Pi(\ell + 1)$ to the position $t'_{\ell+1}$ in $R^\star$, we note that the number of disagreements between $R^\star$ and X involving $R^\star$ does not increase as $t'_{\ell+1}$ is the position returned by Algorithm 1 such that insertion of $\Pi(\ell + 1)$ at that position leads to the least number of disagreements between our ranking and X, note that we are only moving $\Pi(\ell + 1)$ in $R^\star$, so the changes in the Kendall tau distance will only be caused due to $\Pi(\ell + 1)$. Hence, the Kendall tau distance does not increase. Let this new ranking be $\tilde{R}$, we can see that $\tilde{R}$ is an optimal extension of R such that $\tilde{R}|_{C' \cup \Pi_{\ell+1}} = R'_{\ell+1}$.

For the second case where $t_{\ell+1} < t'_{\ell+1}$, we can say that moving $\Pi(\ell + 1)$ and every candidate $\Pi(x)$, $x > \ell + 1$, positioned between $t_{\ell+1}$ and $t'_{\ell+1}$ in $R^\star$ to $t'_{\ell+1}$ in $R^\star$ does not increase the number of disagreements between $R^\star$ and X as a direct consequence of Lemma 2. Note that $t'_{\ell+1}$ is position returned by Algorithm 1 such that insertion of $\Pi(\ell + 1)$ at that position leads to the least number of disagreements between our ranking and X. Let this new ranking be $\tilde{R}$, we can see that $\tilde{R}$ is an optimal extension of R such that $\tilde{R}|_{C' \cup \Pi_{\ell+1}} = R'_{\ell+1}$.

As Claim 2 holds for all $i \in [|C''|]$, we can say that there exists an optimal extension $R^\star$ of R such that $R^\star|_{C' \cup C'' = C} = R'$. This proves that R' returned by Algorithm 1 is an optimal extension to R.

Lemma 3 gives an optimal extension of a ranking in $\mathcal{R}$. We complete the algorithm in the following theorem by extending all the rankings using the same procedure and argue the running time.

Theorem 3. POSSIBLE KEMENY SCORE*can be solved in polynomial time.*

Proof. Let $\mathcal{I} = (\mathcal{C}, \mathcal{R}, X, k)$ be an instance of POSSIBLE KEMENY SCORE. Recall that rankings in $\mathcal{R}$ are over $C' \subseteq \mathcal{C}$. Let $\mathcal{R} = (R_1, R_2, \dots, R_n)$. For every $R_i \in \mathcal{R}$, we find an optimal extension R_i' using Algorithm 1. Let $\mathcal{R}' = (R_1', R_2', \dots, R_n')$ be the set of optimal extensions obtained by applying Algorithm 1 to each ranking in $\mathcal{R}$. If $\mathtt{KT}(X, \mathcal{R}) \leq k$, we return YES; otherwise NO. Next, we prove the correctness of our algorithm. Clearly, if we return YES, then $\mathcal{I}$ is a yes-instance of POSSIBLE KEMENY SCORE. We next argue that if $\mathcal{I}$ is a yes-instance of POSSIBLE KEMENY SCOREwe return an extension $\mathcal{R}'$ such that $\mathtt{KT}(X, \mathcal{R}') \leq k$. Let us suppose that there exists a set of extended rankings $\mathcal{R}^\star = (R_1^\star, R_2^\star, \dots, R_n^\star)$, such that $\mathtt{KT}(X, \mathcal{R}^\star) \leq k$. Due to Lemma 3, we can say that for all $i \in [n]$, $\mathtt{KT}(X, \mathcal{R}_i') \leq \mathtt{KT}(X, R_i^\star)$, which implies that, $\mathtt{KT}(X, \mathcal{R}') = \sum_i \mathtt{KT}(X, \mathcal{R}_i') \leq \sum_i \mathtt{KT}(X, R_i^\star) = \mathtt{KT}(X, \mathcal{R}^\star) \leq k$.

Next, we argue the running time of the algorithm. Note that Algorithm 1 runs in time $\mathcal{O}(m^3)$ and we call Algorithm 1 n times. Thus, the algorithm runs in time $\mathcal{O}(n \cdot m^3)$. Note that in Algorithm 1 at line number 5, the Kendall tau distance calculation runs in time $\mathcal{O}(m)$ because we only need to compute the number of disagreements between $\Pi(i)$ and the candidates of C'.

This completes the proof. □

In our algorithm, we assume that all the rankings in $\mathcal{R}$ are over the subset $C' \subseteq \mathcal{C}$. However, this is only for ease of explanation, and the algorithm works even when rankings in $\mathcal{R}$ are not over the same subset. This is due to the reason that we call Algorithm 1 independently for each partial ranking in $\mathcal{R}$.

4 Dollar-Bribery-Kemeny Score and Ranking Deletion Kemeny Score

We begin with designing a polynomial-time algorithm for \$-Bribery-Kemeny Score. Recall that in \$-Bribery-Kemeny Score we need to change some rankings to X so that X is at most k distance away from the new set of rankings. The problem inherently seems to be closer to the KNAPSACK problem, in which given a set of items, $A = \{a_1, \dots, a_n\}$, a weight function $w\colon A \to \mathbb{N}$, a value function $v\colon A \to \mathbb{N}$, and two natural numbers T, W; the goal is to decide if there exists a subset $S \subseteq A$ such that $\sum_{a \in S} w(a) \leq W$ and $\sum_{a \in S} v(a) \geq T$. We formalize this intuition below by giving a polynomial time reduction to the KNAPSACK problem.

Lemma 4 (⋆). [1] *There is a polynomial time reduction from the* $-Bribery-Kemeny Score *problem to the* Knapsack *problem, where the values are polynomially bounded in the input size.*

Since there is a pseudo-polynomial time algorithm for Knapsack that solves the problem in polynomial time if either weights or values are polynomially bounded [38] and the above reduction is polynomial time, we have the following result.

Theorem 4. $-Bribery-Kemeny Score *can be solved in polynomial time.*

Note that changing a ranking to X is equivalent to deleting this ranking as the contribution of this ranking to Kendall tau distance becomes 0 due to both the operations. Thus, we have the following result due to the same algorithm, with the difference that instead of changing it to X, we delete the ranking.

Theorem 5. Ranking Deletion-Kemeny Score *can be solved in polynomial time.*

5 Swap Bribery-Kemeny Score

In this section, we design a polynomial-time algorithm for Swap Bribery-Kemeny Score problem. Recall that in Swap Bribery-Kemeny Score we need to perform some admissible swaps on the set of rankings $\mathcal{R}$, so that X is at most k distance away from the new set of rankings $\mathcal{R}'$. Let A be a ranking over $\mathcal{C}$. Consider a pair of candidates c, c' such that $c \prec_X c'$ and $c' \prec_A c$. If c, c' are consecutive in A, then we say that $\{c, c'\}$ is an admissible disagreement between A and X, otherwise, it is a non-admissible disagreement. In our algorithm, we swap candidates only when they are in disagreement. Before presenting the algorithm, we first establish an important property regarding admissible disagreements. Specifically, if there exists a non-admissible disagreement $\{a, b\}$ between rankings A and X, then it implies the existence of an admissible disagreement between A and X. This property is crucial because it implies that for any ranking A, either there exists an admissible disagreement or there is no disagreement between A and X (i.e., $\texttt{KT}(X, A) = 0$). Consequently, this ensures that in our algorithm, we can always perform an admissible swap action if $\texttt{KT}(X, A) > 0$. We formalise all these properties below.

Throughout this section, when we refer to *performing a swap action between candidates*, we implicitly mean that the candidates are in disagreement. Throughout the section, after performing a swap action on a ranking R, we reuse the notation R for the new ranking. We begin with the following observation.

Observation 1. *One swap operation in A of an admissible disagreement between A and X reduces the Kendall tau distance between them by exactly one.*

---

[1] The proofs of statements marked by ⋆ can be found in the full version on arXiv: arXiv:2603.28574.

Lemma 5. *The presence of a non-admissible disagreement between rankings A and X implies the existence of an admissible disagreement between A and X.*

Proof. Suppose that there exists a non-admissible disagreement $\{a, b\}$ between A and X. Towards the contradiction, suppose that there are no admissible disagreements between A and X. Since $\{a, b\}$ is a disagreement, let $a \prec_A b$ and $b \prec_X a$. Note that $\{a, b\}$ is a non-admissible disagreement, so there must be some candidates $c_1, c_2, \ldots, c_p$ ranked between a and b in A. Let $A = \ldots a \prec c_1 \prec \ldots \prec c_p \prec b \prec \ldots$. Since there is no admissible disagreement between A and X, we know that $a \prec_X c_1$, $c_i \prec_X c_{i+1}$, for all $i \in [p-1]$, and $c_p \prec_X b$. This implies $a \prec_X b$ due to transitivity in the ranking X, which is a contradiction.

Due to Lemma 5, we have the following useful property.

Corollary 1. *We can always perform an admissible swap action in the ranking A if* $\texttt{KT}(X, A) > 0$.

By performing s swaps in the ranking A, we mean executing s swap operations sequentially, each applied to the updated ranking resulting from the previous swap. It is important to note that a swap which is initially non-admissible may become admissible after performing some admissible swaps, allowing us to perform that swap at a later stage. Due to Observation 1 and Corollary 1, we can always perform a sequence of $0 \leq s \leq \texttt{KT}(X, A)$ admissible swap actions in A and that results in a drop of s in the Kendall tau distance between A and X.

We finally move towards designing our algorithm.

Theorem 6. Swap Bribery-Kemeny Score *can be solved in polynomial time.*

Proof. Let $\mathcal{I} = (\mathcal{C}, \mathcal{R}, X, \texttt{cost}, \texttt{bgt}, k)$ be a given instance of the Swap Bribery-Kemeny Score problem. We design a dynamic programming algorithm to solve this problem. Let $\mathcal{R} = (R_1, R_2, \ldots, R_n)$. We define the dynamic programming table as follows: $T[i, s_1, s_2, j]$ = minimum cost incurred in performing admissible swap actions on the first i rankings such that s_1 swaps are done to R_i, s_2 swaps are done to the set of rankings $(R_1, R_2, \ldots, R_{i-1})$, and the Kendall tau distance between the set of rankings $(R_1, R_2, \ldots, R_i)$ and X is at most j.

For $i = 1$, there are no previous rankings to consider; however, we write $T[1, s_1, s_2, j]$ for brevity, and for $s_2 > 0$, it is an invalid entry. For $1 < i \leq |\mathcal{R}|$, if either $s_1 > \texttt{KT}(X, R_i)$ or $s_2 > \texttt{KT}(X, (R_1, R_2, \ldots, R_{i-1}))$, then also the entry $T[1, s_1, s_2, j]$ is invalid. We store ∞ for the invalid entries or if the allowed number of swaps is insufficient to achieve the desired Kendall tau distance.

We compute the remaining table entries as follows.

Base Case: For $i = 1$, $0 \leq s_1 \leq \texttt{KT}(X, R_1)$, $s_2 = 0$ and $0 \leq j \leq k$, we compute the table as follows.

$$T[1, s_1, 0, j] = \begin{cases} s_1 \cdot \texttt{cost}(R_1) & \text{If } \texttt{KT}(X, R_1) - s_1 \leq j \\ \infty & \text{otherwise.} \end{cases} \tag{1}$$

Recursive Step: For all $1 < i \leq |\mathcal{R}|$, $0 \leq s_1 \leq \texttt{KT}(X, R_i)$, $0 \leq s_2 \leq \texttt{KT}(X, (R_1, R_2, \ldots, R_{i-1}))$, and $0 \leq j \leq k$, we compute the table entries as follows.

$$T[i, s_1, s_2, j] = \min_{s_2'+s_2''=s_2} T[i-1, s_2', s_2'', j - \texttt{KT}(X, R_i) + s_1] + s_1 \cdot \texttt{cost}(R_i) \tag{2}$$

Next, we prove the correctness of this dynamic programming algorithm in the following lemma.

Lemma 6 ($\star$). *For every $i \in [|\mathcal{R}|]$, $0 \leq s_1 \leq \texttt{KT}(X, R_i)$, $0 \leq s_2 \leq \texttt{KT}(X, (R_1, R_2, \ldots, R_{i-1}))$, and $0 \leq j \leq k$, Eqs. 1 and 2 correctly compute $T[i, s_1, s_2, j]$.*

The minimum cost incurred in performing admissible swap actions on $\mathcal{R}$, such that the Kendall tau distance between $\mathcal{R}$ and X is at most j is $\min_{s_1,s_2} T[|\mathcal{R}|, s_1, s_2, k]$. So we return YES if $\min_{s_1,s_2} T[|\mathcal{R}|, s_1, s_2, k] \leq \texttt{bgt}$, otherwise NO. The correctness follows due to Lemma 6

We compute at most $|\mathcal{R}|^2 m^4 k$ entries and each entry can be computed in time $\mathcal{O}(m^2)$. Thus, the algorithm runs in polynomial time. □

6 Candidate Deletion Kemeny Score

In this section, we begin with the case when $k = 0$, and design a polynomial time algorithm by reducing the problem to the HEAVIEST COMMON INCREASING SUBSEQUENCE (HCIS) on permutations problem. In the HCIS problem, given p sequences of numbers, a weight function w on the numbers, and an integer W, the goal is to decide whether there exists a sequence of numbers with a total weight of at least W that is an increasing subsequence of each of the given p sequences. In our reduction, these sequences are permutations.

Lemma 7 ($\star$). *There exists a polynomial time reduction from* CANDIDATE DELETION-KEMENY SCORE*to* HCIS *on permutations when $k = 0$.*

Proof. Let $\mathcal{I} = (\mathcal{C}, \mathcal{R}, X, \texttt{cost}, \texttt{bgt}, k)$ be an instance of CANDIDATE DELETION-KEMENY SCOREwhere $k = 0$. Let $\mathcal{R} = (R_1, \ldots, R_n)$. We define a function $f \colon \mathcal{C} \rightarrow [m]$ as follows: $f(X(i)) = i$. Recall that X is a permutation over $\mathcal{C}$ and $\mathcal{C}$ has m candidates. We construct a set of permutations $J_1, \ldots, J_n$ as follows. Each J_i is an m-length sequence, where for $j \in [m]$, $J_i(j) = f(R_i(j))$. We can observe that $J_i(j) \neq J_i(k)$ when $j \neq k$ as $R_i(j) \neq R_i(k)$ when $j \neq k$ and f is injective, which implies that the elements of J_i are unique for all i and due to the construction the maximum value of f and the length of J_i are both m. Hence J_i is a permutation for all i. The weight of number i is $w(i) = \texttt{cost}(f^{-1}(i))$. Let $W = \sum_{c \in \mathcal{C}} \texttt{cost}(c) - \texttt{bgt}$. Let $\mathcal{J} = (J_1, \ldots, J_n, w, W)$ be an instance of HCIS on permutations. Correctness can be found in appendix. □

Chan et al. [15] designed an algorithm for HCIS with unit weights. The same algorithm can be used for non-unit weights by storing the maximum weight of the common increasing subsequence as the rank of a match instead of the longest length. We present the complete algorithm for completeness.

Lemma 8. HCIS *can be solved in polynomial time when the sequences are permutations.*

Proof. Let $\mathcal{I} = (J_1, J_2, \ldots, J_m, w, W)$ be the given instance of the problem, where for all $i \in [m]$, J_i is a permutation over $[n]$ and for all $x \in [n]$, $w(x) \geq 0$. Let $J_i^{-1}(x)$ denote the position of x in J_i and let J_i^k denote the prefix of J_i with k elements.

We define the notations *match*, *dominating match*, and *rank* as follows. A match is a m-tuple, $(i_1, \ldots, i_m)$ where $J_1(i_1) = J_2(i_2) = \ldots = J_m(i_m)$, the value of this match is $J_1(i_1)$. A match $(\delta_1, \ldots, \delta_m)$ is called a dominating match of another match $(\theta_1, \ldots, \theta_m)$ if $J_1(\delta_1) < J_1(\theta_1)$ and $\delta_j < \theta_j$ for all $1 \leq j \leq m$. Note that Δ_j denotes the match with the value of j and Δ_j is a unique match because our sequences are permutations. The rank of a match $\Delta = (\delta_1, \ldots, \delta_m)$, denoted by $R(\Delta)$, is the weight of the HCIS of $J_1^{\delta_1}, J_2^{\delta_2}, \ldots, J_m^{\delta_m}$ such that $J_1(\delta_1)$ is the last element of the HCIS. For $\Delta_1, \ldots, \Delta_n$, $R(\Delta_j)$ is computed in increasing order of j as follows,

$$R(\Delta_j) = \begin{cases} w(\Delta_j) & \text{if no match dominates } \Delta_j, \\ w(\Delta_j) + \max\{R(\Delta_k) \mid \Delta_k \text{ dominates } \Delta_j\} & \text{otherwise.} \end{cases} \quad (3)$$

It is easy to see that HCIS is $\max_{\Delta_j} R(\Delta_j)$. For the decision version, we accept if and only if $\max_{\Delta_j} R(\Delta_j) \geq W$.

We will now prove the correctness of the dynamic programming solution through induction on j. Note that because the sequences are permutations, there are n matches with values 1, 2, …, n. We can compute all the matches in time $\mathcal{O}(m \cdot n)$ and we process them in the increasing order of their value i.e., for a match with value j, the ranks of all the matches with value $1, \ldots, j-1$ should have been computed first as a match with value j can only be dominated by a match which has a value less than j.

For the base case, $R(\Delta_1) = w(\Delta_1) = w(1)$ as there is no match that can dominate Δ_1 and hence the HCIS ending with value 1 only has one element with weight $w(1)$. Let us suppose that for all $y < j$, $R(\Delta_y)$ is computed correctly. For the first case assume w_{OPT} as the optimal rank of match Δ_j that is the weight of the sequence $OPT = j$ i.e. the HCIS ending at match Δ_j contains only the element j. It is obvious in this case that the rank computed by Eq. 3 $= w_{OPT}$. For the second case assume w_{OPT} as the optimal rank of the match Δ_j that is weight of the sequence $OPT = \ldots, x, j$. We know that the rank of match Δ_j computed by Eq. 3 $\leq w_{OPT}$ as w_{OPT} is the optimal rank of the match Δ_j. Since x is before j in OPT, x has to be before j in every sequence J_i and $x < j$, hence Δ_x dominates Δ_j which means that the rank of match Δ_j computed by Eq. 3 $\geq w(\Delta_j) + R(\Delta_x) \geq w_{OPT}$. Hence the rank of match Δ_j computed by Eq. 3 $= w_{OPT}$. Hence Eq. 3 correctly computes the rank of all matches.

We precompute all the n matches in time $\mathcal{O}(m \cdot n)$, then for each match we check all the n matches for domination in time $\mathcal{O}(m)$, hence the algorithm runs in time $\mathcal{O}(m \cdot n^2)$ □

Due to Lemma 7 and 8, we have the following result.

Theorem 7. CANDIDATE DELETION-KEMENY SCORE*can be solved in polynomial time when* $k = 0$.

Next, we show that for one ranking (i.e., $|\mathcal{R}| = 1$), the problem is equivalent to the PARTIAL VERTEX COVER (WPVC) problem for permutation graphs. In WPVC, given a vertex-weighted graph G with weight function $w\colon V(G) \to \mathbb{N}$, and integers W, t, the goal is to find a subset $S \subseteq V(G)$ of weight at most W that covers at least t edges, i.e., for at least t edges, at least one of the endpoints is in S. A *permutation graph* is a graph whose vertices represent the elements of a permutation, and whose edges represent pairs of elements that are reversed by the permutation, and we say that such a permutation realises the given permutation graph. The complexity of WPVC for permutation graph is not known. However, if WPVC for permutation graph is NP-hard, then CANDIDATE DELETION-KEMENY SCOREis also NP-hard; and if it is polynomial-time solvable, then CANDIDATE DELETION-KEMENY SCOREis polynomial time solvable for one ranking.

Lemma 9. *There is a polynomial time reduction from* WPVC *on permutation graph to* CANDIDATE DELETION-KEMENY SCORE.

Proof. Let $\mathcal{I} = (G, w, W, t)$ be an instance of WPVC where G is a permutation graph. Let Π be a permutation realising the permutation graph G. Let $n = |V(G)|$. Let $\mathcal{C} = V(G)$, $X = 1 \succ 2 \succ \ldots \succ n$, $R = \Pi$, $\texttt{cost} = w$, $\texttt{bgt} = W$, and $k = |E(G)| - t$. Let $\mathcal{J} = (\mathcal{C}, \mathcal{R}, X, \texttt{cost}, \texttt{bgt}, k)$ be an instance of CANDIDATE DELETION-KEMENY SCORE. Next, we prove the equivalence between the two instances. In the forward direction, let Z be a solution to $\mathcal{I}$. We claim that Z is also a solution to $\mathcal{J}$. Note that the number of edges in $E(G - Z)$ is at most $|E(G)| - t$, thus due to the definition of permutation graph, the number of pairs of vertices such that $i < j$ and $\Pi(i) > \Pi(j)$, where $\{\Pi(i), \Pi(j)\} \subseteq G - Z$, is at most $|E(G)| - t$. Thus, $\texttt{KT}(X|_{\mathcal{C}\setminus Z}, R|_{\mathcal{C}\setminus Z}) \leq |E(G)| - t$. Clearly, $\texttt{cost}(Z) \leq \texttt{bgt}$. In the reverse direction, let Z be a solution to $\mathcal{J}$. Then, we claim that Z is also a solution to $\mathcal{I}$. Clearly, $w(Z) \leq W$. Note that $\texttt{KT}(X, R) = |E(G)|$ by the definition of permutation graph. Since $\texttt{KT}(X|_{\mathcal{C}\setminus Z}, R|_{\mathcal{C}\setminus Z}) \leq |E(G)| - t$, for at least t disagreements, one of the candidate is in Z. Thus, Z covers at least t edges in G. □

Due to Lemma 9, if WPVC on a permutation graph is NP-hard, then CANDIDATE DELETION-KEMENY SCOREis also NP-hard. Obtaining a polynomial-time algorithm for WPVC on a permutation graph is also beneficial due to the following result.

Lemma 10 ($\star$). *There is a polynomial time reduction from* CANDIDATE DELETION-KEMENY SCORE*when* $|\mathcal{R}| = 1$ *to* WPVC *on permutation graph.*

Lemma 9 gives a polynomialâĂŘtime reduction from WPVC on permutation graphs to CANDIDATE DELETION-KEMENY SCORE, and the fact that our construction fixes $|R| = 1$ does not weaken the result, any instance of WPVC is still mapped to an equivalent instance of the CANDIDATE DELETION-KEMENY SCORE. Conversely, Lemma 10 reduces that same $|R| = 1$ variant back to WPVC. Because both reductions operate on the identical restricted case, they establish a full polynomial-time equivalence, which not only yields Theorem 8 but also transfers hardness: if WPVC on permutation graphs were shown NP-hard, the same would hold for CANDIDATE DELETION-KEMENY SCOREwith $|R| = 1$ and hence for CANDIDATE DELETION-KEMENY SCOREin general

Thus, due to Lemma 9, if WPVC on a permutation graph is solvable in polynomial time, then CANDIDATE DELETION-KEMENY SCOREis also solvable in polynomial time for one ranking. Thus, due to Lemma 9 and 10, we have the following result.

Theorem 8. CANDIDATE DELETION-KEMENY SCORE*can be solved in polynomial time for one ranking if and only if* WPVC *can be solved in polynomial time for permutation graphs unless* P = NP.

7 Conclusion

In this paper, we studied the Kemeny Score problem under some well-studied bribery schemes. Unlike many other voting rules, we design polynomial-time algorithms for dollar bribery, swap bribery, voter deletion, the special case of candidate deletion when we want Kendall tau distance 0, and possible Kemeny score where we extend the given partial rankings. Our main open question is to resolve the computational complexity of CANDIDATE DELETION-KEMENY SCORE. We believe that it is NP-hard. Another research direction is to study bribery actions for Kemeny winner. It has been studied for candidate/voter addition/deletion in the literature. It would be interesting to resolve the computational complexity of this bribery action.

References

1. Anand, A., Dey, P.: Distance restricted manipulation in voting. Theor. Comput. Sci. **891**, 149–165 (2021)
2. Bałchanowski, M., Boryczka, U.: A comparative study of rank aggregation methods in recommendation systems. Entropy **25**(1), 132 (2023)
3. Bartholdi, J., Tovey, C.A., Trick, M.A.: Voting schemes for which it can be difficult to tell who won the election. Soc. Choice Welf. **6**, 157–165 (1989)

4. Betzler, N., Bredereck, R., Niedermeier, R.: Theoretical and empirical evaluation of data reduction for exact kemeny rank aggregation. Auton. Agents Multi Agent Syst. **28**(5), 721–748 (2014)
5. Betzler, N., Fellows, M.R., Guo, J., Niedermeier, R., Rosamond, F.A.: Fixed-parameter algorithms for kemeny rankings. Theor. Comput. Sci. **410**(45), 4554–4570 (2009)
6. Betzler, N., Fellows, M.R., Guo, J., Niedermeier, R., Rosamond, F.A.: How similarity helps to efficiently compute kemeny rankings. In: Proceedings of (AAMAS 2009), Budapest, Hungary, 10-15 May 2009, Volume 1, pp. 657–664. IFAAMAS (2009)
7. Biedl, T., Brandenburg, F., Deng, X.: On the complexity of crossings in permutations. Discret. Math. **309**(7), 1813–1823 (2009)
8. Boehmer, N., Bredereck, R., Faliszewski, P., Niedermeier, R.: Winner robustness via swap- and shift-bribery: parameterized counting complexity and experiments. In: IJCAI 2021, pp. 52–58. ijcai.org (2021)
9. Brandt, F., Conitzer, V., Endriss, U., Lang, J., Procaccia, A.D.: Handbook of computational social choice, Cambridge University Press (2016)
10. Bredereck, R., Chen, J., Faliszewski, P., Nichterlein, A., Niedermeier, R.: Prices matter for the parameterized complexity of shift bribery. Inf. Comput. **251**, 140–164 (2016)
11. Bredereck, R., Faliszewski, P., Kaczmarczyk, A., Niedermeier, R., Skowron, P., Talmon, N.: Robustness Among Multiwinner Voting Rules. In: Bilò, V., Flammini, M. (eds.) SAGT 2017. LNCS, vol. 10504, pp. 80–92. Springer, Cham (2017). https://doi.org/10.1007/978-3-319-66700-3_7
12. Bredereck, R., Faliszewski, P., Kaczmarczyk, A., Niedermeier, R., Skowron, P., Talmon, N.: Robustness among multiwinner voting rules. Artif. Intell. **290**, 103403 (2021)
13. Bredereck, R., Faliszewski, P., Niedermeier, R., Talmon, N.: Complexity of shift bribery in committee elections. ACM Trans. Comput. Theory **13**(3), 20:1–20:25 (2021)
14. Caragiannis, I., Kaklamanis, C., Karanikolas, N., Krimpas, G.A.: Evaluating approval-based multiwinner voting in terms of robustness to noise. Auton. Agent. Multi-Agent Syst. **36**, 1–22 (2022)
15. Chan, W.-T., Zhang, Y., Fung, S.P.Y., Ye, D., Zhu, H.: Efficient algorithms for finding a longest common increasing subsequence. In: Deng, X., Du, D.-Z. (eds.) ISAAC 2005. LNCS, vol. 3827, pp. 665–674. Springer, Heidelberg (2005). https://doi.org/10.1007/11602613_67
16. Chen, J., Faliszewski, P., Niedermeier, R., Talmon, N.: Elections with few voters: candidate control can be easy. J. Artif. Intell. Res. **60**, 937–1002 (2017)
17. Davenport, A.J., Kalagnanam, J.: A computational study of the kemeny rule for preference aggregation. In: Proceedings of AAAI 2004, pp. 697–702. AAAI Press / The MIT Press (2004)
18. De, K., Mittal, H., Dey, P., Misra, N.: Parameterized aspects of distinct kemeny rank aggregation. In: Algorithms and Discrete Applied Mathematics - 10th International Conference, CALDAM 2024, Bhilai, India, February 15-17, 2024, Proceedings. Lecture Notes in Computer Science, vol. 14508, pp. 14–28. Springer (2024)
19. Dey, P., Misra, N., Narahari, Y.: Complexity of manipulation with partial information in voting. Theor. Comput. Sci. **726**, 78–99 (2018)
20. Dorn, B., Schlotter, I.: Multivariate complexity analysis of swap bribery. Algorithmica **64**(1), 126–151 (2012)

21. Dwork, C., Kumar, R., Naor, M., Sivakumar, D.: Rank aggregation methods for the web. In: Proceedings of WWW 10, pp. 613–622. ACM (2001)
22. Elkind, E., Faliszewski, P., Slinko, A.: Swap Bribery. In: Mavronicolas, M., Papadopoulou, V.G. (eds.) SAGT 2009. LNCS, vol. 5814, pp. 299–310. Springer, Heidelberg (2009). https://doi.org/10.1007/978-3-642-04645-2_27
23. Faliszewski, P., Gawron, G., Kusek, B.: Robustness of greedy approval rules. In: European Conference on Multi-Agent Systems, pp. 116–133. Springer (2022)
24. Faliszewski, P., Hemaspaandra, E., Hemaspaandra, L.A.: How hard is bribery in elections? J. Artif. Intell. Res. **35**, 485–532 (2009)
25. Faliszewski, P., Manurangsi, P., Sornat, K.: Approximation and hardness of shift-bribery. Artif. Intell. **298**, 103520 (2021)
26. Faliszewski, P., Reisch, Y., Rothe, J., Schend, L.: Complexity of manipulation, bribery, and campaign management in bucklin and fallback voting. Auton. Agents Multi. Agent Syst. **29**(6), 1091–1124 (2015)
27. Fitzsimmons, Z., Hemaspaandra, E.: Complexity of manipulative actions when voting with ties. In: Walsh, T. (ed.) ADT 2015. LNCS (LNAI), vol. 9346, pp. 103–119. Springer, Cham (2015). https://doi.org/10.1007/978-3-319-23114-3_7
28. Fitzsimmons, Z., Hemaspaandra, E.: Kemeny consensus complexity. In: Proceedings of IJCAI 2021, pp. 196–202 (2021)
29. Fitzsimmons, Z., Hemaspaandra, E., Hoover, A., Narváez, D.E.: Very hard electoral control problems. In: AAAI 2019, pp. 1933–1940. AAAI Press, Honolulu, Hawaii, USA (2019)
30. Fomin, F.V., Lokshtanov, D., Raman, V., Saurabh, S.: Fast local search algorithm for weighted feedback arc set in tournaments. In: AAAI 2010, pp. 65–70. AAAI Press, Atlanta, Georgia, USA (2010)
31. Gawron, G., Faliszewski, P.: Robustness of approval-based multiwinner voting rules. In: Pekeč, S., Venable, K.B. (eds.) ADT 2019. LNCS (LNAI), vol. 11834, pp. 17–31. Springer, Cham (2019). https://doi.org/10.1007/978-3-030-31489-7_2
32. George, A., Dimitrakakis, C.: Eliciting kemeny rankings. In: AAAI 2024, pp. 12164–12171. Placeholder Publisher, Placeholder Address (2024)
33. de Haan, R.: Complexity results for manipulation, bribery and control of the kemeny judgment aggregation procedure. In: Proceedings of AAMAS 2017, pp. 1151–1159. ACM (2017)
34. Hemaspaandra, E., Spakowski, H., Vogel, J.: The complexity of kemeny elections. Theor. Comput. Sci. **349**(3), 382–391 (2005)
35. Karia, N., Mallick, F., Dey, P.: How hard is safe bribery? In: Proceedings of AAMAS 2022, pp. 714–722. IFAAMAS (2022)
36. Kemeny, J.G.: Mathematics without numbers. Daedalus **88**(4), 577–591 (1959)
37. Kenyon-Mathieu, C., Schudy, W.: How to rank with few errors. In: Proceedings of ACM Symposium on Theory of Computing, pp. 95–103. ACM, San Diego, California, USA (2007)
38. Kleinberg, J.: Algorithm Design. Addison Wesley, Boston, MA (2006)
39. Knop, D., Koutecký, M., Mnich, M.: Voting and bribing in single-exponential time. ACM Trans. Econo. Comput. **8**(3), 12:1–12:28 (2020)
40. Kusek, B., Bredereck, R., Faliszewski, P., Kaczmarczyk, A., Knop, D.: Bribery can get harder in structured multiwinner approval election. In: Proceedings of AAMAS 2023, pp. 1725–1733. ACM (2023)
41. Li, X., Wang, X., Xiao, G.: A comparative study of rank aggregation methods for partial and top ranked lists in genomic applications. Brief. Bioinform. **20**(1), 178–189 (2019)

42. Misra, N., Sonar, C.: Robustness radius for chamberlin-courant on restricted domains. In: Catania, B., Královič, R., Nawrocki, J., Pighizzini, G. (eds.) SOFSEM 2019. LNCS, vol. 11376, pp. 341–353. Springer, Cham (2019). https://doi.org/10.1007/978-3-030-10801-4_27
43. Rico, N., Vela, C.R., Díaz, I.: Reducing the time required to find the kemeny ranking by exploiting a necessary condition for being a winner. Eur. J. Oper. Res. **305**(3), 1323–1336 (2023)
44. Rico, N., Vela, C.R., Díaz, I.: Runtime bounds prediction for the kemeny problem. J. Ambient. Intell. Humaniz. Comput. **15**(1), 175–185 (2024)

Complexity of Eliminating (Majority) Illusion in Directed Networks

Sougata Jana(✉) and Sanjukta Roy

Indian Statistical Institute, Kolkata, India
{sougatajana_r,sanjukta}@isical.ac.in

Abstract. We study illusion elimination problems on directed social networks where each vertex is colored red or blue. A vertex is under *majority illusion* if it has more red out-neighbors than blue out-neighbors when there are more blue vertices than red vertices in the network. In a more general phenomenon of p-illusion, a vertex under p-illusion has more than p-fraction of red out-neighbors (as opposed to 1/2 for majority). In the directed illusion elimination problem, we recolor the minimum number of vertices so that no vertex is under p-illusion, for $p \in (0, 1)$. Unfortunately, the problem is NP-hard for $p = 1/2$ even when the network is a directed grid. Moreover, the problem is NP-hard and W[2]-hard when parameterized by the number of recolorings for each $p \in (0, 1)$ even on bipartite DAGs. Thus, we cannot get a polynomial time algorithm on DAGs, unless P=NP, nor can we get an FPT algorithm even by combining the solution size and directed graph parameters that measure distance from acyclicity, unless FPT=W[2]. Furthermore, the problem is NP-complete in graphs of degree at most three for $p \in (0, \frac{2}{3}]$. We show that the problem can be solved in polynomial time in structured, sparse networks such as outerplanar networks, outward grids, trees, and cycles. Finally, we show tractable algorithms parameterized by treewidth of the underlying undirected graph and maximum deficiency of the graph combined, and by the number of vertices under illusion.

Keywords: Majority illusion · Directed networks · FPT algorithm

1 Introduction

Social networks influence opinions in both practice and theory [9,17,20]. Our perceptions are heavily filtered by those we follow rather than the objective global truth. This vulnerability is often exploited by political parties or marketing brands through *majority illusion* [29], a social phenomenon where a rare opinion appears to be mainstream because it is adopted by a few highly connected agents.

The implications of the majority illusion extend significantly into strategic communication, particularly within the realms of political campaigning, digital advertising, and the optimization of influence [4,34]. Furthermore, the perceptual distortions due to illusion impact voting behavior [14,32] and various collective

P. Lenzner and D. Schmand (Eds.): SAGT 2026, LNCS 16911, pp. 280–299, 2027.
https://doi.org/10.1007/978-3-032-38782-0_16

(a) Every vertex is under majority illusion: has more red out-neighbors than blue

(b) Blue vertices are under p-illusion for every $p \in (0, 1)$ as they have only red out-neighbors

Fig. 1. Illusions in different networks.

decision-making processes [5,9], as well as the equitable distribution of resources through participatory budgeting [27]. Johnson et al. [25] showed the effects of majority illusion in social network in the decision for getting vaccinated. Schrama et al. [30] showed that the majority illusion can push the entire population from an abundant, high-welfare state to a depleted, low-welfare one. Both works highlight the need for network analysis and network-based policies to prevent misinformation-driven convergence to an undesirable state.

We study the complexity of eliminating illusions in social networks by modifying the opinions of the minimum number of agents. The computational complexity of illusion elimination is highly dependent on the network topology. Fioravantes et al. [19] studied networks as undirected graphs and considered the problem of eliminating the majority illusion. However, in social networks, the influence between the agents is usually not symmetric, i.e. the edge relations are not symmetric. Therefore, we model the network as a directed graph G where the set of vertices V is the set of agents, and an *edge* from agent i to agent j implies that i can be *influenced by* j. Moreover, in directed networks, it is natural to assume that agents are influenced by their out-neighbors and may change opinion due to lobbying or bribery [7,15]. The opinion of an agent is represented by a coloring function $f : V \to \{B, R\}$, where B and R denote blue and red, respectively. For example, the two colors can represent a two party election and if there are more blue voters than red, then we say that blue is the majority.[1] A voter is under *majority illusion* if it has strictly more red out-neighbors than blue out-neighbors. There are instances where some or all vertices are under the majority illusion (see Fig. 1(a)).

In this paper, we initiate the study of the computational question of eliminating illusion in directed graphs by recoloring the minimum number of vertices. We assume that blue is the majority. A graph is *majority illusion-free* if none of its vertices is under majority illusion. We ask can G be illusion-free by recoloring at most k vertices? In a *minimum illusion-free recoloring*, a minimum number of vertices are recolored such that the graph G is illusion-free.

[1] It does not restrict the model to the two party case, when there are multiple parties and one party is majority, then the majority can be represented by blue and all the other parties by red.

Directed Illusion-Free Recoloring (Difr):
Input: $G = (V, E)$, a directed graph, a coloring function $f : V \to \{B, R\}$, and a nonnegative integer k.
Question: Does there exist a (recoloring) function $f' : V \to \{B, R\}$ of f such that G is illusion-free under the coloring f', where $|\{v \mid f(v) \neq f'(v)\}| \leq k$?

The majority illusion is often introduced in the context of elections. However, applications like vaccination provide a more compelling motivation to look beyond the majority. Consider a contact network where each agent is colored according to whether they are vaccinated. For many contagious diseases, achieving herd immunity requires a high global vaccination rate (often well above 50%, and in some cases exceeding 90%) [2,18]. This corresponds to a super-majority i.e., we would require almost 90% of a neighborhood should be vaccinated. Conversely, when the goal is accurate perception of underrepresented groups, it is relevant to consider the status of a subset of neighborhood that is strictly smaller than majority. The network structure can systematically distort the beliefs of individuals about the prevalence of minority attributes (e.g. race, sexual orientation, disability status), leading to misperception that are well documented in studies of social networks and the majority illusion [16,29]. These applications require a definition of illusion that is more general than the majority illusion. We define illusion based on a fraction p that takes a value $> 1/2$ for the former example or a value $< 1/2$ for the latter example.

We define a vertex as under *p-illusion* if a strictly less than p fraction of its out neighbors is blue (see Fig. 1(b)). We study the elimination of p-illusion by editing the vertex colors in directed graphs where we do not impose the assumption that the blue vertices form a majority. Given a rational number $p \in [0, 1]$, we ask whether it is possible to ensure that every voter has at least p-fraction of blue out-neighbors? A graph G is *p-illusion-free* if each vertex in the graph is p-illusion-free. Given a rational $p \in [0, 1]$, we define the following problem.

Directed p-Illusion-Free Recoloring (p-Difr):
Input: $G = (V, E)$, a directed graph, a coloring function $f : V \to \{B, R\}$, and a nonnegative integer k.
Question: Does there exist a (recoloring) function $f' : V \to \{B, R\}$ of f such that G is p-illusion-free under the coloring f', where $|\{v \mid f(v) \neq f'(v)\}| \leq k$?

Note that $p = \frac{1}{2}$ with blue as the strict majority is the Difr problem. The p-illusion elimination problem has been studied for undirected graphs where a certain number of edges can be added and/or deleted [13]. Eliminating illusions by editing edges in directed graphs is trivial in the sense that it does not utilize the topology of the network and depends only on deficiency of the vertices.

1.1 Our Contribution

We initiate the study of eliminating the p-illusion by recoloring the vertices. Furthermore, we initiate the analysis of computational complexity of eliminating majority illusion and p-illusion in directed graphs. In directed graphs, when we recolor a vertex, only its in-neighbors can see it; the out-neighbors remain unaffected, unlike the undirected case. Thus, it may appear that a minimum illusion-free recoloring can be easily found. Indeed, that is the case when we add and/or delete edges of the graph to eliminate majority illusion.[2] However, we show that the recoloring problem is harder. We show that the complexity of the problem depends on three aspects: graph class, graph parameters, and the value of p. We systematically study algorithmic complexity by combining these aspects.

Graph Classes. We primarily focus on cycles, grids, planar graphs, trees, and tree-like graphs. Note that, as the influence between the agents can come from their residential neighborhood or can be constrained by spatial or local interactions, it is natural to assume that the network of social interactions is a planar graph or simply a grid. Similarly, a directed tree or out-tree (also known as arborescence) models hierarchical influence, such as mentorship, organizational chains, or follower cascades, where influence flows outward from central sources.

Parameters. We specifically look at two structural parameters: maximum degree and tree-width of the graph; and the problem specific parameters: solution size k, number of vertices under illusion $|X|$, and maximum deficiency of any vertex D. Deficiency indicates how far a vertex is from being illusion-free. Parameter maximum degree measures the maximum number of agents that are known to an agent and is motivated by the observation that each agent typically only knows a few other agents, and therefore if people only follow who they know, then it yields a graph of bounded degrees [3,10]. As we show that the problem is polynomial time solvable for trees, the parameter treewidth measures a distance from easy instances. In addition, it is a standard parameter for understanding the structure of the graph. Furthermore, since the brute-force method would give an XP algorithm parameterized by the solution size, it is natural to ask if that is the best we can do. Deficiency D measures the perception gap that caused the illusion. Thus, we ask if the problem is easy when there are small number of vertices under illusion or if their illusion is caused by small gap in perception.

Values of p. As we focus on the computational question of eliminating p-illusion, unlike previous work on this problem, we need to understand the role of p in its complexity. It can be easily observed that for large values of p, e.g., in a graph

[2] For example, when we are adding edges to eliminate illusion, it does not depend on the graph, the number of edges we need to add is total 'deficiency' of the vertices under illusion, where deficiency of a vertex is the number of extra red out-neighbors.

with maximum degree Δ, when $p > \frac{\Delta-1}{\Delta}$, all the out-neighbors of each vertex must be blue, consequently, the problem is trivial. However, small values of p, do not create such easy instances.

We begin by showing that DIFR is NP-complete on directed grids. Then, we show that solving p-DIFR is NP-hard even for graphs of degree at most 3 for $p \in (0, \frac{2}{3}]$. Towards this we first show that it is NP-hard on graphs of maximum degree 3 when $p \in (1/3, 2/3]$.

Furthermore, we prove a more general result. We show that p-DIFR is NP-complete and W[2]-hard for any $p \in (0, 1)$ even on bipartite acyclic graphs. This implies that we cannot hope to obtain a fixed parameter tractable (FPT) algorithm parameterized by k, i.e. it cannot be solved in time $f(k)|I|^{\mathcal{O}(1)}$, where f is any computable function of k, and $|I|$ denotes the input size, unless W[2] = FPT.

In all of our hardness reductions, each vertex under illusion needs exactly one additional blue out-neighbor to be illusion-free, i.e., we say that the maximum deficiency of any vertex is at most one. Thus, p-DIFR is paraNP-hard[3] with respect to the maximum deficiency of any vertex. Moreover, since it is hard on DAGs, it is paraNP-hard with respect to the distance from acyclicity, including many directed graph parameters such as directed feedback vertex set, feedback arc set, directed treewidth, directed cutwidth, directed bandwidth, or degreewidth, to name a few.

To understand the true causes of the intractability results, we explore the line between easy and hard graph topologies. We show a dichotomy result as we prove that the p-DIFR is polynomial time solvable when the maximum degree $\Delta \leq 2$. We identify orientations of grid graphs where eliminating p-illusion is solvable in polynomial time. We call them *outward grid graphs*, where the edges are oriented from left to right and from top to bottom. Outward grids naturally model hierarchical or layered information flow, where influence propagates directionally from central sources to peripheral nodes. We establish that p-DIFR can be solved in time $\mathcal{O}(mn\sqrt{mn})$ on an $m \times n$ outward grid G.

We show that p-DIFR is polynomial time solvable not only on out-trees but also when the underlying undirected graph is a tree. In search of tractable cases, we further explore structural parameters. Strengthening our results on trees, we obtain fixed-parameter tractable (FPT) algorithm for p-DIFR parameterized by treewidth of the graph when the maximum deficiency of any vertex is bounded. We show that p-DIFR is solvable in time $\mathcal{O}((2D)^{tw}) \cdot n^{\mathcal{O}(1)}$ on a n-vertex directed graph G with deficiency at most D.

Observe that the problem is NP-hard even when $D = 1$. To eliminate illusion for a vertex, we need to bring down the deficiency to zero. For definitions of treewidth and tree decomposition, see [11]. Finally, we use a simple ILP based formulation to show that p-DIFR is FPT parameterized by the number of vertices under illusion, also, parameterized by the treedepth of the primal and the dual LP separately.

---

[3] The problem is NP-hard even when the parameter is constant, i.e., we cannot even expect to get an XP algorithm with respect to this parameter, unless P= NP.

Our results demonstrate that illusion elimination can be done efficiently when the graph is sparse; however, even though the flow of information might be more structured in acyclic graphs, it does not help in identifying the vertices to be recolored to eliminate illusion. Due to the paucity of space, all omitted proofs are deferred to the full version of the paper [24].

1.2 Related Works

Different variants of the majority illusion elimination problem have been studied from the graph-theoretic perspective [31]. Grandi et al. and Dipple et al. [13, 22] studied the computational questions of eliminating the majority illusion, in *undirected graphs* by editing edges (i.e., adding and/or deleting edges). Grandi et al. [22] showed that the problem of eliminating illusion for the q fraction of vertices is NP-complete in general and W[1]-hard when parameterized by the number of modified edges (i.e., the solution size). Dipple et al. [13] showed that eliminating the majority illusion for all agents is solvable in polynomial time. Unlike undirected graphs, eliminating illusions by editing edges in directed graphs is trivial in the sense that it does not utilize the topology of the network and depends only on deficiency of the vertices.

Conditions for the existence of majority illusion in directed networks and how they differ from the undirected case have been studied [1,8,28]. Majority illusion also affects information diffusion, an extremely well studied problem, where a target set is elected to maximize influence [26]. Bredereck and Elkind [7] considered the problem of maximizing opinion diffusion under majority dynamics with the help of bribery (or influence) and established a connection between their model and the target set problem. Furthermore, controlling the election can be easier by influencing agents' opinion in a social network [15,33]. Our problem connects naturally to graph modification problems, where the goal is to identify a minimum size vertex subset such that deleting or modifying it satisfies a desired graph property [11].

2 Preliminaries

This section introduces our social network model and establishes the notations used throughout the paper. We also present several key observations that provide the foundation for the subsequent analysis and results.

A social network is represented by a directed graph $G = (V, E)$ where vertices are the agents and each vertex has a labeling (or color) $f : V(G) \to \{B, R\}$, where B (R resp.) denotes blue (red resp.).

Notation. We use $[n]$ to denote the set $\{1, 2, \ldots, n\}$. Given a directed graph $G = (V, E)$, we use (v, u) to denote the edge from v to u, for $v, u \in V$. Let $R(V) = f^{-1}(R)$ and $B(V) = V \setminus R(V)$ denote the set of red and blue vertices, respectively. For any vertex $v \in V$, we denote its sets of out-neighbors and in-neighbors by $N^+(v) = \{u \in V : (v, u) \in E\}$ and $N^-(v) = \{u \in V : (u, v) \in E\}$, respectively. Let r_v and b_v be the number of red and blue out-neighbors of v defined as $r_v = |N^+(v) \cap R(V)|$ and $b_v = |N^+(v) \cap B(V)|$, respectively.

A vertex v is considered to be *under illusion* if it possesses a surplus of red out-neighbors; that is, if $r_v > b_v$. We define the *deficiency* of a vertex v, denoted by $def(v)$, as: $def(v) = \max\{0, r_v - b_v\}$. Consequently, the set of illusion vertices, denoted by X, consists of all vertices with positive deficiency: $X = \{v \in V : def(v) > 0\}$.

The *p-deficiency* of a vertex v, denoted by $def_p(v)$, is defined by $def_p(v) = \max\{0, \lceil p \cdot |N^+(v)| \rceil - b_v\}$. A vertex v is under *p-illusion* if $def_p(v) > 0$. Consequently, a vertex v is *p-illusion-free* if $b_v \geq \lceil p \cdot |N^+(v)| \rceil$. Note that $def_{\frac{1}{2}}(v) = \left\lceil \frac{def(v)}{2} \right\rceil$. Let X_p denote the set of vertices under p-illusion, called as the p-illusion vertices.

We say that a *recoloring f' of f produces a solution* to the DIFR (p-DIFR, resp.) problem on G if G has no illusion (p-illusion, resp.) vertex under the coloring f'; the solution is the subset of vertices that are recolored, i.e., $\{v \in V(G) : f(v) \neq f'(v)\}$, and solution size k is the size of this set, that is, the number of recolorings.

2.1 Structural Properties

We begin with some basic observations. First note that to eliminate both illusion and p-illusion, we always recolor a red vertex and never recolor a blue vertex.

Observation 1. *Let v be a vertex under illusion in G. Then, illusion of v can be eliminated by recoloring at least $t_v = \left\lceil \frac{def(v)}{2} \right\rceil$ red out-neighbors of v.*

Each recolored vertex in $N^+(v) \cap R(V)$ increases b_v by 1, thus decreasing $def_p(v)$ by 1. Hence we get the following.

Observation 2. *Let v be a vertex under p-illusion in G. Then, p-illusion of v can be eliminated by recoloring at least $def_p(v)$ red out-neighbors of v.*

3 Hardness Reductions

In this section, we provide four hardness reductions for DIFR and p-DIFR. Observe that given a recoloring, the non-existence of majority illusion or p-illusion can be verified in polynomial time. Thus, our problems are in NP. We prove that DIFR remains NP-complete when restricted to grid graphs and p-DIFR is hard even on bipartite DAGs. Thus, we cannot design polynomial time algorithms for acyclic or planar graphs, unless P=NP. Furthermore, we show that p-DIFR is NP-complete on directed graphs of degree at most three for $p \in (0, \frac{2}{3}]$. We start with the reduction on grid graphs.

3.1 NP-Completeness of DIFR on Grid Graphs

We study the DIFR problem on planar graphs, especially on directed grids. Directed grid is a undirected grid with arbitrary orientations of the edges. The DIFR problem is NP-complete for directed grids. The hardness reduction is from PLANAR MONOTONE RECTILINEAR 3-SAT problem, a restricted variant of 3-SAT. In MONOTONE 3-SAT, each clause is monotone, that is, it consists exclusively of either positive or negative literals. An *incidence graph* of a 3-SAT formula is a bipartite graph. Variables and clauses form the two distinct vertex sets, with an edge connecting a variable to a clause if that variable (as a positive or negative literal) appears in the clause. In a standard *rectilinear embedding* of the incidence graph of PLANAR MONOTONE RECTILINEAR 3-SAT [12], variable vertices are arranged along a central horizontal axis; positive clauses are positioned above this axis, while negative clauses are placed below (see Fig. 3(a)). Each clause is depicted as a horizontal segment connected to its corresponding variables via three vertical segments, referred to as legs. The clauses can be nested so that the graph is still planar.

PLANAR MONOTONE RECTILINEAR 3-SAT.
Input. A 3-CNF formula φ, such that every clause of φ is monotone and consists of three literals and the incidence graph of φ has a rectilinear embedding.
Output. Does there exist a satisfying assignment for φ?

This problem is well known to be NP-complete [12]. We also assume that formula φ consists of distinct clauses.

Theorem 1. DIFR *is NP-complete on directed grids.*

Proof (Proof Sketch). Let φ be an instance of the PLANAR MONOTONE RECTILINEAR 3-SAT problem. Let k be the number of variables in φ. We construct an instance $(\hat{G}, f, k')$ of DIFR. We will first construct a graph G that is a subgraph of a grid graph. The vertex set of G is constructed as follows:

(i) For every variable x, we add two sets of variable vertices, namely the positive variable vertices $\{v_x^i | i \in [\ell_x]\}$ and the negative variable vertices $\{v_{\bar{x}}^i | i \in [\ell_x]\}$, where ℓ_x is a positive integer bounded by a polynomial in the size of formula φ for every x. We fix the value of ℓ_x when the grid embedding is done.
(ii) For every variable x, we add another set of vertices v^{xi}, called the *controllers* of x where $i \in [2\ell_x]$.
(iii) For every clause $c \in \varphi$, we add a clause-vertex v_c and an additional vertex v_c^1. This is the clause gadget for clause c.

The initial color assignment f is as follows: for each variable x, all the variable vertices v_x^i and $v_{\bar{x}}^i$ are colored red, for each $i \in [\ell_x]$, and all the other vertices are colored blue.

We add the following directed edges to the graph G:

(i) For each variable x, we construct a gadget by connecting the edges $(v^{x(2i-1)}, v_x^i)$, $(v^{x(2i-1)}, v_{\bar{x}}^i)$, $(v^{x(2i)}, v_{\bar{x}}^i)$, $(v^{x(2i)}, v_x^{i+1})$ for each $i \in [\ell_x]$ where

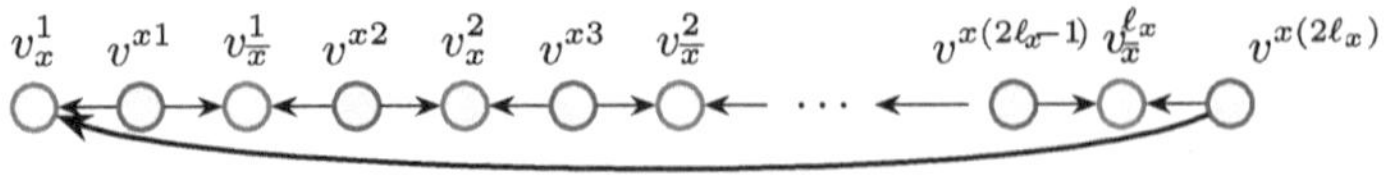

Fig. 2. Variable gadget V_x for variable x.

the index $\ell_x + 1$ is taken modulo ℓ_x (see Fig. 2). Note that the gadget is a cycle in the undirected sense.
We call this undirected cycle so constructed the *variable gadget* associated with the variable x and is denoted by V_x. In this variable gadget, each controller vertex v^{xi} is under illusion.

(ii) For every clause-vertex v_c, if literal x (or $\overline{x}$) is in c, then we add the edge (v_c, v_x^j) (or $(v_c, v_{\overline{x}}^j)$ resp.) for a unique $j \in [\ell_x]$. The value of j depends on the grid embedding; note that v_x^j or $v_{\overline{x}}^j$ are in the variable gadget associated to the variable x.

(iii) Add edge v_c to v_c^1, for every clause-vertex v_c. In clause gadget, the clause-vertex v_c is under illusion.

We show that the constructed graph G is planar by providing the following embedding.

Embedding of G**.** To find a grid embedding of the graph constructed so far, we adapt the planar rectilinear embedding of the incidence graph G_φ of φ. We embed the variable gadget for a variable x along the horizontal and vertical legs connected to x in the rectilinear embedding (see Fig. 3). Note that each clause is monotone, i.e., it is either a positive or negative clause.

Embedding the Clause Gadget. Let c be a clause of size three in formula φ. In the embedding of G, we position the clause vertex v_c at the intersection of the clause's horizontal segment and its central vertical leg in the rectilinear embedding. For example, in Fig. 3(b) vertex v_{c_1} is placed at a coordinate corresponding to the position marked as c_1 in Fig. 3(a). For positive clauses, an auxiliary vertex v_c^1 is placed above v_c (not shown in the figure), while for negative clauses, it is placed below.

Embedding the Variable Gadget. We embed the variable gadget so that it maintains the connection to its clause vertices. The variable gadget V_x for each variable x is routed along the existing connections in the rectilinear embedding to reach each of its clauses. In particular, if the clause is connected to the variable by the central leg, then the variable gadget reaches the same column as the clause vertex and the row immediately below (resp. above) the clause vertex for a positive (resp. a negative) clause. On the other hand, if the clause is connected to the variable by a leg that is left (resp. right) to the variable, then the variable gadget reaches the same row as the clause vertex, and the column immediately left (resp. right) to the clause vertex. For example, suppose that the variable x

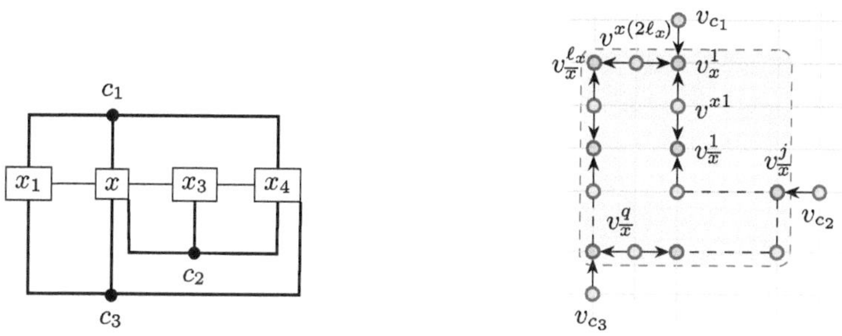

(a) Rectilinear embedding: variable vertex x belongs to a positive clause c_1 and two negative clauses c_2, c_3.

(b) Grid embedding of gadget V_x for variable x (in the left figure). The dashed lines indicate subpaths of the gadget.

Fig. 3. Grid reduction excerpt from Theorem 1.

appears in one positive clause c_1 and two negative clauses c_2 and c_3 (Fig. 3(a)). The construction proceeds as follows (see Fig. 3(b)):

Connecting the Gadget for x to the Clauses Containing x: Without loss of generality, suppose that the vertex v_x^1 is placed at the same column as v_{c_1} and the row immediately below v_{c_1}. Then, the positive literal vertex v_x^1 is connected to the positive clause vertex v_{c_1}, with the variable gadget following the vertical leg from clause c_1 to the variable's horizontal axis.

The path continues along the vertical and horizontal segments to reach the row of the vertex v_{c_2}. Observe that c_2 is connected to x by its left leg. Thus, the path reaches the column immediately left to the column of v_{c_2}. A directed edge $(v_{c_2}, v_{\overline{x}}^j)$ is added from the clause vertex v_{c_2} to the corresponding negative variable literal $v_{\overline{x}}^j$.

The gadget then traverses back along the horizontal lines to reach the column of the vertex v_{c_3} as x and c_3 are in the same column in the rectilinear embedding (in Fig. 3(a)). We add the edge $(v_{c_3}, v_{\overline{x}}^q)$ for some index $q \in [\ell_x]$.

Completing the Variable Gadget of x: Finally, the variable gadget returns via the vertical leg of c_3, running parallel to its initial trajectory along the leg of c_1. The cycle is closed by placing a controller vertex $v^{x(2\ell_x)}$ between $v_{\overline{x}}^{\ell_x}$ and v_x^1, with a directed edge to v_x^1, completing the cycle of the variable gadget of x (see the highlighted part in Fig. 3(b)).

Let us denote the graph constructed using the clause-variable connections as defined above by G.

Properties of G. In the construction of G and f we maintain the following properties. We use these properties to prove structural lemmas for G.

(P1) Each clause vertex and each controller vertex is under majority illusion with deficiency one.

(P2) By construction, the variable gadget for each variable forms a simple cycle (in undirected sense) along the grid lines.

(P3) Each clause vertex is connected to a red vertex corresponding to each literal that appear in it.
(P4) The subpath of a variable gadget that connects two of its clauses is always on odd number of vertices. Moreover, the distance between the clause vertices are large enough to avoid any overlap or intersection between two paths from variable gadgets of two distinct variables. A distance bounded by polynomial in the size of φ is sufficient to maintain this property.
(P5) Given an embedding of G, we define ℓ_x as the number of negative variable vertices i.e., $v^i_{\overline{x}}$ (and equivalently, the number of positive variable vertices i.e., v^i_x) on the variable gadget for variable x. Thus, ℓ_x is bounded by a polynomial in size of φ.
(P6) Each two consecutive columns (and rows) start with different colors, i.e., if one starts with red, the next one starts with blue.

We begin by showing that we are close to constructing a grid.

Lemma 1. *The graph G is a subgraph of a grid; specifically, G can be obtained by deleting a set of vertices and edges from a grid graph. Moreover, in G there are no two consecutive red vertices in a row or in a column.*

Proof. By the above construction, the graph G is embedded into the plane using only orthogonal segments (horizontal and vertical lines). Since all vertices are positioned at the intersections of a discrete rectangular coordinate system and no two edges cross except at these vertices, by (P2) and (P4), the graph G is isomorphic to a subgraph of a sufficiently large rectangular grid.

Now we prove the second part of the statement of the lemma. According to the construction of the variable gadget, every red variable vertex v^i_x or $v^i_{\overline{x}}$ is preceded and followed by a blue controller vertex v^{xj} for each $i \in [\ell_x], j \in [2\ell_x]$. Since we are not allowed to cross two variable gadgets, it is impossible for two red vertices to be next to each other. Additionally, by (P6) of the construction, we know that no two columns (or rows) have red vertex in the same row (resp. column). Hence the Lemma 1 follows. ◇

Therefore, G is a subgraph of a grid. We now construct a grid graph $\hat{G}$ from G.

Construction of the Grid $\hat{G}$: In the graph G, it may be possible that some vertices as well as some edges are missing. To complete the grid, we add a dummy blue vertex (say, d) at an empty position and set d as the out-neighbor of the vertices around it in the grid. Due to second part of Lemma 1, we can add each missing edge with blue vertex as the head (that is, receives the edge). Thus, we ensure that no dummy vertex is under illusion.

We set $k' = \sum_{x \in Var(\varphi)} \ell_x$ where $Var(\varphi)$ denotes the set of variables in the formula φ. Then k' is polynomially bounded by $|\varphi|$, the size of the formula φ using (P5). So, we have the required constructions for the reduction. Thus, the construction can be done in polynomial time. We are left with the prove of equivalence of the DIFR problem and the PLANAR MONOTONE RECTILINEAR 3-SAT problem. The proof of correctness is in the full version. □

We observe that Theorem 1 additionally shows that the undirected version of the problem (as studied in [19]) is NP-hard for subgraphs of grids. However, it is not clear if the undirected version of the problem remains hard on grid graphs. This is because in the construction of Theorem 1, the graph G is a subgraph of grid and removing the orientation of the edges in G does not change if a vertex is under illusion. However, the orientation of edges in the graph $\hat{G}$ is crucial to keep the red vertices illusion-free and the controller vertices under illusion.

Corollary 1. *Given an undirected graph G and a coloring function $f : V(G) \to \{B, R\}$, deciding if recoloring k vertices eliminates majority illusion is NP-hard even when G is a subgraph of a grid.*

3.2 Hardness of P-Difr on Bipartite DAGs

Now we study the computational difficulty of the p-Difr problem. We present a reduction from the classical NP-complete problem Hitting Set. In p-Difr, each vertex under p-illusion requires a certain fraction of its out-neighbors be recolored blue in order to eliminate the p-illusion. These requirements can be viewed as demanding that at least a prescribed number of vertices be chosen from specific neighborhoods, precisely mirroring the hitting requirement in set systems.

Hitting Set.
Input: A universe U, a family $\mathcal{A}$ of sets over U, and a nonnegative integer k.
Question: Does there exist a subset $U' \subseteq U$ of size at most k that has a nonempty intersection with all elements of $\mathcal{A}$?

We have the following result.

Theorem 2. *p-Difr is NP-complete and W[2]-hard for any $p \in (0,1)$ even on acyclic bipartite graphs.*

Proof (Proof Sketch). We show this by providing a polynomial time reduction from Hitting Set to p-Difr that preserves the parameter, solution size. Let $U = \{u_1, u_2, \ldots, u_n\}$ be the universe and $\mathcal{A} = \{A_1, A_2, \ldots, A_m\}$ be the family of sets of sizes $d_1, d_2, \ldots, d_m$ respectively, where $\min_{j\in[m]} d_j > \left\lceil \frac{1}{p} \right\rceil$. Let (U, A, k) be an instance of the Hitting Set. We will now construct the graph for the p-Difr problem (see Fig. 4).

(i) For each element u_i, create a red vertex r_i and for each set A_j, create a blue vertex v_j. Create x dummy blue vertices $b_1, b_2, \ldots, b_x$, where $x = \left\lceil \frac{pd}{1-p} \right\rceil - 1$ and $d = \max_{j\in[m]} d_j$.
(ii) For each $u_i \in A_j$, add edge (v_j, r_i), and add edges (v_j, b_ℓ), for $\ell = 1, 2, \ldots, x_j$, for each $j \in [m]$, where x_j is a natural number such that $\left\lfloor \frac{pd_j - 1}{1-p} \right\rfloor \leq x_j < \left\lceil \frac{pd_j}{1-p} \right\rceil$. Note that the number x_j exists since $p < 1$ and $d_j > \left\lceil \frac{1}{p} \right\rceil$ (i.e., $pd_j - 1 > 0$).

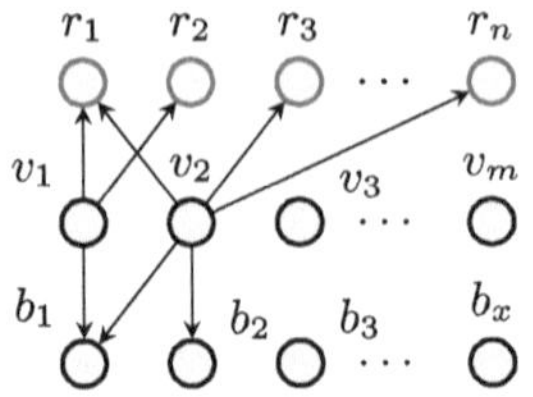

Fig. 4. Construction in Theorem 2, with $A_1 = \{u_1, u_2\}$, $A_2 = \{u_1, u_3, u_n\}$

Let us call the graph so created as $G = (V, E)$. This completes the construction. It can be done in polynomial time. We show the equivalence proof in the full version. □

3.3 p-DIFR for Degree Three Directed Graphs

In Theorem 1, we showed that DIFR is NP-hard for graphs of degree at most four. We strengthen the result and show that p-DIFR is NP-complete for $p \in (0, \frac{1}{3}] \cup (\frac{1}{3}, \frac{2}{3}]$, and is solvable in polynomial time for $p \in (\frac{2}{3}, 1)$, when the degree of each vertex in the graph is at most three. Note that, for $p \in (\frac{2}{3}, 1)$, we need every out-neighbor of a vertex to be blue in order to be p-illusion-free, so p-DIFR is trivially polynomial time solvable in this case. We prove the NP-completeness for $p \in (\frac{1}{3}, \frac{2}{3}]$ by a reduction from the 3-REGULAR VERTEX COVER Problem [21].

We provide a reduction from a 3-regular VERTEX COVER instance H, where in G, we create a red vertex for each vertex in H and a blue edge-vertex for each edge in H. The out-neighbors of an edge-vertex are its endpoints in H and it has a personal blue out-neighbor. We show that a subset of k vertices cover all the edges in H if and only if recoloring the corresponding red vertices in G eliminates the p-illusion of the edge-vertices for $p \in (1/3, 2/3]$.

3-REGULAR VERTEX COVER: *Input*: A 3-regular undirected graph $H = (U, F)$ and a nonnegative integer k.

Question: Does there exist a subset $C \subseteq U$ with $|C| \leq k$ such that every edge has at least one end point in C?

Theorem 3. *p-DIFR is NP-complete on graphs of maximum degree three for $p \in (\frac{1}{3}, \frac{2}{3}]$.*

It remains to show that it is NP-complete when $p \in (0, \frac{1}{3}]$. Note that for $p \in (0, \frac{1}{3}]$, a vertex under p-illusion needs one blue out-neighbor to be p-illusion-free, that is, a vertex is under p-illusion if all its out-neighbors are red. We start from a 3-HITTING SET instance and modify the reduction in Theorem 2 by omitting the vertices $\{b_1, \dots, b_x\}$ in the construction to obtain the following result.

Proposition 1. *p-DIFR is NP-complete on graphs of degree at most 3 for $p \in (0, \frac{1}{3}]$.*

4 Polynomial Time Solvable Topologies

Although the problem is NP-complete on grids, we identify orientations of the grid where the problem can be solved in polynomial time. Furthermore, we obtain a dichotomy by showing that the problem is easy on graphs of maximum degree two, even though the problem is NP-complete on graphs of maximum degree three. We begin by establishing a basic observation for directed cycles, showing that eliminating p-illusions in these structures is straightforward. We then extend our analysis to outward grids and cycles before concluding with a specialized algorithm for trees.

Observe that The p-DIFR problem on directed cycles can be solved by recoloring all red vertices. Before we explain the algorithm for cycles, we state a simple reduction rule that will be used in multiple algorithms.

Reduction Rule 1. *If a vertex in the graph G has only one out-neighbor v that is red, then recolor v.*

Rule 1 is *safe*, as the vertex has only one red out-neighbor, so we need to recolor it to remove the p-illusion of the vertex.

Note that in the graph classes, namely, cycles and outward grids, the number of out-neighbors are bounded by two. This inherent sparsity simplifies the elimination of illusion and p-illusion. We have the following observation.

Observation 3. *Suppose $G = (V, E)$ is a directed graph with $|N^+(v)| \leq 2$ for every $v \in V$. Then,*

(i) For $p > \frac{1}{2}$, the problem becomes trivial, as resolving all illusions merely requires recoloring every red vertex except for the red vertices that have no in-neighbors.
(ii) For $p \leq \frac{1}{2}$, the notions of illusion and p-illusion of a vertex v are equivalent, i.e., a solution for DIFR *yields a solution for p-*DIFR *and vice-versa.*

Thus, we assume $p \leq 1/2$ and solve for DIFR in cycles and outward grids.

Proposition 2. *The p-*DIFR *problem on an n-vertex graph whose underlying undirected graph is a cycle can be solved in time $\mathcal{O}(n)$.*

In contrast to Theorem 1 on grids, we show that not all orientations of grid poses the hardness. We identify a class of oriented grids, called the *outward grids* where the problem is solvable in polynomial time. Recall that an *outward grid* is a directed grid such that it has a planar embedding where the out-neighbors of a vertex v are the vertices to the right of v and below v.

Theorem 4. *Let $G = (V, E)$ be an $m \times n$ outward grid. Then, p-*DIFR *on G can be solved in time $\mathcal{O}(mn\sqrt{mn})$.*

Proof. Given G is an outward grid. Since an outward gird is defined as a directed grid such that it has an embedding where the out-neighbors of a vertex v are the vertices to the right of v and below v. The deficiency of a vertex under illusion is either 1 or 2 since each vertex has at most two in-neighbors and at most two out-neighbors. Observe that a vertex with deficiency 1 has exactly one out-neighbor.

Algorithm.

Step 1 Eliminate illusion of the vertices with deficiency 1 using Rule 1.
Step 2 Construct an auxiliary undirected graph $H = (R(V), E')$, where $R(V)$ is the set of red vertices, and $E' = \{\{a, b\} : N^+(x) = \{a, b\}$ for some $x \in X\}$.
Step 3 Find a minimum vertex cover of H.
Step 4 Recolor the minimum vertex cover.

Correctness. We first eliminate illusion of the vertices with deficiency 1 using Rule 1, which states that if a vertex in the graph G has only one out-neighbor v that is red, then recolor v.

After exhaustively apply Rule 1, each vertex of G that is under illusion has deficiency 2. We remove their illusion in the following way. First, we construct an auxiliary graph H. For every $x \in X$ (set of illusion vertices), we have that $N^+(x) = \{a, b\}$, for some $a, b \in R(V)$, that is, the two out-neighbors of x are red. We construct an undirected graph $H = (R(V), E')$, where $R(V)$ is the set of red vertices, and $E' = \{\{a, b\} : N^+(x) = \{a, b\}$ for some $x \in X\}$. That is, we get E' by connecting the two red out-neighbors for each illusion vertex. In Step 4 of the algorithm we recolor a subset of red vertices that forms a vertex cover of H. We show that it removes illusion for each vertex of X, and does so with the minimum number of recolorings. We need to recolor exactly one red out-neighbor for every vertex under illusion since to remove illusion we must recolor at least $\lceil \frac{def(x)}{2} \rceil$ red out-neighbors for every illusion vertex x (Observation 1). Therefore, by choosing a minimum vertex cover, we are guaranteed that we recolor the minimum number of vertices.

Finally, we show that the vertex cover of H can be found in polynomial time by finding a maximum matching in H as H is a bipartite graph.

Claim. H is acyclic.

Proof. We show that H has no cycle. Observe that no cycle of length two is possible. First we show that H has no 3-cycle (a_1, b_1, a_2). Thus, we show if $N^+(x_1) = \{a_1, b_1\}$, $N^+(x_2) = \{a_2, b_1\}$ for some $x_1, x_2 \in X$ and $a_1, a_2, b_1 \in R(V)$, then there exist no $x_3 \in X$ such that $N^+(x_3) = \{a_1, a_2\}$. We show it by contradiction.

Suppose that a vertex x_3 with the above property exists in X. Then we have the two cases as depicted in Fig. 5: either x_1 is at a higher level than x_2, or x_1 is at a lower level than x_2.

In both the cases, for existence of the vertex $x_3 \in X$ with neighborhood $N^+(x_3) = \{a_1, a_2\}$, we need a_1 and a_2 to be in two consecutive levels, which is not possible. This proves that there is no 3-cycles in H. Similarly, we can show H has no cycle. Thus, we prove the claim. ◇

To complete the proof of the theorem, it remains to show the running time of the algorithm. We Construct H in polynomial time. Then, we find a maximum matching in H using Hopcroft-Karp [23]. Finally, find a minimum vertex cover from the maximum matching (using König's theorem) and recolor the red vertices in the cover. Thus, the algorithm runs in polynomial time. For illusion

Fig. 5. The two cases in the proof of Theorem 4.

vertices with deficiency one, we need $\mathcal{O}(mn)$ time. For illusion vertices with deficiency two, we need $\mathcal{O}(|E'|\sqrt{|R|}) = \mathcal{O}(mn\sqrt{mn})$ time. Hence, the total run time is $\mathcal{O}(mn + mn\sqrt{mn}) = \mathcal{O}(mn\sqrt{mn})$. □

We focus on directed trees. For out-trees (all edges going away from root and from parent to children), we simply need to recolor minimum number of red children for each vertex that is under p-illusion. The problem is more involved when we consider arbitrary directed trees. We devise a dynamic programming algorithm. We consider an arbitrary fixed ordering of the vertices in T, in which in-children of a vertex precedes its out-children.

Proposition 3. *p-DIFR on an n-vertex directed tree can be solved in time $\mathcal{O}(n^4)$.*

5 Parameterized Algorithms

This section establishes the fixed-parameter tractability of p-DIFR under different parameterizations. We first present an FPT algorithm parameterized by the treewidth of the graph and the maximum deficiency. We present a PTAS for the p-DIFR problem on planar graphs. Subsequently, we provide FPT algorithms parameterized by the number of vertices under p-illusion and the treedepth of the constraints matrix of the ILP formulation of p-DIFR separately.

5.1 FPT Algorithm Parameterized by Treewidth and Maximum Deficiency

The NP-hardness even on bipartite DAGs, eliminates the possibility of designing FPT algorithm parameterized by most directed width parameters including directed treewidth, directed cutwidth, digraph bandwidth, degreewidth as all of these measure the distance from acyclicity. We begin with a detailed construction of the treewidth-based algorithm.

Theorem 5. *Let G be an n-vertex directed graph with deficiency at most D and tree width tw. Then the p-DIFR problem on G is solvable in time $\mathcal{O}((2D)^{tw}) \cdot n^{\mathcal{O}(1)}$.*

The above theorem has applications to classes of planar graphs, called the outerplanar graphs. An embedding of a graph $G = (V, E)$ is 1-outerplanar, if it is planar, and all vertices lie on the exterior face. For $\lambda \geq 2$, an embedding of a graph $G = (V, E)$ is λ-outerplanar, if it is planar, and when all vertices on the outer face are deleted, then a $(\lambda - 1)$-outerplanar embedding of the resulting graph is obtained. A graph is λ-outerplanar, if it has a λ-outerplanar embedding. It is known that the treewidth of a λ-outerplanar graph $G = (V, E)$ is at most $3\lambda - 1$ [6]. Thus, we have the following corollary.

Corollary 2. *p-*DIFR *can be solved in polynomial-time on an n-vertex λ-outerplanar graph.*

Proof. The proof follows immediately from Theorem 5. Since the treewidth of a λ-outerplanar graph is at most $3\lambda - 1$, we can solve the p-DIFR problem in time $\mathcal{O}(n^{3\lambda-1})$ (note that here the maximum degree, $\triangle \leq n$). □

5.2 A PTAS for Planar Graphs

We use the classical layering technique introduced by [4] for designing approximation algorithms on planar graphs. On a high level, we break the input graph into layers to solve the problem optimally in each layer. Then we take a union of these solutions to return a feasible solution for the original input. The proof of the following theorem follows directly from [19]. We have a similar result for the DIFR problem.

Theorem 6. *For any given $\varepsilon > 0$, there exists an approximation algorithm which computes the solution of the p-*DIFR *problem on a planar graph in $O(n^{1/\varepsilon})$ time and computes a solution which is $(1+\varepsilon)$-times the optimum.*

5.3 Formulation of ILP and the FPT Algorithms

We show that the p-DIFR problem is fixed-parameter tractable with respect to the number of vertices under p-illusion. We first formulate the problem as an Integer Linear Program (ILP), which serves as the basis for developing the subsequent FPT algorithms.

Let us define a binary variable for every red vertex in the graph.

$$\text{Let } x_u = \begin{cases} 1, \text{if } u \text{ is recolored} \\ 0, \text{otherwise} \end{cases}$$

$$\texttt{ILP-}p\texttt{-DIFR:} \quad \textit{minimize} \quad \sum_{u \in R(V)} x_u$$

Subject to the constraints,

$$\sum_{u \in N^+(v)} x_u \geq def_p(v) \quad \forall\, v \in X_p, \qquad (p\text{-illusion-free})$$

$$x_u \in \{0, 1\} \quad \forall\, u \in R(V). \qquad (\text{feasibility})$$

Inequalities (p-illusion-free) say that among the red out-neighbors of v, at least $def_p(v)$ must be recolored. The inequalities in (feasibility) represent the binary choice of whether or not to recolor a given red vertex.

Observation 4. *The ILP formulated above correctly characterizes the p-DIFR problem, and its optimal solution corresponds to an optimal recoloring.*

Proof. Observation 2 implies that if Equation (p-illusion-free) is satisfied for a vertex v, then v is p-illusion-free. Observe that the feasibility set of the ILP is always non-empty as there always exists an p-illusion-free recoloring by labeling all vertices to blue. Thus, by minimizing the objective function, the above ILP produces an optimal solution. □

Using the defined ILP, we obtain the following result regarding p-DIFR.

Corollary 3. *p-DIFR can be solved in time FPT parameterized by the number of vertices under p-illusion. Furthermore, it is FPT parameterized by the primal treedepth of ILP-p-DIFR.*

6 Conclusion

In this work, we introduce and study majority illusion elimination on directed graphs, by recoloring a minimum number of vertices so that no vertex remains under illusion. We establish that the problem is NP-complete on grids and contrast it with the positive result on an oriented grids, called outward grid. We extend the concept to p-illusion and show it remains W[2]-hard even on DAGs when deficiencies are one. On the other hand, we show a polynomial time algorithm for trees and an FPT algorithm parameterized by treewidth and deficiency. We also showed that the problem is hard on bounded degree graphs. Our work opens several directions for future research. First, is it true that p-DIFR is NP-complete for $p < \frac{\Delta-1}{\Delta}$ for each $\Delta > 3$? Second, can p-DIFR admit FPT algorithm or polynomial kernel with respect to treewidth? Next, what are the best possible approximation algorithms for general graphs? Finally, which additional structures can yield more efficient algorithms, specifically for p-illusion elimination?

Acknowledgment. SR is supported by ANRF ECRG grant ANRF/ECRG/2025/001517/PMS.

References

1. Anastos, M., Lamaison, A., Steiner, R., Szabó, T.: Majority colorings of sparse digraphs. E-JC, P2–31 (2021)
2. Anderson, R.M., May, R.M.: Infectious Diseases of Humans: Dynamics and Control. Oxford University Press, Oxford (1992)

3. Bachrach, Y., Kohli, P., Kolmogorov, V., Zadimoghaddam, M.: Optimal coalition structure generation in cooperative graph games. In: AAAI, pp. 81–87 (2013)
4. Baker, B.S.: Approximation algorithms for np-complete problems on planar graphs. J. ACM (JACM) **41**(1), 153–180 (1994)
5. Bara, O.L., Turrini, P.: Predicting voting outcomes in presence of communities. In: AAMAS, pp. 151–159 (2021)
6. Bodlaender, H.L.: A partial k-arboretum of graphs with bounded treewidth. TCS, **209**(1-2), 1–45 (1998)
7. Bredereck, R., Elkind, E.: Manipulating opinion diffusion in social networks. IJCAI (2017)
8. Broersma, N.: Extending the graph theory of majority illusions. Master's thesis (2025)
9. Castiglioni, M., Ferraioli, D., Gatti, N.: Election control in social networks via edge addition or removal. In: AAAI, vol. 34, pp. 1878–1885 (2020)
10. Cseh, Á., Irving, R.W., Manlove, D.F.: The stable roommates problem with short lists. Theory Comput. Syst. **63**(1), 128–149 (2019)
11. Cygan, M., et al.: Parameterized Algorithms, vol. 5. Springer, Heidelberg (2015). https://doi.org/10.1007/978-3-319-21275-3
12. De Berg, M., Khosravi, A.: Optimal binary space partitions for segments in the plane. IJCGA **22**(03), 187–205 (2012)
13. Dippel, J., La Tour, M.D., Niu, A., Roy, S., Vetta, A.: Eliminating majority illusion is easy. In: AAAI, vol. 39, pp. 13763–13770 (2025)
14. Doucette, J.A., Tsang, A., Hosseini, H., Larson, K., Cohen, R.: Inferring true voting outcomes in homophilic social networks. In: AAMAS, vol. 33, pp. 298–329 (2019)
15. Faliszewski, P., Gonen, R., Koutecký, M., Talmon, N.: Opinion diffusion and campaigning on society graphs. J. Log. Comput. **32**(6), 1162–1194 (2022)
16. Scott, L.: Feld: why your friends have more friends than you do. Am. J. Sociol. **96**(6), 1464–1477 (1991)
17. Ferrara, E.: Twitter spam and false accounts prevalence, detection and characterization: a survey. arXiv preprint arXiv:2211.05913 (2022)
18. Fine, P., Eames, K., Heymann, D.L.: Herd immunity: a rough guide. Clin. Infect. Dis. **52**(7), 911–916 (2011)
19. Fioravantes, F., Lahiri, A., Lauerbach, A., Sabater, L., Sieper, M.D., Wolf, S.: Eliminating majority illusion. In: AAMAS, pp. 749–757 (2025)
20. Fujiwara, T., Müller, K., Schwarz, C.: The effect of social media on elections: evidence from the united states. JEEA **22**, 1495–1539 (2024)
21. Michael, R., Garey, D.S.J.: Computers and intractability: a guide to the theory of np-completeness (1990)
22. Grandi, U., Kanesh, L., Lisowski, G., Sridharan, R., Turrini, P.: Identifying and eliminating majority illusion in social networks. In: AAAI, vol. 37, pp. 5062–5069 (2023)
23. John, E., Hopcroft, R.M.: Karp: an n5/2 algorithm for maximum matchings in bipartite graphs. SIAM J. Comput. **2**(4), 225–231 (1973)
24. Jana, S., Roy, S.: Eliminating illusion in directed networks (2026)
25. Johnson, N.F.: The online competition between pro-and anti-vaccination views. Nature **582**(7811), 230–233 (2020)
26. Kempe, D., Kleinberg, J., Tardos,É.: Influential nodes in a diffusion model for social networks. In: ICALP, pp. 1127–1138. Springer, Heidelberg (2005). https://doi.org/10.1007/11523468_91

27. Kempe, D., Yu, S., Vorobeychik, Y.: Inducing equilibria in networked public goods games through network structure modification. arXiv preprint arXiv:2002.10627 (2020)
28. Kreutzer, S., Oum, S., Seymour, P., van der Zypen, D., Wood, D.R.: Majority colourings of digraphs. E-JC, P2–25 (2017)
29. Lerman, K., Yan, X., Xin-Zeng, W.: The "majority illusion" in social networks. PLoS ONE **11**(2), e0147617 (2016)
30. Schrama, N., Tilman, A.R., Vasconcelos, V.V.: Majority illusion drives the spontaneous emergence of alternative states in common-pool resource games with network-based information. iScience (2025)
31. Venema-Los, M., Christoff, Z., Grossi, D.: On the graph theory of majority illusions. In: EUMAS, pp. 17–31. Springer, Heidelberg (2023). https://doi.org/10.1007/978-3-031-43264-4_2
32. Wilder, B., Vorobeychik, Y.: Controlling elections through social influence. arXiv preprint arXiv:1711.08615 (2017)
33. Wu, J., Estornell, A., Kong, L., Vorobeychik, Y.: Manipulating elections by changing voter perceptions. In: IJCAI, pp. 557–563 (2022)
34. Zhou, X., Zhang, Z.: Maximizing influence of leaders in social networks. In: Proceedings of the 27th ACM SIGKDD Conference on Knowledge Discovery & Data Mining, pp. 2400–2408 (2021)

Leveraging Matchings in Constrained Fair Division with a Conflict Graph

Evangelos Markakis[1,2,3(✉)] and Michalis Samaris[1]

[1] Athens University of Economics and Business, Athens, Greece
{markakis,michsam}@aueb.gr
[2] Archimedes, Athena Research Center, Athens, Greece
[3] Input Output Group (IOG), Athens, Greece

Abstract. We study the problem of allocating indivisible goods under constraints, expressed via a conflict graph G. In such an instance, the m items are the vertices of G and connected items cannot be allocated in the same bundle. Under this model, it is already known that EF1 allocations may not exist. Our main contribution is an analysis parametrized by the maximum degree $\Delta(G) = \Delta$ on the existence and computation of complete EF1 allocations. We address this question in various cases by leveraging results from matching theory. First, we provide a tight existence result for agents with ordered valuations and for the broader class of tiered valuations. We present an algorithm that returns an EF1 allocation when the number of items does not exceed a specific bound. This bound is determined by n and Δ, where n is the number of agents, and it is tight when Δ is greater than $2n/3$. We also construct an approximation algorithm for higher values of m. We then move to general additive valuations, where the problem becomes more challenging. Given the current impossibility results, we focus on the case where m is at most $2n$ and provide an almost complete picture for the instances that admit EF1 allocations, by combining Round Robin with matchings.

Keywords: Fair Division · Conflict Graph · Envy-Freeness · EF1

1 Introduction

Fair Division with indivisible items has attracted significant research interest in the recent years. This can be evidenced by the plethora of new results within the last decade, as exhibited in surveys such as [1], but also by the emergence of motivating applications, including course allocation algorithms [9], and food donation programs [25], among others. The main question in this context is to derive fair allocations of the available resources and several fairness criteria have been proposed, as a way to alleviate the fact that more traditional fairness notions, such as envy-freeness and proportionality fail to exist.

Among the various relaxations of envy-freeness that have been suggested, our work focuses on the well-known EF1 criterion (*envy-freeness up to one good*)

P. Lenzner and D. Schmand (Eds.): SAGT 2026, LNCS 16911, pp. 300–318, 2027.
https://doi.org/10.1007/978-3-032-38782-0_17

defined by [9]. An allocation is said to be EF1 if for any pair of agents i, j, for which agent i envies the bundle of agent j, the envy is eliminated after the hypothetical removal of some item from the bundle of j. This is a concept that can be easily satisfied whenever there are no further constraints on the allocation space. Namely, both a simple round-robin algorithm, as well as the envy cycle elimination algorithm by [21] are guaranteed to produce EF1 assignments.

The status regarding the existence of EF1 allocations however changes drastically when there are additional restrictions on the feasible assignments. Recently, there have been various works that study fair division problems under constraints [27], motivated by different application scenarios. Indicatively, some works examine the division of items into categories, with a constraint on the number of items of each category allocated to each agent [4]. In another model, the items form the vertices of a graph and each bundle must form a connected subgraph [3,8]. We refer to our related work section for further exposition.

Our work focuses on yet another graph-theoretic model of constrained fair division that has been initiated recently, where the constraints are modeled via a *conflict graph*. More precisely, the items correspond to the vertex set of the conflict graph and a bundle is not allowed to contain two items that are connected with an edge. In other words, the bundles allocated to the n agents must constitute a n-coloring in the conflict graph (with each bundle being an independent set). This model turns out to impose severe limitations on the existence of fair allocations, if we want to allocate all items (i.e., have a complete allocation).

Firstly, a complete allocation may simply not exist, even without imposing any fairness criterion. To circumvent this, the mild condition of $\Delta < n$, where Δ is the maximum degree of the graph does guarantee the existence of a complete allocation (since this is sufficient for the existence of a valid n-coloring).

Even under this assumption, counterexamples for the existence of EF1 allocations have already been identified [17,18]. We feel this naturally poses the question of understanding further or characterizing when is it possible to achieve EF1 or other fairness concepts under such constraints.

1.1 Our Contribution

We are interested in the existence and efficient computation of complete, EF1 allocations in the presence of a conflict graph, when the agents have additive valuations. The main contribution of our work is that we explore the effect of the maximum degree of the conflict graph, Δ, on the existence of EF1 allocations. For the cases where we establish existence, we also describe efficient algorithms for computing such allocations. The techniques we use are based on leveraging results from matching theory such as Hall's theorem for perfect matchings or the structure of vertex sets that form violations to Hall's theorem when no perfect matching exists. We derive our results by combining these techniques with algorithmic tools of fair division such as Round Robin and envy cycle elimination procedures.

We start in Sect. 3, where we deal with ordered valuations and the wider class of tiered valuations. Ordered valuations, where the agents agree on the ranking of all items w.r.t. their value has been extensively considered in fair division (e.g. [26]). Tiered valuations form a more natural superclass, where the items are grouped into tiers, and the agents agree on the ranking between the tiers even if they may not agree on the ranking of the items within each tier. and have also been studied in fair division [23]. We consider valuations with tiers of size n, meaning that each tier (except maybe the last one) contains exactly n items (so that agents agree on which are the n most valuable items, then the next n most valuable and so on). For this valuation class we provide in Sect. 3.1 an algorithm that returns an EF1 allocation when the number of items, m, is bounded as: $m \leq n \left\lfloor \frac{n}{\Delta} \right\rfloor + n - \Delta$. We show that this result is tight, i.e., when m exceeds the above bound there may not exist EF1 allocations, and this is proved by extending the counterexample of Igarashi et al. [18]. To alleviate this negative fact when $m > n \left\lfloor \frac{n}{\Delta} \right\rfloor + n - \Delta$, we provide a positive approximation result in Sect. 3.2. Namely, for $\Delta \leq \frac{n}{2}$, and based on our previous algorithm, we provide an approximation algorithm obtaining a $(1 - \frac{2}{r+1})$-EF1 allocation where $r = \left\lfloor \frac{n}{\Delta} \right\rfloor$. Observe that, the ratio of the algorithm approaches 1 as r becomes sufficiently small and tends to 0.

In Sect. 4 we move to general additive valuations. The setting here is much more restrictive, as we exhibit that even with identical valuations, an EF1 allocation may not exist when $m > 2n - \Delta$. We therefore focus on understanding EF1 existence when $m \leq 2n$, for which we provide an almost complete picture. Firstly, we combine the Round Robin algorithm with an appropriately constructed matching to derive an EF1 allocation when either $m \leq 2n - \Delta$ or $m \leq 2n$ and $\Delta \leq \frac{n}{2}$. Our most technical result is that we extend this algorithm to attain EF1 when $m \leq 2n$ and $\Delta \leq \frac{2n}{3}$. As a complementary result, when $\Delta > \frac{2n}{3}$, we can attain EF1, when $m \leq 2n - \Delta + 1$, and G does not have $K_{\Delta, 2n-2\Delta+1}$ as a subgraph. The last 2 results are obtained by a repeated application of matching algorithms, in combination with envy cycle removals.

1.2 Further Related Work

The model of fair division with a conflict graph, that we study here was first introduced by Chiarelli et al. [11], where they focus on a different objective, that of maximizing the lowest total profit of items allocated to any agent. The existence and computation of complete EF1 allocations under this model, which is also the focus of our work, was later studied by Hummel and Hetland [17], where they established both positive results for some special cases, as well as impossibility results for general additive valuations (e.g., non-existence when $\Delta > n$ or when $n \geq 4$ and with lower values of Δ). In the same work they also considered the criteria of MMS and Maximum Nash Welfare under this setting. Igarashi et al. [18] proved that a maximal but not necessarily complete EF1 allocation always exists for two agents and any graph, when the agents have monotone valuations. Moreover, they showed NP-hardness results for finding maximal EF1 allocations for three or more agents. A special case of this problem, that corresponds to interval scheduling was considered by Li et al. [20] and Kumar et al. [19], under the fairness criteria of EF1 and MMS. Additionally,

Kumar et al. [19] also considered the case where the items are chores. Finally, Yoneda and Yoneda [28] studied a setting where the conflict constraints are treated as "soft." In this scenario, allocating adjacent goods to the same agent is allowed and the objective is to find EF1 allocations with a small number of such conflict violations.

There have been several other models of fair division under constraints. Biswas et al. [5] considered a model where items are grouped into categories and each bundle needs to respect a bound on the items received from each category. Another graph-related model involves the allocation of connected bundles, where items are located again in a graph, as studied in [3,8]. Other models concern constraints defined via matroids. For example, [4] considered a setting where the constraints are determined by laminar matroids. Furthermore, Gourves et al. [14] considered a model where the allocated items should form a base of a matroid. Additional results under matroid constraints regarding MMS and other criteria have also been obtained in [13,15]. Yet another model focuses on the scenario where all agents should receive the same number of items (e.g. in assigning shifts) studied in [12] and more recently in [7,22]. . For an overview of problems involving constrained fair division we refer to the survey by Suksompong [27] or to the one by Biswas et al. [6].

When it comes to the unconstrained setting, there is an even bigger volume of research activity within the last decades. The lack of envy-free allocations led over the years to various new criteria including the one we study here, defined by [9], as well as the notions of EFX (envyfreeness up to any good) introduced in [10,15], MMS defined by [9], and groupwise MMS considered in [2]. For an overview, we refer to the survey by [1].

2 Preliminaries

We consider a setting with n agents and m indivisible items to be allocated to the agents. We denote by N the set of agents and by M the set of items. Each agent $i \in N$ has an *additive* valuation function v_i over the items so that for every $S \subseteq M$, $v_i(S) = \sum_{g \in S} v_i(\{g\})$ and $v_i(\emptyset) = 0$. For simplicity, we will use $v_i(g)$ instead of $v_i(\{g\})$, and we also assume that $v_i(g) \geq 0$ for every $g \in M$. We denote by V the set of valuation functions of the n agents, i.e., $V = \{v_i \mid i \in N\}$.

A *complete allocation*, or simply an allocation, denoted by $A = (A_1, A_2, \ldots, A_n)$, is a partition of the items M, where $\bigcup_{i \in [n]} A_i = M$ and $A_i \cap A_{i'} = \emptyset$ for any $i, i' \in [n]$ with $i \neq i'$. The bundle A_i is the set of items assigned to agent i. A *partial allocation* is an allocation over a strict subset of the set of items M.

In the constrained setting we study, certain pairs of items are not allowed to be allocated to the same agent. These pairs are represented via an undirected *conflict graph* $G = (M, E)$, where its vertices are the set of items and for every edge $(u, v) \in E$, the items u and v are conflicting and cannot be assigned to the same bundle. An allocation (complete or partial) is *feasible* if no bundle contains a pair of conflicting items. In other words, a feasible allocation forms a n-coloring of G and each bundle A_i is an independent set of G. The question of interest in our work is to find feasible and complete allocations which also satisfy some fairness criteria.

Definition 1. *We denote by* (N, M, V, G) *an instance of fair allocation with a conflict graph, where*

- N *is the set of* n *agents,*
- M *is the set of* m *items,*
- V *is a set of* n *additive valuation functions, with* $v_i \in V$ *being the valuation function of agent* i*,*
- $G = (M, E)$ *is the conflict graph where the items* M *are the set of vertices and* E *the set of edges.*

Our analysis will make use of the maximum degree $\Delta(G)$, of a vertex in G. For brevity, we will denote the maximum degree by Δ, instead of $\Delta(G)$. Given a partial allocation $A = (A_1, A_2, \ldots, A_n)$, let $C_i(A)$ be the *conflicting items of agent* i defined as the items that have as neighbor in G an item allocated to agent i w.r.t. A, i.e., $C_i(A) = \{u \in M \setminus A_i : (u, v) \in E \text{ for some } v \in A_i\}$.

Feasibility Graph. We define now an additional graph that will be helpful in formalizing some of our algorithms and their analysis. Given a feasible partial allocation A, and the set U of unallocated items in A, the *feasibility graph*, denoted as $F(A, U)$, is a bipartite graph where $V(F(A, U)) = N \cup U$ and $E(F(A, U)) = \{(i, g) \mid g \notin C_i(A)\}$. Hence, in $F(A, U)$ each agent i is connected with the items $g \in U$ such that $A_i \cup \{g\}$ remains feasible. In the feasibility graph, for a subset of vertices S we denote by $\Gamma(S)$ the vertices that are neighbors with at least one vertex belonging to S.

In the sequel, we will often allocate items to agents based on sets of edges of the feasibility graph. For brevity we will be using the procedure below. In particular, given a partial allocation A, and a subset R of edges of $F(A, U)$ such that each $g \in U$ belongs to at most one edge of R, Procedure 1 allocates for each $(i, g) \in R$ the item g to agent i.

Procedure 1. Allocate(A, R)

Input: Partial allocation $A = (A_1, \ldots, A_n)$, $R \subseteq E(F(A, U))$ s.t. every $g \in U$ belongs to at most one edge of R.
1: **for** each $(i, g) \in R$ **do**
2: $\quad A_i = A_i \cup \{g\}$
3: **end for**

Beyond completeness and feasibility, we want allocations that also meet some fairness criterion. The fairness criterion in our work is *envy-freeness up to one item* (EF1). Given an allocation A we say that an agent i *envies* agent j if $v_i(A_i) < v_i(A_j)$. An allocation is *envy-free* (EF) if no agent envies the bundle of some other agent i.e., $v_i(A_i) \geq v_i(A_j)$ for every pair of agents $i, j \in N$. Envy-freeness up to one item is a relaxation of envy-freeness where every agent i is not envious towards any other agent j after the hypothetical removal of some item from the bundle of j. The formal definition of an EF1 allocation is following.

Definition 2. *In an instance (N, M, V, G), an allocation A is envy-free up to one item (EF1) if, for every pair of agents $i, j \in N$, it holds that $v_i(A_i) \geq v_i(A_j \setminus g)$ for some $g \in A_j$.*

Similarly to the above definition, an allocation is said to be α-EF1 if, for every pair of agents $i, j \in N$, $v_i(A_i) \geq \alpha v_i(A_j \setminus g)$ for some $g \in A_j$.

Due to the following known proposition, and since we ask for complete allocations, we only consider instances with $\Delta < n$.

Proposition 1 ([17]). *For any conflict graph $G = (M, E)$ with $\Delta \geq n$ there is an instance (N, M, V, G) that has no EF1 allocation.*

2.1 Definitions and Tools from Matching Theory

Now, we present some preliminary concepts related to matchings, which will be used extensively in the following sections.

In a bipartite graph $G = (X \cup Y, E)$ a *perfect matching* is a matching that matches every vertex in X to a unique vertex in Y and vice versa. For a perfect matching to exist in a bipartite graph, it is necessary that $|X| = |Y|$. If $|X| \leq |Y|$ we say that a matching *saturates* X if every vertex in X is matched to a distinct vertex in Y. In the sequel, we will extensively use the graph theoretic version of Hall's theorem as follows.

Theorem 1 (Hall's theorem, [16]). *A bipartite graph $G = (X \cup Y, E)$ with $|X| \leq |Y|$ has a matching that saturates all vertices in X if and only if for every subset $S \subseteq X$, it holds that $|\Gamma(S)| \geq |S|$.*

Clearly, when $|X| = |Y|$ and Hall's condition holds, the matching is perfect. In a bipartite graph $G = (X \cup Y, E)$, we say that $(S, \Gamma(S))$ is a *Hall violator* if $|S| > |\Gamma(S)|$. Finally, a consequence of Hall's theorem is the following proposition.

Proposition 2. *If in a bipartite graph $G = (X \cup Y, E)$, where $|Y| = n'$ and $|X| \leq n'$, each vertex in Y has degree at least d and each vertex in X has degree at least $n' - d$, then there exists a matching saturating X in G.*

The proof of Proposition 2 along with all missing proofs in the sequel can be found in the full version of our work in [24].

3 Ordered Valuations and Beyond

We say that the agents have *ordered valuations* if there is an ordering of the items, say $g_1, g_2, \ldots, g_m$, such that $v_i(g_1) \geq v_i(g_2) \geq \ldots \geq v_i(g_m)$ for every

$i \in N$. Ordered valuations are motivated by settings where there is a common perception for the ranking of the items, even if the agents do not agree about their precise value. The results we present in this section actually hold for a broader class, that we term *valuations with tiers of size n*. Let k be the integer such that $(k-1)n < m \leq kn$. When the agents have valuations with (common) tiers of size n, the set of items M is partitioned into sets (tiers) $M_1, M_2, \ldots, M_k$. The set M_1 contains the top n most preferred items which are common to all agents, even though they may not agree on the ranking of these items. The set M_2 contains the next n items, and so on. Only M_k may contain strictly less than n items. A formal definition follows.

Definition 3. *The agents have valuations with tiers of size n if there is a partition of the items in tiers $M_1, M_2, \ldots, M_k$, such that*

(i) $|M_j| = n$ *for every* $j \in [k-1]$ *and* $|M_k| \leq n$.
(ii) For any agent i and for all items $g \in M_j$, $g' \in M_{j'}$ *where* $j < j'$ *it holds that* $v_i(g) \geq v_i(g')$.

Ordered valuations form a special case of the above definition, where the items belonging to the same tier M_j are also ranked in the same way by all agents. The following proposition holds for valuations with tiers of size n and thus also for ordered valuations. It says that if every agent has exactly one item from each tier except the last one, and no agent has two or more items from the last tier then the allocation is EF1.

Proposition 3. *Consider an instance as per Definition 3, with tiers* $M_1, M_2, \ldots, M_k$. *Every allocation* $A = (A_1, A_2, \ldots, A_n)$ *such that* $|A_i \cap M_j| = 1$ *for every* $i \in [n]$, $j \in [k-1]$, *and* $|M_k \cap A_i| \leq 1$, *is EF1.*

3.1 EF1 via Tiered Matching

Our main result in this subsection is an algorithm that returns a complete EF1 allocation when the number of items is bounded by $n \left\lfloor \frac{n}{\Delta} \right\rfloor + n - \Delta$.

Our proposed algorithm iteratively allocates the items to the agents via matchings (one per tier) in the feasibility graph. We briefly discuss first for how many agents an unallocated item is feasible with their bundles. For a partial allocation A and a set of unallocated items U, an agent i is not connected with an item $g \in U$ if some item which is a neighbor of g in the conflict graph belongs to A_i, i.e., $g \in C_i(A)$. Since the conflict graph G has maximum degree Δ, even if all of the at most Δ neighbor items of g have already been given to Δ different agents, there are at least $n - \Delta$ agents whose bundle is feasible with item g. Thus, every $g \in U$ is connected with at least $n-\Delta$ agents in $F(A, U)$. We are now in a position to present the *Tiered Matching Algorithm* (Algorithm 1).

Because of Proposition 3, if in each round of Algorithm 1, the matching R is perfect (except the last one, where it needs to saturate M_k), then the resulting allocation is complete and EF1. In what follows, we prove that this condition holds when the number of items does not exceed $n \left\lfloor \frac{n}{\Delta} \right\rfloor + n - \Delta$.

Algorithm 1. Computing an EF1 allocation by assigning each agent one item from each set M_i

Input: (N, M, V, G), with valuations having tiers of size n

Set $A_i = \emptyset$ for every agent i.
Let $M_1, M_2, \ldots, M_k$ be the partition of items into the tiers.
for each j from 1 to k **do**
    Construct $F(A, M_j)$.
    Find a maximum size matching R_j in $F(A, M_j)$.
    Allocate(A, R_j)
end for
return $A = (A_1, A_2, \ldots, A_n)$

Theorem 2. *Algorithm 1 runs in polynomial time and returns a complete EF1 allocation when* $m \leq n \left\lfloor \frac{n}{\Delta} \right\rfloor + n - \Delta$ *and the agents have valuations with tiers of size* n.

Proof. We first assume that $m \leq n \left\lfloor \frac{n}{\Delta} \right\rfloor$.

Then Algorithm 1 would run for at most $\left\lfloor \frac{n}{\Delta} \right\rfloor$ rounds. We prove that it returns a perfect matching in every round except the last one where it returns a matching saturating every item of M_k. In other words, it returns a matching saturating every item in each of at most $\left\lfloor \frac{n}{\Delta} \right\rfloor$ rounds. We proceed by induction. In round 1, since $C_i(A) = \emptyset$ for every agent $i \in N$, we have $F(A, M_1) = K_{n,n}$. Hence, a perfect matching R_1 always exists. Now, let $A = (A_1, A_2, \ldots, A_n)$ be a partial allocation obtained by Algorithm 1 after round r where in each round j, with $j \leq r$, the respective matching R_j is perfect and $r \leq \left\lfloor \frac{n}{\Delta} \right\rfloor - 1$. In the partial allocation A, every agent i has exactly r items in her bundle A_i. Therefore, since each item is represented by a vertex of the graph G whose degree is at most Δ, the conflict set $C_i(A)$ for each agent i has at most $r\Delta \leq (\left\lfloor \frac{n}{\Delta} \right\rfloor - 1)\Delta = \left\lfloor \frac{n}{\Delta} \right\rfloor \Delta - \Delta \leq n - \Delta$ items. In round $r+1$, since $|C_i(A)| \leq n - \Delta$ and $|M_{r+1}| = n$ it is clear that $|M_{r+1} \cap C_i(A)| \leq n - \Delta$, and thus every agent i has degree at least Δ in $F(A, M_{r+1})$. Combining this with the fact that each item has degree at least $n - \Delta$, it follows from Proposition 2 that a matching saturating every vertex of M_{r+1} exists in $F(A, M_{r+1})$. By Proposition 3, this concludes that if $m \leq n \left\lfloor \frac{n}{\Delta} \right\rfloor$, Algorithm 1 returns a complete EF1 allocation.

Now, let $m = n \left\lfloor \frac{n}{\Delta} \right\rfloor + l$ where $1 \leq l \leq n - \Delta$. Each of the l items belonging to $M_{k'}$ where $k' = \left\lfloor \frac{n}{\Delta} \right\rfloor + 1$ is feasible with at least $n - \Delta$ agents and $l \leq n - \Delta$.

Therefore, in $F(A, M_{k'})$ for every $S \subseteq M_{k'}$, it holds that $\Gamma(S)| \geq n - \Delta \geq |S|$. Thus by Theorem 1 a matching saturating every vertex of $M_{k'}$ exists and by Proposition 3 this concludes that Algorithm 1 returns a complete EF1 allocation when $m \leq n \left\lfloor \frac{n}{\Delta} \right\rfloor + n - \Delta$. □

Tightness. Igarashi et al. [18] have shown a counterexample to EF1 existence for any $n \geq 4$ with identical additive valuations and $m = n + 2$. This is not in conflict with our results since the conflict graph in their example is $K_{3,n-1}$ i.e., $\Delta(K_{3,n-1}) = n - 1$. Indeed, for $\Delta = n - 1$, $n \left\lfloor \frac{n}{\Delta} \right\rfloor = n$ and Theorem 2 guarantees that Algorithm 1 returns an EF1 allocation when $m \leq n+n-\Delta = 2n-(n-1) = n+1$. Therefore, since $m = n+2$ in the counterexample by Igarashi et al. [18], this shows that our bound on m, for which Algorithm 1 returns an EF1 allocation is tight. In the following proposition we extend the tightness of Algorithm 1 w.r.t. the number of items, for any $\Delta > \frac{2}{3}n$. In fact, we strengthen this even further, and prove an impossibility result even for approximate EF1 allocations, beyond a certain constant ratio, when m exceeds the bound of Theorem 2.

Proposition 4. *For any $n \geq 4$ and Δ, such that $\frac{2n+1}{3} \leq \Delta \leq n-1$, there is an instance with identical valuations and $m = n\left\lfloor \frac{n}{\Delta} \right\rfloor + n - \Delta + 1$ such that no complete α-EF1 allocation exists for any $\alpha > \frac{\sqrt{2}}{2}$.*

Proof. Since $\frac{2n+1}{3} \leq \Delta \leq n-1$, we have $\left\lfloor \frac{n}{\Delta} \right\rfloor = 1$. The counterexample is $K_{\Delta,2n-2\Delta+1}$. Let M_1 be the part with Δ vertices and M_2 the part with $2n-2\Delta+1$ vertices. Observe that $m = \Delta + 2n - 2\Delta + 1 = 2n - \Delta + 1 = \left\lfloor \frac{n}{\Delta} \right\rfloor n + n - \Delta + 1$. The agents have the same valuation v, where

$$v(j) = \begin{cases} \sqrt{2}, & j \in M_1 \\ 1, & j \in M_2 \end{cases}$$

Let $A = (A_1, A_2, \ldots, A_n)$ be a complete allocation. Since the conflict graph is a complete bipartite graph, it is clear that for every agent i either $A_i \subseteq M_1$ or $A_i \subseteq M_2$ in any feasible allocation.

If the items of M_1 are allocated to Δ agents by giving one item of value $\sqrt{2}$ to each one, then the items of M_2 will be allocated among the remaining $n-\Delta$ agents. By the pigeonhole's principle there will be some agent i who receives at least three items of value 1 among the $2n-2\Delta+1$ items of M_2 i.e., $v(A_i) \geq 3$. Thus, even if one item g of A_i is removed the agents who are allocated one item of M_1 still envy agent i. Moreover, for any agent j of the Δ agents receiving one item from M_1, it holds that $\frac{v(A_j)}{v(A_i \setminus \{g\})} \leq \frac{\sqrt{2}}{2}$. Hence the allocation A can be at most a $\frac{\sqrt{2}}{2}$-EF1 allocation.

The other case is that strictly less than Δ agents are allocated the items of M_1. Then, at least one agent i would receive at least two items of value $\sqrt{2}$, so that $v(A_i) \geq 2\sqrt{2}$. The items of M_2 would be allocated to at least $n-\Delta+1$ agents. Due to the pigeonhole's principle there will be one agent j that would receive at most one item among the $2n-2\Delta+1$ items of M_2. Thus, $v(A_j) \leq 1$ and j still envies i even if one item of A_i is removed. Moreover, it holds that $\frac{v(A_j)}{v(A_i \setminus \{g\})} \leq \frac{1}{\sqrt{2}} = \frac{\sqrt{2}}{2}$.

Therefore, in both cases there is no EF1 allocation and additionally there always exist two agents, i and j, such that $\frac{v(A_j)}{v(A_i \setminus \{g\})} \leq \frac{\sqrt{2}}{2}$. This implies that there is no complete α-EF1 allocation for any $\alpha > \frac{\sqrt{2}}{2}$ in this instance. □

Note that for the construction of Proposition 4, we must have $\Delta \geq \frac{2n+1}{3}$. Otherwise, if $\Delta \leq \frac{2}{3}n$, then the degree of vertices in M_1 would be $2n-2\Delta+1 \geq \frac{2}{3}n+1$ and the maximum degree of the conflict graph $K_{\Delta,2n-2\Delta+1}$ would not be equal to Δ. Thus, the counterexample no longer holds when $\Delta \leq \frac{2}{3}n$.

3.2 Approximation via Tiered Matching

Given the tightness of the previous result when $\Delta > \frac{2n}{3}$, in this subsection, we investigate further the behavior of Algorithm 1 when there is no restriction on the number of items and for lower values of Δ. More precisely, we explore the case where $\Delta \leq \frac{n}{2}$ (with the agents still having valuations with tiers of size n). Note we can still run Algorithm 1, but for $j > \lfloor \frac{n}{\Delta} \rfloor$, there is no guarantee that the matching R_j produced in line 5 of Algorithm 1 will be perfect. If it is not perfect, this implies that there is a Hall violator $(S, \Gamma(S))$ in $F(A, M_j)$ where S is a subset of agents and $|S| > |\Gamma(S)|$. Since every item has degree at least $n - \Delta$ in $F(A, M_j)$, for every subset of agents with size $\Delta + 1$ or greater, each item is connected with at least one agent in the subset. Hence that would mean that $|\Gamma(S)| = n \geq |S|$, which violates the assumption that $(S, \Gamma(S))$ is a Hall violator. Therefore, this implies that $|S| \leq \Delta$. Consequently $|\Gamma(S)| \leq \Delta - 1$ and an agent i that is unmatched in R_j has at least $n - (\Delta - 1) = n - \Delta + 1$ items of M_j in her conflict set. Let $r = \lfloor \frac{n}{\Delta} \rfloor$ and l be the minimum integer such that $m \leq lrn$. When $(l-1)rn < m \leq lrn$, we could add zero valued items without conflicts, and thus assume that $m = lrn$, so that Algorithm 1 runs for lr rounds.

The following lemma shows a lower bound for the number of items each agent i has in her bundle A_i in an allocation A obtained by Algorithm 1. For every $h \in [l]$ we denote by M^h the items of the first hr rounds i.e., $M^h = \bigcup_{j=1}^{hr} M_j$.

Lemma 1. *When $\Delta \leq n/2$,then for every $h \in [l]$ and every agent $i \in N$, if A_i is the bundle given to i by Algorithm 1, it holds that $|M^h \cap A_i| \geq h(r-1)+1$.*

Let U be the set of unallocated items after the execution of Algorithm 1. For every h such that $2 \leq h \leq l$, let U_h be the subset of U obtained from rounds j such that $r(h-1)+1 \leq j \leq rh$, i.e., $U_h = (\bigcup_{r(h-1)+1}^{rh} M_j) \cap U$.

The next algorithm is based on obtaining first an allocation A by Algorithm 1 (which may not be complete) and then figuring out how to allocate the items of U. For every U_h, let N_h be the set of agents who have less items from M^h than the number of rounds rh so far. Algorithm 2 gives priority to the agents of N_h for the unallocated items of U_h. Then, if there are still items in U_h and no such agent is feasible with some of them, they are allocated to the other agents ensuring that every agent has at most $h(r+1)-1$ items from M^h in her bundle.

Lemma 2. *When $\Delta \leq n/2$, the allocation A returned by Algorithm 2 is complete and $h(r-1)+1 \leq |M^h \cap A_i| \leq h(r+1)-1$ for every agent i and every $h \leq l$.*

By Lemmas 1 and 2 the best and the worst case for a bundle A_i of an agent i are as represented in Table 1. Observe that in A_b it holds that $|M^h \cap A_b| = h(r+1)-1$ for every $h \in [l]$. The additional items of A_b arise from the best possible rounds. For every $h \geq 2$ there are two items of round $M_{(h-1)r+1}$ in the bundle of A_b. This implies that the next possible round that A_b may contain an extra item is M_{hr+1}, where there is also one extra item, because of the inequality $|M^h \cap A_b| \leq h(r+1)-1$ and so on. Respectively, for A_w it holds that $|M^h \cap A_w| = h(r-1)+1$ for very $h \in [l]$ and the lost items of A_w occur in the worst possible way satisfying the inequality $|M^h \cap A_w| \geq h(r-1)+1$.

Algorithm 2. Distributing the unallocated items from the execution of Algorithm 1, subject to upper bounds on the items each agent receives

Input: (N, M, V, G)
```
A = Tiered Matching(N, M, V, G).
for h = 2 to l do
    Set N_h = {i | |A_i ∩ M^h| < rh}.
    while U_h ≠ ∅ and ∃g ∈ U_h and i ∈ N_h s.t. g ∉ C_i(A) do
        A_i = A_i ∪ {g} and remove g from U_h.
        if |M^h ∩ A_i| = rh then
            Remove i from N_h.
        end if
    end while
    Set N'_h = ∅.
    while U_h ≠ ∅ and ∃g ∈ U_h and i ∉ N'_h s.t. g ∉ C_i(A) do
        A_i = A_i ∪ {g} and remove g from U_h.
        if |M^h ∩ A_i| = h(r + 1) − 1 then
            Add i to N'_h.
        end if
    end while
end for
return A = (A_1, A_2, ..., A_n)
```

Table 1. The best and the worst case for the bundles A_i. The entries in the columns correspond to $|A_b \cap M_j|$ and $|A_w \cap M_j|$ for the respective column M_j.

	M_1	M_2	...	M_r	M_{r+1}	M_{r+2}	...	M_{2r}	...	$M_{(l-1)r+1}$	$M_{(l-1)r+2}$	...	M_{lr}
A_b	1	1	1	1	2	1	1	1	...	2	1	1	1
A_w	1	1	1	1	0	1	1	1	...	0	1	1	1

Theorem 3. *When $\Delta \leq n/2$ and the agents have valuations with tiers of size n, Algorithm 2 runs in polynomial time and returns an allocation A which is a $(1 - \frac{2}{r+1})$-EF1 where $r = \lfloor \frac{n}{\Delta} \rfloor$.*

Proof. The best and the worst case for a bundle A_i of allocation A returned by Algorithm 2, denoted as A_b and A_w respectively, are shown in Table 1. We will show that $v_i(A_w) \geq (1 - \frac{2}{r+1}) v_i(A_b \setminus \{g\})$ where $A_b \cap M_1 = g$ and i is the agent that A_w is allocated to. Let $A_w^h = \bigcup_{j=(h-1)r+1}^{hr} A_w \cap M_j$ for every $h \in [l]$.

Because of the ordered valuations, for every $h \in [l-1]$ it holds that $v_i(A_b \cap M_{hr+1})| \leq \frac{2}{r-1} v_i(A_w^h))$ since every one of $r-1$ items of A_w^h (r if $h = 1$) has at least as much value as every pair of two items of $A_b \cap M_{hr+1}$. Observe that if we remove the items of $A_b \cap M_{hr+1}$ from A_b for every $h \in [l-1]$ then both agents have exactly one item from each M_j such that $j \notin \{hr + 1 \mid h \in [l-1]\}$. Hence,

$$v_i(A_w) \geq v_i(A_b \setminus \{g\}) - \sum_{h=1}^{l-1} v_i(A_b \cap M_{hr+1})$$

$$v_i(A_w) \geq v_i(A_b \setminus \{g\}) - \sum_{h=1}^{l-1} \frac{2}{r-1} v_i(A_w^h)$$

Observe that $\sum_{h=1}^{l-1} v_i(A_w^h) = v_i(A_w) - v_i(A_w^l) \leq v_i(A_w)$. Then,

$$v_i(A_w) \geq v_i(A_b \setminus \{g\}) - \frac{2}{r-1} v_i(A_w)$$

$$(1 + \frac{2}{r-1}) v_i(A_w) \geq v_i(A_b \setminus \{g\})$$

$$v_i(A_w) \geq (1 - \frac{2}{r+1}) v_i(A_b \setminus \{g\})$$

This completes the proof that A is $(1 - \frac{2}{r+1})$-EF1. □

4 General Additive Valuations

In this section we consider general additive valuations. We know already from the previous section that for exact EF1 allocations, we need $m \leq n \left\lfloor \frac{n}{\Delta} \right\rfloor + n - \Delta$. Notice that when $\Delta > n/2$, this upper bound simplifies to $2n - \Delta$. Here we restrict our study even further to the case of $m \leq 2n$. To motivate this, recall that since $\Delta < n$, Proposition 4 already implies that even when the agents have identical additive valuations, if $\Delta > \frac{2}{3}n$ and $m > 2n - \Delta$, an EF1 allocation may not exist. We therefore find it important to understand EF1 existence in the still non-trivial case when m is bounded by a small multiple of n.

We first show that for general additive valuations, an EF1 allocation can be computed when $m \leq 2n - \Delta$. Recall that this is the tight bound in the number of items for EF1 allocations established in the previous section. In particular, Algorithm 3, which we analyze in the sequel, returns an EF1 allocation when $m \leq 2n - \Delta$ or when $\Delta \leq \frac{n}{2}$ and $m \leq 2n$.

Algorithm 3. A combination of Round-Robin and matchings for general additive valuations

---

Input: (N, M, V, G)
1: Set $A_i = \emptyset$ for every agent i.
2: Run 1 round of Round-Robin so that each agent gets 1 item.
3: Let M_2 be the unallocated items. Construct $F(A, M_2)$.
4: Find a maximum size matching R in $F(A, M_2)$.
5: Allocate(A, R)
6: **return** $A = (A_1, A_2, \ldots, A_n)$

Theorem 4. *For an instance (N, M, V, G) with additive valuations, Algorithm 3 runs in polynomial time and returns an EF1 allocation if one of the following conditions holds:*

(i) $m \leq 2n - \Delta$.
(ii) $\Delta \leq \frac{n}{2}$ *and* $m \leq 2n$.

If $m \geq 2n - \Delta + 1$ and $\Delta > \frac{n}{2}$, Algorithm 3 cannot work. In particular, there is no guarantee that a matching saturating every vertex of M_2 in $F(A, M_2)$ exists in line 4 of Algorithm 3 (a property that is used for the cases handled by the proof of Theorem 4). To remedy this, we propose Algorithm 4, a technically more involved algorithm, as an extension of Algorithm 3, that returns an EF1 allocation when $m \leq 2n$ and $\Delta \leq \frac{2n}{3}$. This results in the following theorem, which is the main technical result of this section.

Theorem 5. *In a (N, M, V, G) instance where $\Delta \leq \frac{2n}{3}$ and $m \leq 2n$, Algorithm 4 runs in polynomial time and returns an EF1 allocation.*

4.1 Prelims to Algorithm 4: Relevant Definitions and Procedures

Before presenting the pseudocode of Algorithm 4, we provide some necessary concepts. In a bipartite graph $G = (X \cup Y, E)$, if no matching exists that saturates all vertices of X, then Hall's condition of Theorem 1 is violated by at least one subset $S \subseteq X$ and its neighborhood $\Gamma(S)$. A Hall violator of maximum deficiency is a Hall violator $(S, \Gamma(S))$ that maximizes $|S| - |\Gamma(S)|$. A Hall violator of maximum deficiency $(S, \Gamma(S))$ is maximal if for every Hall violator $(S', \Gamma(S'))$, where $S \subset S'$, it holds that $|S| - |\Gamma(S)| > |S'| - |\Gamma(S')|$. This implies that if $(S, \Gamma(S))$ is a Hall violator of maximum deficiency that is also maximal, then $|X'| < |\Gamma(X') \cap (Y \setminus \Gamma(S))|$ for every $X' \subseteq X \setminus S$, otherwise S could be extended by X' and would not be maximal.

We refer to a pair of items $p = \{g^1, g^2\}$ as feasible if (g^1, g^2) is not an edge of the conflict graph G. Algorithm 4 is based on constructing the following type of matchings.

Definition 4. *A feasible 2-matching R in $F(A, U)$ w.r.t. S where $S \subseteq U$, is a set of edges of $F(A, U)$ such that*

(i) each $g \in U$ is matched with exactly one agent.
(ii) each agent i is matched with at most 2 items of U.
(iii) if $(i, g), (i, g') \in R$ then $g, g' \in S$ and $(g, g') \notin E(G)$.

The set of feasible pairs of a 2-matching R is the set of pairs of items that matched to the same agent in R.

Another graph that we make use of is the *envy graph* of an allocation A. This is a directed graph, denoted by $EG(A)$, where its vertex set is the set of agents and there is an edge (i, j) from agent i to j whenever $v_i(A_j) > v_i(A_i)$.

Within our algorithm, we make use of Procedure 2 stated below, which receives as input a partial allocation A and a bundle A_f that does not belong to any agent. The agents have the option to swap their bundle with A_f, and when the procedure ends, no agent envies the final remaining bundle, A_f. We also ensure that $EG(A)$ is acyclic at the end (due to the order of the swaps).

Procedure 2. Envy Swap(A, A_f)

```
Input: A = (A_1, ..., A_n), A_f
Transform EG(A) into a DAG by Envy Cycle Elimination [21].
Let 1, 2, ..., n be a topological order of EG(A).
for i = n downto 1 do
    if v_i(A_i) < v_i(A_f) then
        Swap A_i with A_f.
    end if
end for
return A, A_f
```

When each agent has 1 item in her bundle and a matching does not exist, the question is how can we handle the items of the Hall violator S. Algorithm 4 creates pairs of items of S in a feasible manner and each agent has the choice to exchange her bundle with one of these pairs. This is repeated until either the unallocated items can be matched to the agents with a single item so far or no agent is willing to exchange her bundle with such a pair. In the latter case some agents will end up with 3 items in their bundle and others with 1 item.

4.2 Proof Sketch of Theorem 5

We provide here the main skeleton of our proof. Because of Theorem 4, we assume that $\Delta > \frac{n}{2}$ and $m > 2n - \Delta$. If a matching R in line 4 exists, Algorithm 4 does not enter the while loop in lines 10–29. The returned allocation A is EF1. The rest of this part of the proof is as in Theorem 4. Otherwise, there is a Hall violator $(S, \Gamma(S))$.

Since the maximum degree of G is Δ, every vertex of $F(A, M_2)$ has degree at least $n - \Delta$. For the Hall violator when Algorithm 4 enters the while loop in lines 10-29 for the first time, it holds that $n - \Delta \leq |\Gamma(S)| < |S| \leq \Delta$.

In every iteration of the while loop in 10-29, we consider the following four cases for the bundle A_f that is left unallocated by Envy Swap in line 16. We denote by M_s the set of items belonging to the agents of $\Gamma(S)$ and by M_0 the items belonging to the agents of $N' \setminus \Gamma(S)$. These cases are distinguished based on which agent held the bundle before Envy Swap. The cases are the following.

C1: $A_f = \{g\}$, where $g \in M_s$ and g is not feasible with any item of M_0.
C2: $A_f = \{g\}$, where $g \in M_s$ and g is feasible with some item of M_0.
C3: $A_f = \{g\}$, where $g \in M_0$.
C4: $A_f = \{p_i\}$, where p_i is a feasible pair belonging to an agent $i \in N \setminus N'$.

Algorithm 4. Leveraging 2-matchings and the Envy Swap procedure to return an EF1 allocation

Input: (N, M, V, G)
Set $A_i = \emptyset$ for every agent i.
Run 1 round of Round-Robin so that each agent gets 1 item.
Let M_2 be the set of unallocated items. Construct $F(A, M_2)$.
if a maximum size matching R in $F(A, M_2)$ saturating every vertex in M_2 exists **then**
  Allocate(A, R)
else
  Set $A' = A$, $N' = N$.
  Find a maximal Hall violator of maximum deficiency $(S, \Gamma(S))$ where $S \subseteq M_2$ in $F(A', M_2)$.
  $c =$ true
  while $c =$ true **do**
    Compute a feasible 2-matching R' w.r.t. S in $F(A', M_2)$.
    Let P be the set of feasible pairs of R'.
    if $v_h(p) > v_h(A_h)$ for some feasible pair $p \in P$ and some agent $h \in N$ **then**.
      Set $A_f = A_h$.
      $A_h = \{p_h\}$ where $p_h \in P$ and $p_h = \arg\max_{p \in P} v_h(p)$.
      Envy Swap(A, A_f). The new bundle A_f remains unallocated.
      Let $N' = \{i \in N \mid |A_i| = 1\}$ and A' the respective partial allocation for the agents of N'.
      Let M_2 be the set of unallocated items. Construct $F(A', M_2)$.
      if a maximum size matching R in $F(A', M_2)$ saturating every vertex in M_2 exists **then**
        Allocate(A, R)
        $c =$ false
      else
        Compute a maximal Hall violator of maximum deficiency $(S, \Gamma(S))$ in $F(A', M_2)$.
      end if
    else
      Allocate(A, R')
      $c =$ false
    end if
  end while
end if
return A

Observe that in the first three cases the number of agents that are allocated a feasible pair is increased by 1 after the iteration. Moreover, in the first iteration A_f cannot fall into Case C4 since no agent is allocated a feasible pair so far.

To proceed with the proof, we first show that Algorithm 4 is well-defined and always terminates. This is established by Lemma 3 and Claims 1–3. Let

$n_p = |N \setminus N'|$, i.e., the agents that have been already allocated a feasible pair and M_p the set of their items, thus $|M_p| = 2n_p$.

Lemma 3. *A feasible 2-matching R' w.r.t. S in line 11 in each iteration of the while loop within lines 10-29 exists and can be computed in polynomial time.*

To construct the 2-matching in Lemma 3, we use the *auxiliary graph* which is obtained after orienting the edges of the feasibility graph. The direction of each edge depends on whether it belongs to a maximum size matching or not. A procedure that uses the auxiliary graph and extends a maximum size matching in a feasible 2-matching w.r.t. S is provided in the full version of our work [24]. The fact that $\Delta \leq 2n/3$ guarantees the existence of the 2-matching.

The specific construction of the 2-matching, combined with the structure of the feasibility graph implied by the condition that $\Delta \leq \frac{2n}{3}$, ensures the validity of the claims stated below. Claim 1 specifies the conditions under which Algorithm 4 exits the while loop in lines 10-29 and terminates. Claim 2 shows that the items belonging to the agents of $N' \setminus \Gamma(S)$ is a subset of the respective items in the initial iteration. Claim 3 is obtained almost directly by Claim 2.

Claim 1. *Algorithm 4 exits the while loop in lines 10–29 if one of the following holds.*

(i) $v_h(p) \leq v_h(A_h)$ *for every feasible pair* $p \in P$ *and any agent* $h \in N$ *in line 13.*
(ii) $|S| - |\Gamma(S)| = 1$ *and the bundle* A_f *returned by Envy Swap falls in Case C2.*
(iii) $|S| - |\Gamma(S)| = 1$ *and the bundle* A_f *returned by Envy Swap falls in Case C3.*
(iv) $|S| - |\Gamma(S)| = 2$ *and* A_f *returned by Envy Swap falls in Case C3.*

Claim 2. *When Algorithm 4 re-enters the while loop in lines 10–29, the set of items belonging to the agents of* $N' \setminus \Gamma(S)$ *is a subset of the respective set in the previous iteration.*

Claim 3. *If* $|S| = \Delta - 2n_p$ *the bundle* A_f *returned by Envy Swap cannot fall into Case C1.*

The set of items belonging to the agents of $N' \setminus \Gamma(S)$ are connected in the conflict graph with every item belonging to S at some point during the execution of Algorithm 4. Thus, Claim 2 implies that the overall number of items which are elements of S at some iteration is at most Δ. Since $\Delta \leq \frac{2n}{3}$, the number of feasible pairs that can be constructed is $O(n^2)$. Moreover, observe that the value of any agent does not decrease during Algorithm 4 and in every iteration of the while loop at least one agent strictly increases her value. Consequently, in combination with Claim 3, after a polynomial number of iterations the deficiency $|S| - |\Gamma(S)|$ would strictly decrease if Algorithm 4 re-enters the while loop. Thus, because of Claim 1, Algorithm 4 always terminates.

Having established the termination of the algorithm, we can now establish that it produces a desirable allocation.

Lemma 4. *Algorithm 4 returns an EF1 allocation, under the assumptions stated in Theorem 5.*

Finally, we argue that Algorithm 4 runs in polynomial time. A maximal Hall violator of maximum deficiency and a feasible 2-matching can be computed in polynomial time. Since the initial deficiency $|S|-|\Gamma(S)|$ is at most $\Delta-(n-\Delta) \leq \frac{n}{3}$ and after a polynomial number of iterations the deficiency is strictly decreased, then the overall number of iterations for the while loop is polynomial.

4.3 Further Consequences of Algorithm 4

The following theorem shows that when $\Delta > \frac{2n}{3}$ and $m = 2n-\Delta+1$, a necessary condition for the non-existence of EF1 allocations, even with additive valuations, is that $K_{\Delta,2n-2\Delta+1}$ is a subgraph of the conflict graph. Recall that $K_{\Delta,2n-2\Delta+1}$ is the conflict graph of the counterexample in Proposition 4 for every $\Delta > \frac{2n}{3}$.

Theorem 6. *When $m = 2n-\Delta+1$, $\Delta \geq \frac{2n+1}{3}$ and G does not have $K_{\Delta,2n-2\Delta+1}$ as a subgraph, Algorithm 4 returns an EF1 allocation.*

5 Conclusions

We have studied the existence of complete EF1 allocations in constrained fair division with a conflict graph. Our main technical contribution is the use of matching theory (and especially Hall's theorem) for establishing the existence and efficient computation of EF1 allocations for certain classes of valuation functions. An open question arising from our work is for what range of m, when $m > 2n$, an EF1 allocation is guaranteed in the case that $\Delta \leq 2n/3$.

There are also several other important research avenues. The maximum degree Δ provides only partial information about the conflict graph. Focusing on this parameter allows us to establish a robust worst-case analysis, however, a graph with a small number of vertices of degree Δ may differ significantly in the conflicts it generates. Investigating how other structural properties, such as the average degree or vertex connectivity could affect the fairness guarantees is an appealing direction. Furthermore, our work has focused only on the EF1 criterion, which is already quite challenging, but several other fairness notions can also be explored. There has been some progress on this front (e.g., for the MMS criterion in [17]), but we are still far from having a more complete understanding on which notions are more amenable under this constrained model.

Acknowledgment. This work was supported by the project MIS 5154714 of the National Recovery and Resilience Plan "Greece 2.0" funded by the European Union under the NextGenerationEU Program.

Disclosure of Interests. The authors have no competing interests.

References

1. Amanatidis, G., et al.: Fair division of indivisible goods: recent progress and open questions. Artif. Intell. **322**, 103965 (2023)
2. Barman, S., Biswas, A., Murthy, S.K.K., Narahari, Y.: Groupwise maximin fair allocation of indivisible goods. In: Proceedings of the Thirty-Second AAAI Conference on Artificial Intelligence (AAAI 18), pp. 917–924 (2018)
3. Bilò, V., et al.: Almost envy-free allocations with connected bundles. Games Econom. Behav. **131**, 197–221 (2022)
4. Biswas, A., Barman, S.: Fair division under cardinality constraints. In: Proceedings of the 27th International Joint Conference on Artificial Intelligence (IJCAI 18), pp. 91–97 (2018)
5. Biswas, A., Ke, Y., Khuller, S., Liu, Q.C.: An algorithmic approach to address course enrollment challenges. In: 4th Symposium on Foundations of Responsible Computing (FORC 2023). LIPIcs, vol. 256, pp. 8:1–8:23. Schloss Dagstuhl (2023)
6. Biswas, A., Payan, J., Sengupta, R., Viswanathan, V.: The theory of fair allocation under structured set constraints. In: Ethics in Artificial Intelligence: Bias, Fairness and Beyond, pp. 115–129. Springer Nature, Singapore (2023)
7. Bogomolnaia, A., Baklanov, A., Victorova, E.: Teams formation: efficiency and approximate fairness. Games Econom. Behav. (2025)
8. Bouveret, S., Cechlárová, K., Elkind, E., Igarashi, A., Peters, D.: Fair division of a graph. In: Proceedings of the Twenty-Sixth International Joint Conference on Artificial Intelligence (IJCAI-17), pp. 135–141 (2017)
9. Budish, E.: The combinatorial assignment problem: approximate competitive equilibrium from equal incomes. J. Polit. Econ. **119**(6), 1061–1103 (2011)
10. Caragiannis, I., et al.: The unreasonable fairness of maximum Nash welfare. ACM Trans. Econ. Comput. **7**(3) (2019)
11. Chiarelli, N., et al.: Fair packing of independent sets. In: Combinatorial Algorithms: 31st International Workshop (IWOCA 2020), pp. 154–165. Springer-Verlag (2020)
12. Ferraioli, D., Gourvès, L., Monnot, J.: On regular and approximately fair allocations of indivisible goods. In: International Conference on Autonomous Agents and Multi-Agent Systems (AAMAS 14), pp. 997–1004 (2014)
13. Gourvès, L., Monnot, J.: On maximin share allocations in matroids. Theoret. Comput. Sci. **754**, 50–64 (2019)
14. Gourvès, L., Monnot, J., Tlilane, L.: A protocol for cutting matroids like cakes. In: 9th International Conference on Web and Internet Economics (WINE 2013), pp. 216–229. Springer (2013)
15. Gourvès, L., Monnot, J., Tlilane, L.: Near fairness in matroids. In: Proceedings of the Twenty-First European Conference on Artificial Intelligence (ECAI'14), pp. 393–398. IOS Press (2014)
16. Hall, P.: On representatives of subsets. J. Lond. Math. Soc. **1**, 26–30 (1935)
17. Hummel, H., Hetland, M.L.: Fair allocation of conflicting items. Auton. Agent. Multi-Agent Syst. **36**(1), 8 (2021)
18. Igarashi, A., Manurangsi, P., Yoneda, H.: Dividing conflicting items fairly. In: Proceedings of the Thirty-Fourth International Joint Conference on Artificial Intelligence (IJCAI-25), pp. 3908–3915 (2025)
19. Kumar, Y., Equbal, S., Gurjar, R., Nath, S., Vaish, R.: Fair scheduling of indivisible chores. In: Proceedings of the 23rd International Conference on Autonomous Agents and Multiagent Systems (AAMAS '24), pp. 2345–2347 (2024)

20. Li, B., Li, M., Zhang, R.: Fair scheduling for time-dependent resources. In: Advances in Neural Information Processing Systems, vol. 34, pp. 21744–21756. Curran Associates, Inc. (2021)
21. Lipton, R.J., Markakis, E., Mossel, E., Saberi, A.: On approximately fair allocations of indivisible goods. In: Proceedings of the 5th ACM Conference on Electronic Commerce, pp. 125–131 (2004)
22. Mancho, A., Markakis, E., Protopapas, N.: Fairness under equal-sized bundles: Impossibility results and approximation guarantees. In: 18th International Symposium on Algorithmic Game Theory (SAGT 2025), pp. 191–208 (2025)
23. Markakis, E., Santorinaios, C.: Improved EFX approximation guarantees under ordinal-based assumptions. In: Proceedings of the 2023 International Conference on Autonomous Agents and Multiagent Systems (AAMAS '23), pp. 591–599 (2023)
24. Markakis, E., Samaris, M.: Leveraging matchings in constrained fair division with a conflict graph (2026). https://arxiv.org/abs/2606.13083
25. Mertzanidis, M., Psomas, A., Verma, P.: Automating food drop: The power of two choices for dynamic and fair food allocation. In: Proceedings of the 25th ACM Conference on Economics and Computation (EC 24), p. 243 (2024)
26. Plaut, B., Roughgarden, T.: Almost envy-freeness with general valuations. SIAM J. Discret. Math. **34**(2), 1039–1068 (2020)
27. Suksompong, W.: Constraints in fair division. SIGecom Exch. **19**(2), 46–61 (2021)
28. Yoneda, H., Yoneda, M.: Fair division with soft conflicts (2026). https://arxiv.org/abs/2602.20929

Realist Vampire(s) Seeking Consenting Suicidal Person(s)

Fabien Mathieu[1,2](✉)

[1] Swapcard Lab, Paris, France
fabien@swapcard.com
[2] Sorbonne Université, CNRS, LIP6, Paris 75005, France

Abstract. Most people believe that the principal weaknesses of vampires are sunlight, wooden stakes in inconvenient places, and extortionate dentist bills. Most people are mistaken. Being creatures of undeniably aristocratic persuasion, vampires fear social humiliation above all. In particular, exhibiting symptoms of haematological indigestion (typically induced by an incompatible blood type) constitutes a social death sentence, occasionally followed by the literal kind. To preserve gastric decorum within the undead community, we study the *Ghoul Exchange Programme*, an online matching market in which vampires trade ghouls so as to align blood types. We model it as a stochastic matching problem, prove that no policy can stabilise it under a natural symmetry condition on arrivals (called *mirror invariance*), and analyse two ways to recover stability: admitting human volunteers, or tolerating a bounded discard rate. Both yield a trade-off between delay and waste. Our framework maps onto Kidney Exchange Programmes: volunteers become deceased donors, discard becomes wait-list mortality, and any reward-maximising policy is revealed to carry an implicit valuation of patient outcomes, with consequences ranging from the inequitable to the disturbing.

Keywords: Online stochastic matching · Stability · Impossibility result · Kidney exchange · Vampires

1 Introduction

1.1 Motivation

The transformation of a human into a vampire has been exhaustively described in the literature [6,10,23,24,26]. Yet one rather neglected fact remains: even fully drained of its original blood, a vampiric body retains some characteristics of its former blood type, a phenomenon we call "memory of blood", in analogy with the notorious and undisputed "memory of water" [8,15]. Counter-intuitive as it seems, it is thus perfectly meaningful to speak of a vampire's blood type.

This memory manifests itself through an extremely strong digestive intolerance, called *acute haemolytic feeding reaction*, whenever the blood type consumed is incompatible with the vampire's own type [21]. For instance, a vampire

P. Lenzner and D. Schmand (Eds.): SAGT 2026, LNCS 16911, pp. 319–336, 2027.
https://doi.org/10.1007/978-3-032-38782-0_18

with type A^- can safely feed on O^- and A^- victims, but will react rather dramatically to any victim carrying a B antigen or a positive Rhesus factor.

Haemolytic reaction has become a real problem because of the rather precise ritual that is vampiric alimentation: having selected a prospective victim, the vampire hypnotises it into a state of docile subservience. By a slight abuse of notation, such a hypnotised human is termed a *ghoul*. Each ghoul may nourish only one vampire (not necessarily its creator). Like an opened bottle of fine claret, however, a ghoul should be consumed promptly or unceremoniously discarded. Further complications arise from a critical etiquette constraint: a vampire cannot inquire after a human's blood type *prior* to hypnosis, such an inquiry being considered vulgar, bordering on a *faute de goût*. Consequently, vampires frequently find themselves burdened with ghouls unsuitable for personal consumption.

The vampiric society, having spotted a potentially explosive problem, has long sought a solution. The obvious one is to establish a Ghoul Exchange Programme (GEP), where vampires can trade ghouls to find compatible matches. Thanks to the programme, Count X (A^+) no longer needs to endure the social horror of his B^- ghoul whilst Baroness Y (AB^-) bemoans her O^+ surplus (cf. Fig. 1). For a modest inscription fee, members can exchange ghouls civilly, resolving supply-demand imbalances with algorithmic precision. However, the design of such a programme is non-trivial, as it must ensure stability to prevent queues of unmatched ghouls from growing indefinitely[1], while respecting the delicate social norms of the undead community.

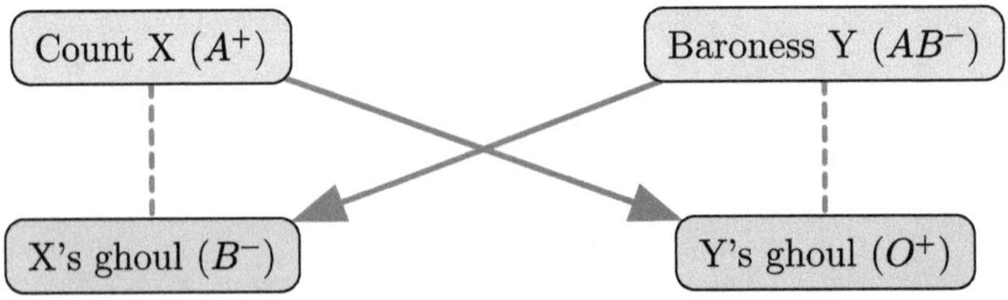

Fig. 1. The *Ghoul Exchange Programme* in action: red dashed lines indicate initial incompatibilities; green solid lines show successful feedings post-exchange.

1.2 Ghoul Exchange Programme Vs Kidney Exchange Programme

The matching problem we study is structurally identical to a Kidney Exchange Programme (KEP) [3,25] restricted to ABO+Rh blood-type compatibility. A vampire-ghoul pair, the vampire in the role of a recipient and the ghoul in that of a donor, plays the role of a (recipient, donor) pair: the recipient is incompatible with their own donor and seeks a partner pair whose ghoul the first vampire can

[1] Which would pose housing issues.

feed on and whose vampire can feed on the first ghoul. Pairwise exchange in the KEP and ghoul swap in the GEP describe the same algorithmic object.

The vampiric framing is more than stylistic. First, it follows a long tradition of using fictional settings to explore algorithmic problems, initiated by the original *stable marriage* problem [12]. Working in the vampiric setting, we set aside the elements of the medical setting that would obscure the model without changing its essence: clinical compatibility beyond ABO+Rh (HLA, crossmatch tests, immunisation), surgical scheduling, the time pressure of patient deterioration, and the consent of all parties. What remains is what matters algorithmically: a compatibility graph derived from marker-set inclusion, stochastic arrival of pairs, and a matching policy with no foresight. The marker count is also reduced for ease of explanation, since a real KEP can involve many more markers (see for example [27]), but our structural results extend without change to any marker count.

Second, the vampiric setting allows us to explore theoretical results that would risk trivialising real human suffering in a strictly KEP framing: any allocation policy implicitly orders patient types, and fairness in a stochastic matching market becomes a choice between competing inequities. Vampires, creatures of fiction, seldom protest these conclusions; humans rightly might.

1.3 Contributions

This article studies the design of the Ghoul Exchange Programme (GEP) from the perspective of online stochastic matching. We make three main contributions.

First, we partition vampire-ghoul pairs into three categories defined by the inclusion relations between their blood-type marker sets: *autarkic* (vampires that can feed directly on their ghoul), *helpless* (those whose ghoul carries strictly more markers), and *swinger* (those who could benefit from an exchange). Theorem 2, our main result, then states that under *mirror invariance* of the arrival distribution, a natural symmetry condition that holds whenever donors and recipients are drawn from a common population, and provided that the population contains at least one non-autarkic type, no matching policy stabilises the GEP. The result persists when compatible hyperedges (*food orgies*) are permitted.

Second, we propose two strategies that recover stability. The first introduces universal *volunteer humans*, who break mirror invariance. The second, called *k-filtering*, relaxes compatibility above a queue-length threshold. Both exhibit the same qualitative delay/waste trade-off observed in [7].

Third, in Sect. 6, we translate our results to real-life KEP: humans correspond to deceased donors, k-filtering to bounded wait-list mortality. We discuss the algorithmic similarities, the ethical specificities, and the implicit valuation of patient outcomes that any reward-maximising policy carries.

All results are grounded in theory and supported by extensive simulations[2], available in an accompanying notebook. Full proofs and additional derivations are deferred to the extended version of this paper [19].

[2] Approval for large-scale clinical trials was unfortunately not granted.

1.4 Roadmap

The remainder of the paper is organised as follows. Section 2 is a self-contained background recap about online stochastic matching. It contains no original result. Section 3 presents the adaptation of the model to the Ghoul Exchange Programme. Section 4 shows a general impossibility result, which is circumvented in Sect. 5. Section 6 bridges GEP and KEP. Section 7 concludes.

2 Online Stochastic Matching

Our journey towards vampiric gastric well-being begins with a brief review of online stochastic matching, whose stability hinges on three ingredients: a compatibility graph, arrival rates, and a matching policy.

2.1 Model

An online stochastic matching model consists of items arriving at random instants to be matched with other items. Matching may occur immediately upon arrival or following a period of queueing. Formally, a matching model is defined by a triple (G, λ, ϕ).

The graph $G = (V, E)$, with $|V| = n$ and $|E| = m$, is the *compatibility graph.* Nodes of V represent item types. An edge $e \in E$ is a non-empty multiset of nodes, and performing the match e removes from the queues one item of each node in e, counted with multiplicity. A *simple edge* is a set of two distinct nodes; a *self-loop* is the singleton $\{v\}$, matching one item of type v with itself; a *hyperedge* is any edge on three or more nodes, where a node may occur several times. G is a *simple graph* when all its edges are simple. We assume every node belongs to at least one edge. Unless otherwise stated, only simple edges and self-loops are considered.

The vector $\lambda \in \mathbb{R}^n_{>0}$ represents *arrival rates* per type, with each type typically following an independent Poisson process. Only types with a positive arrival rate actually participate in the model.

The *matching policy* ϕ is the algorithm that determines which matches are executed. It is invoked upon each arrival and performs at most one match per call[3], with unmatched items remaining in queue.

One central property of matching models is stability, which states that the number of items waiting in the system will not explode with time. Formally, a model (G, λ, ϕ) is *stable* if its evolution forms a positive recurrent Markov chain (ensuring that long-run averages such as matching rates per edge are well-defined). A *matching problem* (G, λ) is *stabilisable* if some policy ϕ stabilises it. Other metrics of interest include delay (related to queue length by Little's law) and matching quality (via edge utilities). In simulations, we use the measured average queue size as a proxy for both stability and delay.

[3] For most reasonable policies, multiple matches per call offer no advantage.

2.2 Main Stability Results

Let $A = (a_{i,j}) \in \mathbb{N}^{n \times m}$ be the incidence matrix of G, where $a_{i,j}$ indicates whether node i is an endpoint of edge j (possibly with multiplicity if j is a hyperedge). Under stability, the matches per edge and unit of time define a *matching rate* $\mu \in \mathbb{R}^m_{\geq 0}$. The arrival rates λ, matching rates μ, and incidence matrix A are then linked by a *conservation equation*:

$$\lambda = A\mu. \tag{1}$$

Note that A defines a linear map from $\mathbb{R}^m$ (edge space) to $\mathbb{R}^n$ (node space). This map may be *surjective*, *injective*, *bijective*, or none of these. For simple graphs, the surjectivity of A is equivalent to the absence of bipartite connected components in G. Remarkably, stability is entirely characterised by Eq. (1) and the surjectivity of a submatrix of A.

Theorem 1 ([7,18]). *A matching problem (G, λ) is stabilisable if and only if Eq. (1) admits a non-negative solution $\mu \in \mathbb{R}^m_{\geq 0}$ such that the restriction of A to the support of μ is surjective.*

When stabilisability is established, an effective policy must be identified. For simple graphs, *longest queue first* stabilises any stabilisable problem [16], so Theorem 1 is an exact criterion. For general structures with hyperedges and self-loops, a universal *virtual queue* policy attains the same characterisation [18]. We stress that our impossibility result (Theorem 2) does *not* rely on this general sufficiency: its hyperedge case is a direct compatibility-score argument (Sect. 4). The sufficiency direction is invoked only to certify the recovered stability of Sect. 5, where self-loops are added to the compatibility structure.

2.3 Related Work

Online stochastic matching emerged from the study of bipartite models. Caldentey, Kaplan, and Weiss [5] introduced the first-come-first-served infinite bipartite matching model, and Bušić, Gupta, and Mairesse [4] established stability conditions in the bipartite case. Mairesse and Moyal [16] extended the stability analysis to non-bipartite graphs. The general theory, including the polytope perspective underlying Theorem 1 and the universal policies mentioned above, is developed in [7].

Beyond stability, a complementary line of research investigates matching quality. Gurvich and Ward [13] study the dynamic control of matching queues with an emphasis on reward optimisation, and Kerimov, Ashlagi, and Gurvich [14] characterise constant-regret policies in dynamic matching. The delay/quality trade-off explored in Sect. 5 belongs to this family; a formal framework for quantifying such trade-offs is provided by [7].

Online stochastic matching arises in any domain where agents arrive over time and must be paired subject to compatibility constraints. The most extensively studied such domain is that of Kidney Exchange Programmes [3,25], where donor-recipient pairs queue for compatible organ transplants.

3 The Ghoul Exchange Programme

We now specialise the online stochastic matching model to the Ghoul Exchange Programme by introducing *vampire-ghoul pairs* (VGs). Each VG is characterised by an ordered pair of blood types, using the notation T_1/T_2: the vampire's type T_1 (left) and the ghoul's type T_2 (right). For instance, A^+/B^- represents an A^+ vampire and their B^- ghoul.

For notational convenience, we refer to the antigens A, B, and the Rh factor + as *markers*[4]. More generally, a system with k binary markers yields 2^k blood types and 2^{2k} VG types; real-world transfusion compatibility involves considerably more markers [27]. Our results apply to any marker system, but we focus on the ABO+Rh system ($k = 3$, marker set $\mathcal{M} = \{A, B, +\}$), and write $M(T) \subseteq \mathcal{M}$ for the marker set of blood type T. A vampire of type T_V can safely feed on a ghoul of type T_G if and only if $M(T_G) \subseteq M(T_V)$.

3.1 Vampire-Ghoul Compatibility Graph

There are $2^3 = 8$ possible blood types, yielding $8^2 = 64$ distinct VG types. Among the VG types, 8 are *symmetric*, i.e. vampire and ghoul share identical blood types. Two VG types are *compatible* if each vampire can feed on the opposing ghoul, as illustrated by Fig. 1. Notably, type T_1/T_2 is always compatible with its mirror type T_2/T_1. This definition extends to hyperedges: a *compatible* hyperedge admits a compatible perfect matching between involved vampires and ghouls.

VG types partition into three categories according to the inclusion relation between $M(T_V)$ and $M(T_G)$:

Autarkic: ($M(T_G) \subseteq M(T_V)$) The vampire can feed directly on their ghoul. Example: AB^-/A^-, since $\{A\} \subseteq \{A, B\}$.
Helpless: ($M(T_V) \subsetneq M(T_G)$) The ghoul carries all the vampire's markers and at least one additional marker. Example: A^+/AB^+, since $\{A, +\} \subsetneq \{A, B, +\}$.
Swinger: ($M(T_V) \parallel M(T_G)$) The vampire and the ghoul have incomparable marker sets. Example: A^+/B^+, since $\{A, +\}$ and $\{B, +\}$ are incomparable (neither can feed on the other).

These categories satisfy the following properties. The mirror of a non-symmetric autarkic is helpless, and conversely. Crucially, a helpless type is compatible *only* with autarkics: if $v = T_V/T_G$ is helpless and compatible with $v' = T'_V/T'_G$, it implies that $M(T'_G) \subseteq M(T_V) \subsetneq M(T_G) \subseteq M(T'_V)$, showing that v' is autarkic. Conversely, every swinger is compatible with at least one other swinger (its mirror, which is a distinct swinger type since swingers are never symmetric).

The category names emphasise the attitude towards the GEP: autarkics lack natural incentive to participate; helpless VGs would starve without autarkic

[4] Medical terminology distinguishes antigens and factors, but this is gastronomically irrelevant.

participation; swingers are the main supporters of the programme, as they both can and must benefit from the exchanges.

Among the 64 VG types, 27 are autarkic, 19 are helpless, and 18 are swingers. Figure 2 illustrates the swinger subgraph of the compatibility graph.

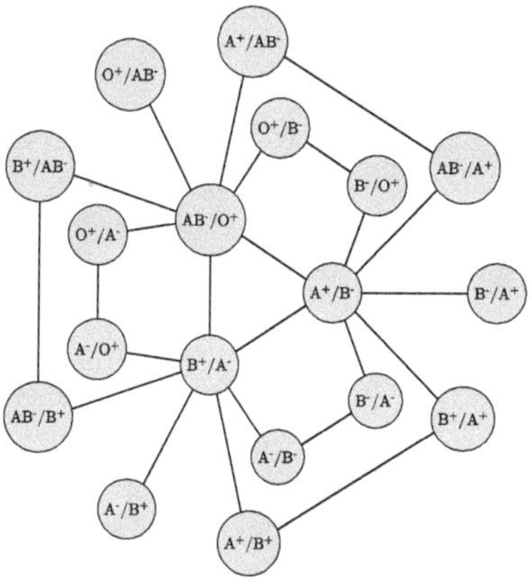

Fig. 2. Restriction of the VG compatibility graph to its swinger component.

3.2 Blood Type Distribution

For numerical experiments, realistic data are desirable. We adopt the US blood type distribution proposed in [11,28][5], shown in Table 1.

Table 1. US Blood Type Distribution, from [28].

O^+	A^+	B^+	AB^+	O^-	A^-	B^-	AB^-
37.4%	35.7%	8.5%	3.4%	6.6%	6.3%	1.5%	0.6%

For VG pairs, unless otherwise stated, we assume vampires and ghouls follow identical independent distributions: VG pairs are sampled independent and identically distributed (i.i.d.) across both components. For instance, the probability of an AB^+/O^- VG is $3.4\% \times 6.6\% \approx 2.2$ ‰.

[5] Specifically, [28] is a Wikipedia page that uses numbers from [11], which focuses on prevalence per ethnicity but ignores possible correlations between Rhesus and antigens. For our fictional purposes, however, vaguely realistic-looking numbers suffice.

3.3 Companion Code

In lieu of clinical trials, all numerical analyses and simulations of the GEP were performed using the Python package *stochastic-matching* [17]. All results, code, and interactive visualisations are available at https://balouf.github.io/stochastic_matching/companion/realist_vampires.html. Each simulation processed 10^9 arrivals.

4 Instability of the Programme

We begin with a broad instability result, then we quantify its practical impact.

4.1 Theoretical Result

Theorem 2. *Consider a matching problem* $(G = (V, E), \lambda)$ *where the types* V *are VG types. Assume that* (V, λ) *is* mirror-invariant*: if* $v_i = T_1/T_2 \in V$*, then* $v_j = T_2/T_1 \in V$ *and* $\lambda_i = \lambda_j$*. Furthermore assume that the support of* λ *contains at least one non-symmetric VG type and that every edge* $e \in E$ *is compatible. Then* (G, λ) *is not stabilisable.*

Mirror invariance amounts to assuming that the joint distribution of (vampire, ghoul) types is symmetric under swapping the vampire and ghoul types, $T_1 \leftrightarrow T_2$. A simple way to achieve it is i.i.d. sampling: draw the vampire type from any distribution π over blood types (e.g. Table 1), then independently draw the ghoul type from the same π. But mirror invariance does not require independence. For instance, a *copy-cat* mixture, in which the ghoul copies the vampire's blood type with some probability p and is drawn independently from π otherwise, also satisfies the hypothesis for any $p \in [0, 1]$. In a real-life KEP context, where donor and recipient are frequently family-related and therefore positively correlated, mixture models of this kind are arguably more realistic than i.i.d., yet they remain mirror-invariant.

Proof (Proof idea (full proof in the extended version [19]*)).* Assign each type a *compatibility score* $s(v) = |M(T_V)| - |M(T_G)|$, non-negative on every compatible edge. By mirror invariance, the cumulative arrival score $W(t) = \sum_{v \in V_t} s(v)$ is a symmetric random walk on $\mathbb{Z}$ with positive per-step variance, while the score $S(t)$ of the pending queue satisfies $S(t) \leq W(t)$. When $W(t) \leq 0$ we have $|S(t)| \geq |W(t)|$, so $\mathbb{E}[\,|S(t)|\,] = \Omega(\sqrt{t})$; since $|W(t)| \to \infty$ in probability and $|s| \leq 3$ bounds each pending score, the queue length cannot stay tight, which a positive recurrent chain would require. Hence no policy stabilises the system. The degenerate case in which every type has score 0 is settled separately through Theorem 1: the swingers split into bipartite mirror pairs whose incidence submatrix is not surjective. □

4.2 Numerical Evaluation

Theoretical impossibility does not mean practical impossibility. Instability need not mean unusability: in the best case the obstruction is only a symmetric random walk, a gentle square-root growth punctuated by returns to zero, and not all VG types suffer equally. We thus benchmark Theorem 2 numerically, gathering results by VG category in Table 2.

Table 2. Measured average queue size per category for different compatibility graphs. Other configurations (Autarkic-only, Helpless-only, Swinger & Helpless) have trivial behaviour and are omitted.

	Autarkic	Helpless	Swinger
Swinger-only	N/A	N/A	43048
All categories	< 0.01	49526	10186
All categories, threesomes allowed	265	21061	7806
Autarkic & Swinger	4.16	N/A	10.75
Autarkic & Helpless	< 0.01	55012	N/A

We first examine the restriction of the programme to swingers (cf. Fig. 2), a natural subgraph since autarkics have little incentive to participate (dooming the helpless by their absence). Instability follows from Theorem 2 but also directly from Theorem 1: the conservation law (1) admits a unique non-negative solution, where each swinger type matches only with its mirror, partitioning the 18 swinger types into 9 bipartite components. Numerically, swingers alone exhibit the predicted $\Omega(\sqrt{t})$ explosion: 43,048, confirming the theorem's grim prognosis.

Assuming that autarkics can be lured into the programme, allowing the matching policy to utilise their self-loops as needed, we next consider the full compatibility graph. In this setting, autarkic queues are near zero, with occasional brief holds due to virtual queue reservations. The waiting time of swingers is notably reduced: autarkic-swinger matchings lighten the bipartite aspect of the internal swinger matching rates. The helpless, on the other hand, are in a tough spot, as they can only match with autarkics, who can match with themselves, swingers, or helpless. They accumulate substantial queues: almost 50,000.

The pair $\{AB^+/O^-, O^-/AB^+\}$ makes this concrete: it carries the maximum score imbalance ($|s| = 3$), and since O^-/AB^+ can match only with the universal AB^+/O^-, every solution of Eq. (1) must route the full AB^+/O^- rate to it, forcing a bipartite component and hence instability.

Vampires being licentious by nature, we next permit ghoul exchanges among more than two VGs; for instance $\{O^-/AB^+, AB^+/A^+, A^+/O^-\}$ forms a compatible hyperedge. Food orgies do not evade Theorem 2: a compatible hyperedge still carries non-negative score, so the score walk underlying the proof is unaffected and the same $\Omega(\sqrt{t})$ obstruction reappears. They do, however, allow feeding in more numerous (if not necessarily better) company. Limiting ourselves to threesomes for tractability, Table 2 shows substantial gains for the helpless and modest ones for swingers, at the cost of larger autarkic queues (aggressive hyperedge reservations).

The two remaining non-trivial, partial-population configurations behave differently. *Autarkic & Swinger* breaks mirror invariance (every non-symmetric autarkic has its mirror in the excluded helpless category), so Theorem 2 does not apply and stability holds. *Autarkic & Helpless* preserves mirror invariance and is unstable by Theorem 2, with helpless queues of the same order as in the full graph.

Excluding the entire helpless population (28.2%) seems, however, a steep price for stability. Our next step proposes subtler alternatives.

5 Stabilising the Programme

To evade Theorem 2, one must violate at least one of its hypotheses. This section explores two avenues: Sect. 5.1 breaks the mirror invariance; Sect. 5.2 relaxes compatibility.

5.1 To Serve Man

A first path to stability skews the type distributions to induce positive drift in the compatibility score. Excluding the helpless works, but targeted decimation suffices: remove a small positive proportion of O^- vampires, or AB^+ ghouls, or merely of O^-/AB^+ VGs, and the system is stable.

In vampire society, decimation needs no Thanos-style finger-snap, only a well-aimed rumour: that AB^+ vampires feeding on O^- humans keep werewolf-adjacent company, and reputational ruin follows overnight. The club baulks at this, deeming it borderline genocidal. Instead, they propose admitting *preghouls*, i.e. regular *humans*, to the exchange programme. Formally, a human is a vampire-ghoul pair where the vampire component is a universal placeholder compatible with any blood type. Humans possess self-loops: if undesired, they exit unharmed.

For any $0 < \alpha < 1$, blending the VG compatibility graph with a proportion α of humans yields a stabilisable problem. This is an immediate consequence of Theorem 1: the universal human self-loops let one exhibit a matching-rate vector of full support (for instance, matching O^- humans uniformly with every VG type), and the incidence matrix restricted to that support is surjective, which is exactly the stabilisability criterion. However, this stability is relative: for small α, queue sizes of the obstructed categories can remain operationally large. The smaller the human inflow, the longer the finite-horizon behaviour resembles the unstable case.

That said, modern technology complicates un-hypnotised human procurement. In the Dark Ages, a swift horse and sturdy net sufficed. Today, the safest method persuades humans (without hypnosis) that mingling with vampires appeals. This requires gothic romance novels wherein the human protagonist discovers that vampires are misunderstood, not bloodthirsty monsters, and falls desperately for a brooding, eternally youthful vampire [20]. In short: with great α comes great romantic absurdity. Vampires, having refined literary tastes, loathe such productions and wish to limit them to a strict minimum.

We thus evaluate the α-queue trade-off numerically; results appear in Fig. 3.

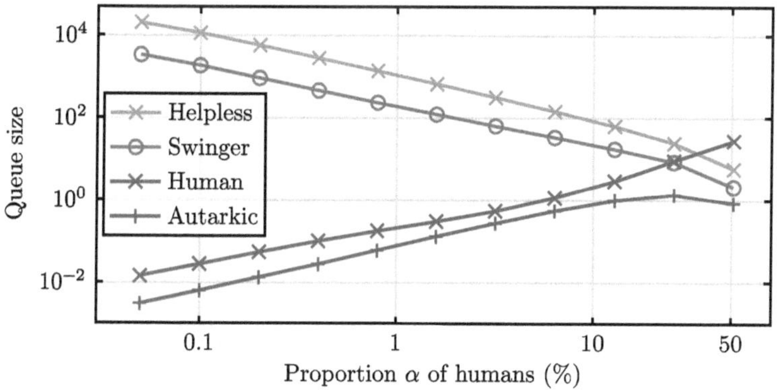

Fig. 3. Delay vs proportion α of regular humans in the exchange programme.

Helpless and swinger queues drop sharply with α, while human and autarkic queues rise modestly (virtual reservations again). Autarkic queues barely exceed 1 even in the worst case.

For $\alpha = 0.1\%$ (a haiku on the sensuality of moonlight over ruined castles), the helpless queue falls to ~ 10000 (vs 50000 without humans). At $\alpha = 1\%$ (fan-fiction of *Gone with the Wind*, vampire edition), it reaches 1000. With $\alpha = 10\%$ (a 5+ tomes trilogy, adaptation rights bought by Netflix), it drops below 100. Using these results, vampiric society can surely balance haematic famine against literary torment.

5.2 Hunger Games

The second escape from Theorem 2 permits, sparingly, incompatible edges. It is a standard approach in online matching: approximate an unstable problem via a parameterised family of stabilisable instances [7].

Here, we render the problem stabilisable by adding self-loops to all non-autarkic types, then deploy a stable policy family minimising their use. Numerous policy families achieve this; we advocate k-filtering for its simplicity and strong empirical performance. The k-filtering mechanism is straightforward: choose a universal matching algorithm, e.g. *virtual queue*; fix parameter k; as long as the largest type-specific queue remains below k, the system is fluid enough and incompatible edges are forbidden; above k, the policy is allowed to select incompatible edges to avert catastrophe.

In practice, selecting an incompatible edge forces the vampire to discard the ghoul and exit hungry, or consume it gambling on negligible gastric repercussions. Most vampires opt for the former.

We evaluate the queue-regret trade-off numerically (Fig. 4), where regret is assessed as follows: assign reward -1 to forbidden edges, $+1$ to autarkic self-loops, and $+2$ to proper exchanges; then compute the observed rate-reward gap against the optimal (unstable) policy that avoids forbidden edges entirely [17].

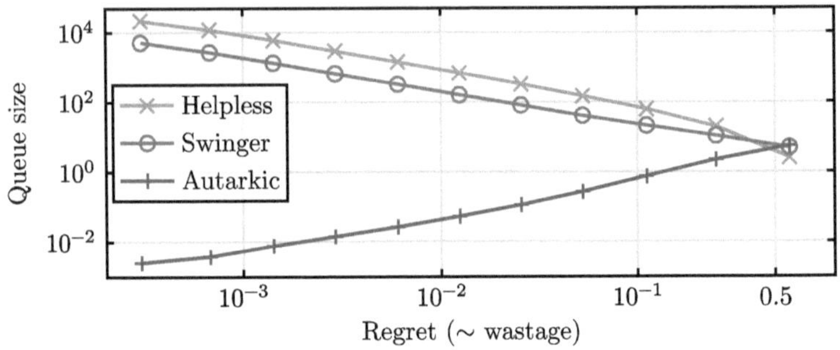

Fig. 4. Delay vs ghoul wastage; cleansing thresholds from $k = 1$ (right) to $k = 1024$ (left).

The profile is very similar to Fig. 3, without the human part: a clear trade-off sharply reduces queues for challenged categories (helpless, swingers), at the cost of wasted ghouls and modestly longer autarkic waits.

5.3 Comparing the Two Approaches

Both techniques exhibit the same qualitative trade-off and achieve comparable queue reductions for similar levels of "waste", unsurprisingly, since such trade-offs are provably unavoidable in similar frameworks [7]. The human approach wastes no food but demands a supply of willing humans, constrained by the pace of romantic fiction production; k-filtering needs no external supply but discards ghouls and leaves vampires hungry. The choice thus depends on whether vampiric society finds romantic fiction or food waste more distasteful, and given the average vampire's literary tastes, neither option is without suffering.

6 Implications for Kidney Exchange Programmes

This section drops the vampiric lore to discuss what our approach says about real-life Kidney Exchange Programmes. The discussion is structural, not prescriptive: we are not health economists and do not recommend any calibrated policy.

6.1 What Changes When Moving from GEP to KEP

A few things separate the fictional GEP from real-life KEP, mainly the compatibility structure, the blood distribution, and the objective.

Markers. The GEP uses the ABO+Rh system, three binary markers. Real-life KEP design considers many more compatibility constraints, including HLA matching and the recipient's history of immunisation; the modelling and optimisation literature on European KEPs is reviewed in [3]. The analogy has clear limits: in kidney transplantation the Rhesus factor is in fact immaterial (it matters for other organs, such as the liver), and the clinically decisive markers, chiefly HLA, are neither few nor binary. Our ABO+Rh coding is thus an algorithmic abstraction, not a clinical compatibility model. For comparison, the related but distinct problem of red-blood-cell transfusion compatibility involves on the order of ten clinically significant antigen systems [27]. Our results extend without modification to any binary marker count $k \geq 2$; what is essential is the *binary* nature of each marker, since the entire analysis rests on marker-set inclusion. It therefore applies to any present-or-absent attribute, but not directly to graded or continuous compatibility. The triangle of score-1 swingers seen in Fig. 2 appears as soon as $k \geq 3$, so the swinger subgraph remains non-bipartite for all marker counts of practical interest.

For any $k \geq 1$ there are 3^k autarkic types, $3^k - 2^k$ helpless, and $4^k - 2 \cdot 3^k + 2^k$ swingers (derivations in the extended version [19]); swingers dominate as k grows, reaching 88.8% at $k = 10$ and 99.4% at $k = 20$.

Blood Distribution. Ghouls and vampires are usually not blood-related, so independent blood types are natural in the GEP. In a KEP, donors and recipients are often family-related and positively correlated; yet, as noted after Theorem 2, mirror invariance does not require independence. Two conditions suffice for it: that needing a transplant is uncorrelated with one's own blood type, and that willingness to donate is symmetric[6]. We neither confirm nor refute these in any specific population. Even when they hold only approximately, the random-walk argument behind Theorem 2 suggests a *near-instability* regime: the chain may be technically positive recurrent, yet the score walk still produces large deviations on operational timescales, so wait-list dynamics can appear unstable even when the Markov chain is not.

Rewards and Optimisation. The operations-research literature on kidney allocation typically optimises Quality-Adjusted Life Expectancy (QALE) [29] and accounts for patient-specific deadlines via wait-list mortality models [1,2]. The full set of trade-offs that real KEP design must weigh (post-transplant quality of life, distributional fairness, time pressure, surgical capacity) is beyond our scope, but we can describe the structural pressure that our framework imposes

[6] If X agrees to donate to Y, then a healthy Y would agree to donate to a sick X.

on any reward profile, whatever the metric. The rest of this section explores that pressure.

6.2 Reading our Framework onto KEP Design

The three points below are not new prescriptions: each corresponds to a feature already known and debated in the KEP literature. Our narrower claim is that a deliberately minimal model already exhibits them in closed form, offering a structural lens rather than practical advice.

Autarkic Participation. Autarkic pairs can arrange a compatible exchange without external help and may at first see no reason to enter a matching programme; our experiments suggest otherwise. In Table 2, without autarkics the helpless have no compatible partner among swingers and cannot be matched at all, while swingers alone queue above 43,000. With autarkics joining, the helpless become matchable, the swinger queue drops four-fold, and autarkics' own queue stays near zero (below 0.01 on pair exchanges, 265 with threesomes); a larger pool may also raise the QALE of each autarkic exchange (Sect. 6.3).

The all-category system stays unstable: Theorem 2 still applies and the helpless queue keeps growing. What changes is the *order of magnitude* of the obstruction: under a wait-list mortality model, a four-fold queue reduction is, by Little's law, a four-fold reduction in expected waiting time, with immediate consequences on mortality.

Non-directed and Deceased Donors. Human volunteers correspond to donors who enter the pool without a paired recipient of their own. The closest real-life analogue is the *non-directed* (altruistic living) donor, who gives without needing to receive; a deceased donor plays the same structural role. Their mathematical role is identical: their self-loops break the mirror invariance of the arrival distribution and lift the obstruction of Theorem 2. As noted in Sect. 5.1, any positive proportion suffices in theory, but a non-trivial inflow is needed in practice (Fig. 3). The vampire struggle to recruit humans with romantic nonsense translates into the real-life tension of promoting altruistic and post-mortem organ donation. Modern KEPs increasingly route such donors through *chains* rather than isolated swaps; extending the mirror-symmetry analysis to chains, and more generally to the longer exchange cycles that we only touch on through food-orgy hyperedges, remains an open direction.

This argues for one concrete design choice. Deceased-donor and KEP pools often operate as parallel pipelines [1,29], with the deceased-donor pool feeding wait-listed recipients and the KEP pool handling living-donor pairs. Our framework confirms that a combined pool, in which a deceased donor entering the system can be allocated either to a wait-listed recipient or to a KEP pair (enabling the KEP donor for another transplantation in the latter), would mutualise inflow and reduce queues on both sides at near-zero added cost.

Bounded Mortality and k-Filtering. The k-filtering policy of Sect. 5.2 discards a pair, via an incompatible match, once queues grow past a threshold k. In real KEPs, no operator explicitly discards a pair: the recipient may simply die on the wait-list, with effective k being their patience for the disease [1,2]. The two mechanisms differ ethically: one decides, the other observes. They produce, however, comparable system-level behaviours, with stabilised queues at the cost of bounded discards and a Pareto-type trade-off between delay and waste.

Wait-list mortality can thus be folded into the matching design via the discard threshold k and the optimisation target, both of which may be made type-specific. The reverse reading is less comfortable: once mortality is part of the model, the choice of objective is no longer purely technical, since it favours some recipients over others. The diamond example below makes this concrete.

6.3 An Ethical Workbench: the Diamond

We illustrate the structural pressure of optimisation with a small fictional running example. The compatibility graph used here, the *diamond*, is one of the simplest stabilisable structures with a non-trivial polytope of stable allocations; a generic version is used in [7] as a running example, and we decorate it with blood-type markers to bring it into the GEP/KEP setting.

Organ-allocation ethics is a field in its own right, spanning bioethics, health economics, and operations research [9,22]. We do not revisit it. Our aim is narrower: to show how a few of its dilemmas surface, in closed form, on the polytope of stable allocations.

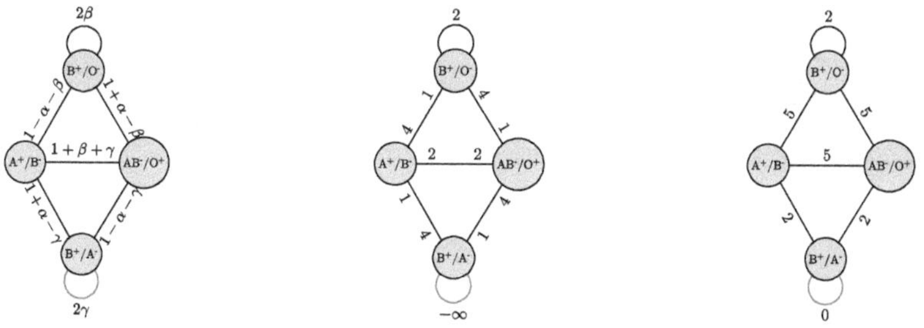

(a) Feasible rates. (b) Asymmetric QALE. (c) Exclusion allowed.

Fig. 5. Ethical variations on a diamond graph. In Fig. 5a assigns asymmetric rewards to perimeter edges, each carrying a separate reward per endpoint (placed nearer the node it rewards), introducing a *stable marriage* flavour. Figure 5c shows weights for which selecting the incompatible loop (without reward) gives a better global optimum.

The Diamond Polytope. Consider the four following type pairs,

$$V = \{B^+/A^-, AB^-/O^+, A^+/B^-, B^+/O^-\},$$

with arrival rates $(\lambda_{B^+/A^-}, \lambda_{AB^-/O^+}, \lambda_{A^+/B^-}, \lambda_{B^+/O^-}) = (2, 3, 3, 2)$. The compatibility graph has five pair-edges and one self-loop on the autarkic type B^+/O^-. In anticipation, we also add a self-loop on B^+/A^-, although it is incompatible. The problem, shown in Fig. 5, is stabilisable: there is no mirror invariance in the joint distribution of donors and recipients so Theorem 2 does not apply.

The non-negative solutions of Eq. (1) can be parameterised by three scalars α, β, γ, as shown in Fig. 5a: α balances the outer edges, while β and γ set the rates of the autarkic and incompatible self-loops. They form a polytope, the convex hull of the vertices $(-1, 0, 0)$, $(1, 0, 0)$, $(0, 1, 0)$, $(0, 0, 1)$, and $(0, 1, 1)$ (in coordinates (α, β, γ)). Feasibility is not stabilisability, though: by Theorem 1, a stable policy realises a rate only where the incidence matrix restricted to its support is surjective. This holds throughout the polytope except at the three vertices $(\pm 1, 0, 0)$ and $(0, 1, 1)$, whose support drops rank; those are reachable only with discards, i.e. by k-filtering.

Given edge-based rewards, the linear objective attains its optimum at a vertex (up to ties); whether a stable policy realises that optimum or only approaches it hinges on the surjectivity above, as the variations below make concrete.

Variation A: Asymmetric Rewards and Blocking Pairs

Reward-based optimisation rests on two convenient assumptions: each edge carries a single reward split evenly between its two endpoints, and a global planner simply sums rewards over matched edges. The first breaks as soon as the two recipients on an edge value the match differently: in a KEP, the survival gain for one recipient need not equal the other's. Figure 5b shows such an allocation, giving each pair-edge a separate reward per endpoint.

For a global planner, every perimeter solution $(\alpha \in [-1, 1], \beta = 0, \gamma = 0)$ is optimal and equivalent, with an aggregate reward of 24 (the four perimeter edges contribute $4 \times 5 = 20$, the central edge 4). Locally, the choice of α is anything but neutral. Each vertex of the West-East axis collects $7 - 3\alpha$, hence 10 at $\alpha = -1$ and 4 at $\alpha = 1$; the North-South axis is its mirror image, rising from 2 to 8. The diamond thus carries a *stable-marriage* flavour [12], the two axes playing the two sides: globally equivalent solutions are locally very different, and either axis can object to a choice that disadvantages it.

The central edge sharpens this into a *blocking-pair* dilemma. Consider the vertex $(\alpha = 0, \beta = 1, \gamma = 1)$, which routes all A^+/B^- and AB^-/O^+ arrivals through the central edge and leaves North and South to their self-loops. The autarkic loop (B^+/O^-) is harmless, but the incompatible loop (B^+/A^-) is used, so the aggregate reward collapses to $-\infty$. Yet each West-East vertex then collects 6, against $7-3\alpha$ on the perimeter: the axis strictly prefers this internal matching whenever $\alpha > 1/3$, and can credibly threaten it to repel any such proposal. Worse, raising the central reward from 2 to 5 lets the internal matching (15 per vertex) beat every perimeter allocation, so a self-interested West-East coalition can drag the planner off the global optimum entirely.

We flag these as potential ethical hazards, not as problems we claim to solve.

Variation B: Type Exclusion

Figure 5c keeps a symmetric reward structure but adds a twist: the incompatible loop on B^+/A^- is allowed, with reward 0. In KEP terms, this is the option to exclude a subset of patients from the matching pool.

The optimum is the vertex ($\alpha = 0, \beta = 0, \gamma = 1$), where all B^+/A^- arrivals are excluded and the remaining three types reorganise into a triangle, for an aggregate reward of 20. Forbidding exclusion ($\gamma = 0$) leaves, as best option, the whole segment $\alpha \in [-1, 1], \beta = 0$, with aggregate reward 19. Exclusion is preferable for the global welfare.

This is the mirror image of Variation A: there the global optimum was indifferent and local preferences imposed an arbitrary choice, here it is strict and prescribes the removal of a type. Both leave a category of recipients with fewer or no transplants, but only the second writes that choice into the global objective. In both, the West-East axis is decisive, defecting *from* the welfare optimum in A and being *recruited* by it in B at the cost of the South; local pivotal power and global prescription point in opposite directions, yet rest on the same fact: any reward-maximising stable policy carries an implicit ranking of recipient types, visible in closed form on this small toy example.

The diamond is, in miniature, a gallery of the ethical pathologies that reward-maximising stability can breed in a Kidney Exchange Programme.

7 Conclusion

We have examined the delicate balance between vampiric etiquette and haematic compatibility. Under mirror invariance, no matching policy can stabilise the Ghoul Exchange Programme (Theorem 2); stability is recoverable either by admitting human volunteers, which break the symmetry, or by discarding ghouls once queues grow too long, at the price of food waste, both exhibiting the same Pareto-style delay/waste trade-off. Carried over to the Kidney Exchange Programme, where many more markers are in play but the impossibility persists, our results raise both thrilling prospects and unsettling ethical implications.

References

1. Anderson, R., Ashlagi, I., Gamarnik, D., Kanoria, Y.: Efficient Dynamic Barter Exchange. Oper. Res. **65**(6), 1446–1459 (2017)
2. Ashlagi, I., Nikzad, A., Strack, P.: Matching in Dynamic Imbalanced Markets. Rev. Econ. Stud. 90(3), 1084-1124 (2023). arXiv:1809.06824
3. Biró, P., et al.: Modelling and optimisation in european kidney exchange programmes. Eur. J. Oper. Res. **291**(2), 447–456 (2021)
4. Bušić, A., Gupta, V., Mairesse, J.: Stability of the bipartite matching model. Adv. Appl. Probab. **45**(2), 351–378 (2013). https://doi.org/10.1239/aap/1370870122
5. Caldentey, R., Kaplan, E.H., Weiss, G.: FCFS infinite bipartite matching of servers and customers. Adv. Appl. Probab. **41**(3), 695–730 (2009). https://doi.org/10.1239/aap/1253281061
6. Carriger, G.: Soulless. The Parasol Protectorate, Orbit, USA (2009)
7. Comte, C., Mathieu, F., Varma, S.M., Bušić, A.: Online stochastic matching: a polytope perspective (2025). https://hal.science/hal-03502084

8. Davenas, E., et al.: Human basophil degranulation triggered by very dilute antiserum against IgE. Nature **333**, 816–818 (1988). https://api.semanticscholar.org/CorpusID:12992106
9. Dickerson, J.P., Procaccia, A.D., Sandholm, T.: Price of fairness in kidney exchange. In: Proceedings of AAMAS 2014, pp. 1013–1020 (2014)
10. Fanu, J.S.L.: Carmilla. British & Colonial Publishing, London (1872)
11. Fung, M.K., Grossman, B.J., Hillyer, C.D., Westhoff, C.M. (eds.): Technical Manual. AABB, Bethesda, MD, 18th edn. (2014)
12. Gale, D., Shapley, L.S.: College admissions and the stability of marriage. Am. Math. Mon. **69**(1), 9–15 (1962). https://doi.org/10.2307/2312726
13. Gurvich, I., Ward, A.: On the Dynamic Control of Matching Queues. Stoch. Syst. **4**(2), 479–523 (2014). https://doi.org/10.1287/13-SSY097
14. Kerimov, S., Ashlagi, I., Gurvich, I.: Dynamic matching: characterizing and achieving constant regret. Manage. Sci. **70**(5), 2799–2822 (2024)
15. Maddox, J., Randi, J., Stewart, W.: "high-dilution" experiments: a delusion. Nature **334**(6180), 287–291 (1988). https://doi.org/10.1038/334287a0
16. Mairesse, J., Moyal, P.: Stability of the stochastic matching model. J. Appl. Probab. **53**(4), 1064–1077 (2016). https://doi.org/10.1017/jpr.2016.65
17. Mathieu, F.: Stochastic Matching (2022). https://pypi.org/project/stochastic-matching/
18. Mathieu, F.: Online stochastic matchings: stability on hypergraphs (2026). https://hal.science/hal-05697834
19. Mathieu, F.: Realist vampire(s) seeking consenting suicidal person(s) (extended version) (2026), https://hal.science/hal-05702926
20. Meyer, S.: Twilight. The Twilight Series, Little, Brown and Company, USA (2005)
21. Panch, S.R., Montemayor-Garcia, C., Klein, H.G.: Hemolytic transfusion reactions. N. Engl. J. Med. **381**(2), 150–162 (2019). https://doi.org/10.1056/NEJMra1802338
22. Persad, G., Wertheimer, A., Emanuel, E.J.: Principles for allocation of scarce medical interventions. Lancet **373**(9661), 423–431 (2009)
23. Pratchett, T.: Carpe Jugulum. Discworld, Doubleday, London (1998)
24. Rice, A.: Interview with the Vampire. The Vampire Chronicles, Knopf, USA (1976)
25. Sharifi, S.: Enhancing kidney transplantation through multi-agent kidney exchange programs: a comprehensive review and optimization models. Int. J. Ind. Eng. Comput. **16**, 483–498 (2025)
26. Stoker, B.: Dracula. Archibald Constable and Company (1897)
27. Wemelsfelder, M., et al.: Extensive red blood cell matching considering patient alloimmunization risk. Vox Sang. **119**(4), 368–376 (2024). https://doi.org/10.1111/vox.13594
28. Wikipedia contributors: blood type distribution by country. https://en.wikipedia.org/wiki/Blood_type_distribution_by_country (2025). Accessed 11 Jan 2026
29. Zenios, S.A., Chertow, G.M., Wein, L.M.: Dynamic allocation of kidneys to candidates on the transplant waiting list. Oper. Res. **48**(4), 549–569 (2000)

Extension of Excess Demand Ascending Auction to Multi-demand Model by Discrete Convex Analysis Approach

Kazuo Murota[1] and Akiyoshi Shioura[2(✉)]

[1] Faculty of Economics and Business Administration, Tokyo Metropolitan University, Tokyo 192-0397, Japan
murota@tmu.ac.jp

[2] Department of Industrial Engineering and Economics, Institute of Science Tokyo, Tokyo 152–8550, Japan
shioura@iee.eng.isct.ac.jp

Abstract. We consider the problem of finding the (unique) minimal Walrasian equilibrium price in multi-item, multi-unit auction models: there are multiple indivisible items for sale, with several units of each item, and a bidder may be interested in buying more than one copy of each item. In its special case with unit-demand bidders, where each bidder demands at most one unit of any item, Andersson, Andersson, and Talman (2013) proposed a general framework of ascending auction algorithms based on the concept of excess-demand item set. This paper extends this approach to the multi-unit case by exploiting the discrete convexity of the Lyapunov function associated with the auction model. In particular, we make use of the facts that (i) the equilibrium price vectors are characterized as the minimizers of the Lyapunov function, (ii) the Lyapunov function is an instance of an $L^\natural$-convex function, and (iii) a concept generalizing "excess-demand item set" can be defined in $L^\natural$-convex function minimization in general.

Keywords: ascending auction · Walrasian equilibrium · indivisible goods · Lyapunov function · discrete optimization · discrete convex analysis

1 Introduction

We consider the problem of finding a Walrasian equilibrium price in multi-item, multi-unit auction models: there are multiple indivisible items (goods) for sale, with several units of each item, and a bidder may be interested in buying more than one copy of each item. We focus on ascending auction algorithms, in which the price vector is increased monotonically to the (unique) minimal Walrasian equilibrium price.

An extensive study has been made on the special case with unit-demand bidders, where each bidder demands at most one unit of any item. It is known

P. Lenzner and D. Schmand (Eds.): SAGT 2026, LNCS 16911, pp. 337–352, 2027.
https://doi.org/10.1007/978-3-032-38782-0_19

that there exists a unique minimum equilibrium price vector and it coincides with the VCG price, which is strategyproof. This property motivates us to compute the minimum equilibrium price.

Demange, Gale, and Sotomayor [6] gave the first ascending auction algorithm for computing the minimum equilibrium price in the unit-demand model. This algorithm repeatedly increases the price vector in the components corresponding to a minimal overdemanded item set, where a set of items is called overdemanded if the number of bidders demanding only items in the set exceeds the number of items in the set. Although this algorithm is guaranteed to compute the minimum equilibrium price, it has drawbacks that a minimal overdemanded set itself is not easy to compute and the number of iterations tends to be large.

These drawbacks are resolved in the algorithm of Mo, Tsai, and Lin [15] (see also [1,24]). Instead of a minimal overdemanded set, this algorithm employs a particular overdemanded set that can be computed with a variant of Ford and Fulkerson's labeling algorithm. This item set is known to be the largest member of the so-called "purely overdemanded sets" ([15, Props. 1 and 2]). Furthermore, it is shown by Andersson and Erlanson [2] and Murota, Shioura, and Yang [21,22], independently, that the number of iterations is the smallest possible.

Andersson et al. [1] introduced the concept of excess-demand sets to present a general framework of ascending auctions for computing the minimum equilibrium price; see (3) for the definition of an excess-demand set. The algorithms of Demange et al. [6] and Mo et al. [15] are both captured in this framework, because a minimal overdemanded set is an excess-demand set (see Prop. 1(2)) and a purely overdemanded set is a synonym of an excess-demand set ([1, p. 29]). The framework of Andersson et al. [1] adds more flexibility in the choice of an item set, possibly at the cost of increasing the number of iterations. The item sets used in the ascending auction for the unit-demand model are summarized in Table 1.

Table 1. Item sets used in the auction algorithm for the unit-demand model

Demange et al. [6]	(any) minimal overdemanded set
Mo et al. [15]	(unique) maximal purely overdemanded set
	= (unique) maximal excess-demand set
Andersson et al. [1]	(any) excess-demand set

The objective of this paper is to show that the flexible "any excess-demand set" framework also applies to the multi-demand setting. Specifically, we extend the auction algorithm framework of Andersson et al. [1] to the multi-demand model with strong gross substitutes valuations by appropriately defining excess-demand sets. We derive this extension by exploiting the $L^\natural$-convexity of the Lyapunov function associated with the auction model, where $L^\natural$-convexity is one of the central concepts in discrete convex analysis [16,18,19] (described in

Sect. 5). We emphasize that this paper is concerned with a structural generalization of the auction algorithm rather than the development of a new, faster algorithm.

The multi-demand model allows bidders to obtain multiple items with several units of each item. To describe the model more precisely, denote by $N = \{1, 2, \ldots, n\}$ the set of item types and by $u(i)$ the number of supplied units of item type $i \in N$. Then the items obtained by a bidder b is represented by a vector $x_b \in \mathbb{Z}^n$ of nonnegative integers, and an allocation of the auction is represented by a set of such vectors $\{x_b\}$ satisfying $\sum_b x_b = u$, where u denotes $(u(1), u(2), \ldots, u(n))$, which is a vector of positive integers. A special case of the multi-demand model in which $u = \mathbf{1}$ $(= (1, 1, \ldots, 1))$ and each x_b is a unit vector ($x_b \in \{0, 1\}^n$, $\|x_b\|_1 = 1$) is nothing but the unit-demand model. Another model, lying between the unit-demand and multi-demand models, is the unit-supply model, in which u is a vector of positive integers and $x_b \in \{0, 1\}^n$ for each b. The unit-supply model is studied more extensively in the literature (e.g., [10,12]) than the (general) multi-demand model.

While an equilibrium always exists in the unit-demand model, this is not the case with the multi-demand model or the unit-supply model. It is known (see Sect. 3.1 for details) that an equilibrium exists in the multi-demand model if bidders' valuation functions satisfy the strong gross substitutes condition, and that this condition is equivalent to $M^\natural$-concavity, which is another discrete convexity concept in discrete convex analysis. Under this condition, there exists a unique minimal member among equilibrium price vectors. While the minimum equilibrium price does not generally coincide with the VCG price in the multi-demand model, it nevertheless has several desirable properties (see, e.g., [11]). In particular, the minimum equilibrium price is the best Pareto-optimal price for bidders. We always assume the strong gross substitutes condition when we consider the multi-demand or unit-supply models.

In this paper, we are interested in extending the algorithms in Table 1 to those for finding the minimal equilibrium price in the multi-demand model. Gul and Stacchetti [11] gave an ascending auction for the unit-supply model and Ausubel [3] for the (general) multi-demand model. When used in the unit-demand model, both of these algorithms produce the same trajectory (ascending sequence) of the price vector as the algorithm of Mo et al. [15]. However, no ascending auctions have been given for the multi-demand model that correspond to the algorithm of Demange et al. [6] or that of Andersson et al. [1] for the unit-demand model.

Our approach is based on the following fundamental connection between auctions and $L^\natural$-convex functions:

- An equilibrium price is characterized as a minimizer of the Lyapunov function associated with the model (Ausubel [3]).
- The Lyapunov function is an $L^\natural$-convex function (Murota et al. [22]).

We thus follow the approach expounded in Murota [18, Sec. 8], [19, Sec. 17.3] and Bichler, Fichtl, and Schwarz [5].

Instead of directly extending the excess-demand auction algorithm, we make a detour to the Lyapunov function minimization to obtain the excess-demand auction algorithm for the multi-item model. We carry out this idea in the following three steps.

1st Step: By reformulating the concepts of excess-demand set in terms of the Lyapunov function, we rewrite the ascending auction algorithm for the unit-demand model to a Lyapunov function minimization algorithm. For each variant of the ascending auction algorithm in Table 1, we obtain a corresponding variant of the Lyapunov function minimization algorithm.

2nd Step: We show that the Lyapunov function minimization algorithms for the unit-demand model (obtained in the 1st step) can be used, without substantial changes, as algorithms to find the minimal minimizer of a general $L^{\natural}$-convex function.

3rd Step: By applying the $L^{\natural}$-convex function minimization algorithm (constructed in the 2nd step) to the Lyapunov function of the multi-demand model, we obtain the Lyapunov function minimization algorithm for finding the minimal equilibrium price in the multi-demand model. Then we turn the Lyapunov function minimization algorithm into an excess-demand auction algorithm by appropriately defining the concepts of deficiency, overdemanded sets, and excess-demand sets in the multi-demand setting in terms of the Lyapunov function.

The organization of this paper is as follows. Section 2 explains the unit-demand auction model, followed by a review on the existing ascending auction algorithms using excess-demand item sets. Section 3 describes the main results of this paper, showing that, by appropriately defining "excess-demand set" in the multi-demand setting, we can extend the existing algorithms for the unit-demand model to those for the multi-demand model. The subsequent three sections, Sects. 4 to 6, are devoted to the justification of the main results with the aid of discrete convex analysis.

Related Work. Several recent papers on auctions make effective use of concepts and techniques in discrete and continuous optimization to improve computational efficiency. Paes Leme and Wong [23] present a polynomial algorithm for equilibrium computation in an aggregate demand oracle model by making judicious use of subgradients as well as another polynomial algorithm in the value oracle model. Eickhoff et al. [7] give a network flow-based algorithm for a specific type of gross substitutes valuation, called a truncated additive valuation. Eickhoff et al. [8] present a primal-dual framework that features the polymatroid sum problem, in place of $L^{\natural}$-convex function minimization, in identifying the minimal maximally overdemanded set (= the minimal maximizer of deficiency δ in (1) in our paper). Baldwin et al. [4] present a polynomial algorithm for computing equilibrium allocations in product-mix auctions, in which the valuations of the bidders are expressed as bid vectors. Fujishige and Yang [9] propose dynamic auctions applicable to valuations of all unimodular demand types, where gross substitutes valuations are a special case of such valuations.

2 Review of Ascending Auctions for Unit-Demand Model

2.1 Unit-Demand Auction Model and Walrasian Equilibrium

In the unit-demand auction model, each bidder demands at most one item. We assume that there are m bidders and n items, and denote the sets of bidders and items as $M = \{1, 2, \ldots, m\}$ and $N = \{1, 2, \ldots, n\}$, respectively. Each item $i \in N$ is available only in one unit, and its value for bidder $b \in M$ is denoted as $v_b(i) \in \mathbb{Z}_+$. In addition, we consider an artificial item 0 that has no value (i.e., $v_b(0) = 0$ for all $b \in M$) and is available in infinite number of units. We denote $N^0 = N \cup \{0\}$.

Given a price vector $p \in \mathbb{Z}^n_+$, each bidder $b \in M$ demands an item $i \in N^0$ that maximizes the value $v_b(i) - p(i)$, where $p(0) = 0$ by convention. For a bidder b and a price vector $p \in \mathbb{Z}^n_+$, define the demand set $\widetilde{D}_b(p)$ as

$$\begin{aligned}\widetilde{D}_b(p) &= \arg\max\{v_b(i) - p(i) \mid i \in N^0\} \\ &= \{i \in N^0 \mid v_b(i) - p(i) \geq v_b(j) - p(j)\ (\forall j \in N^0)\}.\end{aligned}$$

Note that $\widetilde{D}_b(p)$ is a nonempty subset of N^0 for any p.

An *allocation* of items to bidders is defined as a mapping $\pi : M \to N^0$ such that $\pi(b) \neq \pi(b')$ for every distinct $b, b' \in M$ with $\pi(b) \in N$ and $\pi(b') \in N$; this condition means that each item is allocated to at most one bidder. The auctioneer wants to find a pair of a price vector $p^* \in \mathbb{Z}^n_+$ and an allocation π such that $\pi(b) \in \widetilde{D}_b(p^*)$ for every $b \in M$ and $p^*(i) = 0$ for every item $i \in N \setminus \{\pi(b) \mid b \in M\}$. Such a pair is called a *(Walrasian) equilibrium* and p^* is a *(Walrasian) equilibrium price vector.* An equilibrium price vector always exists, and a minimal equilibrium price vector is uniquely determined which is denoted as $p^*_{\min}$ in the following.

2.2 Ascending Auction Algorithms

We start with a generic form of an ascending auction algorithm (Algorithm 1 in [1]). Let $p \in \mathbb{Z}^n_+$ and $Y \subseteq N$. We define

$$O(Y, p) = \{b \in M \mid \widetilde{D}_b(p) \subseteq Y\}, \tag{1}$$

which denotes the set of bidders who only demand items in Y at price p. The *deficiency* of Y is defined as the value of $\delta(Y; p) = |O(Y, p)| - |Y|$.

If the deficiency of Y is positive, that is, $|O(Y, p)| > |Y|$, at least one bidder in $O(Y, p)$ cannot get any item in Y; such an item set Y is said to be *overdemanded* at p. Note that an overdemanded set is necessarily a nonempty set, since $\widetilde{D}_b(p) \neq \emptyset$ for any p and $b \in M$.

The following is a basic ascending auction algorithm, which aims to eliminate overdemanded sets by iteratively increasing the price vector p. For any $X \subseteq N$, we write $\chi_X \in \{0, 1\}^n$ for the characteristic vector of X.

Algorithm Ascending Auction (generic form)
Step 0: Set $p := p^\circ$, where $p^\circ \in \mathbb{Z}_+^n$ is a vector satisfying $p^\circ \leq p^*_{\min}$.
Step 1: If there is no overdemanded set at price p, then stop.
Step 2: Find an item set $X \subseteq N$ that is overdemanded at price p.
Step 3: Set $p := p + \chi_X$ and go to Step 1.

This algorithm, Ascending Auction, terminates after a finite number of iterations since all overdemanded sets disappear when the prices become sufficiently large. However, the vector p obtained at the termination of the algorithm may not be an equilibrium price, since the nonexistence of overdemanded sets does not imply equilibrium.

With a judicious choice of the item set X in Step 2, the minimal equilibrium price vector $p^*_{\min}$ can be obtained by the above algorithm. We explain this in three steps according to the historical development.

Demange et al. [6] proposed selecting a *minimal* overdemanded set for the item set X in Step 2 and showed that this choice yields the minimal equilibrium price $p^*_{\min}$. It is noted that a minimal overdemanded set is not uniquely determined.

Theorem 1 ([6]). *The algorithm* Ascending Auction *finds the minimal equilibrium price vector* $p^*_{\min}$ *if, in each iteration, the item set* X *selected in Step 2 is a minimal overdemanded set at price* p.

Use of excess-demand sets in Ascending Auction was initiated by Mo et al. [15] (see also Sankaran [24] and Andersson et al. [1]). For a price vector $p \in \mathbb{Z}_+^n$ and an item set $Y \subseteq N$, define

$$U(Y, p) = \{b \in M \mid \widetilde{D}_b(p) \cap Y \neq \emptyset\}, \tag{2}$$

which denotes the set of bidders who demand some item in Y at price p. We have $U(Y, p) \supseteq O(Y, p)$ from (1) and (2). A nonempty set $X \subseteq N$ is said to be an *excess-demand set* at price p if it satisfies

$$|U(Z, p) \cap O(X, p)| > |Z| \qquad (\emptyset \neq \forall Z \subseteq X). \tag{3}$$

Here, $|U(Z, p) \cap O(X, p)|$ is the maximum number of items the bidders are willing to take from the set Z ($\subseteq X$), under the assumption that only the bidders in $O(X, p)$ get items in X. Hence, the condition (3) means that for every nonempty subset Z of X, the number of items in Z demanded by the bidders is strictly larger than the size of Z. An alternative expression of the condition (3), without involving $U(\cdot, p)$, is given by

$$|O(X, p)| - |O(X \setminus Z, p)| > |Z| \qquad (\emptyset \neq \forall Z \subseteq X), \tag{4}$$

which is indeed equivalent to (3) since

$$U(Z, p) \cap O(X, p) = O(X, p) \setminus O(X \setminus Z, p), \quad O(X, p) \supseteq O(X \setminus Z, p) \tag{5}$$

for every nonempty subset Z of X. The alternative expression (4) will be used in Sect. 3.2 to extend the notion of excess-demand set to the multi-demand model.

Various properties of excess-demand sets are listed in the following proposition. It is noteworthy that there is a unique maximal excess-demand set, while there may be several different minimal excess-demand sets.

Proposition 1 (cf. [1,13,15]).
(1) *An excess-demand set is an overdemanded set.*
(2) *A minimal overdemanded set is an excess-demand set.*
(3) *An item set is a minimal excess-demand set if and only if it is a minimal overdemanded set. (This is a consequence of* (1) *and* (2) *above.)*
(4) *For every excess-demand sets X and Y, their union $X \cup Y$ is also an excess-demand set. Consequently, the maximal excess-demand set is uniquely determined.*
(5) *An item set X is the unique maximal excess-demand set if and only if it is the unique minimal maximizer of the deficiency $\delta(X; p)$.*

Mo et al. [15] (see also [24]) showed that the minimal equilibrium price vector $p^*_{\min}$ can be obtained by using the unique maximal excess-demand set in each iteration of the algorithm.

Theorem 2 ([15,24]). *The algorithm* Ascending Auction *finds the minimal equilibrium price vector $p^*_{\min}$ if, in each iteration, the item set X selected in Step 2 is the maximal excess-demand set at price p.*

It follows from Theorems 1 and 2 with Proposition 1 that the minimal equilibrium price vector can be obtained by the algorithm Ascending Auction if the set X selected in each iteration is either a minimal excess-demand set or the unique maximal excess-demand set. Andersson et al. [1] showed that the minimality/maximality condition is not needed here.

Theorem 3 ([1]). *The algorithm* Ascending Auction *finds the minimal equilibrium price vector $p^*_{\min}$ if, in each iteration, the item set X selected in Step 2 is an excess-demand set at price p.*

Andersson et al. [1, Example 1] argue that the choice of an excess-demand set in Step 2 is essential for finding $p^*_{\min}$. The behavior of this algorithm is investigated in detail for a concrete instance in [1, Example 2].

3 Ascending Auction Algorithms for Multi-Demand Model

This section conveys the main message of this paper that we can make the algorithm Ascending Auction applicable to the multi-demand model by appropriately defining "overdemanded set" and "excess-demand set."

3.1 Multi-Demand Auction Model

In contrast to the unit-demand model where each bidder is interested in obtaining a single item, the multi-demand model allows bidders to obtain multiple items with several units of each item. In this setting, $N = \{1, 2, \ldots, n\}$ denotes the set of types of items, rather than the set of individual items, and the number of supplied units of item $i \in N$ is denoted by a positive integer $u(i)$. We denote $u = (u(1), u(2), \ldots, u(n))$ and $[\mathbf{0}, u]_{\mathbb{Z}} = \{x \in \mathbb{Z}^n \mid 0 \leq x(i) \leq u(i) \ (i \in N)\}$. Each vector $x \in [\mathbf{0}, u]_{\mathbb{Z}}$ is called a *bundle*; a bundle $x = (x(1), x(2), \ldots, x(n))$ corresponds to a multi-set of items, and $x(i) \in \mathbb{Z}_+$ represents the multiplicity of item $i \in N$. Each bidder $b \in M$ has a valuation function $v_b : [\mathbf{0}, u]_{\mathbb{Z}} \to \mathbb{Z}$, which is monotone nondecreasing with $v_b(\mathbf{0}) = 0$. The number $v_b(x)$ represents the value of the bundle x worth to bidder b. For $b \in M$ and $p \in \mathbb{Z}^n_+$, define the *demand set* as $D_b(p) = \arg\max\{v_b(x) - p^\top x \mid x \in [\mathbf{0}, u]_{\mathbb{Z}}\}$.

An *allocation* of items is defined as a set of bundles $x_1, x_2, \ldots, x_m \in [\mathbf{0}, u]_{\mathbb{Z}}$ satisfying $\sum_{b=1}^{m} x_b = u$. The auctioneer wants to find a pair of a price vector p^* and an allocation $x^*_1, x^*_2, \ldots, x^*_m$ such that $x^*_b \in D_b(p^*)$ for all $b \in M$. Such a pair is called a *(Walrasian) equilibrium* and p^* is a *(Walrasian) equilibrium price vector*.

While an equilibrium always exists in the unit-demand model, it may not in the multi-demand model. For the existence of an equilibrium in the multi-demand model, a property of valuation functions, called *strong gross substitutes condition*, plays a critical role. To be specific, it is known (Milgrom and Strulovici [14, Th. 19]; also Ausubel [3]) that if bidders' valuation functions satisfy the strong gross substitutes condition, an equilibrium exists and moreover, there exists a unique minimal equilibrium price. The condition of strong gross substitutes was introduced by Milgrom and Strulovici [14] as a generalization of the gross substitutes condition by Kelso and Crawford [12] (also Gul and Stacchetti [10]) for valuation functions defined on $\{0, 1\}^n$.

The strong gross substitutes condition is known ([26, Sec. 4]) to be equivalent to M$^\natural$-concavity, which is a fundamental concept in discrete convex analysis. A valuation function $v : [\mathbf{0}, u]_{\mathbb{Z}} \to \mathbb{Z}$ is said to be *M$^\natural$-concave* [16,19] if it satisfies the following exchange axiom:

$$\forall x, y \in [\mathbf{0}, u]_{\mathbb{Z}},\ \forall i \in \mathrm{supp}^+(x - y),\ \exists k \in \mathrm{supp}^-(x - y) \cup \{0\} :$$
$$v(x) + v(y) \leq v(x - \chi_i + \chi_k) + v(y + \chi_i - \chi_k),$$

where for any vector $z \in \mathbb{Z}^n$, we define $\mathrm{supp}^+(z) = \{i \in N \mid z(i) > 0\}$ and $\mathrm{supp}^-(z) = \{i \in N \mid z(i) < 0\}$, and for any $i \in N$, the notation χ_i means the ith unit vector, that is, $\chi_i = \chi_{\{i\}}$, and $\chi_0 = \mathbf{0}$ by convention. Given the equivalence of M$^\natural$-concavity to strong gross substitutability, we can say that an equilibrium exists if the valuation functions v_b $(b \in M)$ are M$^\natural$-concave. In this paper we always assume that valuation functions v_b $(b \in M)$ are M$^\natural$-concave. It is noted that the valuation function underlying the unit-demand model is M$^\natural$-concave (see [16, Note 11.9], [26, Example 2.3]).

3.2 Ascending Auction Algorithm

In this section, we define the notions of "overdemanded set" and "excess-demand set" for the multi-demand model. This enables us to extend the algorithm Ascending Auction of Sect. 2 to the multi-demand setting.

We first define an overdemanded set in the multi-demand model. For $p \in \mathbb{Z}^n_+$ and $X \subseteq N$, define a notation $\mu_b(X;p) = \min\{y(X) \mid y \in D_b(p)\}$ $(b \in M)$. The value $\mu_b(X;p)$ denotes the minimum quantity of item units demanded by bidder b from item set X at price p. Their sum $\sum_{b \in M} \mu_b(X;p)$ is the minimum total quantity of item units demanded from item set X, while $u(X) = \sum_{i \in X} u(i)$ is the maximum quantity of item units that can be allocated to item set X. Hence, it would be natural to say that a set $X \subseteq N$ is *overdemanded* at price p if

$$\textstyle\sum_{b \in M} \mu_b(X;p) > u(X). \tag{6}$$

We refer to

$$\delta(X;p) = \textstyle\sum_{b \in M} \mu_b(X;p) - u(X) \tag{7}$$

as the *deficiency* of X. It can be shown (see Proposition 12(2)) that there exists a unique minimal member among the maximizers of the deficiency $\delta(X;p)$. In the unit-demand model, $\sum_{b \in M} \mu_b(X;p)$ equals $|O(X,p)|$ defined in (1) and $u(X) = |X|$, and therefore, (6) coincides with the inequality $|O(X,p)| > |X|$ defining the overdemandedness.

The algorithm Ascending Auction in Sect. 2 is described in terms of overdemanded sets. Although it was originally meant for the unit-demand model, the algorithm makes sense, at least formally, for the multi-demand model with the above-definition of overdemanded sets in the multi-demand model. The following theorem, which is the first main result of this paper, states that the algorithm thus obtained is indeed valid for the multi-demand model.

Theorem 4. Ascending Auction *applied to the multi-demand model finds the unique minimal equilibrium price vector* $p^*_{\min}$ *if, in each iteration, the set* X *selected in Step 2 is a minimal overdemanded set* (6) *at price* p*, or* X *is the unique minimal maximizer of the deficiency* $\delta(X;p)$ *in* (7).

The proof of Theorem 4 is given in Sect. 6. In Sects. 4 and 5, we introduce the necessary tools for the proof.

Next, we go on to define "excess-demand set" for the multi-demand model. We say that a nonempty item set X is an *excess-demand set* if the following condition is satisfied:

$$\textstyle\sum_{b \in M} (\mu_b(X;p) - \mu_b(X \setminus Z;p)) > u(Z) \qquad (\emptyset \neq \forall Z \subseteq X), \tag{8}$$

where (8) is equivalent to $\delta(X;p) - \delta(X \setminus Z;p) > 0$ $(\emptyset \neq \forall Z \subseteq X)$.

To justify this definition, suppose that each bidder b wants to receive $x_b(X)$ units from item set X and $x_b(X \setminus Z)$ units from item set $X \setminus Z$ simultaneously, subject to the condition that $x_b \in D_b(p)$. Then, $\mu_b(X;p) - \mu_b(X \setminus Z;p)$ is the number of item units demanded by bidder b from the item set Z. Thus the inequality (8) means that the sum of this demand over all bidders exceeds the number of units $u(Z)$ of supply from Z, which is the situation where the demand exceeds the supply. In the unit-demand model, the condition (8) reduces to the alternative expression (4) of the defining condition for excess-demand sets.

An excess-demand set is a special case of an overdemanded set, since the inequality (8) with $Z = X$ coincides with (6). Thus the algorithm Ascending Auction using an excess-demand set in Step 2 is applicable, at least formally, to the multi-demand model. The following theorem, which is the second main result of this paper, states that the algorithm thus obtained is indeed valid for the multi-demand model.

Theorem 5. Ascending Auction *applied to the multi-demand model finds the unique minimal equilibrium price vector* p^*_{min} *if, in each iteration, the set* X *selected in Step 2 is an excess-demand set in the sense of* (8).

The proof of Theorem 5 is given in Sect. 6 after the necessary tools are introduced in Sects. 4 and 5. Theorems 4 and 5 are the multi-demand extensions of Theorems 1 and 3 for the unit-demand model, respectively.

4 Excess-Demand Ascending Auction Viewed as Lyapunov Function Minimization

The following three sections are devoted to the proofs of Theorems 4 and 5. In this section, we present the Lyapunov function approach for the unit-demand auction model. By reformulating the notions of excess-demand set and its extremal cases (minimal and maximal excess-demand sets) in terms of the Lyapunov function, we rewrite the algorithm Ascending Auction to a minimization algorithm for the Lyapunov function.

The *Lyapunov function* for the unit-demand model is a function in price vector $p \in \mathbb{Z}^n_+$ defined as

$$L(p) = \textstyle\sum_{b \in M} \max\left[0, \max_{i \in N}\{v_b(i) - p(i)\}\right] + p(N) \qquad (p \in \mathbb{Z}^n_+). \qquad (9)$$

The set of minimizers of this function coincides with the set of equilibrium price vectors, which is a special case of a well-known result of Ausubel [3].

Proposition 2. *In the unit-demand model, a vector* $p \in \mathbb{Z}^n_+$ *is an equilibrium price vector if and only if it is a minimizer of the Lyapunov function* L *in* (9). *In particular,* $p \in \mathbb{Z}^n_+$ *is the minimal equilibrium price vector if and only if it is the minimal minimizer of* L.

Our next step is to show that Ascending Auction for finding an equilibrium price vector can be regarded as an incremental algorithm for finding a minimizer of the Lyapunov function, where p is repeatedly incremented with a 0–1 vector. In the following, we refer to a 0–1 vector d with $L(p + d) < L(p)$ as a *descent direction* of the function L at p. The next proposition connects the deficiency $\delta(X; p)$ to the value $L(p + \chi_X) - L(p)$.

Proposition 3. *([22, Lem. 5.8]) For $p \in \mathbb{Z}^n_+$ and $X \subseteq N$, we have $L(p+\chi_X) - L(p) = |X| - |O(X,p)|$ $(= -\delta(X;p))$.*

The equation in Proposition 3 enables us to reformulate the notions of overdemanded and excess-demand sets in terms of the Lyapunov function L. It follows immediately from Proposition 3 that an overdemanded set X corresponds to a descent direction $d = \chi_X$ of the function L, as follows.

Proposition 4. *Let $p \in \mathbb{Z}^n_+$. A set $X \subseteq N$ is an overdemanded set at price p (i.e., $|O(Y,p)| > |Y|$) if and only if $L(p+\chi_X) < L(p)$ holds. In particular, X is a minimal overdemanded set at price p if and only if X is a minimal subset of N satisfying $L(p+\chi_X) < L(p)$.*

Based on this relationship, the (generic) algorithm Ascending Auction can be rewritten in terms of the Lyapunov function as follows.

Algorithm Lyapunov Minimization (generic form)
Step 0: Set $p := p^\circ$, where $p^\circ \in \mathbb{Z}^n_+$ is a vector satisfying $p^\circ \leq p^*_{\rm min}$.
Step 1: If $L(p+\chi_X) \geq L(p)$ for all $X \subseteq N$, then stop.
Step 2: Find a set $X \subseteq N$ such that $L(p+\chi_X) < L(p)$.
Step 3: Set $p := p + \chi_X$ and go to Step 1.

We are concerned with how to select the item set X in Step 2 that ensures the minimal equilibrium price vector $p^*_{\rm min}$ at the termination of the algorithm. More specifically, we aim to formulate propositions for Lyapunov Minimization that correspond to those for Ascending Auction stated in Sect. 2, namely, Theorem 1 for the choice of minimal overdemanded sets, Theorem 2 for maximal excess-demand sets, and Theorem 3 for (general) excess-demand sets.

With the characterization of a minimal overdemanded set given in Proposition 4, the following proposition for Lyapunov Minimization is immediate from Theorem 1 for Ascending Auction.

Proposition 5. Lyapunov Minimization *finds the minimal minimizer $p^*_{\rm min}$ of the Lyapunov function L in* (9) *if, in each iteration, the item set X selected in Step 2 is a minimal subset of N satisfying $L(p+\chi_X) < L(p)$.*

The (unique) maximal excess-demand set can be characterized in terms of the Lyapunov function as its minimal steepest descent direction.

Proposition 6. *([22, Lem. 5.6(i)]) Let $p \in \mathbb{Z}^n_+$. A set $X \subseteq N$ is the (unique) maximal excess-demand set* (3) *at price p if and only if X is the (unique) minimal minimizer of $L(p+\chi_X) - L(p)$.*

With this characterization of the maximal excess-demand set, the following proposition for Lyapunov Minimization is immediate from Theorem 2 for Ascending Auction.

Proposition 7. Lyapunov Minimization *finds the minimal minimizer $p^*_{\rm min}$ of the Lyapunov function L in* (9) *if, in each iteration, the item set X selected in Step 2 is the minimal minimizer of $L(p+\chi_X) - L(p)$.*

To characterize excess-demand sets, we consider the condition

$$L(p+\chi_Y) > L(p+\chi_X) \qquad (\forall Y \subsetneq X) \tag{10}$$

for $X \subseteq N$. We say that a nonempty set X is *(L,p)-minimal* if it satisfies (10). First, we observe that (10) for $Y = \emptyset$ implies $L(p) > L(p+\chi_X)$, and that all minimal excess-demand sets and the (unique) maximal excess-demand set at p are (L,p)-minimal. The next proposition shows that every excess-demand set is (L,p)-minimal, and vice versa.

Proposition 8. *Let $p \in \mathbb{Z}^n_+$. A set $X \subseteq N$ is an excess-demand set* (3) *at price p if and only if X is (L,p)-minimal in* (10).

With the characterization of an excess-demand set given in Proposition 8, the following proposition for Lyapunov Minimization is immediate from Theorem 3 for Ascending Auction.

Proposition 9. *The algorithm* Lyapunov Minimization *finds the minimal minimizer $p^*_{\min}$ of the Lyapunov function L in* (9) *if, in each iteration, the item set X selected in Step 2 is (L,p)-minimal in* (10).

5 Minimization of General $L^\natural$-Convex Functions

In Sect. 4 we introduced the Lyapunov function for the unit-demand model and provided conditions guaranteeing the algorithm of Lyapunov Minimization to find the minimal minimizer (Propositions 5, 7, and 9). Motivated by the fact that the Lyapunov function is an $L^\natural$-convex function, we extend, in this section, the algorithm of Lyapunov Minimization to general $L^\natural$-convex functions. This generalization enables us, in Sect. 6, to extend the ascending auction algorithm for the unit-demand model to the one for the multi-demand model described in Sect. 3.

A function $g : \mathbb{Z}^n \to \mathbb{R} \cup \{+\infty\}$ defined on $\mathbb{Z}^n$ is said to be *$L^\natural$-convex* if for every $p, q \in \operatorname{dom} g$ and every nonnegative $\lambda \in \mathbb{Z}_+$, it holds that

$$g(p) + g(q) \geq g((p+\lambda\mathbf{1}) \wedge q) + g(p \vee (q-\lambda\mathbf{1})), \tag{11}$$

where $\operatorname{dom} g = \{p \in \mathbb{Z}^n \mid g(p) < +\infty\}$, $\mathbf{1} = (1,1,\ldots,1)$, and for any $p, q \in \mathbb{Z}^n$, $p \wedge q$ and $p \vee q$ denote, respectively, the vectors of component-wise minimum and maximum of p and q. It follows from (11) with $\lambda = 0$ that an $L^\natural$-convex function is a submodular function, that is, $g(p) + g(q) \geq g(p \wedge q) + g(p \vee q)$ for every $p, q \in \operatorname{dom} g$. The concept of $L^\natural$-convex function plays a primary role in the theory of discrete convex analysis [16,19]. The Lyapunov function L associated with the unit-demand auction model by (9) is known to be $L^\natural$-convex ([21,22]; see also [18,19]), where the function L is integer-valued and $\operatorname{dom} L = \mathbb{Z}^n_+$ in our model.

Throughout this section, we assume that $g : \mathbb{Z}^n \to \mathbb{R} \cup \{+\infty\}$ is an $L^\natural$-convex function such that the set of its minimizers, denoted as $\arg\min g$, is nonempty and bounded from below. Under these conditions, $\arg\min g$ has a unique minimal vector, which is a consequence of the submodularity of g. We denote the unique minimal minimizer of g by $p^{\dagger}_{\min}$. Note that the Lyapunov function L in (9) satisfies the above-mentioned conditions and that the (unique) minimal minimizer of L coincides with the (unique) equilibrium price vector $p^{*}_{\min}$.

The following algorithm is a straightforward generalization of Lyapunov Minimization in Sect. 4 to an arbitrary $L^{\natural}$-convex function g.

Algorithm $L^{\natural}$-convex Minimization (generic form)
Step 0: Set $p := p^{\circ}$, where $p^{\circ} \in \mathrm{dom}\, g$ is a vector satisfying $p^{\circ} \leq p^{\dagger}_{\min}$.
Step 1: If $g(p + \chi_X) \geq g(p)$ for all $X \subseteq N$, then stop.
Step 2: Find a set $X \subseteq N$ such that $g(p + \chi_X) < g(p)$.
Step 3: Set $p := p + \chi_X$ and go to Step 1.

As in Lyapunov minimization, the selection of the set X in Step 2 is crucial in obtaining the minimal minimizer $p^{\dagger}_{\min}$. In analogy to (10) characterizing excess-demand sets, we consider the condition

$$g(p + \chi_Y) > g(p + \chi_X) \qquad (\forall Y \subsetneq X) \tag{12}$$

for $X \subseteq N$ and refer to a nonempty set X satisfying (12) as a *(g,p)-minimal set*. This condition, when imposed on X in Step 2, guarantees that $p^{\dagger}_{\min}$ is found at the termination of the algorithm, which is stated in Theorem 6 below. Note that this theorem corresponds to Propositions 5, 7, and 9 for Lyapunov minimization for the unit-demand model.

Theorem 6. $L^{\natural}$-convex Minimization *finds the minimal minimizer* $p^{\dagger}_{\min}$ *of an* $L^{\natural}$*-convex function* g *if, in each iteration, the set* X *selected in Step 2 is* (g,p)*-minimal in the sense of* (12)*, which is the case if*
(i) X *is a minimal subset of* N *satisfying* $g(p + \chi_X) < g(p)$*, or*
(ii) X *is the unique minimal minimizer of* $g(p + \chi_X) - g(p)$*.*

6 Lyapunov Minimization for Multi-Demand Model

The objective of this section is to complete the proofs of Theorems 4 and 5 on the ascending auction algorithm for the multi-demand model. Our approach is to extend the dual algorithmic view, namely, the equivalence of Ascending Auction and Lyapunov Minimization algorithms discussed in Sect. 4 for the unit-demand model to that for the multi-demand model. Technically, we rely on the general results on $L^{\natural}$-convex Minimization algorithm obtained in Sect. 5.

6.1 Lyapunov Minimization for multi-demand model

For the multi-demand model, the *Lyapunov function* is defined as

$$L(p) = \textstyle\sum_{b \in M} \max_{x \in [\mathbf{0},u]_{\mathbb{Z}}} \{v_b(x) - p^{\top} x\} + p^{\top} u \qquad (p \in \mathbb{Z}^n_+). \tag{13}$$

When the bidders' valuation functions enjoy $M^\natural$-concavity (strong gross substitutability), this Lyapunov function is $L^\natural$-convex and captures the equilibrium prices as its minimizers, as follows.

Proposition 10 ([3,21,22,27]). *Let $L : \mathbb{Z}^n_+ \to \mathbb{Z}$ be the Lyapunov function in* (13) *for the multi-demand model and assume that the valuation functions v_b are $M^\natural$-concave for all $b \in M$.*
(1) *The Lyapunov function L is $L^\natural$-convex.*
(2) *$p \in \mathbb{Z}^n_+$ is an equilibrium price vector if and only if it is a minimizer of L. In particular, $p \in \mathbb{Z}^n_+$ is the unique minimal equilibrium price vector if and only if it is the unique minimal minimizer of L.*

Given the general results (Sect. 5) on $L^\natural$-convex function minimization, Proposition 10 naturally suggests that we apply the Lyapunov Minimization algorithm to the function L in (13). In this case, the key condition (12) for the choice of X in Step 2 of the $L^\natural$-convex Minimization algorithm reads

$$L(p + \chi_Y) > L(p + \chi_X) \qquad (\forall Y \subsetneq X). \tag{14}$$

Recall that a nonempty set X satisfying (14) is called (L, p)-minimal.

Under the assumption of $M^\natural$-concavity of valuation functions, the Lyapunov function L is $L^\natural$-convex by Proposition 10(1). Then we can use Theorem 6 for general $L^\natural$-convex minimization to obtain the following theorem, stating that the output of the algorithm Lyapunov Minimization is indeed the unique minimal minimizer $p^*_{\min}$ of L.

Theorem 7. Lyapunov Minimization *applied to the Lyapunov function L in* (13) *for the multi-demand model with $M^\natural$-concave valuations finds the unique minimal minimizer $p^*_{\min}$ of L if, in each iteration, the item set X selected in Step 2 is (L, p)-minimal in the sense of* (14)*, which is the case if*
(i) *X is a minimal subset of N satisfying $L(p + \chi_X) < L(p)$, or*
(ii) *X is the unique minimal minimizer of $L(p + \chi_X) - L(p)$.*

6.2 Ascending Auction for multi-demand model

In this section we translate the Lyapunov Minimization algorithm in Sect. 6.1 to the form of Ascending Auction by characterizing the deficiency, overdemanded sets, and excess-demand sets in terms of the Lyapunov function L.

First we consider overdemanded sets and deficiency, which are defined, respectively, by (6) and (7).

Proposition 11. *([21, Lem. 1.1]; see also [3]) For $p \in \mathbb{Z}^n_+$ and $X \subseteq N$, it holds that $L(p + \chi_X) - L(p) = u(X) - \sum_{b \in M} \mu_b(X; p) (= -\delta(X; p))$.*

Proposition 12. *Let $p \in \mathbb{Z}^n_+$ and $X \subseteq N$.*
(1) *$L(p + \chi_X) < L(p)$ holds if and only if X is overdemanded in the sense of* (6).
(2) *X is a minimizer of $L(p + \chi_X) - L(p)$ if and only if X is a maximizer of deficiency $\delta(X; p)$ in* (7)*. In particular, the (unique) minimal minimizer of $L(p + \chi_X) - L(p)$ is the (unique) minimal maximizer of the deficiency.*

We next connect excess-demand sets to the Lyapunov function. Recall that a nonempty item set X is called an excess-demand set if (8) is satisfied.

Proposition 13. *Let $p \in \mathbb{Z}^n_+$. A set $X \subseteq N$ is an excess-demand set at price p in the sense of* (8) *if and only if X is (L,p)-minimal in the sense of* (14).

Using Propositions 12 and 13, we can translate Theorem 7 to the following theorem concerning the Ascending Auction algorithm.

Theorem 8. Ascending Auction *applied to the multi-demand model with $M^\natural$-concave valuations finds the unique minimal equilibrium price vector $p^*_{\min}$ if, in each iteration, the item set X selected in Step 2 is an excess-demand set in the sense of* (8)*, which is the case if*
(i) *X is a minimal overdemanded set* (6) *at price p, or*
(ii) *X is the unique minimal maximizer of the deficiency $\delta(X;p)$ in* (7).

The special cases (i) and (ii) of Theorem 8 above correspond to Theorem 4, while the general case of Theorem 8 is nothing but Theorem 5. We have thus completed the proofs of the two main theorems announced in Sect. 3.

Acknowledgment. The authors thank the anonymous referees for their valuable comments. This work was supported by JSPS/MEXT KAKENHI JP23K11001 and JP23K10995, and by JST ERATO Grant Number JPMJER2301, Japan.

References

1. Andersson, T., Andersson, C., Talman, A.J.J.: Sets in excess demand in simple ascending auctions with unit-demand bidders. Ann. Oper. Res. **211**(1), 27–36 (2013). https://doi.org/10.1007/s10479-013-1344-1
2. Andersson, T., Erlanson, A.: Multi-item Vickrey-English-Dutch auctions. Games Econ. Behav. **81**, 116–129 (2013). https://doi.org/10.1016/j.geb.2013.05.001
3. Ausubel, L.M.: An efficient dynamic auction for heterogeneous commodities. Amer. Econ. Rev. **96**(3), 602–629 (2006). https://doi.org/10.1257/aer.96.3.602
4. Baldwin, E., Goldberg, P.W., Klemperer, P., Lock, E.: Solving strong-substitutes product-mix auctions. Math. Oper. Res. **49**(3), 1502–1534 (2024). https://doi.org/10.1287/moor.2019.0248
5. Bichler, M., Fichtl, M., Schwarz, G.: Walrasian equilibria from an optimization perspective: a guide to the literature. Nav. Res. Logist. **68**(4), 496–513 (2021). https://doi.org/10.1002/nav.21963
6. Demange, G., Gale, D., Sotomayor, M.: Multi-item auctions. J. Polit. Econ. **94**(4), 863–872 (1986). https://doi.org/10.1086/261411
7. Eickhoff, K., McCormick, S.T., Peis, B., Rieken, N., Vargas Koch, L.: A flow-based ascending auction to compute buyer-optimal Walrasian prices. Networks **84**(2), 161–180 (2024). https://doi.org/10.1002/net.22218
8. Eickhoff, K., Neuwohner, M., Peis, B., Rieken, N., Vargas Koch, L., Végh, L.A.: Faster dynamic auctions via polymatroid sum. ACM Trans. Econ. Comput. **13**(3), 47 (2025). https://doi.org/10.1145/3729429

9. Fujishige, S., Yang, Z.: A universally efficient dynamic auction for all unimodular demand types. Math. Oper. Res. **51**(1), 829–851 (2026). https://doi.org/10.1287/moor.2023.0127
10. Gul, F., Stacchetti, E.: Walrasian equilibrium with gross substitutes. J. Econ. Theory **87**(1), 95–124 (1999). https://doi.org/10.1006/jeth.1999.2531
11. Gul, F., Stacchetti, E.: The English auction with differentiated commodities. J. Econ. Theory **92**(1), 66–95 (2000). https://doi.org/10.1006/jeth.1999.2580
12. Kelso, A.S., Jr., Crawford, V.P.: Job matching, coalition formation and gross substitutes. Econometrica **50**(6), 1483–1504 (1982). https://doi.org/10.2307/1913392
13. van der Laan, G., Yang, Z.: An ascending multi-item auction with financially constrained bidders. J. Mech. Inst. Des. **1**(1), 109–149 (2016). https://doi.org/10.22574/jmid.2016.12.004
14. Milgrom, P., Strulovici, B.: Substitute goods, auctions, and equilibrium. J. Econ. Theory **144**(1), 212–247 (2009). https://doi.org/10.1016/j.jet.2008.05.002
15. Mo, J.P., Tsai, P.S., Lin, S.C.: Pure and minimal overdemanded sets: a note on Demange. Unpublished Mimeo, Gale and Sotomayor (1988)
16. Murota, K.: Discrete Convex Analysis. SIAM, Philadelphia (2003). https://doi.org/10.1137/1.9780898718508
17. Murota, K.: On steepest descent algorithms for discrete convex functions. SIAM J. Optim. **14**(3), 699–707 (2003). https://doi.org/10.1137/S105262340241900
18. Murota, K.: Discrete convex analysis: a tool for economics and game theory. J. Mech. Inst. Des. **1**(1), 151–273 (2016). https://doi.org/10.22574/jmid.2016.12.005
19. Murota, K.: Discrete Convex Analysis: Extended Theory with Applications (in Japanese). Maruzen Publishing, Tokyo (2024), English version to appear in Mathematical Surveys and Monograph series, American Mathematical Society (2026)
20. Murota, K., Shioura, A.: M-convex function on generalized polymatroid. Math. Oper. Res. **24**(1), 95–105 (1999). https://doi.org/10.1287/moor.24.1.95
21. Murota, K., Shioura, A., Yang, Z.: Computing a Walrasian equilibrium in iterative auctions with multiple differentiated items. In: Cai, L., Cheng, S.W. (eds.) Proceedings of the ISAAC13, pp. 468–478. Springer, Berlin (2013). https://doi.org/10.1007/978-3-642-45030-3_44
22. Murota, K., Shioura, A., Yang, Z.: Time bounds for iterative auctions: a unified approach by discrete convex analysis. Discrete Optim. **19**, 36–62 (2016). https://doi.org/10.1016/j.disopt.2016.01.001
23. Paes Leme, R.P., Wong, S.C.: Computing Walrasian equilibria: fast algorithms and structural properties. Math. Program. **179**(1–2), 343–384 (2020). https://doi.org/10.1007/s10107-018-1334-9
24. Sankaran, J.K.: On a dynamic auction mechanism for a bilateral assignment problem. Math. Social Sci. **28**(2), 143–150 (1994). https://doi.org/10.1016/0165-4896(94)00754-3
25. Shapley, L.S., Shubik, M.: The assignment game I: the core. Int. J. Game Theory **1**, 111–130 (1972). https://doi.org/10.1007/BF01753437
26. Shioura, A., Tamura, A.: Gross substitutes condition and discrete concavity for multi-unit valuations: a survey. J. Oper. Res. Soc. Japan **58**(1), 61–103 (2015). https://doi.org/10.15807/jorsj.58.61
27. Sun, N., Yang, Z.: A double-track adjustment process for discrete markets with substitutes and complements. Econometrica **77**(3), 933–952 (2009). https://doi.org/10.3982/ECTA6514

Simultaneous Ordinal Maximin Share and Envy-Based Guarantees

Hannaneh Akrami[1,2(✉)] and Timo Reichert[2]

[1] Max Planck Institute for Informatics and Saarland Informatics Campus, Saarbrücken, Germany
hakrami@mpi-inf.mpg.de

[2] Hertz Chair for Algorithms and Optimization, University of Bonn, Bonn, Germany
s6tireic@uni-bonn.de

Abstract. We study the fair allocation of indivisible items among agents with additive valuations. The fair division literature has traditionally focused on two broad classes of fairness notions: envy-based notions and share-based notions. Within the share-based framework, most attention has been devoted to the maximin share (MMS) guarantee and its relaxations, while envy-based fairness has primarily centered on EFX and its relaxations. Recent work has shown the existence of allocations that simultaneously satisfy multiplicative approximate MMS and envy-based guarantees such as EF1 or EFX. Motivated by this line of research, we study—for the first time—the compatibility between *ordinal* approximations of MMS, also known as 1-out-of-d MMS, and envy-based fairness notions. 1-out-of-d MMS differs from the classical MMS notion by maximizing the minimum share over all allocations of items to d, rather than n bundles. In particular, we establish the existence of allocations satisfying the following combined guarantees for goods: (i) simultaneous 1-out-of-$\lceil 3n/2 \rceil$ MMS and EFX for ordered instances; (ii) simultaneous 1-out-of-$\lceil 3n/2 \rceil$ MMS and EF1 for top-n instances; and (iii) simultaneous 1-out-of-$4\lceil n/3 \rceil$ MMS and EF1 for ordered instances.

Keywords: Fair division · MMS · EF1

1 Introduction

Fair allocation of resources is a fundamental problem at the intersection of computer science, economics, and social choice theory, and has received significant attention since the seminal work of [38]. The goal is to divide a set M of m items among a set N of n agents, where each agent $i \in N$ has a valuation function $v_i : 2^M \to \mathbb{R}$ over subsets of items. Over the years, a rich collection of fairness notions has been proposed, which can broadly be categorized into *share-based* and *envy-based* notions. Among these, proportionality (and its relaxations) and

A full version of this paper containing all omitted proofs is available at https://arxiv.org/2602.15566.

P. Lenzner and D. Schmand (Eds.): SAGT 2026, LNCS 16911, pp. 353–370, 2027.
https://doi.org/10.1007/978-3-032-38782-0_20

envy-freeness (and its relaxations) are widely regarded as the canonical representatives of share-based and envy-based fairness, respectively. In this work, we focus on the fair allocation of *indivisible* goods among agents with additive valuations.

In the discrete fair division setting, where resources consist of indivisible goods, proportionality is often unattainable. A central relaxation of proportionality in this setting is the *maximin share* (MMS) guarantee [15]. An allocation $A = (A_1, \ldots, A_n)$ is a partition of M into n bundles, where each agent receives exactly one bundle. MMS of each agent i is the maximum value she can obtain by receiving the minimum valued bundle in any allocation. Formally, let Π_n be the set of all possible partitions of M into n bundles. Then

$$\mu_i^n(M) = \max_{A \in \Pi_n} \min_j v_i(A_j).$$

An allocation is MMS if all agents value their bundle at least as much as their MMS.

It is known that exact MMS allocations do not always exist [32], which has led to an extensive line of work on approximate MMS guarantees. Formally, an allocation X is α-MMS, iff $v_i(X_i) \geq \alpha \cdot \mu_i^n(M)$ for all agents i. A long sequence of results has progressively improved the approximation factor, with the current state-of-the-art being the existence of α-MMS allocations for $\alpha = 7/9$ [29].

On the envy-based side, *envy-freeness up to any item* (EFX) has emerged as one of the most prominent relaxations of envy-freeness for indivisible goods. An allocation A is said to be EFX if for all agents $i, j \in N$,

$$v_i(A_i) \geq v_i(A_j \setminus \{g\}) \quad \text{for all } g \in A_j.$$

In contrast to MMS, it remains an open question whether EFX allocations are guaranteed to exist for additive valuations. Nevertheless, a substantial body of work has studied relaxations of EFX, as well as the existence of EFX allocations in more restricted settings (see Sect. 1.3). Another related line of research considers *partial allocations*, in which some items may remain unallocated [17]. In this context, combining EFX guarantee with efficiency notions is crucial in order to avoid highly wasteful outcomes.

While much of the fair division literature focuses on individual fairness notions in isolation, [9] initiated the study of *simultaneously satisfying share-based and envy-based fairness guarantees* for goods under additive valuations. In particular, they established the existence of allocations that are both 0.553-MMS and 0.618-EFX. Subsequent work strengthened this line of results: [20] proved the existence of partial allocations that are simultaneously 1/2-MMS and EFX, which was later improved to 2/3-MMS and EFX by [5]. [10] proved the existence of complete allocations that are MXS (a share-based notion weaker than MMS) and EFL (an envy-based notion weaker than EFX) at the same time. [22] introduced the *residual MMS (RMMS)* notion and proved there exist partial allocations that are RMMS and EFX, and complete allocations that are both RMMS and EFL.

Most of the aforementioned results combine *multiplicative (cardinal) approximations* of MMS with EFX or its relaxations. Another important and well-studied class of relaxations of MMS is given by *ordinal* approximations which was introduced by [15] together with the original definition of MMS. In this relaxation, instead of partitioning the goods into n bundles to obtain agents' desired threshold (MMS), we partition them into $d > n$ bundles. Similarly, we say an allocation A is *1-out-of-d MMS*, iff $v_i(A_i) \geq \mu_i^d(M)$. By setting $d = n$, we get the exact MMS. Ordinal MMS guarantees depend only on the relative ranking of the subsets of goods rather than their exact values [27]. [15] demonstrated that a 1-out-of-$(n + 1)$ MMS allocation can be achieved when *excess goods* are allowed. Absent such excess goods, only weaker guarantees are known. The earliest non-trivial result in the standard setting established the existence of 1-out-of-d MMS allocations with $d = 2n - 2$ [1]. Subsequent work progressively tightened this bound, first to $d = \lceil 3n/2 \rceil$ [26], then to $d = \lfloor 3n/2 \rfloor$ [27], culminating in the best-known guarantee of $d = 4\lceil n/3 \rceil$ [4]. Despite these advances, whether a 1-out-of-$(n+1)$ MMS allocation exists in the standard setting remains unresolved.

1.1 Our Results

In this work, we initiate the study of the *compatibility between ordinal relaxations of MMS and envy-based fairness notions*, such as EFX and its relaxations. To the best of our knowledge, this is the first systematic investigation of how ordinal share-based guarantees interact with envy-based notions in the allocation of indivisible goods.

We primarily focus on *ordered instances*. In such instances, all agents agree on the relative ordering of goods; that is, there exists a renaming of the goods as $g_1, \ldots, g_m$ such that for all $i \in N$, $v_i(g_1) \geq \cdots \geq v_i(g_m)$.

For share-based notions, it is known that any instance can be reduced to an ordered instance without loss of generality [12]. Consequently, when studying share-based guarantees alone, one may assume that the instance is ordered. However, this reduction does not preserve envy-based properties. While a simple envy-cycle elimination algorithm [33], applied by allocating goods in decreasing order of value, guarantees EFX for ordered instances, the existence of EFX allocations for general (non-ordered) instances remains one of the most important open problems in fair division.

Our first main result establishes the existence of *complete* allocations–where all goods are allocated–that are simultaneously EFX and 1-out-of-$\lceil 3n/2 \rceil$ MMS for ordered instances.

Theorem 1. *For every goods instance* $(M, N, (v_i)_{i \in N})$ *that is ordered, there exists a complete allocation that is 1-out-of-*$\lceil 3n/2 \rceil$ *MMS and EFX at the same time.*

Our second main result extends the compatibility of 1-out-of-$\lceil 3n/2 \rceil$ MMS and envy-based fairness to a more general setting, which we call *top-n instances*.

Top-n instances have recently received heightened attention. They were introduced in [36], and further expanded upon in [35]. In this setting, agents agree only on the set of the top n most valuable goods; that is, there exists a renaming of the goods $g_1, \ldots, g_m$ such that

$$v_i(g_j) \geq v_i(g_{j'}) \quad \text{for all } i \in N,\ j \in [n],\ j' \in [m] \setminus [n].$$

This assumption is strictly weaker than full orderedness. Under this setting, we prove the existence of allocations that are simultaneously EF1 and 1-out-of-$\lceil 3n/2 \rceil$ MMS.

Theorem 2. *Given a goods instance I that is top-n, there exists a partial allocation that is both 1-out-of-$\lceil 3n/2 \rceil$ MMS and EFX, and there exists a complete allocation that is both 1-out-of-$\lceil 3n/2 \rceil$ MMS and EF1.*

In our final result for the goods-only instances, we establish the compatibility of weaker envy-based notions with stronger ordinal MMS guarantees for ordered instances:

Theorem 3. *Given a goods instance I that is ordered, there exists a complete allocation that is both 1-out-of-$4\lceil n/3 \rceil$ MMS and EF1.*

Our algorithm for Theorem 3 can be strengthened to admit a Fully Polynomial-Time Approximation Scheme (FPTAS) that computes an EF1 allocation which guarantees each agent i at least $(1-\varepsilon) \cdot \mu_i^{4\lceil n/3 \rceil}$.

We briefly compare our results in the goods setting with analogous work on combining *cardinal* MMS approximations with envy-based guarantees. While existing results for cardinal MMS and EFX (or its relaxations) apply to general instances [5], the best-known guarantees for ordered instances are no stronger. In particular, to the best of our knowledge, the largest value of α for which α-MMS can be guaranteed together with EFX or EF1–even for ordered instances–is $\alpha = 2/3$, despite the fact that the state-of-the-art MMS approximation alone achieves $\alpha = 7/9$ [29].

For ordered instances our result attains the state-of-the-art *ordinal* MMS guarantee of 1-out-of-$4\lceil n/3 \rceil$ while simultaneously satisfying EF1. Moreover, prior results combining α-MMS with EFX apply only to *partial* allocations, whereas Theorem 1 guarantees complete allocations that satisfy EFX.

In Theorem 4, we turn our attention to chores instances and provide the first-ever simultaneous ordinal MMS and EF1 guarantees, even for classes of instances more general than ordered instances.

Theorem 4. *For every chores instance I that is both top-n and top-$2\lfloor 2n/3 \rfloor$, there exists an allocation that is both 1-out-of-$\lfloor 2n/3 \rfloor$ MMS and EF1.*

1.2 Technical Contribution

The main technical challenges addressed in this paper stem from the fact that existing algorithms for 1-out-of-d MMS are largely agnostic to the structural properties required to ensure envy-freeness. Consequently, these algorithms rely on assumptions that cease to be without loss of generality once envy-based guarantees are introduced. Two such assumptions are *orderedness* and *normalization* (see Definition 10) of instances.

To relax the former, we consider the notion of *top-n* instances. Although this property is not without loss of generality, it constitutes a substantially weaker requirement than full orderedness and significantly broadens the class of instances that can be handled by Algorithm 2.

To address the normalization assumption, we propose a novel normalization technique that preserves any given ordering of valuations; see Lemma 9. This construction allows us to decouple the valuations used by Algorithm 3 from those employed in the analysis. As a result, we retain the analytical advantages of working with normalized instances while ensuring that the algorithm operates on the original valuations, which is crucial for guaranteeing EF1.

Finally, the only previously known algorithm achieving 1-out-of-$4\lceil n/3 \rceil$ MMS [4] relies on a bag-filling process that allocates bags in a fixed order and fills them according to a prescribed item order. These properties are incompatible with our setting, as allowing agents who have already received a bag to swap bundles precludes maintaining either order. Consequently, the existing analysis cannot be applied directly. We therefore develop a modified analysis that decouples the performance guarantees from these ordering assumptions, enabling correctness under the additional flexibility required for envy-freeness.

1.3 Further Related Work

In the context of the EFX criterion, [37] established existence for the case of two agents with monotone valuations. For the case of three agents, [19] proved that EFX allocations always exist for three agents when valuations are additive. This was extended to broader valuation classes in a sequence of works [2,14,19] and to three types of additive valuations [30]. Existence has also been shown in several restricted valuation domains, including identical [37], binary [25], and bi-valued [8] preferences.

In parallel, researchers have explored both approximate notions [9,18,20,21] and weakened variants [8,13,14,17,31,34] of EFX, making this an active area within discrete fair division. Motivated by the epistemic perspective introduced by [11,16] proposed a novel relaxation known as *epistemic EFX* (EEFX). It has been shown that EEFX allocations always exist under monotone valuations [6] and admit polynomial-time algorithms in the additive case [16].

More relevant to our setting, Markakis and Santorinaios [36] show that 2/3-EFX allocations can be guaranteed for top-n instances. Additionally, a relaxation of EFX—termed envy-freeness up to any flip—is introduced and studied in this setting by Mancho, Markakis, and Protopapas [35].

In the chores setting, the current best-known guarantees for α-MMS and (1)-out-of-(d) MMS are respectively $\alpha = 13/11$ [29] and $d = \lfloor 9n/11 \rfloor$ [23]. [12] show that for ordered instances, there exists an allocation that is EFX and 4/3-MMS.

For a broader treatment of these results and related work, we refer the reader to the survey by [7]. Closely related is the extensively studied problem of allocating chores rather than goods; see [24] for a comprehensive overview.

2 Definitions and Notation

We denote an instance of fair division by $I = (M, N, (v_i)_{i \in N})$, where M denotes the m indivisible goods, and N the n agents. For every agent, $v_i : 2^M \to \mathbb{R}_{\geq 0}$ denotes an additive valuation function, i.e. $v_i(X) = \sum_{g \in X} v_i(\{g\})$. For ease of notation, we write $v_i(g)$ instead of $v_i(\{g\})$ for goods $g \in M$. Without loss of generality, we can write $M = [m]$ and $N = [n]$, where $[k] = \{1, \ldots, k\}$ for all integers k.

Definition 1. *The* 1-out-of-d MMS *value of an agent* $i \in N$ *is defined by* $\mu_i^d(M) := \max_{A \in \Pi_d(M)} \min_{A_j \in A} v_i(A_j)$, *where* $\Pi_d(M)$ *denotes the partitions of* M *into* d *subsets. If* M *is clear from context, we omit it and write* μ_i^d. *If* $d = n$, *we simply call this the* MMS *value and write* μ_i.

A partition P of M into d bundles is a $\mu^d(M)$ partition for agent i, if $\min_{j \in [d]} v_i(P_j) = \mu_i^d(M)$.

Definition 2. *An allocation* A *is called* 1-out-of-d MMS, *if for all* $i \in N$, $v_i(A_i) \geq \mu_i^d(M)$.

Definition 3. *Given a bundle* B *and a (partial) allocation* $(A_1, \ldots, A_n)$, *we say* i *strongly envies an agent* j *if there exists* $g \in A_j$ *such that* $v_i(A_i) < v_i(A_j \setminus \{g\})$.

Definition 4. *An allocation* A *is called* envy-free up to any good, *or* EFX, *if for any pair of agents* $i \neq j$ *and all* $g \in A_j$, *we have* $v_i(A_i) \geq v_i(A_j \setminus \{g\})$. *In other words, no agent strongly envies another agent.*

Similarly, A *is called* envy-free up to one good, *or* EF1, *if for any pair of agents* $i \neq j$ *we have* $v_i(A_i) \geq v_i(A_j)$, *or there exists* $g \in A_j$ *with* $v_i(A_i) \geq v_i(A_j \setminus \{g\})$.

Definition 5. *Given a bundle* B, *and a (partial) allocation* A, *an agent* i *is called* most envious *of* B, *if there exists a proper subset* $B' \subsetneq B$ *such that* $v_i(B') > v_i(A_i)$, *and no other agent strongly envies* B'.

If there exists an agent who strongly envies B, there is also a most envious agent of B. Namely, let B' be a minimal subset of B envied by some agent. An agent i who envies B' is a most envious agent.

Definition 6. *An instance* $I = (M, N, (v_i)_{i \in N})$ *is called* ordered *if there exists an ordering* $g_1, \ldots, g_m$ *of* M *such that* $v_i(g_1) \geq v_i(g_2) \geq \cdots \geq v_i(g_m)$ *for all agents* $i \in N$. *In this case we assume without loss of generality that* $M = \{1, \ldots, m\}$ *and* $v_i(1) \geq \cdots \geq v_i(m)$ *for all agents* $i \in N$.

Top-k instances have recently received heightened attention. They were introduced in [36], and further expanded upon in [35]:

Definition 7. *An instance $I = (M, N, (v_i)_{i \in N})$ is a* top-k *instance for $k \in [m]$, if the set of the k most valuable goods is identical for all agents. We call goods in this set the* top k *goods of I.*

Note that the agents need not agree on the values, or even the order among the items in the *top k* goods of I.

Remark 1. Definition 7 is weaker than orderedness. In particular, every ordered instance is top-k for any $k \in [m]$. Hence, for share based fairness, any instance can be assumed to be top-k without loss of generality. For envy based notions however, no such reduction is known.

All algorithms presented in this paper for goods instances, only compute partial allocations A at first, i.e. allocations where not all goods are necessarily assigned to agents. If we only wish to achieve an MMS-based guarantee, we can assign the remaining goods to agents arbitrarily. This does not work for envy-based guarantees however. To remedy this, we employ the *envy-cycle elimination algorithm*, first presented in [33]. Briefly summarized, the algorithm successively adds the remaining goods to existing bags in the following way. Consider the digraph G_A where the nodes are agents, and there exists an edge (i, j) if i envies j. If G_A contains an agent i with no incoming edge, we can add the most valuable unassigned item to i's bundle. If G_A contains no such agent, then it must contain a directed cycle C. In this case, we can assign each agent in C the bundle of the next agent along C. We eliminate cycles this way, until we find an agent with no incoming edge to assign the next good to. For a full description of the algorithm, see the full version of this paper. This procedure leads to the following lemma:

Lemma 1. *Let I be an instance, and A be a partial allocation that is EF1. Then there exists a complete allocation A' that is also EF1, and $v_i(A_i) \leq v_i(A'_i)$ for all agents i.*

If additionally I is ordered, A is EFX, and each allocated good is at least as valuable as each unallocated good, there exists a complete allocation A' that is also EFX, and $v_i(A_i) \leq v_i(A'_i)$ for all agents i.

Since all valuation functions we consider here are additive, we can divide $v_i(g)$ by μ_i^d for all $i \in N, g \in M$, and receive an equivalent instance with $\mu_i^d = 1$ for all agents. Note that all the envy-based notions that we study are scale-invariant. Hence, without loss of generality, we assume $\mu_i^d = 1$ for $d = \lceil 3n/2 \rceil$ in Sects. 3 and 4, and $d = 4\lceil n/3 \rceil$ in Sect. 5.

3 1-Out-of-$\lceil 3n/2 \rceil$ MMS Together with EFX for Ordered Instances

In this section, we present an algorithm that gets an ordered instance and outputs an allocation that is 1-out-of-$\lceil 3n/2 \rceil$ MMS and EFX at the same time (Algorithm 1).

Algorithm 1. 1-OUT-OF-$\lceil 3n/2 \rceil$ MMS + EFX

Input: An ordered instance $(M, N, (v_i)_{i \in N})$

Output: A partial allocation that is 1-out-of-$\lceil 3n/2 \rceil$ MMS and EFX

```
k ← 1,  U ← N
while ∃i ∈ U : v_i(k) ≥ 1 do                              // Initialization
    B_k ← {k}
    A_i ← B_k,  U ← U \ {i}
    k ← k + 1
end while
for j from k to n do
    B_j ← {j, 2n − j + 1}
end for
g ← 2n + 2 − k,  L ← {B_1, ..., B_n}
while U ≠ ∅ do                                            // Bag-Filling
    if ∃i ∈ U, B ∈ L : v_i(B) ≥ 1 then
        L ← L \ {B},  U ← U \ {i}
        A_i ← B
    else if ∃i ∈ N \ U, B ∈ L : v_i(B) > v_i(A_i) then
        L ← (L ∪ {A_i}) \ {B}
        A_i ← B
    else
        Let B ∈ L arbitrary: B ← B ∪ {g}
        g ← g + 1
    end if
end while
return (A_1, ..., A_n)
```

Algorithm 1 follows the approach of [4], but is augmented with an additional phase that allows agents to claim a bundle even if they have already been allocated one. As in [5], this extra phase mitigates the myopic behavior that agents would otherwise exhibit. A more subtle yet crucial departure from [4] lies in the initialization of the bags: unlike their approach, we permit bags of size one, a modification that is essential for guaranteeing the EFX property.

We can assume without loss of generality, that $m \geq 2n$.[1] Now consider the bag filling approach shown in Algorithm 1: we first initialize n bags, such that bag B_j contains good j, and possibly also good $2n - j + 1$. Then, we successively add the most valuable leftover good to an arbitrary bag, and allow agents without a bag to claim bags they value at least 1, and agents with a bag to swap for a bag they value more than their current bag. The latter is crucial to ensure EFX.

We first prove that Algorithm 1 produces a partial allocation that is 1-out-of$\lceil 3n/2 \rceil$ MMS, and later that the allocation is also EFX. Since we only assign bags to agents who value them at least 1, if the algorithm allocates a bag to every agent, the allocation is 1-out-of-$\lceil 3n/2 \rceil$ MMS. Towards a contradiction,

[1] Otherwise, we add dummy goods of value 0 to every agent, until this is true.

let us assume that there exists an agent i that does not receive a bag in this process. We call the bag that results from B_j at the end of the algorithm $\hat{B}_j$.

Lemma 2. *For each bag $\hat{B}_j$, let g_j be the second most valuable good in $\hat{B}_j$, if it exists (and $\emptyset$ otherwise). We then have $\sum_{j=1}^{n} v_i(\hat{B}_j \setminus \{g_j\}) < \sum_{j=1}^{n} \max\{1, v_i(j)\}$.*

Lemma 3. *Let $G = \{g \in M \mid v_i(g) > 1\}$, i.e. the items that agent i values more than one. We have $v_i(M \setminus [n+1, 2n]) \geq n + \sum_{g \in G}(v_i(g) - 1)$.*

Remark 2. Lemma 3 needs the assumption that $\mu_i^{\lceil \frac{3n}{2} \rceil} = 1$; hence it is responsible for the value of $d = \lceil \frac{3n}{2} \rceil$ (See the full version of this paper for further details).

Lemma 4. *In Algorithm 1, all agents receive a bundle worth at least 1.*

Proof. Assume that some agent i does not receive a bundle, as we have done throughout this section. Let $G = \{g \in M \mid v_i(g) > 1\}$, and g_j be the second most valuable good in $\hat{B}_j$ if it exists (and $\emptyset$ otherwise) as before. Additionally, let $\bar{M} = M \setminus \{g_j : j \in [n]\}$. Notice that $v_i(\{g_j : j \in [n]\}) \leq v_i(\{n+1, \ldots, 2n\})$. We then have

$$\begin{aligned} v_i(\bar{M}) &\geq v_i(M) - v_i(\{n+1, \ldots, 2n\}) \\ &\geq n + \sum_{g \in G}(v_i(g) - 1) = \sum_{j=1}^{n} \max\{1, v_i(j)\} && \text{(Lemma 3)} \\ &> \sum_{j=1}^{n} v_i(\hat{B}_j \setminus \{g_j\}) = v_i(\bar{M}); && \text{(Lemma 2)} \end{aligned}$$

a contradiction. Hence, every agent receives a bag.

Lemma 5. *The allocation computed by Algorithm 1 is EFX.*

Combining these results, and then applying the envy-cycle elimination algorithm from Lemma 1, we get:

Theorem 1. *For every goods instance $(M, N, (v_i)_{i \in N})$ that is ordered, there exists a complete allocation that is 1-out-of-$\lceil 3n/2 \rceil$ MMS and EFX at the same time.*

4 1-Out-of-$\lceil 3n/2 \rceil$ MMS Together with EF1 for Top-n Instances

In this section, we present an algorithm that gets a top-n instance and outputs a partial allocation that is 1-out-of-$\lceil 3n/2 \rceil$ MMS and EFX at the same time (Algorithm 2), and a way to complete this allocation while maintaining EF1. Algorithm 2 is algorithmically similar to the one presented in [27], but with differences in important details, and differs majorly in its analysis. Firstly, when wanting only the MMS guarantee, our analysis is significantly shorter and simpler. Also, since we do not have orderedness, to achieve an ordinal MMS guarantee, we maintain the additional invariant that every bag created throughout the algorithm contains exactly one of the top n goods of the instance.

In order to state the algorithm, we require the following two definitions:

Algorithm 2. 1-OUT-OF-$\lceil 3n/2 \rceil$ MMS + EFX

Input: A top-n instance $(M, N, (v_i)_{i \in N})$
Output: A partial allocation that is 1-out-of-$\lceil 3n/2 \rceil$ MMS and EFX

1: Set $B_j \leftarrow \emptyset$ for all $j \in N$, $U \leftarrow N$, $L \leftarrow M$
2: **while** $U \neq \emptyset$ **do**
3: Let an arbitrary "lone divider" agent $i \in U$ divide the items in L into $|U|$ bags C_j, each with value ≥ 1 to i and each containing exactly one of the top n goods
4: **for** $j \in U$ **do**
5: Let $C'_j \subseteq C_j$ be inclusion-wise minimal, containing its top n good, such that $\exists i' \in U$ with $v_{i'}(C'_j) \geq 1$
6: **if** $\exists a \in N \setminus U$ such that a strongly envies C'_j **then**
7: Let $C''_j \subseteq C'_j$ be inclusion-wise minimal, containing its top n good, with $v_{a^*}(C''_j) > v_{a^*}(B_{a^*})$ for some agent a^*, and no agent strongly envies C''_j
8: $L \leftarrow L \cup B_{a^*} \setminus C''_j$, $B_{a^*} \leftarrow C''_j$
9: Go to Line 2
10: **end if**
11: **end for**
12: Find a nonempty envy-free matching in the threshold graph $T_{C',1}$ between the bags $C' = (C'_1, \ldots, C'_{|U|})$ and U
13: **for** Agents i matched to a bag C'_j **do**
14: $B_i \leftarrow C'_j$, $U \leftarrow U \setminus \{i\}$, $L \leftarrow L \setminus B_i$
15: **end for**
16: **end while**
17: **return** $(B_1, \ldots, B_n)$

Definition 8. *Given a set of agents U and a partition of (a subset of) the goods $B = (B_i)_{i \in U}$, as well as a threshold vector $t = (t_i)_{i \in U}$, the* threshold graph $T_{B,t}$ *is a bipartite graph with nodes corresponding to agents in U on one side and nodes corresponding to bags in B on the other side, with an edge between an agent i and a bag B_j iff $v_i(B_j) \geq t_i$.*

Definition 9. *Given a threshold graph $T_{B,t}$, a matching M in $T_{B,t}$ is called* envy-free, *if for every matched bag $B_j \in B$ and unmatched agent i, we have $v_i(B_j) < t_i$, i.e. there is no edge from i to B_j.*

The algorithm starts by assigning an arbitrary agent i the role of "lone divider". They are now tasked to divide the goods into bags that i values at least 1, while disregarding other agents' valuations. Next, we compute an envy-free matching. This serves two purposes: it maintains envy-freeness from unmatched agents to the matched ones, while also ensuring that leftover goods still have sufficient value to satisfy the MMS guarantee for the remaining agents. Now we shrink some bags in order to eliminate envy between matched agents. Lastly, we give agents who were assigned a bundle in a previous iteration the option to swap for a bag we have just created. This ensures that envy cannot be created between agents who were assigned in different iterations. If this was not necessary, we assign each agent the bag they were matched to, and iterate this process until every agent receives a bag.

Algorithm 2 relies on finding envy-free matchings in the threshold graph with threshold 1 for all agents, since every agent is meant to receive bag of value at least 1.

Lemma 6 ([5]). *The threshold graph $T_{C',\mathbb{1}}$ from Algorithm 2 always contains a nonempty envy-free matching.*

The main thing left to show is that Line 6 can always be executed, i.e. any given agent i can be a lone divider, as well as that the algorithm terminates.

Lemma 7. *In line 3 of Algorithm 2, any agent $i \in U$ can fulfill the role of lone divider, i.e. can divide the unallocated goods L into $|U|$ bundles of value at least 1, each of which contains exactly one of the top n goods.*

Proof. Let S be the set of agents who are already satisfied at the start of the iteration where i is meant to become a lone divider, let $k = |S|$, and let $(B_j)_{j \in S}$ be the bags of these agents. Also, without loss of generality, we can order the goods in M by non-increasing v_i. In particular, the top n goods are now exactly $[n]$. First observe that $v_i(B_j) < 1$ for all $j \in S$: all matchings up to this point have been envy-free, so all bags allocated in Line 14 have value less than 1.

Bags assigned in Line 8 are proper subsets of C'_j, as some agent a strongly envied C'_j. Now since C'_j was minimal, $v_i(C''_j) < 1$. We also know that exactly $n - k$ of the top n goods are still in L, since every bag created throughout the algorithm contains exactly one of them. We now find a partition of L by using Algorithm 1: we apply the algorithm to L and $n - k$ copies of agent i. Since all agents are identical, this is now an ordered instance with respect to the order we chose. Note in particular that the most valuable good g'_j in each bag $B_j, j \notin S$ is from $[n]$, and since there are exactly $n - k$ many of those left, the second most valuable good g_j in each bag is from $M \setminus [n]$ (if it exists). Let $\bar{L} = L \setminus \{g_j \mid j \notin S\}$, i.e. all leftover items, except the second most valuable in each bag. Define $G = \{g \in L \mid v_i(g) > 1\}$. We now assume that one of the bags at the end of the algorithm has value < 1 to i. This is equivalent to one of the copies of i not receiving a bag. We do however need to modify the proof of Theorem 4 slightly to account for the missing agents and goods:

$$\begin{aligned}
v_i(\bar{L}) &= v_i(M) - v_i(M \setminus L) - \sum_{j \notin S} v_i(g_j) \\
&\geq v_i(M) - v_i(M \setminus L) - v_i([n+1, 2n]) \\
&> v_i(M) - k - v_i([n+1, 2n]) \\
&\geq n - k + \sum_{g \in G} (v_i(g) - 1) && \text{(Lemma 3)} \\
&\geq \sum_{j \notin S} \max\{1, v_i(g'_j)\} > v_i(\bar{L}). && \text{(Lemma 2)}
\end{aligned}$$

This is, again, a contradiction. Hence, i can divide the goods in the way that line 3 of Algorithm 2 requires.

Theorem 2. *Given a goods instance I that is top-n, there exists a partial allocation that is both 1-out-of-$\lceil 3n/2 \rceil$ MMS and EFX, and there exists a complete allocation that is both 1-out-of-$\lceil 3n/2 \rceil$ MMS and EF1.*

The guarantees from Theorem 2 are almost tight, in the sense that Algorithm 2 cannot guarantee an allocation that 1-out-of-$\lfloor 3n/2 \rfloor - 2$ MMS. To see this, we analyze a special case of the worst-case example from [28] in the full version of this paper.

5 1-Out-of-4$\lceil n/3 \rceil$ MMS Together with EF1 for Ordered Instances

In this section we present an algorithm that computes an allocation that is both 1-out-of-4$\lceil n/3 \rceil$ MMS and EF1 for ordered instances (Algorithm 3). It is conceptually similar to the one presented in [4], with significant adjustments that make it compatible with envy based notions.

In this section, we assume n to be a multiple of 3. We can achieve this by copying an arbitrary agent 1 or 2 times. This does not change 4$\lceil n/3 \rceil$, and does not disrupt the ordering condition. Hence, a complete 1-out-of-4$\lceil n/3 \rceil$ MMS and EF1 allocation for this modified instance is a partial allocation with the same guarantees for the original instance. If we wish to obtain a complete allocation of the goods, we need to decide whom to allocate the goods that were previously allocated to the dummy agents. We do this in the detailed proofs in the full version of this paper.

5.1 Working with Normalization

Many state of the art algorithms for computing share based allocations use normalization in their analysis:

Definition 10. *An instance $(M, N, (v_i)_{i \in N})$ of fair division is called d-normalized, if in a μ^d-partition for any agent i, all bundles have value exactly 1.*

This can be assumed without loss of generality if we only want share based fairness guarantees.

Lemma 8 ([3]). *If a share-based fairness result holds for d-normalized instances, it holds for all instances with $\mu_i^d > 0$ for all agents i.*

If we also want to include an envy based guarantee, this normalization condition can no longer be generated this way. In order to adapt algorithms that utilize normalized instances it is still instructive to look into methods for normalization. In particular, since we can not order the input instance ourselves, and instead assume it to be ordered, we have to ensure that the method we use to normalize the instance respects the given order; we can not, as is done in the usual analysis, normalize first, and then order the result.

Lemma 9. *Given an ordered instance $I = (M, N, (v_i)_{i \in N})$ of fair division, there is an instance $I' = (M, N, (\bar{v}_i)_{i \in N})$ that is d-normalized and ordered with respect to the order of I, and has $\bar{v}_i(g) \leq v_i(g)$ for all $g \in M$.*

Proof. We construct a method of normalizing I that respects its ordering. Let $P = (P_1, \ldots, P_d)$ be an μ^d-partition for an agent i. Now let $P_j \in P$ be a bundle with $v_i(P_j) > 1$. Now we continuously and uniformly shrink goods in P_j for agent i until either $\bar{v}_i(P_j) = 1$, in which case we stop and move on to the next bundle, or a good $g \in P_j$ has equal value to any number of goods $h_k \notin P_j$. In that case, we swap g with the good h that has the highest index in the ordering from among the h_k and g. We then continue shrinking P_j.

This method terminates, since the shrinking of a given bundle P_j is only interrupted any time a good in P_j has the same value as a good not in P_j, so at most $\mathcal{O}(m^2)$ times. Hence we have at most $\mathcal{O}(m^2 n)$ swapping steps. It also computes a d-normalized instance, as in the end we have a μ^d-partition where every bundle has value 1. The ordering remains intact by construction.

Remark 3. Since this method does not increase the value of goods, the argument from Lemma 8 still works: For any share based fairness guarantees we can without loss of generality assume that the instance has been normalized in this way.

We have now established that we can assume normalization that respects the given ordering of an instance if we wish to attain an MMS guarantee of some sort, but not if we simultaneously wish for an envy-based guarantee. On the other hand, analysis of the algorithm in Sect. 5.2 requires normalization in its MMS guarantee. To circumvent this, we run Algorithm 3 using the original valuations v_i. During the analysis of the MMS guarantee, we will then consider the normalized valuations $\bar{v}_i$, as given by Lemma 9. Since normalizing in this way cannot increase valuations, if we can prove that every agent receives their μ^d value with respect to $\bar{v}$, they will also receive it with respect to v. On the other hand, whenever we consider envy throughout the algorithm, it will be with respect to the original valuations v, such that normalization can not interfere with our envy-freeness guarantee.

Some notable points to consider for this concept are, that all arguments in the analysis that call upon the ordering can do so before and after normalization, since Lemma 9 guarantees that the order does not change. Furthermore, some bags B might have $v_i(B) \geq 1 > \bar{v}_i(B)$, so the algorithm considers B to be fit for agent i while the analysis does not. Hence we can never consider the valuations of satisfied agents during the MMS part of the analysis. We may only upper bound the value of assigned bags for unsatisfied agents, which works since normalization can only decrease values of goods.

5.2 The Algorithm

Algorithm 3 is a bag-filling procedure, much like Algorithm 1. The only difference is that we no longer allow bags of size 1 in the initialization step; instead, each

Algorithm 3. 1-OUT-OF-$4\lceil n/3 \rceil$ MMS + EF1

Input: An ordered instance $(M, N, (v_i)_{i \in N})$
Output: A partial allocation that is 1-out-of-$4\lceil n/3 \rceil$ MMS and EF1

1: **for** j from 1 to n **do** // Initialization
2: $B_j \leftarrow \{j, 2n - j + 1\}$
3: **end for**
4: $g \leftarrow 2n + 1, \quad L \leftarrow \{B_1, \ldots, B_n\}, \quad U \leftarrow N$
5: **while** $U \neq \emptyset$ **do** // Bag-Filling
6: **if** $\exists i \in U, B \in L : v_i(B) \geq 1$ **then**
7: $L \leftarrow L \setminus \{B\}, \quad U \leftarrow U \setminus \{i\}$
8: $A_i \leftarrow B$
9: **else if** $\exists i \in N \setminus U, B \in L : v_i(B) > v_i(A_i)$ **then**
10: $L \leftarrow (L \cup \{A_i\}) \setminus \{B\}$
11: $A_i \leftarrow B$
12: **else**
13: Let $B \in L$ arbitrary: $B \leftarrow B \cup \{g\}$
14: $g \leftarrow g + 1$
15: **end if**
16: **end while**
17: **return** $(A_1, \ldots, A_n)$

bag is of the form $B_j = \{j, 2n - j + 1\}$. It differs from the one presented in [4] mainly in Line 9. This is a swap step similar to the one seen in Sect. 3. The analysis presented in [4] uses that bags are filled by increasing index of the bags, however. This is a property that is not maintainable throughout the swap step, so we cannot use it without modification. We still consider that analysis, and adapt it in a way that renders this condition redundant.

To show that the allocation produced by Algorithm 3 is in fact 1-out-of-$4\lceil n/3 \rceil$ MMS, we begin by assuming towards a contradiction that some agent i does not receive a bag. This happens if the algorithm runs out of goods to fill bags before agent i is assigned a bag. In particular, there exists an initial bag B_j with $\bar{v}_i(B_j) \leq v_i(B_j) < 1$. Let ℓ^* be the lowest index such that $\bar{v}_i(B_{\ell^*+1}) < 1$. We distinguish the cases $\bar{v}_i(2n - \ell^*) \geq 1/3$ and $\bar{v}_i(2n - \ell^*) < 1/3$.

The first of these cases uses a partition of the bags into three groups. In [4], this partition is dependent on the algorithm filling the bags in increasing order of index. Since the swap step in Algorithm 3 makes this infeasible, we resort to Definition 11. That these groups behave functionally identical becomes clear in the detailed proofs provided in the full version of this paper.

Definition 11. *Let $A^+ = \{B_1, \ldots, B_{\ell^*}\}$. Let A^1 be the set of all bags that receive exactly one item during bag filling before any bag receives two items. Let A^2 be the set of all other bags.*

With minor adjustments to the analysis from [4], concerning the normalization and the aforementioned Definition 11, we achieve the following lemma:

Lemma 10. *If Algorithm 3 does not allocate a bag to some agent i, then $\bar{v}_i(2n-\ell^*) < 1/3$.*

For the second case, we only bound the value of the initial bags B_j. Hence, neither the normalization, nor the deviation from the order of the bags during bag-filling can impact the analysis. All proofs work precisely as they do in [4].

Lemma 11. *([4]). If Algorithm 3 does not allocate a bag to some agent i, then $\bar{v}_i(2n-\ell^*) \geq 1/3$.*

Lemmas 10 and 11 together cover all cases for $\bar{v}_i(2n-\ell^*)$ and lead to a contradiction. Hence, no agent can be left without a bag at the end of Algorithm 3. The last thing towards proving the correctness of Algorithm 3 is to show that the partial allocation is in fact EF1.

Lemma 12. *The allocation computed by Algorithm 3 is EF1.*

Proof. Let i and j be two agents, having been assigned bags A_i, A_j respectively. We show that there exists $g \in A_j$ such that $v_i(A_i) \geq v_i(A_j \setminus \{g\})$. We distinguish three cases:

Case 1: $A_j = B_k = \{k, 2n-k+1\}$, i.e. a bag created during initialization. We can choose to remove good k. Now A_i contains a good from $[n]$, which is more valuable than $2n-k+1$, so $v_i(A_i) \geq v_i(A_j \setminus \{k\})$.

Case 2: A_j has received goods during bag-filling, and j was assigned A_j before i was assigned a bag. In this case, let g be the last good added to A_j. Now $v_i(A_j \setminus \{g\}) < 1 \leq v_i(A_i)$, since otherwise, i would have claimed $A_j \setminus \{g\}$ (before adding g).

Case 3: A_j has received goods during bag-filling, and j was assigned A_j while i was already assigned a bag A at that time. Let g be the last good added to A_j. Now $v_i(A_j \setminus \{g\}) \leq v_i(A)$, since else i would have swapped bags instead of g being added. Also, $v_i(A) \leq v_i(A_i)$, since agents only swap bags for higher value ones. Thus, $v_i(A_j \setminus \{g\}) \leq v_i(A_i)$.

Theorem 3. *Given a goods instance I that is ordered, there exists a complete allocation that is both 1-out-of-$4\lceil n/3 \rceil$ MMS and EF1.*

The guarantees from Theorem 3 are almost tight, in the sense that Algorithm 3 cannot guarantee an allocation that is better than 1-out-of-$\lfloor (4n+1)/3 \rfloor$. This is shown by the worst-case example from [4]. The algorithm analyzed there is almost identical to Algorithm 3, it only misses the swap step. In the example, all valuations are identical, so Algorithm 3 never executes a swap step. As such, the example works with the same proof as in [4].

6 Conclusion

We studied the compatibility between *ordinal* maximin share guarantees and envy-based fairness notions in the allocation of indivisible goods. Focusing on ordered and top-n instances, we showed that strong ordinal MMS guarantees can be achieved simultaneously with EFX and EF1.

Our results highlight the potential of ordinal approaches for reconciling share-based and envy-based fairness. An important direction for future work is to understand whether similar guarantees can be obtained for general instances or with stronger envy-based notions, and to further explore the limits of combining ordinal and envy-based fairness criteria.

References

1. Aigner-Horev, E., Segal-Halevi, E.: Envy-free matchings in bipartite graphs and their applications to fair division. Inf. Sci. **587**, 164–187 (2019)
2. Akrami, H., Alon, N., Chaudhury, B.R., Garg, J., Mehlhorn, K., Mehta, R.: Efx: A simpler approach and an (almost) optimal guarantee via rainbow cycle number. In: Proceedings of the 24th ACM Conference on Economics and Computation, p. 61. EC '23, Association for Computing Machinery, New York, NY, USA (2023)
3. Akrami, H., Garg, J., Sharma, E., Taki, S.: Simplification and improvement of mms approximation. In: Proceedings of the Thirty-Second International Joint Conference on Artificial Intelligence. IJCAI '23 (2023)
4. Akrami, H., Garg, J., Sharma, E., Taki, S.: Improving approximation guarantees for maximin share. In: Proceedings of the 25th ACM Conference on Economics and Comutation, p. 198. EC '24, Association for Computing Machinery (2024)
5. Akrami, H., Rathi, N.: Achieving maximin share and efx/ef1 guarantees simultaneously. In: Proceedings of the Thirty-Ninth AAAI Conference on Artificial Intelligence and Thirty-Seventh Conference on Innovative Applications of Artificial Intelligence and Fifteenth Symposium on Educational Advances in Artificial Intelligence, AAAI Press (2025)
6. Akrami, H., Rathi, N.: Epistemic efx allocations exist for monotone valuations. In: Proceedings of the Thirty-Ninth AAAI Conference on Artificial Intelligence and Thirty-Seventh Conference on Innovative Applications of Artificial Intelligence and Fifteenth Symposium on Educational Advances in Artificial Intelligence. AAAI'25/IAAI'25/EAAI'25, AAAI Press (2025)
7. Amanatidis, G., et al.: Fair division of indivisible goods: Recent progress and open questions. Artif. Intell. **322**, 103965 (2023)
8. Amanatidis, G., Birmpas, G., Filos-Ratsikas, A., Hollender, A., Voudouris, A.A.: Maximum Nash welfare and other stories about EFX. J. Theoret. Comput. Sci. **863**, 69–85 (2021)
9. Amanatidis, G., Markakis, E., Ntokos, A.: Multiple birds with one stone: Beating 1/2 for efx and gmms via envy cycle elimination. Theoret. Comput. Sci. **841**, 94–109 (2020)
10. Ashuri, A., Gkatzelis, V.: Simultaneously Satisfying MXS and EFL, pp. 689–718. Association for Computing Machinery, New York, NY, USA (2025)
11. Aziz, H., Bouveret, S., Caragiannis, I., Giagkousi, I., Lang, J.: Knowledge, fairness, and social constraints. In: Proceedings of the 32nd AAAI Conference on Artificial Intelligence (AAAI), pp. 4638–4645 (2018)
12. Barman, S., Krishnamurthy, S.K.: Approximation algorithms for maximin fair division. ACM Trans. Econ. Comput. (TEAC) **8**(1) (2020)

13. Berendsohn, B.A., Boyadzhiyska, S., Kozma, L.: Fixed-point cycles and approximate EFX allocations. In: 47th International Symposium on Mathematical Foundations of Computer Science, MFCS 2022. LIPIcs, vol. 241, pp. 17:1–17:13. Schloss Dagstuhl - Leibniz-Zentrum für Informatik (2022)
14. Berger, B., Cohen, A., Feldman, M., Fiat, A.: Almost full EFX exists for four agents. In: Proceedings of the 36th AAAI Conference on Artificial Intelligence (AAAI), vol. 36(5), pp. 4826–4833 (2022)
15. Budish, E.: The combinatorial assignment problem: Approximate competitive equilibrium from equal incomes. J. Polit. Econ. **119**(6) (2011)
16. Caragiannis, I., Garg, J., Rathi, N., Sharma, E., Varricchio, G.: New fairness concepts for allocating indivisible items. In: Proceedings of the Thirty-Second International Joint Conference on Artificial Intelligence, IJCAI-23, pp. 2554–2562. International Joint Conferences on Artificial Intelligence Organization (2023)
17. Caragiannis, I., Gravin, N., Huang, X.: Envy-freeness up to any item with high Nash welfare: The virtue of donating items. In: Proceedings of the 20th ACM Conference on Economics and Computation (EC), pp. 527–545 (2019)
18. Chan, H., Chen, J., Li, B., Wu, X.: Maximin-aware allocations of indivisible goods. In: Proceedings of the 28th International Joint Conference on Artificial Intelligence (IJCAI), pp. 137–143 (2019)
19. Chaudhury, B.R., Garg, J., Mehlhorn, K.: EFX exists for three agents. In: Proceedings of the 21st ACM Conference on Economics and Computation (2020)
20. Chaudhury, B.R., Kavitha, T., Mehlhorn, K., Sgouritsa, A.: A little charity guarantees almost envy-freeness. SIAM J. Comput. **50**(4), 1336–1358 (2021)
21. Farhadi, A., Hajiaghayi, M., Latifian, M., Seddighin, M., Yami, H.: Almost envy-freeness, envy-rank, and nash social welfare matchings. In: Proceedings of the AAAI Conference on Artificial Intelligence, vol. 35, pp. 5355–5362. (2021)
22. Feige, U.: The residual maximin share (2025). https://arxiv.org/abs/2505.19961
23. Garg, J., Huang, X., Segal-Halevi, E.: Improved maximin share approximations for chores by bin packing. In: Proceedings of the Thirty-Ninth AAAI Conference on Artificial Intelligence and Thirty-Seventh Conference on Innovative Applications of Artificial Intelligence and Fifteenth Symposium on Educational Advances in Artificial Intelligence, AAAI Press (2025)
24. Guo, H., Li, W., Deng, B.: A survey on fair allocation of chores. Mathematics **11**(16), 3616 (2023)
25. Halpern, D., Procaccia, A.D., Psomas, A., Shah, N.: Fair Division with Binary Valuations: One Rule to Rule Them All. In: Chen, X., Gravin, N., Hoefer, M., Mehta, R. (eds.) WINE 2020. LNCS, vol. 12495, pp. 370–383. Springer, Cham (2020). https://doi.org/10.1007/978-3-030-64946-3_26
26. Hosseini, H., Searns, A.: Guaranteeing maximin shares: Some agents left behind. In: International Joint Conference on Artificial Intelligence (IJCAI), pp. 238–244 (2021). https://doi.org/10.24963/ijcai.2021/34
27. Hosseini, H., Searns, A., Segal-Halevi, E.: Ordinal maximin share approximation for goods. J. Artif. Intell. Res. **74** (2021)
28. Hosseini, H., Searns, A., Segal-Halevi, E.: Ordinal maximin share approximation for chores. In: Proceedings of the 21st International Conference on Autonomous Agents and Multiagent Systems, pp. 597–605. AAMAS '22, International Foundation for Autonomous Agents and Multiagent Systems (2022)
29. Huang, X., Zhou, S.: An fptas for 7/9-approximation to maximin share allocations (2025). https://arxiv.org/abs/2511.13056

30. Hv, V.P., Ghosal, P., Nimbhorkar, P., Varma, N.: Efx exists for three types of agents. In: Proceedings of the 26th ACM Conference on Economics and Computation, pp. 101–128. EC '25, Association for Computing Machinery (2025)
31. Jahan, S.C., Seddighin, M., Javadi, S.M.S., Sharifi, M.: Rainbow cycle number and EFX allocations: (almost) closing the gap. In: Proceedings of the Thirty-Second International Joint Conference on Artificial Intelligence, IJCAI 2023, 19th-25th August 2023, Macao, SAR, China, pp. 2572–2580. ijcai.org (2023)
32. Kurokawa, D., Procaccia, A.D., Wang, J.: Fair enough: Guaranteeing approximate maximin shares. J. ACM **65**(2), 1–27 (2018)
33. Lipton, R.J., Markakis, E., Mossel, E., Saberi, A.: On approximately fair allocations of indivisible goods. In: Proceedings of the 5th ACM Conference on Electronic Commerce, pp. 125–131. ACM (2004)
34. Mahara, R.: Extension of additive valuations to general valuations on the existence of EFX. In: Proceedings of 29th Annual European Symposium on Algorithms (2021)
35. Mancho, A., Markakis, E., Protopapas, N.: Fairness under equal-sized bundles: Impossibility results and;approximation guarantees. In: Lavi, R., Zhang, J. (eds.) Algorithmic Game Theory: 18th International Symposium. SAGT 2025, pp. 191–208. Springer, Cham (2025). https://doi.org/10.1007/978-3-032-03639-1_11
36. Markakis, E., Santorinaios, C.: Improved efx approximation guarantees under ordinal-based assumptions. In: Proceedings of the 2023 International Conference on Autonomous Agents and Multiagent Systems, pp. 591–599. AAMAS '23, International Foundation for Autonomous Agents and Multiagent Systems (2023)
37. Plaut, B., Roughgarden, T.: Almost envy-freeness with general valuations. SIAM J. Discret. Math. **34**(2), 1039–1068 (2020)
38. Steinhaus, H.: The problem of fair division. Econometrica **16**, 101–104 (1948)

Individual Rationality in Constrained Hedonic Games: Friends, Enemies, and Neutrals

Šimon Schierreich[1,2](✉) and Ildikó Schlotter[3,4]

[1] AGH University of Krakow, Krakow, Poland
schiesim@fit.cvut.cz
[2] Czech Technical University in Prague, Prague, Czechia
[3] ELTE Centre for Economic and Regional Studies, Budapest, Hungary
schlotter.ildiko@krtk.elte.hu
[4] Budapest University of Technology and Economics, Budapest, Hungary

Abstract. We study constrained coalition formation in games induced by *friends*, *enemies*, and *neutrals*, under the two standard refinements of additively separable preferences: *friend-oriented* and *enemy-oriented*. We ask for partitions that are *individually rational* (IR), while additionally requiring exactly k non-empty coalitions, each satisfying a prescribed lower and upper bound on its size. Although IR alone is trivial to satisfy for any hedonic game, the size constraints make it computationally intractable to decide whether a feasible partition exists.

The two models tell strikingly different stories. Under enemy-oriented preferences, the problem collapses to size-constrained graph coloring, and its complexity follows accordingly. Under friend-oriented preferences, however, the picture is far more intricate, and is governed by the *enmity structure* rather than the friendships. The complexity is further shaped by two factors: how strict the imposed size requirements are, and whether relationships are *symmetric* or *asymmetric*, with several cases turning out tractable in the symmetric setting but intractable once asymmetry is allowed. Charting this boundary in terms of both classical and parameterized complexity, we provide a complete understanding of which properties of the friend/enemy structure are responsible for hardness.

Keywords: Coalition Formation · Hedonic Games · Friends and Enemies · Individual Rationality · Parameterized Complexity

1 Introduction

Imagine that you are running a summer camp and must assign the arriving children to the camp's cabins for the week. The children are far from indifferent about who they bunk with: some are close friends who would love to stay together, a few pairs genuinely dislike each other and would make life miserable for their whole cabin if put together, and most are simply indifferent to the rest.

P. Lenzner and D. Schmand (Eds.): SAGT 2026, LNCS 16911, pp. 371–389, 2027.
https://doi.org/10.1007/978-3-032-38782-0_21

The assignment is also bound by hard practical limits. Each cabin has a maximum capacity; no cabin should be opened with only a child or two inside, and the number of cabins available for the week is fixed in advance.

This situation, and many others like it, captures the essence of the broader problem of *coalition formation*. The task is to partition a set of agents into *coalitions* so that the resulting configuration is *stable*[1]—that is, no agent would prefer to deviate from their current coalition. If we further assume that the agents are *self-interested* and care only about the composition of their own coalition, we obtain the well-known model of *hedonic games* [4,23]. In this work, we study hedonic games induced by *friends*, *enemies*, and *neutrals* [16,22,36,39]: each agent partitions the others into those they like, those they dislike, and those they are indifferent to. This class is a special case of a more general model of *additively separable hedonic games* (ASHGs) [5,8]. Following the literature, we consider the two canonical refinements of such preferences, *friend-oriented* and *enemy-oriented*, which differ in whether an agent primarily seeks the company of their friends or primarily seeks to avoid their enemies.

The notion of stability we adopt is that of *individual rationality* (IR) [2,20, 38]. Intuitively, IR requires that no agent prefers leaving their current coalition and forming a coalition on their own. Traditionally, any coalition structure is acceptable as long as it meets the chosen stability criterion. In many real-world scenarios, however—from assigning children to camp cabins to forming student project teams or assigning researchers to working groups—we face additional structural constraints on feasible outcomes:

1. We require that the resulting coalition structure consists of exactly k non-empty coalitions. This constraint was introduced by Sless *et al.* [40] and subsequently studied by Waxman *et al.* [41] and Barr *et al.* [6].
2. The size of each of the k coalitions must be within its own lower and upper bound.

It is easy to see that the first constraint is a special case of the second, where the lower bound of each coalition is one, and the upper bound equals the number of agents. The general model combining these constraints with IR was introduced by Fioravantes *et al.* [25] for ASHGs, building on the fixed-size coalitions of Biló *et al.* [7] and a line of related work on fixed- and equal-size coalitions [1,19,35] (see also the recent model of Bullinger *et al.* [13] with global size constraints). The particular structural restrictions we study here were subsequently investigated by Fioravantes *et al.* [26] for anonymous and diversity preferences [10,29].

1.1 Our Contribution

We provide a detailed study of individual rationality under the two structural constraints described above, considering four variants that differ in how the coalition sizes are restricted. In increasing order of generality, these are: the *k-coalition* variant, which only fixes the number of non-empty coalitions; the *balanced-size*

[1] Other desirable criteria are also studied; e.g., various notions of *efficiency* [11,12,30].

Table 1. An overview of our complexity results for friend-oriented preferences. Here, k is the number of desired coalitions, ub $= \max_{j\in[k]} \text{ub}(j)$, r denotes the number of recluses (i.e., agents a with $\mathcal{F}_a = \emptyset$ and $\mathcal{E}_a \neq \emptyset$), vc (and $\text{vc}^{\mathcal{E}}$), tw, and cw the vertex cover number of the relationship graph (the enmity graph, resp.), its treewidth, and its clique-width, and ξ the number of conflicting agents (i.e., agents a with $\mathcal{E}_a \neq \emptyset$); in the rows labeled using $|\mathcal{E}_a|$, the stated bound on $|\mathcal{E}_a|$ applies to all agents $a \in A$. Entries of the form "X / Y" display the complexity for symmetric instances (left of the slash) and for asymmetric instances (right); a single entry applies to both settings. NP-h (W[1]-h) means para-NP-hardness (W[1]-hardness) for the given parameter value.

	IR-FO-k	IR-FO-BSC	IR-FO-FSC	IR-FO-SCC
$k = 1$	P [O2]	P [O2]	P [O2]	P [O2]
$k \geq 2$	NP-h [T2]	NP-h [T2]	NP-h [T2]	NP-h [T2]
ub ≤ 2	N/A	P [T4]	P [T4]	P [T4]
ub ≥ 3	N/A	NP-h [T3]	NP-h [T3]	NP-h [T3]
$r = 0$	P [T8]/NP-h [T9]	NP-h [T3]	NP-h [T3]	NP-h [T3]
$r = 1$	?/NP-h [T9]	NP-h [T3]	NP-h [T3]	NP-h [T3]
$r \geq 2$	NP-h [T2]	NP-h [T3]	NP-h [T3]	NP-h [T3]
vc	FPT [T16]	FPT [T19]	FPT [T19]	?
tw $+k$	FPT [T16]	W[1]-h, XP [T17,T18]	W[1]-h, XP [T17,T18]	W[1]-h, XP [T17,T18]
tw	FPT [T16]	W[1]-h [T18]	W[1]-h [T18]	W[1]-h [T18]
cw	W[1]-h [T18]	NP-h [T18]	NP-h [T18]	NP-h [T18]
$\text{vc}^{\mathcal{E}} = 1$	P [T10]	P [T11]/NP-h [T12]	P [T11]/NP-h [T12]	P [T11]/NP-h [T12]
$\text{vc}^{\mathcal{E}} = 2$	P [T13]/NP-h [T14]	?/NP-h [T14]	?/NP-h [T14]	?/NP-h [T14]
$\text{vc}^{\mathcal{E}} = 3$	P [T13]/NP-h [T14]	NP-h [T14]	NP-h [T14]	NP-h [T14]
$\text{vc}^{\mathcal{E}} \geq 4$	NP-h [T14]	NP-h [T14]	NP-h [T14]	NP-h [T14]
ξ	FPT [T15]	FPT [T15]	FPT [T15]	?
$\|\mathcal{E}_a\| = 0$	P [O1]	P [O1]	P [O1]	P [O1]
$\|\mathcal{E}_a\| = 1$	P [T5]/NP-h [T14]	P [T5]/NP-h [T12]	?/NP-h [T12]	?/NP-h [T12]
$\|\mathcal{E}_a\| = 2$	?/NP-h [T14]	?/NP-h [T12]	?/NP-h [T12]	?/NP-h [T12]
$\|\mathcal{E}_a\| = 3$	?/NP-h [T14]	?/NP-h [T12]	NP-h [T7]	NP-h [T7]
$\|\mathcal{E}_a\| \geq 4$	NP-h [T6]	NP-h [T6]	NP-h [T6]	NP-h [T6]

(BSC) variant, where any two coalition sizes may differ by at most one; the *fixed-size* (FSC) variant, where each coalition must have a prescribed size; and the *size-constrained* (SCC) variant, where each coalition is assigned its own lower and upper bounds. For each of these, we chart the complexity of deciding whether an individually rational outcome exists, as summarized in Table 1. We approach the problem from several dimensions: the number of desired coalitions and the permitted coalition sizes; whether relationships are symmetric or asymmetric;

the maximum number of enemies per agent; the number of conflicting agents (those having enemies); the number of recluses (agents having enemies but no friends); and structural parameters of the underlying relationship and enmity graphs, namely their vertex cover number, treewidth, and clique-width.

Our first finding is that the two preference orientations could hardly behave more differently. Under enemy-oriented preferences, friendships provably play no role: all four variants collapse to size-constrained versions of the classic k-Coloring problem (Sect. 3), and their complexity is thus inherited from the graph-coloring literature. Under friend-oriented preferences, no such collapse occurs—the complexity is governed by the enmity structure in a far subtler way, and charting this landscape constitutes the technical core of the paper.

Since friend-oriented (and enemy-oriented) preferences form a special case of additively separable hedonic games, our results directly extend those of Fioravantes *et al.* [25] to this prominent preference domain. Our techniques, however, are quite different. Whereas Fioravantes *et al.* build their algorithms largely on N-fold integer formulations, we draw on a broad range of tools from the parameterized complexity toolbox—including color coding, bounded search trees, and dynamic programming over nice tree decompositions. On the negative side, our hardness reductions start from a variety of source problems and, owing to the nuanced picture we paint, require careful, technically involved constructions.

1.2 Related Work

Friends-and-enemies games were introduced by Dimitrov *et al.* [22]. Ohta *et al.* [36] later extended the model with neutral agents. The existence and verification of stable outcomes in this domain have since been studied for a range of stability notions [16,33,39]. Importantly, Chen *et al.* [16] studied parameterized complexity of deciding the existence of stable solutions for the friends–enemies–neutrals model. None of these works, however, considers individual rationality and/or structural constraints on the outcome.

Friends-and-enemies games form a subclass of *additively separable hedonic games* (ASHGs) [8] which, together with *fractional hedonic games*, (FHGs) [3] are among the most studied classes of hedonic games; see, e.g., [9,24,37]. As IR is trivially satisfiable in any such game without further restrictions, these works focus on more demanding notions of stability. An exception is the work of Fioravantes *et al.* [25], who studied the same model as we do, albeit for the more general class of ASHGs. Their results, however, do not pertain to our setting: their hardness results do not transfer to a restricted preference domain, and since expressing friend- or enemy-oriented preferences by additive valuations requires weights linear in the number of agents, their algorithmic results—which achieve fixed-parameter tractability only when the maximum weight is taken as an additional parameter—yield at best XP algorithms in our setting. A similar model was also studied by Fioravantes *et al.* [26]; however, for a different preference model incomparable with ours.

More broadly, across the many subclasses of hedonic games, individual rationality is rarely studied as a solution concept: either no coalition is worse than the singleton, so IR is trivially achievable even under our constraints, or it was simply not explored. The one exception we are aware of is the work of Deligkas *et al.* [20], who study IR in *topological distance games* [14]; that model is incomparable to ours, and their (mostly negative) results do not carry over.

Restrictions on the admissible coalition structures other than ours have also been considered. Beyond the k-coalition and fixed-size models discussed above, Wright and Vorobeychik [42] introduced a bounded maximum coalition size, studied further in several follow-ups [24,29,34]. Even under this restriction, however, IR remains trivial, as one may always form arbitrarily many singletons.

2 Preliminaries

We assume the reader is familiar with the basics of graph theory [21] and both classical and parameterized complexity [17].

We consider a set A of n *agents*. Each agent $a \in A$ is associated with a set of *friends* $\mathcal{F}_a \subseteq A \setminus \{a\}$ and a set of *enemies* $\mathcal{E}_a \subseteq A \setminus \{a\}$ so that $\mathcal{F}_a \cap \mathcal{E}_a = \emptyset$. Note that $(\mathcal{F}_a, \mathcal{E}_a)$ is not necessarily a partition of $A \setminus \{a\}$: agents in $A \setminus (\mathcal{F}_a \cup \mathcal{E}_a \cup \{a\})$ are *neutrals* for a; we denote their set as $\mathcal{N}_a$. We can encode the friends–enemies–neutral relations using a directed edge-colored *relationship graph* $G = (A, E, \mathrm{c})$, where for each a and every $b \in \mathcal{F}_a \cup \mathcal{E}_a$, E contains an arc (a, b). This arc is colored *blue* if b is a friend of a and *red* if b is a's enemy. We use $G^{\mathcal{F}}$ to denote the *friendship graph*, i.e., the graph G reduced to the blue arcs, and we use $G^{\mathcal{E}}$ to denote the *enmity graph* constructed from G by leaving only the red arcs. Agents' relations are *symmetric* if $b \in \mathcal{F}_a \iff a \in \mathcal{F}_b$ and $b \in \mathcal{E}_a \iff a \in \mathcal{E}_b$ hold for every $a, b \in A$. In this case, the graph G is undirected.

Any subset $C \subseteq A$ of agents A is called a *coalition*. We say that $C \subseteq A$ is a *singleton* if $|C| = 1$, and C is the *grand coalition* if $C = A$. By $\mathcal{C}_a$ we denote the set of all coalitions that contain agent $a \in A$. The preferences of an agent $a \in A$ is a weak ordering $\succeq_a$ over $\mathcal{C}_a$. For two coalitions $C, D \in \mathcal{C}_a$, we use $C \succ_a D$ to represent that agent a strictly prefers coalition C over D, i.e., $C \succeq_a D$ and $D \not\succeq_a C$. Similarly, we use $C \sim D$ if agent a is indifferent between C and D, that is, $C \succeq_a D$ and $D \succeq_a C$. A list $\mathcal{P} = (\succeq_a)_{a \in A}$ is called the *preference profile*. Throughout the paper, we consider the following two restrictions of agents' preferences based on the sets of friends and enemies:

- A preference profile $\mathcal{P}$ is *friend-oriented* if for every $a \in A$ and each pair of $C, D \in \mathcal{C}_a$ it holds that $C \succeq_a D$ if and only if (1) $|C \cap \mathcal{F}_a| > |D \cap \mathcal{F}_a|$ or (2) $|C \cap \mathcal{F}_a| = |D \cap \mathcal{F}_a|$ and $|C \cap \mathcal{E}_a| \leq |D \cap \mathcal{E}_a|$.
- A preference profile $\mathcal{P}$ is *enemy-oriented* if for every $a \in A$ and each pair of $C, D \in \mathcal{C}_a$ it holds that $C \succeq_a D$ if and only if (1) $|C \cap \mathcal{E}_a| < |D \cap \mathcal{E}_a|$ or (2) $|C \cap \mathcal{E}_a| = |D \cap \mathcal{E}_a|$ and $|C \cap \mathcal{F}_a| \geq |D \cap \mathcal{F}_a|$.

A *coalition structure* $\pi = (\pi_1, \ldots, \pi_k)$ is a partition of agents into coalitions, that is, $\bigcup_{i=1}^{k} \pi_i = A$ and $\pi_i \cap \pi_j = \emptyset$ for each pair of distinct $i, j \in [k]$. For an agent $a \in A$ and a coalition structure π, we use $\pi(a)$ to denote the coalition that agent a is part of. We extend the preferences from coalitions to coalition structures by setting $\pi \succeq_a \pi'$ whenever $\pi(a) \succeq_a \pi'(a)$.

The goal of a *hedonic game* $\Gamma = (A, \mathcal{P})$ is to find a *desirable* coalition structure π, where *desirable* is some well-defined requirement on the solution coalition structure π. In this paper, the desirable coalition structures are those that meet certain *stability* criteria. The notion of stability that we adopt in this work is that of *individual rationality* (IR), which requires that no agent strictly prefers to be in a singleton coalition over staying in their current coalition.

Definition 1. *Let Γ be a hedonic game, and π a coalition structure for Γ. We say that π is* individually rational *(IR) if $\pi(a) \succeq_a \{a\}$ for every agent $a \in A$.*

For our two preference restrictions, individual rationality admits a simple combinatorial characterization, which we use throughout the paper in place of the preference relations themselves.

Observation 1. *Let $\Gamma = (A, \mathcal{P})$ be a hedonic game and π a coalition structure.*

(a) If $\mathcal{P}$ is friend-oriented, then π is IR if and only if for each agent $a \in A$ we have that $\pi(a)$ contains a friend of a or no enemy of a.
(b) If $\mathcal{P}$ is enemy-oriented, then π is IR if and only if for each agent $a \in A$ we have that $\pi(a)$ contains no enemy of a.

Nevertheless, it is trivial to find an individually rational coalition structure for any hedonic game—simply place each agent into a coalition by themselves. Therefore, we consider the following four natural *constraints*:

1. A *hedonic game with size-constrained coalition* (HG-SCC) is a tuple $(A, \mathcal{P}, k, \mathrm{lb}, \mathrm{ub})$ where $k \in [n]$ is the desired number of coalitions, and lb and ub are functions from $[k]$ to $\{0, 1, \ldots, n\}$ setting a lower and upper bound on the size of each coalition. The solution structure π of such a game must satisfy $\pi = (\pi_1, \ldots, \pi_k)$ where $\mathrm{lb}(j) \le |\pi_j| \le \mathrm{ub}(j)$ for each $j \in [k]$.
2. A *hedonic game with k coalitions* (k-HG) is HG-SCC where $\mathrm{lb}(j) = 1$ and $\mathrm{ub}(j) = n$ for every $j \in [k]$.
3. A *hedonic game with fixed-size coalitions* (HG-FSC) is HG-SCC with $\mathrm{lb}(j) = \mathrm{ub}(j)$ for every $j \in [k]$.
4. A *hedonic game with balanced-size coalitions* (HG-BSC) is HG-FSC such that $\mathrm{ub}(j) \in \{\lfloor n/k \rfloor, \lceil n/k \rceil\}$ for every $j \in [k]$.

The relationships between the constraints are as follows: HG-BSC is a special case of HG-FSC, which in turn is a special case of HG-SCC. k-HG is a special case of HG-SCC and is incomparable with any other restriction. Naturally, a hardness result for a special case implies hardness for a more general model, and algorithmic upper bounds are implied in the opposite direction.

Given an HG-SCC Γ with friend-oriented preferences, the problem of deciding whether Γ admits an IR coalition structure is denoted IR-FO-SCC; the problems IR-FO-FSC, IR-FO-BSC, and IR-FO-k, as well as their enemy-oriented variants, are defined analogously. For fixed-size (or balanced-size) coalitions, we will assume that the given sizes sum up to n. Since we can check efficiently whether a coalition structure is IR, all studied problems are in NP.

3 Enemy-Oriented Preferences

Our first result settles the enemy-oriented case completely, by showing that it collapses to a classic coloring problem. Indeed, if preferences are enemy-oriented, then friendships play no role in whether a given coalition structure is IR: being alone is *not* preferred by an agent a to being in a coalition C if and only if a has no enemies in C. Therefore, individual rationality of a coalition structure π is equivalent to each coalition forming an independent set in the enmity graph $G^{\mathcal{E}}$; notice that enmities can be assumed to be symmetric. That is, our problems are equivalent to the size-constrained variants of the classic k-COLORING problem. Since EQUITABLE 3-COLORING is NP-complete already for 4-regular graphs, this immediately implies the following:

Observation 2. *IR-EO-k and* IR-EO-BSC *are NP-complete even if* $k = 3$ *and* $|\mathcal{E}_a| = 4$ *for every* $a \in A$.

By contrast, it is not hard to see that deciding whether a graph H can be 2-colored so that the color classes respect some size constraint can be done in polynomial time, using a simple dynamic programming approach based on the observation that each connected component of H has a unique 2-coloring up to the reversal of the colors. This yields the following result.

Theorem 1. IR-EO-SCC *for* $k = 2$ *is polynomial-time solvable.*

The polynomial equivalence with size-constrained coloring settles the enemy-oriented case: any complexity result for these coloring problems, classical or parameterized, translates directly to our setting, and vice versa. No such collapse is possible under friend-oriented preferences, where friendships can compensate for the presence of enemies; the resulting—much richer—complexity landscape is the subject of the rest of the paper.

4 Friend-Oriented Preferences

Directing our attention to friend-oriented preferences, we investigate how different natural parameters influence the computational complexity of our problems.

4.1 Few or Small Coalitions

We show that our problems are already hard if we aim only for two coalitions, yielding a strict dichotomy in terms of the number of desired coalitions.

Theorem 2. *If* $k = 1$, IR-FO-SCC *can be decided in linear time. IR-FO-k and* IR-FO-BSC *are NP-complete for* $k = 2$*, even if preferences are symmetric, each agent has at most* 8 *friends, and there are only two agents with no friends.*

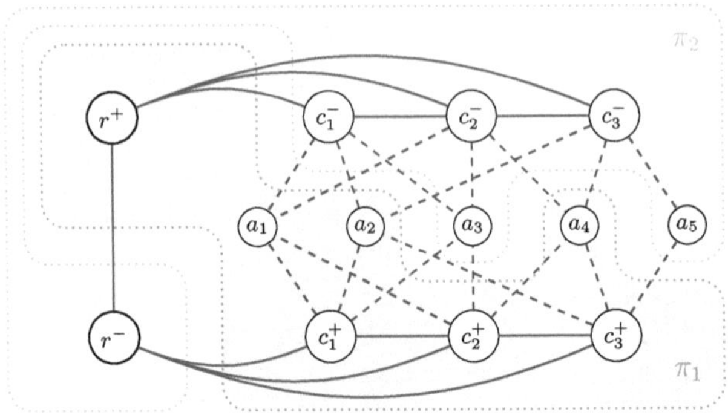

Fig. 1. An illustration of the hardness construction used to prove Theorem 2 for a formula $\varphi = (x_1 \vee x_2 \vee x_3) \wedge (x_1 \vee x_3 \vee x_4) \wedge (x_2 \vee x_4 \vee x_5)$. Red (solid) edges represent that two agents are enemies, while blue (dashed) edges represent friendship. Using colored backgrounds, we highlight one possible IR coalition structure.

Proof sketch. To show NP-hardness of IR-FO-k for $k = 2$, we give a reduction from NP-hard Monotone 4-Regular NAE 3-SAT [18]. The input of this problem is 3-CNF formula $\varphi = C_1 \wedge \cdots \wedge C_m$ over a set $X = \{x_1, \ldots, x_n\}$ of variables such that φ contains no negative literals and each variable appears in exactly four clauses. The question is whether φ admits a *valid* truth assignment, i.e., one in which each clause is satisfied by some but not all of its variables.

Given φ, we construct an equivalent instance $\mathcal{J}$ of FO-k-HG as follows (see Fig. 1 for an illustration of the construction). We have one *variable agent* a_i for every variable $x_i \in X$, and two *clause agents* c_j^+ and c_j^- for every clause C_j. In addition, we create two *guard agents* r^+ and r^-, whom we let be enemies. We also let r^+ be enemies with all clause agents c_j^-, and similarly, r^- be enemies with all clause agents c_j^+. The guard agents have no friends. Furthermore, for each $j \in [m-1]$ the pairs (c_j^-, c_{j+1}^-) and (c_j^+, c_{j+1}^+) of clause agents are also enemies. Each clause agent c_j^+ or c_j^- has three variable agents as their friends, namely the ones corresponding to literals present in the clause C_j. All remaining relations are neutral. To finalize the construction, we set $k = 2$.

For correctness, assume first that α is a valid assignment for φ. Then the coalition structure π defined by $\pi_1 = \{r^+\} \cup \{c_j^+ : j \in [m]\} \cup \{a_i : \alpha(x_i) = \texttt{true}\}$ and $\pi_2 = A \setminus \pi_2$ is IR for $\mathcal{J}$, as can be checked in a straightforward way.

In the opposite direction, let $\pi = (\pi_1, \pi_2)$ be an IR coalition structure for $\mathcal{J}$. We first observe that r^+ and r^- cannot be members of the same coalition, since they do not have friends and are mutual enemies. By the same argument, no clause agent c_j^- can be in the same coalition with r^+, and no clause agent c_j^+ can be in the same coalition as r^-. Hence, without loss of generality, we can assume that $\{r^+, c_1^+, \ldots, c_m^+\} \subseteq \pi_1$ and $\{r^-, c_1^-, \ldots, c_m^-\} \subseteq \pi_2$. We construct an assignment α by setting $\alpha(x_i) = \texttt{true}$ if and only if $a_i \in \pi_1$ for every $i \in [n]$. For contradiction, assume that α is not valid for φ, i.e., there is a clause C_j with either all or none of its literals being true. In the former case, all friends of c_j^- are in π_1. However, c_j^- has at least one enemy in π_2, which contradicts the individual rationality of π. In the latter case, we apply the same argument on c_j^+. Consequently, α is a valid truth assignment, finishing the proof for IR-FO-k. For IR-FO-BSC, we simply add n dummy agents $d_1, \ldots, d_n$ that are neutrals from the perspective of all agents.

Next, we show that aiming for small coalitions does not yield tractability: our problems are hard already if we require each coalition to be of size at most 3. The reduction is from the NP-hard $\{P_3, K_3, K_{1,3}\}$-DECOMPOSITION problem, which is known to be NP-hard even on graphs of maximum degree 3 [15]. Given a graph $H = (W, F)$ with $|F| = 3m$, this problem asks if F can be partitioned into sets $F_1, \ldots, F_m$ of size exactly 3 so that each F_i forms a 3-edge path (P_3), a triangle (K_3), or a star with three edges ($K_{1,3}$). The main idea of our reduction is to introduce an agent corresponding to each edge of the input graph H, with two agents being friends if the corresponding edges share an end-vertex and being enemies otherwise. It is not hard to see that in such a game, a coalition of size 3 is IR iff the corresponding edges in $H \simeq P_3, K_3, K_{1,3}$.

Theorem 3. IR-FO-BSC *is NP-complete even if* $\mathrm{ub}(j) = 3$ *for* $\forall j \in [k]$, *preferences are symmetric,* $|\mathcal{F}_a| \in \{3, 4\}$ *for* $\forall a \in A$, *and there are no neutrals.*

Contrasting Theorem 3, we show that if each coalition must be either a pair of agents or a singleton, then our problems are solvable efficiently. Our algorithm relies on the observation that a coalition formed by two agents is IR if and only if there is no enmity between these two agents (in any direction). By searching for a matching of an appropriate size in the graph where two agents are connected by an edge if and only if neither considers the other an enemy, we can solve our instance in the same time necessary for finding a maximum matching.

Theorem 4. *If* $\mathrm{ub}(j) \leq 2$ *for every* $j \in [k]$, *then* IR-FO-SCC $\in$ P.

4.2 Small Number of Enemies

First, observe that if no agent has enemies, then any coalition structure is IR. Hence, we only need to check whether the size constraints can be respected. In fact, for this, we only need to check whether $n \geq \sum_{i \in [k]} \mathrm{lb}(i)$ and $n \leq \sum_{i \in [k]} \mathrm{ub}(i)$, yielding a linear-time algorithm.

Proposition 1. *If* $|\mathcal{E}_a| = 0$ *for every* $a \in A$, *then* IR-FO-SCC $\in$ P.

If each agent has only one enemy, then we can create a balanced coalition structure (i.e., where all coalition sizes differ by at most 1) using a simple and fast algorithm: It suffices to place each agent that has some enemy into a coalition not shared by their unique mutual enemy. To achieve this, we fix an ordering of the agents so that agents with at least one enemy precede those without enemies, and each agent is next to their enemy (if they have one). Applying the round robin method based on this ordering to place the agents into k coalitions, we obtain an IR coalition structure.

Theorem 5. *If* $|\mathcal{E}_a| \leq 1$ *for every* $a \in A$ *and enmities are symmetric, then* IR-FO-BSC *and IR-FO-k can be solved in polynomial time.*

Theorem 5 is contrasted by our next result, which shows that both IR-FO-BSC and IR-FO-k become intractable once each agent has four enemies, even if the number of coalitions is only $k = 3$. This result follows from the NP-hardness of the classic 3-coloring problem and its equitable variant, where the sizes of the color classes have to differ by at most 1; both of these problems are known to be NP-complete even on 4-regular graphs [28]. Our reduction is very simple: each vertex is represented by an agent with no friends, and two agents are enemies if and only if the corresponding vertices are adjacent in the input graph.

Theorem 6. IR-FO-BSC *and IR-FO-k are NP-complete even if preferences are symmetric,* $k = 3$*, and* $|\mathcal{E}_a| = 4$ *for every* $a \in A$.

For the variant where the coalition structure is not required to be balanced but the coalition sizes are still fixed, the problem remains hard even if each agent has exactly three enemies; to show this, we use a reduction from the NP-complete SEMI-EQUITABLE 3-COLORING problem [27] where the color classes of an n-vertex input graph need to be of size $4n/10$, $3n/10$, and $3n/10$.

Theorem 7. IR-FO-FSC *is NP-complete even if preferences are symmetric,* $k = 3$*, and* $|\mathcal{E}_a| = 3$ *for every* $a \in A$.

4.3 Small Number of Recluses

Notice that under friend-oriented preferences, agents without friends are usually the source of computational intractability, since they must be placed in a coalition that contains none of their enemies, and thus we may need to seek coalitions that form independent sets in the enemy graph—an idea utilized in our reduction from 3-COLORING and its variants in the proofs of Theorem 6 and 7. Hence, it makes sense to study how the number of such agents influences the complexity of our problems, motivating the following definition.

Definition 2. *An agent* $a \in A$ *is called a* recluse *if* $\mathcal{F}_a = \emptyset$ *and* $|\mathcal{E}_a| \geq 1$.

Notice that with upper and lower bounds on the number of coalition sizes, Theorem 3 implies that even symmetric instances with no recluses are intractable. For IR-FO-k, i.e., when only the number of coalitions is given, Theorem 2 shows that even two recluses suffice to cause NP-hardness. By contrast, IR-FO-k can be solved if preferences are symmetric and there are no recluses.

Theorem 8. *If there are no recluses, every symmetric IR-FO-k* Γ *admits an individually rational coalition structure which can be found in polynomial time.*

Proof. Recall that $k \leq n$. We first identify all connected components $K_1, \dots, K_\ell$ of the friendship graph $G^{\mathcal{F}}$. Due to the absence of recluses, each K_j is either of size at least two or contains a single agent that has neither friends nor enemies.

If $k \leq \ell$, then we set $\pi_j = V(K_j)$ for each $j \in [k-1]$ and $\pi_k = \bigcup_{j=k}^{\ell} V(K_j)$. Then π has k non-empty coalitions and is IR due to our previous observation.

If $k > \ell$, then for every component K_j, $j \in [\ell]$, we compute a spanning tree T_j. We start by setting $\pi_j = V(K_j)$ for every $j \in [\ell]$. This is IR as shown above, but coalitions π_j for $j > \ell$ are empty. Hence, we do the following: let π_j be a non-empty coalition of size at least two and $\pi_{j'}$ be an empty coalition. We find agent $a \in \pi_j$ that is a leaf of the spanning tree T_j; we move a from π_j to $\pi_{j'}$. Now, agent a is in a singleton coalition, so $\pi_{j'}$ is IR for a. Since we removed a leaf from the tree of T_j, the coalition $\pi_j \setminus \{a\}$ remains also IR, since each agent of $\pi_j \setminus \{a\}$ still has at least one friend in $\pi_j \setminus \{a\}$—their neighbor in $T_j \setminus \{a\}$. The procedure terminates once all k coalitions are non-empty. The invariant of individual rationality is satisfied after each transfer. □

Unfortunately, the algorithm of Theorem 8 cannot be extended to the asymmetric case, as our next result shows.

Theorem 9. *IR-FO-k is NP-complete even if there are no recluses.*

Proof sketch. We reduce from 3-Coloring. Let H be the input graph. We construct an instance Γ of IR-FO-k as follows. Let us set $K = |V(H)|^2$. For each vertex $u \in V(H)$, we introduce a *vertex-agent* a_u and $K-1$ additional dummy agents; these K agents together will form a directed cycle of length K in the friendship graph $G^{\mathcal{F}}$. In fact, $G^{\mathcal{F}}$ will be the disjoint union of these $|V(H)|$ cycles, which immediately implies that no recluses are contained in our instance, as each agent has exactly one friend. Besides these friendships, we let each dummy agent consider every agent other than their unique friend and themselves an enemy. Each vertex agent considers all dummy agents other than their unique friend as an enemy. Finally, two vertex agents a_u and a_v consider each other mutual enemies if u and v are adjacent in H. Finally, we set $k = (K-1) \cdot |V(H)| + 3$. It is not hard to verify that H is 3-colorable if and only if Γ admits an IR coalition structure with exactly k non-empty coalitions. ⊿

Theorem 8 and 9 leave open only the symmetric case with exactly one recluse.

4.4 Restricting the Enmity Graph

Next, we examine how the structure of the enmity graph influences the tractability of our problems. We consider the vertex cover number of $G^{\mathcal{E}}$, denoted by $\mathrm{vc}(G^{\mathcal{E}})$. We start with a simple algorithm for the case when $\mathrm{vc}(G^{\mathcal{E}}) \leq 1$: the main idea is to place the unique problematic agent—the one incident to all edges in $G^{\mathcal{E}}$—into a singleton.

Theorem 10. *If* $\mathrm{vc}(G^{\mathcal{E}}) \leq 1$, *then IR-FO-k can be solved in linear time.*

For symmetric instances, in the case $\mathrm{vc}(G^{\mathcal{E}}) \leq 1$, a polynomial-time algorithm based on a more careful case analysis can solve the IR-FO-SCC problem.

Theorem 11. *If* $\mathrm{vc}(G^{\mathcal{E}}) \leq 1$, *then* IR-FO-SCC *for symmetric instances can be solved in polynomial time.*

Proof. If there are no enmities, then we can solve the instance by Proposition 1. So we assume $\mathrm{vc}(G^{\mathcal{E}}) = 1$, and let c be the agent covering all edges in $G^{\mathcal{E}}$. We start by first guessing the coalition j containing c and its size $s_j \in [n]$ in a solution π. Next, we guess whether c has an enemy in $\pi_j = \pi(c)$.

If c has no enemies in π_j, then we can put an arbitrary set of $s_j - 1$ agents into a coalition C together with c from among $A \setminus \mathcal{E}_c$, and set C is the j-th coalition; if $|A \setminus \mathcal{E}_c| < s_j$, we can reject the current set of guesses. We can then distribute the remaining agents across the remaining coalitions arbitrarily in a way that respects the lower and upper bounds, if this is possible, since there are no enmities between the remaining agents (see the method in Proposition 1).

If c has some enemies in π_j, then we also guess a friend c' of c in π_j. Next, we start adding agents to a coalition C, which initially contains c and c', as follows: as long as $|C| < s_j$, we try to add an agent to C that either does not consider c an enemy or considers some agent in C a friend. If this procedure stops with $|C| < s_j$, then consider the set X of those remaining agents—all of them enemies of c—that have at least one friend. We aim to find a subset $X' \subseteq X$ of s'_j agents that is *valid*, that is, each of them has at least one friend in X'. Adding a valid set of size s'_j to C yields an IR coalition of size s_j.

Observe that if $s'_j = s_j - |C| > |X|$, then no IR coalition exists of size s_j containing c, since every enemy of c in π_j must have a friend in π_j too; thus, we can reject. Otherwise, it is possible to find a valid set X' unless (i) $s'_j = 1$, or (ii) s'_j is odd, but the subgraph of $G^{\mathcal{F}}$ induced by X is the union of independent edges (i.e., a matching). In these cases, if $C = \{c, c'\}$, then no IR coalition of size s_j contains c, because each edge in $G^{\mathcal{F}}[X]$ must have either 0 or 2 of its endpoints in such a coalition. If $|C| > 2$, then it suffices to remove the agent added at the last step to C, and add to C a valid set of $s'_j + 1$ agents from X, obtaining an IR coalition of size s_j containing c. Since there are no enmities between the remaining agents, we can distribute them respecting the upper and lower bounds of the coalitions (or reject if this is not possible). There are at most n^3 guesses, and each of them can be verified in linear time. □

Unfortunately, the algorithm in Theorem 11 cannot be generalized to the asymmetric case, as shown by the following strong intractability result.

Theorem 12. IR-FO-BSC *is NP-complete even if* $\mathrm{vc}(G^{\mathcal{E}}) = 1$, $k = 2$, *and* $|\mathcal{E}_a| \leq 1$ *and* $|\mathcal{F}_a| \leq 2$ *for each* $a \in A$.

If preferences are symmetric, we can generalize the algorithm of Theorem 10 for a vertex cover of size 3, using an extensive case analysis.

Theorem 13. *If* $\mathrm{vc}(G^{\mathcal{E}}) \leq 3$ *and preferences are symmetric, IR-FO-k can be solved in polynomial time.*

The next three intractability results show that the algorithm for IR-FO-k in Theorem 13 cannot be generalized to (a) deal with asymmetric preferences, even if $\mathrm{vc}(G^{\mathcal{E}}) = 2$ and we ask for $k = 2$ coalitions, (b) solve IR-FO-k for symmetric instances with $\mathrm{vc}(G^{\mathcal{E}}) = 4$, or (c) solve IR-FO-BSC under the same restrictions. These results are obtained by reductions similar to the one of Theorem 2.

Theorem 14. *The followings hold:*

(a) IR-FO-k is NP-complete even if $\mathrm{vc}(G^{\mathcal{E}}) = 2$, $k = 2$ *and* $\max_{a \in A} |\mathcal{E}_a| \leq 1$.
(b) IR-FO-k is NP-complete even if $\mathrm{vc}(G^{\mathcal{E}}) = 4$ *and the instance is symmetric.*
(c) IR-FO-BSC *is NP-complete even on symmetric instances with* $\mathrm{vc}(G^{\mathcal{E}}) = 3$.

We close this section with a result that shows that taking the number ξ of agents that have enemies as a parameter, IR-FO-FSC is fixed-parameter tractable. The result is based on the observation that friendship relations between agents who have no enemies can be removed; hence, the underlying relationship graph is guaranteed to have a vertex cover of size ξ. As we will see in Theorem 19, such instances can be solved in FPT time with respect to ξ.

Theorem 15. IR-FO-FSC *is in FPT when parameterized by the number of conflicting agents* $\xi = |\{a \in A : \mathcal{E}_a \neq \emptyset\}|$.

4.5 Restricting the Relationship Graph

We now turn our attention to the relationship graph G—including both friendships and enmities—to study how classic structural graph parameters such as treewidth and clique-width influence the computational complexity of our problems.
To start with, we develop a fixed-parameter tractable algorithm for IR-FO-k with parameter $\mathrm{tw}(G)$, the treewidth of G. Although our algorithm uses the standard method of dynamic programming along a tree-decomposition of G, the details of the computation and the proof of its correctness are far from trivial.

Theorem 16. *IR-FO-k admits an algorithm with* $2^{\mathcal{O}(\mathrm{tw}(G)\cdot\log \mathrm{tw}(G))} \cdot n$ *running time. Thus, IR-FO-k is in FPT parameterized by the treewidth of G.*

Proof sketch. For the sake of exposition, we assume that $k \leq \mathrm{tw}(G)$ in this proof sketch. We formulate an explicit bottom-up dynamic programming algorithm over a *nice* tree decomposition $\mathcal{T}$ of G—a rooted tree decomposition in a standard normal form whose nodes are of four types (leaf, introduce, forget, and join nodes), simplifying the description of the computation; see the textbook of Cygan *et al.* [17] for a formal definition.

For every node x of $\mathcal{T}$, let $\beta(x)$ denote the agents in the bag of x, and let A^x denote the set of agents in the union of all bags in the subtree of $\mathcal{T}$ rooted at x. We compute a dynamic programming table $\mathrm{DP}_x[p, f, s]$, where $p\colon \beta(x) \to [k]$ is a partition of bag agents between coalitions, $f\colon \beta(x) \to \{-1, 0, 1\}$ assigns to each bag agent a *flag* based on their neighborhood, and $s\colon [k] \to \{0, 1\}$ represents whether the coalition $j \in [k]$ is non-empty. We call the triple (p, f, s) a *signature*. Observe that for each node x, there are at most $k^{\mathcal{O}(\mathrm{tw})} \cdot 3^{\mathcal{O}(\mathrm{tw})} \cdot 2^{\mathcal{O}(k)} = 2^{\mathcal{O}(\mathrm{tw}\cdot\log \mathrm{tw})}$ different signatures. For a signature (p, f, s), the table DP_x stores `true` if there exists a corresponding *partial partition* π' of A^x such that

(i) for every agent $a \in \beta(x)$ we have $\pi'(a) = \pi'_{p(a)}$, that is, each bag agent is allocated to the correct coalition,
(ii) for every agent $a \in \beta(x)$ such that $f(a) = -1$ holds that $|\pi'(a) \cap \mathcal{E}_a| \geq 1$ and $|\pi'(a) \cap \mathcal{F}_a| = 0$,
(iii) for every agent $a \in \beta(x)$ such that $f(a) = 0$ holds that $|\pi'(a) \cap \mathcal{E}_a| = |\pi'(a) \cap \mathcal{F}_a| = 0$,
(iv) for every agent $a \in \beta(x)$ such that $f(a) = 1$ holds that $|\pi'(a) \cap \mathcal{F}_a| \geq 1$,
(v) for every agent $a \in A^x \setminus \beta(x)$ the partition π' is IR, and
(vi) for every $j \in [k]$ it holds that $|\pi_j| \geq 1$ if $s(j) = 1$ and $|\pi_j| = 0$ otherwise.

If no such partial partition exists for (p, f, s), the dynamic programming table stores `false` for this signature.

Assume now that the dynamic programming table is computed correctly for the root node r. By definition, the bag of the root node is empty. Therefore, we ask if $\mathrm{DP}_r[\emptyset, \emptyset, \mathbf{1}]$, where $\emptyset$ represents the function with an empty domain and $\mathbf{1}$ is a constant-1 function, is set to `true`. If it is the case, then there exists a partition of $A^r = A$ which is individually rational for every agent $a \in A$ by property (v) and all coalitions are non-empty by property (vi). So, the algorithm returns *yes*. Otherwise, no such partition exists, and, therefore, the algorithm correctly returns *no*. $\triangle$

We can extend our dynamic programming algorithm on the tree-decomposition of the relationship graph G so that for each coalition that has an agent in the current bag, we store the number of agents contained in a partial solution; this approach yields an XP algorithm for our size-constrained problem variants with parameter $k + \mathrm{tw}(G)$.

Theorem 17. IR-FO-SCC *is in XP parameterized by* $k + \mathrm{tw}(G)$.

Based on our reductions from the q-COLORING problem—the generalization of 3-COLORING in which the vertices must be properly colored using q colors—we can show that our algorithm presented in Theorem 16 has optimal running time, assuming the Exponential Time Hypothesis (ETH) [32]. In addition, the same reduction allows us to observe that IR-FO-k is W[1]-hard when parameterized by the clique-width of G. These intractability results also extend to the IR-FO-BSC problem, due to known results on the EQUITABLE q-COLORING problem.

Theorem 18. *The followings hold:*

(a) Unless ETH fails, no algorithm solves FO-k-HG in $2^{o(\mathrm{tw}(G) \cdot \log \mathrm{tw}(G))} \cdot n$ *time.*
(b) IR-FO-k is W[1]-hard when parameterized by the clique-width of G.
(c) IR-FO-BSC *is W[1]-hard when parameterized by the treewidth of G and the number k of coalitions, combined, and NP-hard when parameterized by the clique-width of G.*

Motivated by the intractability of IR-FO-BSC with respect to treewidth, as shown in Theorem 18, we consider the vertex cover number of the relationship graph as a stronger parameter, leading to an FPT algorithm for IR-FO-FSC.

Theorem 19. *When parameterized by* vc(G), IR-FO-FSC *is in FPT.*

Proof. Let M denote a vertex cover of G of minimum size; we can compute M in $1.25284^{|M|} \cdot (n + |E|)$ time [31]. We will assume that there is an IR coalition structure π for our instance. We call an agent $a \in M$ *lonely* in π if $\mathcal{F}_a \cap \pi(a) = \emptyset$. For each agent $a \in M$ that is not lonely, we fix some agent $a_c \in \mathcal{F}_a \cap \pi(a)$. Let $A' = \{a_c : c \in M, c \text{ is not lonely in } \pi\}$.

Our algorithm makes four guesses in total: the partitioning of M induced by π, the set of lonely agents, an auxiliary graph H, and, later on, an ordering of the parts of the guessed partitioning; the number of possible combinations is bounded in the running-time analysis at the end of the proof. We start by guessing the partitioning $\widetilde{\pi}$ of M induced by π. Next, for each agent a in M, we guess whether a is lonely in π; let M' denote the agents in M that are *not* lonely. Then, we guess the following auxiliary graph H whose vertex set is $M' \cup A'$ and whose edge set is $\{(c, a_c) : c \in M'\}$. For each coalition $\widetilde{C} \in \widetilde{\pi}$, we let $S(\widetilde{C}) = \widetilde{C} \cup \{a_c : c \in M' \cap \widetilde{C}\}$. Assuming that our guesses are correct, we have $S(\widetilde{C}) \subseteq \pi(\widetilde{C})$ where $\pi(\widetilde{C})$ denotes the unique coalition in π that contains all agents in $\widetilde{C}$. Although we do not know the identity of the agents in $S(\widetilde{C})$, we know the cardinality $|S(\widetilde{C})|$.

Next, we decide which coalitions we should allocate the agents of $S(\widetilde{C})$ to. We may assume that $\text{ub}_i \leq \text{ub}_j$ whenever $1 \leq i \leq j \leq k$. Let us now guess the ordering $\widetilde{C}_1, \dots, \widetilde{C}_\ell$ of the sets in $\widetilde{\pi}$ according to the size of the coalitions they are contained in under π, so that $|\pi(\widetilde{C}_i)| \leq |\pi(\widetilde{C}_j)|$ whenever $1 \leq i < j \leq \ell$. Now, we compute a mapping $\mathsf{ind} : [\ell] \to [k]$ as follows. For $i = 1, \dots, \ell$, we find a coalition index $\mathsf{ind}(i) \in [k]$ such that (i) $\mathsf{ind}(i) > \mathsf{ind}(i-1)$ for every $i > 1$, (ii) $\text{ub}_{\mathsf{ind}(i)} \geq |S(\widetilde{C}_i)|$, and (iii) $\text{ub}_{\mathsf{ind}(i)}$ is as small as possible.

Claim 1. *Suppose that an IR coalition structure π exists, and the algorithm made correct guesses with respect to π. Then there exists an IR coalition structure π' where, for each $i \in [\ell]$, the coalition $\pi(\widetilde{C}_i)$ has size* $\text{ub}_{\mathsf{ind}(i)}$.

Due to Claim 1, we may restrict our search for a solution in which $\widetilde{C}_i$ is allocated to the coalition with index $\mathsf{ind}(i)$. To compute a suitable IR coalition structure, we further need to allocate the agents in $A \setminus M$ to the coalition indices so that (i) each non-lonely agent in M has a friend in their coalition (recall that we do not know the identity of agents in $A' \setminus M$), (ii) no lonely agent in M shares their coalition with an enemy, and (iii) the size constraints are respected.

To this end, we construct a flow network N as follows, with source s and target t. Let $I = \{\mathsf{ind}(i) : i \in [\ell]\}$ be the indices of coalitions that will hold conflicting agents. For all coalition index $i \in [\ell]$, we set the *demand* of $\mathsf{ind}(i) \in I$ as $\text{ub}_{\mathsf{ind}(i)} - |S(\widetilde{C}_i)|$, and we set the demand of indices $j \in [k] \setminus I$ simply as ub_j.

First, we create an *agent vertex* u_a for each agent $a \in A \setminus M$. Second, for each coalition index $j \in [k]$, we create a *coalition vertex* v_j. Third, we also define a *guard vertex* $g_{a'}$ for each $a' \in A' \setminus M$.

There is an arc (s, u_a) with capacity 1 for each agent $a \in A$, an arc (v_j, t) for each coalition index j whose capacity is the demand of j. We also add an arc (g_a, t) for each agent $a \in A' \setminus M$ with capacity 1. Now, for each $a \in A \setminus M$, we add an arc of capacity 1 from agent vertex u_a to each coalition vertex v_j where either $j \notin I$ or $j = \mathsf{ind}(i)$ for some $i \in [\ell]$ such that $a \notin \mathcal{E}_c$ for any lonely agent $c \in \widetilde{C}_i$. We also add an arc of capacity 1 from u_a to $g_{a'}$ for some $a' \in A' \setminus M$ if a is *suitable for* a', meaning that a is considered a friend by all agents c for which $a' = a_c$. Recall that even though we do not know the identity of a', we can decide for each $a \in A \setminus M$ whether a is suitable for a' using the guessed auxiliary graph H—hence, our network is well defined. We finish our algorithm by finding a maximum flow in N; if its value is $|A \setminus M|$, we return 'yes'; otherwise, we proceed with our next set of guesses.

Claim 2. *Suppose there exists an IR coalition structure π that, for each $i \in [\ell]$, allocates all agents in $S(\widetilde{C}_i)$ to coalition index $\mathsf{ind}(i)$, and the algorithm made correct guesses with respect to π. Then there exists a flow of size $|A \setminus M|$ in the network N. Conversely, if N admits a flow of size $|A \setminus M|$, then there exists an IR coalition structure π.*

Claim 1 and 2 show the correctness of our algorithm.

Running time. Computing M is in FPT. Guessing the partitioning of M yields $\mathrm{vc}(G)^{\mathrm{vc}(G)}$ possibilities, while guessing the lonely agents yields $2^{\mathrm{vc}(G)}$ possibilities. Guessing the auxiliary graph H results in at most $\mathrm{vc}(G)^{\mathrm{vc}(G)}$ possibilities, since there are at most $|M|$ agents in A', and each agent in M' is connected to exactly one agent in A' in H. Finally, guessing the ordering of the sets in π' yields at most $\mathrm{vc}(G)! = \mathcal{O}(\mathrm{vc}(G)^{\mathrm{vc}(G)})$ possibilities. Hence, the number of possible guesses is $2^{\mathrm{vc}(G)\log(\mathrm{vc}(G))}$. Since for each fixed set of guesses, the bottleneck is to compute a maximum flow with lower bounds, which can be done in polynomial time with standard techniques, the running time of the presented algorithm is indeed fixed-parameter tractable with parameter $\mathrm{vc}(G)$. □

5 Conclusion

We studied individual rationality in friend-oriented and enemy-oriented hedonic games under four variants of size constraints, charting the boundary between tractable and intractable cases across a range of natural parameters.

Two messages emerge from our results. First, under friend-oriented preferences, it is the enmity structure alone that governs the complexity: whenever enmities are scarce or well-structured, tractability can often be recovered, whereas rich friendship structures never cause hardness on their own. Second, symmetry acts as a genuine computational resource: several polynomial-time solvable cases for symmetric relations become NP-hard as soon as asymmetry is allowed.

Beyond resolving the remaining open cases in Table 1—the most intriguing one, in our view, being whether the size-constrained (SCC) variant is fixed-parameter tractable with respect to the vertex cover number of the relationship graph—we see two natural directions for future research. One is to combine the size constraints studied here with more demanding stability notions, such as Nash or core stability, for which even the existence of unconstrained stable outcomes is non-trivial in our preference domain. Another is optimization: among all feasible individually rational coalition structures, find one that maximizes social welfare.

Acknowledgements. This research was supported in part by the National Science Centre, Poland, grant number UMO-2025/58/A/ST6/00371, and co-funded by the European Union under the project Roboprox (reg. no. CZ.02.01.01/00/22_008/0004590). Ildikó Schlotter is supported by the Hungarian Academy of Sciences under its Momentum Programme (LP2021-2) and its János Bolyai Research Scholarship.

References

1. Agarwal, P., Agarwal, H., Raj, V., Nath, S.: Harmonious balanced partitioning of a network of agents. In: AAMAS '25. pp. 41–49 (2025)
2. Ashlagi, I., Roth, A.E.: Individual rationality and participation in large scale, multi-hospital kidney exchange. In: EC '11. pp. 321–322 (2011)
3. Aziz, H., Brandl, F., Brandt, F., Harrenstein, P., Olsen, M., Peters, D.: Fractional hedonic games. ACM Trans. Econ. Comput. 7(2), 6:1–6:29 (2019)
4. Aziz, H., Savani, R.: Hedonic games. In: Handbook of Computational Social Choice, pp. 356–376. Cambridge University Press (2016)
5. Banerjee, S., Konishi, H., Sönmez, T.: Core in a simple coalition formation game. Soc. Choice Welf. **18**(1), 135–153 (2001)
6. Barr, H., Trabelsi, Y., Kraus, S., Roditty, L., Hazon, N.: The complexity of manipulation of k-coalitional games on graphs. In: ECAI '24. pp. 3388–3396 (2024)
7. Bilò, V., Monaco, G., Moscardelli, L.: Hedonic games with fixed-size coalitions. In: AAAI '22. pp. 9287–9295 (2022)
8. Bogomolnaia, A., Jackson, M.O.: The stability of hedonic coalition structures. Games Econ. Behav. **38**(2), 201–230 (2002)
9. Brandt, F., Bullinger, M., Tappe, L.: Stability based on single-agent deviations in additively separable hedonic games. Artif. Intell. **334**, 104160 (2024)
10. Bredereck, R., Elkind, E., Igarashi, A.: Hedonic diversity games. In: AAMAS '19. pp. 565–573 (2019)
11. Bullinger, M.: Pareto-optimality in cardinal hedonic games. In: AAMAS '20. pp. 213–221 (2020)
12. Bullinger, M., Chatziafratis, V., Shahkar, P.: Welfare approximation in additively separable hedonic games. In: AAMAS '25. pp. 418–426 (2025)
13. Bullinger, M., Dunajski, A., Elkind, E., Gilboa, M.: Single-deviation stability in additively separable hedonic games with constrained coalition sizes. In: AAMAS '26. pp. 3624–3626 (2026)
14. Bullinger, M., Suksompong, W.: Topological distance games. Theor. Comput. Sci. 981, 114238 (2024)
15. Bulteau, L., Fertin, G., Labarre, A., Rizzi, R., Rusu, I.: Decomposing subcubic graphs into claws, paths or triangles. J. Graph Theory. 98(4), 557–588 (2021)
16. Chen, J., Csáji, G., Roy, S., Simola, S.: Hedonic games with friends, enemies, and neutrals: Resolving open questions and fine-grained complexity. In: AAMAS '23. pp. 251–259 (2023)

17. Cygan, M., Fomin, F.V., Kowalik, Ł., Lokshtanov, D., Marx, D., Pilipczuk, M., Pilipczuk, M., Saurabh, S.: Parameterized Algorithms. Springer (2015)
18. Darmann, A., Döcker, J.: On a simple hard variant of Not-All-Equal 3-Sat. Theor. Comput. Sci. 815, 147–152 (2020)
19. Deligkas, A., Eiben, E., Ioannidis, S.D., Knop, D., Schierreich, Š.: Balanced and fair partitioning of friends. In: AAAI '25. pp. 13754–13762 (2025)
20. Deligkas, A., Eiben, E., Knop, D., Schierreich, Š.: Individual rationality in topological distance games is surprisingly hard. In: IJCAI '24. pp. 2782–2790 (2024)
21. Diestel, R.: Graph Theory. Springer, Berlin, Heidelberg, 6th edn. (2025)
22. Dimitrov, D., Borm, P., Hendrickx, R., Sung, S.C.: Simple priorities and core stability in hedonic games. Soc. Choice Welf. 26(2), 421–433 (2006)
23. Drèze, J.H., Greenberg, J.: Hedonic coalitions: Optimality and stability. Econometrica 47(4), 987–1003 (1980)
24. Fioravantes, F., Gahlawat, H., Melissinos, N.: Exact algorithms and lower bounds for forming coalitions of constrained maximum size. In: AAAI '25. pp. 13847–13855 (2025)
25. Fioravantes, F., Gahlawat, H., Melissinos, N., Schierreich, Š.: Individual rationality in constrained hedonic games: Additively separable and fractional preferences. In: AAMAS '26. pp. 2848–2857 (2026)
26. Fioravantes, F., Gahlawat, H., Melissinos, N., Schierreich, Š.: "Individual Rationality in Size-Constrained Hedonic Games: Anonymous and Diversity Preferences" and venue is WINE '26. In: GAIW '26 (2026)
27. Furmanczyk, H., Kubale, M.: Equitable coloring of corona products of cubic graphs is harder than ordinary coloring. Ars Math. Contemp. 10(2), 333–347 (2016)
28. Furmanczyk, H., Mkrtchyan, V.: Graph theoretic and algorithmic aspect of the equitable coloring problem in block graphs. Discret. Math. Theor. Comput. Sci. 23(2) (2022)
29. Ganian, R., Hamm, T., Knop, D., Schierreich, Š., Suchý, O.: Hedonic diversity games: A complexity picture with more than two colors. Artif. Intell. 325, 104017 (2023)
30. Ganian, R., Hamm, T., Knop, D., Roy, S., Schierreich, Š., Suchý, O.: Maximizing social welfare in score-based social distance games. In: TARK '23. pp. 272–286 (2023)
31. Harris, D.G., Narayanaswamy, N.S.: A faster algorithm for vertex cover parameterized by solution size. In: STACS '24. pp. 40:1–40:18 (2024)
32. Impagliazzo, R., Paturi, R., Zane, F.: Which problems have strongly exponential complexity? J. Comput. Syst. Sci. 63(4), 512–530 (2001)
33. Lang, J., Rey, A., Rothe, J., Schadrack, H., Schend, L.: Representing and solving hedonic games with ordinal preferences and thresholds. In: AAMAS '15. pp. 1229–1237 (2015)
34. Levinger, C., Azaria, A., Hazon, N.: Social aware coalition formation with bounded coalition size. In: AAMAS '23. pp. 2667–2669 (2023)
35. Li, L., Micha, E., Nikolov, A., Shah, N.: Partitioning friends fairly. In: AAAI '23. pp. 5747–5754 (2023)
36. Ohta, K., Barrot, N., Ismaili, A., Sakurai, Y., Yokoo, M.: Core stability in hedonic games among friends and enemies: Impact of neutrals. In: IJCAI '17. pp. 359–365 (2017)
37. Peters, D., Elkind, E.: Simple causes of complexity in hedonic games. In: IJCAI '15. pp. 617–623 (2015)
38. Roth, A.E.: Individual rationality and Nash's solution to the bargaining problem. Math. Oper. Res. 2(1), 64–65 (1977)

39. Rothe, J., Schadrack, H., Schend, L.: Borda-induced hedonic games with friends, enemies, and neutral players. Math. Soc. Sci. 96, 21–36 (2018)
40. Sless, L., Hazon, N., Kraus, S., Wooldridge, M.J.: Forming k coalitions and facilitating relationships in social networks. Artif. Intell. 259, 217–245 (2018)
41. Waxman, N., Kraus, S., Hazon, N.: Manipulation of k-coalitional games on social networks. In: IJCAI '21. pp. 450–457 (2021)
42. Wright, M., Vorobeychik, Y.: Mechanism design for team formation. In: AAAI '15. pp. 1050–1056 (2015)

Computing Fair and Efficient Indivisible Chore Allocations with Bounded Surplus

Nicholas Teh(✉)

University of Oxford, Oxford, UK
nicholas.teh@cs.ox.ac.uk

Abstract. We study the problem of allocating indivisible chores with additive costs, seeking allocations that are weighted envy-free up to one chore (WEF1) and fractionally Pareto optimal (fPO). Mahara (SODA 2026) recently proved that such allocations always exist, but finding one in polynomial time for general instances remains open. We give a polynomial-time algorithm for the setting with bounded surplus chores: for every fixed constant s, a WEF1 and fPO allocation can be computed whenever the number of chores is at most the number of agents plus s. This guarantee allows for arbitrarily many agents and arbitrarily many distinct cost functions. Our approach works through a prescribed bundle size problem. The key parameter is the number of chores assigned beyond the first chore in each nonempty bundle. When this surplus is S, we decide whether there is a WEF1 and fPO allocation respecting the prescribed bundle sizes, and compute one if it exists, in time $m^S \text{poly}(n, m, L)$, where L is the total input bit length. The algorithm relies on two structural observations: with positive costs and fixed bundle sizes, fPO is equivalent to minimizing the product of assigned costs; and agents who receive at most one chore impose no nontrivial WEF1 constraints. We complement the algorithm with a hardness result showing that the prescribed bundle size problem becomes strongly NP-hard when the surplus is unbounded, even with two agent types and bundle sizes restricted to $\{3, 5\}$.

1 Introduction

Fair division of indivisible items is a central problem in algorithmic game theory and multi-agent systems; see, e.g., [2,4] for recent surveys. It captures settings in which tasks or resources must be divided among agents with heterogeneous preferences. Two desiderata have been especially central in this literature: *fairness* and *efficiency*. A classical fairness notion is *envy-freeness* (EF), which asks that no agent prefer another agent's bundle to her own. For indivisible items, exact EF may be impossible, and much of the literature therefore studies relaxations such as envy-freeness up to one item (EF1) [21]. An orthogonal desideratum is *Pareto optimality* (PO), which requires that there be no alternative allocation that makes some agent better off without making anyone worse off.

P. Lenzner and D. Schmand (Eds.): SAGT 2026, LNCS 16911, pp. 390–407, 2027.
https://doi.org/10.1007/978-3-032-38782-0_22

The combination of approximate envy-freeness and Pareto efficiency has become a standard benchmark in indivisible fair division. For indivisible goods (i.e., items that agents value positively), this benchmark is well understood under additive valuations: maximum Nash welfare allocations are EF1 and PO [9], and subsequent work developed algorithmic and fractional-efficiency refinements [6]. Chores (i.e., items that impose costs rather than create value) are more delicate. Moving a chore away from one agent helps that agent but burdens another, and the structural arguments used for goods do not transfer directly.

In this paper, we study the allocation of indivisible chores under additive costs. The chores may represent undesirable shifts, maintenance tasks, grading duties, service obligations, or administrative work, and agents may incur different costs for performing them. We allow agents to have different entitlements, and use the corresponding weighted version of EF1, called *weighted envy-freeness up to one chore* (WEF1). Informally, after removing her most costly chore from her own bundle, an agent's entitlement-normalized cost should be no larger than her entitlement-normalized cost for any other agent's bundle. For efficiency, we use *fractional Pareto optimality* (fPO), which rules out Pareto improvements even by fractional reallocations of chores and is therefore stronger than ordinary PO.

A recent breakthrough of Mahara [22] shows that every additive chore instance admits an EF1 and fPO allocation, and extends this existence result to the weighted-entitlement setting. This settles the existential question, but leaves open the computational one: can such an allocation be found in polynomial time when both the number of agents and the number of chores are part of the input?

We study this computational question in a small surplus setting, where the number of chores exceeds the number of agents by at most a constant. Similar "few extra items" setting have been studied extensively for goods and mixed manna [8,11,17,19,20,23]. For chores, this setting has a particularly useful EF1 structure. If an agent receives at most one chore, then removing her most costly chore leaves zero cost. Thus, such an agent creates no nontrivial WEF1 constraint. The difficulty is therefore concentrated on agents who receive at least two chores.

To make this precise, let $q = (q_1, \ldots, q_n)$ be a quota vector, where q_i is the number of chores assigned to agent i. We define the *quota surplus* $S(q) := \sum_{i \in N} \max\{q_i - 1, 0\}$. This quantity counts the number of chores assigned beyond the first chore in each nonempty bundle. When $S(q)$ is small, only a small part of the allocation can generate nontrivial WEF1 constraints, even if the number of agents and the number of distinct cost functions are large. This parameter is the basis of our algorithms and hardness results.

1.1 Our Contributions

Our main contribution is a polynomial-time algorithm for computing WEF1 and fPO allocations in the bounded surplus setting, and in particular whenever the number of chores exceeds the number of agents by at most a constant. The result is obtained through a more general prescribed quota algorithm whose running time is controlled by the quota surplus $S(q)$. Table 1 summarizes the algorithmic landscape.

Table 1. Algorithmic landscape. Results labeled by theorem or corollary number are proved in this work; the final row details the remaining general case. FPT means fixed-parameter tractable.

Setting	Status	Remarks
$m \leq n$	Polynomial time	Base case: all nonempty bundles can be singletons, so WEF1 is immediate.
$m \leq n + s$, fixed s	Polynomial time	Theorem 2 for positive costs; Corollary 1 extends this to nonnegative costs.
Prescribed q, fixed $S(q)$	$m^{S(q)}\text{poly}(n, m, L)$ time	Theorem 1.
Prescribed q, p chore types	Polynomial/FPT for the stated parameters	Theorem 3; polynomial for fixed p and fixed number of heavy agents, and FPT in $p + S(q)$.
Prescribed q, unbounded $S(q)$	Strongly NP-hard	Theorem 4, even with two agent types and quotas in $\{3, 5\}$.
General m, n	Computationally open	Existence follows from Mahara [22]; polynomial-time computation remains open.

Fractional Efficiency with Fixed Bundle Sizes. Our first result gives a simple way to identify fractional Pareto optimality once the number of chores assigned to each agent is fixed. With strictly positive additive costs, an allocation is fPO exactly when the product of the individual chore costs, evaluated for the agents who receive those chores, is as small as possible among all allocations with the same bundle sizes. We state and prove this result in Sect. 3.

Prescribed Quota Vectors. We next study the problem in which the bundle sizes are fixed in advance. Given a quota vector q, positive costs, and positive entitlements, we decide whether there is a WEF1 and fPO allocation in which agent i receives exactly q_i chores for every i, and compute one if it exists, in time $m^{S(q)}\text{poly}(n, m, L)$. For each agent who must receive at least two chores, the algorithm guesses all but one chore in that agent's bundle. These guessed chores determine the left-hand side of that agent's WEF1 inequalities. The one remaining chore for each nonempty agent is selected by a minimum-cost perfect matching whose permitted edges ensure WEF1. A final product comparison checks fPO.

Few Extra Chores. The prescribed quota algorithm gives us our main result. For every fixed constant s, a WEF1 and fPO allocation can be computed in polynomial time whenever $m \leq n + s$. This guarantee allows arbitrarily many agents and imposes no restriction on the number of distinct cost functions. The proof uses the fact that, under positive costs, any WEF1 allocation with $m > n$ must assign at least one chore to every agent. Thus, the quota surplus of such an allocation is exactly $m - n$, which is at most s. We enumerate the possible positive quota vectors and apply the prescribed quota algorithm. A zero-cost preprocessing extends the result from positive costs to nonnegative costs.

Few Chore Types. We also give a typed-chores extension. If chores have p cost types, then the prescribed quota algorithm can guess type counts rather than individual chores. This gives a polynomial-time algorithm for fixed p and a fixed number of agents with quota at least two, and an algorithm fixed-parameter tractable in $p + S(q)$.

Hardness for Prescribed Quotas. Finally, we show that the dependence on $S(q)$ is meaningful. When $S(q)$ is unbounded, deciding whether a quota-respecting EF1+PO allocation exists is strongly NP-hard. The hardness holds even with positive integer costs, only two agent types, and quotas restricted to $\{3, 5\}$. The same construction gives strong NP-hardness for EF1+fPO.

1.2 Related Work

Fair and Efficient Allocation of Indivisible Items. The fair allocation of indivisible items is a central topic in algorithmic game theory and multi-agent systems; see, e.g., [2,4] for recent surveys. Since exact envy-freeness can fail for indivisible items, much of the literature focuses on relaxations such as envy-freeness up to one item (EF1). The notion of EF1 was implicit in the work of Lipton et al. [21] and became a standard and well-studied relaxation in many subsequent works. For indivisible goods with additive valuations, the maximum Nash welfare allocation is EF1 and PO [9], and Barman, Krishnamurthy, and Vaish [6] gave a pseudo-polynomial-time algorithm for finding EF1+PO allocations and established the existence of EF1+fPO allocations. However, these positive results for goods do not transfer directly to chores, where the direction of envy and the direction of Pareto improvements interact differently.

Fair and Efficient Chore Allocation. Chores are significantly more delicate than goods. Aziz et al. [3] studied fair allocation of indivisible goods and chores and highlighted the difficulty of combining approximate envy-freeness with efficiency for chores. Several positive results were known for restricted chore instances. Ebadian, Peters, and Shah [10], and independently Garg, Murhekar, and Qin [13] gave polynomial algorithms for EF1+PO in bivalued chore instances. Later, Garg, Murhekar, and Qin [14] obtained EF1+fPO allocations for three agents and for instances with at most two disutility functions, as well as EFX+fPO allocations for three-agent bivalued instances. For instances with two chore types, Aziz et al. [5] gave a polynomial-time algorithm for computing EF1+fPO allocations, as well as a polynomial-time algorithm for EFX allocations. Mahara [22] recently resolved the existential question for general additive chores by proving that an EF1+fPO allocation always exists, with an extension to the weighted setting (i.e., agents with possibly unequal entitlements). This leaves open the computational problem of finding such allocations in polynomial time when both n and m are part of the input. Our work addresses this computational question in a setting not covered by constant-agent or few-type algorithms: both the number of agents and the number of distinct cost functions may be unbounded, but only few chores can be placed beyond the first chore in a nonempty bundle.

Weighted Seting (Entitlements) and Few-Type Restrictions. Weighted envy-freeness captures asymmetric obligations or entitlements. For chores, Wu,

Zhang, and Zhou [26] gave algorithms for WEF1 allocations and studied when weighted picking sequences guarantee stronger properties. Springer, Hajiaghayi, and Yami [24] studied almost envy-free allocations with entitlements for goods and chores. Closest to our weighted setting, Garg, Murhekar, and Qin [15] proved polynomial-time WEF1+PO results for structured instances, including instances with few agent types or few chore types. Our results are orthogonal: we allow arbitrarily many agent types and chore types, but parameterize by the number of chores that can create nontrivial EF1 constraints. Moreover, our positive results target fPO, which is stronger than PO.

Surplus, Balancedness, and Cardinality Constraints. Our use of surplus differs from the k-surplus model of Akrami et al. [1], where extra copies of chores may be introduced. Here no chores are added and feasibility is not relaxed. The surplus $S(q)$ is only a measure of how far the quota vector is from assigning at most one chore to each nonempty agent. Balanced chore allocation is another related direction. Garg, Murhekar, and Qin [16] give a polynomial-time algorithm for computing a balanced fPO allocation; this implies EF1+fPO when $m \leq n$ and EF2+fPO when $m \leq 2n$. Our few extra chores result strengthens the scarce chores setting in a complementary way: for every fixed s, it computes exact EF1+fPO allocations whenever $m \leq n + s$, even though some agents may receive more than two chores. More broadly, fair division under constraints has been studied for goods under category, matroid, and balancedness constraints [7,18,25]. These works impose feasibility constraints on the bundles, often for goods, and typically seek fairness or approximate fairness guarantees under those constraints. Our prescribed quota model instead prescribes the bundle cardinalities for chores and asks whether exact EF1+PO or EF1+fPO can be achieved. The strong NP-hardness result for exact quotas shows that even very simple cardinality prescriptions can make the fair and efficient chore problem computationally intractable when the quota surplus is unbounded.

2 Preliminaries

Let $N = \{1, \ldots, n\}$ be the set of *agents* and $M = \{1, \ldots, m\}$ the set of *chores*. Agent i has an *additive cost function* $c_i : 2^M \to \mathbb{R}_{\geq 0}$, with $c_i(S) = \sum_{j \in S} c_{ij}$.[1] An *allocation* is a tuple $A = (A_1, \ldots, A_n)$ that partitions M. For an allocation A, let $q(A) = (|A_1|, \ldots, |A_n|)$ denote its *quota vector*. For a vector $q \in \mathbb{Z}^n_{\geq 0}$ with $\sum_i q_i = m$, let $\mathcal{A}(q) = \{A : |A_i| = q_i \text{ for every } i \in N\}$ be the set of allocations respecting q. We call an allocation in $\mathcal{A}(q)$ *quota-respecting*.

Definition 1 (Weighted EF1 for chores). *Let $\alpha_i > 0$ be the entitlement of agent i. For a set $S \subseteq M$, define $d_i^-(S) := c_i(S) - \max_{j \in S} c_{ij}$ if $S \neq \varnothing$; and $d_i^-(S) := 0$ otherwise. An allocation A is* weighted envy-free up to one chore (WEF1), *if for every ordered pair of agents i, k, $\frac{d_i^-(A_i)}{\alpha_i} \leq \frac{c_i(A_k)}{\alpha_k}$.*

[1] All numerical inputs in algorithmic statements are rational. In running-time bounds, L denotes the total bit length of the costs and entitlements.

When all entitlements are equal, this is the usual EF1 notion for chores. The definition uses $d_i^-(A_i)$ because, for chores, agent i eliminates as much envy as possible by removing her most costly chore from her own bundle. A fractional allocation is a matrix $x = (x_{ij})_{i \in N, j \in M}$ such that $x_{ij} \geq 0$ for every $i \in N$ and $j \in M$, and

$$\sum_{i \in N} x_{ij} = 1 \quad \text{for every } j \in M.$$

Here, x_{ij} is the fraction of chore j assigned to agent i. For each agent i, denote $x_i = (x_{ij})_{j \in M}$ and define

$$c_i(x_i) := \sum_{j \in M} c_{ij} x_{ij}.$$

Definition 2 (PO and fPO). *An allocation A is* Pareto optimal (PO) *if there is no allocation B such that $c_i(B_i) \leq c_i(A_i)$ for every $i \in N$, with strict inequality for at least one agent. It is* fractionally Pareto optimal (fPO) *if there is no fractional allocation x such that $c_i(x_i) \leq c_i(A_i)$ for every $i \in N$, with strict inequality for at least one agent.*

Clearly fPO implies PO. We use the following standard characterization of fPO for additive costs. It is the chore analogue of the usual weighted social cost characterization of fractional Pareto efficiency.

Proposition 1 (fPO characterization). *Assume $c_{ij} > 0$ for all i, j. An allocation A is fPO if and only if there are weights $\lambda_1, \dots, \lambda_n > 0$ such that, for every $j \in A_i$ and every agent k, $\lambda_i c_{ij} \leq \lambda_k c_{kj}$.*

Equivalently, the same condition can be written as follows: there exist weights $\lambda_1, \dots, \lambda_n > 0$ such that, for every fractional allocation x, $\sum_{i \in N} \lambda_i c_i(A_i) \leq \sum_{i \in N} \lambda_i c_i(x_i)$.

Proof. The "if" direction is immediate: if A minimizes $\sum_i \lambda_i c_i(x_i)$ for some $\lambda_i > 0$, then any fractional allocation that weakly decreases every agent's cost and strictly decreases one agent's cost would have strictly smaller weighted cost, a contradiction. For the converse, let $a_i = c_i(A_i)$, and consider the linear program

$$\begin{aligned} \max \ & \sum_{i \in N} \delta_i \\ \text{s.t.} \ & \sum_{j \in M} c_{ij} x_{ij} + \delta_i \leq a_i \quad \forall i \in N, \\ & \sum_{i \in N} x_{ij} = 1 \quad \forall j \in M, \\ & x_{ij} \geq 0 \quad \forall i, j, \\ & \delta_i \geq 0 \quad \forall i. \end{aligned}$$

A positive objective value is exactly a fractional Pareto improvement over A. Since A is fPO, the optimum is 0; feasibility follows from the fractional allocation corresponding to A, with $\delta_i = 0$ for all i.

The dual, with variables $\lambda_i \geq 0$ for the first set of constraints and free variables for the chore-assignment equalities, can be written as

$$\begin{aligned} \min \sum_{i \in N} \lambda_i a_i - \sum_{j \in M} p_j & \\ \text{s.t. } p_j \leq \lambda_i c_{ij} \quad & \forall i \in N,\ j \in M, \\ \lambda_i \geq 1 \quad & \forall i \in N. \end{aligned}$$

By strong duality, there is an optimal dual solution (λ, p) of value 0. In particular, $\lambda_i > 0$ for every i. Let $\sigma(j)$ be the agent who receives chore j in A. Since $p_j \leq \lambda_{\sigma(j)} c_{\sigma(j)j}$ for every j,

$$\sum_{j \in M} p_j \leq \sum_{j \in M} \lambda_{\sigma(j)} c_{\sigma(j)j} = \sum_{i \in N} \lambda_i c_i(A_i) = \sum_{i \in N} \lambda_i a_i.$$

The dual objective value is 0, so equality must hold throughout. Therefore, for every $j \in A_i$, we have $p_j = \lambda_i c_{ij}$. Since also $p_j \leq \lambda_k c_{kj}$ for every agent k, it follows that $\lambda_i c_{ij} \leq \lambda_k c_{kj}$ for every $j \in A_i$ and every k. The equivalent weighted-cost minimization statement follows because the objective is separable over chores. □

3 Product Minimality at Fixed Quotas

Although fPO is defined against all fractional allocations, it has a simple characterization once the quota vector is fixed. For strictly positive costs, define $\Phi(A) = \sum_{i=1}^{n} \sum_{j \in A_i} \log c_{ij}$. Then, minimizing Φ is equivalent to minimizing the product $\prod_{i=1}^{n} \prod_{j \in A_i} c_{ij}$.

Lemma 1. *Assume $c_{ij} > 0$ for all i, j. An allocation A is fPO if and only if*

$$\Phi(A) = \min\{\Phi(B) : B \in \mathcal{A}(q(A))\}.$$

Equivalently, A minimizes the product of assigned costs among all allocations with quota vector $q(A)$.

Proof. Suppose first that A is fPO. By Proposition 1, there are $\lambda_i > 0$ such that, whenever $j \in A_i$, $\lambda_i c_{ij} \leq \lambda_k c_{kj}$ for every k. Let $B \in \mathcal{A}(q(A))$. If $j \in A_i$ and $j \in B_k$, then $\log \lambda_i + \log c_{ij} \leq \log \lambda_k + \log c_{kj}$. Summing over all chores gives us

$$\sum_i |A_i| \log \lambda_i + \Phi(A) \leq \sum_i |B_i| \log \lambda_i + \Phi(B).$$

Since B has the same quota vector as A, the λ-terms cancel. Thus $\Phi(A) \leq \Phi(B)$. Conversely, suppose A minimizes Φ over $\mathcal{A}(q)$, where $q = q(A)$. Let $\ell_{ij} = \log c_{ij}$ and consider

$$\begin{aligned} \min \sum_{i,j} \ell_{ij} x_{ij} & \\ \text{s.t. } \sum_i x_{ij} = 1 \quad & \forall j \in M, \\ \sum_j x_{ij} = q_i \quad & \forall i \in N, \\ x_{ij} \geq 0 \quad & \forall i, j. \end{aligned}$$

The feasible region is a transportation polytope and hence has integral extreme points. Therefore the LP optimum is attained by an integral allocation in $\mathcal{A}(q)$. Since A minimizes Φ over $\mathcal{A}(q)$, A is an optimal solution of this LP. Its dual is

$$\begin{aligned} \max \sum_j u_j + \sum_i q_i v_i \\ \text{s.t.} \quad u_j + v_i \leq \ell_{ij} \quad \forall i, j. \end{aligned}$$

Let (u, v) be an optimal dual solution. For $j \in A_i$, complementary slackness gives $u_j + v_i = \ell_{ij}$, while dual feasibility gives $u_j + v_k \leq \ell_{kj}$ for every k. Hence, $\ell_{ij} - v_i \leq \ell_{kj} - v_k$. Setting $\lambda_i = e^{-v_i}$ gives $\lambda_i c_{ij} \leq \lambda_k c_{kj}$ for every $j \in A_i$ and every k. Proposition 1 implies that A is fPO. □

Remark 1. The algorithms use the quantities $\log c_{ij}$ only to compare products of assigned costs. They can therefore be implemented in the standard Turing model as follows. Since L denotes the total input bit length, for every allocation A the product $P(A) = \prod_{i \in N} \prod_{j \in A_i} c_{ij}$ has numerator and denominator bit length $O(L)$. Thus, for any two allocations A, B with $P(A) \neq P(B)$, the ratio $P(A)/P(B)$ differs from 1 by at least $2^{-O(L)}$. Thus, in all min-cost flow and matching computations, replacing each $\log c_{ij}$ by a rational approximation with $O(L + \log m)$ bits after the binary point preserves the ordering of all feasible solutions with different products. Exact equality tests, such as $\Phi(A) = \Gamma(q)$, are resolved by comparing the rational products $P(A)$ and $P(B)$ via cross-multiplication using $O(L)$-bit integers.

4 Prescribed Quotas and Quota Surplus

We now consider the problem in which the quota vector q is *prescribed* as part of the input. The goal is to find an allocation in $\mathcal{A}(q)$ that is both WEF1 and fPO, or decide that no such allocation exists.

Definition 3 (Quota surplus). *The quota surplus of q is $S(q) = \sum_{i=1}^{n} \max\{q_i - 1, 0\}$. Let $H(q) = \{i : q_i \geq 2\}$, $R(q) = \{i : q_i = 1\}$, and $E(q) = \{i : q_i = 0\}$. Agents in $H(q)$ are called* heavy agents.

Let $S := S(q)$. Since each agent in $H(q)$ contributes at least one to $S(q)$, we have $|H(q)| \leq S$. Moreover,

$$\sum_{i \in H(q)} q_i = \sum_{i \in H(q)} (q_i - 1) + |H(q)| = S + |H(q)| \leq 2S.$$

Thus, at most $2S$ chores are assigned to heavy agents.

4.1 The Prescribed Quota Algorithm

For a quota vector q, define $\Gamma(q) = \min\{\Phi(A) : A \in \mathcal{A}(q)\}$. By Lemma 1, an allocation respecting q is fPO if and only if it has Φ-value $\Gamma(q)$. The key point is that, for an agent $h \in H(q)$, the algorithm does not need to guess the entire bundle A_h. It guesses only the set $T_h = A_h \setminus \{g_h\}$, where g_h is a chore removed from h's bundle in the EF1 comparison. The chore g_h is chosen later by a matching.

In Algorithm 1, a tuple $(T_h)_{h \in H}$ is a partial allocation of core chores to the heavy agents: the sets $T_h \subseteq M$ are pairwise disjoint and satisfy $|T_h| = q_h - 1$ for every $h \in H$.

Algorithm 1. PRESCRIBEDQUOTA

Require: Positive rational costs c_{ij}, positive entitlements α_i, and a quota vector q with $\sum_i q_i = m$.
Ensure: An allocation $A \in \mathcal{A}(q)$ that is WEF1 and fPO, if one exists.

Compute an allocation $B^q \in \arg\min\{\Phi(B) : B \in \mathcal{A}(q)\}$ by min-cost flow with edge costs $\log c_{ij}$.
Let $H = H(q)$, $R = R(q)$, $E = E(q)$, and $N^+ = H \cup R$.
for all partial allocations $(T_h)_{h \in H}$ of core chores to the agents in H **do**
    for each $h \in H$ **do**
        $\tau_h \leftarrow c_h(T_h)/\alpha_h$ and $\beta_h \leftarrow \max_{j \in T_h} c_{hj}$
    end for
    if $E \neq \varnothing$ and $\tau_h > 0$ for some $h \in H$ **then**
        continue
    end if
    Let $M' = M \setminus \bigcup_{h \in H} T_h$.
    Build a bipartite graph between N^+ and M'.
    for each $j \in M'$ **do**
        for each $r \in R$ **do**
            Allow (r, j) iff $\tau_a \leq \frac{c_{aj}}{\alpha_r}$ for every $a \in H$.
        end for
        for each $k \in H$ **do**
            Allow (k, j) iff $c_{kj} \geq \beta_k$ and $\tau_a \leq \frac{c_a(T_k)+c_{aj}}{\alpha_k}$ for every $a \in H$.
        end for
    end for
    Find a minimum-cost perfect matching μ, using cost $\log c_{ij}$ for edge (i, j).
    if no such matching exists **then**
        continue
    end if
    Define $A_h = T_h \cup \{\mu(h)\}$ $(h \in H)$, $A_r = \{\mu(r)\}$ $(r \in R)$, $A_e = \varnothing$ $(e \in E)$.
    if $\Phi(A) = \Phi(B^q)$ **then**
        return A
    end if
end for
return no quota-respecting WEF1+fPO allocation exists

The prescribed quota problem asks for an allocation $A \in \mathcal{A}(q)$ that is both WEF1 and fPO.

Theorem 1. *For positive rational costs and positive entitlements, the problem of finding a quota-respecting WEF1 and fPO allocation for a prescribed quota vector q, or deciding that none exists, can be solved in time $m^{S(q)}\text{poly}(n, m, L)$.*

Proof. For any candidate allocation $A \in \mathcal{A}(q)$ and any heavy agent $h \in H(q)$, let

$$g_h \in \arg\max_{j \in A_h} c_{hj} \quad \text{and} \quad T_h = A_h \setminus \{g_h\}.$$

Then $d_h^-(A_h) = c_h(T_h)$. Thus the algorithm enumerates all possible choices of these core sets T_h. Once the sets T_h are fixed for all $h \in H(q)$, it remains to choose one guard chore g_h for each heavy agent and one singleton chore for each agent in $R(q)$. Algorithm 1 does exactly this by a minimum-cost perfect matching.

We first prove soundness. Suppose Algorithm 1 outputs an allocation A. Agents in $R \cup E$ receive at most one chore, so $d_i^-(A_i) = 0$ for every $i \in R \cup E$. Hence all WEF1 constraints with such an agent on the left-hand side hold automatically.

Now consider a heavy agent $h \in H$. The matching assigns h the chore $\mu(h)$. Since the edge $(h, \mu(h))$ is allowed, we have $c_{h\mu(h)} \geq \beta_h = \max_{j \in T_h} c_{hj}$. Therefore $\mu(h)$ is a valid guard chore for h, and $d_h^-(A_h) = c_h(T_h)$. Consequently, $\frac{d_h^-(A_h)}{\alpha_h} = \tau_h$.

It remains to check the right-hand side of the WEF1 inequalities. If $e \in E$, then $A_e = \varnothing$, so the empty-agent test in Algorithm 1 verifies the constraints from heavy agents to empty agents. If $r \in R$, then $A_r = \{\mu(r)\}$, and the allowed-edge condition for $(r, \mu(r))$ gives

$$\tau_h \leq \frac{c_{h\mu(r)}}{\alpha_r} = \frac{c_h(A_r)}{\alpha_r} \quad \text{for every } h \in H.$$

If $k \in H$, then $A_k = T_k \cup \{\mu(k)\}$, and the allowed-edge condition for $(k, \mu(k))$ gives

$$\tau_h \leq \frac{c_h(T_k) + c_{h\mu(k)}}{\alpha_k} = \frac{c_h(A_k)}{\alpha_k} \quad \text{for every } h \in H.$$

Thus A is WEF1. The product comparison in the algorithm is equivalent to $\Phi(A) = \Gamma(q)$, because all costs are positive and B^q has minimum Φ-value in $\mathcal{A}(q)$.

We next prove completeness. Let $A^* \in \mathcal{A}(q)$ be any allocation that is WEF1 and fPO. By Lemma 1, $\Phi(A^*) = \Gamma(q)$. For every heavy agent $h \in H$, choose $g_h \in \arg\max_{j \in A_h^*} c_{hj}$ and set $T_h = A_h^* \setminus \{g_h\}$. Then $|T_h| = q_h - 1$, and the algorithm considers the tuple $(T_h)_{h \in H}$.

For this tuple, $\tau_h = \frac{c_h(T_h)}{\alpha_h} = \frac{d_h^-(A_h^*)}{\alpha_h}$. If $E \neq \varnothing$, the WEF1 constraints of A^* toward empty agents imply that the empty-agent test passes. The residual assignment in A^* gives a perfect matching on the graph constructed by the algorithm: each agent $h \in H$ is matched to g_h, and each singleton agent $r \in R$ is matched to its unique chore in A_r^*. The guard condition holds by definition of g_h, and all allowed-edge inequalities are exactly the WEF1 inequalities of A^* from heavy agents to the corresponding target agents.

Therefore a feasible perfect matching exists in this iteration. Let μ be the minimum-cost perfect matching chosen by the algorithm, and let A be the allocation induced by μ and the guessed cores. The matching induced by A^* is feasible, so $\Phi(A) \leq \Phi(A^*) = \Gamma(q)$. On the other hand, $A \in \mathcal{A}(q)$, so by the definition of $\Gamma(q)$, $\Phi(A) \geq \Gamma(q)$. Therefore, $\Phi(A) = \Gamma(q)$, and the algorithm outputs an allocation.

It remains to bound the running time. The algorithm enumerates exactly $\sum_{h \in H}(q_h - 1) = S(q)$ chores across the guessed sets $(T_h)_{h \in H}$. Hence the number of tuples is at most $m^{S(q)}$. For each tuple, the graph construction and the perfect matching computation are polynomial in n, m, and the input bit length. The computation of $\Gamma(q)$ is also polynomial by a minimum-cost flow formulation, with logarithmic costs handled as in Remark 1. Thus the total running time is $m^{S(q)}\text{poly}(n, m, L)$. □

5 Unconstrained Instances with Few Surplus Chores

We next use the prescribed quota algorithm to handle unconstrained instances when the number of surplus chores is small. The key point is that, under strictly positive costs, any WEF1 allocation with more chores than agents must give every agent at least one chore.

Theorem 2. *Assume $c_{ij} > 0$ and $\alpha_i > 0$. For every fixed $s \geq 0$, a WEF1 and fPO allocation can be computed in polynomial time whenever $m \leq n + s$.*

Proof. First suppose $m \leq n$. Compute a minimum-cost matching that assigns each chore to a distinct agent, using edge cost $\log c_{ij}$ for assigning chore j to agent i, implemented as in Remark 1, and let A be the induced allocation. Every agent receives at most one chore, so A is WEF1. Let $q = q(A)$. Since this matching minimizes Φ over all allocations in which every agent receives at most one chore, it in particular minimizes Φ over $\mathcal{A}(q)$. Lemma 1 therefore implies that A is fPO.

Now suppose $m > n$, and write $m = n + s'$ with $1 \leq s' \leq s$. In any WEF1 allocation, every agent must receive at least one chore. Otherwise, if some agent k is empty, then another agent i receives at least two chores, and strict positivity gives us $\frac{d_i^-(A_i)}{\alpha_i} > 0 = \frac{c_i(A_k)}{\alpha_k}$, contradicting WEF1.

By the weighted-entitlement extension of Mahara's EF1+fPO existence theorem [22], there exists a WEF1 and fPO allocation for the given entitlements. Its quota vector q has all entries positive, and thus, we have that

$$S(q) = \sum_i (q_i - 1) = m - n = s'.$$

There are $\binom{n+s'-1}{s'} = n^{O(s')}$ positive quota vectors summing to m. We enumerate them and run Theorem 1 for each. The quota vector of some WEF1+fPO allocation is among the enumerated vectors, so the algorithm outputs an allocation for at least one vector. Since $s' \leq s$, the running time is polynomial for every fixed s. □

The strict positivity assumption can be removed for the unconstrained corollary by a standard zero-cost preprocessing.

Corollary 1 (Nonnegative costs). *For every fixed $s \geq 0$, given nonnegative rational costs c_{ij} and positive rational entitlements α_i, a WEF1 and fPO allocation can be computed in polynomial time whenever $m \leq n + s$.*

Proof. While there is a chore j and an agent i with $c_{ij} = 0$, assign j permanently to i and remove j. If no chore remains, use the empty allocation on the reduced instance. Otherwise, all remaining costs are strictly positive, and the number of remaining chores is still at most $n+s$. Apply Theorem 2 to the reduced instance.

We now add back the removed chores. Consider a removed chore j that was assigned permanently to an agent i with $c_{ij} = 0$. Adding j to i's bundle does not change $c_i(A_i)$, and it also does not change $d_i^-(A_i)$: if A_i already contains a positive-cost chore for i, the maximum i-cost chore is unchanged, while if all chores in $A_i \cup \{j\}$ have zero i-cost, then $d_i^-(A_i \cup \{j\}) = 0$. For any other agent h, the cost $c_h(A_i)$ of i's bundle can only increase, which can only make the WEF1 constraint toward i easier. Thus WEF1 is preserved.

For fPO, let $\bar{A}$ be the allocation computed for the reduced instance, and let A be the final allocation after adding back the removed chores. Suppose for contradiction that a fractional allocation x of the original instance Pareto-dominates A. Let x' be the restriction of x to the chores that remain after the zero-cost removals. Then x' is a feasible fractional allocation of the reduced instance. For every agent a,

$$c_a(x'_a) \leq c_a(x_a) \leq c_a(A_a) = c_a(\bar{A}_a).$$

The first inequality uses nonnegativity of costs, and the equality uses the fact that every removed chore was added back to an agent who has zero cost for it. If x strictly decreases the cost of some agent a relative to A, then the displayed inequality is strict for that same agent. Therefore, x' Pareto-dominates $\bar{A}$, contradicting fPO of $\bar{A}$. □

6 Extensions: Typed and Identical Chores

The prescribed quota algorithm guesses actual chores in the sets T_h. When chores have few cost types, it is enough to guess how many chores of each type appear in each such set. We say that chores have p cost types if M is partitioned into $M_1, \ldots, M_p$ such that, for every type t and every two chores $j, j' \in M_t$, we have $c_{ij} = c_{ij'}$ for all agents i. Let $m_t = |M_t|$, and write $c_{i,t}$ for the cost of a type-t chore to agent i.

Theorem 3. *Assume positive rational costs and positive entitlements. If chores have p cost types, then the prescribed quota WEF1+fPO problem can be solved in time*

$$\left(\prod_{a\in H(q)} \binom{q_a+p-2}{p-1}\right) \operatorname{poly}(n,m,L).$$

In particular, the problem is polynomial-time solvable for fixed p and fixed $|H(q)|$, and is fixed-parameter tractable in $p + S(q)$.

Proof. For each agent $a \in H(q)$, guess the type-count vector

$$z_a = (z_{a,1},\dots,z_{a,p}) \in \mathbb{Z}^p_{\geq 0}, \quad \sum_{t=1}^{p} z_{a,t} = q_a - 1.$$

We only keep guesses satisfying $\sum_{a\in H(q)} z_{a,t} \leq m_t$ for every type t. For a kept guess, we realize the guessed cores by choosing, for every type t, arbitrary disjoint subsets of M_t of sizes $z_{a,t}$ for the heavy agents $a \in H(q)$. This is possible precisely because $\sum_{a\in H(q)} z_{a,t} \leq m_t$. Since chores of the same type have the same cost vector, only these type counts matter for WEF1 and for the product objective. The number of such guesses is at most

$$\prod_{a\in H(q)} \binom{q_a+p-2}{p-1}.$$

Fix one feasible guess $z = (z_a)_{a\in H(q)}$. For any agent i, define $C_i(z_a) = \sum_{t=1}^{p} z_{a,t}c_{i,t}$. For each $a \in H(q)$, define

$$\tau_a = \frac{C_a(z_a)}{\alpha_a} \quad \text{and} \quad \beta_a = \max\{c_{a,t} : z_{a,t} > 0\},$$

where the maximum is well-defined because $a \in H(q)$ implies $\sum_t z_{a,t} = q_a - 1 \geq 1$. If $E(q) \neq \varnothing$ and some $\tau_a > 0$, then this guess cannot lead to a WEF1 allocation, since a heavy agent would WEF1-envy an empty agent.

It remains to choose one residual chore for each agent in $H(q) \cup R(q)$. Let $\rho_t = m_t - \sum_{a\in H(q)} z_{a,t}$ be the number of remaining chores of type t. We build a min-cost flow instance with supply ρ_t at each type t, and demand one at each agent-slot in $H(q) \cup R(q)$.

A type t may be sent to a singleton agent $r \in R(q)$ iff

$$\tau_a \leq \frac{c_{a,t}}{\alpha_r} \quad \text{for every } a \in H(q).$$

A type t may be sent to a heavy agent $b \in H(q)$ iff $c_{b,t} \geq \beta_b$ and

$$\tau_a \leq \frac{C_a(z_b) + c_{a,t}}{\alpha_b} \quad \text{for every } a \in H(q).$$

The first condition says that the chosen residual chore can serve as the guard chore of b. The second condition is exactly the WEF1 constraint from every heavy agent a toward b.

The edge cost of assigning a type-t chore to agent i is $\log c_{i,t}$, implemented as in Remark 1. Since the flow network has integral supplies and demands, an optimal flow is integral and therefore corresponds to an actual residual assignment of chores. If this flow instance is infeasible, we discard the current guess z.

For the fixed guess z, add the core cost $\sum_{a \in H(q)} \sum_{t=1}^{p} z_{a,t} \log c_{a,t}$ to the minimum residual-flow cost. We output the resulting allocation only if this total is $\Gamma(q) = \min\{\Phi(A) : A \in \mathcal{A}(q)\}$, where $\Gamma(q)$ is computed, again as in Remark 1, by the typed transportation problem with type supplies m_t, agent demands q_i, and edge costs $\log c_{i,t}$.

Soundness follows because the allowed edges encode exactly the guard condition and all WEF1 constraints whose left-hand side is nonzero. The equality with $\Gamma(q)$ implies fPO by Lemma 1. Completeness follows by taking any quota-respecting WEF1+fPO allocation, recording the type counts z_a of its EF1 cores, and observing that its residual guard/singleton assignment is a feasible integral flow for the corresponding guess.

The fixed-parameter claim follows since

$$\prod_{a \in H(q)} \binom{q_a + p - 2}{p - 1} \leq \prod_{a \in H(q)} p^{q_a - 1} = p^{S(q)} \leq (p + S(q))^{p + S(q)}.$$

Thus the non-polynomial part of the running time is bounded by a function only of $p + S(q)$. □

Corollary 2 (Identical chores). *Assume all chores have the same positive cost vector: for every agent i, $c_{ij} = c_i$ for all chores j. For a prescribed quota vector q, every allocation in $\mathcal{A}(q)$ is fPO. Moreover, a quota-respecting allocation is WEF1 if and only if*

$$\frac{(q_i - 1)^+}{\alpha_i} \leq \frac{q_k}{\alpha_k} \quad \textit{for every pair of agents } i, k.$$

Thus prescribed quota WEF1+fPO is decidable in $O(n^2)$ time for identical chores.

Proof. Since all chores are identical, every allocation with quota vector q has the same product $\prod_{i \in N} c_i^{q_i}$. Hence every allocation in $\mathcal{A}(q)$ is fPO by Lemma 1. For WEF1, agent i's own EF1 cost is $(q_i - 1)^+ c_i$, while agent i's cost for agent k's bundle is $q_k c_i$. Since $c_i > 0$, the WEF1 inequalities are exactly

$$\frac{(q_i - 1)^+}{\alpha_i} \leq \frac{q_k}{\alpha_k} \quad \forall i, k,$$

as desired. □

7 Hardness for Prescribed Quotas

The algorithm of Theorem 1 is exponential in $S(q)$. We now show that prescribed quotas become hard when this quantity is unbounded. The hardness holds even without entitlements, i.e., for ordinary EF1. Here, two agent types means that there are only two distinct cost functions, although agents of the same type may have separate quotas.

Theorem 4. *It is strongly NP-hard to decide whether there exists an allocation $A \in \mathcal{A}(q)$ that is EF1 and PO, even with positive integer costs, two agent types, and $q_i \in \{3, 5\}$ for every agent i. The same hardness holds for EF1+fPO.*

Proof. We reduce from 3-PARTITION. The input consists of integers $a_1, \ldots, a_{3r}$ with

$$\sum_{t=1}^{3r} a_t = rB \quad \text{and} \quad B/4 < a_t < B/2$$

for every t. It is strongly NP-complete to decide whether these numbers can be partitioned into r triples, each summing to B [12].

Create one distinguished agent d and bin agents $b_1, \ldots, b_r$. Create five special chores $h_1, \ldots, h_5$ and one number chore e_t for each a_t. Set

$$q_d = 5, \quad q_{b_s} = 3 \quad \text{for every } s.$$

For the distinguished agent, set $c_d(h_\ell) = B$ and $c_d(e_t) = 4a_t$. For every bin agent b_s, set $c_{b_s}(h_\ell) = K$ and $c_{b_s}(e_t) = 4a_t$, where $K = 3B$. Since $B/4 < a_t < B/2$, we have $B < 4a_t < 2B < K$. All costs are positive integers, and all bin agents have the same cost function.

We first show that every quota-respecting PO allocation assigns all special chores to d. Suppose some special chore h_ℓ is assigned to a bin agent. Since d has quota five and there are exactly five special chores, d must receive some number chore e_t. Swapping h_ℓ and e_t changes d's cost from $4a_t$ to B, and changes the bin agent's cost from K to $4a_t$. Both agents strictly improve, and all others are unchanged. Thus the original allocation was not PO.

Now suppose a quota-respecting EF1+PO allocation exists. By the previous paragraph, d receives $\{h_1, \ldots, h_5\}$, and every bin receives three number chores. The value of d_d^- on d's bundle is

$$d_d^-(\{h_1, \ldots, h_5\}) = 5B - B = 4B.$$

For d to be EF1 toward bin b_s, we need

$$4B \leq c_d(A_{b_s}) = \sum_{e_t \in A_{b_s}} 4a_t.$$

Thus the three numbers assigned to each bin have sum at least B. Since the total sum is rB, every bin must receive a triple summing exactly to B. Hence the 3-PARTITION instance is a yes-instance.

Conversely, suppose the 3-PARTITION instance has triples $T_1, \dots, T_r$ such that

$$\sum_{t \in T_s} a_t = B \quad \text{for every } s \in [r].$$

Assign all five special chores to d, and assign the number chores in T_s to bin agent b_s.

This allocation is EF1. The self-constraints are immediate from nonnegativity, so consider two distinct agents. Agent d's threshold is $4B$, and d's cost for every bin bundle is $4B$. A bin agent's own bundle has cost $4B$; after removing any one chore, its remaining own cost is at most $4B$. Since every other bin bundle also has cost $4B$ to this agent, the EF1 constraints between bin agents hold. It is also EF1 toward d, because its EF1 threshold is at most $4B$, while its cost for d's bundle is $5K = 15B$.

It remains to prove fPO. By Lemma 1, it is enough to prove quota-wise product optimality. In any quota-respecting allocation where a special chore is assigned to a bin, d must receive some number chore. Swapping such a pair preserves all quotas and changes the product contribution from

$$c_d(e_t)c_{b_s}(h_\ell) = 4a_t K$$

to

$$c_d(h_\ell)c_{b_s}(e_t) = B \cdot 4a_t,$$

which is smaller because $B < K$. Repeating this swap strictly decreases the product until all special chores are assigned to d. Once this holds, the product is $B^5 \prod_{t=1}^{3r} 4a_t$, independent of how the number chores are assigned to the bin agents. Therefore the constructed allocation is quota-wise product-minimizing, and hence fPO. Since fPO implies PO, it is also EF1+PO.

Thus the prescribed quota EF1+PO and EF1+fPO instances are yes-instances exactly when the original 3-PARTITION instance is a yes-instance. The reduction uses only integers bounded by $3B$, so the hardness is strong. □

8 Conclusion

We give a polynomial-time algorithm for computing WEF1 and fPO allocations of indivisible chores whenever $m \leq n + s$ for fixed s. The main structural reason is specific to chores: if an agent receives at most one chore, then $d_i^-(A_i) = 0$, so only agents with at least two chores can create nontrivial WEF1 constraints. Combined with product minimality at fixed quotas, this gives us a prescribed quota algorithm running in time $m^{S(q)}\text{poly}(n, m, L)$.

The hardness result shows that prescribed quotas become strongly NP-hard when $S(q)$ is unbounded, even under severe restrictions on costs and quotas. This leaves two natural open questions. First, can the dependence on $S(q)$ be improved to $f(S(q))\text{poly}(n, m, L)$? Second, can EF1+fPO allocations be computed in polynomial time for general unconstrained chore instances without enumerating quota vectors?

References

1. Akrami, H., Chaudhury, B.R., Garg, J., Mehlhorn, K., Mehta, R.: Fair and efficient allocation of indivisible chores with surplus. In: Proceedings of the 32nd International Joint Conference on Artificial Intelligence (IJCAI), pp. 2494–2502 (2023)
2. Amanatidis, G., et al.: Fair division of indivisible goods: Recent progress and open questions. Artif. Intell. **322**(C) (2023)
3. Aziz, H., Caragiannis, I., Igarashi, A., Walsh, T.: Fair allocation of indivisible goods and chores. Auton. Agents Multi-Agent Syst. **36**(3) (2022)
4. Aziz, H., Li, B., Moulin, H., Xiaowei, W.: Algorithmic fair allocation of indivisible items: A survey and new questions. ACM SIGecom Exchanges **20**(1), 24–40 (2022)
5. Aziz, H., Lindsay, J., Ritossa, A., Suzuki, M.: Fair allocation of two types of chores. In: Proceedings of the 22nd International Conference on Autonomous Agents and Multiagent Systems (AAMAS), pp. 143–151 (2023)
6. Barman, S., Krishnamurthy, S.K., Vaish, R.: Finding fair and efficient allocations. In: Proceedings of the 19th ACM Conference on Economics and Computation (EC), pp. 557–574 (2018)
7. Biswas, A., Barman, S.: Fair division under cardinality constraints. In: Proceedings of the 27th International Joint Conference on Artificial Intelligence (IJCAI), pp. 91–97 (2018)
8. Bouveret, S., Lemaître, M.: Characterizing conflicts in fair division of indivisible goods using a scale of criteria. Auton. Agents Multi-Agent Syst. **30**(2): 259–290 (2016)
9. Caragiannis, I., Kurokawa, D., Moulin, H., Procaccia, A.D., Shah, N., Wang, J.: The unreasonable fairness of maximum Nash welfare. ACM Trans. Econ. Comput. **7**(3), 12:1–12:32 (2019)
10. Ebadian, S., Peters, D., Shah, N.: How to fairly allocate easy and difficult chores. In: Proceedings of the 21st International Conference on Autonomous Agents and Multiagent Systems (AAMAS), pp. 372–380 (2022)
11. Feige, U., Sapir, A., Tauber, L.: A Tight Negative Example for MMS Fair Allocations. In: Feldman, M., Fu, H., Talgam-Cohen, I. (eds.) WINE 2021. LNCS, vol. 13112, pp. 355–372. Springer, Cham (2022). https://doi.org/10.1007/978-3-030-94676-0_20
12. Garey, M.R., Johnson, D.S.: Computers and Intractability; A Guide to the Theory of NP-Completeness. W. H. Freeman & Co. (1979)
13. Garg, J., Murhekar, A., Qin, J.: Fair and efficient allocations of chores under bivalued preferences. In: Proceedings of the 36th AAAI Conference on Artificial Intelligence (AAAI), pp. 5043–5050 (2022)
14. Garg, J., Murhekar, A., Qin, J.: New algorithms for the fair and efficient allocation of indivisible chores. In: Proceedings of the 32nd International Joint Conference on Artificial Intelligence (IJCAI), pp. 2710–2718 (2023)
15. Garg, J., Murhekar, A., Qin, J.: Weighted EF1 and PO allocations with few types of agents or chores. In: Proceedings of the 33rd International Joint Conference on Artificial Intelligence (IJCAI), pp. 2799–2806 (2024)
16. Garg, J., Murhekar, A., Qin, J.: Constant-factor EFX exists for chores. In: Proceedings of the 57th Annual ACM Symposium on Theory of Computing (STOC), pp. 1580–1589 (2025)
17. Hsu, K.: Existence of MMS allocations with mixed manna. arXiv preprint arXiv:2401.07490,2024

18. Kawase, Y., Mahara, R.: Fair and efficient balanced allocation for indivisible goods. In: Proceedings of the 40th AAAI Conference on Artificial Intelligence (AAAI), pp. 17067–17075 (2026)
19. Kurokawa, D., Procaccia, A., Wang, J.: When can the maximin share guarantee be guaranteed? In: Proceedings of the 30th AAAI Conference on Artificial Intelligence (AAAI), pp. 523–529, (2016)
20. Lim, E., Tzeh Yuan Neoh, N., Teh: The cost of efx: Generalized-mean welfare and complexity dichotomies with few surplus items. arXiv preprint arXiv:2601.12849,2026
21. Lipton, R.J., Markakis, E., Mossel, E., Saberi, A.: On approximately fair allocations of indivisible goods. In: Proceedings of the 5th ACM Conference on Electronic Commerce (EC), pp. 125–131 (2004)
22. Mahara, R.: Existence of fair and efficient allocation of indivisible chores. In: Proceedings of the 37th ACM-SIAM Symposium on Discrete Algorithms (SODA), pp. 6742–6766 (2026)
23. Neoh, T.Y., Teh, N.: Understanding efx allocations: Counting and variants. In: Proceedings of the 39th AAAI Conference on Artificial Intelligence (AAAI), pp. 14036–14044 (2025)
24. Springer, M., Hajiaghayi, M., Yami, H.: Almost envy-free allocations of indivisible goods or chores with entitlements. In: Proceedings of the 38th AAAI Conference on Artificial Intelligence (AAAI), pp. 9901–9908 (2024)
25. Suksompong, W.: Constraints in fair division. ACM SIGecom Exchanges **19**(2), 46–61 (2021)
26. Xiaowei, W., Zhang, C., Zhou, S.: Weighted EF1 allocations for indivisible chores. Artif. Intell. **347**, 104386 (2025)

Author Index

P. Lenzner and D. Schmand (Eds.): SAGT 2026, LNCS 16911, pp. 409–410, 2027.
https://doi.org/10.1007/978-3-032-38782-0

FSC
www.fsc.org
MIX
Papier | Fördert
gute Waldnutzung
FSC® C083411

Kolibri 360 GmbH
Ferdinand-Jühlke-Straße 7
99095 Erfurt, Deutschland
produktsicherheit@kolibri360.de